W9-BTK-034

ALISON BING

VENICE & THE VENETO

CITY GUIDE

INTRODUCING VENICE

A fleet of gondoliers, among others, navigates the riches of the Grand Canal (p125)

From the look of it, you'd think Venice spent all its time primping. Bask in the glory of Grand Canal palaces, but make no mistake: this city's a powerhouse.

You may have heard that Venice is an engineering marvel, with marble cathedrals built atop ancient posts driven deep into the *barene* (mud banks) – but the truth is that this city is built on sheer nerve. Reasonable people might blanch at water approaching their doorsteps and flee at the first sign of *acqua alta* (high tide). But reason can't compare to Venetian resolve. Instead of bailing out, Venetians have flooded the world with voluptuous Venetian-red paintings and wines, music, Marco Polo spice-route flavours, and bohemian-chic fashion. And they're not done yet.

VENICE LIFE

With the world's most artistic masterpieces per square kilometre, you'd think the city would take it easy, maybe rest on its laurels. But Venice refuses to retire from the inspiration business. In narrow *calli* (alleyways), you'll glimpse artisans hammering out shoes crested like lagoon birds, cooks whipping up four-star dishes on single-burner hotplates, and musicians lugging 18th-century cellos to riveting baroque concerts played with punk-rock bravado. As you can see, all those 19th-century Romantics got it wrong. Venice is not destined for genteel decay. Billionaire benefactors and cutting-edge biennales are filling up those ancient *palazzi* (palaces) with restored masterpieces and eyebrow-raising contemporary art and architecture, and back-alley galleries and artisan showrooms are springing up in their shadows. Your timing couldn't be better: the people who made walking on water look easy are already well into their next act.

But don't go expecting to have the city to yourself. Even in the foot-stomping chill of January, Venice has its admirers. The upside is that you'll keep fascinating company here. More accessible than ever and surprisingly affordable given its singularity, Venice remains a self-selecting city: it takes a certain imagination to forgo the convenience of cars and highways for slow boats and crooked *calli*. Sculptors, harpsichordists, sushi chefs and dreamers passing as accountants might end up bumping elbows over heaping plates of *risotto di seppie* (squid risotto) along scuffed wooden tables in authentic *osterie* (pub-restaurants). Judging by the crowd, you might think the Art Biennale must be happening – but no, that's just an average Wednesday night in Venice. Venice is best when caught between acts, after the day trippers rush off to beat afternoon traffic, and before cruise ships dump dazed newcomers off in Piazza San Marco with three hours to see all of Venice before lunch. Those visitors may never get to see Venice in its precious downtime, when gondoliers warm up their vocal chords with scorching espresso on their way to work, and mosaic artisans converge at the bar for tesserae shoptalk over a *spritz* (*prosecco*-based drink).

Neither rain nor high tides can dampen high spirits at Venice's twice-daily happy hours, when even the most orthodox fashionistas will gamely pull on *stivali di gomma* (rubber boots) over their stylish artisan-made shoes, and slosh out to the bar to get first dibs on *cicheti* (traditional bar snacks). How come 'happy hour' lasts five hours a day, and why not close at the first high tide signal? 'There's only one Venice', explains one host as he pours another glass of fizzy Veneto *prosecco* well past the mark for *un ombra* (half-glass). 'We might as well enjoy it.'

If you ever did have Venice to yourself, you'd soon be hopelessly lost. When streets suddenly dead-end into canals or you wind up on a ferry with the right number heading in entirely the wrong direction, Venice can seem like a very tricky live-action video game, and you're the hapless character lost in the maze. Once you've found someone who knows the way and points you toward the correct dock, that's it: you've passed your Venice initiation. But do Venetians a favour and consult the signs, your map or a fellow traveller first. If each day tripper asked one local for directions to San Marco, every Venetian would hear the question repeated some 333 times a year. Venetians enjoy searching questions – but try asking something that stirs Venetian passions. What's freshest right now at the Rialto markets, and how should it be cooked? Who should win the Golden Lion at this year's Venice Film Festival? Any thoughts about feeding pigeons in Piazza San Marco?

The most sensitive local subject is still Mose (Modulo Sperimentale Elettromeccanico), the controversial flood barrier system currently under construction. But the combined effects of industrial pollution and global warming are also taken very seriously in this fragile lagoon ecosystem, and any effort you make to help mitigate the impact of travel – stay longer, eat and drink local specialities, support local artisans, tidy up after yourself – makes you a most welcome guest.

Sweeping view of the lagoon city

HIGHLIGHTS

❶

ART MASTERPIECES

Masterpieces await around every canal bend in Venice, where the paint seems fresh on 500-year-old canvases vibrant with Venetian colour, and boats drift past modern sculpture masterpieces from the Palazzo Grassi to the pavilions of the Biennale.

❺

❷

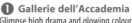

1 Gallerie dell'Accademia
Glimpse high drama and glowing colour that caused sensations – and censorship (p76)

2 Scuola Grande di San Rocco
Chase lightning flashes of insight through Tintoretto's stormy scenes (p85)

3 I Frari
Watch the cathedral glow with Titian's red-hot altarpiece (p84)

4 Peggy Guggenheim Collection
See the future coming at this modern-art showcase (p78)

5 Palazzo Grassi
Experience the shock of the new at Tadao Ando's modernised marvel (p71)

6 Ca' Pesaro
Survey Venice's best buys from the Biennale and finest Asian art imports (p88)

Ca' Pesaro

LOCAL FOOD & DRINK

Garden islands and lagoon aquaculture yield speciality produce and seafood you won't find elsewhere – all highlighted in inventive modern Venetian cuisine, with tantalising traces of ancient spice routes.

❶ Rialto markets
Find all the fixings for Venice's signature dishes at the Rialto markets (p85)

❷ Veneto speciality produce
Taste-test Veneto's best: Sant'Erasmo baby artichokes, feathery *radicchio trevisano* (bitter, red chicory), white Bassano asparagus (p179)

❸ Lagoon-fresh seafood
Food sensations for every season: spider crab, plump prawns, tender octopus, *bottarga* (caviar paste) and more, fresh from the Pescaria (p85)

❹ Roving happy hour
Discover your new drink of choice on a Venetian *giro d'ombra* (roving happy hour) (p202)

❺ Inventive chefs
Fresh local ingredients and trade-route flavours give Venetian cuisine crossover appeal (p179)

ANGELS IN THE ARCHITECTURE

Lift your spirits with landmarks that honour Venice's higher aspirations, with choirs of angels flitting across heavenly baroque halls, streams of sunlight filling lofty Byzantine domes, and engineering marvels in glistening Renaissance marble.

❶ Basilica di San Marco
Gasp at angels shimmering and skipping across gold mosaic domes (p65)

❷ Chiesa di San Giorgio Maggiore
Discover the mood-lifting powers of a Palladio masterpiece (p114)

❸ Ca' Rezzonico
See Tiepolo's trompe l'œil ceilings raise the roof on a baroque palace (p80)

❹ Chiesa di Santa Maria della Salute
Marvel at Baldassare Longhena's monument to survival (p81)

❺ Chiesa di Santa Maria dei Miracoli
Witness the minor marble miracle that launched the Renaissance in Venice (p92)

❻ Cattedrale di Santa Maria Assunta
Bask in the otherworldly glow of Torcello's 12th-century mosaic Madonna (p120)

4

ONE-OF-A-KIND FINDS

Savvy shoppers head to Venice for artisan-made scores at surprisingly reasonable prices: standout statement jewellery, handprinted journals, opera-ready couture from a nonprofit initiative, and signature works by Murano glass-blowers.

3

❶ Murano glass
Blow minds but not necessarily budgets with hand-blown gifts (p174)

❷ Fortuny designs
Go boho-chic with art nouveau patterns (p112)

❸ Custom-made shoes
Put a spring in your step with made-to-measure shoes from stores like Daniela Ghezzo (p165), Gmeiner (p171) and Giovanna Zanella (p174)

❹ Handmade paper
Look good on paper with intricate marbled-paper photo albums from stationers like Cartè (p169)

❺ Prison couture
Look sharp with unique designs from Venice's nonprofit prisoner-retraining program, Banco 10 (p173)

MUSICAL VENICE

This show-stopper city has its own play list in landmark locales: arias soar to gilded ceilings at La Fenice, Vivaldi accompanies Carpaccio masterpieces, chamber music escapes ancient prison cells, and squares and canals swing with jazz and tango.

❶ La Fenice
Shout *brava!* for opera diva encores at Venice's incendiary opera house (p210)

❷ Piazza San Marco
Tango across the square at sunset to musicians playing at Caffè Florian (p199)

❸ Interpreti Veneziani
Hear Vivaldi's *Four Seasons* played with verve as a soundtrack for Venice (p209)

❹ Concerts in Prigioni Nuove
Spend an enjoyable evening in prison with a lively classical concert by Collegium Ducale (p209)

❺ Venice Jazz Club
Hear swinging standards reinvented nightly just off Campo Santa Margherita (p209)

CONTENTS

Alison Bing

When she's not scribbling notes in church pews or methodically eating her way across Venice's *sestieri* (neighbourhoods), Alison contributes to Lonely Planet's *Venice, USA, San Francisco* and *Tuscany & Umbria* guides, as well as architecture, food, and art glossies including *Architectural Record, Cooking Light* and Italy's *Flash Art*. Currently she divides her time between San Francisco and a hilltop town on the border of Lazio and Tuscany with her partner Marco Flavio Marinucci. Alison holds a bachelor's degree in art history and a master's degree from the Fletcher School of Law and Diplomacy, a joint program of Tufts and Harvard Universities – perfectly respectable diplomatic credentials she regularly undermines with opinionated culture commentary for newspapers, magazines, TV and radio.

ALISON'S TOP VENICE DAY

The Venetian *bea vita* (beautiful life) begins with cappuccino overlooking the Piazza San Marco in the company of griffins at the frescoed cafe of the Museo Correr (p69), then cross the square to join the crowds in a collective gasp under the gold domes of the Basilica di San Marco (p65). Afterwards, I brave the gauntlet of boutiques lining the route from the Piazza to the Ponte dell'Accademia – but I can't resist stops at Galleria Rosella Junck and Caterina Tognon Arte Contemporanea to see the latest contemporary art sensations (see p74). The Punta della Dogana (p81) is the next logical stop on a contemporary art binge, to see the latest rotation from François Pinault's collection installed in the fluid gallery spaces Tadao Ando created in Venice's ancient waterfront customs warehouses. From here, it's a leisurely wander up the sunny Zattere and Calle Lunga San Barnaba to a long lunch of Venetian seafood classics at Ristoteca Oniga (p183) and a coffee among artists, fishmongers and arguing philosophy students at Il Caffè Rosso (p201) in Campo Santa Margherita. My old friends Rosalba Carriera and Pietro Longhi greet me with a wink from the walls at Ca' Rezzonico (p80), but I can't stay long: I have a standing date with a red-hot Titian at I Frari (p84), and VizioVirtù (p168) balsamic vinegar chocolates on the way. I take the long way to happy hour at the Rialto via Santa Croce studios to see the newest handmade wonders, and wind up dragging artisans along the Grand Canal for drinks at Al Mercà (p202). Crossing the Rialto as the sun sets, I arrive in time for the last boar-salami *crostini* (sandwich) and a stunning Amarone at I Rusteghi (p182), then hustle off to my Interpreti Veneziani concert (p209). Humming Vivaldi, I return to face the dimly glimmering Basilica di San Marco, and say the word that bears repeating in Venice: *unbelievable.*

LONELY PLANET AUTHORS

Why is our travel information the best in the world? It's simple: our authors are passionate, dedicated travellers. They don't take freebies in exchange for positive coverage so you can see the advice you're given is impartial. They travel widely to all the popular spots, and off the beaten track. They don't research using just the internet or phone. They discover new places not included in any other guidebook. They personally visit thousands of hotels, restaurants, palaces, trails, galleries, temples and more. They speak with dozens of locals every day to make sure you get the kind of insider knowledge only a local could tell you. They take pride in getting all the details right, and in telling it how it is. Think you can do it? Find out how at **lonelyplanet.com**.

GETTING STARTED

Nothing can really prepare you for your first glimpse of Venice, its marble palaces rising above the teal-blue lagoon like a wildly ambitious desert mirage – but for the rest of your Venice vacation, preparations come in handy. To see why the world tends to show up whenever Venice has thrown a party for the past five centuries, plan your visit to coincide with a highlight from Venice's calendar of festivals and events (see opposite), and be sure to book accommodation ahead (see p214). With some advance planning (see below), you can arrive with tickets in hand for opera at La Fenice, skip the queues for museum and event tickets, and slide right into reserved seats at the restaurant of your choice.

While you might come to Venice prepared to splurge on once-in-a-lifetime adventures, you'll also find opportunities to see Venice at its best for far less than you'd expect (see p21). To plan a dream getaway to match your budget, see p20 for average costs and money-saving tips. With fairy-tale charms and year-round attractions, this lagoon wonderland attracts plenty of visitors – but by keeping a few tips in mind for sustainable travel (see p21), you can distinguish yourself as a most welcome guest.

WHEN TO GO

Travellers looking for elbow room for sketching in the Gallerie dell'Accademia, casual conversation with Venetians and spontaneous weekend dinners without reservations would be better off going in Venice's quieter months of October through March. But even solitary types will find that some Venetian experiences are better in a crowd: happy hours, thunderous encores at La Fenice, and the chorus of 'ooh!' as crowds pass through the portals of Basilica di San Marco to glimpse shimmering gold mosaic domes overhead. For a balance of quiet moments and collective euphoria,

stay at least overnight in Venice, so you can see what the city is like after the crowd thins out and the moon rises, and in the morning when the town throws back an espresso and starts the show all over again.

You'll probably pay a premium for the privilege of being in town for masquerade balls during Carnevale, gala art openings for the Biennale, or star-studded premieres at the Venice International Film Festival. But this city has been internationally famed (and notorious) for its party-throwing prowess since the 16th century, and you can see why at any of the city's major shindigs – see Festivals, opposite, and the list of official holidays, p267.

ADVANCE PLANNING

Well Ahead

Before you book your train or plane to Venice, browse Venice accommodation options (p214) online: you'll be surprised how much you can save by going midweek or just before a holiday, and you'll get prime choices in B&Bs and rental apartments if you plan ahead. For major events like the Biennale or Carnevale, you can often book discounted advance tickets online through Venice Tourism Board's VeniceConnected (www.veniceconnected.com) or special passes through Hello Venezia (www.hellovenezia.com). You can also buy La Fenice opera tickets online at www.teatrolafenice.it (p210).

One Week Ahead

Skip the queues for popular attractions by purchasing tickets online through the Venice Tourism Board (www.turismo venezia.it) or last-minute tickets at www.weekendavenezia.com (see p266). If you're planning a dinner out during a holiday, Carnevale or Venice International Film Festival, now would be a good time to book a table.

One or Two Days Ahead

Check special event calendars at www.aguestinvenice.com and www.veneziadavivere.com, and plan an evening around a concert by Venice Jazz Club, Interpreti Veneziani, Musica a Palazzo, or other local music groups (see p208).

Since Venice is gorgeous inside and out, bad weather doesn't have to scuttle your travel plans. The only thing more splendid than your first glimpse of Venice may be the sight of Venice reflected in a puddle – or on very rare occasions, Venice's Gothic arches and gondola prows poking through a white blanket of snow. Bone-chilling weather in January and February can bring crystalline blue skies ideal for photo ops and gooey hot cocoa in Piazza San Marco. The heaviest rains fall from December through March, but you might luck into a freak summer thunderstorm – after you see lightning strikes over the lagoon, you'll have a whole new appreciation of Tintoretto brushstrokes and the thunderous summer movement of Vivaldi's *Four Seasons*. July and August tend to be hot and muggy, but if you get uncomfortable, make like a Venetian on vacation and escape to Lido beaches (see p116) or the Riviera Brenta (p231).

FESTIVALS & EVENTS

Three rules for revellers are posted in major vaporetto stops: no littering in the canals, no defacing historic buildings, and no strutting about bare-breasted. The fact that Venice feels obliged to post that last regulation shows that opportunities for, erm, self-expression don't begin and end with Carnevale.

Whether you like to spend your downtime getting arty, sweaty, mystical, or all of the above, Venice has you covered with Biennales, marathons, and weddings to the sea. The busiest months for traditional festivities are May through September; find out more about many of Venice's upcoming events at Cultura & Spettacolo (www.culturaspettacolovenezia.it, in Italian). Fair warning: this town seems determined to see you dunked. Many festivals entail crossing makeshift pontoon bridges or rowing while standing up, and boozing canalside has obvious risks.

January

REGATA DELLA BEFANA

Witches in Venice don't ride brooms: they row boats, as you can see in this regatta featuring a fleet of brawny male rowers cross-dressed as *befane* (witches). According to Italian legend, La Befana is the good witch who accompanied the three wise men to deliver gifts to baby Jesus, bringing sweets to children along the way. Traditionally, on Epiphany (6 January), La Befana

top picks

WAYS TO CELEBRATE CARNEVALE

- Slide tackle in knee britches at Calcio Storico, the fancy-dress football match in Piazza San Marco.
- Binge on *fritelle veneziane*, the rum-and-raisin doughnuts best eaten when still warm, morning, noon, and night.
- Quadrille the night away at La Fenice's Masked Ball on the second Saturday of Carnevale (tickets start at €200; costume and dance classes not included).
- Grab a spot canalside for the Grand Canal flotilla, where the parade floats actually float.
- Have a historically accurate blast, or DIY trying – make your own mask at Ca' Macana (p167) or master the art of mask acting at Teatro Junghans (p210).

brings sweets to good children and coal for naughty ones. This was once Italy's main gift-giving event, until Babbo Natale (Father Christmas) stole La Befana's thunder. But on Epiphany in Venice, La Befana still has the honour of kicking off the first of more than 100 annual regattas on the lagoon.

February

CARNEVALE
www.carnevale.venezia.it

Ten days and nights of masquerade madness – or until your liver twitches and wig itches – rage on in February before Lent begins on Ash Wednesday. Even Napoleon and Mussolini couldn't stop Venice's signature event, when masqueraders revel in the streets and occasionally stumble into canals wearing long-nosed plague masks and *commedia dell'arte* costumes. If you're feeling a tad hung over after a week or so, imagine how you would have felt in the 18th century, when the party lasted two months!

March

SALONE NAUTICO DI VENEZIA
www.festivaldelmare.com

Since 2002 the Stazione Marittima (Ferry Terminal) has hosted the popular Venice International Boat Show, with regattas at Stazione Marittima and 100 historic vessels on display at the Arsenale.

top picks

FOR FIRST-TIME VISITORS

- Basilica di San Marco (p65) Experience the awe of ages under glittering gold mosaic domes.
- Grand Canal (p125) The world's grandest boulevard is a shimmering stretch of water lined with gleaming Venetian Gothic marble palaces.
- Gallerie dell'Accademia (p76) A multiplex of masterpieces, packed with action, romance, catastrophe, redemption and controversy.
- I Frari (Chiesa di Santa Maria Gloriosa dei Frari; p84) This Gothic cathedral is lined with priceless art, but Titian's red-hot altarpiece gives it an otherworldly glow.
- Scuola Grande di San Rocco (p85) Lightning-strike streaks of paint illuminate floor-to-ceiling masterpieces by Venice's master of stormy drama, Tintoretto.

April

FESTA DI SAN MARCO
www.comune.venezia.it
Join the celebration of Venice's patron saint on 25 April, when Venetian men carry a *bocolo* (rosebud) in processions through Piazza San Marco, then bestow them on the women they love.

May

VOGALONGA
www.turismovenezia.it
Not a race so much as a show of endurance, this 32km 'long row' starts with the launch of 1000 boats in front of the Palazzo Ducale, loops past Burano and Murano, and ends with cheers, sweat and enormous blisters at Punta della Dogana.

FESTA DELLA SENSA
www.sevenonline.it/sensa
Venice loves its lagoon so much, it has renewed its wedding vows to the water every year since 998. On the Feast of the Ascension on the second Sunday in May, the city gave Venice's fleet a grand send-off as it sailed off to reclaim Dalmatia in 998. The fleet returned triumphant, and ever since, the city has celebrated the Feast of the Ascension with the Sposalizio del Mar (Wedding with the Sea) ceremony, when the city's leader

(first the doge, now the mayor) tosses a gold ring in the waters near San Nicolò on the Lido. Got your scuba gear?

PALIO DELLE QUATTRO ANTICHE REPUBBLICHE MARINARE
www.comune.venezia.it
A glorious grudge match: the former maritime republics of Amalfi, Genoa, Pisa and Venice take turns hosting the historic Regatta of the Four Ancient Maritime Republics, when four galleons, crewed by eight oarsmen and one at the tiller, compete for maritime boating bragging rights. Costumed processions re-enact each republic's great naval victories, and honour the Palio winners. As any Venetian will be quick to point out, since the Palio's inception in 1954, Venice has won 30 matches to nine by Amalfi, six by Pisa, and eight by historic rival Genoa. The challenge will be held in Venice again in 2011.

June

VENEZIA SUONA
www.veneziasuona.it, in Italian
Hear medieval *campi* (squares) and baroque *palazzi* (palaces) echo with the latest sounds from around the world over a glorious June weekend. Most performances run from 4pm to 10pm.

FESTA DI SAN PIETRO DI CASTELLO
www.comune.venezia.it
The Festival of St Peter of Castello takes place during the last week of June, with music, revelry and food stalls at the steps of the church that was once the city's cathedral. The ancient festival begins with traditional religious veneration, and has all the hallmarks of a proper Italian *sagra* (feast): games for kids, hearty rustic fare, and Abba tribute bands.

LA BIENNALE DI VENEZIA
www.labiennale.org
Venice's international showcase for the arts and architecture has been a show-stopper for a century. In odd-numbered years the Art Biennale usually runs from June to November, and in even years the Architecture Biennale kicks off in September – but every summer the Biennale features avant-garde dance, theatre, cinema and music. The Art Biennale is headquartered in permanent

pavilions in the Giardini Pubblici (p104), with special exhibitions at locations across Venice. In alternate years the Architecture Biennale is staged in the Arsenale, with occasional installations in other parts of the city. The Festival Internazionale di Danza Contemporanea (International Festival of Contemporary Dance) is held annually starting in mid-June, and runs for about six weeks.

July

FESTA DEL REDENTORE
www.turismovenezia.it
Walk on water across the Canale della Giudecca to Chiesa del SS Redentore (p112) via a bobbing, wobbly pontoon bridge during the Feast of the Redeemer, the third weekend in July. Yet another regatta is held on the Grand Canal, but the real action is at the Redentore and on the Canale della Giudecca, where crowds picnic in boats and watch fireworks. Every year since 1577, Venice has commemorated its reprieve from the plague by crossing the pontoon bridge to give thanks at the church – a joyous and only occasionally soaking wet event.

SUGGESTIVO
www.culturaspettacolovenezia.it, in Italian
The annual summer fest seems to go by a different name every year, but live jazz, theatre and dance are recurring themes from Giudecca to mainland Mestre. The highlight is the Venice Jazz Festival, with jazz legends such as Wynton Marsalis and the Lincoln Center Jazz Orchestra bringing down the house at La Fenice, and Italian stars like Paolo Conte playing Piazza San Marco with La Fenice's orchestra. Pick up programs from tourist offices; events often continue into September.

August

VENICE INTERNATIONAL FILM FESTIVAL
www.labiennale.org/en/cinema
The only thing hotter than Lido beaches in August is the red carpet at this star-studded event, which runs from the last weekend in August through the first week of September at the Palazzo della Mostra del Cinema on the Lido. When the Venice Biennale Internazionale d'Arte announced its first annual film showcase in 1932, the scandal threatened to sink Venice. 'What kind of a city would risk its reputation on popular entertainment?', sniffed Cannes, New York and Toronto. But once Greta Garbo, Joan Crawford, Clark Gable and 25,000 people showed up for screenings, the showcase and its 'Golden Lion' awards ceremony proved a winning formula of art and celebrity. Never an indie film showcase, the Venice International Film Festival often rewards directors who should have won Oscars on creative merit, including Darren Aronofsky (The Wrestler), Spike Jonze (Being John Malkovich), Antoine Fuqua (Training Day), and Ang Lee (Brokeback Mountain), as well as perennial favourites Woody Allen, Takeshi Kitano, Martin Scorsese and Zhang Yimou.

September

REGATA STORICA
www.comune.venezia.it
Never mind who's winning, check out the fantastic gear: 16th-century costumes, eight-oared gondolas, and ceremonial barks all feature in a historical procession re-enacting the arrival of the Queen of Cyprus. On the first Sunday of the month, a floating parade is followed by a series of four races that start at Castello and proceed west up the Grand Canal to the former convent of Santa Chiara, where the boats turn around a bricola (pylon) and pound back down to the finishing line at Ca' Foscari. Kids, women and gondolieri take turns rowing fast and furiously for top honours at the macchina, the Historical Regatta's trophy stand.

VENICE VIDEOART FAIR
www.venicevideoartfair.org
Poetic, lovely and weird, Italy's premier video art fair features 25 booths of new-media art in the anachronistic island setting of San Servolo (p124), a ferry ride away from the Biennale gardens.

SAGRA DEL PESCE
www.comune.venezia.it
The sleepy island of Burano (p119) roars to life during September's annual Fish Festival, when crowds enjoy fish, polenta and white wine accompanied by traditional music. In the afternoon the city's only mixed men's and women's rowing regatta takes place off

the island – and since this is the last serious match of the regatta season, rowers go all out for a definitive win.

October

FESTA DEL MOSTO

www.comune.venezia.it

A genuine country fair, held on an island. On Venice's 'garden isle' of Sant'Erasmo (p122), northeast of the city, the wine grape harvest is celebrated on the first Sunday in October with a parade of floats, farmers market, gourmet food stalls, live music, and wine.

VENICE MARATHON

www.venicemarathon.com

Six thousand runners work up a sweat over 42km of spectacular scenery, dashing along the River Brenta past Palladian villas before crossing into Venice and heading to Piazza San Marco via a 160m floating bridge. Mind your step…

November

FESTA DELLA MADONNA DELLA SALUTE

www.turismovenezia.it

If you'd survived plague, floods and Austrian invasion, you'd throw a party too. Every 21 November since the 17th century, Venetians have crossed a pontoon bridge across the Grand Canal to give thanks at the Chiesa di Santa Maria della Salute (p81) and splurge on sweets.

COSTS & MONEY

The splendours of Venice do not always come cheap – though when you consider that supplies have to be brought in by boats and lugged over footbridges, prices for basic food, drink and lodging can seem surprisingly reasonable. Rome and Milan often charge just as much or more, minus the Grand Canal views, stellar selection of Veneto wines, and lagoon-fresh seafood.

To reduce your entry fees, check out ticket prices on different days available online through the Venice Tourism Board's new VeniceConnected (www.veniceconnected.com) service, which sells reduced-price advance combined or solo tickets for transportation, city museums and parking.

Accommodation, meals, transport and sight entry fees will be your main expenses. A basic double is hard to find for less than €80 a night, especially in high season. With some planning during the November to March low season, you might find a charming, central B&B for as little as €65, hostel bunks with frescoes or canal views for even less, or apartment rentals by the week starting at around €300. For midrange rates as low as €100 (in low season) or €160 in high season, you might score a room in a sleek boutique B&B or an actual palace.

A full sit-down meal (three courses, with dessert and house wine) quickly heads upwards of €25 to €30, but cicheti (Venetian snacks, or 'small plates') are a budget gourmet delight: under €10 gets you two to four orders of meatballs, crostini (open-face sandwiches) even seafood delicacies at the bar with a glass of wine. Most bars sell panini (sandwiches) and similar snacks costing €3 to €5, and pizza starts at about €2 a slice or €7 for a generous personal-sized pie. As is true across Italy, coffee and snacks at the bar are cheaper than at a table. Self-catering is another budget eating option; see p185.

It pays to stay longer in Venice when it comes to public transport, because tickets for unlimited travel for 24 to 72 hours are a much better deal than one-way tickets. For details, see the Transport chapter, p257.

The more you see, the less you pay per site with multivenue entry passes to Venice's museums and churches. For passes and combined entry tickets, see p266, and the individual venue listings.

Given these basic costs, a backpacker sticking religiously to youth hostels, walking rather than taking vaporetti (public ferries), enjoying meals of cicheti, panini and house wine, and making good use of museum and church passes, could get by on €50 to €60 per day. A midrange budget varies widely depending on food, lodging and season, ranging from €100 to €250 a day.

HOW MUCH?

Espresso coffee at the bar €0.90 to €1

Cicheti (Venetian bar snacks) €1 to €4 each

Chorus Pass (good for entry to 16 churches) €9

Hand-blown Murano glass ring €10 to €30

Handmade marble-paper travel journal €15 to €25

12-hour vaporetto ticket €16

Bicycle hire per day on the Lido €10

TOP 10 SIGNATURE SPLURGES & BEST BARGAINS

With some savvy and the plentiful options in this book, you can maximise your Venice experience and minimise the bill. Check out these signature Venice experiences, and best-value Venetian alternatives.

- Splurge: sip an authentic Bellini (*prosecco*-and-peach cocktail) where it was invented, at Harry's Bar (€15; p199). Bargain: toast the good life with a strong spritz (*prosecco*-and-bitters cocktail) for €1.50 to €3 at an authentic neighbourhood *osteria* (pub-restaurant) – see p198 for options near you.
- Splurge: explore Venice and discover your own romantic side on a 40-minute gondola ride (€80, not including tip or extras, like singing; see also p259). Bargain: take the ultimate Venetian transit dare and stand up like a local on a €1 traghetto (commuter gondola) ride across the Grand Canal (see p261).
- Splurge: drift off under frescoed ceilings in a kingly antique bed at a 1540 palace, Palazzo Abadessa (double €145 to €325; p222). Bargain: drift off under 18th-century frescoes in a €22 dorm bed at Foresteria Valdese (p224), a hostel housed in a 17th-century palace.
- Splurge: indulge in decadent dining at Michelin-starred Met (two courses €70-plus, not including wine; p191). Bargain: go all out with €10 to €20 for a five-star *cicheti* (bar snacks) feast at All'Arco (p188), including a glass or two of DOC Veneto wine.
- Splurge: score opening-night box seats to opera performances that raise the gilded roof at Teatro La Fenice (tickets €153; p210). Bargain: even on the day of performances, you may still be able to score €24 tickets to an Interpreti Veneziani concert at historic San Vidal (p209).
- Splurge: make a summer getaway to Lido beaches with a private cabana (€17 plus vaporetto transport; p116). Bargain: lounge dockside along the Zattere with Da Nico's *gianduiotto*, a slab of hazelnut *gelato* (ice cream) submerged under whipped cream (€8; p184).
- Splurge: purchase a highly collectable signed work by the world's leading glass artisans at Murano Collezioni (artworks €300-plus; p119). Bargain: score unsigned rings and beads by emerging Murano glass artisans for €7 to €15 from Linea Arte Vetro (p175).
- Splurge: linger over luxurious hot chocolate at Caffè Florian (hot chocolate €10, plus €6 music surcharge for outdoor seating in Piazza San Marco; p199). Bargain: sip €2 artisanal hot chocolate served hot and gooey from a chocolate fountain, at VizioVirtù, (p168).
- Splurge: reserve prime-time tickets to Venice International Film Festival screenings in the Lido's Palazzo della Mostra del Cinema (tickets €40; p19). Bargain: book daytime Venice International Film Festival screenings at the Lido's PalaBiennale (€8), behind the Palazzo della Mostra del Cinema.
- Splurge: soak your cares away with a milk, honey and rose bath in a Palladian landmark at eco-friendly Bauer Palladio Hotel & Spa (p224). Bargain: soak up the sun with a chilled €4 *prosecco* (sparkling white wine) in the Carlo Scarpa–designed garden at Palazzo Querini-Stampalia (p105).

INTERNET RESOURCES

To find out what's on the calendar in Venice during your visit, drop by the APT tourism office (p274) to pick up this month's printed *Eventi* brochure, or click on the Calendar button at www.comune.venezia.it. As well as the obvious www.lonelyplanet.com, sites offering handy information, listings and deals include the following:

A Guest in Venice (www.aguestinvenice.com) Hotelier association provides information on upcoming exhibits, events, and lectures.

Venezia da Vivere (The Creative Guide to Contemporary Venice; www.veneziadavivere.com) The guide to what's hip and happening in Venice now: music performances, art openings, nightlife, new designers and more.

Venice Explorer (http://venicexplorer.net) Provides calendar listings and locator maps for Venice venues, bars and attractions.

Venice Tourism Board (Azienda Promozione Turistica di Venezia, or APT; www.turismovenezia.it) Sells tickets to major city attractions online, covers upcoming cultural events and lists hundreds of B&Bs, hotels and other accommodation options.

Weekend a Venezia (http://en.venezia.waf.it) Offers discounted and last-minute tickets to major tourist attractions.

SUSTAINABLE VENICE

Look up at Venice's towering church domes, grand Gothic archways and arching footbridges, then look at what's directly below: the teal waters of Venice's lagoon. With only 7.6 sq km of land punctuating 267km of sparkling lagoon waters and canals, this city is more water than land. But make no mistake: without Venetians' careful custodianship of this lagoon for over 1000 years, there would be no land left to support these landmarks.

Reclaiming those 7.6km from the lagoon was hard work Venetians accomplished over several centuries, digging deeper channels in the shallow lagoon to drain the waters around tiny islands. To extend the islands, platforms were built of pine pylons rammed into the muddy lagoon floor topped by layers of Istrian stone. Over the centuries, the seawater gradually mineralised the wood and hardened the structure, while the upper stone layers remained impervious to the tides. On top of these ingenious platforms, Venetians built incredible monuments that have stood the test of time, including Baldassare Longhena's domed 1630 Chiesa di Santa Maria della Salute (p81), a spectacular domed structure supported by at least 100,000 pylons at the tip of Dorsoduro island.

You may have heard that Venice is sinking, but that's not entirely accurate. The city's wooden foundations have held up miraculously well, despite the rise and fall of tides and periodic flooding over centuries. But the foundations are taking a pounding as never before, with new stresses from industrial pollutants and the wakes of speeding motorboats. At the same time, the dredging of deeper channels to accommodate ferries, tankers and cruise ships has contributed to a doubling in water levels since 1900. Back then, Piazza San Marco flooded about 10 times a year; now it's closer to 60. Venice is trying to control the tides by building new mobile barriers at the edges of the lagoon, called Mose (see p36). But even if the Mose project can alleviate some flood conditions, other threats remain to the fragile lagoon ecosystem that keeps Venice afloat. Since the 1960s, Venetians have taken bold steps to reverse the toll on the lagoon from industrialisation, enforcing new rules around waste from the Porta Marghera chemical plants inland and new speed rules for boats.

But when it comes to shoring up complex environmental concerns, 90,000 Venetians can't reverse the tide of wear and tear on the lagoon by themselves – which is where your help comes in handy. With 22 million visitors a year, even a minor adjustment in travel patterns can lighten the burden of upkeep for Venetians, and make a sea change in the life of the lagoon. You can be the next hero of Venice's story with a few thoughtful decisions:

Take the train to Venice Long-haul ferries and cruise ships have an outsize environmental impact on tiny Venice and its fragile lagoon aquaculture, exposing Venice's ancient foundations to degradation from high-speed *motoschiaffi* (wakes) and leakage of wastewater from the bilge, ballast and flushing of on-board toilets. Sulphur emissions from cruise ships eat away the city's stonework, leaving lacy Gothic balconies to crumble as marble and stone turn to powder. Take the lower-impact train instead, and Venice will be most grateful – and within Italy, the train is more time- and cost-efficient, too.

Stay overnight Fewer than one-third of Venice's visitors stay the night and enjoy Venetian dinners, concerts, happy hours and hospitality. Venetians try not to take this personally, but it does put a strain on local–visitor relations and tax revenues for essential services like garbage collection and bridge maintenance. Your choice to stay for a night or more gives Venice a chance to show off its legendary hospitality, and lightens the burden for Venetians for all that upkeep.

Go with the slow flow Ask water-taxi drivers to go slower to avoid kicking up a wake to protect Venice's foundations, and gondoliers will sing your praises. If you take your sweet time getting around town on foot, you'll be more likely to discover Venetian artisans, *gelaterie* (ice-cream shops), and off-the-beaten-path *osterie* (pub-restaurants) that don't often benefit from tourism.

Pick up and pack out trash You'll be admired for recycling and tidying as you go through Venice – and when receptacles are scarce or full, pack out your trash.

Ask for acqua del rubinetto (tap water) Drinking tap water instead of bottled water helps spare the city the cost and effort of recycling some 20–60 million water bottles annually.

Spend time and money in local businesses You'll be assuring your Venetian hosts that all their effort to keep Venice afloat is worthwhile, and personally appreciated.

BACKGROUND

HISTORY

Imagine the audacity of people deciding to build a city of marble palaces on a lagoon. But not content with conquering the known world, Venice sailed mighty ships right off the map to establish new eastern trade routes. When the maritime empire passed its high-water mark, Venice refused to concede defeat on the world stage. Instead Venetians flooded the world with vivid painting in Venetian reds, baroque music and modern opera, independent thinkers, and parties without parallel. In its audacious thousand-year history, Venice has not only risen above sea level, but repeatedly risen to the occasion.

FROM SWAMP TO EMPIRE

A malarial swamp seems like a strange place to found an empire, unless you consider the circumstances: from the 5th to 8th century AD, Huns, Goths, and sundry other barbarians repeatedly sacked Roman Veneto towns along the Adriatic, and made murky wetlands off the coast seem comparatively hospitable. Celtic Veneti had lived in the area relatively peacefully since 1500 BC and had been Roman citizens since 49 BC, and were not in the habit of war. When Alaric led a Visigoth invasion through the province of Venetia in AD 402, many Veneti fled to marshy islands in the lagoon that stretches along the province's Adriatic coast. Some Veneti tentatively returned to the mainland when the Visigoths left, but after Attila, king of the Huns, attacked in 452, many refugees came to stay on the islands for good.

The nascent island communities elected tribunes and in 466 met in Grado, south of Aquileia, forming a loose federation. When Emperor Justinian claimed Italy's northeast coast for the Holy Roman Empire in 540, Venetia (roughly today's Veneto region) and the islands elected representatives to local Byzantine government in Ravenna, which reported to the central authority in Constantinople. But when warring French Lombards swept across the Po plains eastward in 568, Veneti refugees headed for the islands in unprecedented numbers, and the marsh began to look like a city. Thousands settled on the commercial centre of Torcello; others headed to the now submerged island of Malamocco, bucolic Chioggia, and the fishing and local trading centre of Rivoalto (colloquially known as Rialto).

Crafty Venetian settlers soon rose above their swampy circumstances, residing on land lifted above tides with wooden pylons driven into some 100 feet of soft silt. When the Byzantine grip slipped, Venice seized the moment: in 726 the people of Venice elected Orso Ipato as their *dux* (Latin for leader), or doge (duke) in Venetian dialect, the first of 118 elected Venetian dogi that would lead the city for more than 1000 years. Like some of his successors, Orso tried to turn his appointment into a hereditary monarchy. He was assassinated for overstepping his bounds; some later dogi with aspirations to absolute power were merely blinded. At first, no one was able to stay in the doge's hot seat for long: Orso's successor, Teodato,

top picks

BOOKS IN/ABOUT VENICE

- *Shakespeare in Venice* by Alberto Toso Fei – a captivating guide to the Venetian inspirations for Shakespeare's dramas, including *Othello* and *Merchant of Venice*.
- *The Passion* by Jeanette Winterson – Napoleon's cook pursues a card-dealing Venetian woman of mystery in this magic-realist fable.
- *History of Venice* by John Julius Norwich – massive, engrossing epic, if a bit long on naval battles and short on recent history.
- *Corto Maltese in Fables of Venice* – Italian comic-book legend Hugo Pratt's cosmopolitan sea captain cracks the mysteries of the *calli* (alleyways).
- *Wings of the Dove* by Henry James – a con man and sickly heiress meet in Venice, with predictable outcomes but gorgeous storytelling.

PIRATE BRIDES

Today the only pirates you're likely to spot in Venice are the ones selling knock-off Prada handbags at the Ponte dell'Accademia, but for centuries pirate ships prowled the waters around the Lido. In 944, a bevy of wealthy Venetian brides sparkling with golden dowries were sailing off into the sunset to weddings on the Lido when their boat was intercepted by pirates. The women were whisked off to a nearby harbour at Caorle, but Venetians in hot pursuit discovered the lair, slaughtered the pirates and delivered the rattled brides to weddings that must have seemed comparatively anticlimactic. The event was long commemorated with the annual Festa delle Marie (Feast of the Marys), in which Venice's 12 wealthiest families presented money for dowries to 12 poor but beautiful young women. Today the 'Marys' are remembered during Carnevale with a procession and a beauty pageant crowning the most beautiful of the 12 Marys.

managed to transfer the ducal seat to Malamocco in 742 before being deposed. Gradually the office of the doge was understood as an elected office, which was kept in check by two councillors and the Arengo (a popular assembly).

The Lombards had failed to conquer the lagoon, but the Franks were determined to succeed. When they invaded the lagoon, the Franks were surprised by capable resistance led by Agnello Partecipazio from Rivoalto, a shallow area of the lagoon virtually unnavigable by large seafaring vessels unless they knew how to navigate the maze of deep-water channels criss-crossing the lagoon basin. Partecipazio was elected doge in 809, and the cluster of islets around Rivoalto became the focus of community development. Land was drained, canals cleared, and Partecipazio built a fortress on what would later be the site of the Palazzo Ducale. The duchy launched commercial and naval fleets that would become the envy of the Adriatic, with Venetian ships trading as far away as Egypt.

THE STOLEN SAINT

Venice had all the makings of an independent trading centre – plenty of ports, a defensible position against Charlemagne and the Huns, leadership to settle the inevitable trade disputes – but no glorious shrine to mark Venice's place on the world map. So Venice did what any ambitious, God-fearing medieval city would do: it procured a patron saint. Under Byzantine rule, St Theodore (San Teodoro) had been the patron saint. But according to local legend, the evangelist St Mark (San Marco) had once visited the lagoon islands and been told by an angel that his body would rest there – and some Venetian merchants decided to make the prophecy come true.

In 828, Venetian smugglers stole St Mark's body from its resting place in Alexandria, Egypt, apparently hiding the holy corpse in a load of pork to deter inspection by Muslim customs officials. Venice summoned the best artisans from Byzantium and beyond to enshrine these relics in an official church of the doge that would impress visitors with the power and glory of Venice. The usual medieval construction setbacks of riots and fires thrice destroyed exterior mosaics and weakened the underlying structure. Occasionally higher purpose got clouded over in construction dust: St Mark's bones were misplaced twice. But even while the basilica was under construction, the winged lion of St Mark was adopted as the official emblem of the Venetian empire, symbolically setting Venice apart from Constantinople and claiming St Mark as the patron saint of an independent empire.

c 1500 BC	AD 726	828
Celtic Veneti tribes, possibly from Anatolia (in present-day Turkey), arrive in northeast Italy to inhabit the region now known as the Veneto.	Orso Ipato becomes the first elected Venetian doge. The Byzantines consider Ipato's election an act of rebellion, and if not actually behind it, are certainly not devastated by Ipato's assassination in 737.	According to legend, the corpse of St Mark the Evangelist is smuggled from Alexandria (Egypt) to Venice in a shipment of pork. St Mark is adopted as the patron saint of Venice.

DUTY & BOOTY

Once terra firma was established, Venice set about shoring up its business interests. When consummate diplomat Pietro Orseolo was elected doge in 991, he positioned Venice as a neutral party between the western Holy Roman Empire and eastern territories controlled by Constantinople, and won the medieval equivalent of most-favoured-nation status from both competing empires.

Even at the outset of the Crusades, Venice maintained its strategic neutrality, continuing to trade with Muslim leaders from Syria to Spain while its port served as the launching pad for crusaders bent on wresting the Holy Land from Muslim control. With rivals Genoa and Pisa vying to equip crusaders, Venice established the Arsenale shipyards in Castello that would become the greatest industrial site in medieval Europe. But while the Arsenale was quick to supply warships, La Serenissima (The Most Serene) preferred to remain above the fray, joining crusading naval operations only sporadically – and almost always in return for trade concessions.

Constantinople knew full well who was supplying the crusaders' ships, and in the wake of the First Crusade in 1095, Venice's relations with Byzantium were strained. Savvy Byzantine emperor Manuele Comnenus played on Venetian–Genoese rivalries, staging an 1171 assault on Constantinople's Genoese colony and blaming it on the Venetians, who were promptly clapped into irons. Venice sent a fleet to the rescue, but the crew contracted plague from stowaway rats, and the ships limped home without having fired a shot.

Meanwhile, Venice was under threat by land from Holy Roman Emperor Frederick Barbarossa's plans to force Italy and the Pope to recognise his authority. Back in 1154, Barbarossa's strategy must have seemed like an easy win: divide and conquer Italian city states long at odds with one another and frequently on the outs with the papacy. But after several strikes, Barbarossa discovered that northern Italy was a tough territory to control. When his army was struck by plague in 1167, Barbarossa was forced to withdraw to Pavia, only to discover that 15 Italian city states, including Venice, had formed the Lombard League against him. Barbarossa met with spectacular defeat, and when things couldn't get any worse, he was excommunicated. Venice quickly recognised that it could only handle being in the middle of one holy war at a time, and through nimble diplomatic manoeuvres, convinced Pope Alexander III and the repentant emperor to make peace in Venice in 1177.

But for fast talking, even the shrewdest Venetian merchant couldn't top Doge Enrico Dandolo. The doddering nonagenarian doge who'd lost his sight years before might initially have seemed like an easy mark to Franks seeking Venice's support in the Fourth Crusade. But Doge Dandolo drove a hard bargain: Venice would provide a fleet to carry 30,000 Crusaders, but not for less than 84,000 silver marks – approximately double the yearly income of the king of England at the time.

Only one-third of the proposed Frankish forces turned up in Venice the following year, and their leaders couldn't pay. But Venice had the ships ready, so as far as it was concerned, it had kept its side of the bargain. To cover the balance due, Doge Dandolo suggested the Crusaders might help Venice out with a few tasks of its own on the way to Palestine. This included invading Dalmatia and a detour to Constantinople in 1203 that would last a year, while Venetian and Frankish forces thoroughly pillaged the place.

Finally Doge Dandolo claimed that Constantinople had been suitably claimed for Christendom, and at age 96 declared himself 'Lord of a Quarter and a Half-Quarter of the Roman

1094	1171	1204
The Basilica di San Marco is consecrated. Capped with shimmering gold mosaic domes, the doge's spectacular 'Chiesa d'Oro' (Church of Gold) stands for the glory of Venice, St Mark and a brains trust of Mediterranean artisans.	After staging an attack on the Genoese in Constantinople and pointing the finger at Venice, Byzantium orders the arrest of all Venetians in the Byzantine Empire. A noticeable chill sets in over the Adriatic.	Doge Dandolo leads a Venetian fleet hired to take Frankish holy warriors to the Fourth Crusade on a detour to Constantinople, where Venetian-led armies massacre and pillage before heading back to Venice laden with booty.

TRENDSETTERS & TROUBLEMAKERS: VENETIANS WHO CHANGED HISTORY

Doge Marin Falier (1285–1355)

Claim to fame The hot-headed doge was in power for eight months. After a Venetian courtier apparently made a joke at his expense, the doge plotted to overthrow Venice's noble council. Details leaked out and he was arrested and beheaded within the hour. Legacy In the Palazzo Ducale's Sala del Maggior Consiglio, Doge Falier's portrait is blacked out, and his sarcophagus was emptied and used as a washbasin in Venice's public hospital. The thwarted coup justified consolidation of power by Venice's security service, the Consiglio dei Dieci (Council of Ten), which encouraged Venetians to spy on their neighbours.

Isotta Nogarola (c 1418–1466)

Claim to fame The Verona-born teenage prodigy corresponded in Latin with Renaissance philosophers and was widely published in Rome and Venice. An envious anonymous critic published attacks against women intellectuals, claiming 'an eloquent woman is never chaste' and accusing Nogarola of incest in 1439. Venetian scholars rose to Nogarola's defence, and she continued her correspondence with leading humanists. Legacy With Venetian diplomat Ludovico Foscarini, Nogarola published one of Europe's influential early feminist tracts: a 1453 dialog asserting that since Eve and Adam were jointly responsible for expulsion from Paradise, women and men must be equals.

Paolo Sarpi (1552–1623)

Claim to fame When the Pope excommunicated the republic of Venice in 1606 for ignoring Rome's rulings, Servite monk Paolo Sarpi defended Venice's 'God-given' right to govern its people. Under Sarpi's direction, Venice ordered churches to ignore the excommunication, and Venetian religious orders that failed to hold Mass were closed and had their property seized. The excommunication was lifted a year later. Legacy Six months after Rome recanted, five assassins stabbed Sarpi in Campo Santa Fosca and fled to papal territories. Sarpi survived, writing legal and scientific tracts for 13 more years. Venice raised a monument in Sarpi's honour on the site of the attempted assassination (see p153).

Sara Copia Sullam (1592–1641)

Claim to fame A leading Jewish intellectual involved with Venice's Accademia degli Incogniti literary salon, Sullam was admired for her poetry and spirited correspondence with a monk from Modena. A critic accused her of denying the immortality of the soul, a heresy punishable by death under the Inquisition. Sullam responded with a treatise on immortality written in two days; her manifesto became a bestseller. Legacy Sullam's writings remain in publication as key works of early modern Italian literature, and her work is credited with broadening public perceptions of Venice's Jewish community.

Daniele Manin (1804–1857)

Claim to fame After suggesting reforms to Austrian rulers, this young Venetian lawyer was arrested for treason. On 22 March 1848, fellow Venetians rescued him from jail to lead an insurrection. Manin was declared president of Venice, and for 17 months the republic survived Austrian bombardment, starvation and cholera. Manin negotiated favourable terms for surrender, with amnesty granted to all Venetians except himself. Legacy Manin was exiled to France, where he agitated for independent Italy. Manin did not live to see his dream fulfilled, but in 1868, his remains were returned to Venice for a state funeral. Today, Via Lunga XXII Marzo (March 22 St) commemorates the Venice uprising.

1271	c 1295	1297
Traders Nicolò and Matteo Polo set sail for Xanadu, the court of Kublai Khan, with Nicolò's 20-year-old son, Marco. The Polos make a fortune in the jewellery business in Asia.	Upon his return home to Venice, Marco Polo hits the real jackpot: memoirs. Critics claim Marco's tales are exaggerated, but that doesn't stop readers from enjoying them for the next 700-plus years.	Venice ends constitutional monarchy and closes the Grand Council, allowing only Venetians descended from noble families to participate in the new Assembly – until Venice runs low on funds, and allows merchants to buy noble titles.

Yet inside the red velvet cloak of its ruling elite, Venice was hiding an iron hand. Venice's shadowy secret service, the Consiglio dei Dieci (Council of Ten), thwarted conspiracies by deploying a host of James Bonds throughout Venice and major European capitals. Venice had no qualms about spying on its own citizens to ensure a balance of power, and trials, torture and executions were generally carried out in secret. Still, compared with its neighbours at the time, Venice remained a haven of tolerance.

Occasionally, the Council made examples of lawbreakers. Denunciations of wrongdoers were nailed to the door of the Palazzo Ducale and published by Venice's presses – and when that failed to convey the message, the Council of Ten ordered the bludgeoning or decapitation of those found guilty of crimes against the doge. Severed heads were placed atop columns outside the Palazzo Ducale and sundry parts distributed for display in the *sestieri* (neighbourhoods) for exactly three nights and four days, until they started to smell.

ALL SMILES, WITH BARED TEETH

As it turns out, overripe heads were the least of Venice's public health problems. Never mind that Venice sacked Constantinople, or that Constantinople sided with Genoa against Venice: warfare wasn't enough to deter the two maritime powers from doing brisk business with one another for centuries. When Constantinople fell to Ottoman rule in 1453, business with Venice carried on as usual. The rival powers seemed to understand one another very well; the Venetian language was widely spoken across the eastern Mediterranean.

There were some awkward moments in diplomatic relations, however. Both sides periodically took prisoners of war, and seldom released them. Prisoners were routinely forced into servitude and/or conversion. In 1428 Venice established a special prison in Dorsoduro to convert Muslim Turkish women prisoners to Christianity. Ottomans tended to hold Venetians for ransom, though it wasn't always an especially profitable gambit. Though Venice officially installed collection boxes in churches in 1586 to raise funds for POW ransom, they remained mostly empty.

After Suleiman the Magnificent took over Cyprus in 1571, Venice felt its maritime power slipping, and allied with the papal states, Spain and even archrival Genoa to keep the Ottoman sultan at bay. The same year a huge allied fleet (much of it provided by Venice) routed the Turks off Lepanto, in Greece, and Sebastiano Venier and his Venetian fleet sailed home with 100 Turkish women as war trophies.

Legend has it that when Turkish troops took over the island of Paros, the POWs included Cecilia Venier-Baffo, who was apparently the illegitimate daughter of Venice's noble Venier family, a niece of the doge, and possibly the cousin of Sebastiano (of Lepanto fame). Cecilia became the favourite wife of Sultan Salim II in Constantinople (now called Istanbul), and when he died in 1574 she took control as Sultana Nurbani (Princess of Light), mother and regent of Sultan Murad III and faithful pen pal of Queen Elizabeth I of Britain and Catherine de Medici of France. According to historian Alberto Toso Fei, the Sultana's policies were so favourable to Venetian interests that the Venetian senate set aside special funds to fulfil her wishes for Venetian specialities, from lapdogs to golden cushions. Genoa wasn't pleased by her favouritism, and in 1582 she was poisoned to death by what appears to have been Genoese assassins.

1508	1630	1678
The Holy Roman Empire, Papal States, Spain and France form the League of Cambrai against Venice – but with Venice cutting side deals, the Northern Italian map looks much the same after eight years of war.	The plague strikes again, killing about a third of the population within 16 months. With so few left to lead the city, the Assembly allows wealthy Venetians to buy their way into the Golden Book of nobles.	Venetian scholar Eleonora Lucrezia Corner Piscopia becomes the first woman to receive a university degree, earning the title Doctor of Philosophy at the University of Padua – and a plaque near Venice's city hall.

THE AGE OF DECADENCE

While Italy's city states continued to plot against one another, they were increasingly eclipsed by mega-merger-marriages cementing alliances among France, Henry VIII's England and the Habsburg Empire. As it lost ground to these European nation states and the seas to pirates and Ottomans, Venice took a different tack, and began conquering Europe by charm.

Venice's star attractions were its parties, music, art and women, not necessarily in that order. Nunneries in Venice held soirées to rival those in its *ridotti* (casinos), and Carnevale lasted up to three months. Claudio Monteverdi was hired as choir director of San Marco in 1613, introducing multipart harmonies and historical operas with crowd-pleasing tragicomic scenes. In Monteverdi's new modern style, opera caught on: by the end of the 17th century, Venice's opera season included as many as 30 different operas, including 10 brand-new operas composed for Venetian venues.

All of these new orchestras required musicians, but Venice came up with a ready answer: orphan girls. Circumstances conspired to produce an unprecedented number of Venetian orphans: on the one hand were plague and snake-oil cures, and on the other were scandalous masquerade parties and flourishing prostitution. Funds poured in from anonymous donors to support *ospedaletti*, or orphanages, and the great baroque composers Antonio Vivaldi and Domenico Cimarosa were hired to lead orphan orchestras (see the boxed text, p107). The Venetian state took on the care and musical training of the city's orphan girls, who in turn earned their keep by performing at public functions and *ospedaletti* fund-

PRINCE OF PLEASURE

Never was a hedonist born at a better time and in a more appropriate place. Eighteenth-century Venice had retired from the arduous business of running a maritime empire, and was well into its new career as the pleasure capital of Europe. Into this decadent demi-monde world, Giacomo Casanova was born in 1725. He was abandoned as a young boy, and became a gambler and rake on the make while studying law in Padua. He graduated by age 17 to take up a position with the church in Venice, but adventuring soon became Casanova's primary career, with minor sidelines in penning love letters for cardinals, looking good in a military uniform, and playing violin badly in an orchestra of drunkards. His charm won him warm welcomes into the homes of wealthy patrons – and the beds of their wives, lovers and daughters.

Venice was a licentious place, but some political limits still applied. Though Casanova's escapades may have been dangerous to marriages, his dalliances with Freemasonry and banned books were considered nothing less than a threat to the state. After an evening of foursomes with the French ambassador and a couple of nuns, Casanova was arrested on the nebulous charge of 'outrages against religion' and dragged to the Piombi, the Palazzo Ducale's dreaded attic prison. Sentenced to five years in a sweltering, flea-infested cell, Casanova complained bitterly, and carved an escape hatch through the wooden floor – but just when he was ready to make his getaway, a sympathetic warden had him moved to a more comfortable cell. But Casanova soon devised plan B: he escaped through the roof of his new cell, entered the palace, and casually breezed past the guards in the morning.

Casanova fled Venice to make his fortune in Paris and serve briefly as a French spy. But his extracurricular habits caused him no end of trouble: he went broke in Germany, survived a duel in Poland, fathered and abandoned several children (possibly including a child by one of his daughters), and contracted venereal diseases in England (despite occasional use of a linen condom prototype). Late in life, he returned to Venice as a celebrity, and served the government as a spy – but he was exiled for publishing a satire of the nobility. He wound up as a librarian in an isolated castle in Bohemia, where boredom drove him to finally write his memoirs. In the end, he concludes, 'I can say I have lived.'

1703–40	1718	1807
Antonio Vivaldi serves as the musical director at La Pietà, where he teaches and composes hundred of concerti for orchestras of orphan girls. He is fired in 1709 but swiftly recalled, to Venice's immense credit.	Venice and Austria sign the Treaty of Passarowitz with the Ottoman Empire, dividing up prime coastal territory among themselves, and leaving once-powerful Venice with only nominal control over the Dalmatian coast and a smattering of Ionian islands.	Napoleon suppresses religious orders in Venice to quell dissent. Yet dissent continues until Independence, when some churches are reconsecrated. Many remain abandoned today, serving as archives or tourist attractions instead.

raising galas. Visiting dignitaries treated to orphan concerts were well advised to tip the orphan performers: you never know whose illegitimate daughter you might be insulting otherwise.

Socialities began gifting snuffboxes and portraits painted by Venetian artists as fashionable tokens of their esteem, and salon habitués across Europe became accustomed to seeing mythological and biblical themes painted in sensuous Venetian styles, with the unmistakable city on the water as a backdrop. On baroque church ceilings across Venice, frescoed angels play heavenly music on lutes and trumpets – instruments officially banned from churches by Rome. Venetian art became incredibly daring with Titian and Veronese, bringing voluptuous colour and sly social commentary to familiar religious subjects.

Church authorities were not amused by Venetian antics. Rome repeatedly censured Venice for depicting holy subjects in an earthy, Venetian light, and playing toe-tapping tunes in churches – but such censorship was largely ignored within Venice. Finally, after Rome issued its umpteenth official reprimand of Venice, the Venetian state decided to do some paperwork of its own. Venice conducted an official 1767 audit of 11 million golden ducats in revenues rendered to Rome in the previous decade, and decided to cut its losses: 127 Veneto monasteries and convents were promptly closed, cutting the local clerical population in half and redirecting millions of ducats to Venice's coffers.

RED LIGHTS, WHITE WIDOWS & GREY AREAS

While Roman clerics furiously scribbled their disapproval, Venetian trends stealthily took over drawing rooms across the continent, and Grand Canal *palazzi* (palaces) and Veneto villas clustered around the River Brenta became playgrounds for Europe's upper crust.

Venetian women's lavish finery, staggering platform shoes up to 50cm high and masculine quiff hairdos scandalised visiting European nobility, until Venice felt obliged to enact sumptuary laws preventing women from adopting manly hairstyles and blinding displays of jewels on dipping décolletages. Venetian noblewomen complained to the doge and the Pope, and the restrictions were soon dropped.

With maritime trade revenues dipping and the value of the Venetian ducat slipping in the 16th century, Venice's fleshpots brought in far too much valuable foreign currency to be outlawed. Instead, Venice opted for regulation and taxation. Rather than baring all in the rough-and-ready streets around the Rialto, prostitutes could only display their wares from the waist up in windows, or sit bare-legged on windowsills. Venice decreed that to distinguish themselves from noblewomen who increasingly dressed like them, ladies of the night should ride in gondolas with red lights. By the end of the 16th century, the town was flush with some 12,000 registered prostitutes, creating a literal red-light district. Today red beacons mostly signal construction, but you can enjoy a decadent dinner at Antiche Carampane (Old Streetwalkers; see p185) near Ponte delle Tette (Tits Bridge).

Beyond red lights ringing the Rialto, 16th- to 18th-century visitors encountered broad grey areas in Venetian social mores. Far from being shunned by polite society, Venice's 'honest' courtesans became widely admired as poets, musicians and tastemakers (see the boxed text, p32). As free-spirited, financially independent Venetian women took lovers and accepted lavish gifts from admirers in the 16th to 18th centuries, there became a certain

1846	1848	1866
The first train crosses the new rail bridge from Venice to the mainland. The feat was bittersweet: churches were demolished for the station, trains brought more occupying Austrian troops, and Venetians footed the bill.	Daniele Manin leads an anti-Austrian rebellion and declares Venice a republic again for 17 months. The Austrians retake the city in 1849, and Venice remains under somewhat skittish Austrian control for the next 17 years.	Venice and the Veneto join the new Kingdom of Italy. The unification of Italy was nearly complete: Rome, the major obstacle to Italian unity, was made the capital of Italy in 1870.

VENICE'S 'HONEST COURTESANS'

High praise, high pay and even high honours: Venice's *cortigiane oneste* were no ordinary strumpets. An 'honest courtesan' earned the title not by offering a fair price, but by providing added value with style, education and wit that reflected well on her patrons. They were not always beautiful or young, but *cortigiane oneste* were expected to be well educated, the better to dazzle their admirers with poetry, music, philosophical insights and apt social critiques. In the 16th century, some Venetian families of limited means spared no expense on their daughters' educations: beyond an advantageous marriage or modest trade, educated women might aspire to become *cortigiane oneste*, commanding a price 60 times that of the average *cortigiana di lume* (literally, 'courtesan of the lamp', or streetwalker).

Far from hiding their trade in back alleys, a catalogue of 210 of Venice's '*piu honorate cortigiane*' (most honoured courtesans) was published in 1565, listing contact information and going rates, payable directly to the courtesan's servant, her mother, or occasionally her husband. A *cortigiana onesta* might circulate in Venetian society as the known mistress of one or more devoted admirers, who compensated her for the privilege of her company rather than services rendered, and with an allowance rather than pay per hour – though on rare occasion, an exceptionally clever Petrarchan sonnet might win her favours. Syphilis was an occupational hazard, and special hospices were founded for infirm courtesans.

One courtesan listed at the top of the pay scale in the 1565 catalogue was Veronica Franco (1546–91), the daughter of a *cortigiana onesta* who married a wealthy doctor and had a child as a teenager, but left her stormy marriage to become a courtesan by age 20. By age 30 Franco's exclusive patrons included King Henry III of France, and she'd published an acclaimed volume of her poetry. But when an outbreak of the plague forced Franco to flee the city in 1575, her home was looted, and she returned to the city two years later to provide for her six children and orphaned relatives only to face Inquisition accusations of witchcraft. Franco defended herself successfully, and went on to publish 50 of her letters (including two sonnets to Henry III) in 1580. With the proceeds, she established a charity for courtesans and their children.

fluidity surrounding the definition of a *cortigiana* (courtesan). Historians continue to debate the livelihood of Venetian intellectual Gaspara Stampa (c 1523–54), famed as a lute player, literary salon organiser, and author of published Petrarchan sonnets openly dedicated to her lovers. With their husbands at sea for months or years, Venice's 'white widows' took young, handsome *cicisbei* (manservants) to tend their needs. Not coincidentally, Venetian ladies occasionally fell into religious fervours entailing a trimester-long seclusion.

During winter masquerades and Carnevale, Venice's nobility regularly escaped the tedium of salons and official duties under masks and cloaks, generating enough gossip to last until the summer social season in Riviera Brenta villas provided fresh scandal. Some Venetians dropped the mask of propriety altogether, openly cohabiting with lovers year-round and acknowledging illegitimate heirs in their wills. By the 18th century, less than 40% of Venetian nobles bothered with the formality of marriage, and the regularity of Venetian annulments scandalised even visiting French courtiers.

REVOLTS

When Napoleon arrived in 1797, Venice had been reduced by plague and circumstances from 175,000 to fewer than 100,000 people, and its reputation as fierce partiers did nothing to prevent the French and Austrians from handing the city back and forth as a war trophy.

1895	1902	1918
Venice hosts its first Biennale to reassert Venice's role as global tastemaker. Other nations are eventually invited to participate, though initially with caution – a provocative Picasso is removed from the Spanish Pavilion in 1910.	The San Marco campanile (bell tower) suddenly collapses in a heap of bricks. Miraculously, the only casualty is the caretaker's cat. A replica of the tower is built by 1912; restorations continue, just in case.	Austro-Hungarian planes drop almost 300 bombs on Venice, but their aim is off, resulting in mercifully little loss of life or damage.

Venice declared its neutrality in the war between France and Austria, but that didn't deter Napoleon. Venetian warships managed to deter one French ship by the Lido, but when Napoleon made it clear he intended to destroy the city if it resisted, the Maggior Consiglio (Grand Council) decreed the end of the Republic. The doge doffed the signature cap of his office, claiming, 'I won't be needing this anymore.' Rioting citizens were incensed by such cowardice, but French forces soon ended the insurrection, and began the systematic plundering of the city.

Though Napoleon only controlled Venice sporadically for a total of about 11 years, the impact of his reign is still visible. Napoleon grabbed any Venetian art masterpiece that wasn't nailed down, and displaced religious orders to make room for museums and trophy galleries in the Gallerie dell'Accademia and Museo Correr. Napoleon's city planners lifted restrictions on the Jewish Ghetto, filled in canals and widened city streets to facilitate movement of troops and loot; his decorators established a taste for gaudy gold cornices and spare, whimsical grotesques. Napoleon lost control of Venice in 1814, and two years later one-quarter of Venice's population was destitute.

But Austria had grand plans for Venice, and expected impoverished Venetians to foot the bill. They were obliged to house Austrian soldiers, who spent off-duty hours carousing in the *campi* (squares) with bullfights and beer gardens and their new happy hour invention, the *spritz* (a *prosecco*-and-bitters cocktail). Finding their way back home afterwards was a challenge in Venetian *calli* (alleyways), so the Austrians implemented a street-numbering system. To bring in reinforcements and supplies, they dredged and deepened entrances to the lagoon for ease of shipping access and began a train bridge in 1841 – all with Venetian labour and special Venetian taxes. To make way for the new train station in 1846, *scuole*, convents, and a palace were demolished.

With no say in the Austrian puppet government running Venice, many Venetians voted with their feet: under the Austrians, the population fell from 138,000 to 99,000. When a young lawyer named Daniele Manin suggested reforms to Venice's puppet government in 1848, he was tossed in prison – sparking a popular uprising against the Austrians that would last 17 months (see the boxed text, p26). Austria responded by bombarding and blockading the city. In July, Austria began a 24-day artillery bombardment raining some 23,000 shells down on the city and its increasingly famished and cholera-stricken populace, until Manin finally managed to negotiate the surrender to Austria with a guarantee of no reprisals. Yet the indignity of Austria's suppression continued to fester, and when presented with the option in 1866, the people of Venice and the Veneto voted to join the new independent kingdom of Italy under King Vittorio Emanuele II.

LIFE DURING WARTIME

Glamorous Venice gradually took on a workaday aspect in the 19th century, with factories springing up on Giudecca and around Mestre and Padua, and textile industries setting up shop around Vicenza and Treviso. As an increasingly strategic industrial area, Venice began to seem like a port worth reclaiming. But when Austro-Hungarian forces advanced on Venice, they were confronted by Italy's navy marines. Two days after Italy declared war on Austria in 1915, air raids on the city began, and would continue intermittently throughout WWI until 1918. Venice was lucky: the bombardments caused little damage or loss of life.

1933	1948	1966
Mussolini opens the Ponte della Libertà (Freedom Bridge) from Mestre to Venice, creating another land link to the mainland. The 3.85km-long, two-lane highway remains the only access to Venice by car or bus.	American heiress Peggy Guggenheim arrives in Venice, an entourage of lap dogs and major modernists in tow. She revitalizes interest in Italian art post-war, reclaiming Futurism from the Fascists and championing Venetian abstract expressionism.	Record floods cause widespread damage and unleash debate on measures needed to protect Venice. Venice's admirers around the world rally to save the city, and rescue its treasures from the muck of the lagoon.

When Mussolini rose to power after WWI, he was determined to turn the Veneto into a modern industrial powerhouse and a model Fascist society – despite Venice's famously laissez-faire reputation. Mussolini constructed a roadway from the mainland to Venice, literally bringing the province into line with the rest of Italy. While Italy's largest Fascist rallies, with up to 300,000 participants, were held in the boulevards of Padua, Italian Resistance leaders met in Padua's parks to plot uprisings throughout northern Italy. When Mussolini's grip on the region began to weaken, partisans joined Allied troops to wrest Veneto from Fascist control.

Venice emerged relatively unscathed by Allied bombing campaigns that targeted mainland industrial sites, and was liberated by New Zealand troops in 1945 – but the mass deportation of Venice's historic Jewish population in 1943–44 shook Venice to its very moorings. When the Veneto began to rebound after the war, many Venetians left for the mainland, Milan and other postwar economic centres. The legendary lagoon city seemed mired in the mud, unable to reconcile its recent history with its past grandeur, and unsure of its future.

ACQUE ALTE

On 4 November 1966, disaster struck. Record floods poured into 16,000 Venetian homes in terrifying waves, and residents were stranded in the wreckage of 1400 years of civilisation. Venice's cosmopolitan nature was a saving grace: assistance from admirers poured in from Mexico to Australia, millionaires and pensioners alike, and Unesco coordinated some 27 private organisations to redress the ravages of the flood. Photographs of the era (available online at www.albumdivenezia.it) show Venetians drying ancient books one page at a time and gondolas gliding into bars for a *spritz,* served by bartenders in hip-high waders.

Venice's *acque alte* (high tides) bravado may be its saving grace. Today, with 60,000 official residents easily outnumbered by day trippers, Venetians may seem scarce in their own city. Yet despite dire predictions, Venice has not yet become a Carnavale-masked parody of itself or a lost Atlantis. The city remains relevant and realistic, continuing to produce new music, art and crafts even as it seeks sustainable solutions to rising water levels. Venice remains anchored not merely by ancient pylons, but by the people who put them there: the Venetians.

RECENT EVENTS

Look around: all those splendid palaces, paintings and churches were created by a handful of Venetians. In the city's entire history, there have only been about three million Venetians who can claim grandparents from Venice. With 60,000 official residents easily outnumbered by visitors on any given day, Venetians may seem like a rarity in their own city. The population has halved in size since 1848, and 25% of the population is aged over 65. But there are 2000 children still playing tag in Venice's *campi,* and local universities keep the city young and full of ideas. If you don't always encounter locals on the main thoroughfares, that's because Venetians prefer to *'andare per le fodere'* – 'go by the inner linings' of a city with some 3000 backstreets.

Despite its reputation, this is not just a city of the idle rich. Most Venetians live in flats, and 1000 Venetian palaces are now used as hotels and B&Bs. With modest means, Venetians pursue artisanal occupations that might sound esoteric: paper-marbling, glass-blowing, octopus fishing. But Venetians are constantly reinventing these traditions, and in tiny storefront studios you'll glimpse artisans turning paper into a purse, glass into jewellery, and baby octopi into brilliant

1996	2003	2006
La Fenice burns to the ground for the second time; two disgruntled electricians are eventually found guilty of arson. The city completes a €90 million replica of the 19th century opera house in 2003.	After decades of debate, Silvio Berlusconi officially launches the construction of Modulo Sperimentale Elettromeccanico (Mose), with the aim of preventing disastrous floods caused by rising sea levels. Completion is set for 2014.	François Pinault moves his world-class contemporary art collection to Palazzo Grassi galleries, redesigned by Tadao Ando. Pinault and Ando transform abandoned Punta della Dogana warehouses into gallery extensions in 2009.

NOALTRÌ VS VOALTRÌ (US VERSUS THEM)

The usual outside–insider dynamic doesn't quite wash in historically cosmopolitan Venice, whose excellent taste in imports ranges from Byzantine mosaics to the Venice International Film Festival. Bringing a world-class art collection with you is one way to fit in, as Peggy Guggenheim and François Pinault (owner of Palazzo Grassi and Punta Dogana) discovered. But you don't have to be a mogul to *Venexianàrse*, or 'become Venetian'. Of the 20 million visitors to Venice each year, only some three million stay overnight, and staying in a locally run B&B or inn is a chance to experience Venice among Venetians. You can eat like a Venetian, attempt a few words of Venet, or learn a Venetian craft. But the surest way to win over Venetians is to express curiosity about them and their city – so few rushed day trippers stop to make polite conversation that the attempt is received with surprise and appreciation. As you'll find out, those other 17 million visitors are missing out on excellent company.

cicheti (Venetian bar snacks). Resting on past glories would be easy, and topping them seems impossible, but as usual, Venetians are opting for the impossible.

Even as the city thinks ahead, preservation remains both a blessing and burden in Venice. Tax revenues are mostly routed to the federal government in Rome, so as Venetians are often quick to point out, revenues collected in Venice effectively subsidise public works in other parts of Italy rather than covering the considerable costs of upkeep in Venice proper. In 2007 the national government in Rome promised that extra finances and special planning for Venice would help meet the high costs of dealing with mass tourism, but with Italy's current economic crisis, Venetian officials are still waiting. International and nonprofit organisations have generously provided funds to keep Venice afloat, but often their grants are earmarked for high-visibility pet projects preserving Venice's monuments and masterpieces rather than on projects essential to Venice as a living city, such as public works maintenance or support for Venetian artisans.

To cover the costs of upkeep, Venice has taken some controversial measures. Recently, the city has raised public transport costs and relaxed some historic preservation rules. Chain stores are still banned from taking over the waterfront, but due to an apparent lapse in funding and judgment, the city allowed corporate sponsors and German ad agency Plakativ Media to drape palaces undergoing restoration with glaringly anachronistic ad banners. There may be more banners to come: in March 2007, Mayor Massimo Cacciari announced that he would seek sponsors to build a new bridge to replace the creaky timber Ponte dell'Accademia.

But ambitious city planners see an alternative to more banners: you. With an ever-expanding calendar of concerts, culinary courses, art openings and events, Venice hopes to attract more overnight visitors, whose hotel, restaurant and retail taxes lighten Venice's burden. Visitors who take the time to *Venexianàrse* (enjoy life as a Venetian; see the boxed text, above), may yet allow Venice to throw off the shroud of advertising and reveal its legendary charms.

THE FRAGILE LAGOON

With 400 bridges connecting 117 islets across more than 150 canals, Venice's natural setting is extraordinary – and extraordinarily fragile. The lagoon is a great shallow dish, criss-crossed by a series of navigable channels, where ocean tides meet the flow of freshwater streams from alpine rivers. Gazing across the lagoon to the distant horizon, the lagoon may look like an extension of the sea – but its delicate balance of salty and fresh water, *barene* (mud banks) and grassy marshes, solid ground and shifting sand support a unique aquaculture. White ibis perch on rock outcroppings, piles of lagoon crab are hauled in at the Pescaria, and the waters gleam an uncanny teal blue. Visitors often consider Venice to be a man-made marvel, but Venetians pass along the compliment to the lagoon, a wonder of nature that has sustained them for a millennium.

Life in the lagoon is protected by a slender arc of islands halting the Adriatic's advances. Interrupting this bulwark of narrow sandbanks strung north to south in a 50km arc between Punta Sabbioni and Chioggia are three *bocche di porto* (port entrances), which allow the Adriatic a way into the lagoon. Now that deep channels have been dug to accommodate tanker traffic to inland industries and cruise ships bound for Venice, the Adriatic has more routes to rush into the lagoon during seasonal *acque alte* (see below), when sirocco winds push ocean waves toward the Venetian gulf, or when *seiche* (long waves) gently unroll along the Adriatic coast.

You probably won't be sloshing through incoming seawater while you're in Venice – extremely high tides happen only about once in three to five years – but they're a threat to Venice all the same. The lagoon's salt content is rising, and corroding stone foundations. Gaping holes have appeared along waterside walkways, and the Punta della Dogana had to be shored up with injected cement. In 2003 work got under way to protect Piazza San Marco, one of the lowest spots in the city, raising the banks to 1.1m above mean sea level and repairing subterranean rainwater drains. Engineers estimate that, with the aid of technology, Venice may be able to withstand a 26cm to 60cm rise in water levels in the 21st century – great news, except that an intergovernmental panel on climate change recently forecasted increases as high as 88cm.

TO MOSE, OR NOT TO MOSE...

The hot topic of the last 30 years in Venice is a mobile flood barrier project known as Mose (Modulo Sperimentale Elettromeccanico, or Experimental Electromechanical Module). Currently in the works and with a planned completion date of 2014, these inflatable barriers 100ft high and 65ft wide are intended to seal the three entrances to Venice's lagoon whenever rising sea levels approach dangerous levels. The estimated cost is £1.5 billion for what is described even by its supporters as only a partial solution, since flooding is also caused by excessive rain, run-off and swollen inland rivers. But Mose proponents say the city must be saved at any cost, and ever since the great flood of 1966, many Unesco-affiliated agencies have been urgently concerned about the jewel box of a city containing the world's great art treasures.

But as many Venetians are quick to point out, the city is their home, not just a treasure chest, and any stopgap measure must be considered for its public impact. Would flood barriers fill the lagoon with stagnant water, creating public health risks and driving away tourists? Could Mose change local aquaculture, and end fishing on the lagoon? Will it delay solutions to underlying problems? The debate rages on as Mose construction gets under way.

Meanwhile, Venetians have made progress in preserving lagoon life. Industrial operations in Porto Marghera have been reduced over the years, and water is cleaner today than in the 1980s. The Venice city council has convinced most cruise lines to use fuel that emits less sulphur when

---

THE TIDE IS HIGH

Sirens in the calm of a winter's night don't send Venetians into bomb shelters or panics over alien invasions – though they might sport rubber boots at happy hour. The alarm from 16 sirens throughout the city is a warning that within three to four hours, *acque alte* (high tides), are expected to reach the city. The sirens aren't heard that often: water levels only reach 110cm above normal lagoon levels four to five times a year, usually in the rainy season between November and April. When the alarms do sound, it's not an emergency situation like a flood, but an expected seasonal tide that may only affect low-lying areas of the city, and usually subsides within hours.

The siren song of Venice's high tides is highly informative, if you listen closely. The tone indicates the anticipated maximum height the waters might reach above normal lagoon levels: one even tone means up to 110cm, two rising tones means up to 120cm, three rising tones means 130cm, and four rising tones means 140cm and up. A single blast might not even warrant a pause in happy-hour conversation, while the quadruple blast usually inspires shopkeepers to close up early, sliding low flood barriers into place at their doorsteps.

Even at peak high tide, Venetians are usually able to slosh through low areas of the city in boots and go about their business as usual. According to Venetian social etiquette, *acque alte* may be a valid excuse for tardiness and damp handshakes, but it's no excuse for breaking dates. Venice's official website (www.comune.venezia.it) shows areas where *passarelle* (elevated wooden walkways) are in use, and which areas of the city remain high and dry. When *acque alte* exceed 120cm, you might need *stivali di gomma* (Wellington boots or rubber boots). Adventurous visitors might don a pair and grab their cameras: the reflection of Venice's landmarks in spreading puddles can be peculiarly thrilling.

entering port to reduce degradation of stone buildings. Plans have been drawn up to convert inland industrial complexes into hi-tech parks, sustainable fisheries and wetland preserves.

TREADING LIGHTLY ON THE LAGOON

Given all the talk about Mose, and dramatic photos of *acque alte* flooding in the media, it may be surprising to hear that subsidence is a major environmental challenge to the lagoon. Pollution and silt have filled in areas of the shallow lagoon. With water levels dipping and the not-so-gentle slap of speeding motorboat wakes, Venice's ancient foundations are suddenly being exposed to the air – and rot. Algae takes root and takes over, threatening foundations and choking out other marine life. Since 1930 an estimated 20% of birdlife has disappeared, 80% of lagoon flora is gone, and lagoon water transparency has dropped 60%. The birds on their rocks, the plentiful crabs, the gleaming teal waters: all the distinctive features of Venice's remarkable setting are very much at risk.

Solutions aren't easy, but simple gestures are. See p21 for a few ways to make your visit more sustainable. Choosing to eat line-caught, rather than trawled, lagoon seafood and locally grown and organic (*biologico,* or *bio*) foods in Venice not only reduces your carbon footprint, it also provides critical support for sustainable fishing and farming practices that have kept this lagoon's aquaculture intact for a millennium. The things you already do at home to conserve water – using soaps and products without chemical detergents, reusing your linens, taking shorter showers – will make a real difference to the life of the lagoon.

To change Venice travel patterns for the greener, consider supporting Venetian restaurants, tour companies and businesses (see the GreenDex, p299): your vote of confidence rewards more thoughtful approaches, proving there is a growing demand for more responsible travel options in Venice, and raises spirits and standards in Venice. You can explore the lagoon without getting your feet wet at Punto Laguna (☎ 041 529 35 82; www.salve.it; Campo Santo Stefano, San Marco 2949; 🕑 2.30 5.30pm Mon Fri, closed Aug), with multimedia displays and initiatives to safeguard the future of this extraordinary ecosystem.

THE ARTS & ARCHITECTURE

THE ARTS

By the 13th century, Venice had already accomplished the impossible: building a maritime empire on a shallow lagoon, with palaces rising majestically from mud banks. Yet Venice's golden age of arts and architecture did not coincide with the peak of its powers. Brutal bouts of plague beginning in 1348–49 repeatedly decimated the city, new trade routes to the New World to the west bypassed Venice and its tax collectors, and the Ottoman Empire became a world power to the east by the middle of the 15th century. But when the empire could no longer prevail by wealth or force, Venice lived by its wits, making its reputation still greater with new forms of art, music, theatre and poetry. For all the effort La Serenissima had poured into shipbuilding and rivalries with Genoa and Constantinople, its final, definitive triumphs would not be on the battlefield or the high seas, but indoors in galleries, churches, libraries and concert halls.

VISUAL ARTS

The sheer number of masterpieces packed into Venice might make you wonder if there's something in the water here, but the reason may be more simple: historically, Venice tended not to starve its artists and architects. Rather than suffering for their art, many Venetian artists and architects did quite well by it. Multiyear commissions from wealthy private patrons, the city, and the Church gave them some sense of security. Artists were granted extraordinary opportunities to create new artwork without interference, with the city declining to enforce the edicts and censorship of the Inquisition.

If Venice's greatest talents faced a challenge, it wasn't that of disinterest or lack of ideas, but stiff competition. Instead of dying young, destitute and out of favour, painters such as Titian and Giovanni Bellini and architects including Jacopo Sansovino and Baldassare Longhena all survived into their 80s to produce late, great works. Especially in painting, this creative outpouring would lead to new innovations, styles so distinct that they would come to distinguish Venice from the rest of Italy, and Europe.

Early Venetian Painting

Once you've seen the mosaics at the Basilica di San Marco and Santa Maria Assunta in Torcello, you'll recognise some key aspects of early Venetian painting: wide eyes and serene expressions on larger-than-life religious figures floating on gold backgrounds or hovering above Gothic thrones. Byzantine influence can be seen in the *Madonna and Child with Two Votaries* painted c 1325 by Paolo Veneziano (c 1300–62) in the Gallerie dell'Accademia (p76): like stagehands parting theatre curtains, two angels pull back the edges of a starry red cloak to reveal a hulking Madonna and golden baby Jesus, as two tiny patrons kneel before her throne. But for all its similarities to Byzantine icons, this painting has some hallmarks of later Venetian painting: glowing colour, heightened drama, and every working artist's essential skill, the ability to flatter patrons without pandering too much.

By the early 15th century, Venice had a number of painters skilled in such otherworldly, International Gothic religious paintings, with Gentile da Fabriano, Pisanello, Jacobello del Fiore and Michele Giambono supplying paintings that reflected and complemented Venetian Gothic architecture. Meanwhile in Padua, the university was becoming a magnet for humanist philosophers from across Italy, and Florentine artists such as Donatello and Filippo Lippi found work in this forward-thinking city. Padua's Andrea Mantegna (1431–1506) took the new Florentine Renaissance rules of realism and perspective to extremes, showing bystanders in his biblical scenes reacting to unfolding miracles and martyrdoms with shock, anxiety, ambivalence, awe, anger, even inappropriate laughter (see also p247).

In Venice, painters were gently breaking with Byzantine convention. The *Madonna with Child* c 1455 by Jacopo Bellini (c 1396–1470) in the Accademia is an image any parent might relate to: the bright-eyed baby Jesus reaches one sandaled foot over the edge of the balcony, while an apparently sleep-deprived Mary patiently pulls him away from the ledge. Tuscan painter Gentile da Fabriano was in Venice as he was beginning his transition from the International Gothic style to Renaissance realism, and apparently influenced the young Murano-born painter Antonio Vivarini (c 1415–80), whose *Passion* polyptych in the Ca' d'Oro shows tremendous pathos. Antonio's brother, Bartolomeo Vivarini (c 1432–99), created an altarpiece in I Frari that shows a playful baby Jesus wriggling out of his mother's arms. Instead of floating among angels in a golden heaven, the Madonna is squarely seated on her marble Renaissance throne, with blue skies in the background.

Venice's Red-Hot Renaissance

Jacopo Bellini's sons Gentile (1429–1507) and Giovanni (c1430–1516) would nudge Venice into a Renaissance blaze of glory. Gentile's 1500 *Miracle of the Cross at the Bridge of San Lorenzo* at the Accademia shows a religious figure not high on a throne or adrift in the heavens, but floating in the Grand Canal, with crowds of bystanders stopped in their tracks in astonishment. In a work completed the same year in the Accademia, his brother Giovanni's *Annunciation* takes an entirely different approach to the canvas, using glowing reds and oranges to focus attention on the solitary figure of the kneeling Madonna in a marble-panelled room, with the angel arriving in a rush of rumpled drapery. Giovanni's luminous colour was a revelation achieved not in traditional tempera (pigment mixed with egg yolk and water), but with a new medium that would revolutionise Venetian painting: oil paints.

After centuries of artisan anonymity, Venice's painters came into their own during the Renaissance with signed works in highly individual styles. From Venice's guild of house painters emerged some of art history's greatest names, starting with Giovanni Bellini, who passed on his tremendous skills with human expression and dramatic colour to two rather apt pupils: Giorgione (1477–1510) and Titian (c 1488–1576), whose works can be compared in the Accademia. The two worked together on the frescoes that once covered the Fondaco dei Tedeschi (of which only a few fragments remain in the Ca' d'Oro, p74), with teenage Titian following Giorgione's lead. Giorgione was a Renaissance man who wrote poetry and music, is credited with inventing the easel, and preferred to paint from inspiration without sketching out his subject first, as in his enigmatic 1508 masterpiece *La Tempesta* (The Storm; Gallerie dell'Accademia p76). With its mysterious expressions and evocative landscape, this work shows the influence of another visitor to Venice c 1500: Leonardo da Vinci.

When Giorgione died at 33, probably of the plague, his collaborator Titian finished some of his works – but young Titian soon set himself apart with brushstrokes that brought his subjects to life, while increasingly taking on a life of their own. At the Chiesa di Santa Maria della Salute, you'll notice Titian started out a measured, methodical painter in his 1510 *St Marco Enthroned*, though his brushwork was already loose enough and vermillion-vibrant enough to add dynamism to a straightforward scene. After seeing Michelangelo's writhing, expressive *Last Judgment* Titian let it rip, and in his final 1576 *Pietà* his expressive urgency is palpable in paint smeared onto canvas with his bare hands.

But even for a man of many masterpieces, Titian's 1518 *Assunta* (Ascension) at I Frari is an astonishing accomplishment. Vittore Carpaccio (1460–1526) rivalled Titian's reds with his own sanguine hues – hence the dish of bloody beef cheekily named in his honour by Harry's Bar – but it was Titian's *Assunta* that cemented Venice's reputation for glorious colour. Titian has captured the instant when Madonna has risen beyond the grasp

top picks

VENETIAN PAINTINGS THAT CHANGED PAINTING

- *Feast in the House of Levi* (Veronese, Gallerie dell'Accademia, p76)
- *Assunta* (Titian, I Frari, p84)
- *Crucifixion* (Tintoretto, Scuola Grande di San Rocco, p85)
- *La Tempesta* (Giorgione, Gallerie dell'Accademia, p76)
- *Madonna with Child Between Saints Caterina and Maddalena* (Giovanni Bellini, Gallerie dell'Accademia, p76)

of the lowly mortals below, and angels are putting their backs into the final push. This altarpiece seems to fill the nave with the radiant warmth of the Madonna's red robes, and according to Venetian legend, her pale wrist revealed by a slipping sleeve has caused more than one priest to become too hot and bothered to pray in her presence.

Not Minding Their Manners: Venice's Mannerists

Although art history tends to insist on a division of labour between Venice and Florence – Venice had the colour, Florence the ideas – the Venetian School had plenty of ideas that repeatedly got it into trouble. Titian was a hard act to follow for impact, but he had fierce competition from Venice's Jacopo Robusti, aka Tintoretto (1518–94), and Paolo Caliari from Verona, known as Veronese (1528–88). Tintoretto earned key public commissions, but his lightning-bolt brushwork drawing out human drama even in religious scenes proved controversial. His subject matter was typically dictated by patrons – biblical scenes, mythical allegories, odes to the greats of Venice – but he made them new with Mannerist hallmarks: careful spotlighting, stormy backdrops, and vertigo-inducing perspective.

A crash course in Tintoretto begins at his preserved *bottega* (workshop) in Cannaregio (p152), and nips around the corner to Chiesa della Madonna dell'Orto, his parish church and the serene brick backdrop for his action-packed 1546 *Last Judgment* (p95). True-blue Venetian that he is, Tintoretto shows the final purge as a teal tidal wave, which lost souls are vainly trying to hold back, like human Mose barriers. A dive-bombing angel swoops in to save one last person – a riveting image Tintoretto reprised in the upper floor of the Scuola Grande di San Rocco (p85). Tintoretto spent some 15 years creating works for San Rocco, and his biblical scenes read like a modern graphic novel. Backdrops fade to black to capture the cataclysmic drama of Jesus's final days and the Black Death, with Tintoretto's streaky white rays of hope. Tintoretto sometimes used special effects to get his point across and, like other Venetian artists of the time, sometimes enhanced his colours with a widely available local material: finely crushed glass.

The colours of Veronese have a luminosity entirely their own, earning him ducal commissions, room to run riot inside Chiesa di San Sebastiano (p81) and shades of pink and green named in his honour – but his choice of subjects got him into trouble with some very important clients. When Veronese was commissioned to paint the *Last Supper*, his masterpiece ended up looking suspiciously like a Venetian dinner party, with apostles dressed like Venetians mingling freely with Turkish merchants, Jewish guests, serving wenches, dwarves, begging lapdogs and (most shocking of all) Protestant Germans. The Inquisition took none too kindly to this depiction of a sacred event in an earthy Venetian light, and demanded that Veronese change the painting. Veronese not only refused to remove the offending Germans, but altered scarcely a stroke of paint, simply changing the title to *Feast in the House of Levi*. In an early victory for freedom of expression, Venice stood by the decision, bringing to a head a centuries-long stand-off between Venice and the Church over high art and higher authority.

The next generation of Mannerists included Palma il Giovane (1544–1628), grandson of the noted painter from Cremona, Palma il Vecchio (1480–1528). Palma il Giovane finished Titian's final work, the *Pietà*, took a turn towards Tintoretto with brooding lighting and action-packed brushwork, and in his later years fused Titian's early naturalism with Tintoretto's drama. The Oratorio dei Crociferi (p97) is a showplace for his accomplishments. Another Titian acolyte who adopted Tintoretto's dramatic Mannerist lighting effects was Jacopo da Ponte (1517–92), aka Bassano because his family hailed from Bassano del

THE ULTIMATE PARTY PLANNING COMMITTEE

Venice party planners outdid themselves for the 1574 reception of young King Henry III of France. As he approached the city on a royal barge rowed by 400 oarsmen, glass-blowers blew molten glass on rafts alongside the ship for his entertainment (sure beats balloon animals). The king was greeted by a bevy of Venetian beauties dressed in white, and dripping family jewels into deep décolletages. Then came dinner: 1200 dishes, 300 bonbons, with flatware and napkins made of spun sugar. But the masterstroke was the all-star decorations committee of Palladio, Veronese and Tintoretto, who built and painted triumphal arches for the occasion. Try topping that at your next office party.

Grappa. Jacopo's father Francesco Bassano il Vecchio was a painter of some note whose four sons took up his trade with Mannerist verve, including Jacopo, Francesco Bassano il Giovane (c 1549–92), Leandro (1557–1622) and Gerolamo (1566–1621). Jacopo's work can be seen in the Gallerie dell'Accademia (p76), Chiesa di San Giorgio Maggiore (p114), and the Museo Civico (p246) in Bassano del Grappa.

top picks

VENICE VIEWS INDOORS

- *Procession in San Marco* (1496, Gentile Bellini; Gallerie dell'Accademia, p76)
- *Rio dei Mendicanti* (1723–24, Canaletto; Ca' Rezzonico, p80)
- *Piazza San Marco, Mass After the Victory* (1918, Emma Ciardi; Museo Correr, p69)
- *The San Marco Basin with San Giorgio and Giudecca* (1770–74, Francesco Guardi; Gallerie dell'Accademia, p76)
- *Rio dei Mendicanti with the Scuola di San Marco* (1738–40, Bernardo Bellotto; Gallerie dell'Accademia, p76)

Going for Baroque

By the 18th century, Venice had lived through plague, defended itself against Turkish invasion, and saw its world-domination ambitions dashed – but Venice was determined to make light of a dire situation, and its tragicomic tendency is captured in 18th-century arts. Pietro Longhi (1701–85) dispensed with the premise of lofty subject matter and painted wickedly witty Venetian social satires, while Giambattista Tiepolo (1696–1770) turned religious themes into a premise for dizzying ceilings covered with ročoco sunbursts – and the Ca' Rezzonico (p80) became a showplace for both their talents. An entire salon is dedicated to Pietro Longhi's drawing-room scenarios, including *The Morning Chocolate* (1775), which shows fashionable Venetians bingeing on trendy cocoa and doughnuts at the risk of popping waistcoat buttons, and upsetting a disapproving lapdog. Giambattista Tiepolo covered the Ca' Rezzonico's ceilings with shameless flattery, showing Ludovico Rezzonico and his bride surrounded by Fame, Wisdom, and Merit – but these trompe l'œil domes are so clever, colourful and overtly theatrical that it seems Tiepolo was gleefully showing off.

Instead of popes on thrones, portraitist Rosalba Carriera (1675–1757) captured her socialite sitters on snuff-boxes, and painted in a medium she pioneered: pastels. Her portraits at Ca' Rezzonico walk a fine line between Tiepolo's flattery and Longhi's satire, revealing her sitter's every quirk and wrinkle, but also sly smirks that make them look like the life of any 18th-century party. Her own late self-portrait in the Accademia is no more merciful, and no less revealing – the crows' feet around her eyes seem to call out their twinkle.

As the 18th-century party wound down, the Mannerists' brooding theatricality was merged with Tiepolo's pastel beauty by Tiepolo's son, Giandomenico (1727–1804). His early 1747–49 *Stations of the Cross* in the Chiesa di San Polo (p89) takes a dim view of humanity in light colours, illuminating the jeering faces of Jesus's tormenters. Giandomenico used a lighter touch working alongside his father on the frescoes at Villa Valmarana 'ai Nani' (p245) outside Vicenza, covering the walls with Chinese motifs, rural scenes and carnival characters.

EVERY ROOM WITH A VIEW: THE VEDUTISTI

Many Venetian artists turned their attention from the heavens to the local landscape in the 18th century, notably Antonio Canal, also known as Canaletto (1697–1768). He became the leading figure of the *vedutisti* (landscape artists) with minutely detailed *vedute* (views) of Venice that leave admiring viewers with vicarious hand cramps. Compare your snapshots of Venice to Canaletto's paintings, and you might be struck how closely Canalettos resemble actual photos – and in fact, Canaletto creating his works with the aid of a forerunner to the photographic camera, the *camera oscura* (camera obscura). Light entered this instrument and reflected the image on to a sheet of glass, which Canaletto then traced. After he had the outlines down, he could concentrate on filling in the details, from passers-by to lagoon algae exposed by fluctuating tides.

As Venice's fortunes waned, it increasingly relied on admirers to get by – and the works of the *vedutisti* sold well to Venice visitors as a kind of rich man's postcards. Canaletto was backed by the English collector John Smith, who lived most of his life in Venice and introduced the artist to a steady English clientele. Canaletto's success with foreigners was such that only a few of his paintings can be seen in Venice today, including one in the Gallerie dell'Accademia (p76) and a couple in Ca' Rezzonico (p80).

Canaletto's nephew Bernardo Bellotto (1721–80) also adopted the *camera oscura* in his painting process, though his landscapes are less photographic than expressionistic, with strong chiaroscuro (shadow and light) contrasts. A couple of his paintings hang in the Gallerie dell'Accademia, near work by another notable *vedutista*, Francesco Guardi (1712–93): *The San Marco Basin with San Giorgio and Giudecca*. Instead of focusing on details, Guardi opted for an impressionistic approach, capturing Venice's glories reflected in the lagoon. Among the last great *vedutisti* was Venetian Impressionist Emma Ciardi (1879–1933), who captured unfolding Venetian mysteries amid shimmering mists: with early morning fog lifting to reveal Carnevale revellers slinking off home. Her work is on view at the Ca' Rezzonico (p80) and Ca' Pesaro (p88).

Lucky Stiffs: Venetian Funerary Sculpture

Bookending Venice's accomplishments in painting are its masterpieces in sculpture, especially commemorative works. Venice kept its Gothic sculptors busy with more than 200 churches needing altars, the fire-prone Palazzo Ducale requiring near-constant rebuilding for some 300 years, and tombs required for dogi (dukes) and nobles whose diplomatic careers were cut short by advancing age, plague and intrigue. Sculptors were brought in to complete special commemorative commissions, such as the tombs of Doge Marco Corner in Zanipolo (p99) done by Nino Pisano (c 1300–68) from Pisa. Pisano's sprawling wall monument featuring the massive, serenely snoozing doge somewhat exaggerated the doge's career: Corner was doge for under three years.

Pisano's outsized accomplishment is upstaged by Pietro Lombardo (1435–1515) and his sons Tullio (1460–1532) and Antonio (1458–1516), who created tombs to several dogi in the same church. Elderly dogi often expired after only a couple years in Venice's hot seat, so the Lombardi were kept busy with heroic, classical monuments to Nicolo Marcello, doge for a year from 1473 to 1474, Pietro Mocenigo, who hung on as doge from 1474 to 1476, and Andrea Vendramin, doge from 1476 to 1478. This last monument was probably completed under the leadership of Tullio, who seems to have taken some short cuts to completing the vast, gilded marble tomb: he sculpted the figures in half-relief, and chopped away part of Pisano's Corner tomb to make room for Vendramin. Complex monuments meant to be viewed from afar weren't Tullio's strong suit: his particular talent was the ideal beauty of his faces, as you can see in his bust of a young male saint in the cloister at Chiesa di Santo Stefano (p71). This figure's limpid eyes, slightly parting lips and tumble of wavy hair from his upturned head are so arrestingly gorgeous, they are said to have inspired Titian's Madonna in his masterful *Assunta* in I Frari.

Thanks to some clever curation in the Santo Stefano cloister, the influence of Tullio Lombardo's beautiful boy can be even more clearly seen in the work of Antonio Canova (1757–1822), the most prominent sculptor to emerge from the Veneto. In the cloister you can see Canova's trial runs for his great relief intended for Titian's pyramid tomb at I Frari (Chiesa di Santa Maria Gloriosa dei Frari), which would become his own funerary monument. Mourners hang their heads and clutch onto one another in their grief, scarcely aware that their diaphanous garments are slipping off, and even the great winged lion of St Mark is curled up in grief at the entry of the tomb (p84). Don't let this work or his glistening Orpheus and Eurydice in the Museo Correr (p69) fool you: Canova's seamless perfection in glistening marble was achieved through diligent work and rough drafts modelled in gypsum. Canova's creative process can be seen at his studio, the Gipsoteca Canoviana (p235), outside his hometown of Possagno, Veneto.

Not Strictly Academic: Venetian Modernism

The arrival of Napoleon in 1797 was a disaster for Venice and its art. In the few years of his Kingdom of Italy (1806–14), Napoleon and his forces made short work of centuries of Venetian artistic accomplishments, knocking down churches for monument to the glory of the emperor and systematically plundering Venice and the region of its artistic treasures. Some works have been restored to Venice, including bronze horses that probably belong in Istanbul, since technically they were pilfered from Constantinople – but unless you want an earful, don't even get Venetians started on the mother lode of Venetian art that remains in the Louvre. Yet even under 19th-century occupation, Venice remained a highlight of the Grand Tour, and European and American notables flocked to the city to draw inspiration from its monuments – often literally, yielding memorable Venice cityscapes by visiting artists (see the boxed text, below).

After joining the newly unified Italy in 1866, Venice's signature contribution to the new nation's art history was Francesco Hayez (1791–1882). The Venetian painter paid his dues with society portraits and Venetian historical tableaux, but is best remembered for Romanticism and frank sexuality beginning with such audacious early works as *Rinaldo and Armida* (1814) in the Gallerie dell'Accademia.

Never shy about self-promotion, Venice held its first Biennale (Biennial International Art Exhibition; see p18) in 1895 as a promotional showcase to reassert Venice's role as global tastemaker, and provide an essential corrective to the brutality of the Industrial Revolution and decades under military occupation. A grand garden pavilion provided a self-promoting, studiously inoffensive take on Italy's latest artistic achievements – principally lovely ladies, pretty flowers, and lovely ladies wearing pretty flowers. Other nations were granted pavilions in 1907, but the Biennale retained strict control, and had a Picasso removed from the Spanish pavilion in 1910 so as not to shock the public with modernity.

But a backlash to Venetian conservatism arose from the ranks of Venetian painters, whose early experiments in modern styles were a reaction to what they saw as a stifling insistence on academic art. Shows of young artists backed by the Duchess Felicita Bevilaqua La Masa found a permanent home in 1902, when the Duchess gifted the Ca' Pesaro to the city (p88) as a modern art museum. A leader of the Ca' Pesaro crowd was Gino Rossi (1884–1947), whose brilliant blues and potent symbolism bring to mind Gauguin, Matisse and the Fauvists, and whose later work shifted toward Cubism. Often called the Venetian Van Gogh, Rossi spent many years in psychiatric institutions, where he finally died. Another important figure of the Ca' Pesaro group was sculptor Arturo Martini (1889–1947), whose works in Ca' Pesaro ranged from the rough-edged terracotta *Prostitute* c 1913 to a radically streamlined 1919 gesso bust.

TOP FIVE ARTISTS IN RESIDENCE

- Albrecht Dürer (1471–1528) left his native Nuremberg for Venice in 1494, hoping to see with his own eyes the startling Venetian experiments in perspective and colour that were becoming the talk of Europe. Giovanni Bellini took him under his wing, and once Dürer returned to Germany in 1495, he began his evolution from Gothic painter into Renaissance artist. By the time Dürer returned to Venice in 1505, he was feted as a visionary by the local German community.
- William Turner (1775–1851) was drawn to Venice three times (in 1819, 1833 and 1840), fascinated by the once-powerful merchant empire that, like his native England, had built its greatness on its command of the sea. Turner's hazy portraits of the city are studies in light at different times of day, capturing Venice's uninhibited spirit rather than its majestic skyline. As he explained to John Ruskin, 'atmosphere is my style'. Ruskin applauded the effort, but in London many critics loathed Turner's work.
- James Whistler (1834–1903) arrived in Venice in 1879, bankrupt and exhausted after a failed libel case brought against unrelenting art critic John Ruskin. The American painter rediscovered his verve and brush in prolific paintings of the lagoon city, returning to London in 1880 with a formidable portfolio that re-established him.
- John Singer Sargent (1856–1925) was a lifelong American admirer of Venice, starting with visits at a young age and becoming a part-time resident from 1880 to 1913. Sargent's intimate knowledge of the city shows in his paintings, which capture new angles on familiar panoramas and illuminate overlooked details on neglected monuments.
- Claude Monet (1840–1926) turned up in Venice in 1908, and immediately found Impressionist inspiration in architecture that seemed to dissolve into lagoon mists and shimmering waters. Major works by the French painter in Venice include paintings of Ca' Dario and San Giorgio Maggiore at dusk.

Future Perfect: From Futurism to Fluidity

Meanwhile across town, Filippo Tommaso Marinetti (1876–1944) threw packets of his manifesto from the Torre dell'Orologio in 1910 promoting a new vision for art and literature: futurism. In the days of the doge, Marinetti would have been accused of heresy for his declaration that Venice (a 'magnificent sore of the past') should be wiped out and replaced with a vigorous new industrial city to dominate the Adriatic. The futurists embraced the cultural catalysts of industry and technology and its muscular, streamlined look – a style that Mussolini co-opted in the 1930s for his vision of a monolithic, modern Italy. Futurism would continue to be conflated with Mussolini's brutal imposition of artificial order until it was championed in Venice by a heroine of the avant-garde and refugee from the Nazis, American expat art collector Peggy Guggenheim, who saw in futurism the radical fluidity and flux of modern life.

Venice had never been quick to conform to Rome's dictates on what constituted appropriate art, and artistic dissidents emerged to Mussolini's square-jawed, iron-willed aesthetics. Emilio Vedova (1919–2006) joined the *Corrente* movement of artists, who openly opposed Fascist trends in a magazine that was shut down by the Fascists in 1940. In the postwar years, Vedova veered towards the abstract. Some of his works can be seen in the Peggy Guggenheim Collection (p78) and the Galleria d'Arte Moderna at Ca' Pesaro (p89). Giovanni Pontini (1915–70) was a worker who painted in his downtime until 1947, when he took research trips around Europe to explore the works of Kokoshka, van Gogh and Roualt. You might glimpse these influences in his empathic paintings of fishermen at work and landscapes of ramshackle housing, painted with brushes loaded with expressionist emerald green and cobalt blue.

While Italy was at war with France, Venetian painter Giuseppe Santomaso (1907–1990) painted his way out of the classicist rigidity of Fascism with lyrical, unbounded abstract landscapes in deep teals and brilliant blues, inspired by modern French painters and his lagoon. After the war, Santomaso founded the Italian group Fronte Nuovo delle Arti (New Arts Front), increasingly drawing structural inspiration from Palladio and architectural silhouettes in pared-down, essentialist abstracts. Rigidity and liquidity became the twin fascinations of another avant-garde Italian artist, Bologna-born and Venice-trained Fabrizio Plessi (b 1940). This Unesco-acclaimed video artist and part-time Venice resident whose art evolved from 1970s Arte Povera (Poor Art) experiments in humble materials to multimedia installations featuring the humblest and most glorious material Venice has to offer: water. The signature fluidity that has characterised Venice and its art for centuries is now carrying it into the 21st century, with new art galleries in San Marco and Giudecca showing a range of landscapes, abstraction, video and installation art.

VENICE'S MINIMALIST MAKEUNDER

Paris is still burning with indignation over French billionaire François Pinault's decision to showcase his vast art collection not in the Parisian suburbs, but in Venice. In 2006 Pinault bought the Palazzo Grassi from the Fiat Group, and hired celebrated Japanese minimalist architect Tadao Ando to update the galleries to accommodate Pinault's personal contemporary art collection and ambitious reappraisals of art history. The results are startling and sensuous: Ando's stark partitions are capped with original frescoed ceilings and perfect halos of lighting, illuminating a past worth reconsidering and a future worth turning the next corner to find. For their next trick Ando and Pinault transformed Venice's customs warehouses at the Punta della Dogana into cutting-edge galleries for Pinault's contemporary collection. Ando flooded exposed-brick, wood-beamed warehouses with light through glass-sealed water gates and polished-concrete channels inspired by Carlo Scarpa's designs for Palazzo Querini-Stampalia. The creatively repurposed galleries were inaugurated in 2009 with an exploration of contemporary artists' working processes.

But there's more to these modern museums than stunning exhibition spaces and clever curation. At the Grassi, the 1st-floor cafe is actually an installation art piece that serves espresso, with conceptual decor reinvented by a contemporary artist to reflect each show's theme. The Grassi and Punta della Dogana have waterfront piers used as platforms for rotating sculpture installations, so gondola riders drifting down the Grand Canal might be startled by works like Charles Ray's 8ft *Boy with Frog*, or Subodh Gupta's *Very Hungry God*, a gigantic skull made entirely of aluminium cookware.

MUSIC

Over the centuries, Venetian musicians developed a reputation for playing music as though their lives depended on it, which at times wasn't that far from the truth. In its trade-empire heyday, La Serenissima had official musicians and distinct party music soundtracks, and the distinguished directorship of Flemish Adrian Willaert (1490–1562) for 35 years at the Capella Ducale. But when the city fell on hard times in the 17th to 18th century, it discovered its musical calling. With shrinking trade revenues, the state took the rather quixotic step of underwriting the musical education of orphan girls, and the investment yielded unfathomable returns.

top picks

HISTORIC PERFORMANCE VENUES

- Teatro La Fenice (p210) Opera in a blaze of glory.
- Interpreti Veneziani in Chiesa di San Vidal (p209) Baroque among masterpieces
- Musica a Palazzo in Palazzo Barbarigo-Minotto (p209) Arias in a rococo bedroom.
- Venice Chamber Music Orchestra at Ca' Rezzonico (p80) Classics in a Longhena palace.
- Collegium Ducale at Palazzo delle Prigioni (p209) Symphonies in prison.

Among the maestri hired to conduct these orchestras was one Antonio Vivaldi, who in the course of his 30-year tenure created works performed and sung by orphan girls, wrote hundreds of concerti, and popularised Venetian baroque music across Europe. Visitors spread word of extraordinary performances by orphan girls, and Venice's reputation for musical entertainment made the city a magnet for moneyed socialites. Today's televised talent searches can't compare to Venice's ability to discover talents like Claudio Monteverdi (1567–1643), who was named the musical director of the Basilica di San Marco and went on to launch modern opera.

Modern visitors to Venice can still see music and opera performed in much the same venues as in Vivaldi's day – *palazzi* (palaces), churches, and *ospedaletti* (orphanages) – sometimes with original 18th-century instruments. But rather than playing classical music or opera as period pieces, Venice's leading interpreters perform with verve and wit, keeping up their end of a musical conversation begun centuries ago.

Opera

No matter what's on the bill at La Fenice on any given night, there's bound to be drama. Before the doors open, the buzz begins at cafes around the piazza, where tousled artists and coiffed socialites gather to toss back *prosecco* (sparkling white wine) with an espresso chaser. Once inside, wraps are shed in lower-tier boxes to reveal Murano glass baubles, while in the cheap seats of the top-tier *loggie* (balconies), the *loggione* (opera critics) predict which singers will be in good voice, and which understudies may be due for a promotion. But when the overture begins, all voices hush, and the air turns electric with anticipation. No one wants to miss a note of a performance that could compare with historic premieres by Stravinsky, Rossini, Prokofiev, and Britten, and of course Giuseppe Verdi's *Rigoletto* and *La Traviata*.

Today, opera reverberates inside La Fenice and across town in churches, concert halls and *palazzi* – but until 1637 you would have been able to hear opera only by special invitation. Opera and most chamber music were the preserve of the nobility, and usually performed in private salons. The soundtrack for modern life would change when Venice threw open the doors of the first public opera houses. Between 1637 and 1700, some 358 operas were staged in 16 theatres to meet the musical demands of a population of 140,000. As the only composer with any experience in the genre, the elderly Monteverdi wrote the two stand-out operas of this era, *Il Ritorno di Ulisse al suo Paese* (The Return of Ulysses) and *L'Incoronazione di Poppea* (The Coronation of Poppea). In each, Monteverdi created an astonishing range of plot and subplot, with strong characterisation and powerful music, and the critical response couldn't have been better: he was buried with honours in I Frari.

Later composers diversified the local opera scene. A singer at the Basilica di San Marco under Monteverdi's direction, Pier Francesco Cavalli (1602–76) went on to become the outstanding Italian composer of opera of the 17th century, with 42 operas. With his frequent collaborator Carlo Goldoni (p50), Baldassare Galuppi (1706–84) applied a light touch to *opera buffa* (comic opera) favourites like *Il Filosofo di Campagna* (The Country Philosopher).

THE ARTS & ARCHITECTURE THE ARTS

LOCAL VOICE: DAVIDE AMADIO

Fish and art on Giudecca A couple of decades ago, Giudecca was mostly fishermen. Now you can find art shows, theatre, musicians – and still plenty of fish.

How baroque is like punk Baroque composers experienced all the same emotions we do – fear, passion, violence – back when people lived short, intense lives. We can play politely, or we can be true to the spirit of their work.

Jamming on a 1787 cello This instrument was made for Venetian churches, with their perfect humidity and generous acoustics. When we travel, the wood dries and contracts, and I have to adjust how I play to get the right sound.

Musical DNA I come from a family of musicians; my father [Gianni] plays double bass and my sister [Sonia] plays viola in Interpreti Veneziani. You know how some siblings look different from one another, but have similar gestures? We have different instruments and styles, but I've been told that when we play, somehow you can tell we're related.

Davide Amadia is an Interpreti Veneziani (p209) cellist with a rock-star following on YouTube.

Classical

Are you ready to baroque-n-roll? Venetian classical musicians are leading a revival of 'early music' from the medieval through Renaissance and baroque periods, with historically accurate arrangements played *con brio* (with verve) on period instruments. Audiences accustomed to thinking of classical works as soothing background music may be surprised by funky Renaissance dance tunes at Carnevale, and baroque solos banged out on a harpsichord like a piano break from Chuck Berry's 'Johnny B. Goode'.

The comparison is more apt than it might seem on paper. Venetian baroque was the rebel music of its day, openly defying edicts from Rome deciding which instruments could accompany sermons and what kinds of rhythms and melodies were suitable for moral uplift. Venetians kept right on playing stringed instruments in churches, singing along to bawdy *opera buffa* and capturing the full range of human experience in compositions that were both soulful and sensual. Modern misconceptions about baroque being a nice soundtrack to accompany wedding ceremonies are smashed by baroque 'early music' ensembles like Venice Baroque Opera, commanding international followings with original 18th-century instruments and fresh, shockingly contemporary interpretations.

Venice's best-loved composer is Antonio Vivaldi (1678–1741), who left a vast repertoire of some 500 concertos that established the three-movement concerto form while leaving room for virtuoso displays. Though his still-popular *Four Seasons* may be instantly recognisable from hotel lobbies and ringtones, you haven't heard summer-lightning strike and spring threaten to flood the room until you've heard Vivaldi played by Interpreti Veneziani (p209).

Look also for program featuring Venetian baroque composer Tomaso Albinoni (1671–1750), especially the exquisite *Sinfonie e Concerti a 5*. From scores for movies as diverse as *Gallipoli, Flashdance* and *The Doors,* you may recognise the *Adagio in G Minor* long attributed to Albinoni – though we now know it was written by his biographer in 1958. For a more avant-garde take on classical music, look for works by Bruno Maderna (1920–73) or Luigi Nono (1924–90). Also, consider the venue: any classical performance in the intimate Casa di Goldoni (p90), the Tiepolo-bedecked Ca' Rezzonico (p80), and the Ospedaletto (p107) will transport you to the 18th century in one movement, and catapult you into the 21st with the next.

Leggera (Pop)

Most of the music you'll hear booming out of water-taxis and *bacari* (old-style bars) is *musica leggera* (light music). This term covers homegrown rock, jazz, folk and hip-hop talents, as well as perpetrators of perniciously catchy dance tunes and pop ballads. The San Remo Music Festival (televised on RAI 1) annually honours Italy's best songs and mercifully weeds out the worst early on, unlike the wildly popular Italian version of *X Factor*.

Besides major Italian and international radio-play fare and the odd reality-show winner, Venice has an indie music scene in jazz, reggae and ska. The Venice Jazz Club (p209) offers improvised sessions and tribute nights, and you may luck into a performance by Venetian jazz saxophonist Pietro Tonolo or Venetian trumpeter/musicologist Massimo Donà. With an natural affinity for island music, Venice loves Jamaican reggae and local 'reggae-n-roll' band Ciuke e I Aquarasa, and skanks to local ska bands SkaJ – you might catch these and other bands and reggae DJs at Torino@Notte (p199). For reviews of live-music venues, see p208.

LITERATURE

Given its prime port position, Venice seemed predestined to become a shipping empire – but in surprising 15th-century plot twist, it also became a publishing empire. Johannes Gutenberg cranked out his first Bible with a movable-type press in 1455, and Venice became an early adopter of this cutting-edge technology. Venetian records show printing presses in operation as early as the 1470s, and soon thereafter, lawyers settling copyright claims. Venetian publishers printed not just religious texts, but histories, poetry, textbooks, plays, musical scores, pamphlets and manifestos.

One early Renaissance champion was Pietro Bembo (1470–1547), librarian, city historian, diplomat and poet, who in his *Rime* (Rhymes) and other works defined the concept of platonic love and gave lasting form to Italian grammar. Blame him if you must for the tricky Italian imperfect subjunctive tense, but Bembo must be praised for his collaboration with Aldo Manuzio on the invention that would revolutionise reading and democratise learning: the Aldine Press, which introduced italics and published paperbacks. Manuzio's family became the most important publishing dynasty in Europe, producing the first printed editions of many Latin and Greek classics and relatively cheap volumes of literature, including Dante's *La Divina Commedia* (The Divine Comedy). By 1500, nearly one in six books published in Europe was printed in Venice.

At a time when women were scarcely in print elsewhere in Europe, Venetian women became prolific and bestselling published authors in subjects ranging from mathematics to politics, and over 100 Venetian women authors from the 15th to 18th centuries remain in circulation today. Given the chance for an education in letters, girl prodigies emerged in Venice, including Eleonora Lucrezia Corner Piscopia, who became the first female university graduate in Europe in 1678 at the University of Padua. Among the luminaries of their era were the philosopher Isotta Nogarola (c 1418–66; see p26), musician and Petrarchan sonneteer Gaspara Stampa (1523–54) and poet and Jewish philosopher Sara Copia Sullam (1592–1641; see p26) who bested their critics and thwarted Inquisition inquiries to achieve immortality in print.

Poetry

The mother tongue of Venice isn't Italian or Venetian but poetry, the language of duels, politics and, of course, romance. Shakespeare may be known for his sonnets, but the Bard has competition for technical prowess from Petrarch (aka Francesco Petrarca; 1304–74), who added wow to Italian woo with his eponymous sonnets. Writing in Italian and Latin, Petrarch applied a strict structure of rhythm (14 lines, with two quatrains to describe a desire and a sestet to attain it) and rhyme (no more than five rhymes per sonnet) to romance the idealised Laura. He might have tried chocolates instead: Laura never returned the sentiment. Petrarch lived for years in Venice, but retired outside Padua in the rhyming town of Arquà Petrarca (p241), a literary pilgrimage site visited by the likes of Rilke, Byron and Mozart.

Posthumously, Petrarch became the darling of Venice's most esteemed *cortigiane oneste* (well-educated 'honest courtesans'). Among the acknowledged mistresses of the Petrarchan sonnet was Tullia d'Aragona, whose sharp-witted sonnets wooed men senseless: noblemen divulged state secrets, kings risked their thrones to beg her hand in marriage, and much ink was spilled in panegyric praise of her hooked nose.

Written with wit and recited with passion, a good poem might win you a free date with a high-end courtesan or get you killed, whichever happened first. Leonardo Giustinian (1388–1446) was a member of the Consiglio dei Dieci (Council of Ten) who spent his time off from spying on his neighbours writing poetry in elegant Venetian-inflected Italian, including *Canzonette* (Songs) and *Strambotti* (Ditties). One of Italy's greatest poets, Ugo Foscolo (1778–1827) studied in Padua and arrived in Venice as a teenager amid political upheavals.

top picks

BOOKS BY VENICE VISITORS

- **Watermark** (1993) Russian-born American Nobel Laureate Joseph Brodsky's 17-year fascination with Venice spills onto the page with meditations on night-time lagoon sounds and Venice's resident poet and Mussolini supporter, Ezra Pound.

- **Where Angels Fear to Tread** (1905) EM Forster's first published novel was a comedy of Anglo-Italian relations: a young English widow flits off on the Grand Tour, marries an Italian a dozen years younger (tut tut), dies tragically and leaves behind a young child being raised, much to the family's horror, as an Italian.

- **The Comfort of Strangers** (1981) Booker Prize winner Ian McEwan's tense, twisted bestseller focuses on a holidaying couple who accept the hospitality of a local couple, only to have the evening take a turn for the perverse.

- **Night Letters** (1997) In Robert Dessaix's story, a man just diagnosed with an incurable disease writes a letter every night for 20 nights en route from Zurich to Venice. Marco Polo and Casanova emerge, past and present collide, and fiction illuminates truth.

- **Death in Venice** (1912) Nobel Prize winner Thomas Mann tells a slow but enthralling tale of a German author holidaying on the Lido gripped by an impossible obsession, even as a mysterious epidemic strikes the city.

Young Foscolo threw in his literary lot with Napoleon in a 1797 ode to the general, hoping he would revive the Venetian Republic, and later even joined the French army. But Napoleon considered Foscolo a dangerous mind, and Foscolo ended his days in exile in London.

Not all Venetian poetry was so highbrow. Giorgio Baffo (1694–1768) was a friend of Casanova's whose risqué odes to the posterior might have affected his political career elsewhere – but in Venice, he became a state senator. For bawdy poetry in the Baffo tradition, don't look in libraries: head to any Venetian *osteria* (pub-restaurant), where by night's end cheap wine may well inspire raunchy rhymes sung in dialect.

Memoirs

Life on the lagoon has always been stranger than fiction, and Venetian memoirists have found a ready audience for possibly true tales as tall as the San Marco campanile. Venice-born Marco Polo (1254–1324) was a trader whose adventures across central Asia and Chine were captured in his c 1299 memoirs entitled *Il Milione,* as told to Rustichello da Pisa and written in French. The book achieved bestseller status even before the invention of the printing press, with each volume copied by hand. Some details seemed to have been embellished somewhat in its many European-language translations, but his tales of Kublai Khan's court are riveting reading. In a more recent account by a returned voyager, *Venezia, la Città Ritrovata* (Venice Rediscovered; 1998), engineer Paolo Barbaro captures reverse culture shock as he struggles to come to terms with the wintry lagoon city after several years' absence.

Memoirs with sex and a whiff of scandal sold well in Venice: 'honest courtesan' Veronica Franco (1546–91; see p32) kissed and told in her bestselling memoir, but for sheer braggadocio it's hard to top the memoirs of Casanova (1725–1798; see p30).

Francesco Gritti (1740–1811) parodied the decadent Venetian aristocracy in vicious, delicious dialect in *Poesie in Dialetto Veneziano* (Poetry in the Venetian Dialect) and satirised the Venetian fashion for memoirs with his exaggerated adventure novel *My Story: The Memoirs of Signor Tommasino Written by Him, a Narcotic Work by Dr. Pifpuf.*

Modern Fiction

Venice may not be the publishing empire it once was, but some Venetian authors have remained at the forefront of modern Italian fiction. The enduring quality of Camillo Boito's 1883 short story *Senso* (Sense), a twisted tale of love and betrayal in Austrian-occupied Venice, made it a prime subject for celebrated director Luchino Visconti in 1954. Mysterious Venice proved the ideal setting for Venice's resident expat American mystery novelist Donna Leon, whose inspector Guido Brunetti uncovers the shadowy subcultures of Venice, from island fishing communities (*A Sea of Troubles*) to environmental protestors (*Through a Glass Darkly*). Leon has not allowed her novels to be published in Italian, because she prefers to remain relatively anonymous in her adopted hometown. But the pride of Venice's literary scene is Tiziano Scarpa (b 1963), who earned the 2009 Strega Prize, Italy's top literary honour, for *Stabat Mater,* the story of an orphaned Venetian girl learning to play violin under Antonio Vivaldi.

FILM

Back in the 1980s, a Venice film archive found that the city had appeared in one form or another in 380,000 films – feature films, shorts, documentaries, you name it. But Venice's photogenic looks have proved a mixed blessing. This city is too distinctive to fade into the background, so the city tends to upstage its co-stars. Venice remains the most memorable part of many forgettable films, and more than holds its own in a few worthy flicks.

Since Casanova's escapades and a couple of Shakespearean dramas unfolded in Venice, the lagoon city was a natural choice of location for movie versions of these classic Venice stories. In the Casanova category, two excellent accounts of the legendary Lothario are Alexandre Volkoff's 1927 *Casanova* and Federico Fellini's 1977 *Casanova,* starring Donald Sutherland. Oliver Parker directed a 1995 version of *Othello,* but the definitive version remains Orson Welles' 1952 *Othello,* shot partly in Venice, but mostly on location in Morocco. Later adaptations of silver-screen classics haven't lived up to the original, including Michael Radford's 1994 *The Merchant of Venice* starring Al Pacino as Shylock, and Swedish director Lasse Hallström's 2005 *Casanova,* with a nonsensical plot but a charmingly rumpled and rakish Heath Ledger in the title role.

Some of the earliest movies set in Venice weren't actually shot in the city, but on Hollywood backlots by German directors who fled Hitler in the 1930s. Ernst Lubitsch's *Trouble in Paradise* (1932) takes odd Germanic Hollywood liberties with the lagoon city, showing a gondolier singing the Neapolitan song *O Sole Mio,* in a splendid voice that may sound familiar: the great Neapolitan tenor Enrico Caruso did the dubbing. Today, many Venetian gondoliers claim they'll sing anything – *Volare,* Elvis, U2 – just not that Neapolitan tune that's been haunting Venice since the 1930s.

After WWII, Hollywood came to Venice in search of romance, and the city delivered as the backdrop for Katherine Hepburn's midlife Italian love affair in David Lean's 1955 *Summertime.* Of all his films, Lean claimed this was his favourite, above *Lawrence of Arabia* and *Doctor Zhivago.* Gorgeous Venice set pieces compensated for some dubious singing in Woody Allen's musical romantic comedy *Everyone Says I Love You* (1996). But the most winsome Venetian romance is Silvio Soldini's *Pane e Tulipani* (Bread and Tulips; 1999), a tale of an Italian housewife who restarts her life as a woman of mystery in Venice, trying to dodge the detective-novel-reading plumber hot on her trail.

More often than not, though, romance seems to go horribly wrong in films set in Venice. It turns to obsession in *Morte a Venezia* (Death in Venice), Luchino Visconti's 1971 adaptation of the Thomas Mann novel, and again in *The Comfort of Strangers* (1990). Harold Pinter wrote the screenplay adaptation of Ian McEwan's novel, but director Paul Schrader turned it into an implausible film in which lovers Natasha Richardson and Rupert Everett inexplicably follow the ever-creepy Christopher Walken into shadowy Venetian alleyways. A better adaptation of a lesser novel, *The Wings of the Dove* (1997) was based on the Henry James novel and mostly shot in the UK, though you can scarcely notice behind Helena Bonham-Carter's hair.

Venice has done its best to shock moviegoers over the years, and did the trick with Nicolas Roeg's riveting *Don't Look Now* (1973) starring Donald Sutherland, Julie Christie, and Venice at its most ominous and depraved. *Dangerous Beauty* (1998) is raunchier but sillier, a missed opportunity to show 16th-century Venice through the eyes of a courtesan. Venice-born Tinto Brass has directed some pseudo skin-flicks against a Venetian backdrop that make you wish the actors would quit blocking your view, including *Monamour!* (2005), a title that combined French *mon amour* (my love) with Venetian *mona* (a reference to female genitals, with the double meaning of 'fool').

Always ready for action, Venice made appearances in *Indiana Jones and the Last Crusade* (1989) and the James Bond/Daniel Craig vehicle *Casino Royale* (2006), whose Grand Canal finale was shot in Venice with some help from CGI – no Gothic architecture was harmed in the making of that blockbuster. To see the latest big film to make a splash in Venice, don't miss the Venice International Film Festival (p19).

THEATRE & PERFORMING ARTS

Venice is a theatre, and whenever you arrive, you're just in time for a show. Sit on the major *campi* (squares), and the commedia dell'arte (archetypal improvisational comedy) commences, with its set of stock characters improvising variations on familiar themes: the tourists giddy from the novelty of *prosecco* at lunch, the kid with the pistachio gelato that falls off the cone, and the oblivious students smooching on a bench so as not to bother their roommates. *Opera buffa* unfolds in the *calli* (alleyways), as graduating students lurch toward another round of toasts at the next pub and neighbours hanging out laundry trade opinions on economic crises and last night's reality TV show. Along the Grand Canal, fairy-tale premises seem plausible, with cursed palaces and balconies set for romance and tragedy. Once you've seen Venice, you'll have a whole new appreciation for its theatrical innovations.

Commedia dell'Arte

During Carnevale, commedia dell'arte conventions take over, and all of Venice acts out with masks, extravagant costumes and exaggerated gestures. It may seem fantastical today, but for centuries, this was Italy's dominant form of theatre. Scholars attribute some of Molière's running gags and Shakespeare's romantic plots to the influence of commedia dell'arte – although Shakespeare would have been shocked to note that in Italy, women's parts were typically played by women. But if gags and rom-com plots tend to wear thin after a 90-minute film, it's no wonder that 18th-century Venice was beginning to tire of slapstick shtick and increasingly bawdy premises after a couple solid centuries of commedia dell'arte. Sophisticated improvisations had been reduced to farce and caricature, robbing the theatre of its subversive zing.

Comedy & Opera Buffa

Enter Carlo Goldoni (1707–93), a prolific jack-of-all-trades who was by turns a doctor's apprentice, a lawyer, and a librettist who attempted to write serious tragic opera, which was much in demand among nobility. But of his 160 plays and 80 or so libretti written under his own name or anagrams (eg Carlindo Grolo), he remains best loved for *opera buffa* and unmasked social satires that remain ripe and delicious: battles of the sexes, self-important socialites getting their comeuppance, and the impossibility of pleasing one's boss.

Goldoni was light-hearted, but by no means a lightweight; his comic genius would permanently change Italian theatre. Instead of flowery verse, Goldoni made the most of Italian prose and Venetian dialect with word games and double meanings. His *Pamela* (1750) was the first play to dispense with masks altogether, and his characters didn't fall into good or evil archetypes: everyone was flawed, often hilariously so. Some of his most winsome roles were reserved for women and *castrati* (male soprano countertenors), from his early 1735 adaptation of Apostolo Zeno's *Griselda* (based on Bocaccio's *Decameron*, with a score by Vivaldi) to his celebrated 1763 *Le Donne Vendicate* (Revenge of the Women). The princess Cecilia Mahony Giustiniani commissioned this latter work, in which two women show a preening chauvinist the error of his ways with lethally witty retorts and comparatively harmless co-ed swordplay. His comedies played with the cheap seats and the society set, each convinced that the other was being mocked.

top picks

FILMS IN/ABOUT VENICE

- **Pane e Tulipani** (Bread and Tulips) An AWOL housewife starts life anew in Venice.
- **Casanova** The Fellini version of the philanderer's life with Donald Sutherland, not Lasse Hallström's take (despite winsome Heath Ledger).
- **Don't Look Now** Julie Christie and Donald Sutherland's demons follow them to Venice in Nicolas Roeg's taut thriller.
- **Casino Royale** The action-packed finale takes Bond down the Grand Canal (don't worry, that palace survived).
- **Death in Venice** Visconti takes on Thomas Mann's story of a Mahleresque composer, an infatuation, and a deadly outbreak.

But one Venetian dramatist was not amused. Carlo Gozzi (1720–1806) believed that theatre should be fantastical and sublime, invitations to consider the impossible. Gozzi believed that Goldoni's Molière-influenced comedies of middle-class manners were prosaic, and staged a searing 1761 parody of Goldoni that was wildly popular – so much so that it drove Goldoni to France in disgust, never to return to Venice. Gozzi went on to minor success with his staging of fairy-tale scenarios, one of which would inspire the Puccini opera *Turandot*. But Gozzi's fantasias had little staying power, and eventually he turned to…comedy.

Meanwhile, Goldoni fell on hard times in France, after a pension granted to him by King Louis XVI upon his marriage to Marie Antoinette was revoked by the Revolution. He died impoverished, but not entirely forgotten: at his French colleagues' insistence, the French state granted his pension to his widow. While Gozzi's works are rarely staged, Goldoni continues to get top billing with regular stagings at the city's main theatre, the Teatro Goldoni (p210), along with Shakespeare's Venice set-pieces, *The Merchant of Venice* and *Othello*.

Contemporary Performing Arts

The modern performing arts scene is not all Goldoni and Shakespeare reruns. Avant-garde troupes and experimental theatres such as Teatro Junghans (p210) bring new plays, performance art and choreography to Venetian stages. Elements of commedia dell'arte ballet periodically enjoy revivals on the contemporary dance scene, and since 2003 contemporary dance has received a thorough workout during the Biennale arts and architecture extravaganzas with the Festival Internazionale di Danza Contemporanea (International Festival of Contemporary Dance; see p18). Dance is also championed by the Fondazione Giorgio Cini (p115), which periodically hosts performances and workshops on contemporary dance from around the world.

ARCHITECTURE

Lulls in Venetian happy-hour conversation are easily resolved with one innocent question: so what is Venetian architecture? Everyone has a pet period in Venice's chequered architectural history, and hardly anyone agrees which is Venice's defining moment. Ruskin waxed rhapsodic about Byzantine Gothic Basilica di San Marco and detested Palladio and his San Giorgio Maggiore; Palladians rebuffed rococo; fans of Ca' Rezzonico's regal rococo were scandalised by the Lido's bohemian Liberty style (*stile liberty*, the Italian version of art nouveau); and pretty much everyone was horrified by the inclinations of industry to strip Venice of its ornamentation.

After Giudecca's baroque buildings were torn down for factories and the Ferrovia (train station) was built, the city took decades to recover from the shock. Venice reverted to 19th-century *venezianità*, the tendency to tack on exaggerated Venetian elements from a range of periods – a Gothic trefoil arch here, a baroque cupola there. Rather than harmonising these disparate architectural elements, interiors were swagged in silk damask and mood-lit with Murano chandeliers. The resulting hodge-podge seemed to signal the end of Venice's architectural glory days. Then came the flood of 1966, and it seemed all of Venice's architectural patrimony would be lost. Architecture aficionados around the globe put aside their differences, and aided Venetians in bailing out *palazzi* and reinforcing foundations across the city.

Over the centuries, Venetian architecture has evolved into such a dazzling composite of materials, styles and influences that you might overlook its singular defining feature: it floats. Ornamental preferences aside, critics agree that Venice is a marvel of engineering. Thousands of wood pylons sunk into lagoon mud support stone foundations, built up with elegant brickwork and rustic ceiling beams, low *sotoportegi* (passageways) and lofty loggias, grand water gates and hidden *cortile* (courtyards). Instead of disguising or wallpapering over these essential Venetian structural elements, modern architects have begun highlighting them. With this approach, the Fondazione Giorgio Cini (p115) converted a naval academy into a gallery, and Tadao Ando turned Punta della Dogana (p81) customs houses into a contemporary art showplace. Venice's new-old architecture is as fresh and vital as ever.

TOP FIVE CONTROVERSIAL BRIDGES

- **Ponte di Calatrava** (p97) – officially known as Ponte della Costituzione (Constitution Bridge), Spanish architect Santiago Calatrava's modern bridge between Piazzale Roma and Ferrovia was commissioned for €4 million in 1999, and for a decade was variously denounced as unnecessary, flawed and wheelchair inaccessible. Since the construction received private backing by retailers hoping to open an upscale shopping mall in the old railway offices at the foot of the bridge, some Venetians refer to it as 'Benetton Bridge'. The bridge has cost almost triple the original estimate, but now that it's mostly complete, foot traffic is noticeably diverting over this minimalist arc of steel, glass and stone.

- **Ponte di Rialto** – the main bridge across the Grand Canal was disaster-prone for centuries: the original 1255 wooden structure burned during a 1310 revolt, and its replacement collapsed under spectators watching a 1444 wedding parade. The state couldn't gather funds for a 1551 stone bridge project which was pitched for by Palladio, Sansovino, or Michelangelo, and the task fell to Antonio da Ponte in 1588. Cost overruns were enormous: as the stonework settled, the bridge cracked, and legend has it that only a deal with the devil allowed da Ponte to finish by 1592. Architect Vincenzo Scamozzi sniffed that the structure was doomed, but da Ponte's bridge remains a diabolically clever masterpiece of engineering.

- **Ponte dei Pugni** (Bridge of the Fists) – turf battles were regularly fought on this pugnacious bridge between residents of Venice's north end, the Nicolotti, and its south end, the Castellani. Deadly brawls evolved into full-contact boxing matches, with starting footholds marked in the corners of the bridge (which was restored in 2005). It was all fun and games even after someone's eye was put out; bouts ended with fighters bloodied, bruised and bobbing in the canal. King Henry III of France apparently enjoyed the spectacle, but escalation into deadly knife fights in 1705 ended the practice, and today Venetians compete for neighbourhood bragging rights with regattas.

- **Ponte delle Tette** – 'Tits Bridge' got its name in the late 15th century, when neighbourhood prostitutes were encouraged to display their wares in the windows of buildings above the bridge instead of taking their marketing campaigns to the streets. According to local lore (and rather bizarre logic), this display was intended to curb a dramatic increase in sodomy. The bridge leads to Rio Terà delle Carampane, named after a noble family's house (Ca' Rampani) that became a notorious hangout for local streetwalkers (dubbed *carampane*).

- **Ponte dei Sospiri** (Bridge of Sighs) Built by Antonio Contino in 1600 and nicknamed by Lord Byron, the bridge connects the upper storeys of the Palazzo Ducale and Prigioni Nuove (New Prisons). According to Byron's conceit, doomed prisoners would sigh at their last glimpse of Venice through the bridge's windows – but as you'll notice on Palazzo Ducale tours, the lagoon is scarcely visible through the stonework-screened windows. Legend has it that couples kissing under the bridge will remain in love forever, but no doubt Venice's prisoners took a less romantic view of the construction.

VENETO-BYZANTINE

If Venice seems to have unfair aesthetic advantages, it did have an early start: cosmopolitan flair has made Venetian architecture a standout since the 7th century. While Venice proper was still a motley, muddy outpost of refugee settlements, the nearby island of Torcello was a booming Byzantine trade hub of 20,000. At its spiritual centre was the Cattedrale di Santa Maria Assunta (p120), which from afar looks like a Byzantine-style basilica on loan from Ravenna. But look closely: those 7th to 9th century apses have Romanesque arches, and the iconostasis separating the central nave from the presbytery is straight out of an Eastern Orthodox church. Back in Torcello's heyday, traders from France, Greece or Turkey could have stepped off their boats and into this church, and all felt at home.

But to signal to visitors that they had arrived in a powerful trading centre, Santa Maria Assunta glitters with 12th- to 13th-century golden mosaics. Recent excavations reveal Torcello glassworks dating from the 7th century, and those furnaces would have been kept glowing through the night to produce the thousands of tiny glass tesserae (tiles) needed to create the mesmerising Madonna with child keeping company with saints over the altar – not to mention the rather alarmingly detailed *Last Judgment* mosaic, with hellfire licking at the dancing feet of the damned.

When Venice made its definitive break with the Byzantine empire in the 9th century, it needed a landmark to set the city apart, and a platform to launch its golden age of maritime commerce. The Basilica di San Marco (p65) captures Venice's grand designs in five vast gold mosaic domes, refracting stray sunbeams like an indoor fireworks display – even today, the sight elicits audible gasps from crowds of international admirers. The Basilica began with a triple nave in the 9th century but, after a fire, two wings were added to form a Greek cross, in an idea borrowed from Church of the Holy Apostles in Constantinople. The East-meets-West style was the ideal showcase for Venice's position as the new powerhouse in the Adriatic. The finest artisans from around the Mediterranean were brought in to raise the Basilica's dazzle factor to mind-boggling, from 11th- to 13th-century marble relief masterpieces over the Romanesque entry arches to the intricate Islamic geometry of the 12th- to 13th-century inlaid semiprecious stone floors.

Since the basilica was the official chapel of the doge, every time Venice conquered new territory by commerce or force, the Basilica displayed the doge's share of the loot – hence the walls of polychrome marble pilfered from Egypt, and 2nd-century Roman bronze horses looted from Constantinople's hippodrome in 1204. The Basilica's ornament changed over the centuries with architectural tastes that swung from Gothic to Renaissance, but the message to visiting dignitaries remained the same: the glory above may be God's, but the power below rested with the doge.

ROMANESQUE

Romanesque was all the rage across Western Europe in the 9th century, from the Lombard plains to Tuscany, southern France to northeast Spain, and later, Germany and England. While the materials ranged from basic brick to elaborate marble, the rounded archways, barrel-vaulted ceilings, triple nave and calming cloisters came to define medieval church architecture. This austere, classical style was a deliberate reference to the Roman empire and early martyrs that sacrificed all for the Church, reminding the faithful of their own duty through the Crusades. But in case the architecture failed to send the message, sculptural reliefs were added, heralding heroism on entry portals and putting the fear of the devil into unbelievers with angels and demons carved into stone capitals in creepy crypts.

As Venice became a maritime empire in the 13th century, many of the city's smaller Byzantine and early Romanesque buildings were swept away to make room for International Gothic grandeur. The finest examples of Romanesque in the Veneto – and possibly in Northern Italy – are Verona's vast 12th- to 14th-century Basilica di San Zeno Maggiore (p247) and Padua's frescoed jewel of a Romanesque Baptistry (p238). Within Venice, you can admire Romanesque simplicity in the Chiesa di San Giacomo dell'Orio (p89) and its bell tower, or the pretty cloister at the Museo Diocesano d'Arte Sacra (p110).

VENETIAN GOTHIC

Soaring spires and flying buttresses rose above Paris in the 12th century, making the rest of Europe suddenly seem small and squat by comparison. Soon every European capital was trying to top Paris with Gothic marvels of their own, featuring deceptively delicate ribbed cross-vaulting that distributed the weight of stone walls and allowed openings for vast stained glass windows.

Europe's medieval superpowers used this grand international style to showcase their splendour and status – but Venice one-upped its neighbours not with height, but by inventing its own version of Gothic. Venice had been trading across the Mediterranean with partners from Lebanon to North Africa for centuries, and the constant exchange of building materials, engineering innovations and aesthetic ideals led to a creative cross-pollination in Western and Middle Eastern architecture. Instead of framing windows with the ordinary ogive (pointed) arch common to France and Germany, Venice added an elegantly tapered,

top picks

DIVINE ARCHITECTURAL EXPERIENCES

- Basilica di San Marco (p65) Mosaics.
- Chiesa di San Giorgio Maggiore (p114) Palladio's expansive, effortlessly uplifting interiors.
- Scuola Grande dei Carmini (p81) Longhena's stairway to heaven.
- Chiesa di Santa Maria dei Miracoli (p92) The Renaissance miracle in polychrome marble.
- Schola Spagnola (Spanish Synagogue) (p92) Lofty, elliptical women's gallery.

Moorish flourish to its arches, with a trilobate shape that became a signature of Venetian Gothic.

While Tuscany used marble for Gothic cathedrals like France and Germany, Venice showcased a more austere, cerebral style with clever brickwork and a Latin cross plan at I Frari (p84), completed in 1443 after a century's work, and Zanipolo (p99), consecrated in 1430. The more fanciful brick Madonna dell'Orto (p95) was built on 10th-century foundations, but its facade was lightened up with lacy white porphyry ornament in 1460–64. This play of white stone edging against red brick may have Middle Eastern origins: the style is pronounced in Yemen, where Venice's Marco Polo established trade relations in the 13th century.

Gothic architecture was so complicated and expensive that it was usually reserved for cathedrals in wealthy parishes – but Venice decided that if it was good enough for God, then it was good enough for the doge. A rare and extravagant secular Gothic construction, the Palazzo Ducale (p66) was built in grand Venetian Gothic style beginning in 1340, with refinements and extensions continuing through the 15th century. The palace was just finished when a fire swept through the building in 1577, leaving Venice with a tricky choice: rebuild in the original *gotico fiorito* (flamboyant Gothic) style, or go with the trendy new Renaissance style proposed by Palladio and his peers. The choice was Gothic, but instead of using brick, the facade was a puzzle work of white Istrian stone and pink Veronese marble with a lofty, lacy white loggia facing the Grand Canal. In 1853 critic and unabashed Gothic architecture partisan John Ruskin called the Palazzo Ducale the 'central building of the world'.

While the doge's palace is a show-stopper, many Venetian nobles weren't living too shabbily themselves by the 14th century – even stripped of its original gilding, the Ca' d'Oro (p96) is a Grand Canal highlight. The typical Venetian noble family's *palazzo* (palace) had a water gate that gave access from boats to a courtyard or ground floor, with the grand reception hall on the *piano nobile* (noble floor), usually the 1st floor. The *piano nobile* was built to impress, with light streaming through double-height loggia windows and balustraded balconies. The 2nd floor might also feature an elegant arcade topped with Venetian Gothic marble arches and trefoils, with decorative crenellation crowning the roofline.

RENAISSANCE

For centuries Gothic cathedrals soared into the skies, pointing the eye and aspirations heavenward – but as the Renaissance ushered in an era of reason and humanism, architecture became more easy to relate to and rational. Venice wasn't immediately sold on this radical new Tuscan

GREAT ARCHITECTURE, GRATIS

Free Walking Tour

Begin with a walkable world tour of modern architecture in the gardens of the Biennale (p104), from the Secessionist Austro-Hungarian Pavilion to the post-industrial South Korea Pavilion in a converted electrical plant. Next, stroll up the canalside boardwalk for splendid views of Chiesa di San Giorgio Maggiore (p114) to Basilica di San Marco (p65), and see priceless mosaics gratis. Exiting the Piazza San Marco to the west, follow the Calle Larga 22 Marzo designer-window-displays westward to Chiesa di Santo Stefano (p71), where you can wander through the Gothic portals to admire 15th-century Venetian boat-builders' craftsmanship in the vast *carena di nave* (ship's hull) ceiling.

Head northeast to Campo Manin, and duck into the courtyard of the Palazzo Contarini del Bovolo for a peek at a hidden Renaissance jewel, the Scala del Bovolo (p71) spiral staircase. Back on Campo Manin, head east to Campo San Luca, then jog north and east onto Calle del Teatro, which turns into Merceria 2 Aprile. Ignore the Rialto-bound crowds and head north across Campo san Bartolomeo across two small bridges, then swing right onto Salizada San Cancian. The fourth *calle* (alleyway) on your right leads to Campo San Maria Nova, where you'll spot the point of this pilgrimage: the multicoloured marble wonder of the Renaissance Chiesa di Santa Maria dei Miracoli (p92). Return to the Ponte di Rialto in time to see Antonio da Ponte's marble bridge awash in golden afternoon sunlight, then walk under the frescoed arcade of the Fabbriche Vecchia along Ruga degli Orefici. By now, you've earned your bargain-priced happy-hour *ombra* (glass of wine) and *cicheti* (traditional bar snacks) at nearby Al Mercà (p202), with tantalising glimpses of the Grand Canal just beyond Sansovino's Fabbriche Nuove. *Cin-cin* (bottoms up)– here's to Venetian architecture.

world view, but the revival of classical ideals gradually took root through Padua University and Venetian publishing houses.

With study of classical philosophy came a fresh appreciation for strict classical order, harmonious geometry and human-scale proportions. A prime early example in Venice is the 1489 Chiesa di Santa Maria dei Miracoli (p92), a small church and great achievement by sculptor-architect Pietro Lombardo (1435–1515), with his sons Tullio and Antonio. The exterior is a near-riot of wildly veined multicolour marbles, kept in check by a steady rhythm of Corinthian pilasters. The stark marble interiors set off a joyous profusion of finely worked sculpture, and the coffered ceiling is filled in with portraits of saints in contemporary Venetian dress: this is ecclesiastical architecture come down to earth, intimate and approachable.

Born in Florence and well-versed in classical architecture in Rome, Jacopo Sansovino (1486–1570) was a champion of the Renaissance as Venice's *proto* (official city architect) whose best works reveal not just a shift in aesthetics, but a sea change in thinking. While the Gothic ideal was a staggeringly tall spire topped by a cross, his Libreria Nazionale Marciana (p133) is an ideal Renaissance landmark: a low, flat-roofed monument to learning, topped by statues of great men. Great men are also the theme of Sansovino's Scala dei Giganti in the Palazzo Ducale (p66), a staircase reserved for Venetian dignitaries and unmistakable metaphorical reminder that in order to ascend to the heights of power, one must stand on the shoulders of giants.

Instead of striving for the skies, Renaissance architecture reached for the horizon. Sansovino changed the skyline of Venice with his work on 15 buildings, including the serenely splendid Chiesa di San Francesco della Vigna (p103), completed with a colonnaded facade by Palladio and sculptural flourishes by Pietro and Tullio Lombardo. But thankfully, one of Sansovino's most ambitious projects never came to fruition: his plan to turn Piazza San Marco into a Roman forum.

As the Renaissance swept into Venice, the changes became noticeable along the Grand Canal: pointed Gothic arcades relaxed into rounded archways, repeated geometric forms and serene order replaced Gothic trefoils, and palaces became anchored by bevelled blocks of rough-hewn, rusticated marble. One Grand Canal trendsetter was Bergamo-born Mauro Codussi (c 1440–1504), who first made his mark in Venice with the gracious Chiesa di San Michele (p117), but whose pleasing classical vocabulary translated just as easily to secular monuments and pleasure palaces. Codussi built the 15th-century Torre dell'Orologio (p71) and several stand-out *palazzi*, including Palazzo Vendramin-Calergi (p97) along the Grand Canal.

Michele Sanmicheli (1484–1559) was from Verona but, like Sansovino, he worked in Rome until the sack of that city in 1527 spurred him to flee to Venice. The Venetian Republic kept him busy engineering defence works for the city, including the Forte Sant'Andrea (see p122), also known as the Castello da Mar (Sea Castle). Even Sanmicheli's private commissions have an imposing imperial Roman grandeur; the Palazzo Grimani (built 1557–59), along the Grand Canal in San Marco, incorporates a triumphal arch on the ground floor, and feels more suited to its current use as the city's appeal court than a 16th-century pleasure palace.

As the baroque began to add flourishes and curlicues to basic Renaissance shapes, Padua-born Andrea Palladio (1508–80) carefully stripped them away, and in doing so laid the basis for modern architecture. His facades are an open-book study of classical architecture, with rigorously elemental geometry – a triangular pediment supported by round columns atop a rectangle of stairs – that lends an irresistible logic to the stunning exteriors of San Giorgio Maggiore and Redentore.

Critic John Ruskin detested Renaissance architecture in general and Palladio in particular, and ranted about San Giorgio Maggiore in his book *The Stones of Venice*: 'It is impossible to conceive a design more gross, more barbarous, more childish in conception, more servile in plagiarism, more insipid in result, more contemptible under every point of rational regard…The interior of the church is like a large assembly room, and would have been undeserving of a moment's attention, but that it contains some most precious pictures'. But don't take his word for it: Palladio's blinding white Istrian facades may seem stoic from afar, but up close they become personal, with billowing ceilings and easy grace that anticipated baroque and high modernism.

BAROQUE & NEOCLASSICAL

In other parts of Europe, baroque architecture seemed lightweight: an assemblage of frills and thrills, with no underlying Renaissance reason or gravitas. But baroque's buoyant spirits made perfect sense along the Grand Canal, where white stone party palaces bedecked with tiers of ornament looked like floating wedding cakes. Baldassare Longhena (1598–1682) stepped into the role as the city's official architect at a moment when the city was breathing a sigh of relief at surviving the Black Death, and Longhena provided the architectural antidote to Venice's dark days with the gleaming white dome of Chiesa di Santa Maria della Salute (p81).

Architectural historians chalk up this unusual octagonal dome to the influence of Roman shrines, Cabbala diagrams, and Palladio's soaring classical lines, but Longhena unleashes pure imagination on Santa Maria della Salute's exterior decoration, with exultant statues posing on the facade and reclining over the main entrance. The building has provided fodder for landscape artists from Turner to Monet, leading baroque-baiting Ruskin to concede that 'an architect trained in the worst schools, and utterly devoid of all meaning or purpose in his work may yet have such natural gift of massing and grouping as will render all his structures effective when seen from a distance'. Longhena's fanciful facade of giant sculptures at the Ospedaletto Ruskin deemed 'monstrous'; baroque fans will think otherwise. Longhena's marvel was Ca' Rezzonico, sunny salons built for the good life with spectacular Tiepolo ceilings.

Venice never lost track of Renaissance harmonies completely under all that ornament, and in the 18th century, bombastic neoclassicism came into vogue. Inspired by Palladio, Giorgio Massari (c 1686–1766) created the Chiesa dei Gesuati as high theatre (setting the stage for Tiepolo's trompe l'œil ceilings), built the gracious Palazzo Grassi with salons around a balustraded central light well, and brought to completion Longhena's Ca' Rezzonico on the Grand Canal.

Napoleon burst into Venice like a bully in 1797, ready to rearrange its face. The emperor's first order of architectural business was demolishing Sansovino's Chiesa di Geminiano to construct a monument in his own glory by Giovanni Antonio Selva (1753–1819), the Ala Napoleonica (see Museo Correr, p69). Napoleon had an entire district with four churches bulldozed to make way for the Giardini Pubblici (aka Biennale) and Via Garibaldi in Castello. Though Napoleon ruled Venice for only 11 years, French boulevards appeared where there were once churches across the city – Sant'Angelo, San Basilio, Santa Croce, Santa Maria Nova, Santa Marina, San Mattio, San Paterniano, San Severo, San Stin, Santa Ternita, San Vito and more disappeared under Napoleon.

THE 20TH CENTURY

After nearly a century dominated by French and Austrian influence, Venice was ready to let loose on the Lido with the easygoing elegance of *stile liberty*. Ironwork vegetation wound around balconies of seaside villas and wild fantasy took root at grand hotels, including Giovanni Sardi's 1898–1908 Byzantine-Moorish Excelsior and Guido Sullam's Hungaria Palace Hotel. Eclectic references to Japanese art, organic patterns from nature and past Venetian styles in *stile liberty* tiles, stained glass, ironwork and murals give Lido buildings cosmopolitan flair and bohemian decadence.

In the 1930s the Fascists arrived to lay down the law on the Lido, applying a strict, functional neoclassicism even to entertainment venues such as the 1937–38 Palazzo Della Mostra Del Cinema and former Casinò (now used for congresses). Fascist architecture makes occasional awkward appearances in central Venice too, notably the Hotel Bauer and the extension to the Hotel Danieli (p223), which represent an architectural oxymoron: the luxury Fascist-deco hotel.

The Biennale introduced new international architecture to Venice (see p104), but high modernism remained mostly an imported style until it was championed by Venice's own Carlo Scarpa (1906–78). In-

top picks

MODERN ARCHITECTURE LANDMARKS

- Biennale Pavilions (p104) High modernist pavilion architecture often steals the show at Art Biennales.
- Punta della Dogana (p81) Customs houses are creatively repurposed as a contemporary art showcase by Tadao Ando.
- Palazzo Querini Stampalia (p105) Carlo Scarpa and his one-time student Mario Botta add street-level smarts to this posh palace.
- Fondazione Giorgio Cini (p115) Former naval academy rocks the boat as an avant-garde art gallery.
- Palazzo Grassi (p71) Tadao Ando's minimalism rescues Massari's palace from neoclassical ornament overload.

stead of creating seamless modern surfaces, Scarpa frequently exposed underlying structural elements and added an unexpectedly poetic twist: water channels run through the floor, slabs of rough concrete are applied to walls as lovingly as marble, terraces are suspended mid-air like diving boards into the infinite. Scarpa's concrete-slab Venezuela Pavilion (p157) was ahead of its time by a full half-century and remains a star attraction even between Art Biennales, while high modernist architecture aficionados make pilgrimages outside of Venice to see Scarpa's Brioni Tomb (p234) near Asolo and Castelvecchio (p250) in Verona. Scarpa's smaller works can be spotted all over Venice: the cricket-shaped former ticket booth at the Biennale (p157), the entry and gardens of the Palazzo Querini Stampalia, and spare restorations to the Accademia.

CONTEMPORARY VENICE: WORKS IN PROGRESS

Preservationist impulses curbed some modern construction in Venice, but there's more modern architecture here than you might think: fully one-third of all buildings in Venice have been raised since 1919, though not without controversy. Among the modern architecture projects that never left the drawing board are a 1953 design for student housing on the Grand Canal by Frank Lloyd Wright, Le Corbusier's 1964 plans for a hospital in Cannaregio, and Luis Kahn's 1968 Palazzo dei Congressi project for the Giardini Pubblici. The decade-long Ponte di Calatrava furore (see boxed text, p52) overlapped with raging debates over the reconstruction of the Teatro Fenice after a 1996 arson – architecture critics lobbied for an avant-garde design by Gae Aulenti, but instead the city opted for a painstaking €90 million replica of the 19th-century opera house, completed in 2003.

But what's far more startling are the number of avant-garde projects that have been realised in Venice, given strict building codes and the challenges of construction with materials that have to be transported by boat, gingerly lifted by crane and hauled by handcart. With support from the city and financing from his own deep pockets, French luxury-goods magnate and art collector François Pinault hired Japanese minimalist architect Tadao Ando to repurpose two historic buildings into austere yet evocative galleries suitable for his contemporary art collection: Giorgio Masari's 1749 neoclassical Palazzo Grassi and the Dogana da Mar warehouses at the Punta della Dogana, built c 1675 and vacated in 2002 (see boxed text, p44).

Meanwhile, MIT-trained Italian architect Cino Zucci kicked off the creative revival of Giudecca in 1995 with his conversion of 19th-century brick factories and waterfront warehouses into art spaces and studio lofts. A triangular bunker-warehouse for bombs during WWII has been transformed into Teatro Junghans, inaugurated in 2005 as Venice's hotspot for experimental theatre, video art, and performance workshops (see p210). Ernest Wullekopf's 1896 Molino Stucky flour mill has been reincarnated as a megacomfort Hilton hotel, with a full-service spa and rooftop poolside bar (see p113).

New projects are cropping up in unlikely places around the lagoon. On the cemetery island of San Michele, David Chipperfield Architects are building extensions that will echo the firm's completed Courtyard of the Four Evangelists (see Cimitero, p117). Tronchetto is mostly an island of parking lots, but is due for a transformation with the arrival of the shiny new People Mover monorail system (p262). The historic Arsenale shipyards now house the Architecture Biennale, with a sleek new courtyard cafe and vast warehouses that once served as a medieval assembly line for galleys now used as interlinked galleries. Within Venice proper, the glam-rock-deco interiors of upscale Ca' Pisani kicked off a design hotel trend. Most recently, architect Alvin Grassi has refashioned the Grand Canal's Palazzo Barbarigo into a modern luxe hotel, creatively repurposing the ground-floor water-gate entry into a sleek deco watering-hole with a full-service bar (see p220).

In the years ahead, Venice will be a space to watch for contemporary architecture. On the Lido, plans for a brand-new conference and cinema complex to host the Venice International Film Festival is underway, since the current cinema is too small and – let's be honest – looks like a Fascist airport. Venice's other drab airport structure, Marco Polo Airport, will get a facelift and much-needed new marina as part of a planned Venice Gateway complex by starchitect Frank Gehry.

NEIGHBOURHOODS

top picks

- **Basilica di San Marco** (p65) A monument to the dazzling imagination of a singular city.
- **Gallerie dell'Accademia** (p76) Packed with plot twists, beauty and gore.
- **Palazzo Ducale** (p66) Pretty pink Gothic powerhouse behind the Venetian Republic.
- **I Frari** (p84) Stern Gothic cathedral lit up by Titian's *Assunta*.
- **Scuola Grande di San Rocco** (p85) Wall-to-wall Tintorettos.
- **Ca' Rezzonico** (p80) *Bea vita* (beautiful life) under Tiepolo skies.
- **Palazzo Grassi** (p71) Contemporary art meets baroque grandeur.
- **Biennale** (p104) International pavilions for modern art and architecture.
- **Burano** (p119) Vibrantly coloured houses cast hypnotic reflections in lagoon waters.
- **Torcello** (p120) Glimpse an ancient empire captured in shimmering mosaics.

What's your recommendation? www.lonelyplanet.com/venice

The winged lion of St Mark was once the universally recognised emblem of Venice, but these days the city is better known to most visitors by a different symbol: a yellow traffic sign reading 'Piazza San Marco', with an arrow pointed in two opposite directions. Almost anywhere you go in Venice you'll find these telltale signs helpfully pointing the routes to San Marco, bypassing a maze of *calli* (alleyways), *sotoportegi* (covered passageways) and canals. Here's the secret to any great Venetian adventure: *ignore those signs*. Plunge into Venice's labyrinth instead, and you'll discover the city behind the Grand Canal facades.

'Plunge into Venice's labyrinth…and you'll discover the city behind the Grand Canal facades'

Pity the cruise-ship crowds dropped off with two hours to take in Venice. That's about enough time for one long gasp at show-stopping Piazza San Marco, but not nearly enough to see what else Venice is hiding behind its Moorish Venetian Gothic portals. You can dine like a local in hidden *cortile* (courtyards), stay overnight in a *palazzo* (palace), and instead of being rudely awoken by an urban roar of gunning engines and blasting car horns, you'll be lulled by the gentle rhythms of this canal city – the splash of gondolier's oars, or the padding of Veronese spaniels over footbridges.

Impossible though it seems, Venice is built on 117 small islands connected by 400 bridges over more than 150 canals. Four *ponti* (bridges) cross the Grand Canal: Ponte di Calatrava, Ponte dei Scalzi, Ponte di Rialto and Ponte dell'Accademia. Since 1171, Venice has been divided into six *sestieri* (districts): Cannaregio, Castello and San Marco on the northeast side of the Grand Canal, and Dorsoduro, San Polo and Santa Croce on the opposite side. Although you can arrive by train, bus or car, the only ways to navigate the *sestieri* are on foot or by boat (see p259).

Yet island fever isn't a problem in Venice; the *sestieri* are different enough that you can just cross a couple of bridges or hop on a vaporetto to get a fresh perspective on the city. Overwhelmed with Byzantine glitz, Bellinis and shoe shopping in San Marco? Head to Santa Croce, where artisans work, wine comes straight from the cask, and talk revolves around boats and Berlusconi. If you hit church overload in San Polo, explore synagogues in Cannaregio instead. When the exacting handiwork of Venetian artisans leaves your brain boggled, Castello offers a vast swath of greenery to clear your head, and big, bold Biennale architecture on the horizon to refocus your long-distance vision. After a day on your feet shuttling from one monument to the next, Dorsoduro's Zattere waterfront lets you rest those museum legs along the Canale della Giudecca with a large bowl of gelato.

For the most dramatic change of pace, head for open waters and islands dotting the horizon. To the east, the 10km Lido di Venezia serves as a breakwater and beach getaway for Venice, and to the south Palladio's white marble edifices gleam from San Giorgio Maggiore and Giudecca. Once an island of exile for misbehaving Venetian nobles, Giudecca is now attracting admirers with galleries and affordable restaurants along the waterfront, experimental theatre in converted munitions warehouses, and swanky hotels in repurposed nunneries and factories. The Lido offers seaside leisure and star-quality style along generous stretches of sand and the breezy balconies of *stile liberty* (liberty style; Italian art nouveau) villas. When the Lido beachfront gets crowded with fashionistas in giant hats, there's more to explore on islands across the expanse of shallow waters of the Laguna Veneta to the north: red-hot blown glass in Murano, fresh fish and high-contrast decor schemes in Burano, and gold mosaic treasures in the wilderness of Torcello.

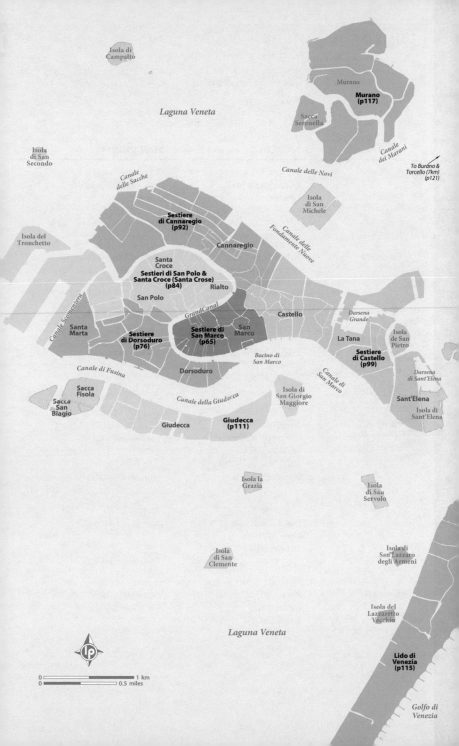

ITINERARY BUILDER

There are many ways to approach Venice, but more than in any other city, you'll be doing it on foot. This table provides some quick hints to main attractions, and tips on where to chill out, chow down and snap up Venetian finds.

AREA	ACTIVITIES	Sights	Shopping
	San Marco	Basilica di San Marco (p65) Palazzo Ducale (p66) Palazzo Grassi (p71)	Venetia Studium (p164) Antica Modisteria Giuliana Longo (p165) Millevini (p165)
	Dorsoduro	Gallerie dell'Accademia (p76) Peggy Guggenheim Collection (p78) Punta della Dogana (p81)	Marina e Susanna Sent p167) Madera (p167) Arras (p166) Drogheria Mascari (p170)
	San Polo & Santa Croce (Santa Crose)	I Frari (p84) Scuola Grande di San Rocco (p85) Ca' Pesaro (p88)	Cartè (p169) Gilberto Penzo (p168) De Rossi (p172)
	Cannaregio	Jewish Ghetto (p92) Chiesa della Madonna dell'Orto (p95) Chiesa di Santa Maria dei Miracoli (p92)	Gianni Basso (p172) Dolceamaro (p172) Giovanna Zanella (p174)
	Castello	Zanipolo (p99) Chiesa di San Francesco della Vigna (p103) Biennale (p104)	Banco 10 (p173) Sigfrido Cipolato (p173) Orovetro Murano (p175)
	Around the Lagoon	Murano (p117) Burano (p119) Torcello (p120)	Cesare Sent (p174) NasonMoretti (p175)

HOW TO USE THIS TABLE

The table below allows you to plan a day's worth of activities in any area of the city. Simply select which area you wish to explore, and then mix and match from the corresponding listings to build your day. The first item in each cell represents a well-known highlight of the area, while the other items are more off-the-beaten-track gems.

Eating	Drinking
Sangal (p181) Cavatappi (p181) I Rusteghi (p182)	Caffè Florian (p199) B Bar (p200) Aurora (p199)
Ristoteca Oniga (p183) Enoteca Ai Artisti (p183) Ristorante La Bitta (p183)	Cantinone Già Schiavi (p201) Il Caffè Rosso (p201) El Chioschetto (p201)
All'Arco (p188) Vecio Fritolin (p184) Antiche Carampane (p185)	Al Mercà (p202) Ai Postali (p202) Sacro e Profano (p203)
Osteria Alla Vedova (p190) Anice Stellato (p190) Taverna del Campiello Remer (p189)	Al Timon (p204) Ardidos (p204) Un Mondo di Vino (p204)
Met (p191) Trattoria Corte Sconta (p191) Il Ridotto (p192)	Bar Terazzo Daniele (p205) QCoffee Bar (p206) Paradiso (p206)
Al Gatto Nero (p195) I Figli delle Stelle (p194) La Favorita (p195)	Colony Bar (p206) Harry's Dolci (p206) Locanda Cipriani (p226)

GREATER VENICE

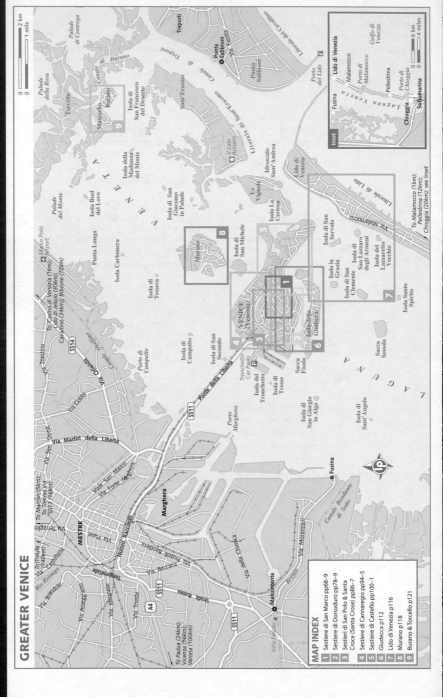

MAP INDEX

1	Sestiere di San Marco pp68–9
2	Sestiere di Dorsoduro pp78–9
3	Sestieri di San Polo & Santa Croce (Santa Crose) pp86–7
4	Sestiere di Cannaregio pp94–5
5	Sestiere di Castello pp100–1
6	Giudecca p112
7	Lido di Venezia p116
8	Murano p118
9	Burano & Torcello p121

SESTIERE DI SAN MARCO

Eating p181; Shopping p163; Sleeping p216

Today visitors to Venice arrive by train, bus and car in Piazzale Roma, but for centuries the point of embarkation was Piazza San Marco. And what an entrance it is: fronted with palaces, ringed with arcades, and capped with the golden domes of the Basilica di San Marco.

Once you recover from the unabashed glory of Piazza San Marco – it could take a few hours or decades – there's more to the *sestiere* to discover beyond its namesake square. For centuries merchants in Venice on official business headed directly from Piazza San Marco to the historic financial centre around the Rialto, but Venice didn't make it easy: the web of lanes known as the Marzarie (or Mercerie) is among the city's most labyrinthine, and remains full of tempting *bacari* (bars) and artisans working molten glass into shimmering dragonflies before your eyes. Major thoroughfares around Piazza San Marco are lined with brand-name distractions, including major designers along Calle Frezzaria and Calle Largo XXII Marzo – plus enough Carnevale-mask refrigerator magnets to cover a cruise ship.

But it would be unfair to dismiss San Marco as a tourist trap. Far from being a dusty museum piece, San Marco is packed with contemporary art galleries, buzzing cafes and *osterie* (pub-restaurants) that celebrate the end of the workday with *ombre* (glasses of wine) and impressive spreads of *cicheti* (traditional bar snacks) after the crowds clear out. And why deny yourself the pleasure of La Fenice, Palazzo Grassi and the Palazzo Ducale just to be contrary? Far from resting on their world-class reputations, San Marco's cultural landmarks are continuing to earn them, one gobsmacked visitor at a time.

The serpentine Grand Canal forms a spectacular natural southwestern boundary to San Marco. To the east San Marco is separated from Castello by the waterways of Rio di Palazzo della Paglia, which runs just behind the Palazzo Ducale and Basilica di San Marco. On the northeast side, San Marco is bordered by Rio di San Zulian, Rio della Fava and finally Rio del Fontego dei Tedeschi, which empties into the Grand Canal just north of the Ponte di Rialto. Vaporetti 1 and N stop along the Grand Canal at several stops along San Marco, including Rialto, Sant'Angelo, San Samuele, Santa Maria del Giglio and Vallaresso.

BASILICA DI SAN MARCO Map pp68–9

☎ 041 522 56 97; www.basilicasanmarco.it; Piazza San Marco; basilica admission free, Pala d'Oro/Loggia dei Cavalli & Museum/Treasury admission €2/3/2; ◷ 9.45am-5pm Mon-Sat, 2-4pm Sun & holidays; ⚓ Vallaresso, San Marco, San Zaccaria

Luminous angels trumpet the way into San Marco in glittering mosaics above vast portals. Inside, the soaring stone structure still sets standards for razzle-dazzle, from the intricate geometry of 12th-century polychrome marble floors to 11th- to 15th-century mosaic domes glittering with millions of gilt-glass tesserae (tiles).

This show-stopper took a brains trust of Mediterranean artisans almost 800 years and grand larceny to complete. Legend has it that Venetian merchants smuggled the corpse of St Mark out of Egypt in 828; the arrival of St Mark's body in Venice is depicted in mosaics dating from 1270 on the left of the facade. Riots and fires thrice destroyed exterior mosaics and weakened the basilica's underlying structure, so Jacopo Sansovino and other church architects grafted on supports and every precious marble available by purchase or pillage. Occasionally higher purpose got clouded over by construction dust: St Mark's bones were misplaced twice. Church authorities in Rome took a dim view of Venice's tendency to glorify itself and God in the same breath, but Venice finished San Marco in its own East-meets-West style: Eastern onion-bulb domes, a Greek cross layout, Gothic arches, and Egyptian porphyry walls.

The roped-off circuit of the church is free and takes about 15 minutes to walk. In niches flanking the main door as you enter the narthex (vestibule) are glittering Apostles with the Madonna, who looks stunning for her age: at more than 950 years old, these are the oldest mosaics in the basilica. Another medieval masterpiece is the Dome of Genesis, which depicts the separation of sky and water and angels with surprisingly abstract, conceptual motifs that anticipate modern art by 650 years. The golden central dome is the 13th-century Cupola of the Ascension, where you'll note angels swirling overhead and dreamy-eyed St Mark on the pendentive (dome support).

BASILICA DI SAN MARCO

0 ⸺ 30 m

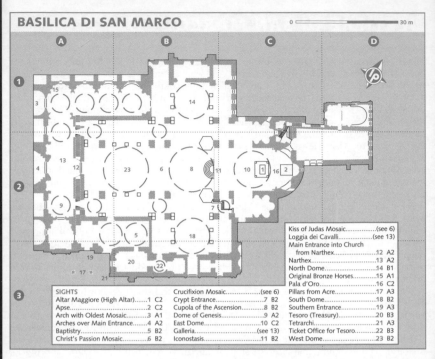

SIGHTS			
Altar Maggiore (High Altar)......1 C2	Crucifixion Mosaic.................(see 6)	Kiss of Judas Mosaic.................(see 6)	
Apse................................2 C2	Crypt Entrance......................7 B2	Loggia dei Cavalli.................(see 13)	
Arch with Oldest Mosaic..........3 A1	Cupola of the Ascension..........8 B2	Main Entrance to Church	
Arches over Main Entrance.......4 A2	Dome of Genesis....................9 A2	from Narthex......................12 A2	
Baptistry.............................5 B2	East Dome..........................10 C2	Narthex............................13 A2	
Christ's Passion Mosaic..........6 B2	Galleria.............................(see 13)	North Dome........................14 B1	
	Iconostasis.........................11 B2	Original Bronze Horses..........15 A1	
		Pala d'Oro.........................16 C2	
		Pillars from Acre.................17 A3	
		South Dome.......................18 B2	
		Southern Entrance..............19 A3	
		Tesoro (Treasury)................20 B3	
		Tetrarchi..........................21 A3	
		Ticket Office for Tesoro........22 B3	
		West Dome.......................23 B2	

Alabaster chalices, icons and other Crusades booty in the Tesoro (Treasury; admission €3; ☽ 9.45am-5pm Mon-Sat Apr-Oct, 9.45am-4pm Mon-Sat Nov-Mar, 2-4pm Sun & holidays) can't quite compare with the bejewelled Pala d'Oro (admission €2; ☽ 9.45am-5pm Mon-Sat Apr-Oct) altarpiece. Tucked behind the high altar that towers above St Mark's sarcophagus, this hidden treasure contains almost 2000 emeralds, amethysts, sapphires, rubies, pearls and other gemstones. More impressive still are the minuscule saints' portraits and lively biblical scenes in vibrant cloisonné, begun in Constantinople in 976 and elaborated by Venetian goldsmiths in 1209.

San Marco was officially the doge's (duke's) chapel until 1807, and the doge's far-reaching influence is highlighted by gilt bronze horses upstairs in the Galleria (Museo di San Marco; admission €4; ☽ same as basilica). Through the Galleria you can access the Loggia dei Cavalli, where reproductions of the bronze horses gallop off the balcony over Piazza San Marco. Note that you'll need to be dressed modestly (ie knees and shoulders covered) to enter the basilica, and large bags must be left around the corner off Piazzetta San Marco dei Leoni at Ateneo

di San Basso, where you'll find free one-hour baggage storage (☽ 9.30am-5.30pm daily).

PALAZZO DUCALE Map pp68–9

Ducal Palace; ☎ 041 271 59 11; www.museicivici veneziani.it; Piazzetta di San Marco 52; admission incl Museo Correr plus 1 civic museum of choice with/ without discount pass €8/13; ☽ 9am-7pm Apr-Oct, 9am-5pm Nov-Mar; ⚓ Vallaresso, San Marco
Don't be fooled by its Gothic elegance: this building was all business, from medieval carved stone capitals depicting key Venetian guilds along the arcade, to Giovanni and Bartolomeo Bon's 15th-century Porta della Carta (Paper Door), the bulletin board for government decrees facing the piazza. The building was damaged by fire in 1577, but Antonio da Ponte (who designed the Ponte di Rialto) restored it.

Entering through the colonnaded courtyard, you'll spot Sansovino's statues of Mars and Neptune flanking the Scala dei Giganti (Giants' Staircase), which Antonio Rizzo built as a suitably grand entrance for Venice's dignitaries and which is currently undergoing restoration. Climb the Scala dei Censori (Censors' Staircase) and Sansovino's lavish gilt stuccowork Scala d'Oro (Golden Staircase), and emerge into 3rd-floor rooms covered with gorgeous propaganda.

In the Sala delle Quattro Porte (Hall of the Four Doors), ambassadors awaited ducal audiences under a Palladio-designed ceiling frescoed by Tintoretto, showing Justice presenting sword and scales to Venice's Doge Girolamo Priuli. Other convincing shows of Venetian superiority include Titian's 1576 *Doge Antonio Grimani Kneeling before Faith* and Giambattista Tiepolo's 1740s *Venice Receiving Gifts of the Sea from Neptune*, where Venice is a gorgeous blonde casually leaning on a lion. Special delegations waited in the Anticollegio (College Antechamber), where Tintoretto drew not-so-subtle parallels between Roman gods and Venetian government: *Vulcan and Cyclops Forging Weapons for Venice, Mercury and the Three Graces* rewarding Venice's industriousness with beauty, and *Minerva Dismissing Mars* in a Venetian triumph of savvy over brute force. Also in the room is a vivid reminder of diplomatic behaviour to avoid: Paolo Veronese's *Rape of Europe*.

Few were granted audience in the Palladio-designed Collegio (Council Room), with Veronese's quintessentially rosy view of Venice in his 1578–82 *Virtues of the Republic* ceiling panels. Tintoretto attempted similar flattery in *The Triumph of Venice* on the ceiling of the adjoining Senato (Senate Hall), but his dark palette hints at the shadowy side of Venetian politics. The Trial Chambers of the Council of Ten features Veronese's positively glowing ceiling panel of *Juno Bestowing her Gifts on Venice*, while in the dark, carved-wood corner is a slot where accusations of treason were slipped to Venice's dreaded secret service.

On the 2nd floor, the cavernous 1419 Sala del Maggior Consiglio (Grand Council Hall) features the doge's throne with a 22m-by-7m backdrop of *Paradise* by Tintoretto's son Domenico that's more politically correct than pretty: heaven is crammed with 500 prominent Venetians, including several Tintoretto patrons. Veronese's political posturing is more elegant in his oval ceiling panel *The Apotheosis of Venice*, where gods marvel at Venice's coronation by angels, with foreign dignitaries and Venetian blondes rubbernecking from the balcony below.

Only the Itinerari Segreti access the Council of Ten headquarters and Piombi attic prison (see the boxed text, below), but visitors can take a detour on the doges' dark side down the hall from the Sala del Maggior Consiglio. Stop by the chamber featuring ominous scenes by the master of apocalyptic visions, Hieronymus Bosch, then follow the path of condemned prisoners across the covered Ponte dei Sospiri (Bridge of Sighs) to Venice's 16th-century Prigioni Nuove (New Prisons), with dank cells covered with graffitied protestations of innocence.

TEATRO LA FENICE Map pp68–9

☎ 041 78 65 11, reservations 041 24 24; www .teatrolafenice.it; Campo San Fantin 1965; tours adult/student & senior €7/5; ☼ vary; ⚓ Santa Maria del Giglio

Venice ushered in the age of opera in the 17th century, hiring as San Marco choirmaster Claudio Monteverdi, the father of modern opera, and opening La Fenice (literally, 'The Phoenix') opera house to much fanfare in 1792 (for more information, see p45 and p138). In the 19th century, Venice's great families were largely ruined and could not afford heating in their enormous *palazzi* (palaces or mansions), so La Fenice served as a members-only club where, in winter especially, they would spend

STATE SECRETS REVEALED: ITINERARI SEGRETI

The Palazzo Ducale's darkest secrets can be found through a passageway disguised as a filing cabinet in the Sala del Consiglio dei Dieci (Chamber of the Council of Ten), festooned with happy cherubim and Veronese's optimistic *Triumph of Virtue over Vice*. Fascinating 1½-hour Itinerari Segreti (Secret Tours; ☎ 041 520 90 70; adult/student/under 6yr €16/7/free; ☼ tours in English 9.55am, 10.45am & 11.35am, Italian 9.30am & 11.10am, French 10.20am, noon & 12.25pm) guide visitors into the cramped, unadorned Council of Ten headquarters, upstairs to a trial chamber lined with top-secret files, and into a windowless room with a single rope, used in perversely imaginative ways to extract information. Purchase tickets where you enter the Palazzo Ducale. To Venice's credit, the room was largely disused by the 17th century – but the same cannot be said for the studded cells of the Piombi, Venice's notorious attic prison. In 1756, Casanova was condemned to five years' confinement here on charges of corrupting nuns, and a more serious suspicion of spreading Freemasonry – but after a matter of months, he slipped past the guards.

See Sestiere di San Polo &
Santa Croce (Santa Crose)
Map pp86–7

See Sestiere
di Dorsoduro
Map pp78–9

much of the day gambling, gossiping and
providing running commentary during
performances. La Fenice audiences were
so notoriously chatty that when he first
performed in Venice, German composer
Richard Wagner miffed Venetians by insist-
ing on total silence during performances.

Rossini and Bellini had staged operas at the house that was the talk of
Europe when the building went up in

flames in 1836. Venice without opera
was unthinkable, and within a year, the
opera house was rebuilt in grand form.
Verdi premiered *Rigoletto* and *La Traviata*
at La Fenice, and international greats
Stravinsky, Prokofiev and Britten composed for the house. But La Fenice was
again reduced to ashes in 1996 by arson;
two electricians found guilty of the crime
were apparently behind on their repair

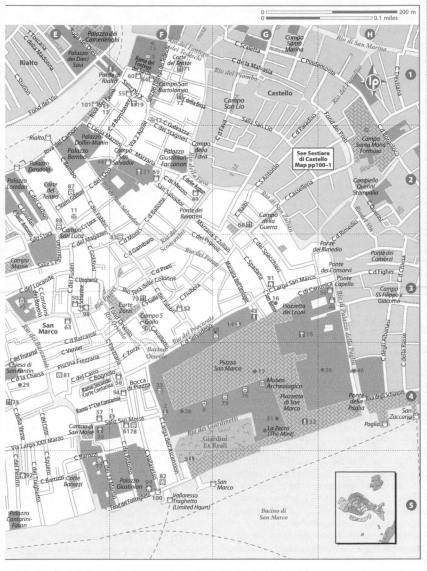

work. A painstaking €90 million replica of the 19th-century opera house reopened in late 2003, and though architectural reviews were mixed – some critics had lobbied for a more avant-garde design by Gae Aulenti – the reprise performance of *La Traviata* was a sensation. The house remains packed in opera season; book ahead for online performances and tours (see p210 for details).

MUSEO CORRER Map pp68–9

☎ 041 240 52 11; www.museiciviciveneziani.it; Piazza San Marco 52; admission incl Palazzo Ducale plus 1 civic museum of choice with/without discount pass €8/13; 🕙 10am-7pm Apr-Oct, 9am-5pm Nov-Mar; 🚊 Vallaresso, San Marco

Napoleon mowed down a church on this spot to make way for a grand ballroom, but he didn't have long to kick up his

SESTIERE DI SAN MARCO

boots in his Ala Napoleonica (p135) – within a couple years of the building's completion, the Austrians took over Venice. When Venice won its independence, it also gained these imperial digs with all the trimmings: ancient maps, Graeco-Roman statuary and splendid medieval paintings. Stride through these salons towards the Palazzo Ducale, and at the end you'll reach Jacopo Sansovino's spectacular 16th-century Libreria Nazionale Marciana (p133), with representations of wisdom by Veronese and Titian. Temporary shows in the neoclassical ballroom on such themes as futurism and Italian architecture are hit-and-miss, but Antonio Canova's 1777 statues of star-crossed lovers Orpheus and Eurydice are permanent scene stealers. Museum entry grants access to the Correr's Caffè dell'Art, which

offers €5 DOC (denominazione d'origine controllata) Veneto merlot in an anteroom frescoed with splendid grotesques and an emperor's-eye view of Basilica di San Marco.

PONTE DELL'ACCADEMIA Map pp68–9
btwn Campo di San Vidal & Campo della Carità;
🚤 **Accademia**
The wooden Ponte dell'Accademia, with a high arch like a cat's back, was built in 1933 as a temporary replacement for an 1854 iron bridge, but it remains a beloved landmark. Engineer Eugenio Miozzi moved onto bigger Fascist monuments such as the Lido casino and the Ponte della Libertà bridge to the mainland, but none has stood the test of time quite like this elegant little footbridge. Renovations

scheduled to begin in 2010/11 are long overdue, but the city is quick to reassure the bridge's ardent admirers that changes will be overwhelmingly structural.

PALAZZO GRASSI Map pp68–9

☎ 041 523 16 80; www.palazzograssi.it; Campo San Samuele 3231; adult/student €15/6; ☺ 10am-7pm daily; ⛴ San Samuele

Paris is still burning with indignation over French luxury goods magnate François Pinault's decision to host world-class art exhibitions and works from his own stand-out collection of contemporary art collection not in a Paris suburb, but in a baroque Grand Canal palace (see p137 and p131). But just have a look around at the 2005 gallery renovation, and even the most patriotic Parisian could hardly blame the guy. Giorgio Massari's 1749 neoclassical palace has become a glorious anachronism in the hands of minimalist architect Tadao Ando, whose movable panels, backlit scrims, and strategic pools of light allow viewers to focus on illuminating art and ideas without eclipsing frescoed ceilings and marble arcades. Expect sublime curation and shameless name-dropping: Pinault regularly parks sculpture by the likes of Jeff Koons on the dock out front, and in 2009 celebrated his marriage with Salma Hayek at the Grassi among A-list guests Bono, Charlize Theron, Ed Norton and Javier Bardem. You'll see more constellations of contemporary art stars at the Punta della Dogana (p81), ancient customs houses renovated by Ando and relaunched in 2009 as a permanent showcase for Pinault's collection of more than 2000 artworks.

TORRE DELL'OROLOGIO Map pp68–9

Clock Tower; ☎ 041 520 90 70; www.museicivici veneziani.it; Piazza San Marco; adult/VENICEcard-holders €12/7; ☺ prebooked tours only, in English 10am, 11am & 1pm Mon-Wed, 1, 2 & 3pm daily, Italian noon & 4pm daily, French 1pm, 2pm & 3pm Mon-Wed; ⛴ Vallaresso, San Marco

Legend has it that as thanks for services rendered, the inventors of this gold-leafed timepiece tracking lunar phases and astrological shifts were blinded so that no city but Venice could boast a similar engineering marvel. Tours of Mauro Codussi's 1496–99 tower (see p135) climb up a steep, claustrophobia-triggering four-storey spiral staircase to the terrace, where the Two Moors statues strike the hour on a bell. Three kings and an angel emerge on Epiphany and the Feast of the Assumption (p267). Tour tickets include entrance to the Museo Correr, where you can book your tour. Children under six not permitted.

PALAZZO CONTARINI DEL BOVOLO Map pp68–9

☎ 041 532 29 20; Calle Contarini del Bovolo 4299; open courtyard admission free; ☺ 10am-6pm daily; ⛴ Rialto

This 15th-century *palazzo* is a hidden jewel of Renaissance architecture with an external spiral *bovolo* (snail-shell) staircase that was closed for restoration at the time of writing, and a shady courtyard that offers privacy for smooches and stirring views of the staircase (see p139).

CHIESA DI SANTO STEFANO Map pp68–9

Campo Santo Stefano 2773; church admission free, museum admission €3 or Chorus Pass; ☺ 10am-5pm Mon-Sat, 1-5pm Sun; ⛴ Accademia

This Gothic church has a bell tower that leans disconcertingly (see p136) and a vast wood-ribbed *carena di nave* (ship's hull) ceiling that looks like an upturned Noah's ark. Enter the cloisters museum (admission €3 or Chorus Pass) to see Canova's 1808 funerary stelae featuring gorgeous women dabbing their eyes with their mourning

top picks

VENICE FOR FREE

- Basilica di San Marco (p65) Glimpse San Marco's golden heavens on a free 15-minute circuit of the church – proof that the best things in life sometimes are free.
- Gallery-hopping (see the boxed text, p74) See exciting contemporary art before it hits the big time at the Biennale.
- Museo della Musica (p73) Take a tour through Venice's musical milestones, and emerge humming.
- Museo della Follia (p124) Thank your lucky stars for modern medicine after seeing the quack psychiatry of yesteryear at this madhouse-turned-museum.
- Palazzo Contarini del Bovolo (above) Get a sneak peek at a Renaissance staircase inside a romantic hidden courtyard.

VENETIAN ROAD RULES

Even though there are no cars in Venice, some pedestrian traffic rules apply:

- Walk single file and keep to the right along narrow streets to let people pass in either direction, and make way for anyone who says *permesso* ('excuse me') – usually a local rushing to or from work or school.
- Pull over to the side if you want to check out a shop window or snap a photo, but don't linger for long: this is the pedestrian equivalent of double-parking your car.
- Snap away on the Rialto and Accademia bridges – everyone loves photographing these Grand Canal views, including locals – but keep moving on smaller bridges, where stalled shutterbugs can cause traffic jams.
- If you see someone struggling with a stroller or heavy bag on a bridge, offer to lend a hand, and you'll earn a grateful *Grazie!*

cloaks, Tulio Lombardo's wide-eyed 1505 saint that Titian is said to have referenced for his *Assunta* at I Frari (p84), and three brooding Tintoretto canvases: *Last Supper,* with a ghostly dog begging for bread; the gathering gloom of *Agony in the Garden;* and the almost-abstract, mostly black *Washing of the Feet.*

CHIESA DI SANTA MARIA DEL GIGLIO
Map pp68–9

Campo di Santa Maria del Giglio 2541; admission €3 or Chorus Pass; 10am-5pm Mon-Sat, 1-5pm Sun; Santa Maria del Giglio

Known in Venetian dialect as Santa Maria Zobenigo, this polyglot church features a 10th-century Byzantine layout, a baroque facade featuring maps of European regions conquered by Venice in the 17th century (see p136), and three intriguing masterpieces by a range of European masters. Hiding behind the altar is Veronese's *Madonna with Child,* with Tintoretto's *Four Evangelists* flanking the organ, and Mary with St John and a charmingly chubby baby Jesus in the Molin Chapel by Northern master Peter Paul Reubens.

CAMPANILE Map pp68–9

Bell Tower; 041 522 52 05; www.basilicasan marco.it; admission €8; 9am-9pm daily Jul-Sep, 9am-7pm Apr-Jun & Oct, 9.30am-3.45pm Nov-Mar; Vallaresso, San Marco

The 30m-tall bell tower has been rebuilt twice since its initial construction in 888, and was long used as the city's main lighthouse. Critics have called the tower squat and ungainly, but when it suddenly collapsed in 1902, Venetians rebuilt the tower exactly as it was, brick by brick (see p134). Entry to the tower leads through the ground-floor Loggetta, a light Renaissance touch by Sansovino and, when the

tower is open to the public, a lift whisks visitors to the top for spectacular panoramas over the city. But you may have to admire it from below: due to ongoing stabilisation efforts, the bell tower may be closed on your visit.

PALAZZO FORTUNY Map pp68–9

041 520 90 70; www.museicivicieneziani.it; Campo San Beneto 3958; adult/VENICEcard-holder €8/5; 10am-6pm Wed-Mon; Sant'Angelo

The not-so-humble home studio of outrageous art nouveau Spanish-Venetian designer Mariano Fortuny y Madrazo features three floors swagged with Fortuny's printed textiles, mood-lit with his signature patterned glass lanterns. Today these sumptuous halls host rotating exhibits by modern artisans, inevitably upstaged by Fortuny's preserved top-floor studio and 1910 sketches of bohemian goddess frocks that could rule red carpets today. If these salons inspire decor schemes of your own, check out Fortuny Tessuti Artistici (p112) in Giudecca, where wall coverings are still hand-printed according to Fortuny's top-secret methods. See also p138.

CHIESA DI SAN SALVADOR Map pp68–9

041 523 67 17; www.chiesasansalvador.it; Campo San Salvador 4835; admission free; 9am-noon & 4-6pm Mon-Sat, 4-6pm Sun Jun-Aug, 9am-noon & 3-6pm Mon-Sat, 3-6pm Sun Sep-May; Rialto

A dream made real, San Salvador was conceived in the 7th century when Jesus appeared to a sleeping Bishop Magnus and pointed out the exact spot on a lagoon map where he should build a church. There was, however, a minor technical glitch: the city of Venice didn't exist yet, and the area was mostly mud banks. But Bishop Magnus had faith that once the church was built the parishioners would follow – and today this church perched on a bustling *campo* (square) proves his point. Built on a plan of three Greek crosses laid end to end, San Salvador has been embellished many times over the centuries, with the present facade erected in 1663. Among the noteworthy works inside are two Titians: the *Transfiguration* behind the main altar, and at Sansovino's altar (third on the right as you approach the main altar), his spectacular *Annunciation,* with a radiant dove overseeing the blushing young angel eagerly delivering the news to a startled Mary.

PALAZZO FRANCHETTI Map pp68–9

☎ 041 240 77 11; www.istitutoveneto.it; Campo Santo Stefano 2842; exhibits adult/student €9/6, cafe admission free; ☻ 10am-7pm daily; ⓐ Accademia

Makeover madness hasn't diminished the essential charms of one of Venice's most admired Grand Canal palaces. No fewer than three extended Venetian families originally lived under one Gothic roof at this 16th-century mansion, and apparently they didn't always see eye to eye on decor. When archduke Frederick of Austria snapped up this Gothic palace in the 19th century, he attempted to unify competing styles with a spare, modern makeover. The Franchetti family lived here for decades after independence, and commissioned architect Camillo Boito to reinstall a retro-Gothic look, plus a formal garden and a grand art nouveau staircase. The palace was home to a private bank from 1922 until 1999, when the Istituto Veneto di Scienze, Lettere ed Arti (Veneto Institute of the Sciences, Letters and Arts) moved in and brought the galleries up to date for expositions and conferences (see website for listings). The latest addition is the 2009 Palazzo Franchetti Caffè (p200) in the enclosed garden cloisters, with intricately patterned window screens that harmonise the palace's Gothic, modern and art nouveau design schemes. See also p137.

CHIESA DI SAN MOISÈ Map pp68–9

☎ 041 528 58 40; Campo di San Moisè; admission free; ☻ 9.30am-12.30pm Mon-Sat; ⓐ Vallaresso, San Marco

Scrumptious icing flourishes of carved-stone ornament across the 1660s facade make this church appear positively lick-able, though 19th-century architecture critic John Ruskin found its wedding-cake appearance indigestible: 'one of the basest examples of the basest schools of the Renaissance', gagged the outspoken advocate for spare Venetian Gothic. This may seem a tad excessive, but from an engineering perspective Ruskin had a point: several of the facade statues had to be removed in the 19th century to prevent the facade from collapsing under their combined weight. The remaining statuary by Flemish sculptor Heinrich Meyring (aka Merengo in Italian) includes scant devotional works, but a sycophantic number of tributes to the Fini family of generous church patrons. Still, compared with the naked, full-frontal Fascist facade of the Bauer Hotel beside it, San Moisè's exuberant partisanship seems much more palatable. Among the scene-stealing works inside are Tintoretto's *The Washing of the Feet,* in the sanctuary to the left of the main altar, and Palma il Giovane's *The Supper,* on the right side of the church.

CHIESA DI SAN VIDAL Map pp68–9

Campo di San Vidal 2862; admission free; ☻ 9am-noon & 3.30-6pm Mon-Sat; ⓐ Accademia

No longer a functioning church, San Vidal has found a use as a concert hall for Interpreti Veneziani (p209), Venice's premier interpreters of Vivaldi, played on original 18th- to 19th-century instruments. Built as a monument to the glories of God and two Venetian dogi (see p137), this stately church is best known for the masterpiece behind the main altar: *St Vitale on Horseback and Eight Saints,* an uncharacteristically gore-free work by Vittore Carpaccio featuring traces of his signature traffic-light red and a miniaturist's attention to detail.

MUSEO DELLA MUSICA Map pp68–9

☎ 041 241 18 40; Campo San Maurizio 2761; admission free; ☻ 9.30am-7.30pm daily; ⓐ Santa Maria del Giglio

Housed in the restored neoclassical Chiesa di San Maurizio, this collection of rare and often very curious instruments spans the 17th to 19th centuries and is accompanied by informative panels on the life and times of Antonio Vivaldi (see p136 and p45). To hear how these instruments sound in action, check out the kiosk with a range of

GALLERY-HOP SAN MARCO

For all its splendours of bygone eras, San Marco is not just a museum piece. Slip into the backstreets behind Santa Maria del Giglio and you'll jump ahead of the art curve in galleries showcasing the next generation of artistic breakthroughs from Italian and international artists, in media ranging from glass sculpture to video installation. Entry is free and inspiration abundant at these five San Marco galleries:

- Caterina Tognon Arte Contemporanea (Map pp68–9; ☎ 041 520 78 59; www.caterinatognon.com; Campo San Maurizio 2671; ☑ 3-7pm Mon-Sat, plus by appointment; ☒ Santa Maria del Giglio) Don't be fooled by the small storefront space: Tognon makes a big splash with a spirited mix of emerging and established contemporary artists here and at the adjacent stART space in 17th-century Palazzo da Ponte. A major recent show of avant-garde glassworks featured Kiki Smith's visceral vessels and Roberta Silva's single exhalation captured for poetic posterity in a glass bubble. See also p136.
- Galleria Rosella Junck (Map pp68–9; ☎ 041 521 07 59; www.rossellajunck.it; Calle Larga XXII Marzo 2360; ☑ 10am-12.30pm & 4-7.30pm Mon-Sat; ☒ Santa Maria del Giglio) Step into this darkened gallery from the bright boutique street, and you'll sense you've entered an aquarium: on walls lined with glass cases, spotlit art-glass objects radiate an ethereal, underwater light. Some combination of miracles and high shelves have preserved fragile 16th- to 18th-century wonders, including a shell pitcher with a sea-dragon handle and a delicate vase shaped like a hedgehog. Alongside turn-of-the-century art glass by historic Murano makers Salviati and Fratelli Toso are exceptional contemporary pieces: Donald Robertson's frosted glass warrior helmets, Marie Aimée Grimaldi's filigreed Hamlet-in-Murano crystal skull, and Xavier Le Normand's column vases with trilobite-shaped cutaways. See also p136.
- La Galleria van der Koelen (Map pp68–9; ☎ 041 520 74 15; www.galerie.vanderkoelen.de; Ramo Primo dei Calegheri 2566; ☑ 10am-12.30pm & 3.30-6.30pm Mon-Sat; ☒ Santa Maria del Giglio) Quiet minimalism keeps a low profile behind the loud, proud Teatro La Fenice. Shows here strike a delicate balance between high-concept and visceral appeal, as with Günther Uecker's delicately brutal embossed-paper nails and detailed drawings of glass shards. Between the onslaught of colour and drama that is the Gallerie dell'Accademia and the whirlwind of spiritual uplift of Basilica di San Marco, La Galleria van der Koelen is the calm eye in the centre of Venice's aesthetic storm. See also p138.
- Galleria Traghetto (Map pp68–9; ☎ 041 522 11 88; www.galleriatraghetto.it; Campo Santa Maria del Giglio 2543; ☑ 3-7pm Mon-Sat; ☒ Santa Maria del Giglio) This place holds gutsy shows of young Italian and international artists on the brink of breakthroughs. Look for Rome-based Serafino Maiorano's artfully blurred digital photographs with bleeding reds that evoke Carpaccio, and Lithuanian painter Andrius Zakarauskas' history paintings cleverly reduced to salutes, finger pointing, and other highly charged gestures.
- Jarach Gallery (Map pp68–9; ☎ 041 522 19 38; www.jarachgallery.com; Campo San Fantin 1997; ☑ 10am-1pm & 2.30-7.30pm Tue-Sat; ☒ Santa Maria del Giglio) While diva La Fenice holds centre stage in this piazza, contemporary photography waits in the wings for discovery through a shadowy sotoportego (passageway). Quiet drama and compelling mystery unfold in this ancient courtyard gallery, with shows like Giorgio Barrera's staged crimes in progress glimpsed through Venetian Gothic windows. See also p138.

early-music CDs and ticket point for Interpreti Veneziani, who fund this museum and play museum-piece instruments with modern verve around the corner at San Vidal.

FONDACO DEI TEDESCHI Map pp68–9
Salizada del Fontego dei Tedeschi 5346; admission free; ☑ 8.30am-6.30pm Mon-Sat; ☒ Rialto
Stamps are the main commodity traded near the ancient well in the sombre courtyard of this former fondacho (trading house), where Venice's central post office was installed in 1937. But imagine how this place must have looked during its 13th- to 17th-century heyday as the Wall Street of Venice's German community, before the creeping damp destroyed the exterior frescoes by Giorgione and Titian – only a few fragments remain in the Ca' d'Oro (p96). The traders here drove a hard bargain: when Giorgione and Titian showed up to collect their payment of 150 ducats for the work, they were told their work was worth only 130 ducats. Incensed, they insisted on an independent appraisal, which confirmed the original figure – but the artists were told they could take it or leave it.

CHIESA DI SAN BARTOLOMEO
Map pp68–9
Campo San Bartolomeo 5178; admission free; ☑ 10am-noon Tue, Thu & Sat; ☒ Rialto

German traders didn't have to stray far from the trading floor of the Fondaco dei Tedeschi to pray for an upswing in the market for their goods. Through several incarnations and shifting fortunes, this church attended to the spiritual needs of Venice's active German trading community. Originally a three-aisled church built in 1170, San Bartolomeo's style was cramped by the buildings that cropped up around it after the Rialto bridge was completed. The current look is the result of a 1723 reworking by Giovanni Scalfarotto, whose sombre approach to exterior decoration was befitting a church dedicated to a martyr who was skinned alive – note the grimacing figure above the door to the 1755 bell tower, capped with a Bavarian onion dome. If you find it open for visits or concerts, you may be surprised by the crystalline colours of Palma il Giovane paintings inside; other key works have been moved to the Gallerie dell'Accademia (p76).

SESTIERE DI DORSODURO

Eating p182; Shopping p166; Sleeping p218

Minds blown by the sight of San Marco require a bracing espresso, restorative *gelato* (ice cream) and possibly a Hail Mary before taking on artistically inclined Dorsoduro. Veronese lavished his tiny parish church of San Sebastian with masterpieces; Tiepolo and Baldassare Longhena worked wonders on both the Grand Canal palace of Ca' Rezzonico and the Scuola Grande dei Carmini convent that doubled as a hostel; and minimalist maestro Tadao Ando transformed Punta della Dogana from warehouse customs dock to contemporary art showplace.

Unlike arty neighbourhoods in other cities, grunge doesn't always come with the territory in Dorsoduro, where the reflections of whitewashed houses and the freshly scrubbed Chiesa di Santa Maria delle Salute sparkle along the canals – though locals did complain when a particularly artful patina of grime was removed from Chiesa dell'Arcangelo Raffaele. Dorsoduro's high-powered art backers include François Pinault, Peggy Guggenheim and Napoleon, who elbowed aside a convent to make room for a haul of Venetian art trophies looted from across the Veneto at the Gallerie dell'Accademia.

But somehow, this lavish attention hasn't gone to Dorsoduro's head. The neighbourhood still convenes nightly in Campo Santa Margherita for the mandatory happy hour, queues up along the Zattere boardwalk for *gelato* on sunny days, and haggles over the price of tomatoes at the produce barge pulled alongside the pugnacious Ponte dei Pugni (see p52). Once you've mastered the trick of leaning over the barge without falling in the canal, you've officially gotten the hang of Dorsoduro.

This *sestiere* points into the lagoon like a bent, factory-reject gondola prow, with the Grand Canal on the northeast side and the Canale della Giudecca and Canale di Fusina to the southwest. To the north are the bars and eateries of boisterous Campo Santa Margherita – but in the west, the area becomes eerily quiet, except where the university faculties breathe student life into the district around the Chiesa di San Nicolò dei Mendicoli. All Grand Canal vaporetti stop at Accademia, while vaporetto 1 also calls at Ca' Rezzonico and Salute. A branch line of vaporetto 82 and the N night vaporetto call at Zattere and San Basilio. Numbers 51, 52, 61 and 62 also call at Zattere and San Basilio.

GALLERIE DELL'ACCADEMIA

Map pp78–9

☎ 041 522 22 47, bookings 041 520 03 45; www .gallerieaccademia.org; Campo della Carità 1050; adult/EU citizen 18-25yr/under 12yr & EU citizen under 18yr or over 65yr €6.50/3.25/free, video/ audio guide €6/4; ⏱ 8.15am-2pm Mon, 8.15am-7.15pm Tue-Sun, last entry 45min before closing; 🚣 Accademia

Hardly academic, these galleries contain more murderous intrigue, forbidden romance, shameless politicking and near-riots than the most outrageous Venetian parties. The walls of the former Santa Maria della Carità convent complex maintained their serene composure for centuries, with the outstanding architectural assistance of Bartolomeo Bon, Palladio and Carlo Scarpa (see p140) – but ever since Napoleon installed his haul of Venetian art trophies in this convent in 1807, there's been nonstop visual drama inside these walls.

To guide you through the ocular onslaught, visits are loosely organised by style, theme and painter from the 14th to 18th centuries, beginning with Paolo Veneziano's c 1350 *Coronation of Mary,* which shows Jesus bestowing the crown on his mother with a gentle pat on the head as an angelic orchestra performs overhead. For shimmering gore that seems alarmingly fresh, there's no topping Carpaccio's *Crucifixion and Glorification of the Ten Thousand Martyrs of Mount Ararat* in Room 2 – Harry's Bar (p199) was quite correct in naming its bloody raw beef dish after this painter.

Andrea Mantegna's 1466 haughtily handsome *St George* and Giovanni Bellini's sweet-faced *Madonna and Child* haloed by neon-red cherubs highlight Venice's twin artistic tendencies: high drama and glowing colour. Rooms 6 to 10 include such Renaissance-Mannerist masterpieces as Tintoretto's *Creation of the Animals,* a fantastical bestiary that suggests that God put forth his best efforts inventing Venetian seafood (no arguments here), and one of Titian's last efforts possibly finished posthumously by Palma il Giovane: a 1576 *Pietà* where form is secondary to raw emotion, with smears of paint Titian applied with bare hands (see p39).

The Accademia's scene stealer dominates Room 10: Paolo Veronese's controversial *Feast in the House of Levi*, originally called *Last Supper* until Church Inquisition leaders condemned Veronese for showing drunkards, dwarves, dogs and (most alarming of all) Reformation-minded Germans cavorting amid the apostles. Veronese refused to change a thing about his painting besides the title, and Venice stood by this act of artistic defiance against Rome. Follow the exchanges, gestures and eye contact among the characters here, and you'll concede that not one Moorish trader, stumbling servant, gambler or bright-eyed lapdog could have been painted over without losing an essential piece of this Venetian puzzle.

At this point you're only halfway through Venice's contributions to art history – phew – but don't skip rooms 16 to 18, which feature Canaletto's sweeping views of Venice, and Giorgione's 1508 *The Storm (La Tempesta)*, a highly charged scenario involving a nursing mother, a passing soldier and a bolt of summer lightning. Adjoining portrait galleries can scarcely contain larger-than-life Venetian characters, including Giorgione's decidedly un-Botoxed *Old Woman,* Lorenzo Lotto's 1525 soul-searching *Portrait of a Young Scholar,* Rosalba Carriera's brutally honest self-portrait c 1730 (see p41), and

TOP ATTRACTIONS & TERRIFIC ALTERNATIVES

Gallerie dell'Accademia

Attraction See for yourself how Venetian Renaissance painting emerged as the colourful counterpart to formal Florentine painting, and made biblical figures look flash; opposite.

Dilemma Mind the neck strain from trying to glimpse a Tintoretto or Titian amid all the field-tripping art history classes…

Alternative Follow Tintoretto into some very sketchy situations at Scuola Grande di San Rocco (p85), and swoon over Titian in top form at I Frari (p84).

Gondolas

Attraction Those floating red velvet love seats are the world's best way to get from point A to B with Xs and Os en route; p259.

Dilemma At €80 for 40 minutes, plus tip and surcharges for songs, this isn't exactly free love.

Alternative Anyone with a daring streak – and good balance – should take a €1 *traghetto* (commuter gondola) ride (see the boxed text, p261) across the Grand Canal, standing up in the long gondola as Venetians do. Toast your success with sunset drinks at Bar Terazza Danieli (p205), overlooking gondolas pulling in for the night along the quay at San Marco.

Teatro la Fenice

Attraction Be one of the lucky few to see the world's biggest opera divas make their mark on this postage stamp of a stage; p67.

Dilemma With limited runs of bravura performances and a snug 900-seat venue, tickets sell out faster than you can say 'bravo!'

Alternative Opera isn't the only soundtrack in town – see www.hellovenezia.it for concerts in historic venues featuring ancient Venetian party music played on Renaissance-era instruments.

Ponte di Rialto

Attraction Antonio da Ponte's historic stone bridge offers some of the grandest views of the Grand Canal; p87.

Dilemma Haggling souvenir shoppers along the bridge create foot-traffic jams and stiff competition for a view.

Alternative The Rialto is actually best appreciated from the Grand Canal, and the best way to do that (without getting wet) is to hop onto the line 1 vaporetto (p259) down the Grand Canal in the afternoon, as the Istrian stone bridge begins to blush with the sunset.

SESTIERE DI DORSODURO

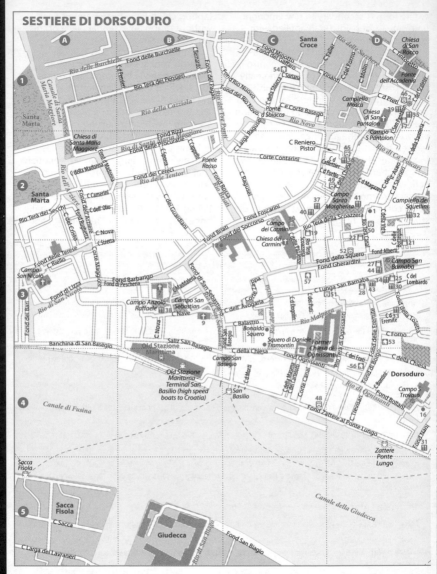

Gian Battista Piazzetta's saucy socialite in his 1740 *Fortune-Teller*. Room 20 reprises Gentile Bellini and Vittore Carpaccio with multi-culti crowds of Venetian merchants embedded in Venetian versions of *Miracles of the True Cross*, before the grand finale: Titian's 1534–39 *Presentation of the Virgin*, with the young Madonna dutifully trudging up an intimidating staircase as onlookers point to her example.

PEGGY GUGGENHEIM COLLECTION
Map pp78–9

☎ 041 240 54 11; www.guggenheim-venice.it; Palazzo Venier dei Leoni 701; adult/over 65yr/student with ID to 26yr/under 10yr €10/8/5/free; ☼ 10am–6pm Wed-Mon; ☐ Accademia

After tragically losing her father on the *Titanic*, heiress Peggy Guggenheim befriended Dadaists, dodged Nazis, and amassed avant-garde works by 200 mod-

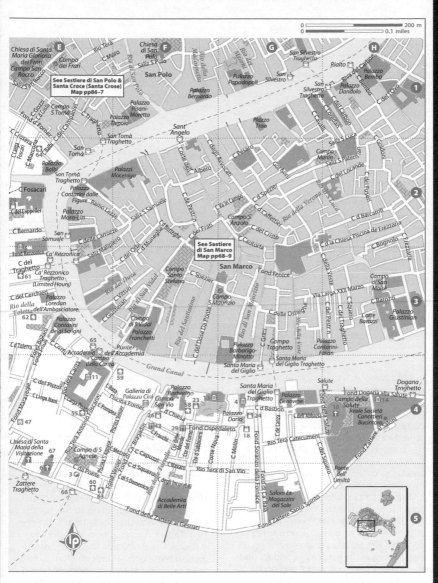

ern artists at her palatial home on the Grand Canal (see also p141). Peggy's **Palazzo Venier dei Leoni** became a modernist shrine, chronicling surrealism, Italian futurism, and abstract expressionism, with a subtext of Peggy's romantic pursuits – the collection includes key works by Peggy's ex-husband Max Ernst and Jackson Pollock, among Peggy's many rumoured lovers. Peggy collected according to her own convictions rather than for prestige or style, so her collection includes inspired folk art and lesser-known local artists alongside artists recognised internationally by just one name, including Kandinsky, Picasso, Rothko, Klee, Brancusi, Mondrian and Dali.

Peggy was more than a mere tastemaker; her spirited advocacy sparked renewed interest in Italian art, which had largely gone

79

SESTIERE DI DORSODURO

out of favour with the rise of Mussolini and the partisan politics of WWII. For this Jewish American champion of Italian art who'd witnessed the dangers of censorship and party-line dictates, serious artwork deserved to be seen and judged on its merits. Her support led to reappraisals of Umberto Boccioni, Giorgio Morandi, Giacomo Balla and Giorgio de Chirico, and aided Venice's own Emilio Vedova.

Wander around works by Moore, Giacometti and Arp in the sculpture garden, where the city of Venice granted Peggy honorary dispensation to be buried alongside her pet dogs in 1979. Espresso is served among art installations at the garden cafe, and around the corner from the museum on Fondamenta Venier dei Leoni is the museum bookstore, selling art books in several languages and replicas of Peggy's signature glasses – winged, like the lion of San Marco.

CA' REZZONICO (MUSEO DEL SETTECENTO VENEZIANO) Map pp78–9
☎ 041 241 01 00; www.musei civiciveneziani .it; Fondamenta Rezzonico 3136; adult/student & child €6.50/4.50; 🕙 10am-6pm Wed-Mon Apr-Oct,

10am-5pm Wed-Mon Nov-Mar, last entry 1hr before closing; 🚊 Ca' Rezzonico
Other museums may illuminate, but this one sparkles. This period-piece Longhena palace showcases 18th-century arts in lavish music salons, sumptuous boudoirs, even a pharmacy with medicinal scorpions. Several salons are crowned with ceiling masterpieces by Giambattista Tiepolo, in rare form with sensuous beauty and shameless flattery. The Throne Room shows gorgeous Merit ascending to the Temple of Glory clutching the Golden Book of Venetian nobles' names – including Tiepolo's patrons, the Rezzonico family. Other collection highlights include the Pietro Longhi Salon satirising of society antics observed by disapproving lapdogs (see p41); the Sala Rosalba Carriera, with her unvarnished pastel portraits of socialites that aren't strictly pretty, but look like they'd be life of any party (see p41); and on the top floor, the Vedustisti galleries (p41) featuring Emma Ciardi's moody canal views. Check the schedule downstairs for Venice Chamber Music Orchestra concerts, played in the proper period splendour of the frescoed ballroom.

CHIESA DI SANTA MARIA DELLA SALUTE Map pp78–9

☎ 041 522 55 58; www.marcianum.it/salute, in Italian; Campo della Salute 1b; sacristy admission €1.50; ⏰ 9am-noon & 3-5.30pm daily; 🚊 Salute

Shows of appreciation don't get much more monumental than Venice's magnificent baroque church to the Sainted Mary of Health, dedicated by Venice's Senate to the Madonna for sparing the city further devastation after a brutal 1630–31 bout of plague killed a third of the city's population in 18 months. At least 100,000 pylons had to be driven deep into the *barene* (mud banks) to shore up the tip of Dorsoduro and support the weight of this baroque engineering marvel (see p141). Baldassare Longhena's unusual domed octagon is an inspired design that architectural scholars have compared to Graeco-Roman temples and Jewish cabbala diagrams, and the site of Venetians' annual pilgrimage to pray for health (see p20). Inside, you'll spot Tintoretto's surprisingly upbeat *The Wedding Feast of Cana* en route to the sacristy, which features no fewer than 12 Titians, including a vivid self-portrait in the guise of St Matthew, and his earliest known work, the precocious vermilion *Saint Mark on the Throne* from 1510.

CHIESA DI SAN SEBASTIAN Map pp78–9

☎ 041 528 24 87; Campo San Sebastian 1687; admission €3 or Chorus Pass; ⏰ 10am-4.45pm Mon-Sat; 🚊 San Basilio

A hidden treasure of Venetian art in the heart of Dorsoduro, this otherwise stark neighbourhood church was embellished with floor-to-ceiling masterpieces by Paolo Veronese over three decades (see p144). Veronese's horses rear over the frames of the coffered ceiling; the organ doors are covered inside and out with episodes from the life of Christ in vivid Veronese colour; and in Veronese's *Martyrdom of Saint Sebastian* near the altar, the bound saint stares down his tormentors amid a Venetian crowd of socialites, turbaned traders and Veronese's signature frisky spaniel. This last work may have held some personal significance for Veronese. According to popular local legend, Veronese found sanctuary at San Sebastian in 1555 after fleeing murder charges in Verona, and his works here deliver lavish thanks to the parish and an especially brilliant poke in the eye of his accusers. Only

work of this magnitude could manage to upstage the superb Titian *San Nicolò* (St Nicholas), on the right as you enter.

PUNTA DELLA DOGANA

☎ 199 139 139; www.palazzograssi.it; Punta della Dogana, Dorsoduro; adult/12-18yr, senior & disabled/under 11yr €15/10/free, with ticket to Peggy Guggenheim within 3 days of visit/combined ticket with Palazzo Grassi €12/20; ⏰ 10am-7pm Wed-Mon; 🚊 Salute

Fortuna, the weathervane atop Punta della Dogana, swung Venice's way when bureaucratic hassles in Paris convinced billionaire art collector François Pinault to create a gallery extension at the Palazzo Grassi (p71) and transfer his world-class collection to the Punta della Dogana (see p141). At the ship's-prow end of Dorsoduro, Venice's historic 17th-century customs house was relaunched in 2009 after a three-year reinvention by architect Tadao Ando as Venice's splashiest contemporary art space (see the boxed text, p44). The inaugural show traced the creative processes of Takashi Murakami, Jeff Koons, Cindy Sherman and other contemporary art stars from rough drafts to end products, installed in converted warehouses flooded with light through polished-concrete channels and water gates – an astute homage to Carlo Scarpa's designs for Palazzo Querini Stampalia (p105) and the Biennale (see p104 and p18).

SCUOLA GRANDE DEI CARMINI Map pp78–9

☎ 041 528 94 20; Campo Santa Margherita 2617; adult/senior & student €5/4; ⏰ 9am-5pm Mon-Sat & 9am-4pm Sun Apr-Oct, 9am-4pm Nov-Mar; 🚊 Ca' Rezzonico

Eighteenth-century backpackers must have thought they'd died and gone to heaven at the Scuola Grande dei Carmini, a shelter run by Carmelite nuns with interiors by Tiepolo and Longhena worthy of a doge (see also p144). Longhena designed the stuccoed stairway to heaven, glimpsed in Tiepolo's nine-panel ceiling of a resplendent *Virgin in Glory* upstairs before you enter the high-ceilinged hostel room itself, a wonder of *boiserie* (carved woodwork). Sadly, cots are no longer available in this jewel-box building, but the Venice Opera (www.venice-opera.com) sometimes stages performances here.

CHIESA DI SAN NICOLÒ DEI MENDICOLI Map pp78–9

☎ 041 528 45 65; Campo San Nicolò 1907;
⏱ 10am-noon & 4-6pm Mon-Sat; ⚓ San Basilio

Other churches in town may be grander and glitzier, but San Nicolò dei Mendicoli earns a special spot in local hearts for being the most essentially Venetian. From the outside, this low, spare brick Veneto-Gothic church dedicated to serving the poor hasn't changed much since the 12th century, when its cloisters functioned as a women's shelter and its portico sheltered *mendicoli* (beggars). The tiny, picturesque *campo* out front is a Venice in miniature, surrounded on three sides by canals and bearing a pylon bearing the winged lion of St Mark, one of the few in Venice to have escaped target practice by Napoleon's troops.

Dim interiors are illuminated by a golden arcade and a profusion of clerestory paintings, including a work that's among the most memorable of Palma Il Giovane's many works in Venice: a *Resurrection* showing onlookers taking cover in terror and amazement, as Jesus leaps from his tomb in a blaze of dazzling golden light. The right-hand chapel is a typically Venetian response to persistent orders from Rome to limit music in Venetian churches: Madonna in glory, thoroughly enjoying a concert of angels on flutes, lutes and violins, singled out by Roman authorities as dangerously secular. The parish's seafaring livelihood is honoured in Leonardo Corona's 16th-century ceiling panel *San Niccolo Guiding some Sailors through a Storm*, which shows the saint shedding a beacon of light, guiding sailors rowing furiously through a storm.

CHIESA DEI GESUATI Map pp78–9

☎ 041 523 06 25; Fondamenta delle Zattere 918;
admission €3 or Chorus Pass; ⏱ 10am-5pm Mon-Sat; ⚓ Zattere

If you're not yet sold on baroque art, just duck inside Giorgio Massari's 1735 high baroque church and look up. On ceiling panels completed in 1737–39, Tiepolo tells stories in the life of St Dominic in trompe l'œil skies with such brilliantly sunny colour, you may momentarily wonder if you're wearing enough sunscreen. Fellow Venetian virtuoso of luminosity Sebastiano Ricci painted the crystalline, 1730–33 *Saints Peter and Thomas with Pope Pius V* on the right side of the nave – quite a contrast to

Tintoretto's adjacent 1565 *Crucifixion*, with mere hints of deep red and green amid the gathering gloom.

If you find the side door to the cloisters open, you might be able to peek into the little-visited Chiesa di Santa Maria della Visitazione. Better known as Chiesa di Santa Maria degli Artigianelli for its role as the spiritual home to Venice's artisans, the otherwise modest church boasts a fine 15th-century chessboard ceiling embedded with scenes of the Visitation. The religious order operates a cultural centre where you might catch the occasional show dedicated to Burano lace or other local crafts, plus a religious guesthouse (see www.donorione-venezia.it/ing/home.htm for details and booking).

CA' DARIO Map pp78–9

Ramo Ca' Dario 352; ⚓ Salute

Grand Canal palaces rank among the world's most prime real estate, except for the perfectly gorgeous 1487 Ca' Dario. Its striking multicoloured marble facade casts a mesmerising reflection in the Grand Canal, captured by no less than Claude Monet – but there's a catch. Starting with the daughter of its original owner, Giovanni Dario, an unusual number of its owners have met mysterious or miserable ends, lost fortunes and/or become frightfully ill, which local gossips claim was enough to dissuade Woody Allen from buying the place in the 1990s. The former manager of The Who and then owner of the building committed suicide there, and one week after renting the place for a holiday in 2002, The Who's bass player, John Entwhistle, died of a heart attack. Though Peggy Guggenheim shows are sometimes held on the premises, Ca' Dario remains unsold; any takers? See also p141.

SQUERO DI SAN TROVASO

Campo San Trovaso 1097; ⚓ Zattere

When it's time for a tune-up, *gondolieri* head to the *squero* (small-scale shipyard). The wood cabin on the corner of the Rio di San Trovaso may look like a misplaced ski chalet, but it's actually part of one of the city's three working *squeri*. From the right bank, you can see refinished gondolas drying in the yard. If you find the door open during working hours, you can poke your head inside in exchange for a donation left in the can by the door – but no flash photography is allowed, as it might startle the gondola builders as they're completing a tricky bit of woodwork with sharp tools.

PALAZZO ZENOBIO Map pp78–9

☎ 041 522 87 70; www.collegioarmeno.com; Fondamenta del Soccorso 2597; admission €5; 🕙 10am-5pm Mon-Sat; 🚊 San Basilio

A baroque beauty that serves as a grand monument to Venetian multiculturalism, Antonio Gaspari's 1690 gilded palace features extravagant French rococo frescoes of Greek myths alongside Armenian religious artefacts – for centuries, this was home to the Collegio Armeno dei Padri Mechitaristi (Armenian College of Mechitarist Fathers). Upstairs in the Sala della Musica – also called the Sala dei Specchi (Hall of Mirrors) – gilded mirrors fogged with age are interrupted by architectural niches apparently stuffed to overflowing with fresh flowers in classical urns, but it's all a very clever trompe l'œil ruse by Louis Dorigny. Turn the corner to the left, and you've suddenly entered a more sombre, studious world, with portraits of Armenian clergy and theologians to inspire scholastic pursuits. Downstairs, you can wander into Venice's largest, most lushly overgrown formal gardens, which are an idyllic spot for a picnic. Better yet, the adjoining wing that once served as a dorm has recently been reopened by the Armenian Mechitarists as a hostel, with private rooms at nominal rates (see p219).

CHIESA DELL'ARCANGELO RAFFAELE Map pp78–9

☎ 041 522 85 48; Campo Anzolo Raffaele 1721; donation suggested; 🕙 9am-noon & 4-6pm Mon-Sat; 🚊 San Basilio

The neighbours called, and they want their grime back: when a recent cleaning to the 17th facade removed centuries of accumulated dirt on carved stone angels' wings above the portals, it caused a local uproar. Had Venice lost its respect for the patina of age? But there's been no similar argument raised about the restoration of the interiors, where in the baptistry behind the altar Francesco Fontebasso's newly restored baroque frescoes seem to emit the early light of dawn in shades of pink, gold and pale green. The cycle of paintings inside above the main altar has been attributed to the Guardi brothers, but no one is sure which one – the *vedutista* (landscape artist) Francesco or his lesser-known elder brother Gian Antonio (1699–1760). In the afternoons, the organist stays in practice with a fugue or two; ask the guardian about upcoming concerts.

SESTIERI DI SAN POLO & SANTA CROCE (SANTA CROSE)

Eating p184; Shopping p168; Sleeping p220

Heavenly devotion and earthly delights are neighbours in San Polo and Santa Croce (Santa Crose), where you'll find truly divine art and the city's ancient red-light district, now home to artisans' workshops and excellent *osterie*. San Polo is the more gregarious, outgoing *sestiere*, with *bacari* convivially clustered around the Rialto markets. Photographers and foodies rub elbows over glistening fish artfully balanced on their tails atop hillocks of ice at the Pescaria (fish market), alongside produce stalls heaped with rare, exotic vegetables from marshy lagoon gardens that look like offerings to the gourmet gods. San Polo has bragging rights to fraternal twin masterpieces that couldn't be more different: Titian's glowing, gorgeous Madonna at the Frari and action-packed, turbulent Tintorettos at Scuola Grande di San Rocco.

Find out what Venice does when it isn't busy entertaining in Santa Croce, where you'll find kids ripping around Romanesque churches on tricycles while parents sip *prosecco* (sparkling white wine), pizza joints doubling as alternative-culture outposts, and mosaic artisans gingerly tapping glass into tiny tiles. In Santa Croce artisans' studios around Campo Santa Maria Mater Domini and San Polo studios around Calle dei Botteri, you can watch ordinary paper fashioned into ingenious purses, statement necklaces, and tiny classical friezes that look like the Elgin Marbles left in a dryer.

Since this is Venice, after all, there are a few charmingly quirky museum collections in historic Grand Canal *palazzi*: modern art and Japanese antiques at Ca' Pesaro, original baroque fashion at Palazzo Mocenigo, and, yes, dinosaurs at the Fondaco dei Turchi. But beyond these museums and a few intriguing churches amid the jumble of lanes and houses, there's not much to see here of major tourist interest, which is what makes it an ideal place to really unwind. No traffic or souvenir salesmanship here: just the murmur of idle chatter in backstreet *bacari,* water lapping at the *fondamenta* (street beside a canal), and unhurried footsteps along single-file *calli.*

Together these two *sestieri* fit together like an oddly shaped oyster, with Santa Croce as the western side and San Polo the eastern end. The oyster is wedged in diagonally along the Grand Canal between Piazzale Roma and the Ponte di Rialto. Though the districts may seem far from the sightseeing crowds, they're surprisingly central. To the south, both districts are within easy reach of the nightlife of Dorsoduro's Campo Santa Margherita, and just across the northwestern Ponte dei Scalzi is Cannaregio and the Ferrovia (train station). Just don't expect to keep your sense of direction once you enter into these twisting, narrow lanes, some hardly wider than an arm span. But when you get lost here, you'll often be rewarded by stumbling upon an ancient *palazzo,* a church forgotten by time, or a scrumptious *osteria* (pub-restaurant) in a secluded *campo.*

Most vaporetti call at Piazzale Roma or Ferrovia at the northwest corner of Santa Croce. In San Polo, the Rialto stop is serviced by lines 1, 4 and N. Line 1 also calls at Riva de Biasio, San Stae (the N stops here too), San Silvestro and San Tomà (the N stops here as well). The Rialto Mercato stop (line 1) is in use during the day only.

I FRARI (CHIESA DI SANTA MARIA GLORIOSA DEI FRARI) Map pp86–7

Campo dei Frari, San Polo 3004; admission €3 or Chorus Pass; ✆ 9am-6pm Mon-Sat, 1-6pm Sun; ⚐ San Tomà

Like moths to an eternal flame, visitors are inexorably drawn to the front of this cavernous, dimly lit Gothic church by a small altarpiece that seems to come equipped with its own sunlight. This is Titian's 1518 *Assunta* (aka *Madonna of the Ascension*), capturing the split second the radiant Madonna reaches heavenward, her sig-

nature Titian-red robe in glorious disarray as she finds her footing on a cloud. Both inside and outside the painting, onlookers below gasp and point out the ascending Madonna to one another.

As if this weren't too much to handle already, the lofty brick Gothic I Frari (or Chiesa di Santa Maria Gloriosa dei Frari) has other fascinating features: minuscule puzzlework marquetry in the *coro* (choir stalls), Bellini's achingly sweet *Madonna with Child* triptych in the sacristy, Titian's *Ca' Pesaro Madonna* to the left of the choir, and Canova's marble pyramid mausoleum,

VENICE FOR CHILDREN

Adults think Venice is meant for them; kids know better. This is where every fairy tale comes to life, with attic prisons inside pink palaces (see Palazzo Ducale, p66), dragon's bones hidden in church walls (see Chiesa dei SS Maria e Donato, p118), master craftsmen carving pocket-sized gondolas (see Gilberto Penzo, p168) and fish balancing on their tails as though spellbound (see Rialto markets, below): top that, JK Rowling.

To wear out hyperactive parents, ruthless kids make them climb the Torre dell'Orologio (p71) or the bell tower of the Chiesa di San Giorgio Maggiore (p114). Kids might occasionally indulge their adults with a push on the swings in the Giardini Pubblici (p104), a nap on a Lido beach (p116) or a *gelato* (ice cream) at Alaska Gelateria (p189) – and double-dare them to try the artichoke and lemon flavours. But if parents are very good, they might be allowed a *prosecco* (sparkling white wine) in the Campo San Giacomo dell'Orio (p202), and the chance to learn how tag is played in Venice.

which he had originally intended as a monument to Titian. The great painter was lost to the plague at 90 in 1576, but legend has it that in light of his contribution to the church, Venice's strict rules of quarantine were bent to allow burial in the Frari. Built for the Franciscans in the 14th and 15th centuries of brick rather than stone, the Frari is bereft of flying buttresses, pinnacles and the gargoyles typical of International Gothic – but its soaring vaulted ceilings and broad triple-nave, Latin-cross floor plan give this church a cathedral grandeur befitting its art masterpieces.

SCUOLA GRANDE DI SAN ROCCO
Map pp86–7

☎ 041 523 48 64; www.scuolagrandisanrocco.it; Campo San Rocco, San Polo 3052; adult/18-26yr/under 18yr €7/5/free; ☿ 9am-5.30pm Easter-Oct, 10am-5pm Nov-Easter; ☷ San Tomà

You'll swear the paint is still fresh on the 50 action-packed Tintorettos painted between 1575 and 1587 for the Scuola Grande di San Rocco. Everyone wanted the commission to paint this building dedicated to the patron saint of the plague-stricken, so Tintoretto cheated a little: instead of producing sketches like his rival Veronese, Tintoretto painted a magnificent *tondo* (ceiling panel) and dedicated it to the saint, knowing such a gift couldn't be refused or matched by other artists.

Take the Scarpagnino staircase to the Sala Grande Superiore, in which Tintoretto covered the ceilings with Old Testament scenes that read like a modern graphic novel. Grab a handglass (mirror) to avoid the otherwise inevitable neck strain as you ogle Tintoretto's riveting ceilings – you can almost hear the swoop overhead as an angel dives down to feed an ailing Elijah. Unlike Vene-

tian colourists, Tintoretto concentrated on dynamic lines for his New Testament wall scenes, foreshadowing abstract expressionism by centuries. Against the shadowy backdrop of the Black Death, Tintoretto highlights his subjects in lightning streaks of hope.

Downstairs, the assembly hall contains a handful of works by other artists including Titian, Giorgione and Tiepolo, and illuminates the story of the Virgin Mary. The story begins on the left wall with the *Annunciation* and ends with the *Ascension* opposite – dark and cataclysmic, compared with Titian's glowing version at I Frari.

Scarpagnino's buoyant, proto-baroque Renaissance facade (see p145) puts a brave face on the confraternity dedicated to San Rocco, who at age 20 in 1315 began wandering southern France and northern Italy helping plague victims until his death at 32. His body was transferred to Venice as a plague-prevention talisman in 1485, providing backup to the new system of vigorous quarantine pioneered by Venice with inspections and waiting periods for incoming ships at Lazaretto (see p27). Between the two, Venice managed to escape the worst of the bouts of plague that wracked Europe and devastated Italy for centuries.

RIALTO MARKETS Map pp86–7
Rialto Mercato; ☷ Rialto

Cutting-edge restaurants worldwide are catching on to a secret that Rialto markets have kept out in the open for 700 years: food tastes better when it's fresh, seasonal and local. More vital to Venetian cuisine than any top chef are the fishmongers at the Pescaria (fish market; ☿ 7am-2pm). This is any foodie's first stop in Venice to admire Venetian specialities in the making: glistening mountains of *moscardini* (baby octopus), crabs ranging from tiny *moeche* (soft-shell crabs) to *granseole* (spider crab), and inky *seppie* (squid) of all sizes. To find out what's next on the seasonal menu, see p179.

Sustainable fishing practices are not a new idea at the Pescaria, where marble plaques show regulations set centuries ago for minimum allowable sizes for lagoon fish. But read stall placards carefully, and

you'll notice seafood flown in from Latin America and Asia, and trawled, endangered bluefin tuna on offer alongside line-caught lagoon fish. Keeping up with gourmet demands isn't easy, given depleted Mediterranean fish stocks (see p35). But savvy diners can make a difference: note the freshest, line-caught lagoon seafood here, and you'll recognise tasty, sustainable options on dinner menus.

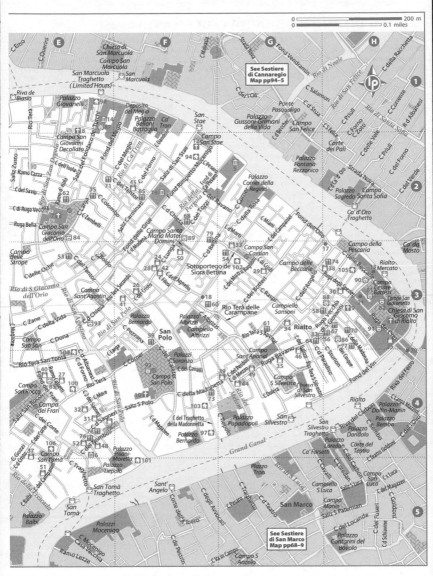

Compared with the tame specimens you'd find at your average supermarket, the Veneto veggies on canalside produce stands look like they just landed from another planet. Tiny purplish Sant'Erasmo *castraure* (baby artichokes) look like alien heads, white Bassano asparagus is eerily spectral and *radicchio trevisano* (bitter red chicory) looks like a mutant Martian flower. Even familiar food goes wild here: suggestively shaped tomatoes and red peppers seem very fresh indeed, and those saucy little strawberries could make grown men cry.

PONTE DI RIALTO Map pp86–7

🚊 Rialto

An amazing feat of engineering in its day, Antonio da Ponte's 1592 marble bridge was for centuries the only land link across the Grand Canal. The construction cost

SESTIERE DI SAN POLO & SANTA CROCE (SANTA CROSE)

250,000 gold ducats, a staggering sum that puts cost overruns for the new Calatrava bridge into perspective. Now that the Rialto is clogged with kiosks and foot-traffic jams, locals go out of their way to avoid it, or zip up the less scenic northern side of the bridge. The southern side faces San Marco, and when crowds of shutter-bugs and tour groups clear out around sunset, it offers a romantic long view of gondolas pulling up to Grand Canal *pal-*

azzi, at striped moorings that look like floating barber poles.

CA' PESARO Map pp86–7
☎ 041 72 11 27; www.museiciviciveneziani
.it; Fondamenta di Ca' Pesaro, Santa Croce 2076;
adult/senior, student & child €5.50/3; ☼ 10am-6pm Tue-Sun Apr-Oct, 10am-5pm Tue-Sun Nov-Mar;
🚤 San Stae

Eclectic collections ranging from a Klimt masterpiece to samurai swords span three floors of this Baldassare Longhena–designed 1710 *palazzo*. When the palace was donated to the city as a showcase for new ideas in 1902, the Galleria d'Arte Moderna began with the boosterish early days of the Biennale, showcasing Venetian landscapes, Venetian painters (notably Giacomo Favretto), and Venetian socialites embodying mythological virtues. But savvy Biennale collectors soon diversified, snapping up pivotal works such as Gustav Klimt's 1909 *Judith II* (Salome) and Marc Chagall's *Rabbi of Vitebsk* (1914–22). The De Lisi Bequest in 1961 added Kandinskys and Morandis to the modernist mix of De Chiricos, Mirós and Moores.

Upstairs, step back in time through the phalanx of samurai warriors at the quirky Museo d'Arte Orientale, evidence of Prince Enricodi Borbone's 1887–89 souvenir shopping spree across Asia preserved for posterity in vintage curio cabinets. The prince reached Japan when Edo art was discounted in favour of modern Meiji, and Edo-era swords, netsukes, and a lacquerware palanquin are his standout acquisitions in this collection of 30,000 objets d'art. The collection has been left much as it was organised in 1928, setting a retro scene perfect for an *Indiana Jones* sequel. See also (p148).

PALAZZO MOCENIGO Map pp86–7

☎ 041 72 17 98; www.museiciviciveneziani.it; Salizada di San Stae 1992; admission with/without discount pass €2.50/4; ☷ 10am-5pm Tue-Sun Apr-Oct, 10am-4pm Tue-Sun Nov-Mar; ⚑ San Stae
Costume dramas unfold in swanky 18th-century salons of this Grand Canal palace with displays of original baroque costumes. Necklines plunge in the Red Living Room, lethal corsets come undone in the Contessa's Bedroom, and deep red procurators' robes hide deep pockets and expanding waistlines in the Dining Room. It's easy to imagine romance blossoming under the ceiling fresco to nuptial bliss in the Green Drawing Room, and doge elections being negotiated in the Count's Library – seven Mocenigo family members served as dogi. The five big portraits are of Mocenigo allies and sometime party guests, such as Charles II of England. But even at the most extravagant parties in these drawing rooms, guests were well advised to mind their tongues: philosopher and Mocenigo house guest Giordano Bruno was turned over to the Inquisition for heresy by his hosts (see p148).

PONTE DELLE TETTE
⚑ Rialto
'Tits Bridge' got its name in the late 15th century, when neighbourhood prostitutes were encouraged to display their wares in windows instead of taking their marketing campaigns to the streets (see p149). Crossing over the bridge, you'll reach Rio Terà delle Carampane, named after a noble family's house (Ca' Rampani) that became notorious as a meeting place for local streetwalkers, who to this day are known as *carampane*. Instead of hanging out in windows, more-ambitious working girls might be found studying: for educated conversation, courtesans might charge 60 times the basic rates of the average *carampane* (see the boxed text, p32).

CHIESA DI SAN POLO Map pp86–7
Campo San Polo, San Polo 2118; admission €3 or Chorus Pass; ☷ 10am-5pm Mon-Sat; ⚑ San Tomà
Most travellers speed past San Polo without realising it's there, because the 9th-century Byzantine church kept a low profile over the centuries while housing cropped up around it. With a high ship's-keel ceiling and 14th- to 15th-century stained glass windows, San Polo is surprisingly airy inside, if a little dark – and the same is true of the art. Tintoretto's *Last Supper* is rife with tension, as apostles react with outrage, hurt and anger at Jesus' news that one of them will betray him. In the sacristy, Giandominico Tiepolo (son of baroque ceiling maestro Giambattista) shows dark sides of humanity in his *Stations of the Cross*: jeering onlookers torment Jesus, his blood-stained rags a perverse contrast with their baroque finery. Literally and figuratively, Tiepolo lays it on thick, so that when a lushly painted Jesus leaps from his tomb on the gold ceiling, it's the ultimate comeuppance.

CHIESA DI SAN GIACOMO DELL'ORIO
Map pp86–7
Campo San Giacomo dell'Orio, Santa Croce 1457; admission €2.50 or Chorus Pass; ☷ 10am-5pm Mon-Sat, 1-5pm Sun; ⚑ Riva de Biasio
La Serenissima seems as serene as ever inside the cool gloom of this 13th-century Romanesque church. You can trace Venice's early maritime conquests in the haul of trophies dragged here from far-flung Venetian territories: a Byzantine column in green marble possibly stolen from Constan-

tinople, a 13th-century baptismal font and a Lombard pulpit perched on a 6th-century column from Ravenna. The main 14th-century Gothic addition is the remarkable wooden *carena di nave* ceiling, but some later art oddities are also worth noting: the wooden crucifix by Veronese and a rare work by Lorenzo Lotto, *Madonna with Child and Saints*. See also p147.

CASA DI GOLDONI Map pp86–7

☎ 041 275 93 25; www.museicivicivenezian.it; Calle dei Nomboli, San Polo 2794; adult/senior, student & child €2.50/1.50; ☽ 10am-5pm Mon-Sat Apr-Oct, 10am-4pm Mon-Sat Nov-Mar; 🚇 San Tomà

Comedians, musicians and writers will feel inspiration bubbling up like a belly laugh from the stone floors at the birthplace of Carlo Goldoni (1707–93), Venice's greatest playwright and a maestro of delicious social satire and *opera buffa* (comic opera; see p50). As the 1st-floor display explains (in Italian), Goldoni was a master of second and third acts: he was a doctor's apprentice before switching to law, a backup career that proved handy when some comedies didn't sell. But Goldoni had the last laugh, with salon sitcoms that made socialites laugh at themselves. The main draws in the museum are the 18th-century marionettes and puppet theatre, but don't miss the chamber-music concerts held here (see website for schedule). Otherwise, the entrance is the most striking part of the 15th-century Gothic house, with its quiet courtyard, private well and stairway in Istrian stone.

SCUOLA GRANDE DI SAN GIOVANNI EVANGELISTA Map pp86–7

☎ 041 71 82 34; Campiello della Scuola 2454; admission €3; ☽ vary; 🚇 Ferrovia

Political power had its perks for this influential Venetian confraternity, including a lavish 1st-floor meeting hall designed in 1729 by Giorgio Massari, a Codussi-designed double staircase, and Pietro Lombardo's 1481 courtyard entry arch that tops any red carpet for impressive entrances (see p146). Bellini and Titian turned out world-class works for the *scuola* (religious confraternity) that have been moved to the Gallerie dell'Accademia (p76) – but Palma Il Giovane's works still illuminate the Sala d'Albergo, and Pietro Longhi's charming *Adoration of the Wise Men* is still here, with

its bright-eyed, wriggling baby Jesus. With the Council of Ten among his clients in the *scuola*, Giandomenico Tiepolo was obliged to finish contracts left unfinished by his father Giambattista when he left for Spain. Today the *scuola* functions as a conference opens, and opens occasionally to the public.

Opposite the *scuola* stands the deconsecrated Chiesa di San Giovanni Evangelista, sometimes open for temporary art exhibitions, with a *Crucifixion* by Tintoretto. A private chapel founded by the Badoer family in 970 includes a wonderful image by Pietro Vecchia of St John the Evangelist holding a pen, awaiting dictation from God, who's hoisting a globe over the altar.

FONDACO DEI TURCHI Map pp86–7

☎ 041 275 02 06; www.museicivicivenezian.it; Salizada del Fontego dei Turchi, Santa Croce 1730; admission free; ☽ 9am-12.30pm Tue-Fri, 10am-3.30pm Sat & Sun; 🚇 San Stae

The dukes of Ferrara had the run of this 12th-century mansion until they were elbowed aside in 1621 to make room for Venice's most important trading partner: Turkey (see p29). For centuries the building served as a way station and warehouse for Turkish merchants, who were a constant in Venice throughout the on-again, off-again relationship between maritime powers, celebrated with favoured-nation trading status and inter-Adriatic weddings, and marred by occasional acts of piracy, invasion and looting. The Fondaco dei Turchi remained rented out to the Turks until 1858, after which the place underwent a disastrous modernisation that left few reminders of its medieval origins. Original features in the facade were sacrificed to the architectural fancies of the time, including odd crenellations that made the gracious Gothic buidling look more like a prison.

Today it houses a scientific library and the rather half-hearted Museo Civico di Storia Naturale (Natural History Museum), which consists of two main displays. The first is on the ground floor: a rather small, sad fish tank containing Venetian coastal specimens bubbling for attention. On the 2nd floor is a more exciting display of dinosaurs, including an *ouransaurus* from the Sahara, a 12m-long prehistoric crocodile skeleton, and a 120-million-year-old *psittacosaurus mongoliensis*, a 0.5m-long skeleton of a baby dinosaur found in the Gobi Desert.

CHIESA DI SAN GIOVANNI ELEMOSINARIO Map pp86–7

Ruga Vecchia di San Giovanni, San Polo 477; admission €2.50 or Chorus Pass; 🕙 **10am-5pm Mon-Sat, 1-5pm Sun;** 🚤 **Rialto**

You could easily stride right past this Renaissance brick church, built by Scarpagnino (aka Antonio Abbondi) after a disastrous fire in 1514 destroyed much of the Rialto area. The church and its separate bell tower are camouflaged by surrounding houses and tucked behind kiosks selling T-shirts with 'Venezia' spelled out in rhinestones, so their sober, soaring presence comes as a surprise – but a Titian of the namesake *St John the Almsgiver* (freshly restored and returned from the Accademia) and a Mannerist altarpiece and recently restored dome frescoes by Pordenone are brilliant finds.

CHIESA DI SAN ROCCO Map pp86–7

☎ **041 523 48 64; Campo San Rocco, San Polo 3053; admission free;** 🕙 **8am-12.30pm & 3-5.30pm daily;** 🚤 **San Tomà**

After staggering out of the Scuola Grande di San Rocco (p85) thunderstruck by Tintoretto, you might want to take a moment to regain sensation in your ocular nerves inside the cheery pink walls of this church across the way. Here a couple of comparatively quiet Tintorettos are safely tucked away on the main-entrance wall and around the altar. Although built at about the same time as the *scuola*, the church was completely overhauled in the 18th century – hence the bold baroque facade, its portal flanked with statues by Giovanni Marchiori. See also p145.

CHIESA DI SAN STAE Map pp86–7

Campo San Stae, Santa Croce 1981; admission €3 or Chorus Pass; 🕙 **10am-5pm Mon-Sat, 1-5pm Sun;** 🚤 **San Stae**

An aficionado of Venetian light, English painter William Turner loved painting the sun-washed Palladian exterior of this church, with its facade dotted by statues of angels and cardinal virtues. You can see what a painter obsessed with light effects might admire in this church: for all its gleaming white classical grandeur, it retains a languid seaside air, with early-morning lagoon mists that collect mystically around its base. The church was founded in 966 but finished in 1709, and though the interiors are surprisingly spare for a baroque edifice, there are a couple of notable works: Giambattista Tiepolo's *The Martyrdom of St Bartholomew* and Sebastiano Ricci's *The Liberation of St Peter*. See also p148.

CHIESA DI SAN GIOVANNI DECOLLATO Map pp86–7

☎ **041 97 25 83; Campo San Giovanni Decollato, Santa Croce;** 🕙 **10am-noon Mon-Sat;** 🚤 **Riva de Biasio**

Heady rumours swirl like canal mists around this long-abandoned church named for San Zan Degolà, or St John the Headless, known rather less dramatically in English as St John the Baptist. On the south wall facing the *campo* is a sculpted medallion of a freshly severed head that presumably represents St John after his head was lopped off by Salome. But according to Venetian urban legend, this is an effigy of Biagio (aka Biasio) Cargnio, who had a butcher shop near here in the 16th century where the sausages contained a secret ingredient: children. When his recipe was discovered, he was promptly beheaded and quartered by the authorities, and his house and shop were demolished – yet somehow, one of the most pleasant waterfront walks along the Grand Canal remains named after him, not far from this church.

After WWII, the church was retired from its job as a warehouse, and restorations uncovered a wooden ship's-keel ceiling and some 11th- to 13th-century Veneto-Byzantine frescoes – best to see them now, since the damp interiors are steadily affecting their condition. In 1994, the church reopened with Russian Orthodox services.

SESTIERE DI CANNAREGIO

Eating p189; Shopping p172; Sleeping p221

Anyone could adore Venice on looks alone, but in Cannaregio you'll fall for its personality. Located between extroverted San Marco and introverted Santa Croce, tough Castello and saintly San Polo, Cannaregio combines all its neighbours' personality quirks. Day trippers race along broad Strada Nuova en route from the train to the Rialto, while just a few streets over, footsteps echo along moody stretches of Fondamenta della Misericordia without a T-shirt kiosk in sight. The Jewish Ghetto is a tribute to a community that thrived against the odds in these malarial swamps, with iconic top-floor synagogues that are an integral part of the scenery alongside neighbouring Gothic beauty Chiesa della Madonna dell'Orto, Renaissance gem Chiesa di Santa Maria dei Miracoli, and the big, brash, baroque I Gesuiti.

But some Cannaregio characters aren't shy about making a splash. Wagnerian dramas continue to unfold nightly at the Casino di Venezia tables a century after Wagner finished his Ring cycle on the premises, and Ca' d'Oro remains one of the most splendid Grand Canal *palazzi*, with a Venetian art collection donated by Baron Franchetti and reclaimed from Napoleon. At night, visitors and the neighbourhood's biggest personalities – students from nearby Foscari University – loath to leave converge on local *osterie* along the Fondamenta degli Ormesini for drinks, gossip and some of Venice's least-known and best-priced meals.

At the northwestern edge of Venice, Cannaregio fronts a stretch of lagoon to the east interrupted by Murano and the Isola di San Michele (Venice's cemetery). Cannaregio bumps into San Marco at the Rialto to the south and Castello at Zanipolo to the east. Apart from the busy Ferrovia stop, there are only two Grand Canal stops: San Marcuola (lines 1 and 82 and N) and Ca' d'Oro (1 and N). Lines 41, 42, 51 and 52 wing around from Ferrovia into the Canale di Cannaregio and Canale delle Fondamente Nuove. Ferries head from Fondamente Nuove to the northern islands, including San Michele, Murano, Burano, Le Vignole and Sant'Erasmo.

CHIESA DI SANTA MARIA DEI MIRACOLI Map pp94–5

Campo dei Miracoli 6074; admission €2.50 or Chorus Pass; ⏰ 10am-5pm Mon-Sat, 1-5pm Sun; 🚤 Fondamente Nuove

When Nicolò di Pietro's Madonna icon started miraculously weeping in its outdoor shrine around 1480, crowd control became impossible in this cramped corner of Cannaregio. Out of deference to her holiness – and possibly to disperse foot-traffic jams – the neighbours took up a collection to build a chapel to house the painting and its ecstatic admirers. But there was another miracle in store for the neighbourhood: Pietro and Tullio Lombardo's design, which completely ignored then-current Gothic in favour of a simpler, more classical approach that would come to be known as Renaissance architecture.

Although frequently described as a 'jewel box', the church is not especially flashy inside: it's simply clad with glistening marble, keeping the focus on the miraculous icon at the front of the church. But look closely at the chancel staircase and you'll notice that angels and the Madonna have been carved right into the railings by Tullio Lombardo. In a prime example of

Renaissance humanism, Pier Maria Pennacchi filled each of the 50 wooden coffered ceiling panels with a bright-eyed portrait of a saint or prophet dressed as a Venetian. The church that began as a modest chapel became a true icon of Venetian ingenuity, and a monument to community. See also p153.

MUSEO EBRAICO & JEWISH GHETTO Map pp94–5

☎ 041 71 53 59; www.museoebraico.it; Campo di Ghetto Nuovo 2902b; adult/student €3/2, tours incl admission €8.50/7; ⏰ 10am-7pm Sun-Fri except Jewish holidays Jun-Sep, 10am-6pm Sun-Fri Oct-May; 🚤 Guglie

This area in Venice was once a *getto* (foundry) on an island away from the main area of Cannaregio to contain the risk of fire – but its role as the designated Jewish quarter from the 16th to 18th centuries gave the word a whole new meaning. In accordance with the Venetian Republic's 1516 decree, Jewish artisans and lenders stocked and funded Venice's commercial enterprises by day, while at night and on Christian holidays, they were restricted to the gated island of the Ghetto Nuovo.

If you scan the top floors of the buildings ringing the Campo di Ghetto Nuovo, you

A BRIEF HISTORY OF JEWISH VENICE

In other premodern European cities, Jewish communities remained distinct from mainstream culture – but from the 10th century onwards, the history of Venice and its Jewish community were deeply intertwined. As with foreigners of any faith, German Jewish arrivals in Venice were initially allowed only limited residence permits. But war with Genoa had depleted Venice's resources and, to raise capital, in 1382 the Maggior Consiglio (Grand Council) granted licences to the Jewish community to operate as moneylenders.

With refugees of various nationalities crowding into Venice after war with the Papal States, the Republic decreed on 29 March 1516 that the 1000 Jews residing in Venice should relocate to one area. The concept of an officially defined Jewish neighbourhood was already centuries old in Spain, but as an incentive Venice's Jewish community was granted 10-year renewable residency permits.

Living conditions weren't easy in Venice's Getto Novo (New Foundry; Ghetto Nuovo in Italian), an island in the mosquito-infected marshes of Cannaregio. Though Jewish residents were free to conduct business throughout the city by day, they were initially required to wear distinguishing caps or badges, and gates around the Ghetto Nuovo were shut by Christian guards from midnight until dawn.

Despite these constraints, Jewish intellectuals had a remarkable impact on Venetian culture, from Sara Copia Sullam's influential literary salons (see p26) to Leon Modena's sermons at the Schola Italiana (Italian Synagogue; see p151) delivered in Italian to accommodate Christian crowds who came to hear him speak. Sephardic Jewish doctors, privy to the considerable medical advancements of the Arab world, were allowed to leave the Ghetto to attend to Gentile patients any time, day or night.

Venice's Jewish community could also freely practise its religion. In 1541, Jewish refugees fleeing persecution from the Inquisition in Spain and Portugal found safe harbour in Venice's Ghetto, and the already crowded buildings soon turned into six-storey medieval skyscrapers. Many new arrivals were wealthy merchants, bringing crucial new business to Venice when its shipping fortunes were on the wane. Venice granted additional zones to the growing Jewish community: the Getto Vecio (or Ghetto Vecchio; Old Foundry) and the Calle del Ghetto Nuovissimo (Very New Ghetto Street).

In the middle of the 16th century, the Jewish community was thriving, and Venice came into its own as a cultural hub of Europe. Jewish printers established Venice's reputation for publishing – the first ever printed version of the Talmud was published in Venice – and helped launch Venice as the early literary hub of Europe. This was the heady heyday of humanists like Veronese and Tintoretto, who painted Jewish characters in biblical narratives not as caricatures, but as individuals able to be related to as neighbours and intellectual peers.

Venice's creative licence with conventional interfaith divisions did not always sit well with the authorities in Rome. Pope Julian cracked down on publishers; Tintoretto was critiqued as depicting holy subjects in too earthy a light; and the Inquisition commanded Veronese to change his depiction of Protestants, Turks and Jews mingling freely at the *Last Supper*. Yet Venice continued to publish books, Tintoretto's human dramas found favour, and Veronese merely changed the title of his masterpiece to *Feast in the House of Levi* (see p76). When a papal bull excommunicated Venice in 1606 for ignoring Church rulings, Venice began closing religious orders; the bull was rescinded within the year.

In 1797 Napoleon abolished all restrictions on Jews and opened the Ghetto. Initially, rabbis opposed the opening, fearing the community would become disperse. But civil liberties continued expanding, and after Venice was annexed to the Kingdom of Italy in 1866, all citizens were guaranteed quality under the law and freedom of religious expression.

Mussolini's rise to power was a throwback to the early days of the Ghetto, with 1938 race laws that revived restrictions and yellow badges. In November 1943 his puppet Fascist government of Salò declared Jews enemies of the state, and some 1670 Jewish Venetians were sent to the Italian concentration camp of Fossoli; 289 were sent onward to Nazi death camps.

Some 420 Jewish Venetians are registered residents today, though most choose to live outside the Ghetto – the memory of 1943 still haunts Venice. Urban legend has it that a ghostly rabbi spotted in the Campo di Ghetto Nuovo after WWII deportations mysteriously reappeared in the 1990s; some say it's Leon Modena, reminding Venice to be tolerant.

can spot three synagogues, or *schole* (literally, 'schools'), distinguished from the residential housing by the small domes that indicate the position of the pulpit. A plain wood cupola in the corner of the *campo* marks the location of the Schola Canton (Corner Synagogue). Next door is the Schola Tedesca (German Synagogue), recognisable by rows of five larger windows.

When Jewish merchants fled the Spanish Inquisition for Venice in 1541, there was no place to go but up: around the Campo

SESTIERE DI CANNAREGIO

di Ghetto Nuovo and the adjacent Campo di Ghetto Vecchio, additional storeys atop existing buildings housed new arrivals and publishers. Jewish refugees from Portugal and Spain raised two synagogues in the Campo di Ghetto Vecchio that are considered among the most beautiful in northern Italy, with interiors renovated in the 17th century that may be the work of Baldassare Longhena. The Schola Levantina (Levantine Synagogue) has a magnificent 17th-century woodworked pulpit, while the main hall of the Schola Spagnola (Spanish Synagogue) is reached by a sweeping staircase. On the Campo di Ghetto Nuovo, the rooftop Schola Italiana (Italian Synagogue) is a simple synagogue built by newly arrived and largely destitute Italian Jews, who had fled from what was then Spanish-controlled southern Italy.

After Napoleon lifted restrictions in 1797, Ghetto residents gained standing as Venetian citizens. But Mussolini's 1938 race laws were throwbacks to the 16th century, and in 1943 most of the 1670 Jews in Venice were rounded up and sent to concentration camps; only 37 returned. Today Venice's Jewish community numbers around 400, including a few families in the Ghetto.

A starting point to explore this pivotal community in Venetian arts, architecture and commerce is the Museo Ebraico (Jewish Museum), where English-language tours leave every half-hour starting at 10.30am, and head inside three of the Ghetto synagogues, including the Schola Canton, Schola Italiana and either the Schola Levantina during summer or the Schola Spagnola in winter. Opened in 1955, the

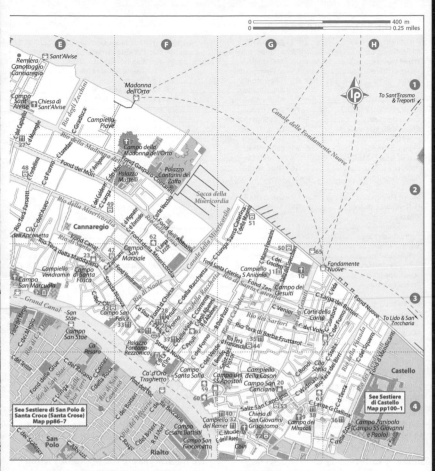

museum has a small collection of finely worked silverware and other Judaica art objects used in private prayer and to decorate synagogues. You can also inquire at the museum about guided tours to the Antico Cimitero Israelitico (Old Jewish Cemetery; p116) on the Lido. For more information on the Ghetto and a walking tour through the area, see p150. For more on Jewish history in Venice, see History, p23, and the boxed text, p93.

CHIESA DELLA MADONNA DELL'ORTO Map pp94–5
Campo della Madonna dell'Orto 3520; admission €3 or Chorus Pass; ☺ 10am-5pm Mon-Sat, 1-5pm Sun; 🚊 Madonna dell'Orto
One of Venice's best-kept secrets, this elegantly spare 1365 brick Gothic cathedral

dedicated to ferrymen, merchants and travellers (hey, that's you) was the object of Tintoretto's attention for decades. No wonder: he lived just over the footbridge from here (see p152). Tintoretto and his family were buried in the corner chapel, and he saved some of his best work for the apse here. His golden-tinged *Presentation of the Virgin in the Temple* shows throngs of star-struck angels and mortals vying for a glimpse of Mary, while in his 1546 *Last Judgment,* lost souls attempt to hold back a teal tidal wave while an angel rescues one last person from the ultimate *acque alte* (high tides). Tintoretto is not usually considered a great Venetian colourist, but this evocative use of colour to heighten his signature drama reveals Titianesque talents. See also p152.

SESTIERE DI CANNAREGIO

CA' D'ORO Map pp94–5

Golden House; ☎ 041 522 23 49; www.cadoro .org, in Italian; Calle di Ca' d'Oro 3932; adult/EU student under 26yr/EU citizen under 18yr or over 65yr €5/2.50/free; 8.15am-2pm Mon, 8.15am-7.15pm Tue-Sun; Ca' d'Oro

Along the Grand Canal, you can't miss the stunning 15th-century Ca' d'Oro, its lacy Gothic facade resplendent even without the original gold-leaf details that gave the palace its name ('Golden House'). Ca' d'Oro was donated to Venice with an impressive art collection by Baron Franchetti (of Palazzo Franchetti fame; see p73). Today it houses these works in the 2nd-floor Galleria Franchetti, plus a jackpot of artwork downstairs plundered from Veneto churches during Napoleon's Italy conquest. Napoleon had excellent taste in souvenirs, as the 1st floor reveals: bronzes, tapestries, paintings and sculpture ripped (sometimes literally) from Veneto churches were warehoused at Milan's Brera Museum as Napoleonic war trophies, until they were reclaimed by Venice for display here.

Collection highlights on the 2nd floor include Andrea Mantegna's teeth-baring, arrow-riddled *Saint Sebastian* altarpiece, Pietro Lombardo's tender *Madonna and Child* in glistening Carrara marble, and pieces of Titian frescoes along with a faded but still sensuous nude fresco fragment by Giorgione saved from the outside of the Fondaco dei Tedeschi (p74). A big incentive for visiting are the photo ops along the loggia balconies over the Grand Canal, with arty angles through lacy stonework. See also p153.

I GESUITI Map pp94–5

☎ 041 528 65 79; Salizada dei Specchieri 4880; 10am-noon & 4-6pm daily; Fondamente Nuove

Giddily over the top even by rococo standards, this gaudy, glitzy 18th-century Jesuit church is difficult to take in all at once, with a staggering spaceship of a pulpit and undulating marble walls. The church is lavishly decorated with white-and-gold stucco, white-and-green marble floors, and marble flourishes filling in any blank space. Gravity is provided by Titian's uncharacteristically dark, gloomy *Martyrdom of St Lawrence*, on the left as you enter the church. Also playing against type here is Tintoretto's *Assumption of the Virgin,* in the northern transept. This image is the antithesis of his dark images in the Scuola Grande di San Rocco (p85), showing the Virgin on her merry way to heaven, suffused with a rosy glow that nods at Titian and a nimble lightness that leans towards Tiepolo.

PONTE DI CALATRAVA Map pp94–5
🚊 Piazzale Roma, Ferrovia

Modern Spanish architect Santiago Calatrava's 2008 bridge over the Grand Canal between Santo Croce and Cannaregio has been called many things: a fish tail, a glass-and-steel fantasy, unnecessary, overdue, pleasingly streamlined and displeasingly wheelchair inaccessible. Its detractors point out that its costs surpassed triple the original 2001 estimate, and engineers are still working to correct a 4cm tolerance to ensure its stability. Even among its supporters, there is disagreement. Some claim the bridge is best seen at night, when it looks from afar like a meteoric streak of light across the Grand Canal; and others prefer it by day, when you can appreciate the red ribbed steel underbelly. Judge for yourself whether the time and money paid off, and you can join the ongoing debates on the bridge's relative merits at happy hours across Venice.

PALAZZO VENDRAMIN-CALERGI
Map pp94–5

☎ 041 529 71 11, Wagner museum 041 276 04 07; www.casinovenezia.it; Palazzo Vendramin-Calergi 2040; admission €5; 🕑 casino 3pm-2.30am Sun-Thu, 3pm-3am Fri & Sat, museum tours 10.30am Tue & Sat, 2.30pm Thu; 🚊 San Marcuola

High Renaissance meets high risk at this 16th-century palace, which for centuries has served as the city's casino (see p208). This might seem like an odd place to convalesce, but composer Richard Wagner was no stranger to drama, and chose to retreat here in 1882–83 to recover from an apparent bout of heart trouble and complete the 20-year effort on this Ring cycle. He succeeded, only to die of a heart attack here within a few months. You can wander into the ground-floor area during casino hours, but unless you're staying in a high-end hotel that offers free passes,

you'll have to don formal attire and pay to see the gaming rooms.

Three of the salons Wagner occupied have been set aside as the Wagner Museum. The museum offers tours three times a week by prior reservation at least 24 hours in advance. The first room is dominated by a Bechstein piano and varied Wagneriana, including early editions of his *Parsifal.* The second room was Wagner's study and lounge, and in a rather macabre touch, a copy of the sofa on which he had his fatal heart attack occupies one corner. There are also copies of scores Wagner created in the 1830s – since the originals are now worth some €700 a page, keeping them lying around here would be too much of a gamble, even for a casino. The third room was Wagner's bedroom, where you can see letters and other documents, including a request from Wagner's wife to the Hotel de l'Europe to deliver 12 *demi-bouteilles* (half-bottles) of Moet & Chandon to their gondolier – keep the Wagners in mind next time you tip for a song.

ORATORIO DEI CROCIFERI Map pp94–5
☎ 041 532 29 20; Campo dei Gesuiti 4095; admission €3; 🕑 3.30-6.30pm Fri & Sat Apr-Oct; 🚊 Fondamente Nuove

Humble though it may seem from the outside – especially after the opulence of I Gesuiti across the street – this simple 12th-century oratory is positively plastered on the inside with 16th-century masterpieces by Palma Il Giovane. The oratory was originally part of a hospice set up by brothers of the Crociferi order to give shelter to pilgrims and provide assistance to the sick, and found a powerful benefactor in the 13th century: Doge Renier Zen. Doge Pasquale Cicogna ordered the place frescoed in honour of the Crociferi, Doge Zen, Venice, and (of course) himself. With works like his 1585 *Doge Renier Zen and the Endowment of the Crociferi,* Palma Il Giovane set the walls ablaze with sunset shades of golden yellow and rose red.

CHIESA DEI SCALZI Map pp94–5
Fondamenta dei Scalzi 55-57; admission free; 🕑 7-11.45am & 4-6.45pm Mon-Sat, 7.45am-12.30pm & 4-7pm Sun & holidays; 🚊 Ferrovia

An unexpected outburst of baroque extravagance next to the dour Ferrovia, this

Longhena-designed church has a facade by Giuseppe Sardi rippling with columns and statues in niches. This is an unusual departure for Venice, where baroque ebullience was usually reserved for interiors of Renaissance-leaning buildings – and in fact it was a deliberate echo of a style often employed in Rome, intended to help make the Carmelites posted here from Rome feel more at home. Sadly, the vault frescoes by Tiepolo in two of the side chapels are damaged. Before the main altar on your left, you might spot the tomb of Venice's last doge, Ludovico Manin, who presided over the dissolution of the Republic in 1797 before the threat of Napoleon and died in ignominy five years later.

CHIESA DI SAN MARCUOLA
Map pp94–5

☎ 041 71 38 72; Campo San Marcuola 1758; admission free; ⊗ 3-6pm Mon-Sat; 🚢 San Marcuola

The right hand of John the Baptist was once housed in this church founded in the 9th century, but the church burned in the 14th century, and what you see was cobbled together (and not quite completed) in the 18th century by architects Giorgio Massari and Antonio Gaspari. Inside is Tintoretto's 1547 *Last Supper,* with Christ and apostles ominously spotlit against a black background in what looks like a mystery theatre version of the New Testament story.

Eating p191; Shopping p172; Sleeping p223

Sailors, saints and modern artists have made Castello what it is today: a waterfront home to earthy *osterie*, ethereal icons and the show-stopper that is the Biennale. Several churches here are gilt to the hilt, historic four-star hotels sprawl out along the Grand Canal waterfront, and the Biennale pavilions are showpieces of modern architecture. Venice's Armenian community and the largest Greek community outside Greece lived in these winding lanes alongside Turkish and Syrian merchants, bringing cosmopolitan flair to local restaurants and even more glittering icons to the neighbourhood. But Castello proves that it's possible to be refined in the extreme without losing vital roughness around the edges. Some 5000 shipbuilders once worked here at the Arsenale, building the fleet that extended Venice's empire to Constantinople, and traces of those glory days can be seen in the Museo Navale and heard in the bawdy humour you might overhear at happy hour.

Just behind the grand facades of the Basilica di San Marco and Palazzo Ducale runs a canal that marks the division between the Sestiere di San Marco and Sestiere di Castello. Walking away to the east or north, you quickly notice a thinning of the crowds. One of the last seriously packed walkways is Salizada San Lio. Already in Campo Santa Maria Formosa, you get the feeling that locals are still at least partly in control. To the very north, the single grandest monument of the district is Zanipolo (Chiesa dei SS Giovanni e Paolo), with the city hospital next door in the church's one-time convent complex. The next psychological marker, if you will, is the north–south Rio di San Lorenzo, beyond which tourists are reduced to a trickle as you wind your way towards the Arsenale, the industrial powerhouse of medieval Venice.

The southern entrance to the Arsenale brings you close to the waterfront and from anywhere along it you have splendid views of the Canale di San Marco. Upmarket hotels lap up these views at the San Marco end of the esplanade, but as you walk further away towards the Giardini Pubblici, a peaceful air descends. Along Via Giuseppe Garibaldi and in its fishbone net of alleys, local folks go about their lives in about as undisturbed a fashion as they can manage. Overrun by interlopers during the Biennale art festival, the area is otherwise intriguing as a taste of the 'real' Venice, full of simple shops, local eateries, vociferous families and the sounds of the Venetian dialect. Beyond, the district trails out into leafy Sant'Elena and sleepy Isola de San Pietro.

Vaporetti 41 and 42 run clockwise and anticlockwise around the Castello district on their circular routes. Vaporetti 51 and 52 do the same thing but include the Lido. They call at San Zaccaria, the main Castello stop near Piazza San Marco (where many other lines also stop). The Biennale stop operates only during the festival; at other times, Giardini is the main stop for the Biennale grounds.

ZANIPOLO (CHIESA DEI SS GIOVANNI E PAOLO) Map pp100–1

☎ 041 523 59 13; Campo SS Giovanni e Paolo; admission €2.50; ☷ 9.30am-6pm Mon-Sat, 1-6pm Sun; 🚊 Ospedale

Who does brick Gothic best? When the Dominicans undertook the 100-year effort to build Zanipolo in 1333 to rival the Franciscans' Chiesa di Santa Maria Gloriosa dei Frari (p84), the church stirred passions and partisanship more common to Serie A football than architecture. Both have red-brick facades with high-contrast detailing in white stone. But since Zanipolo's facade remains unfinished, the Frari won a decisive early decision over Zanipolo with its soaring grace – and with Titian's *Assunta* altarpiece front and centre, the Frari seemed impossible to surpass.

Over the centuries, Zanipolo may have at least tied the score with the sheer scale and variety of its masterpieces. For starters, it has more dogi – 25 of them, in lavish tombs by such notable sculptors as Nino Pisano and Tullio Lombardo. In the transept, a vast 15th-century Murano stained-glass window is currently undergoing restoration to illuminate designs by Bartolomeo Vivarini and Girolamo Mocetto. And in the Cappella del Rosario, off the north arm of the transept, Paolo Veronese's own *Assunta* ceiling depicts the rosy Virgin ascending a staggering staircase to be crowned by cherubs, while angels flip with the joy of it all.

Given masterpieces by Bellini, Canova and Titian at the Frari, the artistic match is tough – not to mention the Chiesa della Madonna dell'Orto (p95) as a contender for brick

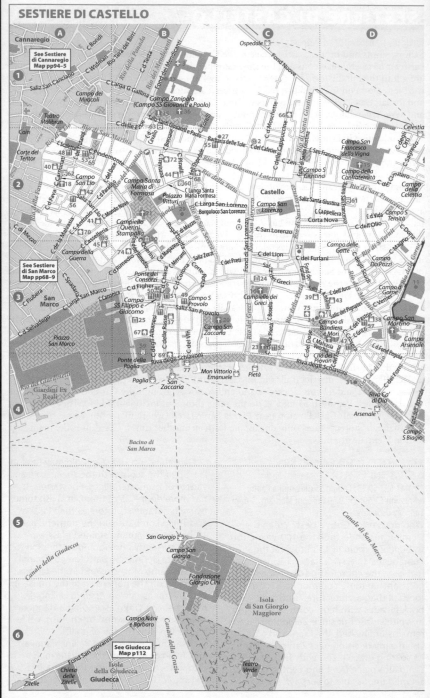

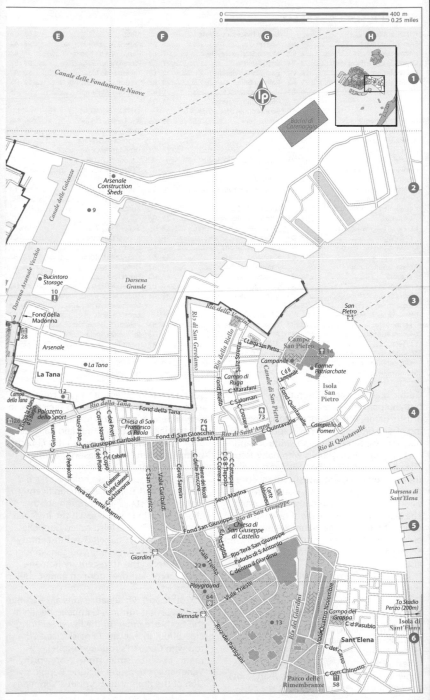

0   400 m
0   0.25 miles

E   **F**   **G**   **H**

1

Canale delle Fondamente Nuove

Bacini di
Carenaggio

2

Arsenale
Construction
Sheds

● 9

Canale delle Galeazze

Darsena Arsenale Vecchio

Bucintoro
Storage

10

Darsena
Grande

Fond della
Madonna

Rio di San Gerolamo

Rio della Riello

Rio delle Vergini

San
Pietro

3

Arsenale

● La Tana

La Tana

C Larga San Pietro

Campo
San Pietro

Campanile

C d'l
Lanzonile

Former
Patriarchate

Fond Quintavalle

Isola
San
Pietro

Campo
della Tana

● 12

Rio della Tana

Fond della Tana

Fond Rielo

Campo di
Ruga

C Marafani

C Saloman

C Crosera

Canale di San Pietro

28

Palazetto
dello Sport

C Grimana

C dei Preti

Corte Nova

C dei Pistor

C Copo

Chiesa di San
Francesco
di Paola

Fond di San Gioacchin
Fond di Sant'Anna

76

Rio di Sant'Anna

73

Quintavalle

Campiello d'
Pomeri

Rio di Quintavalle

4

26

Via Giuseppe Garibaldi

C Cobotti

C Colonne
Corte Colonne
C Schiavona

C Pedrocchi

Riva dei Sette Martiri

C San Domenico

Viale Garibaldi

Corte Saresin

Rena dei Nicoli
delle Ancore

Cattapan
C G B Tiepolo
Correra

Seco Marina

Corte
Solisonda

Darsena di
Sant'Elena

5

Fond San Giuseppe

Rio di San Giuseppe

Chiesa di
San Giuseppe
di Castello

C de Solda

Rio Tera San Giuseppe
Paludo di S Antonio
C dentro il Giardino

Viale Trento

Giardini

● 22

Playground

64

Viale Trieste

Biennale

● 13

Rio dei Giardini

Viale Quattro Novembre

To Stadio
Penzo (200m)

Campo del
Grappa

C d'Pasubio

Isola di
Sant'Elena

6

Sant'Elena

C del Carso

C Gen Chinotto

Rio dei Partigiani

Parco delle
Rimembranze

58

SESTIERE DI CASTELLO

Gothic grandeur and Tintorettos – but Zanipolo shows a lot of heart in its artistic game. Guido Reni's baroque painting of *San Giuseppe* is a rare expression of holy father-son bonding, showing Joseph exchanging adoring looks with baby Jesus. The chapel dome on the southwest end of the nave boasts Giambattista Lorenzetti's *Jesus the Navigator*, where Jesus scans the skies like an anxious Venetian sea captain. The acknowledged master of heartstring-pulling tenderness, Giovanni Bellini, has a polyptych of *San Vincenzo Ferreri* (St Vincent Ferrer) over the second altar of the right aisle.

For more information on the Zanipolo, see p154.

CHIESA DI SAN ZACCARIA Map pp100–1

☎ 041 522 12 57; Campo San Zaccaria 4693;
🕙 10am-noon & 4-6pm Mon-Sat, 4-6pm Sun;
🚤 San Zaccaria

When 15th-century Venetian Paris Hiltons showed more interest in sailors than saints, they might be sent for a stint at the con-vent adjoining Chiesa di San Zaccaria; Venice's spoiled daughters passed their time in prayer here, with breaks for concerts and occasionally scandalous masked balls (see p159). The wealth showered on this church by their grateful (or at least hopeful) parents is evident. To your right as you enter, the Cappella di Sant'Anastasia holds works by Tintoretto and Tiepolo and magnificently crafted choir stalls, and through another chapel from here you'll reach the frescoed Cappella di San Tarasion (also called Cappella d'Oro or Golden Chapel). Twelfth-century mosaics also survive, and you can wander downstairs to the 10th-century Romanesque crypt, left over from an earlier church on the site.

Gothic and Renaissance fans alike admire the facade that Antonio Gambello began in the Gothic manner on the lower sections, crescendoing into the Renaissance at the top with Codussi's rounded embellishments in white Istrian stone. Noteworthy Venetian art treasures include Tiepolo's version of the flight into Egypt in a Venetian boat; Bellini's *Virgin Enthroned with Jesus, an Angel Musician and Saints,* glowing like it's plugged into an outlet; and Antonio Vivarini's 1443 painting of St Sabina, keeping her cool as angels buzz around her head like lagoon mosquitoes.

PALAZZO GRIMANI Map pp100–1

☎ 041 521 05 77; www.palazzogrimani.org; Ramo Grimani 4858; adult/student & senior €9/5; ☯ guided tour in Italian 9.30am, 11.30am & 1.30pm Tue-Sun

Hang a right off Ruga Giuffa, and you'll wind up in ancient Rome by way of Renaissance Venice and Tuscany. Closed to the public for 27 years (see p159), this palace has finally been restored to the eye-blinking grandeur initiated by Doge Antonio Grimani, whose reign was brief (1521–23) but his legacy lavish. The Grimani family were Renaissance trendsetters: they'd collected Graeco-Roman archaeological curiosities since before they became cool in the 14th century, and some of their best pieces can be glimpsed today in the Museo Correr (p69). To make their house a suitable setting for such splendours, the Grimani went all out: floors paved with dizzying polychrome marble patterns, the grand entry staircase that is attributed to Palladio, and walls edged with gilded stucco friezes of dancing nymphs.

But best of all, in 1540 the Grimani hired a dream team of fresco painters specialised in fanciful grotesques and vibrant, Pompeii-style mythological scenes. Francesco Salviati applied the glowing, Raphael-style colours he'd used for Florence's Palazzo Vecchio and Rome's Palazzo Farnese, alongside Francesco Menzocchi, responsible for Vatican frescoes, and Roman painter Giovanni da Udine, considered among the brightest pupils of Raphael and (along with Titian) Giorgione. Their frescoed ceilings are simply staggering: a lagoon duck swoops down from a forest of

trees springing up between vaulted arches, a marble atrium is capped with a trompe l'œil coffered vault, and an inner circle of gilded mythological greats gets completely upstaged by irreverent grotesques in the ceiling corners. Visits are currently possible by prebooked tours in Italian only – but 'Ooooooh!' requires no translation.

CHIESA DI SAN FRANCESCO DELLA VIGNA Map pp100–1

☎ 041 520 61 02; Campo San Francesco della Vigna 2787; ☯ 8am-12.30pm & 3-7pm daily; ⛴ Celestia

Designed and built by Jacopo Sansovino with a facade by a precocious Palladio in his first church commission, this enchanting Franciscan church is one of Venice's most underrated attractions (see also p155). The Madonna positively glows in Bellini's 1507 *Madonna and Saints* in the Capella Santa just off the flower-carpeted cloister courtyard, while swimming angels and strutting birds steal the scene in Antonio da Negroponte's c 1460–70 delightful *Virgin Enthroned.*

Palladio and the Madonna are tough acts to follow, but father–son sculptors Pietro and Tullio Lombardo's 15th-century marble reliefs of saints and the life of Christ, housed in the Cappella Giustiniani, in the north transept left of the altar, are storytelling triumphs. Keep your eye on the expressive reactions of minor figures in these biblical narratives that provide a running commentary on the action, down to the startled mule. Breezes seem to ripple through the Lombardos' carved-marble trees, and lifelike lions seem prepared to pounce right off the wall.

Outside, the bell tower out back looks like the long-lost twin of the Campanile di San Marco, and facing north, a couple of steps leading to a portico of classical columns make the *campo* look like a proper ancient Roman agora. This makes a sociable setting for Venice's best annual block party,

HORSES & HEELS

The street behind Zanipolo became nicknamed Calle Cavallerizza, after stables that once stood here and quartered up to 70 horses. These were mostly reserved for noblemen, who didn't enjoy appreciate getting their silks muddy during *acque altae* (high tides), as well as baroque fashionistas and high-end courtesans, who couldn't walk far in stylish 50cm-high Venetian heels (see p31). The secluded *calle* (alleyway) became notorious for streetwalkers, and in the early 20th century there was a booming black-market street trade here in penicillin, the sought after syphilis cure. Not surprisingly, this street was frequented by the biggest heel of all: Giacomo Casanova. In 1755 he was arrested here on charges of corrupting nuns, and was led off to the rooftop prisons of the Palazzo Ducale to languish – at least until his daring escape (see the boxed text, p67).

the Festa di Francesco della Vigna, with wine and rustic fare served in the stately shadow of Palladio; usually held the third week in June.

GIARDINI PUBBLICI & BIENNALE
Map pp100–1

🚉 Giardini, Biennale

Modern angles and swing sets jutting out amid the greenery signal that you're entering the Giardini, home to Venice's Art Biennale (see La Biennale di Venezia, p18). During the Art Biennale's June–September run in odd years, curators and connoisseurs swarming national showcases ranging from Geza Rintel Maroti's 1909 Secessionist-era Hungarian Pavilion, glittering with mosaics, to Peter Cox's 1988 boxy yellow Australian Pavilion (p158), frequently mistaken for a construction trailer. Carlo Scarpa contributed in one way or another from 1948 to 1972, trying to make the best of Duilio Torres' Fascist 1932 Italian Pavilion (now the Palazzo delle Esposizione) and building the entrance courtyard, the daring 1956 raw-concrete-and-glass Venezuelan Pavilion, and the winsome, bug-shaped Biglietteria (Ticket Office). In even years between Art Biennales, you can wander the gardens in peace and admire the facades of the organic 1958 Canadian Pavilion, a kind of retro ski lodge design with a tree growing right through it, and the postmodern 1996 Korean Pavilion, in an ingeniously converted electrical plant.

During the Art Biennale, it may be hard to see the forest for the tree-art installations in these gardens – but this is the broadest swath of green space in Venice, with shaded benches, a few giostre (swings and other playground equipment) and waterfront snack bar-restaurant Paradiso (p206). The Giardini came about in 1807, when Napoleon decided he needed a little breathing space, and ordered them built here. Never mind that there was an entire residential district here, including four churches: the emperor needed his shrubbery. But he didn't have long to enjoy the scenery, since they were completed just three years before his demise in 1811.

SCUOLA GRANDE DI SAN MARCO
Map pp100–1

☎ 041 529 43 23; Fondamente dei Mendicanti 6776; admission free; ⏰ 8.30am-2pm daily; 🚉 Ospedale

Instead of a simple Saturday father–son handyman project, sculptor Pietro Lombardo and his sons had something more ambitious in mind: a high Renaissance polychrome marble facade for the most important confraternity in Venice (see p155). Instead of ending with panicked calls to a plumber, the results are stunningly obvious in the marble frontage standing at right angles to the Zanipolo (p99) – though Codussi was brought in to put the finishing touches on this Renaissance gem. Below the magnificent lions of St Mark prowling above the portals, don't miss the sculpted trompe l'œil perspectives on the lower half of the facade.

The scuola is the main entrance to the Ospedale Civile, with a beamed ceiling held up by two ranks of five columns. Beyond this point is the hospital proper, in what were once the Convento dei Domenicani and the Chiesa di San Lazzaro dei Mendicanti. But it's best not to enter without health-related reasons, since sightseeing among the sick is considered poor form.

RIVA DEGLI SCHIAVONI Map pp100–1

🚉 San Zaccaria

The waterside walkway west from Rio Ca' di Dio to the Palazzo Ducale in San Marco is Venice's stone boardwalk, the Riva degli Schiavoni. Schiavoni (literally, 'Slavs') refers to the fishermen from Dalmatia in the region of the former Yugoslavia who arrived in Venice in medieval times, and found this a handy spot for casting their nets.

For centuries, vessels would dock and disembark here right into the heart of Venice – if they could find a parking space between galleons and gondolas. A Rosetta Stone's worth of languages were spoken here, as traders, dignitaries, sailors and servants arrived from ports around the Mediterranean and beyond. Paolo Veronese's Feast in the House of Levi, in the Gallerie dell'Accademia (p76), gives you some idea of how the crowd might have looked and dressed, with Turkish, German, North African and Greek merchants wheeling and dealing along the banks from the moment they stepped off ship. The great poet Petrarch found lodgings and inspiration at No 4175, east of Rio della Pietà.

Today the scene is as busy as ever, with some adjustments. The gondolas are still here, but vaporetti have mostly replaced galleons – though you might spot the Italian navy's tall ship *Amerigo Vespucci* docked down by the Arsenale. Tourists hail from even further afield than the merchants of yesteryear, and their main challenge is negotiating tourist menus in San Marco (hint: skip them all and order à la carte). Some of the grand old mansions now function as pricey hotels, so you too can bunk in here, and wait for the sonnets to come to you.

PALAZZO QUERINI STAMPALIA
Map pp100–1

☎ 041 271 14 11; www.querinistampalia.it, in Italian; Campiello Querini Stampalia 5252; adult/ student & senior €8/6; 🕙 10am-8pm Tue-Thu, 10am-10pm Fri & Sat, 10am-7pm Sun; 🚇 San Zaccaria

Design-savvy drinkers take their spritz (*prosecco* cocktail) with a twist of high modernism in the Carlo Scarpa–designed courtyard garden or Mario Botta–designed cafe of 16th-century Palazzo Querini Stampalia. The outer shell of this building dates from the first half of the 16th century, but the inside could not be more surprising: a 1963 bridge, 1940s entrance and garden, and 1959 1st-floor library all designed by Scarpa, with noteworthy 1990s Botta embellishments.

Enter through the Botta-designed bookstore to get a free pass to the cafe and its garden, or buy a ticket to head upstairs to the 2nd-floor Museo della Fondazione Querini Stampalia. In a series of sumptuous, well-preserved 18th-century salons with period furniture mostly left where it was put by the Querinis c 1868, you'll find some 400 paintings, mostly minor works and portraits of illustrious family members. The clear standout is Giovanni Bellini's arresting *Presentation of Jesus at the Temple*, where the hapless child looks like a toddler mummy, standing up in tightly wrapped swaddling clothes. In a small annexe off a large hall before the Bellini is *Scenes of Venetian Life*, a series of some 70 folksy paintings by Gabriele Bella (1730–99). Rotating contemporary art installations add another element of the unexpected to these silk-draped salons and the top-floor gallery, and concerts and lectures held in the baroque music room on Fridays and Saturdays draw Venetian hipsters and old-timers alike (see website for upcoming events).

See also p159.

ARSENALE Map pp100–1
☎ 041 270 95 46; www.labiennale.org; Campo Arsenale 2407; admission depends on exhibitions; 🕙 vary; 🚇 Arsenale

Founded in 1104, the Arsenale soon became the greatest medieval shipyard in Europe, home to 300 shipping companies employing up to 16,000 people, and capable of turning out a new galley in a day. Venice's navy remained unbeatable for centuries, but now arty types invade the shipyards during Venice's Art and Architecture Biennales (see p18).

At its peak, the Arsenale covered 46 hectares and must have made an enormous impression, with its boiling black pitch, metalworking and timber-cutting. Dante used it as a model scene for hell in his *Divina Commedia* (Divine Comedy; Canto XXI, lines 7 to 21). At the core was the Arsenale Vecchio (Old Arsenal), which had a storage area for the *bucintoro*, the doge's ceremonial galley. In 1303–04 came the first expansion, known as La Tana. Occupying almost the whole length of the southern side of the Arsenale and performing essential rope-making work – sometimes by children – it was refashioned in 1579 by Antonio da Ponte (of Rialto bridge fame). The Arsenale Nuovo (New Arsenal) was added in 1325, followed in 1473 by the Arsenale Nuovissimo (Very New Arsenal). In the 16th century, production of *galeazze* (large war vessels with a deep draught) required further workshops and construction sheds, along with the creations of a deeper Canale delle Galeazze.

Capped by the lion of St Mark that eluded destruction by Napoleon's troops, the Arsenale's land gateway is considered by many to be the earliest example of Renaissance architecture in Venice; it was probably executed in 1460. A plaque was installed commemorating the 1571 victory at Lepanto, and the fenced-in terrace was added in 1692. Below the statues is a row of carved lions; the biggest one, regally seated, was taken as booty by Francesco Morosini from the Greek port of Piraeus, which must have taken some doing. On the right flank of the lion, you'll notice some Viking runes, which are said to be a kind of 11th-century war trophy inscription left behind by Norwegian mercenaries boasting of their role helping Byzantium quell a Greek rebellion – the mercenary equivalent of leaving behind a resumé.

VENICE'S SECRET WEAPON: ARSENALOTI

The basic approach used to build everything from cars and websites today was established not during the Industrial Revolution, but in medieval Venice. In early assembly-line fashion, each ship progressed through sequenced design phases in a series of sheds, staffed by *arsenaloti* (Arsenale workers) specialised in a particular aspect of construction, ranging from hull assembly through pitch application to sail rigging. Women specialised in sails; children started apprenticeships at age 10, and did their part twisting hemp into rope.

But this wasn't a low-paid, low-status job. The *arsenaloti* were well paid, and had special privileges even the aristocracy didn't enjoy. They remained faithful to the doge and the state throughout the history of the Republic, proving their loyalty and brawn on several occasions when they were called to arms in times of unrest or rebellion. Using their proven shipbuilding techniques, they also constructed the vast *carena di nave* (ship's keel) ceilings you see in Venetian churches and in the Palazzo Ducale's Sala del Maggior Consiglio (see p66).

Job requirements for *arsenaloti* included skills, strength and silence. Even in raucous Castello *bacari* (old-style bars), *arsenaloti* remained carefully vague about specifics in their workday, in an 'I could tell you, but then I'd have to kill you' kind of way. The process was top secret, and industrial espionage was considered an act of high treason. For centuries the crenellated walls of the Arsenale hid from view the feverish activity of the city's shipwrights, churning out galleys, merchant ships and other vessels.

If other maritime powers had learned to make warships as fast and fleet as Venice, the tiny lagoon republic might have lost its outsized advantage, and been obliterated by its foes. In 1379, when Venetian commander Carlo Zeno's fleet was otherwise engaged, maritime rival Genoa surrounded Venice and tried to starve it into submission. But Genoa hadn't counted on the *arsenaloti*, who worked furiously to produce a fleet able to sustain a counter-attack until Zeno arrived on the horizon.

In 1570, when requested to produce as many ships as possible for an emergency fleet, the *arsenaloti* put out an astounding 100 galleys in just two months – despite a fire that had decimated the Arsenale the previous year. From then on, things went downhill. A bout of plague wiped out a third of the city's population, including *arsenaloti*, and Venice's maritime rivals Austria and the Ottoman Empire discovered their own secret weapon: free trade agreements that excluded Venice. By 1797 naval production had all but ceased, and La Serenissima surrendered to Napoleon without a fight.

The Arsenale pulled double duty as a shipyard and naval base, and even today part of the area remains in the Italian navy's hands. An emergency reserve fleet of at least 25 vessels was always kept ready to set sail from inside the Arsenale, either as a war or merchant fleet. As the centuries progressed, the shortage of raw materials (especially timber) became a problem, and the Republic began having trouble finding crews to hire for tough rowing and sailing gigs that required months, even years, at sea. Eventually, Venice resorted to employing slaves, prisoners and press gangs.

Over the past few years, large, long-neglected swaths of the Arsenale have been taken over and partly restored by the city's Biennale organisation for use as exhibition space. Now Architecture and Art Biennale exhibitions are mounted in the construction sheds of the Arsenale, with a Herculaean effort involving boats, hand-carrying materials, and tight organisation that harkens back to earlier times. Shows often offer peeks inside, including the former Corderia (where ships' cables were made), the Artiglierie (guns) and various wharves. More creative repurpos-

ing lies ahead: ongoing work to transform the entire Arsenale will create modern ship maintenance areas, shops, restaurants, exhibition spaces, a study centre and more.

SCUOLA DI SAN GIORGIO DEGLI SCHIAVONI Map pp100–1

☎ 041 522 88 28; Calle dei Furlani 3259a; admission €3; ☺ 9am-1pm & 2.45-6pm Tue-Sat, 9am-1pm Sun, 2.45-6pm Mon; 🚊 San Zaccaria

By the 15th century, the Slavic community in Castello was so sizeable that its religious confraternity was dedicated not to one, but three patron saints: George, Tryphone and Jerome of Dalmatia. This building was constructed in the 16th century, and the Renaissance interiors remain more or less intact.

Venice's Dalmatian community was so influential that the virtuoso painter Vittore Carpaccio himself painted the 1502–07 cycle of the lives of the saints on the ground floor. Though he never left Venice, Carpaccio clearly did his research: his scenes with Dalmatian backdrops are so minutely detailed that some Slavic visitors claim to recognise the locations as their home region. Carpaccio's imagined worlds are so convincing that in his images of St George with the dragon, the dragon looks like something that might be hauled in with the day's catch at the Pescaria. Carpaccio took any opportunity to load his paintbrush with red for glistening gore, so scattered about before the dragon are remnants of its victims – sundry limbs, bones and the half-eaten corpse of a young woman.

OSPEDALETTO Map pp100–1

☎ 041 270 90 12, 041 532 29 20; Barbaria delle Tole 6691; guided visit to Sala da Musica €3; ⏱ 3.30-6.30pm Thu-Sat Apr-Oct, 3-6pm Thu-Sat Nov-Mar; ⚓ Ospedale

So much for Rome's attempt to limit Venice's love affair with music: a musical theme runs right through the 1664 Baldassare Longhena–designed chapel and adjacent music room at this historic hospice and home for orphans (see p155). The chapel is uplifting by design, with a trumpeting angel who flits overhead, and a mirror image of the mighty organ painted on the ceiling to draw the eye upward. Jacopo Guarana painted the elegant frescoes that cover the Sala da Musica, where orphan girls performed in celebrated concerts (see below).

MUSEO STORICO NAVALE Map pp100–1

☎ 041 520 02 76; Riva San Biagio 2148; admission €3; ⏱ 8.45am-1.30pm Mon-Fri, 8.45am-1pm Sat; ⚓ Arsenale

Maritime madness spans four storeys and 42 rooms at this museum of Venice's seafaring history, featuring full-scale boats including the ducal barge, Peggy Guggenheim's not-so-minimalist gondola, ocean liners, and WWII battleships (see p157). Your first port of call on the ground floor are sprawling galleries of fearsome weaponry – cannons, blunderbusses, swords and sabres – with hardly any noticeable bloodstains. These big guns were rarely needed in Venice, since the shallow, difficult-to-sail lagoon itself was Venice's best protection against invaders. Check out the 17th-century diorama maps, which show the incredible span of Venetian ports and forts across the Adriatic and Mediterranean.

Among the many large-scale model sailing vessels on the 1st floor, you'll find a model of the sumptuous *bucintoro,* the doge's ceremonial barge – Napoleon's French troops destroyed the real thing in 1798. The 2nd floor covers Italian naval history and memorabilia, from unification to the present day, and on the 3rd floor is a room especially for gondolas, including Peggy Guggenheim's swanky gondola. A small room set above the 3rd floor is dedicated to – wait for it – Swedish naval history.

The ticket also gets you entrance to the Padiglione delle Navi (Ships Pavilion; Fondamenta della Madonna), near the entrance to the Arsenale. Of the many boats on display, the most eye-catching is the *Scalé Reale,* an early-19th-century ceremonial vessel used to

VENICE'S ORPHAN ORCHESTRAS

Not often does a shipping crisis change the course of musical history. But in the 17th century, La Serenissima's maritime empire was in decline, with wood supplies in the Veneto running scarce for shipbuilding and the plague decimating crews. With the state running at a deficit, Venice took steps that today might sound radical and a tad quixotic: in four *ospedaletti* (orphanages) around the city, basic room, board and musical education would be provided by Venice for orphaned and abandoned girls in exchange for periodic performances.

The *putte* (little angels) or *figlie del coro* (choir girls) were a peculiarly Venetian phenomenon that drew music lovers, socialites and curiosity seekers from across Europe to Venice. But these were serious concerts, not musical sideshows. Cimarosa was briefly hired at the Ospedaletto, and Vivaldi found steady employment for decades as the concert master at La Pietà (p110), where he wrote pieces specifically for *putte.* The orchestras set new standards for baroque music, and sparked a craze for all things Venetian that helped keep the Republic's economy afloat. Venice's modest investment in girls' education paid off lavishly.

In concert, orphan orchestras sometimes performed behind screens, which by some accounts was meant to shield them from distracting lascivious glances – though some legends say it was to protect performers with visible birth defects from being treated as a carnival sideshow. But rather conveniently, the screens prevented the performers from seeing their audiences, which on any given night might include the birth parents who'd abandoned these girls. After orchestral proof that their daughters were alive and thriving musically, guilt-ridden parents might leave large tips or anonymous donations before slipping away.

ferry King Vittorio Emanuele to Piazza San Marco in 1866 when Venice joined the nascent Kingdom of Italy. The ship last set sail in 1959, when it brought the body of the Venetian Pope Pius X to rest at the Basilica di San Marco.

CATTEDRALE DI SAN PIETRO DI CASTELLO Map pp100–1

☎ 041 520 61 02; Campo San Pietro 2787; ☻ 8am-12.30pm & 3-7pm daily; 🚢 San Pietro

Unlikely though it may seem, this sleepy church on the far-flung island of San Pietro was Venice's cathedral from 1451 to 1807 – not the more attention-seeking and conveniently located Basilica di San Marco, which was the doge's chapel. But the island of San Pietro (originally known as Olivolo) was among the first to be inhabited in Venice, and the original church here was the seat of a bishopric as early as 775.

The present church is an almost-but-not-quite Palladio design. Palladio had been awarded the contract in the 1550s, but the death of the patriarch when the architect was two years into the project led to a project hiatus that lasted beyond the genius's own demise. Palladio's successors largely respected his initial ideas, taking their cue from Giudecca's Chiesa del Redentore (p112) to complete the monumental facade by the end of the 16th century. Note the fine work on the expansive 54m dome, which rivals Michelangelo's at the Vatican for size. Inside, Baldassare Longhena is responsible for the baroque main altar.

Between the second and third altars on the right side of the church, you'll spot a chair with an intricately carved stone back referred to as 'St Peter's Throne'. According to one of Venice's many architectural urban legends, the impressive chair was used by the Apostle Peter in Antioch, and the Holy Grail was later hidden in it. This story has all the makings of an *Indiana Jones* sequel, but very little truth to it: the seat back is made from a scavenged Muslim tombstone that postdates the Apostle's death by some centuries.

Also on the premises, you'll spot San Pietro's blinding white bell tower of Istrian stone by Codussi (finished in 1490) leaning at an odd angle. Next door is the crumbling former patriarchate, retired from its use as military barracks and now partly occupied by apartments.

MUSEO DELLE ICONE Map pp100–1

☎ 041 522 65 81; www.istitutoellenico.org; Campiello dei Greci 3412; adult/student €4/2; ☻ 9am-12.30pm & 1.30-4.30pm Mon-Sat, 9am-5pm Sun; 🚢 San Zaccaria

Glowing colours and all-seeing eyes fill the gallery of the Museum of Icons, a treasure box of some 80 Greek icons made in 14th- to 17th-century Italy – especially the expressive *San Giovanni Climaco*, which shows the saintly author of a Greek spiritual guide distracted from his work by visions of souls diving into hell. The museum goes by a confusing variety of names: it's also known as the *Museo dei Dipinti Sacri Bizantini* (Museum of Holy Byzantine Paintings), attached to the Chiesa di San Giorgio dei Greci, and technically, it's housed in the Istituto Ellenico (Hellenic Institute). This seat of Venice's Greek Orthodox community was built by Baldassare Longhena, served as a hospital for the poor into the 20th century, and stands as a monument to the city's ethnic diversity and religious tolerance.

CHIESA DI SAN GIORGIO DEI GRECI Map pp100–1

☎ 041 522 65 81; Campiello dei Greci 3412; admission free; ☻ 9am-12.30pm & 2.30-4.30pm Wed-Sat & Mon, 9am-1pm Sun; 🚢 San Zaccaria

Greek Orthodox refugees who fled to Venice from Turkey with the rise of the Ottoman Empire built a church here in 1536, with the aid of a special dispensation from Venice to collect taxes on incoming Greek ships (see p158). Nicknamed 'St George of the Greeks', the little church has an impressive iconostasis and a range of Byzantine icons and fine incense still in use at services. The separate, slender bell tower was completed in 1603 and began to lean right from the start; by now it seems poised to dive into the canal.

CHIESA DI SAN GIOVANNI IN BRAGORA Map pp100–1

☎ 041 520 59 06; Campo di Bandiera e Mori 3790; admission free; ☻ 9-11am & 3.30-5.30pm Mon-Sat; 🚢 Arsenale

This serene 15th-century brick church may keep a straight face, but inside the place looks lively with Bartolomeo Vivarini's 1478 *Enthroned Madonna with St Andrew and John the Baptist,* which shows the Madonna bouncing a delighted baby Jesus on her knee. Bartolomeo's nephew

Alvise Vivarini shows Jesus in later years in his splendidly restored 1494 *Saviour Blessing,* with a cloudlike beard and eyes that seem to follow you around the room. This church harmonises Gothic and Renaissance, ancient and avant-garde styles with apparent ease, setting the tone for a young Antonio Vivaldi, who was baptised here. See also p156.

CHIESA DI SAN MARTINO Map pp100–1

☎ 041 523 04 87; Campo San Martino 2298; admission free; ⏲ 9am-noon & 4.30-7.30pm daily; 🚊 Arsenale

Stick your hand into the lion's mouth by the door, and say something nice about your neighbours: maybe that will help atone for all the dangerous rumours spread through the years via this *bocca di leoni* (the mouth of the lion of San Marco). Venetians were encouraged to slip anonymous denunciations of their neighbours through these slots, reporting unholy acts ranging from cursing (forgivable) to Freemasonry (punishable by death) for investigation by Venice's dread security service, the Council of Ten.

The theme of persecution continues indoors with Palma Il Giovane's canvases of Jesus being flogged and on the way to Calvary, which are hung almost out of sight in the choir stalls but can be glimpsed in front of the altar. But the namesake saint, St Martin of Tours (AD 316–97), was actually the first Christian saint to die a natural death and not as a martyr – he was a Hungarian priest who experienced a conversion experience after serving the Roman army in Gaul (France). Sansovino designed the present church in 1654, with the present facade in Istrian marble added much later in 1897.

See also p156.

CHIESA DI SANTA MARIA FORMOSA Map pp100–1

Campo Santa Maria Formosa 5267; admission €3 or Chorus Pass; ⏲ 10am-5pm Mon-Sat, 1-5pm Sun; 🚊 San Zaccaria

Rebuilt in 1492 by Mauro Codussi on the site of a 7th-century church, this house of worship bears a curious name (Curvaceous St Mary) that has spawned two local legends. One claims the name was caused by confusion over a confusingly abbreviated listing and address for a local courtesan in a Venice guidebook in the dark, pre–Lonely Planet days of the early 16th century

(see p159). The other tells the story of San Magno, Bishop of Oderzo, who is said to have had a vision of the Virgin Mary on this spot. Unlike standard views of Our Lady, this Venetian vision was beautiful and *formosa.*

The inside of the church was damaged when an Austrian bomb went off in 1916, but among the works of art to survive is an altarpiece by Palma il Vecchio depicting St Barbara, a bevy of saints, and the body of Christ in his mother's arms. Just to the right of the main door (as you face it from the inside) is a 16th-century Byzantine icon of *St Mary of Lepanto.* Next to the first chapel on the same side of the church is an 8th-century Egyptian Coptic garment, said to be the veil of St Marina – a rare relic of the saint's namesake church demolished in the nearby Campo Santa Marina.

STATUE OF BARTOLOMEO COLLEONI Map pp100–1

Campo SS Giovanni e Paolo; 🚊 Ospedale

You'll know you've crossed from Cannaregio into Castello when you spot Bartolomeo Colleoni galloping out to meet you (see p153). The bronze equestrian statue is one of only two such public monuments in Venice, commemorating one of Venice's more loyal mercenary mainland commanders. From 1448, Colleoni commanded armies for the Republic – though in true mercenary form he switched sides a couple of times when he felt he'd been stiffed on pay or promotions. On his death in 1474, he bequeathed 216,000 gold and silver ducats and even more in property to Venice, on one condition: that the city erect a commemorative statue to him in Piazza San Marco. Since not even a doge had ever won such pride of place in Venice, the Senate found a loophole by reading a clause into the contract: the grand statue would be placed in the Piazza in front of the Scuola Grande di San Marco instead. At least Colleoni can rest easy that the Republic didn't scrimp on the statue, sculpted with imposing grandeur by Verrocchio (1435–88).

SOTOPORTEGO DEI PRETI Map pp100–1

off Salizada Pignater, cnr Campo di Bandiera e Mori; 🚊 Arsenale

Down these steps and under the arch of this *sotoportego* (passageway), there's a reddish stone the size of a hand that's heart-shaped. Legend has it that couples who touch it together will remain in love forever – but if you're not ready to commit just yet, it's a nice private spot for a smooch.

MUSEO DIOCESANO D'ARTE SACRA
Map pp100–1

☎ 041 522 91 66; www.museodiocesanovenezia.it; Chiostro di Sant'Apollonia 4312; admission depends on exhibitions; ☺ 10am-12.30pm Mon-Sat; 🚊 San Zaccaria

Housed in a former Benedictine monastery dedicated to Sant'Apollonia, this museum has a fairly predictable collection of religious art and the occasional standout temporary show – but the exquisite Romanesque cloister you cross to reach the museum is a rare example of the genre in Venice, and it's often open much longer hours than the museum. The adjoining building was a church until 1906, and now houses exhibition spaces.

CHIESA DI SAN LIO Map pp100–1
Campo San Lio; admission free; ☺ 3-6pm Mon-Sat; 🚊 Rialto

Giandomenico Tiepolo sure did know how to light up a room. If you find this 11th-century church open, duck into the atmospheric gloom and as your eyes adjust to the light, look up at Tiepolo's magnificent ceiling fresco, *The Glory of the Cross and St Leon IX.* On your left by the main door is Titian's *Apostle James the Great,* but this church is better known for another Venetian artist: the great *vedutista* (landscapist) Canaletto, who was baptised and buried in this, his parish church. See also left.

LA PIETÀ Map pp100–1
☎ 041 523 10 96; Riva degli Schiavoni 4149; ☺ for concerts only; 🚊 San Zaccaria

Originally called Chiesa di Santa Maria della Visitazione but fondly nicknamed La Pietà, this Giorgio Massari–designed church is best known for its association with the composer Vivaldi, who was concertmaster here in the early 18th century – hence its current sporadic use as a concert hall. The original church was located next door, and a few fragments of it are visible in the Hotel Metropole (see p158).

Eating p194; Shopping p174; Sleeping p224

Other cities have suburban sprawl and malls; Venice has a teal-blue lagoon dotted with photogenic islands, beachfront villas and rare wildlife. Outlying islands range from deserted nunneries to luxury resorts and from bustling modern glass-blowing centres to ancient Byzantine capitals sometimes divided only by a narrow channel.

The closest island is Giudecca, a former industrial and prison district and garden retreat for Venetian nobility that's become Venice's unofficial seventh *sestiere*. Now the warehouses host avant-garde theatre and art shows, and luxury travellers unwind in waterfront spa-hotels – and the prison grows organic vegetables. Next door is Isola di San Giorgio Maggiore, dominated by Palladio's church of the same name and home to the Giorgio Cini Foundation's centre for contemporary art and culture.

A short 10- to 15-minute vaporetto ride whisks you to the Lido, Venice's long strip of beachfront property that's dotted with grand hotels, *stile liberty* villas beneath the pines, and the sleepy fishing town of Malamocco along a protective sea wall. As well as sand, the Lido has two things you won't find in central Venice: the Venice International Film Festival, complete with A-list red-carpet action, and cars, complete with traffic jams. Further along the lagoon is another sleek barrier island, Pellestrina, which reaches like a bony finger down to the mainland.

North of Venice are three of the lagoon's most visited islands. Serious shoppers head directly to Murano, snapping up limited-edition modern pieces created with glass-making techniques in use locally since the 8th century. Spot mohawked storks balancing thoughtfully on one leg and cormorants holding their wings out to dry in the sun after a fish dinner – then get your own seafood meal on the fishing isle of Burano, amid the cheerful riot of saturated-colour houses. On the nearly abandoned island of Torcello, Santa Maria Assunta's golden mosaics end lagoon adventures on a heavenly note. Escapists might prefer lazy days boating on the lagoon, watching lagoon ibis perch on shallow *barene* and drifting past the island madhouse of San Servolo to the Armenian monastery isle of San Lazzaro degli Armeni to an overgrown plague quarantine station at Lazaretto.

Lines 41, 42 and N serve Giudecca regularly, the easiest approaches being from Ferrovia, Piazzale Roma and San Zaccaria. You can reach the Lido by vaporetti 1, 51, 52, 61, 62 and N from various stops. To Murano, the most regular services are the 41 and 42. For Burano, take the LN from Fondamente Nuove via Murano and Mazzorbo. From Burano, the T vaporetto runs every half-hour to Torcello. Line 13 serves Le Vignole and Sant'Erasmo, while line 20 tootles to San Servolo and San Lazzaro.

GIUDECCA

Originally known as the *spina longa* (long fishbone) because of its shape, Giudecca has survived many trials without losing its spirit. Venice's Jewish community lived here prior to the creation of the Ghetto, but contrary to urban legend, Giudecca isn't related to the word 'Jewish' (*hebrei* in Italian). Giudecca is likely derived from Zudega, from *giudicato*, or 'the judged', the name given to rebellious Venetian nobles banished to Giudecca.

The banishments backfired. Giudecca became fashionable, and elite Venetian families (such as the Dandolos, Mocenigos and Vendramins) bought up land to build garden villas with sweeping views of Venice to the north and south to the open lagoon. By the 16th century, the island had been extended through land reclamation to reach something approaching its present form. Merchants set up warehouses, and a flourishing local commercial life made Giudecca a prime piece of real estate. Several religious orders established convents and monasteries here.

But weekend homes were the first to be abandoned during times of plague and war, and when the Republic fell in 1797, everything changed. The religious orders were suppressed, and in 1857, a convent and hospice for reformed prostitutes became a women's prison. Gardens were filled in with barracks, factories and apartments for workers. Down Fondamenta Rio di Sant'Eufemia, the onetime church and convent of SS Cosma e Damiano were turned into a factory and the bell tower into a smokestack. When art nouveau boho designer Fortuny wanted to expand his business, he moved his workshop into a garden villa along the Fondamenta San Biagio.

GIUDECCA

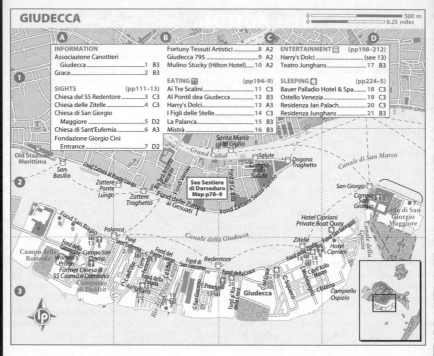

INFORMATION			Fortuny Tessuti Artistici.......8 A2	ENTERTAINMENT 🎭 (pp198–212)
Associazione Canottieri			Giudecca 795...............9 A2	Harry's Dolci.................(see 13)
Giudecca...........................1	B3		Mulino Stucky (Hilton Hotel)..10 A2	Teatro Junghans............17 B3
Grace................................2	B3			
			EATING 🍴 (pp194–9)	SLEEPING 🛏 (pp224–5)
SIGHTS	(pp111–13)		Ai Tre Scalini.............11 C3	Bauer Palladio Hotel & Spa....18 C3
Chiesa del SS Redentore.......3	C3		Al Pontil dea Giudecca....12 B3	Ostello Venezia............19 C3
Chiesa delle Zitelle..............4	C3		Harry's Dolci...............13 A3	Residenza Jan Palach......20 C3
Chiesa di San Giorgio			I Figli delle Stelle........14 C3	Residenza Junghans.......21 B3
Maggiore.......................5	D2		La Palanca.................15 B3	
Chiesa di Sant'Eufemia........6	A3		Mistrà.....................16 B3	
Fondazione Giorgio Cini				
Entrance.........................7	D2			

Today Giudecca is entering its third act, and this one you won't want to miss. The ex-convent of SS Cosma e Damiano has been beautifully restored as live/work loft spaces, and at studios in the former cloisters, you can buy glass, handmade paper, and perfumes from artisans-in-residence. Nearby, a munitions depot is now a cutting-edge theatre, the Teatro Junghans (see p210). Galleries are taking over warehouses alongside Fortuny on the Fondamenta San Biagio, and the convent/orphanage designed by Palladio around his classical white-marble Zitelle church is now the high-end, green-minded Bauer Palladio Hotel & Spa (p224). Some of the city's finest organic vegetables (see the boxed text, p185) and all the chic tapestry handbags at Banco 10 (p173) come from job retraining programs at the Giudecca women's prison, and Elton John and his partner recently bought a Giudecca villa not far from the surprisingly bucolic prison. Giudecca is no longer an island – it's an independent streak in the middle of a lagoon.

Some things haven't changed: gondolas are still custom-made in the Giudecca *squero*, and if you've got a bet riding on the annual Regatta Storica (see p19), the smart money's almost always on Giudecca. You won't find fresher *fritto*

misto (fried seafood), and with the exception of Harry's Dolci (see p194), Giudecca's restaurants are among Venice's most reasonable – and sparkling lagoon views come gratis.

Vaporetti 41, 42, 82 and N (night) make Giudecca an easy hop from San Marco or Dorsoduro, and handy to Piazzale Roma and the Lido.

FORTUNY TESSUTI ARTISTICI Map p112
☎ 041 522 40 78; www.fortuny.com; Fondamenta San Biagio 805; ⏰ 9am-1pm & 2-6pm Mon-Fri, 9-11am & 2-6pm Sat & Sun; 🚤 Palanca

Marcel Proust waxed rhapsodic over Fortuny's silken cottons printed with boho-chic art nouveau patterns, and here you can see why. Visitors can browse 260 textile designs in the gated showroom, but fabrication methods have been jealously guarded in the garden studio for a century. To see more of Fortuny's original designs and his home studio, head to Palazzo Fortuny (p72).

CHIESA DEL SS REDENTORE Map p112
Campo del SS Redentore 194; admission €3 or Chorus Pass; ⏰ 10am-5pm Mon-Sat, 1-5pm Sun; 🚤 Redentore

Even from afar, you can't miss Palladio's 1577 Il Redentore, a triumph of white marble along the Grand Canal celebrating the city's deliverance from the Black Death. Work on this magnificent edifice was completed under Antonio da Ponte (of Rialto bridge fame) in 1592. Inside the church are a few works by Tintoretto, Veronese and Vivarini, but the most striking work is often overlooked. Inside over the portal, Paolo Piazza's strikingly modern 1619 *Gratitude of Venice for Liberation from the Plague* shows the city held aloft by angels in sobering shades of grey. Survival is never taken for granted in this tidal town, and to give thanks during the Festa del Redentore (Feast of the Redeemer; p19), Venetians have been making the wobbly annual pilgrimage across the Giudecca Canal on a shaky pontoon bridge from the Zattere since 1578.

MULINO STUCKY Map p112

☎ 041 522 12 67; www.hilton.com; Fondamenta San Biagio 753; 🚢 Palanca

The striking neo-Gothic hulk of the best-known factory complex on the island, the Mulino Stucky, was built in the late 19th century and employed 1500 people. It shut in 1954, and languished along the lagoon until 2000, when it was narrowly saved from the wrecking ball by the Hilton Hotel chain. Renovated and relaunched in 2007, the Molino Stucky Hilton has 380 rooms, a conference centre and a fabulous lounge by the rooftop pool. The original facade has been preserved and it's beautifully lit at night – who knew a factory could be so romantic?

CHIESA DELLE ZITELLE Map p112

☎ 041 260 19 74; Fondamenta delle Zitelle; 🚢 Zitelle

Designed by Palladio in the late 16th century, the Chiesa di Santa Maria della Presentazione, known as the Zitelle, was a church and hospice for orphans and poor young women (*zitelle* is old local slang for 'old maids'). The church bell only rings on Sundays and the doors are rarely open, but you can get a spa treatment in the adjoining convent and sleep in the orphanage – no, seriously. The Palladio Hotel & Spa (p224) has creatively tweaked the original structure without altering Palladio's blueprint, marble walls, beamed ceilings, or the original cloisters garden, transforming the premises into a memorable high-end spa-hotel.

CHIESA DI SANT'EUFEMIA Map p112

☎ 041 522 58 48; Fondamenta Sant'Eufemia 680; 🕑 9am-noon & 3.30-5pm daily; 🚢 Palanca

Four women saints were crowded under the roof of the original AD 890 church here, but Sts Dorothy, Tecla and Erasma weren't as big a draw as Byzantine Christian martyr Euphemia. She was thrown to hungry lions, but after biting off her hand, the lions refused to eat her holy virgin flesh. The simple Veneto-Byzantine structure you see today dates from the 14th century, with some capitals and columns inside preserved from the 11th century. The pleasing Doric portico attributed to Michele Sanmicheli was added c 1596.

GIUDECCA 795 Map p112

☎ 340 8798327; www.giudecca795.com; Fondamenta San Biagio 795; 🕑 during shows 3-8pm Tue-Fri, Sat & Sun 11am-8pm; 🚢 Palanca

Do you follow the Titian colourists or go with the Tintoretto flow? Either way, Giudecca 795 has you in mind, featuring contemporary artists with a strong sense of colour and dynamic line. Look for Vito Campanelli's high-impact all-red paintings and Guitamachi's graphic train-track cityscapes.

top picks

SUNDAY ISLAND-HOPPING

- Lido (p115) Take a 15-minute vaporetto ride to beaches, bicycling and tours of the Antico Cimitero Israelitico.
- Murano (p117) Many shops are closed, but major attractions are open: Museo del Vetro, Murano Collezioni and Chiesa dei SS Maria e Donato.
- Burano (p119) Find photo ops galore amid the artist's palette of brightly coloured houses, enjoy a leisurely lunch at Trattoria al Gatto Nero, and loll the day away in Mazzorbo.
- Torcello (p120) Discover a glittering hidden treasure in the wilds of Torcello at Cattedrale di Santa Maria Assunta and Museo di Torcello, and get cosy in Hemingway's room at Locanda Cipriani.
- Le Vignole (p122) Drift the day away on a boat trip with Terra e Acqua (p271), with lunch moored along the canal and a hike to Venice's deserted island fortress.

PALLADIO: ARCHITECTURAL PROZAC

Before virtually every pillared bank and cupola-capped manor in the British Empire modelled itself on his designs, Andrea Palladio (1508–80) created churches and villas of surpassing lightness and strength in his native Veneto. Palladian facades across the Veneto were scrubbed until gleaming for the 500th anniversary of his birth in 2008, so now is prime time to see his signature white marble edifices in all their near-blinding glory, with striking shapes that seem purpose-built for spiritual uplift and romantic reflection in Venetian canals and the Veneto's Brenta Riviera.

While romantics may be content to contemplate the moonlit facades of Chiesa di San Giorgio Maggiore (below) or Chiesa del SS Redentore (p112) from across the canal at night, architecture aficionados will want to get up close to appreciate multifaceted buildings that appear flat from afar, and step inside to see how judicious use of vaulting, roof trusses and high windows create generous, light-washed interiors. Note the scrolled-paper capitals and the spare, clean surfaces, and you'll see precocious hints of the rococo and the historically attuned high modernism of Le Corbusier and Tadao Ando.

Even on a smaller scale in *palazzi* (palaces) in Vicenza and villas along the Brenta, Palladio makes interior space seem expansive, airy and haloed in light. Legend has it that the Palladio-built Villa Foscari (p231) was nicknamed La Malcontenta, The Unhappy One, for a lady caught in flagrante delicto by her husband and sent here from Venice to learn the error of her cheating ways. But though there are weeping willows out front, banishment to this pleasure dome arising from the banks of the Brenta frescoed with cavorting mythological figures seems more like an encouragement.

Palladio was made Venice's official architect on the death of Jacopo Sansovino in 1570, but the conservative authorities had no intention of letting him loose in central Venice to replace existing structures with big, bold, modern-antique buildings. Palladio had better luck in Vicenza, where his grand designs define the city centre. Seen close together, Palladio's palaces, government buildings and Teatro Olimpico (p244) brought an easy grace to the city – though neighbouring *palazzi* inevitably look squat and ungainly in the long shadow of Palladio. The architect died before finishing many of his projects in and around Vicenza, but Vincenzo Scamozzi (1552–1616) faithfully carried out Palladio's plans.

ISOLA DI SAN GIORGIO MAGGIORE

Architecture binges have brought visitors to this corner of the lagoon for centuries, and no wonder: have you seen the Palladios? Just east of Giudecca's Zitelle and Redentore is Palladio's grandest church, San Giorgio Maggiore, a vision in white from across the water in San Marco.

You'd never know it today, but this island had become a ramshackle mess by the mid-20th century. The church was covered in the grime of ages, and the buildings that had once housed gracious cloisters and an important naval academy and marina had fallen into alarming disrepair. But not everyone was resigned to the demise of this particular Palladio. After escaping the Dachau internment camp with his son Giorgio, Vittorio Cini returned to Venice on a mission to save San Giorgio Maggiore in 1949. With interests in the Porto Marghera industrial complex and Adriatic shipping, the Cinis were able to gather the means to buy the island in 1951. Over the ensuing decades, the Cini Foundation has restored the island into a cultural centre, hosting cutting-edge art and design shows in its gallery and avant-garde theatre in its gardens.

CHIESA DI SAN GIORGIO MAGGIORE
Map p112

☎ 041 522 78 27; Isola di San Giorgio Maggiore;
🕙 9.30am-12.30pm & 2.30-6.30pm Mon-Sat May-Sep, 9.30am-12.30pm & 2.30-4.30pm Oct-Apr;
🚤 San Giorgio

Sunglasses become essential as you approach San Giorgio in a vaporetto, because Palladio's 1565–80 masterpiece is set to dazzle. The white Istrian marble facade is almost blinding head-on, but close up you'll notice the depth of the massive columns that support the triangular tympanum, with echoing triangles to represent the Holy Trinity. These strict, elegant classical proportions immediately evoke ancient Roman temples, rather than the bombastic baroque trendy in Palladio's day. Inside, this is the only Venetian church where you'll have to remind yourself to look at the paintings. Ceilings billow over the generous nave, with high windows distributing filtered sunshine and easy grace. The black, white and red inlaid stone floor draws the eye toward an altar flanked by Tintoretto's *Collecting the Manna* and *Last Supper,* with his *Deposition* nearby in the Cappella dei Morti. Take the lift (€3) to the top of the 60m-high bell tower for a stirring panorama that takes in Giudecca, San Marco, and the lagoon beyond.

FONDAZIONE GIORGIO CINI Map p112

☎ 041 271 02 80; www.cini.it; Isola di San Giorgio Maggiore; adult/senior & student/student 7-12yr/ under 7yr €12/10/8/free; ⏲ 10am-6.30pm Mon-Sat; 🚢 San Giorgio

A defunct naval academy has been cleverly converted into a shipshape gallery for the Fondazione Giorgio Cini, preserving the original double-height timber ceiling and going for a weatherbeaten-high-design look with luminous stairs in glass and rusted iron. The gallery hosts high-profile international and Italian shows, ranging from a mind-bending avant-garde Japanese typography show to a retrospective of Venice's own poetic abstractionist, Giuseppe Santomaso – including his *Letters to Palladio,* paintings of envelopes with Palladian proportions.

Behind Palladio's grand church extend the grounds of the former monastery with a long history, beginning in the 10th century with its Benedictine founders and finishing with the staircase and library built by Longhena in the 1640s. The Chiostro dei Cipressi (named after the four cypress trees in the cloister) is the oldest extant part of the complex, completed in 1526 in an early-Renaissance style. One side is flanked by the cells of 56 Benedictine monks who long lived here. A stroll through the gardens leads to the outdoor Teatro Verde, built in the 1950s and sometimes used for summer performances.

The Chiostro del Palladio (designed by the Renaissance star) is on the site of a grand library that had been destroyed by fire. It was donated by Cosimo de' Medici in thanks for his stay here during his exile from Florence in 1433.

Palladio also designed the monumental refectory, where a Veronese masterpiece, *Nozze di Cana* (Wedding at Cana), took pride of place – at least until Napoleon came to town. He liked what he saw, so naturally he cut it in two, rolled it up and shipped it off to Paris, where it remains in the Louvre today. But in 2009, filmmaker Peter Greenaway's celebrated video art projections of Veronese's painting 'reinstalled' the work in its rightful place. The work was the scene stealer of the Biennale, with digital enhancements that made the video versions truer to Veronese's signature colours and seamless composition than the degraded, patched-together Louvre canvas.

LIDO DI VENEZIA

When Karl Lagerfeld was looking for an appropriate location for Chanel's 2009 couture resort collection, the choice was obvious: the Lido. This svelte barrier island has brought glamour to the beach since the late 19th century, when Venice's upper crust escaped hot, crowded Venetian summers for breezy *stile liberty* villas – some 200 still rise graciously through the Lido's windswept pines today. Thomas Mann's melancholy novel *Death in Venice* was set in turn-of-the-century Lido, and you'll spot wrought-iron balconies and seaside resorts that date from those elegantly decadent days.

Lido beaches remain a major draw, especially on the Adriatic side, where cleaner water makes for maximum sun-umbrella density on sunny days. This is where you'll find the grand old luxury hotels, including the sprawling splendours of the Hotel des Bains (see p225), with its wonderful verandah bar (Colony Bar; p206). The tanning crowd thins out and rates drop a couple of euros after 2pm, but to avoid amenities fees and throngs of weekenders, rent a bicycle by the vaporetto stop at Lido on Bike and head south to Alberoni and other pristine, windswept beaches. Mind the traffic – after a few days in Venice, cars brought here via ferry from Tronchetto may come as a shock.

The biggest event on the Lido social calendar arrives each September, when starlets and socialites attempt to blind paparazzi with Italian couture at the Venice International Film Festival (aka Mostra del Cinema di Venezia; see p19). Events are held at the 1930s Palazzo della Mostra del Cinema, which looks like a Fascist airport. If you're planning to stay on the Lido during the event, plan ahead and come prepared to splash out. You'll probably be competing with Brangelina's entire entourage for rooms and restaurant reservations, and prices shoot up to double the usual high-season summer rates at hotels.

Only 15 minutes by vaporetti numbers 1, 51, 52, 61, 62, 82 and N from San Marco, the Lido forms a land barrier between the lagoon and the Adriatic Sea. A bicycle or bus B near the vaporetto stop at Gran Viale Santa Maria Elisabetta will take you to Malamocco in the south of the island. On the lagoon side, you can see the nearby Isola di San Lazzaro degli Armeni (see p123), while closer to the shore is the former leper colony and plague quarantine island of Isola del Lazzaretto Vecchio.

LIDO BEACHES off Map p116

Lido di Venezia; deposit/chair/umbrella & chair/hut €5/6/11/17; ⏰ **most beaches 9.30am-7pm May-Sep;** 🚤 **Lido**

Beach chairs and bronzed lifeguards may seem a world apart from muggy, ripe Venice in summer, but they're only a 15-minute ferry ride away. Most Lido beaches charge for chair, umbrella and hut rental, but the tanning crowd thins out and rates drop a couple of euros after 2pm. To avoid obligatory amenities fees and throngs of Italian weekenders, rent a bike and head south to Alberoni and other more pristine beaches.

LIDO ON BIKE Map p116

☎ **041 526 80 19; www.lidoonbike.it; Gran Viale 21b; single/double/family bikes per hr €3/7/14, tandem €6-18, per day single/tandem €9/8;** ⏰ **9am-7pm daily, weather permitting, Mar-Oct;** 🚤 **Lido**

To tour the Lido at your own pace, you might want to get a set of wheels from this friendly bike-rental place right near the Lido vaporetto stop, with reasonable prices and a map thrown in gratis. You must have official identification showing you're at least 18 to rent. And remember to mind the traffic.

MALAMOCCO off Map p116

🚤 **Lido**

Pass over Ponte di Borge to explore the canals and *calli* of a less overwhelming lagoon town, with just a couple of *campi*, churches, *osterie,* and grand *palazzi* with Gothic facades. A miniature version of Venice complete with lions of St Mark carved into medieval facades, Malamocco was actually the lagoon capital from 742 to 811 before Venice took over. But ancient stories also refer to another settlement of Malamocco, which was besieged by the Frankish ruler Pepin in the early years of the Republic and then – poof! – disappeared. Some believe this Venetian Atlantis is still intact, sunk deep into the waters of the lagoon.

ANTICO CIMITERO ISRAELITICO Map p116

☎ **041 71 53 59; admission through Museo Ebraico adult/student €8.50/7;** ⏰ **1hr Italian & English tours 2.30pm Sun Apr-Sep;** 🚤 **Lido**

Epic poems seem to write themselves in this quiet, overgrown garden that was Venice's main Jewish community cemetery from 1386 until the 18th century. The bulk

LIDO DI VENEZIA

0 ____ 1 km
0 ____ 0.5 miles

of the tombstones were discovered by construction workers in the late 19th century, and it was decided to set them up in some sort of orderly fashion. The tombstones range in design from Venetian Gothic to distinctly Ottoman, and one-hour tours organised by the Museo Ebraico (p92) provide insights into the life and times of those buried here. English-language tours are usually held on the last Sunday of the month only.

PALAZZO DELLA MOSTRA DEL CINEMA Map p116

🔊 Lido

A seaside Fascist monument, this rigid airport-terminal structure seems as ill-suited to the playboy Lido as a woolly bathing suit. But once the red carpets are rolled out and the stars arrive for the Venice International Film Festival (see p19), it all makes sense: more than a party venue, the 'palace of cinema' is a movie-launching platform. But when stripped of its red carpet, C+S Associates' 2003 'Wave' entrance begs for a skateboard. Next door is the former casino, another blinding-white monstrosity that replaced the original 1527 Palladio-built casino in a regrettable 1930s Fascist building spree.

PELLESTRINA

Separated from the southern tip of the Lido by the Porto di Malamocco, pastoral Pellestrina (off Map p64) is one of the three sea gates between the Adriatic and the lagoon. The 11km-long barrier island is dotted with villages sparsely populated by farming and fishing families (population about 2900). A handful of small family restaurants serve excellent seafood, and lagoon birds hover overhead for their share of the day's catch. Towards the Chioggia end of the island, you'll find a bird-watching sanctuary in the region of Ca' Roman.

On the seaward side are the Murazzi, a remarkable feat of 18th-century engineering. Although they may not seem immediately impressive to modern eyes accustomed to large-scale construction, these massive sea walls represent Herculean handiwork completed without the benefit of cranes or mechanisation. They are monumental in scale in order to keep high seas from crashing into the lagoon, and extensive in length to be an effective breakwater even today. The Pellestrina stretch and part of the Lido wall remain, but the Murazzi once extended without interruption some 20km from the southern tip of Pellestrina to a point halfway up the coast of the Lido. The disastrous floods of 1966 (see p34) caused significant damage, though the walls were partially restored in the 1970s. On calm days, long stretches of sparsely populated grey-sand beaches separate the Murazzi from the sea; in rough weather, the waves crash against the stones.

This is about as out of the way as you can get for a true taste of Venetian lagoon life, and the sea breezes and sparse traffic here make for a terrific long bicycle ride from the Lido (see opposite). Otherwise, you can take a Pellestrina-bound bus 11 from the Lido vaporetto stop.

ISOLA DI SAN MICHELE

This tranquil cemetery island features a charming Renaissance church and is the final resting place of many illustrious figures, local and foreign. Vaporetti 41 and 42 from Fondamente Nuove stop here en route to Murano.

CIMITERO

☎ 041 72 98 11; admission free; ⏱ 7.30am-6pm daily Apr-Sep, 7.30am-4pm Oct-Mar; 🔊 Cimitero

The city's cemetery was established on Isola di San Michele under Napoleon. Until then, Venetians had been buried in parish plots across town – not the most salubrious solution, as Napoleon's inspectors realised. Today, Goths, incorrigible romantics, and music lovers pause here to visit the final resting places of Ezra Pound, Sergei Diaghilev and Igor Stravinsky. Look for their graves in the (signposted) northeast sector of the island; they are in the 'acatholic' (read Protestant and Orthodox) sections.

Architecture buffs stop by to see the high Renaissance, white Istrian stone Chiesa di San Michele in Isola begun by Codussi in 1469. Cemetery extensions are in the works by David Chipperfield Architects, based on the firm's completed Courtyard of the Four Evangelists: a rather gloomy bunker, with a concrete colonnade and basalt-clad walls engraved with the gospels.

MURANO

Venetians have been working in crystal and glass since the 10th century, but because of the inherent fire hazards of glass-blowing, the industry was moved to the island of Murano in the 13th century. Woe betide

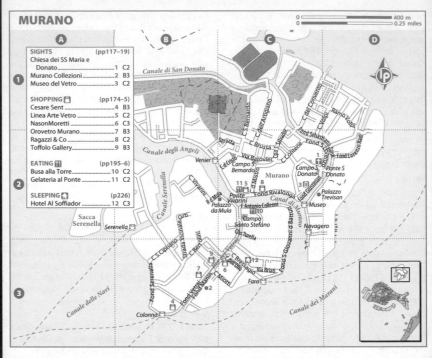

MURANO

| 0 | 400 m |
| 0 | 0.25 miles |

SIGHTS	(pp117–19)
Chiesa dei SS Maria e	
Donato	1 C2
Murano Collezioni	2 B3
Museo del Vetro	3 C2

SHOPPING	(pp174–5)
Cesare Sent	4 B3
Linea Arte Vetro	5 C2
NasonMoretti	6 C3
Orovetro Murano	7 B3
Ragazzi & Co	8 C2
Toffolo Gallery	9 B3

EATING	(pp195–6)
Busa alla Torre	10 C2
Gelateria al Ponte	11 C2

SLEEPING	(p226)
Hotel Al Soffiador	12 C3

the glassblower with wanderlust: trade secrets were so jealously guarded that any glass-worker who left the city was considered guilty of treason and subject to assassination. For a short (not crash!) course in glass, don't miss the Museo del Vetro, which strategically stays open a little later than the glass showrooms so that you can shop first, and ask questions later.

Today glass artisans quite openly ply their trade at workshops along Murano's Fondamenta dei Vetrai marked by 'Fornace' (Furnace) signs, secure in the knowledge that their wares set a standard that can't be replicated elsewhere. To ensure that glass you buy in Venice is handmade in Murano and not factory-fabricated elsewhere, look for the heart-shaped seal guarantee.

Except for the grand glass showrooms and studios, Murano doesn't have a lot of landmarks. The Chiesa dei SS Maria e Donato features some suitably splendid medieval glass mosaics, while you might spot some modern glass-sculpture installations dotting the island. Along the Canal Grande di Murano near the Ponte Vivarini, the Palazzo da Mula (Map p118), sometimes plays host to exhibitions, usually on a familiar subject: glass. Across Canale di San Donato is one of the few private mansions of any note on the island, the 16th-century Palazzo Trevisan.

Once the showrooms and glass studios close up shop for the evening around 5pm to 6pm, the streets clear out fast, and there's a minor stampede on major vaporetto stops. Glassblowers are no longer obliged to live near the *fornaci* (furnaces) to stoke the flames, and many now live in Mestre or Venice instead. At night, Murano seems all but deserted.

CHIESA DEI SS MARIA E DONATO
Map p118

☎ 041 73 90 56; Campo San Donato; ⌚ 9am-noon & 3.30-7pm Mon-Sat, 3.30-7pm Sun; 🚊 Museo Murano's devotion and its glass-making prowess are showcased in one singular monument: Chiesa dei SS Maria e Donato, best known for its 12th-century Virgin Mary apse mosaic, shimmering with gilt-glass tesserae. The other masterpiece here is underfoot: a Byzantine-style, 12th-century mosaic pavement. The church was founded in the 7th century but rededicated to San Donato after his bones were brought here from Cephalonia, along with four bones from a dragon he supposedly killed that now hang behind the altar. Save the church visit until after the museum and stores close around 5pm to 6pm.

MUSEO DEL VETRO Map p118

Museum of Glass; ☎ 041 73 95 86; www.musei civiciveneziani.it; Fondamenta Giustinian 8; adult/EU senior & student 6-14yr/with Museum Pass or VENICE-card & under 6yr €5.50/3/free; ☿ 10am-6pm Thu-Tue Apr-Oct, 10am-4pm Thu-Tue Nov-Mar; ☮ Museo

Murano has displayed its glass-making prowess at the Museo del Vetro since 1861. Downstairs, 3rd-century iridescent Roman glass is featured alongside Maria Grazia Rosin's 1992 postmodern detergent jug in impeccably blown glass. Upstairs, technical explanations detail the process for making *murrine,* the technique used in making Venetian trade beads. The section on glass mosaics explains the mineral sources and chemical reactions that produce specific colours, and by way of example, shows miniature portraits in glass that are outsized masterworks of technique. To the left is the frescoed Salone Maggiore (Grand Salon), with displays ranging from 17th-century winged goblets to Carlo Scarpa's 1930 octopus.

The museum building itself is a noteworthy 15th-century mansion with a peaceful garden. It served as the seat of the Torcello bishopric from 1659 until its dissolution in the early 19th century, when it briefly became Murano's town hall.

MURANO COLLEZIONI Map p118

☎ 041 73 62 72; www.muranocollezioni.com; Fondamenta Manin 1c-d; ☿ 10am-5pm Tue-Sun; ☮ Colonna

Like divas at Teatro La Fenice, signature glass pieces show perfect poise on elegantly spotlit pedestals in this darkened brick warehouse showroom. Famed Murano glass designers Barovier & Toso, Carlo Moretti and Venini are all represented here, and even if you're not in the market for such high-end glass you're welcome to stop in and admire their luminous designs in a range of techniques.

BURANO & MAZZORBO

After bingeing on Venice's Gothic ornament, Burano brings you back to your senses with a shock of colour. You can spot the island coming long before you arrive, with houses painted in primary-colour paint schemes chosen by local fisherfolk, who wanted to be able to spot their own houses on the horizon when heading home from a day at sea. But with more than one red-roofed, cobalt-blue house on a block, Burano residents are now having to make an extra effort to set their homes apart – an orange awning, say, or a window box blazing with neon-red geraniums. The brick Chiesa di San Martino seems downright drab by comparison. With exposure to lagoon humidity and salty seaside air, paint doesn't stay on long, so the local landscape is a constantly changing patchwork of textures, patinas, and (look out where you lean!) fresh paint.

The 40-minute LN ferry ride from the Fondamente Nuove is packed with photographers who bound into Burano's backstreets, snapping away at green stockings hung to dry between pink and orange houses. Either some secret colour-theory ordinance requires locals to choose skivvies to complement their home decor schemes, or Burano is naturally the most artistically inclined fishing village in the Mediterranean basin.

Come for the colours, stay for the cookies: Burano's vaguely lemony, vanilla crumbling biscuits in rings and S shapes are ideal

LOCAL VOICE: MARINA SENT

Shattering the glass ceiling My family have been glass designers in Murano for generations. But back in the 1980s, glassblowing was a profession dominated by men, and my background was in architecture. So when my sister and I began working in glass, it was just for fun, to see what we could do. Glass jewellery wasn't part of the family tradition, and we wanted to make something new.

Spicing it up Anyone interested in glass should visit the Museo del Vetro (above), and explore Murano to look inside laboratories and hear the furnaces. But design inspiration is everywhere in Venice: lately I've been inspired by spices, the piles of paprika and cinnamon at the Rialto markets (p85).

Angels in the architecture Since medieval artisans paid for the capitals along the Palazzo Ducale (p66), we financed the restoration of the statue of Virtue on the side of the building – it's our honour to continue the artisans' tradition in the heart of Venice.

Marina Sent is an architect turned pioneering modern Murano glass designer (see p167).

for dunking in dessert wines. The seafood here is as fresh as you can get without your own fishing pole, and the simple, stellar fare at Trattoria al Gatto Nero (see p195) draws Slow Foodies here from across Italy – reserve ahead.

Burano is traditionally famed for its lace, but at the time of writing the Museo del Merletto (Lace Museum; ☎ 041 73 0034, www.museiciviciveneziani .it) at Piazza Galuppi 187 remained closed for restoration, and much of the stock for sale in Buranelli boutiques was imported – be sure to ask for a guarantee of authenticity. On sunny days, you may still see women chatting and tatting a lacy edge for a pillowcase in parks and *campi*.

When lace-crazed tour groups descend, cross the wooden bridge to neighbouring Mazzorbo to find plenty of green space, a playground, and a seemingly sacrilegious public toilet in the apse of a former chapel. Give yourself time to wander into the quietest corners, and you'll discover a couple of waterfront trattorie, a Byzantine church under restoration, and simple scrollwork houses amid large market gardens (artichokes are a local speciality). A peaceful snooze in the grass takes you light years from the marvels and bustle of Venice.

CHIESA DI SAN MARTINO Map p121
☎ 041 73 00 96; Piazza Galuppi; admission free; ☼ 8am-noon & 3-7pm Mon-Sat; ⚓ Burano
This 16th-century church is worth a quick look, in particular for the *Crocifissione* by Giambattista Tiepolo. The church's tilting brick bell tower sprouts a thin green patch of weeds on top, and serves as a local landmark to stay oriented when wandering the colourful *calli*. Alongside the church, you'll find a quiet *campo* with a single tree that seems more sombre than the others, and was recently renamed to commemorate a tragedy with ripple effects all the way to Burano: Corte Settembre 11, 2001.

TORCELLO
On the pastoral island of Torcello, a three-minute T line ferry hop from Burano, sheep easily outnumber the 20 or so human residents. But this bucolic backwater was once a Byzantine metropolis of 20,000, and has the stunning mosaics to prove it inside Cattedrale di Santa Maria Assunta. Rivalry with Venice and a succession of malaria epidemics systematically reduced its splendour and population, until all

that remained were romantic ruins and lagoon *anatra* (wild duck). Hemingway enjoyed both immensely, and retreated to Locanda Cipriani (see p226) to write in the 1930s.

When you get off the ferry, follow the path along the canal, Fondamenta Borgognoni, which leads you on a 10-minute walk to the heart of the island. Around the central square huddles all that remains of old Torcello: the archives, quarters for clergy and a couple of antique shops amid the few remaining historic homes. Looking around the sparse, scruffy-looking buildings and monuments in the *campo* through the eyes of Hemingway, you can almost picture this place at its peak from the mid-7th century to the 13th century, when it was the seat of the bishop of mainland Altinum (modern Altino). Time permitting before the last T ferry departure, head across the *campo* to take a peek at bronzes and stone relics from Torcello's Byzantine heyday at the quirky Museo di Torcello.

CATTEDRALE DI SANTA MARIA ASSUNTA Map p121
☎ 041 296 06 30; Piazza Torcello; cathedral €4, bell tower €2, incl both plus museum €6; ☼ 10.30am-6pm Mar-Oct, 10am-5pm Nov-Feb, last entry to church/bell tower 30min/1hr before closing; ⚓ Torcello
Founded in the 7th century, Santa Maria Assunta captures the glory of Venice's Byzantine empire days. The Madonna rises like the sun in an eastern apse shimmering with gold mosaics, high above a phalanx of saints on the iconostasis.

On the western wall, a mosaic Last Judgment shows the Adriatic as a sea nymph ushering souls lost at sea towards St Peter, who's jangling the keys to Paradise like God's own bouncer. The alternative these mosaics present is enough to make a medieval believer shudder, and even modern horror movie fans blanch: a blue devil gloats over skewered souls and skulls squirming with worms.

The structure you see today dates from the first expansion of the church in 824 and rebuilding in 1008, making it about the oldest Venetian monument in its original Byzantine-Romanesque condition. Climb the bell tower for a long view over the lagoon and animals that no longer have to fear Ernest Hemingway's hunting parties. From March to October the tower closes half an hour before the church does.

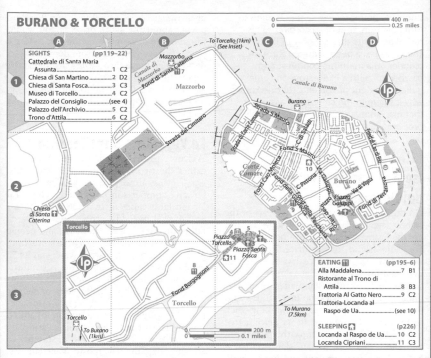

In front of the cathedral entrance are the excavated remains of the 7th-century circular baptistry, demolished and replaced several times before it fell into disuse, and was forgotten for centuries before its rediscovery in the 19th century. Steps lead down into a small pool, a standard early-Christian model for baptisteries. Fragmentary remains of construction on the site of the baptistry go back to the 4th century, indicating that the island was already inhabited under the Roman Empire.

Adjacent to the cathedral, the Chiesa di Santa Fosca (10am-4.30pm daily) was founded in the 11th century to house the body of St Fosca. How this Roman girl raised in Libya wound up a saint a tragic tale: when Fosca announced her conversion to Christianity at 15, her enraged father turned the teenager over to local authorities, but an angel frightened the soldiers away. Fosca calmly turned herself in, and was tortured and bled to death with a sword. After Libya was conquered by the Muslim Ummayads in 655, a Venetian sailor named Vitale brought her remains to Torcello.

MUSEO DI TORCELLO Map p121

041 270 24 64; Piazza Torcello; admission €3, incl cathedral, bell tower €6; 10.30am-5.30pm Tue-Sun Mar-Oct, 10am-5pm Tue-Sun Nov-Feb; Torcello

Across the square from the cathedral in the 13th-century Palazzo del Consiglio is this museum dedicated to the island. On the ground floor are some sculptural fragments from the cathedral, a 6th-century holy-water font and a curious display of Byzantine objects from Constantinople. Upstairs, you'll find a series of surprisingly dark religious paintings from the workshops of Veronese, and sundry ancient office supplies from Torcello's bureaucracy, including a 7th-century lead seal that must have made paperwork downright toxic.

The museum's ancient artefacts are held in the Palazzo dell'Archivio, opposite the Palazzo del Consiglio. They include Roman bronze implements and figurines, and some statuary and funerary stelae (inscribed, stone columns). The Roman items were mostly unearthed at the now-vanished Altino.

The rough-hewn stone chair outside is known as the Trono d'Attila (Attila's Throne). Legend has it that this uncomfortable and singularly unimpressive seat belonged to Attila the Hun, though according to historical accounts this is highly unlikely. The chair may have been acquired through plunder on a maritime conquest and pawned off with a likely story on some gullible resident of Torcello. No one knows why it's here in the *campo;* it's assumed that magistrates sat here to make public proclamations.

MINOR ISLANDS
Isola di San Francesco del Deserto

On this island wilderness in the heart of the lagoon (see Map p64), the only souls around are the Franciscans who have been caretakers of the island for centuries. Evidence of an early Roman presence has been found here, and legend has it that Francis of Assisi sought shelter on the island after a long, arduous journey to Palestine in 1220. It's said that gentle saint planted his walking stick in the ground here, and in its place a tree grew. The Franciscans took this as a sign, and chose this spot for an island retreat – but with malaria rampant and harsh living conditions, in 1420 the surviving monks were forced to desert the island (hence the name).

Another branch of the order determined to make a go of it reoccupied the island later that century, and found conditions as trying as ever. In the 18th century, they were succeeded by yet another reforming branch of the Franciscans. Pope Leo XIII united these groups in the 19th century, creating the order of the Frati Minori. With newfound strength in numbers, the order has remained on the island ever since, except for an interruption under Napoleon.

Today visits to the island are possible by prior arrangement with the monastery (☎ 041 528 68 63; www.isola-sanfrancescodeldeserto.it; admission free, donations appreciated; ☯ 9-11am & 3-5pm Tue-Sun by prior arrangement). Phone ahead, since tours are subject to the availability of a Franciscan brother to usher you through grounds that retain some of its 13th-century elements, including the first cloister. Visitors are kindly requested to speak in hushed tones, as this remains a sacred space of prayer and contemplation.

Getting there is another matter. You may be able to arrange a visit as part of a day trip boating on the lagoon with Terra e Acqua (p271)

or Città d'Acqua (p271). Otherwise, you'll end up paying about the same price as you would for an entire day on the lagoon just to hire a private boat or water taxi from Burano. If you decide to go the taxi route, ask around at the vaporetto stop on Burano, and expect to pay about €80 to €100 for up to four passengers for the return trip and a 40-minute to an hour wait time.

Le Vignole & Sant'Erasmo

Welcome to the Venetian countryside! Together the two islands of Vignole Vecchie and Vignole Nuove almost equal Venice in size, but any comparison ends there. The rural lagoon landscapes of Le Vignole (see Map p64) are covered in fields, groves and vineyards rather than endless monuments, and people are few and far between. The islands long produced most of the doge's wine, and its 50 inhabitants still live mainly from agriculture. The southeastern end of the island remains a military zone, though after long periods of disuse, it's become something of a bird sanctuary. A couple of *osterie* on the inhabited southwestern tip of the island occasionally open on sunny weekends and in summer to accommodate the few, mostly Venetian visitors who find their way here.

A promontory off the southeastern part of Le Vignole ends in the Isola di Sant'Andrea, which has the best-preserved old fort on the lagoon: the 16th-century Forte Sant'Andrea. Built by Michele Sanmicheli and commonly known as the Castello da Mar (Sea Castle), the fort features low-level cannons pointing out to sea. The last time these guns were fired, they managed to dissuade one of Napoleon's warships in 1797. There was also once a chain from the fort across to the (now gone) Forte di San Nicolò on the Lido, rendering entry into the heart of the lagoon by enemy warships virtually impossible. But the guns and chain were rarely needed, since the lagoon was notoriously difficult to navigate without insider knowledge.

The Venetian Municipality is slowly reclaiming the disused military zone on the Isola Sant'Andrea as a park, and you'll find a well-kept path and informational signage already in place amid the ruins of the fort and barracks behind it. Otherwise, this area remains a wilderness, and the only spot for mooring is on the west side of the island. Visits to the fort are possible on boat trips arranged by Terra e Acqua (p271), which may include lunch stops moored along the island and short hikes through the park to the Castello. Laguna Eco Adventures (p271) and Città d'Acqua (p271) may also include a stop at Le Vignole on a boating itinerary.

Together with Le Vignole, Sant'Erasmo (see Map p64) is known as the *orto di Venezia* (Venice's garden). About 750 people live on the island, many around the Chiesa ferry stop. According to the Roman chronicler Martial, Sant'Erasmo was once dotted with country villas belonging to well-to-do citizens of the now-disappeared mainland centre of Altinum (Altino). Until the 1800s, the island bore the direct brunt of waves rolling in from the Adriatic, but the subsequent construction of dikes at the Porto del Lido lagoon entrance led to a build-up of sediment that created Punta Sabbioni. Between the dikes and the Punta Sabbioni, Sant'Erasmo is now buffered from the full force of sea tides.

It's a half-hour walk from the Chiesa stop to the more southern Capannone stop, and another 15 minutes east to what remains of the round Torre Massimiliana, a 19th-century Austrian defensive fort now occasionally used for temporary exhibitions. The small beach and restaurant nearby have become a summer weekend getaway for young and restless Venetians, who rev their speedboats to impress one another. Il Lato Azzurro (p226) is a favourite retreat for artists visiting Venice in summer, offering onsite cultural events and inexpensive lodging near the lagoon, which is just a 25-minute ferry ride from the Biennale.

Vaporetto 13 runs to Le Vignole and Sant'Erasmo from Fondamente Nuove via Murano (Faro stop).

Isola La Certosa

Once home to Carthusian monks (hence the island's name), La Certosa (see Map p64) served as a military zone from about the time Napoleon waltzed into Venice until after WWII. Lately, this long-abandoned island is being revived as an art centre, marina, and park. Since 2007, the Istituto Europeo di Design (p265) has brought students of design, fashion and photography to the island, for coursework ranging from three- to four-week intensive classes to full masters' degree programs.

The island also serves Venice with a much-needed marina. Vento di Venezia (☎ 041 520 85 88; www.ventodivenezia.it) offers moorings for 100 visiting yachts, to be expanded to 400 in coming years. The marina also offers a range of services, including fully equipped boat repair and restoration shops, a hotel with 18 spacious rooms and a restaurant-bar, a boat-charter service, and sailing classes for all levels. The rest of the island (which has a bit of a rabbit problem) is being revamped as urban parkland.

Vaporetto 41 and 42 connect Certosa with Castello stops at San Pietro and Sant'Elena, but schedules are subject to season (see p260).

Isola di San Lazzaro degli Armeni

In 1717 the Armenian order of the Mechitarist Fathers (named after the founding father, Mechitar) was granted use of this island, which had been the site of a Benedictine hospice for pilgrims and then served as a leper colony. The Mechitarist monastery (Map p116; ☎ 041 526 01 04; adult/student & child €6/4.50; ☺ tours 3.25-5pm daily) became an important centre of learning and repository of Armenian culture, which it remains to this day. The order also runs a hostel in a frescoed former school at Palazzo Zenobio in Dorsoduro (see p219).

Access to the island is by tour only. After wandering around the cloister you are taken to the church, sparkling with mosaics and stuffed with paintings; the Armenian monastery was the only one in Venice spared Napoleon's pillaging. After the 18th-century refectory, you'll head upstairs to the library, which is divided into several rooms with curio cabinets of antiquities from Ancient Egypt, Sumeria and India, plus precious book collections. One room is reserved for Armenian art and artefacts.

An Egyptian mummy and a 15th-century Indian throne are the rather quirky main features of the room dedicated to the memory of Lord Byron, who stayed on the island in search of inner peace. True to his eccentric nature, he could often be seen swimming from the island to the Grand Canal – Byron was never one to let a canal come between him and a hot date. Lastly, a circular room contains precious manuscripts, many of them Armenian and one dating to the 6th century.

For San Lazzaro, take vaporetto 20 from San Zaccaria.

Isola di San Clemente & San Servolo

The island of San Clemente (see Map p64) was once the site of a hospice for pilgrims returning from the Middle East. Later, a convent was built and from 1522 it was a quarantine station. The plague that devastated Venice in 1630 was blamed by some on a carpenter who worked on San Clemente, and who became infected and brought the disease to the city. The Austrians turned the building into a mental hospital for women (the first in Europe), and until 1992 it still operated in part as a psychiatric hospital.

Today the entire island is a luxury hotel, and if you check yourself into San Clemente Palace (see p226) you'll find walls padded with silk damask, spa treatments, a golf course, and no shock therapy (except for maybe the bill). But to Venetians 'going to San Clemente' still means only one thing: you've gone around the bend, in more ways than one.

San Servolo (see Map p64) shared these hospital functions from the 18th century until 1978. From the 7th to the 17th centuries Benedictine monks had a monastery here, and you can glimpse some architectural elements dating from those early days in the former hospital. The hospital has been partly opened as the Museo della Follia (Museum of Madness; ☎ 041 524 01 19; www.fondazionesanservolo.it; admission free; ☷ phone bookings 9.30am-5.30pm Mon-Thu, 9.30am-3.30pm Fri).

Two intriguing rooms are full of paraphernalia and explanations of the days when being sent to San Servolo was hardly a guaranteed cure. In the first room is a series of before/after photos of 19th-century inmates, many of whose chief malady was extreme poverty, with hallucinations and non-specific symptoms resulting from bad nutrition and vitamin deficiency. In the main room are instruments used for electro-shock therapy, while in an annexe are other 'therapeutic' instruments, including chains and straitjackets.

Of particular interest is the ancient pharmacy, where for centuries many of Venice's medicines were concocted – including various possible cures for syphilis, a common cause of mental health problems in Venice even after the discovery of penicillin as a cure. Since most penicillin in Italy was set aside for the military well into the 20th century, it remained the most-sought-after street drug sold behind Zanipolo (see the boxed text, p103). The guided tour of the island, which must be booked in advance, also takes in the park and modest church.

Venice International University (p265) is also headquartered on the island, and offers accredited university coursework through reciprocal arrangements with several European, US and Japanese universities. Program strengths are art history, musicology and history.

For San Servolo, take vaporetto 20 from San Zaccaria; the hotel on Isola di San Clemente operates a shuttle service.

GRAND CANAL

Sorry, Champs Élysées, you never stood a chance: in the 15th century, French writer Philippe de Commines proclaimed the Grand Canal 'the finest street in the world, with the finest houses'. Comparing other boulevards to the Grand Canal seems unfair, given teal-blue water in place of asphalt and fleets of gondolas that make rush hour seem romantic.

The Grand Canal looms larger in the imagination than in reality: this stretch of water is only 40m to 100m wide, 3.8km long and about 6m deep. Yet, this backwards-S-shaped canal could cause architectural whiplash, with 185 monuments and 15 religious buildings purpose-built to reflect Venice's glory. Ships laden with treasure pulled up to the grand water gates of *fondachi* (trading houses), and visiting dignitaries alighted on Grand Canal piers suitably stunned by the grandiose Gothic *palazzi* (palaces).

Today you don't have to be a Greek sea captain or Turkish princess to navigate the Grand Canal, though the magnificent ride may make you feel like one. Public transport doesn't get more glamorous than the vaporetto 1 ride from the Piazzale Roma to San Marco. Along the leisurely 45-minute commute, you'll spot some 50 *palazzi*, six churches, four bridges, two open-air markets and other landmarks recognisable from scene-stealing cameos in four James Bond films.

Cruising down the finest 'street' in the world, the Grand Canal

Hurtle through time along the Grand Canal, from a futuristic bridge past a 13th-century Turkish trading post and Wagner's Renaissance residence to a modern-art showcase.

1 Ponte di Calatrava

The Grand Canal starts with controversy: Spanish architect Santiago Calatrava's 2008 luminous glass-and-steel bridge (p97) gracing gritty Piazzale Roma. With costs triple the original €4 million estimates, work to correct a 4cm tolerance, and wheelchair accessibility concerns, some Venetians are grudging in their admiration.

2 Stazione di Santa Lucia

The first trains rumbled from the mainland into Venice in 1846, and a convent dedicated to Santa Lucia was demolished to make way for this train station, built in 1865.

3 Ponte dei Scalzi

Eugenio Miozzi's 1934 Istrian stone-and-iron bridge (p150) connects the train station with the southwestern half of the city.

4 Fondaco dei Turchi

The former Turkish trading centre (p90) features a polychrome marble double colonnade with 13th-century capitals. The watchtowers are mostly decorative: though Venice pillaged Constantinople and Turks and Venetians skirmished at sea, trade triumphed over tension within Venice.

5 Deposito del Megio

Before its conversion into a school in 1922, this silo stored millet for famines and sieges, and saved the city in 1559. Gracing the edifice is Venice's lion of St Mark, a copy of an original chipped off by Napoleon.

6 Palazzo Vendramin-Calergi

Though Mauro Cordussi's Renaissance palace now houses the city's casino (p208), it wasn't exactly lucky for composer Richard Wagner, who retreated here with his family in 1882–83 only to drop dead on the premises.

7 Chiesa di San Stae

Built in 1709 on the site of an older church, this statue-bedecked white church (p91) keeps a straight Palladian face while winking at baroque ornament with its tiered statuary.

8 Ca' Pesaro

With a grand double arcade atop a faceted marble base, this *palazzo* (p88), completed in 1710, houses the Galleria d'Arte Moderna and Museo d'Arte Orientale.

CA' D'ORO TO CA' FOSCARI

Explore a sensational stretch of water between two Gothic palaces, passing open-air markets, the Rialto bridge, mansions inhabited by monkeys and heretics, and a town hall that makes bureaucracy look beautiful.

① Ca' d'Oro

The gilding is long gone from the facade of the 'Golden House' (p96), but the majesty of this 1430 Venetian-Gothic marvel remains. Two tiers of lacy arcades feature peekaboo quatrefoil portholes, crowned by rooftop crenellation that looks like a tiara.

② Pescaria

Before you see it coming on your right, you'll probably hear this fish market (p85), built in 1907 on the site where fishmongers have sung the praises of lagoon seafood for 700 years.

③ Rialto markets

At the neighbouring produce market (p85), Venetian vendors brag shamelessly about local seasonal produce.

④ Fondaco dei Tedeschi

Today a post office, this *fondacho* (p74), once the most important trading house on the canal, used to house German traders. Of the Titian and Giorgione frescoes that once covered the exterior, only a few faded fragments remain, displayed at the Ca' d'Oro (p96).

⑤ Ponte di Rialto

Tourists hang off this bridge (p87) like gargoyles to snap photos of Antonio da Ponte's 1592 engineering marvel. Though final construction costs spiralled to 250,000 Venetian ducats – some €19 million today – this marble arc has a glow rivalling gold around sunset.

⑥ Ca' Farsetti & Palazzo Loredan

Before becoming Venice's city hall in 1826, Ca' Farsetti (p139) served as a noble family residence, an art school where Canova studied and a hotel. Neighbouring Palazzo Loredan makes bureaucracy seem elegant, with city offices behind a 13th-century portico and 1st-floor loggia.

⑦ Palazzi Mocenigo

This Gothic complex (p89) today houses luxury holiday apartments, but it used to host more controversial guests: Thomas Moore sojourned here, philosopher Giordano Bruno retreated here after accusations of heresy, and Byron occupied one house with his two monkeys and 14 servants.

⑧ Ca' Foscari

Turn right to spot the quatrefoil arcades of Doge Francesco Foscari's 15th-century Gothic mansion, converted into a trade school in 1866 and restored in 2006 as the seat of Venice's Foscari University, famed for (fittingly) its architecture program.

The grand finale of this canal is packed with more drama than a La Fenice opera: modern art attacks, prowling lions, stark nakedness, terrifying curses, black plague and a pink prison.

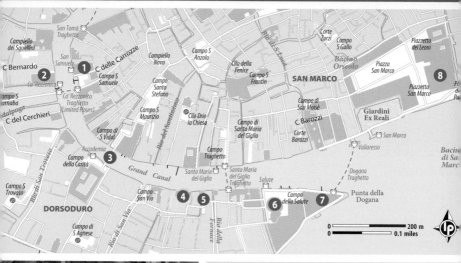

❶ Palazzo Grassi

Expect the unexpected at 18th-century Palazzo Grassi (p71): a car painted by Richard Prince, or a skull sculpted by Subodh Gupta from cooking pots. With ingenious exhibition design by Japanese minimalist Tadao Ando, this museum features blockbuster shows and François Pinault's contemporary art collection.

❷ Ca' Rezzonico

Baldassare Longhena's jewel-box palace (p80) was once used for official ceremonies, and now houses Venice's baroque art treasures. Through its see-and-be-seen windows, you might catch a glimpse of heavenly Tiepolo ceilings.

❸ Ponte dell'Accademia

Built in the 1930s as a temporary replacement for a 19th-century metal bridge, this wooden bridge (p70) arched like a cat's back is an enduring novelty. At the foot of the bridge is the Gallerie dell'Accademia (p76).

❹ Palazzo Venier dei Leoni

Stone lions and Calder sculpture flank this *palazzo*, home to the Peggy Guggenheim Collection (p78). Between the lions, Marino Marini's 1948 naked bronze *Angel of the City* on horseback is evidently excited by his view of the Grand Canal.

❺ Ca' Dario

This 1487 *palazzo* (p82) fascinated Monet, but dark superstitions linger behind this multicoloured marble facade. According to Venetian urban legends, anyone who lives here is cursed with a terrible death, which local gossips claim dissuaded Woody Allen from buying the place.

❻ Chiesa di Santa Maria della Salute

Baldassare Longhena's octagonal domed church (p81) gives thanks to the Madonna for sparing Venice from the plague; it's propped up by 100,000 wood pylons underfoot.

❼ Punta della Dogana

The tip of Dorsoduro is the Punta della Dogana (p81), a historic customs warehouse reimagined by Tadao Ando as a public showcase for François Pinault's contemporary art collection.

❽ Palazzo Ducale

The Grand Canal's grand finale is this pink Gothic *palazzo* (p66) and its Ponte dei Sospiri (Bridge of Sighs) leading the condemned to prison. Recently, preservationists have sighed over the advertising draped over these landmarks while undergoing restoration. Given wide-ranging outcry, the Palazzo Ducale might retire from its brief, inglorious career hawking Swatches.

The Ponte dei Sospiri (Bridge of Sighs) connects the Palazzo Ducale and Prigioni Nuove

Perhaps more than any other city, Venice is best discovered on foot. The following walks cover the *sestieri* that make up the city: San Marco, Dorsoduro, San Polo, Santa Croce (Santa Crose), Cannaregio and Castello. The suggested walking times allow for a leisurely pace but not for peeking inside museums, getting caught up in conversation with an artisan, or pausing for a proper two-hour *pranzo* (lunch), all highly recommended activities that could easily stretch your walking tour out to a day or week.

Consider each itinerary a loose outline, and don't feel obliged to cover the proverbial waterfront. Skip any sights that don't capture your interest and follow your bliss instead, and you'll never feel lost in Venice.

SESTIERE DI SAN MARCO
Piazzetta di San Marco to Torre dell'Orologio

1 Columns of San Marco Careful where you stand: these red-and-grey granite columns standing solo at the San Marco quay are considered unlucky, and many Venetians hurry past them. This isn't an idle superstition, but a long memory: for centuries, public executions took place between the two columns. Afterwards, the corpses were drawn and quartered here, and the chunks were displayed at four points around the city as a caution to would-be criminals until they began to reek (three days, possibly less in fine weather). Erected in 1172, the intended purpose of the columns is unclear, other than to bear the emblems of Venice's patron saints: the winged lion of St Mark, and St Theodore standing calmly atop a dragon that looks like a crocodile. Apparently a third column was brought to complete the set, but when it was being lifted from the boat to the quay, it slipped into the lagoon and was never retrieved.

2 Palazzo Ducale (p66) Pink, pretty, and a powerhouse of empire, the official palace of the doge has its share of dark secrets. Despite its recently restored rosy countenance, the palace has been blackened and levelled by fires several times since its establishment in the 9th century – sometimes under rather suspicious circumstances. The lagoon-facing section with the meeting hall of the Maggior Consiglio (Great Council) was finished in 1419, but after yet another fire raged through the building in 1577, the city considered Palladio's offer to build one of his signature neoclassical temples in its place. Instead, Antonio da Ponte won the commission to restore the magnificent Gothic facades in white Istrian stone and pink Veronese marble. The loggia running along the *piazzetta* (little square) may

seem like a fanciful architectural flourish, but it served a solemn purpose: death sentences were solemnly read out between the ninth and tenth columns from the left. These pillars are easy to recognise: both of them are ominously darker than the others along the loggia. Occasionally the condemned were spared the rope, and instead led upstairs to languish in the dread Piombi attic prison, tucked under the roof of the Palazzo Ducale.

3 Libreria Nazionale Marciana (p70) Facing the Palazzo Ducale across the Piazzetta di San Marco is another arcaded building, but with a very different purpose. The first Venetian library open to the public, this forward-thinking Renaissance building built by Jacopo Sansovino in the 16th century contains centuries of collected Venetian knowledge, including ancient codices in Greek and Latin, musical scores and operas, Marco Polo's last will and testament, and books published in Venice in the 15th century, when the printing press was the newfangled technology most of Europe doubted would ever catch on.

4 Basilica di San Marco (p65) Take a moment to appreciate San Marco from the sides, where the original brickwork has over the centuries been almost entirely covered with an extraordinary patchwork of veined marbles from across Venice's trading routes and ancient classical friezes lifted wholesale from Greek colonies. Inset into the southwest corner of the church is *The Four Tetrarchs,* an Egyptian porphyry statue looted from Constantinople supposedly representing four emperors of ancient Rome under Emperor Diocletian. Rather than hiding this stolen statue, as furtive art thieves might do, Venice made it a cornerstone of the official doge's chapel. The message was clear: Rome laid some useful groundwork, and Constantinople had its moment of glory, but eternity would belong to Venice.

5 Campanile (p72) Another monument that Venetians with long memories give a wide berth, the bell tower of San Marco was sometimes used as a convenient post for (what else?) stringing up criminals, before its abrupt collapse in 1902. Yet Venetians with peculiar affection for this brick monument rebuilt a new model along the lines of the old bell tower, only a little wider at the base to avoid future collapse – though just to be on the safe side, some locals prefer not to linger too long in its shadow.

6 Procuratie Vecchie Stretching west away from the basilica on the north side of the Piazza San Marco, these elegant three-tiered 16th-century arcades designed by Mauro Codussi once housed the residence and offices of the Procurators of St Mark, responsible for the basilica's upkeep and the administration of prime real estate belonging to the basilica. Even today it is considered a mighty honour to be named a Procurator of St Mark, although these days real estate brokering is no longer included in the job description, and living at the office is not required.

7 Procuratie Nuove Opposite Codussi's arcade is the Procuratie Nuove, designed by Jacopo Sansovino and completed by Vincenzo Scamozzi and Baldassare Longhena; it has more classical Renaissance elements than Codussi's Venetian Gothic–arched Procuratie. This was a palace fit for an emperor – or so Napoleon thought when he invaded Venice in 1797, and briefly took up residence here. Today the Museo Correr (p69) takes up most of the first and second storeys of the Procuratie Nuove with displays of

SESTIERE DI SAN MARCO

ancient maps, weaponry, wonderful early Italian devotional paintings, and other Napoleonic loot.

8 Ala Napoleonica (p70) The palace that occupies the third side of the square was built by Napoleon, who decided that what this square really needed was a third side connecting the two Procuratie, and a grand ballroom to entertain imperial guests – never mind that the

WALK FACTS

Start Piazzetta di San Marco
End Torre dell'Orologio
Distance 4km
Time 1½ hours, not including food, drink and photo-op stops
Fuel stops Enoteca Il Volto, Cavatappi

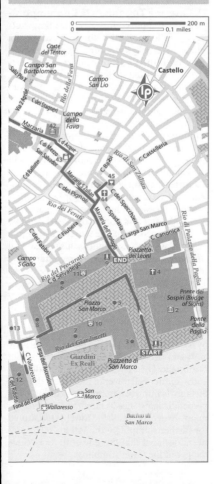

church of San Geminiano was already occupying the location he had in mind. The church was demolished and a classical palace befitting a Roman emperor soon built, but the ballroom was barely finished before the Austrians waltzed in and took over the place. Today the Ala Napoleonica houses the Museo Correr (p69), with a terrific cafe overlooking the square.

9 Torre dell'Orologio (p71) When the clock strikes the hour, look up: two bronze figures are hard at work, hammering away at a huge bell on the small terrace atop this tower. Due to some peculiarity in their Renaissance robot circuitry, these characters strike the bell no fewer than 132 times at noon or midnight. For centuries, San Marco's hardest-working duo have been known as 'I Mori' (the Moors) due to their patina – these figures predate political correctness. Beneath their feet, an archway shows the entrance to the Marzarie (or Mercerie), the web of streets connecting the power-politickers of San Marco to the money-makers of Rialto.

10 Caffè Florian (p199) You might hear this 18th-century cafe before you see its plush red-velvet salons stashed away under the arcade of the Procuratie Nuove. The Florian house orchestra provides the soundtrack to afternoons in the Piazza San Marco, and though you'll pay for the privilege of a musical coffee break with Piazza seating, it's a prime spot for viewing the sunset light displays on the mosaic facade of the Basilica.

11 Caffè Quadri (p200) A second 18th-1century cafe faces Florian across the piazza, with morning sun illuminating its painted baroque drawing-room interiors. This cafe was favoured by the Austrians during their occupation of Venice, which left a bitter aftertaste in the mouths of some Venetians – but Quadri's extra-rich house hot chocolate with whipped cream may yet cure that condition.

West of Piazza San Marco

12 Teatro al Ridotto Housed in what is today the Hotel Monaco & Grand Canal (p216) complex at Calle Vallaresso 1332, the Ridotto earned its notoriety as the city's premier gaming house in the 1700s. During the twilight years of La Serenissima, Venetian nobles wiped out their fortunes at these gaming tables. The state took a cut of the house's take, but eventually this proved insufficient compensation for the ruin wrought on an already shaky local economy. In November 1774 the Ridotto was shut *per tutti i tempi*

NEIGHBOURHOODS WALKING TOURS

ed anni avvenire (for all time and years to come). 'All time' was a relative term: less than 20 years later it was back in business. By the time Napoleon arrived, more than 130 registered *ridotti* were serving Venice's gambling habit. Concerned for their tax base and distracted troops, the Austrian occupation shut the Ridotto decisively in the early 19th century. But if you wander into the hotel's entrance and look to the right, you'll see a staircase sweeping up to the lavishly decorated theatre, now used for conferences and banquets. A secret passage bypassing the main entrance has been closed, since visitors no longer have a regular need to hide from their creditors and spouses.

13 Frezzaria Back on Salizada San Moisè, you'll pass a busy shopping street on your right as you approach Campo di San Moisè. In medieval days, the product that flew off shelves in these storefronts wasn't fashion but *frecce* (arrows), because adult Venetian men had to undertake regular archery practice on the Lido and be ready to sail to war.

14 Marina e Susanna Sent (p167) To your right as you head over the bridge, a watery glimmer from this shop window might catch your eye. On closer inspection, waterfalls turn out to be necklaces of matte teal-green Murano glass, and ice cubes and bubbles are actually clear glass beads strung into elementally chic collars.

15 Palazzo Contarini-Fasan Follow Calle Larga XXII Marzo, commemorating the short-lived Austrian surrender to Venetian rebels on 22 March 1848, then duck left down Calle del Pestrin to this forlorn palace. According to a local legend aided and abetted by gondoliers who ply the waters of the canal out front, this was once the home of Desdemona, wife to Othello and victim of his jealousy in Shakespeare's play.

16 Galleria Rosella Junck (see p74) Back on Calle Larga XXII Marzo as you turn the corner, you never know what fragile beauty will show up next in this picture window: a braying donkey in rose-tinted glass by Seguso c 1950, or a frosted glass warrior's helmet that rather seems to defeat the purpose. These are hints of a glass collection that ranges from 13th-century goblets to contemporary art-glass skulls, and if you're a Murano glass fan without the time to see the Museo del Vetro (p119) on Murano, it's a quick detour through glass-making history.

17 Chiesa di Santa Maria del Giglio (p72) Turning onto Calle delle Ostreghe, you'll soon reach the *campo* fronted by this baroque church, covered in peculiar maps of vaguely familiar locations. This facade represents cartographers' best guesses at the outlines of Venetian vassal states c 1678–81, including Crete, Croatia, Corfu and Padua. Standing tall among these possessions is a statue of Admiral Antonio Barbaro, who commissioned the reconstruction of the original 9th-century church by Giuseppe Sardi for the glory of the Virgin, Venice, and of course himself. This largely secular and self-glorifying architectural audacity enraged 19th-century architectural critic John Ruskin, who called Barbaro's church a 'manifestation of insolent atheism'. In the middle of the *campo,* you'll stumble on an out-of-place brick structure: this is the stump of the church's bell tower, knocked down in 1775 because, like the Basilica di San Marco's Campanile, it was in danger of falling over of its own accord.

18 Caterina Tognon Arte Contemporanea (see the boxed text, p74) Heading westward, you'll emerge in Campo San Maurizio, where this small, smart corner gallery wedged between 14th- and 15th-century *palazzi* displays eye-opening contemporary art and glass, ranging from visceral vessels by art star Kiki Smith to dancing glass devils by Attombri (p170). For ambitious large-scale installations and artists' residencies, the gallery uses an exhibition space around the corner on Calle del Dose, on the 1st floor of Palazzo da Ponte – ask gallery staff if the exhibition continues in the Palazzo, and they'll point the way.

19 Museo della Musica (p73) When Napoleon mowed down the church of San Geminiano to make way for his ballroom in Piazza San Marco, Venice was none too pleased – but by way of compensation, the 9th-century church of San Maurizio was rebuilt as this neoclassical structure in 1806–28. It was a nice gesture, anyway: the new church was soon deconsecrated. Today it houses a rather fascinating museum of baroque music, with original 18th-century instruments and well-researched accounts of the role of music in Venetian life – and as a neat tie-in, a desk selling CDs of music played by local musicians and tickets to concerts by Interpreti Veneziani (p209). Behind the Museo in Campiello Drio la Chiesa, you'll notice the 15th-century bell tower of the Chiesa di Santo Stefano, leaning two metres from its intended perpendicular stance like it's had one spritz too many. Every six hours, the tower is monitored for further slumping – though in 2007, engineers declared that there was no foreseeable danger of the tower tumbling.

20 Chiesa di Santo Stefano (p71) Towering over the broad expanse of Campo Santo Stefano is this massive and rather austere brick church, with just a touch of Gothic around its portals. It's free to peek inside at the impressive *carena di nave* ceiling, which looks like a Venetian galley turned upside down because it more or less was: according to available architectural records, it was probably constructed in pieces at the Arsenale by shipbuilders and assembled on site. If you have time and a Chorus Pass (p266), the sacristy and cloisters feature some thunderous Tintorettos and tear-jerking Canovas.

21 Chiesa di San Vidal (p73) Another church that did double duty as a monument to Venice's naval victories, San Vidal is on your right as you pass through the business end of Campo Santo Stefano to reach the Ponte dell'Accademia to the west. Doge Vitale Falier built the original 11th-century version of this church in honour of his namesake saint, but Antonio Gaspari was commissioned to build this grander 17th-century version to celebrate Francesco Morosoni's triumph over Turkish foes in Morea. After Morosoni became doge, the church still seemed insufficiently grand, so a Palladian facade was tacked on in 1706–14 by Tirali. The church has been deconsecrated, and now serves as the chief venue and ticket point for Interpreti Veneziani concerts. Entry is free if you want a peek at Carpaccio's suitably stately painting, *San Vidal on Horseback.*

22 Palazzo Franchetti (p73) Enter the iron gates across from San Vidal for a breath of fresh air in the gardens of this 16th-century palace, which briefly served as a bank before finding its calling as the home of the Istituto Veneto di Scienze, Lettere ed Arti (Veneto Institute of the Sciences, Letters and Arts). Founded by the Austrians in 1838, this scholastic institute hosts lectures and conferences, and if you utter the magic word 'caffè' to the guard at the front door, you'll be pointed in the direction of a restorative espresso in the recently restored cloisters cafe.

Santo Stefano to Ponte di Rialto

23 Ca' del Duca Backtracking the southwest end of Campo Santo Stefano, Calle Fruttarol follows a winding route northwest towards the Palazzo Grassi and shows you the backsides of several Grand Canal palaces. Following this road, you'll immediately cross a narrow canal and then another, the Rio del Duca. The building on the northwest bank is a palace you may have glimpsed from a vaporetto ride down the Grand Canal; the Ca' del Duca (Duke's House), which the Corner family sold to Francesco Sforza, Duke of Milan, in 1461. The mansion was largely rebuilt in the 19th century, but you can glimpse some of the original faceted Istrian stonework on the ground floor. During Architecture Biennales, this place sometimes hosts exhibitions – most recently, Luxembourg's official entry, a meditation on modern architecture by a dozen Europeans, manifested in a series of minimalist Palladian-white planks.

24 Palazzo Malipiero Turn left into Calle del Teatro, named for a long-gone theatre that once premiered works by Carlo Goldoni (see p50), then swing right, and as you dead-end into Salizada Malipiero, note the plaque on the wall pointing out that in a house along this lane, Giacomo Casanova was born in 1725. Within 15 years, Casanova would begin setting the all-time standard for belt-notching Lotharios at Palazzo Malipiero. The serene palace betrays none of its romantic notoriety, given a placidly classical 18th-century once-over to an underlying 13th-century house repeatedly expanded and updated in the 16th to 17th centuries – though you can glimpse the wild medieval garden out back from the Grand Canal.

25 Palazzo Grassi (p71) Palazzo Malipiero gazes across Campo San Samuele at a larger, grander palace built by Giorgio Massari: the Palazzo Grassi. From the outside, the only hint of this baroque palace's recent reincarnation as a cutting-edge museum by art collector François Pinault and minimalist architect Tadao Ando is the occasional avant-garde sculpture installation plunked on the *campo* or perched on a gangplank sticking into the Grand Canal – a Subodh Gupta skull made of cooking pots, say, or Jeff Koons' giant pink balloon dog. With works from Pinault's collection now installed at new galleries of the Punta Dogana, Palazzo Grassi hosts contemporary art shows as well as ambitious exhibitions comparing ancient Roman and Barbarian art or tracing the development of modern art movements in Italy. A visit here can easily absorb a couple hours, including an obligatory stop at the 1st-floor cafe – more accurately described as a changing art installation that serves a mean espresso with views over the Grand Canal.

26 Salizada San Samuele 3337 Head east along Calle delle Carrozze and into Salizada San Samuele, lined with antique shops and contemporary art galleries – it's anyone's guess what Paolo Veronese, who lived at No 3337, would have thought of it all. Probably he wouldn't have been too shocked, since back in his day this street was a red-light district, along with a back alley cheekily named Calle delle Muneghe (Alley of the Nuns). If you experience a sudden surge of inspiration on this auspicious spot, you can head around the corner to pick up some Veronese rose and green pigments at Arcobaleno (p163), and get cracking on your own masterpiece.

27 Campiello Novo Like most locations dubbed 'Novo' in Venice, this peaceful square actually dates back several centuries. Until Napoleon put an end to the practice in the 18th century, local dead were buried beneath the flagstones in this ancient plaza, then known as Campiello dei Morti (Square of the Dead). Napoleon's city planners correctly recognised that tossing disease-ridden corpses into canals and burying them behind churches near canals and *pozzi* (wells) constituted a public health hazard, and ordered bodies hauled off to the new cemetery at Isola di San Michele instead.

28 La Galleria van der Koelen (see p74) A rather Byzantine byway leads to this contemporary gallery quietly hiding behind La Fenice across the Rio della Veste. Hang a right off the Campiello to Calle de Pestrin, then a left onto Calle dei Frati, and cross the bridge over Rio di Sant'Angelo into the Campo Sant'Anzolo (the Venetian spelling for Angelo). On your right is Calle Caotorta, which you'll follow to the right and over a footbridge to reach the space that for three decades has presented evocative minimalist works – recently, sails without a boat, and mosaics made of gold and torn paper.

29 Teatro La Fenice (p67) Back on Calle Caotorta, cross the first bridge to your right, and hang a left along the rear flank of La Fenice and then right into Calle della Fenice. Another left and you end up in tiny Campiello della Fenice, where a hotel is covered in cannonballs used by the Austrians in their campaign to retake control of the city in 1849. Follow this arc around to Campo San Fantin, where from January to July and September to October, you'll spot opera lovers in rustling

silks and patched corduroy jackets casually milling about with glasses of *prosecco* – until the curtains-up signal dings, starting the mad whoosh up the grand stairway not to miss the overture.

30 Chiesa di San Fantin Opposite the Teatro La Fenice on Campo San Fantin is this plain but pleasing Istrian marble church. Scarpagnino began the church in 1506, but died before it was finished, leaving Sansovino to cap off the project with a domed apse c 1564. Local pastry purveyors helped pay for the construction of this church in honour of San Fantin, the patron saint of sweets. Inside, the 15th-century crucifix isn't a fixed relic: it was carried in processions of condemned criminals to their hangings at the columns of San Marco.

31 Ateneo Veneto The other main building on Campo San Fantin, the Ateneo houses the humanities academy of the University of Venice, but remains fondly remembered as the Scuola di San Fantin or 'dei Picai' (the Hanged), headquarters for the confraternity of San Girolamo and Santa Maria della Giustizia, whose members accompanied criminals on death-row in their final hours before execution. Inside the ground-floor Aula Magna meeting room is a splendid coffered ceiling offering cautionary glimpses of Purgatory by Palma Il Giovane c 1600.

32 Jarach Gallery (see p74) At the end of a shadowy passageway off Campo San Fantin, you might notice the flicker of video art screened in this contemporary art and photography gallery. Even familiar images take on fresh meaning inside this ancient Venetian courtyard mansion, where gallery artist Robert Polidori's photos of flood-ravaged New Orleans strike a deep local chord.

33 Palazzo Fortuny (p72) Follow Calle della Verona north, and veer left onto Rio Terà dei Assassini, where corpses were once frequently found in the shadows. In medieval times murder was such a common nocturnal activity around here that in 1128 the government banned the wearing of certain 'Greek-style' full beards that criminals sometimes used to mask their identities. The devotional niches you may spot around town were often originally created to hold lamps that burned all night as an early crime-prevention measure. At Calle della Mandola, jog left and right into Rio Terà della Mandola, which bumps right into the side of the splendid Palazzo Fortuny, a 15th-century Gothic palace named after the eccentric designer from Granada who moved here with his mother and sister in the 19th century, and in his top-floor studio established bohemian fashion standards still in vogue today – especially his dramatic goddess dresses. Back in the days of corsets and stays, Fortuny's free-flowing gowns worn with little or nothing underneath were an outrage to strict Victorian sensibilities, but a revelation to international trendsetters like dancer Isadora Duncan. The dancer's fashion sense proved unerring, and fatal: she was killed when her signature long, flowing scarf caught in the wheel axle of a moving car.

34 Daniele Manin statue Dogi get their due and then some in Venice, but so too do Venice's independent-minded rebels – hence this grand *campo* named after the ringleader of the anti-Austrian revolt of 1848–49 (see p26), and the towering statue in his honour. To get here from Palazzo Fortuny, drop south along Calle del Teatro Goldoni and turn left at the junction into Calle della Cortesia. Manin lived in a house just on the other side of Rio di San Luca.

35 Palazzo Contarini del Bovolo (p71) Snogging in public *campi* is such a long-established Venetian pastime down the centuries that it's surprising the dogi didn't find a way of regulating and taxing it – but the sweetest kisses are still stolen at this Renaissance palace courtyard hidden down Calle della Vida. The palace is nicknamed Bovolo ('Snail') for its grand open spiral staircase, which at the time of writing was closed to the public for climbing but still open to admiration from the courtyard below.

36 Enoteca Il Volto (p182) Heading north through the Campo Manin, pass through Campiello San Luca to Calle Cavalli, where you'll find this historic wine bar. Pause for an *ombra* of one of the hundreds of varieties of wines at the bar, or trust your host to pair a selection with a generous plate of pasta in the seating nook at the back.

37 Ca' Farsetti Blinking in the light of day after your sojourn at Enoteca Il Volto, head toward the Grand Canal along the side of this grand 12th-century *fondacho* (trading house). Ca' Farsetti is a classic example of a *fondacho*, which was the trendy live/work loft of medieval times: the family lived upstairs on the *piano nobile* ('noble floor', usually the 1st floor), while the ground floor had a grand entrance on the canal used for the loading, unloading and steady influx of valuable trading commodities that kept patrician families of Venice in grand style. In 1826 the town hall moved its offices to Ca' Farsetti from the Palazzo Ducale.

38 Palazzo Loredan Next door to Ca' Farsetti, Palazzo Loredan occupies a key spot on the Riva del Carbon (Coal Quay), which until well into the 19th century was the main unloading point for the city's coal supply – and a point of entry into a red-light district. The area began to clean up its act once official functions were transferred to Ca' Farsetti. In 1868 the city of Venice acquired Palazzo Loredan, and on weekdays you can wander into the foyer to have a look around. On the corner of Calle del Carbon, you'll find a plaque honouring Venetian scholar Eleonora Lucrezia Corner Piscopia as the first woman to receive a university degree, earning the title Doctor of Philosophy at the university of Padua in 1678.

39 Palazzo Dandolo Northeast towards the Ponte di Rialto from Calle del Carbon, you may notice this narrow, 14th-century Gothic mansion. The house belonged to blind doge Enrico Dandolo, whose fleet was commissioned to transport the Franks to the Fourth Crusade in 1204 on their quest to fight the infidels in the Holy Land. Instead, Doge Dandolo led the Franks to Constantinople and proceeded to pillage the place, killing fellow Christians and desecrating the sacred Byzantine cathedral of Hagia Sofia in the process. The doge was supposedly buried in the church under the stone bearing his name, but he was never quite forgiven his trespasses: when the Byzantines regained Constantinople 57 years later, the faithful spat on his tombstone (see Duty & Booty, p25).

40 Palazzo Bembo Wedged in between Calle Bembo and Rio di San Salvador is the birthplace of Pietro Bembo, cardinal, poet, historian and founding father of standard Italian grammar – but unlike the subjunctive tense, this elegant, harmonious 15th- to 17th-century red Gothic facade isn't the least irregular.

41 Palazzo Dolfin-Manin On the other side of Rio di San Salvador, you'll spot the grand portico of this palace, designed by Sansovino and completed in 1547. The neighbouring Bembos and Dandolos objected to this towering addition to the neighbourhood by the Dolfin family, and perhaps their curses worked: the Dolfin family fell on hard times by the 17th century, and was forced to rent and eventually sell the palace to the Pesaro family, who then sold it to the Manins. Venice's last doge, Ludovico Manin, died here in 1802, not long after Venice was forced to surrender to Napoleon under threat of bombardment in 1797. As legend has it, Doge Manin handed his doge's cap to Napoleon's guard with a sigh, saying, 'I won't be needing this anymore' – and two days later, retreated to this palace to live out his days in seclusion.

Back to Piazza San Marco

42 Palazzo Giustinian-Faccanon Heading south, dive into the narrow lanes that lead to Piazza San Marco, collectively called the Marzaria (Mercerie in Italian) after the merchants who plied this route from the quays of San Marco to the *fondachi* (trading houses) of the Rialto. Follow the Marzaria San Salvador around the northern edge of this urban labyrinth, and where the street runs into a canal, you can see the late-15th-century Gothic Palazzo Giustinian-Faccanon. This romantic palace is a gorgeous place to push paper: after serving as a post office and workplace for the editorial team of the city's main newspaper, *Il Gazzettino,* it now serves as the bureaucratic headquarters for ACTV, the city's ferry company.

43 Camuffo (p164) Pause for a moment in the midstream rush of the Marzaria to see if you might catch Signor Camuffo at his desk, coaxing a lump of nondescript glass into a gossamer, spindly-legged dragonfly using little more than a blowtorch, tweezers, his imagination, and very steady hands.

44 Chiesa di San Zulian Let yourself be carried along by the crowds heading south towards San Marco – but before you cross the footbridge over the Rio dei Ferati, turn left to reach this church (☎ 041 523 53 83; ☯ 9am-6.30pm Mon-Sat, 9am-7.30pm Sun) dedicated to San Zulian. Where Marzaria dell'Orologio begins, you'll notice this church, founded in 829, and later sheathed in Istrian stone by Sansovino on a commission from the wealthy physician Tomasso Rangone, who made his fortune selling syphilis cures and a book revealing the secrets to living past 100 (he died at 84). The good doctor is immortalised in bronze over the portal, holding sarsaparilla – apparently a key ingredient to his miracle cure for VD. Inside are some worthwhile works by Palma il Giovane and, on the right as you enter, Paolo Veronese's *The Dead Christ and Saints.*

45 Cavatappi (p181) Now that you've survived the streets of San Marco – no longer crawling with assassins, granted, but still dangerous gauntlets of designer temptations – a drink is in order. Cross Campo della Guerra and sidle up to the bar by 6.30pm, and you just might beat the local crowds to the first choice of *cicheti* here, including *crostini sopressa con carciofi* (open-faced salami sandwiches with artichokes).

Backtrack to Marzaria dell'Orologio, and proceed south towards the arch under the Torre dell'Orologio. Just before you reach the clock tower, you might notice a simple stone carved with the Roman numerals XV.VI.MCCCX. This refers to 1310, the year conspirators plotted to overthrow Doge Pietro Gradenigo but were thwarted by a woman who dropped her kitchen mortar on the head of the rebel leader. Above Sotoportego e Calle del Cappello is a bas-relief of the cook who saved the republic. Once you pass through the arch, you're back in Piazza San Marco – and if you timed your arrival for sunset, you'll catch the last rays of sunlight as they set the golden portal mosaics ablaze.

SESTIERE DI DORSODURO
Accademia to Punta della Dogana

1 Gallerie dell'Accademia (p76) The buildings you bump into on crossing the Ponte dell'Accademia over the Grand Canal from San Marco represent Venice's single most important art collection – and the work of several of its finest architects. Bartolomeo Bon completed the spare, Gothic-edged Santa Maria della Carità facade in 1448; in 1561 Palladio took a classical approach to the Convento dei Canonici Lateranensi, a convent later absorbed into the Accademia; and modernist Carlo Scarpa (a graduate of and professor at the Accademia) took a minimalist approach to restorations from 1949 to 1954, taking care not to upset the delicate symmetries achieved among architects over the centuries.

2 Palazzo Barbarigo Cross two footbridges into skinny Campo San Vio, one of a handful of squares that back onto the Grand Canal, and on its eastern edge you'll find Palazzo Barbarigo. The facade is strikingly decorated with mosaics against a gold background as a kind of monumental advertisement for Compagnia Venezia e Murano, a glass and mosaics manufacturer that moved in here towards the end of the 19th century. You can't really see it from the square without leaning dangerously over the Grand Canal, but keep an eye out when you chug down the canal on vaporetto 1.

3 Peggy Guggenheim Collection (p78) Calle della Chiesa and then Fondamenta Venier dei Leoni lead you to Venice's 20th-century modern art showcase. The Palazzo Venier dei Leoni was never finished, but that didn't stop Peggy Guggenheim from making art history with the available wall space and garden: Jackson Pollock, Marcel Duchamp, René Magritte, Salvador Dali, Henry Moore, and her former husband Max Ernst were among the artists Peggy Guggenheim championed.

The American heiress narrowly escaped Paris two days before the Nazis marched into the city, and arrived in Venice in 1948 to find the city's historically buoyant spirits broken by Mussolini and the ensuing civil war. In her position as leading modern art collector, Peggy stirred interest in postwar Venetian and Italian art and resurrected the reputation of key Italian futurists, whose dynamic style had been coopted to make Fascism more visually palatable. Peggy's affection for Venice was mutual: the city granted special dispensation for her wish to be buried in her sculpture garden, among Giacomettis and her dearly departed lapdogs.

A visit to the museum could take an hour, unless it's a sunny day in the garden – in which case you might be sorely tempted to cancel afternoon plans, and settle into the cafe for the duration.

4 Ca' Dario (p82) Exuberant gardens drip over the walls along Rio delle Toreselle, just around the corner from Peggy's place. But plants may be the only living things that thrive within these exquisite 15th-century polychrome marble walls: according to local legend, Ca' Dario is under a century-old curse. Since 1800, its owners have variously committed suicide, been murdered by lovers and drug dealers, and died penniless due to the cost of upkeep. Not surprisingly, the palace has been up for sale for some time without a buyer being found. Finally in 2005, the Guggenheim Collection struck a deal with the current owner (still alive and solvent, thank you very much) to host periodic exhibitions on the premises.

5 Chiesa di Santa Maria della Salute (p81) What an entrance: emerging through the rough-hewn *sotoportego* (passageway) of narrow Calle dell'Abbazia, Baldassare Longhena's dazzling white monolith suddenly fills your field of vision. This experience of a light at the end of the tunnel is an architectural metaphor masterfully executed by Longhena, whose luminous white dome at the end of Dorsoduro represents the salvation of Venice from the Black Death. Construction was begun in 1631, making good on an official 1630 appeal by the Venetian Senate directly to the Madonna herself, promising her a church in exchange for her intervention on behalf of Venice. Over 50 years the magnificent temple gradually took shape: a mighty dome atop an unusual octagonal base, which architectural scholars have noted conforms in its spatial ratios with mystical numerology diagrams found in arcane Christian texts and the cabbala. Entry to the main church is free, but Titian fans gladly pay the nominal admission to the sacristy, which contains some of the Venetian master's precocious early works.

6 Punta della Dogana (p81) Once the low-slung buildings along the tip of Dorsoduro served as Venice's customs houses, ensuring that no ship could enter the Grand Canal without paying Venice its dues. But in 2007–09, these buildings were reinvented by architect Tadao Ando as a showcase for François Pinault's world-class contemporary art collection, so that Venice gets its due as a hot spot for contemporary art between Biennales. Ando's creative repurposing isn't obvious from the outside of the warehouses, which retains their historic character – but inside, concrete channels and glassed-in water doors create puddles and floods of light at strategic points in the galleries. Depending on the show and the capricious tides of personal interest, a visit could take under an hour or an entire afternoon.

7 Fortuna Giuseppe Benoni designed the Punta della Dogana in 1677 to look like the prow of a ship heading to sea, capped with a watchtower. Atop the tower, two bronze Atlases bend beneath the weight of the world, while balancing on top of the world is capricious (Fortuna) Fortune, twisting and turning with the changing winds. Capricious though she seems, Fortune has served Venice well for centuries: this sculpture is an elaborate weathervane.

Fondamenta Zattere to Chiesa di San Nicolò dei Mendicoli

8 Saloni Ex-Magazzini del Sale Heading around the tip of Dorsoduro to face the Canale della Giudecca, you'll find yourself on Fondamenta Zattere, a wide stone boardwalk that runs along the south side of Dorsoduro all the way to the Stazione Marittima. Today its primary functions are as a prime sunbathing location in summer and favourite route for the *passeggiata* (the near-obligatory Italian evening stroll). But centuries ago, this area did most of Venice's heavy lifting, unloading timber from the mainland onto giant *zattere* (rafts) – hence the name – and keeping warehouses well stocked with precious salt at the *magazzini del sale* (salt warehouses). Although the fa-

cade is a neoclassical job from the 1830s, these nine warehouses were built in the 14th century, and established the monopoly on the all-important salt trade that was one of the foundations of medieval Venice's wealth. In the days before fridges and electricity, the only way to preserve foodstuffs was to cure or pack them in salt – and since preserved foods were essential for ocean voyages, salt became crucial to maritime commerce. Today, a couple of these warehouses are used by the Bucintoro rowing club for storage, while others have been recently restored to serve the city as social centres, environmental initiative labs and temporary exhibition spaces.

9 Ospedale degli Incurabili The hulking building was constructed in the 16th century to address a problem spreading rapidly

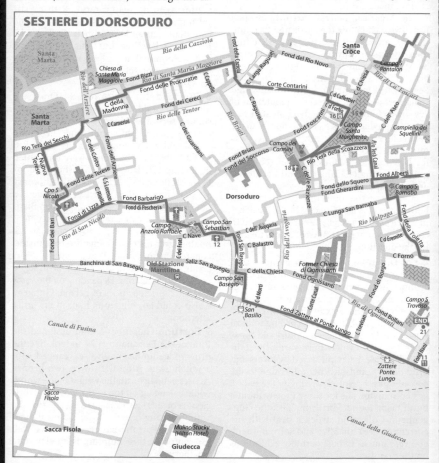

SESTIERE DI DORSODURO

through Europe's nether regions. Euphemistically called the 'French sickness', syphilis had officially become a Venetian problem. With no known cure at the time and blindness and insanity common side effects, Venetians began to petition the state to set aside a hospice for *incurabili* (incurables) and the orphans they left behind – some of whom were also afflicted. Among the most outspoken lobbyists for this effort were women, and funds were pledged early on by prostitutes and brothel madams with a particular interest in the problem. Venice was ahead of its time in dedicating public funds to this public health effort, though at times even this large building was sometimes overcrowded. With the development of penicillin as a cure, such a facility was happily rendered obsolete, and since 2003 the building has housed the Accademia delle Belle Arti (Fine Arts School) that was formerly located in the Gallerie dell'Accademia building.

10 Chiesa dei Gesuati (p87) After crossing a couple of bridges, you end up in front of the imposing 18th-century facade of this church designed by Giorgio Massari. But the real wonder is inside: Tiepolo's trompe l'œil

WALK FACTS

Start Ponte dell'Accademia
End Squero San Trovaso
Distance 4.5km
Time 1½ hours, not including food, drink and photo-op stops
Fuel stops Da Nico, Il Caffè Rosso, Cantinone Già Schiavi

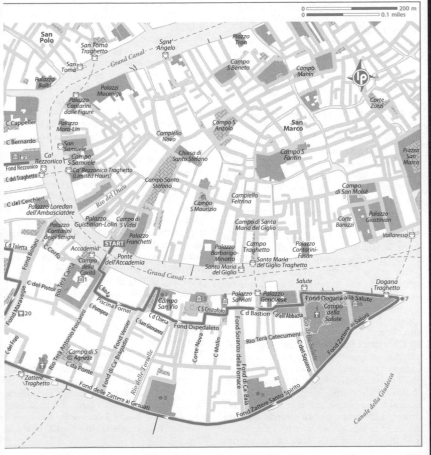

ceilings of St Dominic ascending to heaven in a such a glorious blast of sunshine, you may forget that you're actually indoors.

11 Da Nico (p184) Cravings for ice cream are only natural after all that sunshine along the Zattere and inside Gesuati, and Nico will load you up a cone at the bar or serve you an ambitious bowl of *gelato* at a table on a sunny floating dock.

12 Chiesa di San Sebastian (p81)Almost at the end of the Zattere, across from the San Basilio vaporetto dock, follow the *calle* to your right inland through Campo San Basegio to Fondamenta di San Sebastiano. Follow along the canal to the next footbridge to your left, and cross it to face San Sebastian. Antonio Scarpignano's 1508–48 relatively austere classical facade for this modest parish church creates a sense of false modesty from the outside, because inside, the interior decor goes wild. For 26 years, Paolo Veronese painted the place floor to ceiling, right over the organ and around the pillars. This was Veronese's wall-to-wall masterpiece, and he knew it: he was buried here, according to his wishes. Only in this context could works by Titian and Palma Il Giovane seem so minor – break out that Chorus Pass to enter, and lose minutes (hours, days…) in amazement.

13 Chiesa dell'Arcangelo Raffaele (p83) Wander dazed out of San Sebastian and through the interlinked squares with grass springing up between ancient flagstones, and you'll wind up in front of Chiesa di San Basilio, better known as Chiesa dell'Arcangelo Raffaele. This church may have been founded as early as the 7th century, making it one of Venice's oldest – but since it was rebuilt in the 12th century and again in the 17th and recently cleaned, its facade lies about its age. Francesco Contino built the stark white front to cast a dramatic reflection in the canal. Entry is free, and a friendly guardian will proudly usher you to the recently restored baptistry frescoes by Francesco Fontebasso, in glowing, mood-elevating hues of green and pink apparently borrowed from Veronese around the corner.

14 Chiesa di San Nicolò dei Mendicoli (p82) As you cross the bridge to the north of Campo Anzolo Rafeaele and look left (west), you'll spot the bell tower of the Chiesa di San Nicolò dei Mendicoli. Follow the *fondamenta* around to the *campo,* and take a look at this striking 12th-century brick church, built on the site of an even earlier church that may date from the 7th century. Dedicated to the patron

saint of the poor, located in an ancient working-class neighbourhood of fishermen, the church served as a women's shelter and kept adornment to a minimum outside despite 18th-century embellishments (including a golden arcade indoors). You might recognise it from the Julie Christie thriller *Don't Look Now* as the church Donald Sutherland was assigned to restore – no small task.

Campo Santa Margherita to Fondamenta San Trovaso

15 Campo Santa Margherita The suggested route takes you on a stroll along the canal banks via Fondamenta delle Procuratie, where as early as the 16th century the Procurators of St Mark provided low-income rental housing. Heading across the footbridge onto Corte Contarini, you're suddenly surrounded by Foscari University buildings, and you can follow the flow of student foot traffic into Campo Santa Margherita. This is Venice's late-night hot spot, and a magnet for political protests, flea markets and fishmongers.

16 Il Caffè Rosso (p201) Coffee is highly recommended at this point before further sightseeing, and Caffè Rosso makes an espresso that opens eyes like a rip cord on Venetian blinds. Take a seat in the piazza and brace for impact.

17 Scuola Grande dei Carmini (p81) Seek out the *campo*'s southwest corner, and you'll find this retreat for Carmelite nuns that seems austere outside, with a modest entryway, and a series of intriguing monochrome paintings downstairs. But once you ascend the cloudlike white, stuccoed Baldassare Longhena staircase, you're entering another world, edged with lavish carved *boiseries* (woodwork) and topped with a Tieopolo ceiling showing the Madonna illuminated in the rosy light of dawn. These are standout works by two masters for an order of nuns dedicated to the welfare of travellers – definitely worth dropping by to pay respects.

18 Chiesa dei Carmini In comparison with the adjacent *scuola,* the church (🕙 12:30-5pm Mon-Sat) is relatively plain, with a brick Venetian Renaissance exterior. The inside lightens up a bit with swirls of stucco over the altar and frescoed ceiling by Sebastiano Ricci of two angels taking flight. Entry is free.

19 Ca' Rezzonico (p80) Once you've had enough austerity, head directly to the opposite end of the spectrum at Ca' Rezzonico. The original grand entry of Baldassare Longhena's dashingly handsome palace is along the Grand Canal, but the side entryway now in use opens onto a small courtyard garden where you can picnic (rare in Venice) and take in the view from the rear. Inside are three floors of 18th-century art and social graces, capped with Tiepolo's ceiling masterpieces. The Rezzonicos bought their way into Venice's Golden Book of nobility, and Tiepolo's unabashedly splendid trompe l'œil ceilings promise continued upward mobility, showing Fame and Fortune awaiting the Rezzonicos in heaven. If you head inside, you'll float out a couple of hours later, feeling distinctly light-headed.

20 Cantinone Già Schiavi (p201) Make a beeline from the baroque to the bar, where you'll find *cicheti* and *pallotine* (small bottles of beer) waiting your arrival, plus the rest of the neighbourhood.

21 Squero di San Trovaso (p82) Join the crowds milling sociably outside on the *fondamenta*, and make room at the bar when the thirsty gondola-builders across the canal at the Squero San Trovaso call it a day. Once you've lingered by the door during the day and caught a glimpse of these artisans planing down the side of a gondola, you'll realise that no Dorsoduro scene is truly complete without their handiwork.

SESTIERI DI SAN POLO & SANTA CROCE
San Rocco to San Giacomo dell'Orio

1 Chiesa di San Rocco (p91) The gleaming, upbeat baroque facade of this church (🕑 8am-12.30pm & 3-5pm Mon-Sat) understandably gets short shrift from visitors thunderstruck by the stormy Tintorettos at the affiliated Scuola across the way, but the church was purpose-built to retain its cheer in adversity. After the city had survived a brutal bout of the Black Death, funds poured in to build a church to house the remains of San Rocco (aka St Roch), patron saint of plague victims. The original church was built by Bartolomeo Bon in 1489–1508, but once Tintoretto undertook his 1564–88 painting cycle for the Scuola, Bon's church was immediately down-

graded to has-been status. The church was given a facelift in 1765–71 to make its facade look more like the Scuola, and Bon's rose window that once fronted the building was moved to the side of the church – it's been recently restored, along with Bon's original side door. After the action-packed canvases at the Scuola, you may be surprised to find quietly tender Tintorettos inside the church's Sala dell'Albergo, including *San Rocco Healing the Animals*.

2 Scuola Grande di San Rocco (p85) Pity the architects of this carefully composed classical building for the confraternity of St Roch: their work has been steadily ignored for centuries, even before it was completed. Bartolomeo Bon began this *scuola* in 1517, and at least three other architects were called in to finish the work by 1588 – but once Tintoretto's painting cycle began to streak across the upstairs walls like indoor fireworks, it hardly mattered what the outside looked like anymore. The facade is an impressive display of architectural handiwork: inlaid, veined marble framing the windows and doors, figures leaning out from atop the capitals to greet visitors, and flowering garlands around pillars providing welcome signs of life after plague. Take a moment to appreciate the architecture before you go in, though, because Tintoretto's art installation masterpiece is a near-impossible act to follow.

3 I Frari (p84) Across the street from the Scuola Grande di San Rocco, rest your eyes on the austere brick Gothic facade of the Frari, which you access from around the corner in Campo dei Frari. As you've no doubt heard, there's a Titian – make that *the* Titian – altarpiece here, but the 14th-century structure itself is a towering achievement. The facade facing the canal is an impressive expanse of red brick with delicate scalloping under the roofline, contrasting red-and-white mouldings around windows and arches, and a repeating circle motif of oculi (porthole windows) around a high rosette window. The tall bell tower has managed to remain upright since 1386 – a rare feat, given the shifting *barene* of Venice – its bell-ringer is Venice's most insistent (and probably hard of hearing by now). The cool light of the interior takes a moment's adjustment, but Titian's *Assunta* seems to shed its own sunlight in the apse, and Canova's ethereal white marble tomb seems permanently moonlit.

4 Archivio di Stato Next door to the great church spread the buildings and peaceful cloisters of the Franciscan Convento dei

Frari, which like other religious orders in Venice, was suppressed in 1807 by Napoleon to quell dissent. Since 1815 this sober classical structure has housed the city's archives – a treasure-trove of some 15 million documents, covering 70km of shelves and the breadth of Venice's history dating from the 9th century onward. About 500 requests are handled here each year to help people trace their Italian ancestry, and on rare occasions such as 1 May (Labour Day), the cloisters are open to the public; for research requests and upcoming opening days, see the website (www.archivio distatodivenezia.org).

5 Chiesa di San Giovanni Evangelista

Cross the footbridges into the nondescript Campo San Stin, take the western exit off the *campo* and turn right: almost immediately on the left you'll see a magnificent marble arch-

way by Pietro Lomabardo, topped by the eagle of patron saint John the Baptist. Behind it, two impressive facades give onto a courtyard. Through the portal is a bell tower and church, founded in the 10th century but spiffed up in the 15th and 18th centuries without losing its refined proportions.

6 Scuola Grande di San Giovanni Evangelista

(p90) Opposite is one of the six major Venetian *scuole,* founded in 1261 by an order of *battuti* (flagellants) and later a favoured confraternity of the Council of Ten, Venice's dread secret service. The *scuola* was once a humble hospice, but as it rose in political prominence, the *scuola* acquired a relic of the cross, and its upstairs hall was decked out by a litany of Venetian greats: Massari designed the Sala Capitolare with 11m ceilings and polychrome marble, Palma Il Giovane

SESTIERE DI SAN POLO & SANTA CROCE (SANTA CROSE)

painted the four works gracing the walls of the Sala d'Albergo, and Titian and Bellini painted works for the *scuola* that are now in museum collections. The order was suppressed by Napoleon, and today the *scuola* hosts conferences, but is occasionally open to visitors for a nominal €2 to €3 entry fee. If you get the chance to visit the *scuola*, ask at the front desk afterwards if you can look inside the chapel across the street too.

7 Palazzo Soranzo-Cappello Before you head northeast of Rio Marin to Campo San Giacomo dell'Orio, turn to face west and gaze across the Rio Marin at this 15th-century Gothic mansion, also called Palazzo Soranzo van Axel after a Dutch family that bought the place c 1628. Lush courtyard gardens are closed to the public behind ancient walls, with two Gothic staircases leading to the loggia of the *piano nobile* This palace is said to be among the finest examples of Venetian Gothic mansions, and since it's currently for sale, many Venetians hope that it will be purchased by a foundation and opened to the public at last.

8 Chiesa di San Giacomo dell'Orio (p89) Head east down Calle della Croce, turn right then left into Campo San Nazario Sauro, and keep heading east down Ruga Bella to reach Campo San Giacomo dell'Orio, one of Venice's most charming, easygoing *campi*. The namesake church was founded as early as the 9th or 10th centuries, but was built in its current Romanesque form by 1225, with a modest entrance along the canal wedged in among housing. The basic blueprint is a Latin cross, but it's hardly strict: chapels bubble along the edges, and pillars were added seemingly at random inside for decorative value. Lurking in the dark, cool interior are some notable 14th- to 18th-century artworks, including the 14th-century ship's keel roof, a rare Veronese crucifix, and Gaetano Zompini's macabre *Miracle of the Virgin,* which shows a rabble-rouser rudely interrupting the Virgin's funeral procession, only to have his hands miraculously fall off when he touches her coffin.

San Giacomo dell'Orio to San Polo

9 Osteria La Zucca (p186) Switch culinary gears from traditional Venetian seafood to creative Mediterranean fare at La Zucca, where Rialto market vegetables and spice-route flavours are co-stars on small plates. From the *campo,* take Calle Larga north, and the restaurant is to the right over a footbridge.

10 Mosalco! (p171) The Byzantine splendours of Basilica di San Marco are all the more impressive once you see how the glass mosaics are made at this working mosaic studio,

WALK FACTS

Start Chiesa di San Rocco

End Al Mercà

Distance 4km

Duration Two hours, not including food, drink and photo-op stops

Fuel stops Osteria La Zucca, Gelateria San Stae, Al Mercà

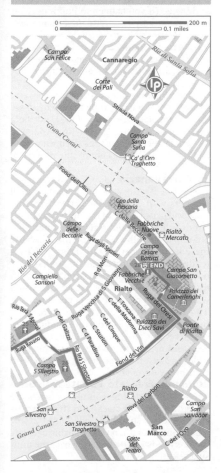

located at Calle del Tentor 1864. Raw glass is gently tapped with a tiny hammer into miniature tesserae, each cut to fit snugly into place in mosaic tableaux. The studio also does restoration work, scale replicas of Byzantine and Roman mosaics, and (a tempting thought) custom designs.

11 Gelateria San Stae (p188) Vanilla is definitely not a synonym for ordinary at this gourmet *gelateria* (ice-cream shop), where high-end ingredients like Madagascar vanilla beans add another level of decadence to a midday treat – but prices are delightfully average, mostly under €2.

12 Palazzo Mocenigo (p89) Dressing the part helped noble Venetian families like the Mocenigos stay relevant and influential for centuries, as you can see in this fascinating palace museum showcasing the fashions of Venice's power elite. Doges' robes, hobblingly high heels, and daring décolletages are displayed here in lavishly furnished period rooms – but for all the social graces of these salons, they saw their share of backstabbing. The Mocenigo family hosted 16th-century philosopher Giordano Bruno here for some time before handing him over to the Inquisition, which subsequently tortured and burnt the betrayed philosopher at the stake in Rome. Lesson learned: never wear out your welcome with the Mocenigos.

13 Chiesa di San Stae (p91) Though its stark white baroque facade is plenty gracious, this church was built in honour of a saint who may be fictitious. According to the legend, San Stae (St Eustace) was a Roman martyr who converted to Christianity, lost everything, then was restored to his position – but when he refused to carry out a pagan sacrifice, Emperor Hadrian condemned him to be roasted alive with his family inside a bronze statue of a bull. Suddenly the Mocenigos don't seem quite as scary.

14 Scuola dei Tiraoro e Battioro With prime real estate along the Grand Canal that must have been the envy of other *scuole,* the goldsmith confraternity was long headquartered next door to San Stae at No 1980. The privileged position is no accident: leading artisans enjoyed prominence in society among nobility and church leaders, and started fashion trends that were closely followed by the jet set across Europe.

15 Ca' Pesaro (p88) Cross two bridges to enter the modern era at this baroque palace, where savvy Biennale purchases form the basis of an eclectic 20th-century painting and sculpture collection. Take an unexpected detour to Edo-era Japan on the top floor, where a haul of Asian applied arts overflows curio cases and a phalanx of samurai armour lines the stairs. From the land entrance, this Baldassare Longhena–designed baroque palace isn't as impressive as it is from the Grand Canal, where you can get the full impact of its restrained, Renaissance-influenced grandeur.

16 Chiesa di Santa Maria Mater Domini Walking southwest away from Ca' Pesaro down a narrow *calle,* you could walk right past this church (⊗ 3.30-5.30pm Mon, 10am-12.30pm Tue, 10am-12.30pm & 3.30-5.30pm Wed, 10am-noon Thu, 10am-12.30pm & 3.30-5.30pm Fri) rebuilt c 1524 on the site of a 10th-century church. Sansovino and Scarpagnino are alternately given credit for the stark but soaring Istrian stone facade, and inside (if you happen to find it open) is an early work by Tintoretto, *Invenzione della Croce* (Invention of the Cross).

17 Veneziastampa (p171) Campo Santa Maria Mater Domini is ringed with well-preserved late-Byzantine and Gothic buildings, and in a 13th-century edifice at No 2174 is a printmaking studio from another era. Mornings are the best time to stop by to see the ancient blackened gears of the Heidelberg machine in action – but anytime you stop by, you'll smell printer's ink drying and find fresh racks of etchings hot off the proverbial press.

18 CartaVenezia (p169) Calle Lunga is a street lined with artisans working small wonders with elemental materials like iron, glass and paper. None of the cotton-rag paper handmade at this studio at Calle Lunga 2125 is compatible with a laser-jet printer, because these luxuriant, raw-edged sheets aren't intended for word-processing. Instead, they're bound into sketchbooks and embossed with mythological friezes destined to give you a whole new appreciation for paperwork.

19 Artistica Ferro (p169) Gondola prows are made to order at this ironwork studio down the street at Calle Lunga 2137, but you can also find artisan-made bowls in a range of styles and bell-like acoustics to resonate with your home decor style.

20 Marco Franzato Vetrate Artistiche (p170) Handmade Murano glass objects are piled into teetering stacks and strewn across shelves at this studio at Calle Lunga 2155a, where time flies when you're poring over jars of glass beads and deliberating over the unusual selection of glass clocks.

21 Ponte delle Tette (p89) 'Tits Bridge' has long since retired from its central role in the local flesh trade, but from the 14th to 18th centuries, streetwalkers displayed their wares from windows, doors, and passageways in this designated red-light zone. Prostitution wasn't banned by La Serenissima, but it was heavily regulated: fees were set by the state and posted in Rialto brothels (soap cost extra) and the rates of high-end *cortigiane* (courtesans) were published in a catalogue extolling their various merits (see p31). Church authorities and French dignitaries repeatedly professed dismay at Venice's lax attitudes towards prostitution, but Venice's idea of a crackdown was to prevent women prostitutes from luring clients by cross-dressing (aka false advertising) and to ban prostitutes from riding in two-oared boats – lucky that gondolas only require one oar.

22 Palazzo Albrizzi From Ponte delle Tette, look south down Rio di San Cassiano, and you'll notice a high, wrought-iron walkway linking two private gardens. The 16th-century mansion on the southeast bank was the site of a celebrated 18th-century salon organised by writer Isabella Teotochi Albrizzi, with sculptor Antonio Canova and writers Walter Scott and Ugo Foscolo among her guests. In Venice, it wasn't such a stretch for brothels and high-culture outposts to share the same block, and sometimes they were one and the same: high-end courtesans debated philosophy and produced some of the city's finest poetry, and occasionally accepted sonnets in exchange for their attentions.

23 Palazzi Soranzo Heading into the broad Campo San Polo, this pair of 14th- to 15th-century Gothic palaces with lacy loggias stand out on your right among the plain, later buildings lining the square. Look closely, and you'll notice some medieval touches, like human heads peeking out of the capitals and coats of arms. Legend has it that Giorgione frescoes once covered this building, and a small moat separating the building from the *campo* served as a hazard for drunkards until it was filled a few decades back.

24 Chiesa di San Polo (p89) Apartment buildings crowded around this 9th-century brick Byzantine church camouflage it, but a ship's-keel ceiling and the riveting, sinister *Stations of the Cross* cycle by Giandomenico

Tiepolo (son of baroque ceiling maestro Giambattista) make it worth your while to locate the door on the side of the building.

Campo San Polo to Rialto

25 Chiesa di Sant'Aponal From Campo San Polo, take Calle della Madonnetta and follow it to Campo Sant'Aponal, where you'll notice a simple Gothic facade topped by five statues and a freestanding Romanesque bell tower. This church was founded c 1034 by refugees fleeing Byzantine authority in Ravenna, and in a twist of political fate, was converted by Napoleon as a jail for political prisoners opposing French occupation. The church was reconsecrated and restored after independence, but fell into disuse, and today is primarily used as an archive for marriage licences.

26 Chiesa di San Silvestro Turn right down Rio Terà San Silvestro, and you'll pass this church (⏲ 7-11am & 4-6pm Mon-Sat) founded in the 9th century, but with a rather dangerous tendency to slump. The structure had to be completely overhauled several times, most recently in the 20th century – hence the rather bland but reassuringly solid neoclassical facade. Inside is Tintoretto's recently restored *Baptism of Christ*, which once was part of the altarpiece. Turn onto the former wine docks on the Grand Canal, the Fondamenta del Vin, and you'll see the Ponte di Rialto just ahead.

27 Il Gobbo Pass the arcaded Fabbriche Vecchie (Old Buildings) along the Ruga degli Orefici, and cross the square toward the Fabbriche Nuove (New Buildings), and you'll spot an iron railing around the 1541 statue of Il Gobbo (The Hunchback) propping up a step. This was a podium for official proclamations and punishment: those found guilty of misdemeanours might be forced to run a gauntlet of jeering citizens from Piazza San Marco to the Rialto, but the minute they touched Il Gobbo, their punishment was complete. Rubbing Il Gobbo was believed to confer luck, to the point that a railing was put up to save the hunchback from being worn out by his admirers.

28 Al Mercà (p202) As with any Venetian accomplishment – a university diploma, a good haul of lagoon crab, waking up in the morning – the completion of your walking tour calls for a drink at the Rialto. Take your *prosecco* from Al Mercà down to the docks, and watch the sunlight fade along the Grand Canal.

SESTIERE DI CANNAREGIO
Ponte dei Scalzi to Madonna dell'Orto

1 Ponte dei Scalzi Not the most beautiful bridge over the Grand Canal (that would be the Rialto) and no longer the newest (that's the Ponte di Calatrava, to your left past the train station), the 1934 Istrian stone Ponte dei Scalzi replaced an iron bridge built by the Austrians in 1858. The bridge's chief engineer, Eugenio Miozzi, redeemed himself with the more modest and widely beloved wooden Ponte dell'Accademia, but was also responsible for three of the ugliest landscape features in Venice: the Piazzale Roma car park, the Lido's Fascist Casino, and the Ponte della Libertà bridge to the mainland.

2 Ponte delle Guglie A 1580 span in brick and contrasting white Istrian stone, 'Needles Bridge' is named after the peculiar obelisks at each end, tacked onto the bridge in 1832 during a redecorating binge by the new Austrian authorities.

3 Schola Spagnola Turn left after the bridge and right into the Calle del Ghetto Vecchio, and on a wall to your left on house No 1131, you'll see an official 1704 decree of the Republic carved in stone. This announcement forbids Jews converted to Christianity entry into the Ghetto or into Jewish homes on pain of punishment that might include 'the rope [hanging], prison, galleys, flogging…and other greater punishments, depending on the judgment of their excellencies (the Executors Against Blasphemy)'. The announcement encourages residents to report their neighbours,

SESTIERE DI CANNAREGIO

adding, 'secret denunciations may be deposited in the usual receptacles. The accusers will be entitled to a bounty of 100 ducats, to be taken from the property of the accused…'. Such laws were summarily abolished under Napoleon, but reprised under Mussolini's 1938 Racial Laws and subsequent deportation orders for Venice's Jewish community.

WALK FACTS

Start Ponte dei Scalzi

End Osteria Al Ponte

Distance 3km

Duration one to 1½ hours

Fuel stops Ardidos, Osteria Al Ponte

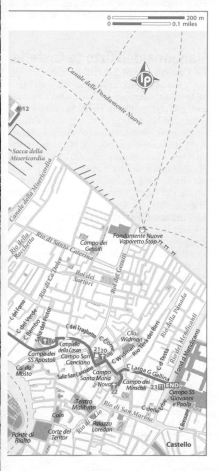

Further along the *calle,* you'll emerge into a small square bordered by two of the Ghetto's five synagogues, also known as *schole* because they were used for scripture studies. Today, entry to *schole* is possible on daily tours organised by the Museo Ebraico (p92) or for worship. The existence of five places of worship within the Ghetto reflected the density and diversity of Venice's Jewish community. When the Inquisition forced Jewish communities out of Spain, some found refuge in Venice, and built the sombre 16th-century Schola Spagnola, with additions including a 1635 update attributed to Baldassare Longhena, and a splendid elliptical women's gallery. This is the building with high arched windows at the square's southern end, near a plaque commemorating Italian Jewish victims of the Holocaust.

4 Schola Levantina Founded in 1583 and splendidly updated in 1683–1700, this Sephardic synagogue was also built by Jewish refugees from Spain, but the confident baroque style of the building shows how decidedly Venetian the community had become: the classical influence of Baldassare Longhena is clearly felt in its elegant proportions and repeating geometric details. Inside, the marble and carved wood interiors are exuberantly baroque, especially the pulpit. The Schola Levantina is used for Saturday prayers in winter (it has heating), while the Schola Spagnola is used in summer.

5 Schola Italiana Calle del Ghetto Vecchio proceeds northeast over a bridge into the heart of Venice's Jewish community, Campo di Ghetto Nuovo. According to official orders c 1516, these bridges were closed at midnight. On the *campo,* look up: atop a pile of private apartments is the wood cupola of the 1575 Schola Italiana. The Italians were the poorest community in the Ghetto, and their synagogue is simple and sunny, with beautifully carved woodwork. In the 17th century, the Schola's learned rabbi Leon Modena was so widely respected as a thinker and scientist that Christians began attending his services, and Modena accommodated them by delivering his sermons in Italian. The rabbi had a weakness for gambling and died penniless, his grave in the Lido's Jewish cemetery marked by a simple flagstone.

6 Schola Tedesca Recognisable from the square from its five long windows, the 'German' synagogue has been the spiritual home of Venice's Ashkenazi community since 1529. According to 16th-century Venetian law, only the German Jewish community was allowed to lend money, and the success of this trade shows in the handsome decor updates here. The interiors are stately, with a baroque pulpit and carved benches downstairs topped by an elliptical women's gallery.

7 Museo Ebraico (p92) Next door to the Schola Tedesca is a modest entryway that leads into a small but significant collection of Venetian Judaica, including illuminated marriage contracts, worked silver menorahs, and Seder plates used for Passover celebrations. Anyone with an interest in Venice's multiethnic, interfaith history should time a visit to coincide with the museum's fascinating tours of three of the Ghetto's *schole* (offered in English several times daily).

8 Schola Canton Look up above the Schola Tedesca in the corner of the *campo*, and you'll see the wooden cupola of this *schola*, built c 1532 with interiors updated in the 18th century with gilded rococo ornament. Though European synagogues typically avoid figurative imagery, this little synagogue takes exception to the rule with eight scenes from Exodus.

9 Bottega del Tintoretto Cross the bridge north out of the Ghetto, and follow the Fondamenta degli Ormesini all the way to Calle dei Mori. Follow it to the next canal and turn right down Fondamenta dei Mori to No 3399, where you'll notice a plaque announcing that this was Tintoretto's home studio. If you feel a sudden surge of inspiration coming on, you're in luck: you can take art classes at the Bottega (p265).

10 Palazzo Mastelli Back at the corner of the Calle dei Mori, you might notice a statue of a man wearing an outsized turban. This is one of four such figures on the building facades ringing the Campo dei Mori (Square of the Moors). This name is a misnomer, since these statues are thought to represent not Middle Eastern or African figures but rather the Greek Mastelli family (the one on the corner is known as Sior Rioba), 12th-century merchants from Morea. The Mastelli brothers were notorious as shady merchants and ruthless participants in Doge Dandolo's sack of Constantinople, and according to Venetian legend, Mary Magdalene herself turned them into stone for their hard-hearted business dealings. The Palazzo Mastelli is also called the Palazzo del Cammello after the distinctive bas-relief of a camel on the facade facing Rio della Madonna dell'Orto.

11 Chiesa della Madonna dell'Orto (p95) A sublime Italian Gothic church in red brick edged in white and bedecked with statuary, this church and its adjoining monastery were originally intended in the 1360s to honour St Christopher, the patron saint of gondoliers and travellers. But when the Madonna statue parked in the monastery's kitchen *orto* (garden) began to work miracles, the statue won pride of place at the altar and the design gradually upgraded to cathedral quality with a doorway designed by Bartolomeo Bon. The monastery had difficulty keeping monks in this remote corner of Cannaregio, and the church was eventually downgraded to a parish church and allowed to deteriorate in the 18th and 19th centuries. Yet even after the Madonna dell'Orto's initial tide of admirers had ebbed, Tintoretto fans made their way to his parish church to see his spectacular *Final Judgment* and a *Presentation of the Virgin* that rivals Titian's more famous version in the Accademia with flushed, luscious reds – Tintoretto had a reputation for nocturnal drama, but he could handle colour with the best Venetian painters.

Madonna dell'Orto to Castello

12 Casinò degli Spiriti Zigzag through the gardens flanking Madonna dell'Orto to this 16th-century casino, where literati and glitterati with the right contacts would gather for learned chitchat and a few drinks. In Venetian terms, a casino was not a gambling parlour like a *ridotto*, but a salon for intimate conversation and serious political discussion among friends – preferably without the lurking presence of the doge's spies, whose job description included detailed debriefings on parties.

13 Palazzo Contarini del Zaffo Backtrack towards the Madonna dell'Orto and turn left along Fondamenta Gasparo Contarini, where you'll find a long, low stretch of blinding white 16th-century palace. The Renaissance design is strikingly simple, punctuated only by the occasional Contarini family coat of arms or carved head over a doorway. The frescoed interiors upstairs include a Tiepolo ceiling, but the palace is now divided into an office building and a hospital.

14 Rio dei Muti Squero Cross Rio della Madonna dell'Orto, follow Corte Vecchia southwest to Rio della Sensa, and turn around to the right to see the remains of a former gondola *squero*, complete with slipways into Rio dei Muti.

15 Chiesa di San Marziale The whitewashed Venetian facade of this church (4-6.30pm Mon-Sat) is impressive not for its exterior ornament – there isn't much to speak of – but because of how its dramatic shape looks reflected in the canal. Inside, the interiors are surprisingly lavish, with a delightful Sebastiano Ricci image of the namesake saint on the ceiling and Tintoretto's first commissioned altarpiece, but the church is rarely open. Stop on the first bridge you cross, Ponte di Santa Fosca, where *guerre dei pugni* (organised fist-fights) once took place. There were no set rules, except that when you fell into the canal, you lost.

16 Paolo Sarpi statue The bronze statue on the square opposite is of La Serenissima's defender and free thinker. Sarpi was an orphan who rose to prominence as a learned scholar and a monk who refused to cut off ties with Galileo Galilei and other thinkers accused of heresy, and successfully defended Venice when Pope Paul V excommunicated the entire city. The pope was not pleased at being upstaged, and on this *campo,* assassins from papal states stabbed Sarpi several times. But Sarpi was not a man to be taken down easily; he survived the attack and continued to serve Venice faithfully.

17 Ardidos (p204) Hang a left at Sarpi onto Strada Nuova, a boulevard bulldozed through the area after the rail link was opened in the 19th century. Over the next footbridge on Campiello dei Fiori at No 2282 is a splashy new cafe, with gourmet beans from far-flung trade routes – Cannaregio-born Marco Polo would surely approve.

18 Ca' d'Oro (p96) Beyond Strada Nuova on your right is a parade of Venetian mansions, but you'd never know it – they present their photogenic profiles only to the Grand Canal, and most are privately owned. The glorious exception is the Ca' d'Oro, with grace notes at every level: polychrome marble mosaic at the ground-floor water gate, ecclesiastical artworks reclaimed from Napoleon on the first floor, and a remarkable St Sebastian by Mantegna and Grand Canal views through the Gothic-arched balcony.

19 Chiesa dei Santi Apostoli Strada Nuova then leads into the pleasing Campo dei SS Apostoli, where the church (7.30-11.30am & 5-7pm Mon-Sat, 8.30am-noon & 4-6.30pm Sun) is worth visiting for the 15th-century Cappella Corner by Mauro Codussi, which features a Tiepolo altarpiece of St Lucy, bearing her limpid eye balls on a platter. The plain brick exterior is rather rudely interrupted by apartment buildings, but as John Ruskin put it rather bluntly, 'The exterior is nothing'.

20 Chiesa di San Canzian Turning right through the Campiello della Cason and across the Rio dei Santi Apostoli, you can see what Henry James meant when he wrote of Venice that 'with its little winding ways where people crowd together, where voices sound as in the corridors of a house…the place has the character of an immense collective apartment' (*The Aspern Papers,* 1888). As you emerge on Campo San Canzian, this sun-washed 1706 church designed by Antonio Gaspari is off to the right (northwest), with pleasing pink interiors and a high cupola.

21 Dolceamaro (p172) Take a break for artisan-made chocolates disguised as salami and cheeses and 20 flavours of chocolate truffles at this gourmet shop, adjacent to San Canzian at No 6051.

22 Chiesa di Santa Maria dei Miracoli (p92) Just when you thought you'd seen enough marvels for the day/decade, you'll spot this multicoloured marble proto-Renaissance beauty across the Santa Maria Nova. Cross the footbridge and walk around to the front of the 1481–89 Miracoli; note the careful placement of each coloured marble panel, creating a rhythmic rippling across the building's exterior. Inside is more wonderful stonework by Pietro and Tullio Lombardo, and a coffered ceiling framing portraits of saints dressed as Venetians, like a class photo in a school yearbook.

23 Osteria Al Ponte (p191) As you reach the edge of Cannaregio, a red door marks the perch *al ponte* (at the bridge) by the Rio dei Mendicanti that's always good for an *ombra, cicheti* at the bar, and generous plates of pasta if you luck into a valuable patch of table real estate. Raise your glass in a toast *a Cannaregio!* for showing you a side of Venice few visitors ever see.

SESTIERE DI CASTELLO
Zanipolo to Campo di Bandiera e Mori

1 Bartolomeo Colleoni statue (p109) Presiding over Campo Zanipolo (Campo SS Giovanni e Paolo) is the proud figure of Bartolomeo Colleoni, the distinguished 15th-century *condottiero* (professional mercenary commander) who claimed Verona for Venice and recaptured Venetian territories from the Milanese. After Milan captured and imprisoned Venice's secret weapon, Duke Francesco Sforza freed him to lead Milanese troops – but in a rare case of mercenary loyalty, Colleoni switched back to Venice's side.

When a promotion was not forthcoming, however, Colleoni began working for Sforza again, and it took a generous signing bonus for Venice to win him back. For Colleoni, war was business, not personal: he was known for fair fights, and since he made a practice of not plundering defeated foes, he didn't make personal enemies – which greatly increased his employment options. Upon his death, Colleoni left a generous sum to Venice to fight the Turks, on the condition that a statue would be erected in his honour in Piazza San Marco. Venice took the money but changed the terms of the agreement slightly, erecting the statue instead in front of the Scuola Grande di San Marco (across the square).

2 Zanipolo (p99) Around the mercenary commander rises the imposing edifice of this 14th-century Dominican church, with

splendid brickwork on the sides and a portal Bartolomeo Bon built with pillars scavenged from Torcello. The facade was intended to top the Franciscan I Frari (p84), but it remained unfinished, so the Franciscans come out ahead on that score. Zanipolo's own Titians and Bellinis burned in an 1867 fire in the Capella del Rosario, though the apparently splendid gilded ceiling by Tintoretto has been replaced with standout works by Paolo Veronese – including a staggering *Assumption* showing the Madonna nimbly ascending a cloudbank. Zanipolo is an engineering marvel, with clever cross-beaming to prevent the vast roof from collapsing. Wildly eclectic interior embellishments range from Tullio and Pietro Lombardo's sculpted tombs of doges who seem eerily alive to Bartolomeo Vivarini's vibrant Mu-

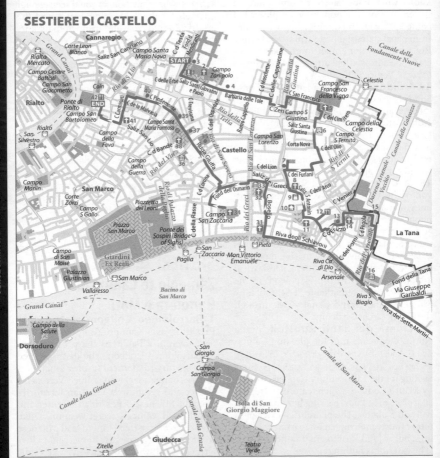

rano stained-glass window, which looks like an action-packed comic. Zanipolo is often referred to in standard Italian as Chiesa dei Santi Giovanni e Paolo, but the namesake John and Paul are neither the apostles, nor (as some Venetians like to joke) the Beatles: this grand church honours two rather obscure Christian martyrs named Giovanni and Paolo, depicted in the stained-glass window.

lonelyplanet.com

WALK FACTS

Start Campo Zanipolo (Campo SS Giovanni e Paolo)
End I Rusteghi
Distance 6.5km
Duration three hours
Fuel stops Paradiso, QCoffee Bar, I Rusteghi

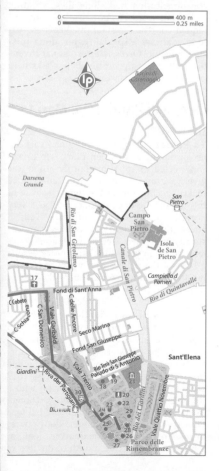

3 Scuola Grande di San Marco (p104) A lion is loose in the Campo Zanipolo (Campo SS Giovanni e Paolo): above an impressive trompe l'œil marble portal, you'll spot the winged lion of St Mark, prowling on his pillared podium. Once the entry to the city's most important religious confraternity, this is now an entry to Venice's main city hospital. Bartolomeo Bon may have begun the 15th-century construction, but after a devastating 1485 fire, father–son sculptors Pietro and Tullio Lombardo took on the project, eventually completed by Codussi. As with their Santa Maria dei Miracoli (p92) just a couple of footbridges away from here, the Lombardi accomplished a small Renaissance wonder at a time when Venice's signature style was still Gothic. The facade upstages Zanipolo's and compares with great 15th-century Tuscan Renaissance edifices, making the grand style accessible, and on a more intimate scale.

4 Ospedaletto (p107) From the Renaissance Scuola, the high baroque awaits a block away at the 1664 Chiesa di Santa Maria dei Derelitti (aka the Ospedaletto, or Little Hospital), a lavish former orphanage designed by Palladio but finished by Baldassare Longhena, with burly statuary looming off the facade over the *calle* like heavenly bouncers. Boys had to leave as teenagers, but girls were allowed to stay, and earned their keep by playing in early fundraising concerts that attracted crowds of Venetian socialites. Their donations were not always as generous as they seemed: among the many orphans housed in Venice's *ospedaletti* were the illegitimate daughters of Venetian nobles, courtesans and well-to-do 'white widows' whose husbands were at sea for years at a time.

5 Chiesa di San Francesco della Vigna (p103) After a quiet stroll east along narrow residential streets, you emerge in Campo San Francesco della Vigna, where the sudden appearance of Palladio's massive 1560 facade comes as a shock. Behind the white marble columns that kicked off Palladio's illustrious career as an architect, Sansovino's 1534 building is full of easy graces and Platonic proportions. Pietro and Tullio Lombardo's reliefs depicting the life of Christ and the four evangelists are masterpieces of marble storytelling that read like gripping graphic novels, while Antonio da Negroponte's serene 1460–70 Madonna remains unperturbed by rising lagoon waters and flocks of Venetian angels who are, naturally, excellent swimmers.

6 Laboratorio Occupato Morion (p209) Skip ahead to the future at this avant-garde cultural centre and contemporary art laboratory,

NEIGHBOURHOODS WALKING TOURS

where alternative biennales are staged and performance art is often in progress. Check the schedule for upcoming live music shows and other events.

7 Scuola di San Giorgio degli Schiavoni (p106) When you reach Campo delle Gatte, turn right, and a quick dogleg will take you to Rio di San Lorenzo. Just before the bridge, on the right, you'll find the Dalmatian community's religious school since the 16th century. Vittore Carpaccio's original 1502–07 paintings for the school are still here, in all their gory glory.

8 Chiesa di Sant'Antonin Follow the canal around the corner to this church, dedicated as early as the 7th century to the patron saint of pigs – though for centuries it served double duty as a pigpen for monks. Foodies may feel duty-bound to pay their respects to the so-called saint of *sopressata* (Venetian salami), but the church was de-consecrated in 1982. Lord Byron relates a popular legend about a carnival elephant that broke free from its cage and went on a rampage in Castello *calli* (must've been a skinny elephant). It was finally trapped in this church and put down with cannon fire – a metaphor used by Venetian poet Pietro Buratti to criticise the Austrian occupation of Venice. *Elefanteide* (The True Story of an Elephant) earned its author a month in prison; the story is still available from Venetian publishers today.

9 Banco 10 (p173) Prison sentences in Venice used to mean confinement in the stifling attic of the Palazzo Ducale, with no opportunity for reform or concern for recidivism rates – but today, the women's prison on Giudecca provides job retraining programs to help prisoners reintegrate into Venetian society upon their release, including apprenticeships in organic farming (see the boxed text, p185) and fashion design. With fine fabrics donated by artisan textile-maker Bevilacqua (p163) and the tutelage of local fashion designers, inmates created the fabulous tapestry handbags and velvet tailcoats in this volunteer-run boutique.

10 Palazzo Soderini (p223) Follow the main street south into Campo di Bandiera e Mori, named for the Venetian brothers Bandiera, who lived in the grand palazzo at No 3611, and their friend Domenico Moro, who lived nearby – all of whom were executed by troops of the Bourbon Kingdom of the Two Sicilies, after a failed 1844 insurrection in favour of Italian unity in Cosenza (Calab-

ria). In Venice, the rebels were honoured as patriots with tombs in Zanipolo.

11 Chiesa di San Giovanni in Bragora (p108) On the corner of the *campo* is a striking 15th-century brick church (☽ 3.30-5pm Mon-Sat) that's a missing link between the Venetian brick Gothic of Zanipolo and the high Renaissance of Mauro Codussi's Chiesa di San Zaccharia (see p102). The meaning of *bragora* remains a mystery, though it may be a reference to a once slow-moving *rio* (waterway) behind the church that unless regularly dredged, quickly became a clogged, stinky *gora* (stagnant canal). Vivaldi was baptised here, and the architect Massari is buried in a quiet corner near some 15th-century fresco fragments.

12 Trattoria Corte Sconta (p191) Castello is good at keeping secrets – hence all the conspiracies hatched along these winding *calli* – but word has gotten out about this hidden courtyard restaurant. Venetian seafood is always a speciality, but don't miss chef Eugenio Oro's latest seasonal inventions, dreamed up on his daily walks here from the Rialto markets.

Campo di Bandiera e Mori to Biennale

13 Palazzo Erizzo A doge had to keep up appearances, so when Francesco Erizzo was elected in 1631, his family home was given a grand 17th-century Renaissance makeover. But for all the light elegance of this facade, the doge's workload was a very heavy burden – several dogi died of sudden attacks that we might now call heart attacks shortly after their elections. Doge Erizzo's term lasted 15 years in relative peace despite a bout of the plague that wracked Venice, but he died as war broke out with Turkey, incited by the capture of a boatload of Turkish pilgrims headed for Mecca.

14 Chiesa di San Martino (p109) Erizzo was rewarded for his service as doge with a grand Renaissance tomb in this peaceful church (☽ 11am-noon & 5-6.30 Mon-Sat), right across the bridge from his family palace. Founded in the 10th century, it was rebuilt by 1619 according to a design by Sansovino with a Romanesque-Renaissance austerity. Though the facade was later redesigned with baroque flourishes, Sansovino's modest doorway remains. To the right of the doorway, look for the *bocca di leoni* (the mouth of the lion of

San Marco), where Venetians were encouraged to slip anonymous denunciations of their neighbours for crimes ranging from cursing to heresy (punishable by death).

15 Arsenale (p105) Down the street is the face that launched a thousand ships: the facade of the Arsenale, Venice's legendary shipyards. During the Architecture Biennale (p18), the warehouses that once could churn out a formidable naval fleet in a month become launching pads for experimental architecture. Memorable recent designs have included a towering mud hut designed by Frank Gehry and dresses that convert into isolation pods for sleeping on Tokyo subways. If you find it open during the summer or periodic exhibitions, have a look around some 1.5km of buildings, and collapse into an architect-designed chair in the stylish courtyard cafe with an espresso.

16 Museo Storico Navale (p107) A vast converted grain silo is scarcely enough room to contain the Venetian enthusiasm for boats of all kinds, from (of course) Venetian gondolas to Asian warships and Swedish vessels (a whole floor of them). The museum traces the maritime history of the city and Italy. Dreams of sailing off into the sunset begin here, and anyone with an interest in seafaring stories should leave a couple of hours to cover four floors of boats, models, maps and navigation instruments.

17 Chiesa di San Francesco di Paola Heading east, you soon enter very-few-tourists territory, and discover a true Venetian boulevard: Via Giuseppe Garibaldi. Along the street is a stark white church (8am-noon & 4-7pm) founded in the 16th century and remodelled in the 18th, containing a painting of the namesake saint healing a man possessed by demons, thought to be by Giandomenico Tiepolo. According to the clock painted on the outside for reasons unknown, it's always 9.30, and the beginning of a new day.

18 Biennale Bookstore After hours of cobblestones, your feet will naturally gravitate towards the greenery of the Giardini Publicci off Via Garibaldi. Follow the paths through the park towards a group of trees on the horizon, with some rooflines at odd angles. These are the pavilions of the Biennale, and though they are closed in even years between iterations of the Art Biennale, you can still walk around and admire some spectacular modern architecture specifically built as national showcases for forward-thinking ideas. Front and centre is the Book Pavilion, which architect James Stirling built in 1991 as a delightful modernist mushroom with an oxidised green copper roof.

19 Scarpa Ticket Booth Like a grasshopper that's momentarily alighted on a concrete pedestal, Carlo Scarpa's 1952 ticket booth has a slender glass oval body under a winged roof that seems miraculously well balanced on its spindly wooden legs. Today ticket sales have moved more functionally (if prosaically) online, but with talk of reopening this booth as a souvenir shop, you might be able to get a Biennale postcard straight from the belly of the beast.

20 Hungarian Pavilion Built when the Austro-Hungarian empire was a European power to be reckoned with and the Vienna Secession was the controversial cutting edge of modern architecture, Geza Rintel Maroti's 1909 Hungarian Pavilion gleams with golden mosaics worthy of Gustav Klimt around its recessed entryway arch. This was one of the Biennale's first national pavilions – not surprising, given Austria's 19th-century rule over Venice and its continuing financial interests there – and has yet to be surpassed for sheer dazzle.

21 Palazzo delle Esposizione The bloated white Fascist Italian pavilion has provided many awkward moments for Italy since its stark new facade was unveiled by Duilio Torres in 1932. Not every Italian artist is comfortable showing in what is essentially a monument to Mussolini's Italy, and its sprawling presence seems a little redundant when, in fact, all of Venice is a monument to Italy's artistic achievement. Now that the pavilion has been opened up to international participation as an Exposition Hall, the world seems smaller and the space much more generous.

22 USA Pavilion Predictable though it may seem, this mini-Monticello is actually very apt in Venice – after all, Palladio designed Vicenza's La Rotunda, the villa that provided the basic blueprint for Thomas Jefferson's Palladian mansion.

23 Nordic Countries Pavilion While other pavilions seem determined to turn the Giardini into a modern industrial park, Sverre Fehn's 1958–62 design for a pavilion to represent Scandinavian countries (minus Finland) takes its cue from the trees. Cool light filters through a slatted ceiling as through a Nordic forest canopy, and three majestic trees burst through the floor and grow right through specially designed holes in the plastic roof.

24 Venezuelan Pavilion Decades before concrete was cool and industrial chic was a dominant design trend, avant-garde Venetian architect Carlo Scarpa built this soaring 1956 structure in slabs of rough concrete around a *cortile* (courtyard). Entering the main gallery is like being suddenly submerged in a swimming pool, flooded with light through high clerestory windows that bend into skylights.

25 Korean Pavilion Seuk Chul Kim's 1996 design transformed an old electrical plant into a cutting-edge pavilion for Korean art, opening up the industrial building to nature with windows and adding balconies overlooking the canal in a nod to Grand Canal architecture. Scrims and leafy screens create an ideal space where function and fantasy overlap, and boundaries need not apply.

26 Great Britain Pavilion Imagine the scandal: an English country home seems to have fled Derbyshire for a bohemian existence hosting artists along a canal in Venice. Edwin Alfred Rickards' 1909 pavilion brings neo-Palladian architecture home, but without losing its British sense of restraint – which may seem like a pity, except that it provides a deadpan backdrop to daring shows by such controversial British artists as Tracy Emin and Steve McQueen.

27 Canadian Pavilion Part ski lodge, part terrarium, and completely ahead of its time, the 1958 Canada Pavilion designed by Milanese architecture firm BBPR revolves around an oak tree growing in a glass atrium right through the centre of this soaring wooden building. The snail-shell blueprint subtly references its lagoon location, the Palazzo Contarini del Bovolo (p71) staircase and the Fibonacci sequence, without ever looking like it's trying too hard.

28 French Pavilion France takes its 1912 Faust Finzi–designed pavilion not at face value but as a point of departure, which in recent years has meant inviting artists to scrawl poetry on its doors, poster it like Situationists, and install a fully functioning commune with a sauna and garden on the roof. Without getting too existentialist about it, the irreverence toward institutions displayed here is true to the intentions of art – making this pavilion simultaneously the most and least traditional art pavilion in the Giardini.

29 Australian Pavilion Hidden away in the bush behind the derrière of the French Pavilion, the 1988 Peter Cox–designed Australian Pavilion has managed to draw attention to this obscure location with architectural controversy: the low, rectangular box shape is often compared with a mobile

home, and it's painted a shade of yellow that must keep the birds in surrounding trees up at night. To be fair, the arched breezeway entry and canalside location gives it more of a beach-house look, but some Australian visitors seem to love to hate their national pavilion. 'Bogan beach house, more like,' scoffed one Australian critic overheard on a recent visit.

30 Paradiso (p206) Party like an art star at this bar perched at the edge of the Biennale, which serves a respectable *ombra* of *prosecco* as you chill out on designer patio couches, and a potent espresso to get you up and going again. The Biennale vaporetto stop is right out front of Paradiso, so at this point you could hop on a circle line vaporetto 42 or 52 to San Zaccaria to continue this itinerary, or take the 1 up the Grand Canal for seated sightseeing. Otherwise, it's a pleasant and leafy walk through the Giardini Pubblici along the waterfront to the boardwalk known as Riva degli Schiavoni.

Biennale to Rialto

31 La Pietà (p110) Just at the point where you turn inland is the Giorgio Massari–designed church known formally as Chiesa di Santa Maria della Visitazione, but more simply as La Pietà. From 1703 to 1740, Antonio Vivaldi was the musical director at the adjoining *ospedaletto,* where he taught and wrote several pieces for resident orchestras of orphan girls. Massari's church was finished after Vivaldi's death in 1760, but there's a certain harmony to its classical proportions, and the oval-shaped hall is ideal for its current use as a concert hall.

32 Chiesa di San Giorgio dei Greci (p108) Taxes on incoming Greek ships helped finance this small yet majestic Orthodox church, built in 1573 to serve Venice's sizeable Greek community. To enter, head around the church to reach the main entrance alongside Rio dei Greci; inside you'll find a lofty classical women's gallery and a wealth of icons. As you look down the river from afar, you'll notice the church's cupola-topped bell tower leaning over the river.

33 Museo delle Icone (p108) Next door to the church and behind a wall designed by Baldassare Longhena is the Longhena–designed Scuola di San Nicolo, which was long a hospice for the poor and today houses more than 80 works of devotional art in the Hellenic Institute's Museum of Icons.

34 Chiesa di San Zaccaria (p102) Cross the bridge and stroll the *fondamenta,* and as you pass Carnevale mask shops, you'll sense you're heading towards Piazza San Marco. Instead, swing left under a Gothic arch depicting the Virgin Mary and Jesus, thought to have been crafted by a Tuscan sculptor around 1430. Beyond, you'll arrive in Campo San Zaccaria and stand before Mauro Codussi's splendid Renaissance facade for the Chiesa di San Zaccaria. This church is pure fascination inside and out, from the unburied mosaic treasure in the 9th- to 12th-century crypt to Giovanni Bellini's 1505 *Madonna and the Four Saints* and Andrea del Castagno's mid-15th-century ceiling frescoes for the Gothic side chapel.

Outside the church, you may notice a sign from 1620 etched in stone above the souvenir shop at No 4967 by the Most Illustrious and Excellent Executors for Blasphemy, warning that 'all games, tumultuous behaviour, loud talk, uttering obscene language, committing acts of dishonesty, dirtying, putting up boat masts or other such objects, leaving refuse or any other kind of things is strictly forbidden on pain of the most severe penalties…'. This decree was intended to steer rowdies away from the convent adjoining Chiesa di San Zaccaria, although this may have been a lost cause. In those days, wayward daughters of wealthy Venetians were sent to San Zaccaria to learn the error of their ways, but instead the convent became notorious for masquerades.

35 Palazzo Grimani (p103) Retrace your steps to the *fondamenta,* and head over the footbridge and up Ruga Giuffa, and before you reach the next canal you will notice a turn-off on your right into Ramo Grimani. The land entry to the sprawling Renaissance Palazzo Grimani is at No 4858, with a much grander facade facing Rio di San Severo. Initially the home of Doge Antonio Grimani (who reigned from 1521 to 1523), the palace now belongs to the city but it was closed to the public for 27 years while painstaking efforts were made to restore its outlandish flights of Venetian-Roman fancy. Finally, the palace is open to visitors on guided tours, and what a sight it is: mythological frescoes and grotesques cover the walls and ceilings, and amid the expanses of polychrome marble is a spiral staircase attributed to Palladio.

36 Palazzo Querini Stampalia (p105) As you cross the next footbridge into Campo

Santa Maria Formosa, hang a sharp left, and you'll find a surprisingly modern footbridge clamped onto the marble *fondamenta,* leading back over the canal into a 16th-century *palazzo.* Carlo Scarpa's 1963 bridge is your first hint that this is not your usual Venetian palace. The residence remained in the Querini family until the last descendent donated it to the city in 1869, and though the *piano nobile* salons were preserved in their 18th-century grandeur with minor works by Bellini and Tiepolo, Scarpa was brought in to rethink the ground floor. Instead of keeping water out – a constant battle in Venetian *palazzi* – Scarpa cheekily invited it in through a system of Islamic-style *khattara* (channels) in rough concrete, introducing trough water features in the courtyard garden. Scarpa's one-time pupil and mega-modernist Mario Botta developed a library and ground-floor QCoffee Bar (p206) with bands of glossy marble and repeating geometric shapes – a fine stop for an architecturally inclined spritz.

37 Palazzo Vitturi Heading into the Campo Santa Maria Formosa, this palace on your right is a classic example of 13th- to 14th-century Veneto-Byzantine style, with a row of pointed arches along the *piano nobile* topped with reliefs in small discs.

38 Chiesa di Santa Maria Formosa (p109) According to local legend, the unusual name of this church (Church of Curvaceous St Mary) comes not from the shape of the church, but from a case of mistaken identity. One of Venice's best-remembered courtesans, Veronica Franco, lived in a house on this *campo.*

A poet who counted among her intimate circle France's King Henry III, she was listed in the city's 16th-century guidebook to high-class escorts as: 'Vero. Franco a Santa Mar. Formosa. Pieza so mare. Scudi 2.' The abbreviated entry probably intended to express that Veronica lived at St Mary's, had womanly curves, and offered services ranging from intelligent conversation to horizontal folk dancing for the (rather hefty) rate of 2 scudi. When confused guidebook readers came looking for an address called Santa Maria Formosa (curvy St Mary), the name so entertained locals that it stuck.

39 Palazzi Donà At the top of the *campo* are these 15th-century houses, which veer in style from Gothic to late Gothic with row upon row of tall, skinny limestone arches. The storefront and large Renaissance entryway are practical additions that came later.

40 Campo Santa Marina Following Calle Pindemonte northwest out of the *campo*, you'll cross a bridge and end up in Campo Santa Marina, with the 13th-century Gothic Palazzo Dolfin along the canal to your right. But what's most noticeable here is what's missing: the namesake church was destroyed in 1820 to make way for public housing, which now serves as a hotel.

41 Chiesa di San Lio (p110) Coming out of the square to the west, head south along Calle Carminati, which brings you into Campo San Lio. Not much of Pietro Lombardo's original 16th-century design for this church

(🕙 9am-noon Mon-Sat) remains after its 18th-century restoration on the outside, except for the portal – but inside, the lovely Gussoni chapel is Lombardo's work, including fresco fragments recently uncovered in the cupola. Look up to spot ceilings by Giandomenico Tiepolo and a Palma Il Giovane altarpiece.

42 I Rusteghi (p182) Leave Castello and the entire world behind at this secluded *enoteca*, where your sommelier Giovane d'Este will set you up with *cicheti*, your next new favourite wine, and a few vintage stories of his own about Castello, where he was born and raised.

top picks

SHOPPING

Between world-famous museums and churches, many visitors miss Venice's best-kept secret: shhhh, it's the shopping. Venice is a highlight of any illustrious shopping career, specialising in the signature artisan-made find. All those kiosks hawking porcelain masks and souvenir tees are just there to throw less dedicated shoppers off the scent of the big score (though hey, those striped gondolier shirts can be quite hip out of context).

For your travelling companions who aren't sold on shopping, here's a convincing argument: consider it an educational experience. In backstreet studios you'll meet the Venetian artisans who are keeping centuries-old crafts traditions alive, and adding new twists: a mod handbag made using bookbinding techniques, custom shoes with sculpted-leather heels, a waterfall of glass worn as a necklace. The person who shows it to you may be very person who made it, and will be most pleased to hear you say 'Complimenti!' (My compliments!) on impressive pieces. While crafts traditions across the industrialised world have disappeared or fossilised into relics of bygone eras, Venice remains an outpost of originality.

COSTS

Bargain-hunters will be gratified to hear Venetian treasures cost less than you'd think. From hand-blown *murrine* glass beads that individually make sensational pendants (€1 to €3) to custom chandeliers (€300-plus), Venice's handcrafted goods are quite reasonably priced for the highly specialised labour involved, and local couture costs less than mass-produced designer merchandise. Shops included in this chapter deliver good value for money spent, and standout Venetian values are highlighted in the boxed text, opposite.

Shipping & Taxes

Chandeliers, antique steamer-trunks and other such cumbersome or fragile items may need to be shipped home. Many stores will take care of this for you for modest shipping costs – ask before you buy. For information on VAT sales tax refunds for visitors from outside the EU, see p272.

OPENING HOURS

Most shops open around 9am to 1pm and 3.30pm to 7pm (or 4pm to 7.30pm), Monday to Saturday. Though some shops in tourist areas stay open 9am or 10am to 7pm daily, shops off the main thoroughfares may remain closed on Monday morning, Wednesday afternoon or Saturday afternoon. Many shops close for major Italian holidays (p267), and for all or part of August. In the following reviews, opening hours are provided only where they differ considerably from these general hours.

SHOPPING AREAS

Mall shopping can't compare to the thrill of treasure-hunting in Venice. Here's where to find Venetian specialities:

- Antiques – hidden gems surface in open-air markets in Campo Santa Maria dei Miracoli and Campo Santa Margarita; otherwise, troll shops in the backstreets of Castello and Dorsoduro, especially along Calle delle Bottege.
- Artisan-made originals – studios cluster together in Venice, so to find unique pieces wander along the artisan areas of San Polo around Calle dei Saoneri; Santa Croce around Calle Lunga and Calle del Tentor; Dorsoduro around the Peggy Guggenheim Collection; and Murano.
- Contemporary art – between Biennales, Venice's contemporary art galleries make passers-by stop and stare around Campo San Maurizio and Salizada San Samuele in San Marco and along Fondamenta San Biagio on Giudecca. For recommended galleries within these areas, see p60.
- Gourmet supplies – depending on your airplane's carry-on policy, Venetian edibles and wines from gourmet shops near the Rialto markets in San Polo make tasty souvenirs. Foodie gift recommendations are covered on p185.
- Italian designers – along Calle Larga XXII Marzo and Calle dei Fabbri in San Marco, Venice has all the standard Italian designer brands you can find back home, from Armani to Zegna. Unless your visit coincides with January winter clearance sales or July/August summer sales, you won't find bargains here – but the window-shopping is sensational.

SESTIERE DI SAN MARCO

Once you see San Marco store shelves laden with boulder-sized Murano glass paperweights (perfect gifts for your ogre friends) and souvenir packages of tricolour pasta (because Italian flags are famously delicious), you may sense you're entering a tourist trap. But the farther you get from the main thoroughfares and familiar logos, the closer you are to Venetian shopping scores: handcrafted hats, ultraplush tapestry pillows and tubes of luscious Titian-red oil paint.

ANTIQUUS Map pp68–9 Antiques
☎ 041 520 63 95; Calle Crosera 3131; 🚊 San Samuele
Pirates and doge descendants would feel right at home among the bejewelled chalices and twinkle-eyed baroque portraits in this heirloom showcase. Even if you're not in the market for a €5,000 silver coffee service, these Venetian splendours are worth a peek – especially that necklace of golden pomegranates with ruby seeds.

ARCOBALENO Map pp68–9 Art Supplies
☎ 041 523 68 18; 3457 Calle delle Botteghe; 🚊 Accademia
After umpteen Venetian art masterpieces, anyone's fingers will start twitching for a paint brush. Arcobaleno provides all the raw materials needed to start your own Venetian art movement, with shelves fully stocked with jars of all the essential pigments: Titian red, Tiepolo sky-blue, Veronese rose and Tintoretto teal.

LIBRERIA STUDIUM Map pp68–9 Books
☎ 041 522 23 82; Calle di Canonica 337; 🕑 9am-7.30pm Mon-Sat, 9.30am-1.30pm Sun; 🚊 San Zaccaria
Consult bibliophile staff for worthy vacation reads, page-turning Venetian history, and top picks from shelves groaning under the weight of Italian cookbooks. Many titles are available in English and French, and there's a respectably vast Lonely Planet section (not that we're biased).

MONDADORI Map pp60–9 Books
☎ 041 522 50 68; Salizada San Moisè 1346; 🕑 10am-8pm Mon-Sat, 11am-7.30pm Sun; 🚊 Vallaresso, San Marco

top picks

GIFTS UNDER €25

- Il Pavone de Paolo Pelosin (p169) Marbled-paper travel journals
- Linea Arte Vetro (p175) Murano glass rings
- Drogheria Mascari (p170) Local-producer wines
- VizioVirtù (p168) Artisan chocolates
- Penny Lane Vintage (p169) Fellini-worthy vintage

The city's broadest selections of guidebooks and Italian literature are major draws at this multistorey literary megastore, run by one of Italy's most prominent book chains (majority shareholders are the Fininvest group, a Berlusconi family venture). Check for upcoming author events, and take your must-read-now novel to the hip Bacaro (p200).

OTTICA CARRARO Map pp68–9 Eyeglasses
☎ 041 520 42 58; www.otticacarraro.it; Calle della Mandola 3706; 🚊 Sant'Angelo
Lost your sunglasses on the Lido? Never fear. Ottica Carraro can make you a custom pair within 24 hours. The store has its own signature 'Venice' line, which ranges from retro-1980s shades with caution-yellow rims to arty matt-rubber frames in bronze and grape.

BEVILACQUA Map pp68–9 Fabrics
☎ 041 528 75 81; www.bevilacquatessuti.com; Fondamenta Canonica 337b; 🕑 10am-7pm Mon-Sat, 10am-5pm Sun; 🚊 San Zaccaria
TV dens become grand salons with Venetian swagger at Bevilacqua, producers of Venetian brocades, damasks, and silken tassels since 1800. Fabrics are woven in time-honoured fashion at the workshop here and at its branch (Campo di Santa Maria del Giglio 2520, San Marco; 🚊 Santa Maria del Giglio).

FIORELLA GALLERY Map pp68–9 Fashion
☎ 041 520 92 28; www.fiorellagallery.com; Campo Santo Stefano 2806; 🕑 9.30am-1.30pm & 3.30-7pm Tue-Sat, 3-7pm Mon; 🚊 Accademia
Groupies are the only accessory needed for Fiorella's rock-star fashions. Crushed-velvet smoking jackets in louche shades of lavender and blood red are printed by hand with baroque wallpaper patterns and a Fiorella signature: wide-eyed rats. Prices start in the hundreds of euros, but check out your

CLOTHING SIZES

Women's clothing

Aus/UK	8	10	12	14	16	18
Europe	36	38	40	42	44	46
Japan	5	7	9	11	13	15
USA	6	8	10	12	14	16

Women's shoes

Aus/USA	5	6	7	8	9	10
Europe	35	36	37	38	39	40
France only	35	36	38	39	40	42
Japan	22	23	24	25	26	27
UK	3½	4½	5½	6½	7½	8½

Men's clothing

Aus	92	96	100	104	108	112
Europe	46	48	50	52	54	56
Japan	S		M	M		L
UK/USA	35	36	37	38	39	40

Men's shirts (collar sizes)

Aus/Japan	38	39	40	41	42	43
Europe	38	39	40	41	42	43
UK/USA	15	15½	16	16½	17	17½

Men's shoes

Aus/UK	7	8	9	10	11	12
Europe	41	42	43	44½	46	47
Japan	26	27	27½	28	29	30
USA	7½	8½	9½	10½	11½	12½

Measurements approximate only; try before you buy

reflection in the graffitied Ettore Sotsass mirror and pretend you're not impressed.

POT-POURRI Map pp68–9   Fashion

☎ 041 522 13 32; www.potpourri.it; Ramo dei Fuseri 1810; 🚊 Vallaresso, San Marco
Unexpected invitations to high tea on the Grand Canal call for an emergency run on Pot-Pourri, where unerring fashionista shop-assistants will suggest a crisp Italian-made baby-blue linen jacket, or shapely white jacquard silk shift that whispers when you walk. High-end service and excellent alterations at off-the-rack prices.

PROMOD Map pp68–9   Fashion

☎ 041 241 06 68; www.promod.eu; Campo San Bartolomeo; 🕑 9.30am-8pm Mon-Sat, 11am-7.30pm Sun; 🚊 Rialto
When lagoon mists catch you without a cardigan on a Sunday afternoon, Promod offers a range of options, right by the Rialto. A snappy continental comeback to

H&M and Topshop, this womenswear chain offers similar prices, with more intriguing colour combinations and richer fabrics.

VENETIA STUDIUM Map pp68–9   Fashion

☎ 041 523 69 53; www.venetiastudium.com; Palazzo Zuccato 2425; 🕑 10am-7pm Mon-Sat; 🚊 Santa Maria del Giglio
Get that 'just got in from Monaco for my art opening' look beloved of bohemians who marry well. The high-drama Delphos tunic dresses make anyone look like a high-maintenance modern dancer or heiress (Isadora Duncan and Peggy Guggenheim were both fans), and the hand-stamped silk-velvet bags are more arty than ostentatious (prices run from €25 to €120).

LE BOTTEGHE Map pp68–9   Gifts, Housewares

☎ 041 522 75 45; Rialto 5164; 🕑 10am-7pm Mon-Sat; 🚊 Rialto
Italian design sensibilities meet global awareness at this fair-trade boutique on the steps of the Rialto. Gondola rides call for foldable straw hats, made by a Bangladeshi collective, in rich shades of saffron and fuchsia, while kids expecting gifts back home will be suitably impressed by recycled cans fashioned into toy airplanes and clever coin-purses by West African artisans.

CAMUFFO Map pp68–9   Glass

Calle delle Acque 4992; 🚊 Vallaresso, San Marco
Kids, entomologists and glass collectors troop over the bridge, under the portico and into the second calle (alleyway) on the left to arrive at the city's finest selection of lampworked glass beetles and dragonflies. With a miniature blowtorch and the patience of a saint, Signor Camuffo adds metallic foils to molten glass to make shimmering wings. Between bugs, he'll chat about his work and sell you strands of Murano glass beads at excellent prices.

L'ISOLA Map pp68–9   Glass

☎ 041 523 19 73; www.lisola.com; Campo San Moisè 1468; 🚊 Vallaresso, San Marco
Backlit chalices and spotlit vases emit an otherworldly glow at this shrine to Murano modernist glass master Carlo Moretti. Strict shapes contain freeform swirls of orange and red, and glasses etched with fish-scale patterns add wit and a wink to high-minded modernism. Prices for signature water glasses start at €47.

MA.RE Map pp68–9

Glass

☎ 041 523 11 91; www.mareglass.com; Via XXII Marzo 2088; ☽ 10am-7pm Mon-Sat; ♨ Vallaresso, San Marco

Form meets function in the blown, etched, boldly coloured modern glassware by one of Murano's biggest names, Salviati. With those cross-etched champagne flutes, your table will be set to receive heads of state – as long as they promise to raise toasts carefully.

DAVINIA DESIGN

Map pp68–9

Glass, Jewellery

☎ 041 520 57 54; www.daviniadesign.com; Calle dei Fuseri 4457; ☽ 10am-1pm & 3-7pm Mon-Sat, 11am-7pm Sun; ♨ Rialto

Less is more at this working studio of simple, dramatic Murano brick-red glass pendants and cufflinks that look like tiny sea urchins clinging to your wrists. You'll usually find transplanted Belgian artisan Davinia at work here fashioning clever, understated daisy stud earrings that look more elegant but cost less than flowery fantasias you'll find around Piazza San Marco – there's a good range from €19 to €37.

ANTICA MODISTERIA GIULIANA LONGO Map pp68–9

Hats

☎ 041 522 64 54; www.giulianalongo.com; Calle l'Ovo 4813; ♨ Rialto

Shoe closets are for amateurs: Giuliana's shop is the dream hat-cupboard of any true sartorialist, with styles that range from handmade Montecristi panama hats with an extra fine weave to a modern hot-pink felt number that looks like a doge's cap for Peggy Guggenheim. Giuliana is here most days, polishing leather aviator hats or affixing a broad band to a *bareteri,* the wide-brimmed gondolier's hat best worn with a rakish tilt.

EPICENTRO Map pp68–9

Housewares

☎ 041 522 68 64; Calle dei Fabbri 932; ☽ 9.30am-1.30pm & 3-7pm Tue-Sat, 3-7pm Mon; ♨ Vallaresso

All the secrets to a perfect Italian espresso are here: stove-top espresso makers with built-in pressure valves, rechargeable milk frothers, and espresso cups in futurist shapes. This boutique is even smaller than cramped Venetian kitchens, but its steel racks are loaded with an Alessi catalogue of monkey-shaped creamers and toothbrush-hugging trolls.

GLORIA ASTOLFO Map pp68–9

Jewellery

☎ 041 520 68 27; www.gloriastolfo.com; Frezzeria 1581; ♨ Vallareso

Take your fashion cues from Venetian painting masterpieces at this Venetian bead artisan's showcase. Garlands of beaded tiger lilies make open-necked T-shirts instantly glamorous, and those baroque pearl earrings would gently tickle your shoulders if you started to nod off at La Fenice. Prices starting at €35 are surprisingly down-to-earth for jewellery this original, especially so close to Piazza San Marco.

MATERIALMENTE

Map pp68–9

Jewellery, Decor

☎ 041 528 68 81; www.materialmente.it; Mercerie San Salvador 4850; ☽ 10am-7pm Mon-Sat ♨ Rialto

No Venetian palace would be complete without opulent mirrors and lavish tapestries, and Maddelena Venier and her brother Alessandro Salvadori have cleverly combined these luxe effects in modern mirrors hand-silkscreened with baroque patterns. The prolific siblings also create whimsical lamps that look like birdcages and signet rings ideal for sealing love letters in wax.

DANIELA GHEZZO Map pp68–9

Shoes

☎ 041 522 21 15; Calle dei Fuseri 4365; ♨ Rialto

A gold chain is pulled across the doorway, but not because Daniela is out: she's chatting with a customer about shoe preferences while taking foot measurements. In the atelier once run by the legendary Segalin-family cobblers, maestra Ghezzo continues the tradition of custom-making every pair to measure, so you'll never see your oxblood ankle boots on another art collector, or your Florentine brown wingtips on a rival titan of industry.

MILLEVINI Map pp68–9

Wine

☎ 041 520 60 90; Ramo del Fontego dei Turchi 5362; ♨ Rialto

For the price of a souvenir T-shirt, a top-notch Veneto vintage recommended by well-versed staff could become a highlight of your visit – beyond DOC *prosecco,* there are Veneto Merlots with gumption, and surprisingly velvety Valpollicellas. This brick wine-cellar is right at the foot of the Rialto bridge, a convenient stop if you want to toast the sunset on your hotel terrace.

SESTIERE DI DORSODURO

Your grandmother would hardly recognise the Venetian handicrafts coming out of Dorsoduro's cutting-edge artisan outlets: teapots with foam-rubber handles, a lagoon-green paper necklace anchored with a blown-glass purple bead, scarves that swirl like seaweed at high tide. But Dorsoduro hasn't lost its sense of history – along these backstreets, you might luck into Bakelite brooches or vintage Ferragamo heels.

ANTIQUARIATO CLAUDIA CANESTRELLI

Map pp78–9   Antiques, Jewellery

☎ 041 522 70 72; Campiello Barbaro 364a; 🚤 Salute

Sunburst mirrors and hand-coloured lithographs of prehistoric-looking lagoon fish are charming souvenirs of Venice's bygone glories, but collector and artisan Claudia Canestrelli is bringing back baroque elegance with her repurposed-antique earrings. Claudia collects stray glass-mosaic roses, winking citrines and freeform baroque pearls from broken diadems, and refashions them into one-of-a-kind heirloom pieces with a romantic, modern sensibility – her earrings would look just as striking worn with jeans or ball gowns.

3856

Map pp78–9   Fashion

☎ 041 72 05 95; Calle San Pantalon 3749; 🚤 San Tomà

Venice is usually more casual and warmer than visitors expect, so 3856 comes in handy with breezy, effortlessly hip boat-neck tees, casual printed sundresses and shapely cotton jackets for women and kids. Priced like sportswear but resort-collection style, these pieces are good to go from day to night with the addition of a Murano glass necklace.

VINTAGE A GO GO

Map pp78–9   Fashion

☎ 041 277 78 95; www.vintagegogo.altervista.org; Calle Lunga San Barnaba 2755; 🚤 Ca' Rezzonico

Mix and match decades into a signature look in this walk-in closet of vintage, which packs a solid selection of romantic '50s vintage cashmere cardigans, psychedelic '60s' Pucci loungewear, '70s leather trenches and screaming '80s turquoise pumps. Prices are above thrift, but below eBay resale values.

ARRAS

Map pp78–9   Fashion, Accessories

☎ 041 522 64 60; Campiello del Squellini 3235; 🚤 Ca' Rezzonico

The handwoven silk wraps piled high on Arras shelves are beyond fabulous: each plush, luxurious textile represents the combined efforts of this weaving cooperative, which offers vocational workshops for people with disabilities. Hand-woven wool jackets are draped for maximum gallery-opening effect by cooperative designers, warding off the evening chill along the canals in true local style.

LE FORCOLE DI SAVERIO PASTOR

Map pp78–9   Forcole

☎ 041 522 56 99; www.forcole.com; Fondamenta Soranzo detta Fornace 341; 🕑 8.30am-12.30pm & 2.30-6pm Mon-Sat; 🚤 Salute

---

HEIRLOOM SOUVENIRS

On sunny summer weekends in Venice, you'll stumble into outdoor markets so crammed with baroque mirrors, tapestry hangings and other Venetian set pieces you might think La Fenice's prop department is having a fire sale. On Campo Santa Margherita, treasures culled from local palace attics can be found amid the usual junk at the mercato delle pulci (flea market). On the same campo (square), the occasional Doctors without Borders (Médecins sans Frontières) jumble sale fundraiser is organised by two dapper Venetian brothers who decided 'retirement is boring, and the world needs all the help it can get'. Savvy shoppers might spot antique cordial glasses, Murano glass seahorse pendants, and vintage Italian cookbooks containing long-lost culinary secrets, all for under €10. For artisan ceramics collectors, the annual Bochaleri in Campo (www.bochaleri.it; Campo San Maurizio, San Marco; 🕑 9am-5pm, last weekend in May) covers styles and eras from classic Renaissance portrait plates to freeform raku sculpture. Savvy vendors at the Mercantino dei Miracoli (Campo Santa Maria Nova or Via Garibaldi; 🕑 9am-1pm & 3.30-7.30pm, 1st weekend of every month; 🚤 Ca' d'Oro) and Mercantino dell'Antiquaria (☎ 333 965 99 94; Campo San Maurizio; 🕑 9am-5pm, last weekend of every month) sell exquisite enamelled lockets, vintage Vespa ads, and '50s sunglasses worthy of Marcello Mastroianni at prices that occasionally approach Sotheby's – but honestly, where else are you going to buy a gondola prow, only slightly dinged?

Mick Jagger had his *forcola* made to measure here – and no, that's not as naughty as it sounds. A *forcola* is a forked tongue of wood where the gondola oar rests, hand-carved from acacia and hard oak, and each one must be made to match a gondolier's exact height and weight so as not to upset a gondola's delicate balance. Sounds like a job for Saverio Pastor, who makes *forcole* that twist and lean in perfect balance – ideal for budding gondoliers, or as customised sculpture.

AQUA ALTRA Map pp78–9   Gifts, Housewares

☎ 041 521 12 59; www.aquaaltra.it; Campo Santa Margherita 2898; ☾ 9.30am-12.30pm & 4-7.30pm Tue-Sat, 4-7.30pm Mon; ⚓ Ca' Rezzonico

Global-minded but with Italian tastes firmly in mind, this volunteer-run fair trade co-op sells single-origin chocolate from Sierra Leone growers' collectives, mod graphite-silver sandals made by Palestinian artisans and match-standard footballs made by a Pakistani cooperative. The group also occasionally organises organic food stalls around town, including near Piazzale Roma.

MADERA Map pp78–9   Gifts, Housewares

☎ 041 522 41 81; www.maderavenezia.it; Campo San Barnaba 2762; ☾ 10am-1pm & 3-6pm Tue-Sat; ⚓ Ca' Rezzonico

Double-takes are a given at this modern design showcase, where wooden spoons look like tongues, elegant pasta bowls are made of recycled plastic bags and teapots in foam-rubber tea cosies look like they're wearing scuba gear. Most pieces are by owner-designer Francesca Meratti and other Italian designers, with some Scandinavian and Japanese influences, in a well-curated collection of original design objects starting at €15.

MARINA E SUSANNA SENT

Map pp78–9   Glass, Jewellery

☎ 041 520 8136; www.marinaesusannasent.com; Campo San Vio 669; ☾ 10am-1pm & 3-6.30pm Tue-Sat, 3-6.30pm Mon; ⚓ Accademia

Statement jewellery has taken over Milan runways, but the iced-glass waterfall necklaces produced by pioneering sister glass artisans Marina and Susanna Sent are show-stoppers. Museum shops around Venice feature their work, including the striped glass brooches in the shape of the shield of Fortitude from the Palazzo Ducale and their signature 'soap' necklaces: frothy strands of big, clear glass bubbles that make

the wearer look both stylish and freshly scrubbed. There's also a branch at Ponte San Moisè (see San Marco Walking Tour, p136). For an interview with Marina Sent, see p119).

GUALTI Map pp78–9   Jewellery, Accessories

☎ 041 520 1731; www.gualti.it; Rio Terà Canal 3111; ⚓ Ca' Rezzonico

Either a shooting star just landed on your shoulder, or you've been to Gualti, where iridescent orange glass bursts from clear resin stems on an interstellar brooch. Gualti's pleated-silk evening wraps are curled at the edges, like fans of lagoon seaweed swaying with the current. Gualti doesn't like to repeat himself, but his prices are often less than you'd expect for one-off designs, starting at €80.

CA' MACANA Map pp78–9   Masks, Costumes

☎ 041 277 61 42; www.camacana.com; Calle delle Botteghe 3172; ☾ 10am-6.30pm Sun-Fri, 10am-8pm Sat; ⚓ Ca' Rezzonico

Glimpse the talents behind the Venetian Carnevale masks that apparently so impressed Stanley Kubrick he placed a rather large order for his last picture, *Eyes Wide Shut*. Choose your own papier mâché persona from the selection of long-nosed plague doctors' disguises or fine-featured courtesans' camouflage, or make your own at Ca' Macana's mask-making workshops.

IL PAVONE DI FABIO PELOSIN

Map pp78–9   Stationery

☎ 041 523 45 17; Fondamenta Venier dai Leoni 721; ☾ 10am-1pm & 2.30-6pm Tue-Sat; ⚓ Accademia

Baccalà mantecato (Venice's signature fish pâté) is bound to come out better when captured in a handmade recipe book stamped with Venetian Gothic architectural patterns. Il Pavone's recipe books, travel logs and day planners are printed with traces of metallic pigments, but don't just judge them by their shimmering covers. Inside they're well organised with tabs and headings for meal planning, trip highlights and upcoming birthdays.

SIGNOR BLOOM

Map pp78–9   Toys, Woodcrafts

☎ 041 522 63 67; Campo San Barnaba 2840; ⚓ Ca' Rezzonico

Kids may have to drag adults away from these brightly coloured 2D wooden puzzles of the Rialto bridge and grinning wooden duckies, because these clever handmade toys make grown-ups squeal with nostalgia. That Calder-esque mobile made of carved red gondola prows would seem equally at home in an arty foyer or a nursery.

SESTIERI DI SAN POLO & SANTA CROCE (SANTA CROSE)

If you're going to get lost in Venice, this is the place to do it. Artisan ateliers await discovery in the crooked lanes of Santa Croce; gourmet finds lurk in the shadow of the Rialto markets; and high fashion can be found at prices within reach along lanes connecting I Frari to the Rialto Bridge.

SERENA VIANELLO Map pp86–7   Accessories

☎ 041 522 33 51; www.serenavianello.com; Campo Sant'Aponal 1226, San Polo; 🚢 San Silvestro
Opulent Como silks and minute finishing set these timeless Venetian designs apart from the faddish crowd. Two-tone silk handbags utilise Tiepolo colour schemes of sky blues and golds, and a silk jacket with gossamer green tones and terracotta piping evokes a walk through Venice.

CAMPIELLO CA' ZEN

Map pp86–7   Antiques
☎ 041 71 48 71; www.campiellocazen.com; Campiello Zen 2581; 🕙 9am-1pm & 3-7pm Mon-Sat; 🚢 San Tomà
Antique Murano glass lamps are the last thing you'd want to cram in your luggage – or so you thought before you saw the 1940s Salviati smoky silver chandelier and the

LOOKING SHARP: VENICE'S AVANT-GARDE EYEWEAR

Centuries before geek chic, the first eyeglasses known to Europe were worn in the Veneto c 1348, and Venetian opticians have been hand-grinding lenses and stylish frames ever since. To get limited-edition prescription shades, bring your prescription to any of the eyewear specialists in this chapter, or snap up a replica of Peggy Guggenheim's outrageous frames at the Collection gift shop (p78).

ultramod Venini vase. That cobalt-blue hand-blown chalice seems practical in comparison, but here's a dangerous thought: they ship.

GILBERTO PENZO Map pp86–7   Boats

☎ 041 71 93 72; www.veniceboats.com; Calle 2 dei Saoneri 2681, San Polo; 🕙 9am-12.30pm & 3-6pm Mon-Sat; 🚢 San Tomà
Yes, you actually can take a gondola home in your pocket. Anyone fascinated by the models at the Museo Storico Navale (p107) will go wild here amid handmade wooden models of all kinds of Venetian boats, including some that are seaworthy (or at least bathtub-worthy). Signor Penzo creates kits, so crafty types and kids can have a crack at it themselves.

MARE DI CARTA

Map pp86–7   Books, Navigational Aids
☎ 041 71 63 04; www.maredicarta.com; Fondamenta dei Tolentini 222, Santa Croce; 🚢 Ferrovia
Sailors, pirates and armchair seafarers should navigate their way to this canal-side storefront, where you'll find every maritime map and DIY boating aid needed for lagoon exploration, boat upkeep and spotting local sea life. If you're considering rowing lessons or a sailboat excursion – and who doesn't after a few days on the lagoon? – stop here first to check out the schedule of boating classes and trips.

BOTTEGA DEGLI ANGELI

Map pp86–7   Ceramics
☎ 041 71 08 66; www.bottegangeli.com; Calle del Cristo 2224, Santa Croce; 🕙 10am-1pm & 3-8pm Mon-Sat; 🚢 Rialto
Matt stoneware vases with a deep-red stained-glass pattern, tiles with shy fish hiding behind seaweed, and '70s mod ceramic sunburst pendants: there's something for every taste and carry-on limit here. Styles range from stark modernist shapes to Japanese anime–inspired frogs, but the signature is a bright red glaze that (as any ceramist will tell you) is quite difficult to achieve.

VIZIOVIRTÙ Map pp86–7   Chocolate

☎ 041 275 01 49; www.viziovirtu.com; Calle del Campaniel 2898a, Santa Croce; 🕙 10am-6.30pm; 🚢 Ca' Rezzonico
Work your way through Venice's most decadent vices and tasty virtues with repeat visits to the Willy-Wonkaesque hot-chocolate fountain, summertime house-made gelato and chocolates filled with ganache

in a five-course meal of flavours: Barolo wine, blueberry and violet, olive oil, *aceto balsamico* (balsamic vinegar) and 'Freud' (which tastes like a cigar, naturally).

ARTISTICA FERRO Map pp86–7 Crafts
☎ 041 520 0490; Calle Lunga 2137, Santa Croce; 🚊 San Stae

Iron becomes red-hot decor at this atelier, where handcrafted metalwork showpieces include fireplace sets, cast-iron sugar bowls that resonate like a bell when struck with a tiny spoon, and a full-scale *fero de prova,* the classic iron hood-ornament for a gondola, with six teeth to represent the six *sestieri* (neighbourhoods) of Venice.

CARTAVENEZIA Map pp86–7 Crafts
☎ 041 524 12 83; Calle Lunga 2125, Santa Croce; 🕐 11am-1pm & 3.30-7.30pm Tue-Sat, 3.30-7.30pm Mon; 🚊 San Stae

Paper is anything but two-dimensional here: instead of being marbled, as has been the custom in Venice for 150 years, CartaVenezia embosses and sculpts handmade cotton paper into seamless raw-edged bowls and lampshades, hand-bound sketchbooks and paper versions of marble friezes that would seem equally at home in a Greek temple or modern loft.

IL GUFO ARTIGIANO Map pp86–7 Crafts
☎ 041 523 4030; Ruga degli Speziali 299, San Polo; 🚊 Rialto

Hot copper and extremely careful handling is the secret to the embossed leather designs gracing journals, handbags, and wallets in this artisan's atelier. Ancient ironwork patterns in Venetian windows and balconies inspire the swirling designs, with vibrantly coloured leather adding an unexpected modern twist: orange satchels, saffron-yellow photo albums and verdant day planners.

CARTÈ Map pp86–7 Crafts, Stationery
☎ 320 024 87 76; Calle di Cristi 1731, San Polo; 🚊 San Tomà

Gondola wakes and lagoon ripples mysteriously appear on hand-bound portfolios and paper necklaces, thanks to the steady hands and restless imagination of marble-paper *maestra* Rosanna Corrò. After years restoring ancient Venetian manuscripts and books, Rosanna decided to work on making something entirely original, and here you have it: bookbound purses in woodgrain

designs, swirling yellow Op art earrings, and photo albums in opulent peacock-eye patterns to showcase your best Venice photos.

IL PAVONE DE PAOLO PELOSIN
Map pp86–7 Crafts, Stationery
☎ 041 522 42 96; Campiello dei Meoni 1478, San Polo; 🚊 San Silvestro

Consider Paolo's hand-bound marbled-paper journals and photo albums a challenge: now it's up to you to come up with Venice memories worthy of such inspired workmanship. Restaurant review books come in scrumptious violet and gold Art Deco patterns, lagoon-swirled blue sketchbooks inspire sudden seascapes, and paper-wrapped pen sets seem to catch fire with flickers of orange and red.

OTTICA VASCELLARI
Map pp86–7 Eyeglasses
☎ 041 522 93 88; www.otticavascellari.it; Ruga Rialto 1030, San Polo; 🚊 Rialto

Second-generation opticians and first-class eyewear stylists, the Vascellari family intuit eyewear needs with a glance at your prescription and a long look to assess your face shape and personal style. Angular features demand Vascellari's signature bold architectural eyewear line with two-tone laminates, delicate features are set off with sleek satin-finish specs, and fabulous gold-rimmed sunglasses will have the crowds parting for you at the Venice Film Festival.

HIBISCUS Map pp86–7 Fashion
☎ 041 520 89 89; Ruga Rialto 1060, San Polo; 10am-6.30pm; 🚊 San Silvestro

Blend right in at the Biennale with Venice's creative crossroads style, layered piece by distinctive piece at Hibiscus: easygoing Italian linen sailor pants, one-of-a-kind jackets with vintage silk embroidery panels, Japanese watercolour-patterned socks and a Maria Calderara ring that looks like a coral reef wrapped around your finger.

PENNY LANE VINTAGE
Map pp86–7 Fashion
☎ 041 524 41 34; Salizada San Pantalon 39, Santa Croce; 🕐 9.30am 1pm & 3.30 6.30pm Mon-Sat, 🚊 Ferrovia

If oversized vintage Italian shades are more your style than Carnevale masks, Penny Lane is your fashion destination. The admiration is mutual here between Venice and London, from the Yellow Submarine decor and Ben Sherman shirts to lagoon lightning-bolt tees and skin-tight nautical striped sweaters for men and women. Vintage-inspired new clothing is displayed up front, but the back room has the major vintage steals – think €10 for a clear vinyl mac and €5 for an Italian intellectual turtleneck sweater c 1970.

ZAZU Map pp86–7   Fashion
☎ 041 71 54 26; Calle dei Saoneri 2750, San Polo; ⏰ 9.30am-1.30pm & 2.30-7.30pm Tue-Sat, 2.30-7.30pm Mon; 🚊 San Tomà

Be Ms Marco Polo of the fashion world, with forays into Italian-designed tapestry bags, one-of-a-kind dresses from Barcelona and chic Japanese wrap tops. Prices are above sportswear but below couture, and the sale rack in the back usually has great pieces for €50 to €100.

DROGHERIA MASCARI
Map pp86–7   Food, Wine
☎ 041 522 97 62; www.imascari.com; Ruga degli Spezieri 381, San Polo; ⏰ 8am-1pm & 4-7.30pm Mon-Tue & Thu-Sat, 8am-1pm Wed; 🚊 San Silvestro

Ziggurat-shaped piles of cayenne, leaning towers of star anise and ranks of estate-grown olive oils attract crowds of awestruck foodies to Drogheria Mascari's windows. Indoors, customers clutch tiny jars of white truffles like holy relics, and staff help dazed first-timers navigate the selection of Sicilian capers and 50 kinds of aromatic honeys. For memorable small-production Italian wines starting at €7, don't miss the backroom *enoteca* (wine bar).

I VETRI A LUME DI AMADI
Map pp86–7   Glass
☎ 041 523 80 89; Calle Saoneri 2747, San Polo; ⏰ 9am-12.30pm & 3-6pm Mon-Sat; 🚊 San Silvestro

Glass menageries don't get more fascinating than the one created before your eyes by Signor Amadi. Fierce little glass crabs approach pink-tipped sea anemones, and glass peas spill from a speckled peapod. You might be tempted to swat at eerily lifelike glass mosquitoes, and the outlines of galloping horses in blue glass would do Picasso proud.

MARCO FRANZATO VETRATE ARTISTICHE Map pp86–7   Glass, Jewellery
☎ 041 24 07 70; Calle Lunga 2155a, Santa Croce; 🚊 San Stae

Slumped, fused and foiled again: glass goes wild in this experimental co-op gallery of emerging glass designers. Mod glass clocks are the work of studio ringleader Marco Franzato, who also stocks a well-priced selection of necklaces of matt glass discs that look like UFOs orbiting around the neck, and jars of handmade Murano beads embedded with rosebuds or stars starting at €0.40 each.

GIUSEPPE TINTI Map pp86–7   Glass, Lamps
☎ 041 524 12 57; www.tintimuranoglass.com; Campo San Cassian 2343, Santa Croce; ⏰ 9am-1pm & 3-7pm Mon-Sat

Look on the bright side with Victor Vasarely-style Murano glass lamps inset with Op art squares, or orange and red striped lamps inspired by commedia dell'arte costumes. Lamps run to about €155 plus shipping; for highly portable, affordable souvenirs, check out Tinti's signature cartoony glass fish magnets (€4 to €7).

FANNY Map pp86–7   Gloves, Leather
☎ 041 522 82 66; Calle dei Saoneri 2723, San Polo; ⏰ 10am-7.30pm 🚊 San Tomà

Quit snickering about the name – when that Venice chill hits your extremities, you'll be seriously glad you found this trove of local artisan-crafted leather gloves. No need to sacrifice style for warmth here: check out the cashmere-lined chocolate pair with ice-blue piping, or those polka-dotted purple numbers. At these prices, you may have to upgrade to that square cherry-red leather tote bag to haul around your glove purchases.

SABBIE E NEBBIE
Map pp86–7   Housewares, Gifts
☎ 041 71 90 73; Calle dei Nomboli 2768a, San Polo; ⏰ 10am-12.30pm & 4-7.30pm Mon-Sat; 🚊 San Tomà

The latest East-West trade-route trends begin here, with Japanese-inspired Rina Menardi ceramics, woven opera wraps that are saffron on one side and paprika on the other, and handmade books from Bologna made with Japanese paper-marbling techniques.

ATTOMBRI Map pp86–7   Jewellery
☎ 041 521 25 24; www.attombri.com; Sotoportego Oresi 74, San Polo; 🚊 Rialto

Bold enough to get noticed on Milan catwalks, Attombri's original sculpted wire collars and bracelets frame glass cameos, crest into beaded green waves and burst into precious garnet blooms. With prices starting at around €40, Attombri jewellery may be among the best designer values to ever grace the pages of Italian *Vogue*.

LA BOTTEGA DI GIO

☎ 041 71 46 64; www.labottegadigio.it; Fondamenta dei Frari 2559a, San Polo; 🚊 San Tomà
Murano glass necklaces you see in the shops not quite your style? Make your own with lampworked Murano glass beads beginning at €1 and your choice of coloured wire, silk thread or leather cord from this DIY jewellery shop. To contain your creations, try a hand-stitched jewellery pouch graced with a glass bead (€15 to €25).

LABERINTHO Map pp86–7   Jewellery

☎ 041 71 00 17; www.laberintho.it; Calle del Scaleter 2236, San Polo; 🚊 San Stae
A token jewel in the window is a tantalising hint of the original custom jewellery this versatile goldsmiths' atelier can create for you: a square gold ring secretly lined with ebony, a necklace of iridescent glass and gold links, or a gold band inlaid top and bottom with opal and turquoise.

MOSAICO! Map pp86–7   Mosaics

☎ 349 520 08 92; www.mosaicoavenezia.it; Calle del Tentor 1864, Santa Croce; ⌚ 8.30am-noon & 2-6pm Mon-Sat; 🚊 San Stae
Marta Bertaggia plies Venice's ancient artisan trade with similar tools used for San Marco's mosaics a millennium ago: a tiny hammer and rods of raw glass. The glass is gently tapped into square *tesserae* (small tiles) and painstakingly set into shimmering mosaic vases, mirror frames, a stunning masquerade mask, the lion of San Marco heraldic emblem and careful recreations of Egon Schiele paintings. Custom pieces can be commissioned here too, so you can capture your own mosaic memory of Venice.

MILLE E UNA NOTA

☎ 041 523 18 22; Calle di Mezzo 1235, San Polo; 🚊 San Tomà
The same thought occurs to almost everyone after hearing a concert in Venice: Is it too late to take up an instrument? The easiest would be the harmonica, and Mille e Una Nota has an impressive range of vintage and modern ones from the Italian Alps. If you're feeling very ambitious, you can pick up some Albinoni sheet music and a lute here too.

GMEINER Map pp86–7   Shoes

☎ 338 896 21 89; www.gabrielegmeiner.com; Campiello del Sol 951, San Polo; 🚊 Rialto
London, Paris, Toyko: Gabriele Gmeiner honed her shoemaking craft in sartorial centres around the globe, and jet-setters now seek out her hidden Venice workshop for ultrasleek Oxfords with hidden 'bent' seams and brogues minutely detailed with hand-stitching, all made to measure for men and women. If Gabriele's not stitching on-site, she's probably at the women's prison on Giudecca, where she leads a job training program in shoe design.

VENEZIASTAMPA Map pp86–7   Stationery

☎ 041 71 54 55; www.veneziastampa.com; Campo Santa Maria Mater Domini 2173, Santa Croce; ⌚ 8.30am-12.30pm & 2.30-7.30pm Mon-Fri, 8.30am-12.30pm Sat; 🚊 San Stae
The squeak and grind of the old Heidelberg press in action is a thrilling throwback to another time, when postcards were gorgeously lithographed, custom bookplates gently reminded book borrowers of their rightful owners and Casanovas invited dates upstairs to 'look at my etchings'. Pick up original hand-stamped stationery with your choice of potent, yet ambiguous, symbols – a muscled arm, a leaking faucet, an ostrich plume – or invitation cards and posters with spry commedia dell'arte figures, by local artists.

IL BAULE BLU Map pp86–7   Toys, Vintage

☎ 041 71 94 48; www.ilbauleblu.com; Campo San Tomà 2916a, San Polo; ⌚ 10.30am-12.30pm & 4-7.30pm Mon-Sat; 🚊 San Tomà
A curiosity cabinet of elusive treasures, which on recent inspection included antique Steiff teddy bears, grey patent leather Miu Miu shoes, vintage Murano *murrine* (glass beads) and a striking yellow glass Scarpa column lamp. If travel has proved tough on your kid's favourite toy, first aid and kind words will be administered at the in-house teddy hospital.

SESTIERE DI CANNAREGIO

Chain stores and tourist souvenir shops line the main shopping strip in Cannaregio between the Ferrovia (train station) and Rialto. But among the Italia football jerseys and nautical-striped singlets for baby gondoliers, you'll spot some stand out artisans.

GIUNTI AL PUNTO Map pp94–5 Books
☎ 041 275 01 52; Campo San Geremia 282; ⏰ 9am-8pm Mon-Wed, 9am-10pm Thu, 9am-midnight Fri & Sat, 10am-10pm Sun; 🚊 Guglie
Late hours, decent paperbacks in several languages, useful cookbooks and maps of Venice make this a handy outlet for information and vacation reading.

SOLARIS Map pp94–5 Comics
☎ 041 524 10 98; www.libreriasolaris.com; Rio Terà de la Maddelena 2332; ⏰ 10am-12.30pm & 4.30-7.30pm Mon-Sat, 4.30-7pm Sun; 🚊 San Marcuola
The plot thickens at Venice's landmark bookstore for comics, mysteries, and science fiction. The tiny store is packed with DVDs, books, and periodicals with a back wall that's one big curved bookcase, and there's an entire section just for Corto Maltese, the detective graphic novel set in Venice by Italian comics master Hugo Pratt.

DOLCEAMARO Map pp94–5 Food, Wine
☎ 041 523 87 08; Campo San Canciano 6051; ⏰ 10am-1pm & 4-7.30pm Mon-Sat, 11.30am-1.30pm & 4.40-7.30pm Sun 🚊 Rialto
For the well-travelled foodie who's been there, eaten that, here's something original: a miniature platter of Italian cheeses and cured meats, made out of artisan chocolate. Dolceamaro also stocks wines, speciality Veneto grappa (spirits), and other gourmet temptations, including aged balsamic vinegars and whole truffles.

DE ROSSI Map pp94–5 Glass Lanterns
☎ 041 522 24 36; Strada Nuova 4311; www.derossiferrobattuto.com; 🚊 Ca' d'Oro
To set a romantic Venetian mood in your own backyard, try an authentic fisherman's lantern, a bubble of glass in a forged-iron frame. This family workshop is among the last, best Venetian lantern-makers, producing traditional and new styles with coloured and matt glass in shapes that range from zucca (pumpkin) to mid-century modernist styles.

GIANNI BASSO Map pp94–5 Printer
☎ 041 523 46 81; Calle del Fumo 5306; 9am-1pm & 2-6pm Mon-Sat; 🚊 Fondamente Nuove
All the advertising Signor Basso needs for his letter-pressing services are the calling cards crowding his small front window with familiar names and fitting symbols. Restaurant critic Gale Greene's title is framed by a knife and fork; prolific mystery writer Scott Turow's name balances atop a pile of books; and Hugh Grant's moniker appears next to a surprisingly tame lion. Bring cash if you want to commission your own business cards, menus or invitations, and trust him to deliver via post if need be – his posted hours aren't always accurate.

SESTIERE DI CASTELLO

Castello is more of a residential area than a tourist zone, so the artisans you'll find in these quiet alleyways are less beholden to

FAIR & DIRECT TRADE IN VENICE

Back in its maritime empire days, Venice wasn't always the fairest trading partner – hence all the pilfered Egyptian marble and Turkish treasures you'll see in Venetian monuments and museums. But lately, Venice is championing a new approach with fair-trade boutiques like Le Botteghe (p164) and Aqua Altra (p167), where purchases of a Sofia Loren–style sun hat or decadent Venetian hot chocolate mix directly supports the artisans' collectives who made them in developing countries.

But the most direct trade in Venice is buying from Venice's many resident artisans.

Local artisans and artisans' collectives who do most of their work in their Venice studios and make a special effort to give back to their community or use local, sustainable or salvaged materials are highlighted in the GreenDex (p299). Any purchase you make from a local artisan has a positive ripple effect around the lagoon and beyond, directly supporting Venetian families, reducing industrial waste, minimising carbon emissions from transport and providing a creative alternative to mass production. In a world of mindless knock offs and cookie-cutter culture, your support for Venice's vital handicrafts tradition is a vote for Venice's enduring originality.

the mainstream tourist trade, and freer to experiment.

QUESTOEQUEO Map pp100–1 — Books

☎ 041 522 37 43; www.questoequeo.it; Calle San Antonin 3542b; ⏰ 10.30am-12.30pm; 🚉 San Zaccaria

Serve up some Venetian architecture with dessert, on cake plates painted with Gothic rosettes worthy of a Grand Canal balcony. Ceramic artisan Martina Purisiol has developed a distinctive marbling effect and colour gradations that echo San Marco's inlaid marble floors, and will do your cooking proud.

ATELIER ALESSANDRO MERLIN

Map pp100–1 — Ceramics

☎ 041 522 58 95; Calle del Pestrin 3876; 🚉 Arsenale

Enjoy your breakfast in the nude, on a horse or atop a jellyfish – Alessandro Merlin paints them all on striking black and white cappuccino cups and saucers. His expressive characters are modern, but his sgraffito technique dates back to Roman times: designs are scratched white lines against a black background.

BANCO 10 Map pp100–1 — Fashion

☎ 041 522 14 39; Salizada Sant'Antonin 3478a; 🚉 San Zaccaria

Prison orange is out and plum silk velvet is in at this nonprofit boutique: all those sumptuous high-fashion velvet tailcoats and cocktail dresses were created as part of a job retraining program at the women's prison on Giudecca. La Fenice has dressed its divas in ensembles made through this program, which uses opulent silks, velvets and tapestry, donated by Fortuny (p72) and Bevilaqua (p163) for smartly tailored jackets and handbags designed by women inmates. Volunteers run the boutique, and purchases fund the women prisoners' continuing career training and reintegration into society after their release.

ARTE VETRO MURANO

Map pp100–1 — Glass, Jewellery

☎ 041 523 75 14; www.artevetromurano.com; Calle delle Rasse 4613; ⏰ 10am 1pm & 3 6pm Mon-Sat; 🚉 San Zaccaria

Shatter glass conventions with new styles by emerging Murano glass designers. Davide Penso makes a necklace of flat

top picks

VENETIAN FASHION

- Giovanna Zanella (p174) Custom shoes
- Ottica Carraro (p163) Sunglasses
- Marina e Susanna Sent (p167) Glass jewellery
- Banco 10 (left) Couture jackets
- Cartè (p169) Paper handbags

puddles of orange glass that have a molten-lava look about them, and Artematte's mismatched yet complementary lampwork glass earrings will earn you double-takes at Biennale art openings.

SIGFRIDO CIPOLATO

Map pp100–1 — Jewellery

☎ 041 522 84 37; San Lio Caselleria 5336; 🚉 San Zaccaria

Booty worthy of pirate royalty is displayed in this fishbowl-sized window display: a constellation of diamonds in star settings on a ring, a tiny enamelled green snake sinking its fangs into a pearl and diamond drop earrings that end in enamelled gold skulls. Though they look like heirlooms, these small wonders were worked on the premises by master jeweller Sigfridio – and you'll pay half the price here than you would at the high-end jewellery showrooms near San Marco which carry Cipolato's work.

SCHEGGE Map pp100–1 — Masks

☎ 041 522 57 89; Calle Lunga Maria Formosa 6185; ⏰ 10am-9pm Mon-Sat; 🚉 Rialto

Go incognito in style, with highly original masquerade masks revealing influences as diverse as Gothic architecture and Modigliani. Well into the night, you'll find this dedicated mother-daughter team wielding tiny paintbrushes, coaxing minute baroque tendrils into bloom along the side of a Klimt mask.

PAROLE E MUSICA Map pp100–1 — Music

☎ 041 523 50 10; www.intermusic.biz; Salizada San Lio 5673; ⏰ 10am-7.30pm Mon-Sat, 11am-7.30pm Sun; 🚉 Rialto

Take Venice's musical inspiration home with you at this store specialising in Italian pop, classical and opera, including new Italian recordings and European indie labels that are hard to find elsewhere.

LOCAL VOICE: GIOVANNA ZANELLA

Starting from the ground up I started my career in fashion, but after 10 years studying under a master shoemaker to understand the contact between the foot and the pavement, now I can say I'm a shoemaker. My shoes sometimes take on architectural or sculptural forms, but there's a fundamental difference: shoes are essentially containers for feet, and you can't just impose shapes on them. They must support the foot, or in a place like Venice where you walk everywhere, you'll immediately start to resent them.

These shoes are made for walking Get lost down the side streets and you'll see artisans at work and people on the move. Venice isn't a Disney production. People are still thinking, still contributing ideas, and that's what gives Venice its continued relevance in the world.

Soundtrack for living I live in San Marco and work near the Rialto, where I can hear the foghorns and the noises of many languages spoken at once. My hammering is part of the city's living symphony.

Bea vita Life is good in Venice, and that joy appears in my shoes. Sometimes I leave, not because I miss discotheques or traffic, just to get a different point of view. But I always come back.

Giovanna Zanella is an avant-garde calzolaia (shoe-maker) and reviver of tired feet (below).

GIOVANNA ZANELLA Map pp100–1   Shoes
☎ 041 523 55 00; Calle Carminati 5641;
🕑 9.30am-1pm & 3-7pm Mon-Sat; 🚊 Rialto
Woven, sculpted and crested like lagoon birds: Zanella's shoes practically demand that red carpets unfurl before you. The Venetian designer makes shoes custom, so the answer is always: yes, you can get those peep-toe numbers in yellow and grey, size 12, extra narrow. It'll cost you of course, but at least you won't be upstaged by Angelina Jolie in the same pair at the Venice Film Festival.

KALIMALA CUOIERIA
Map pp100–1   Shoes, Crafts
☎ 041 528 35 96; www.kalimala.it; Salizada San Lio 5387; 🚊 Rialto
Sleekly supple belts with brushed-steel buckles, modern satchels and man-bags, and knee-high red boots: Kalimala makes leather goods with comfort and modern style in mind. Extra bounce in your step

comes from the natural rubber soles of chocolate-brown desert boots – and from the prices, which start under €75 for artisan-made shoes.

AROUND THE LAGOON

Venice's outlying islands have their artisanal specialities: Murano is world-renowned for glass (look for the seal of authenticity); Burano is famed for its lace; and Giudecca boasts the Fortuny fabric workshop (p112). Watch redhot home decor emerge from the fiery glass *fornace* (furnaces) of Murano, hidden behind glitzy showrooms along Fondamenta Vetrai and Ramo di Mula. Showroom staff let you handle pieces if you ask first, but wield large parcels and handbags with care to avoid glass mishaps. On sunny Burano days, you might glimpse local ladies tatting lace on brightly painted front stoops. The island's main drag, Via Galuppi, is, ahem, laced with lace shops – but look for a seal guaranteeing *'fatto a Burano'* (made in Burano), since much stock is imported.

MURANO

CESARE SENT Map p118   Glass
☎ 041 527 47 52; www.cesaresent.com; Fondamenta Vetrai 8b, Murano; 🕑 10am-6pm Mon-Sat;
🚊 Colonna
Amid the blitz of glitz along the Fondamenta Vetrai, Cesare Sent's matt-glass modernism and restrained palette of black, brick-red and deep purple stand out. Even the prices are pleasingly minimalist: sculptural matt-glass rings start at €20, and rectangular platters with amoeba-shaped *murrine* (glass insets; usually stars or flowers) start at €75.

top picks

VENETIAN HOME DECOR

- Campiello Ca' Zen (p168) Antique Murano chandeliers
- Atelier Alessandro Merlin (p173) Sea-creature cappuccino cups
- de Rossi (p172) Fishermen's lanterns
- Madera (p167) Teapots with scuba-material cosies
- Fortuny (p112) Wall coverings

LINEA ARTE VETRO Map p118 — Glass

☎ 041 73 68 56; Fondamenta Rivalonga 30, Murano; ⊗ 10.30am-5.30pm Mon-Tue & Thu-Sat; 🏛 Museo

Mounds of flaming orange beads and shelves of octopus-tentacle glass rings keep DIY designers and bargain shoppers enthralled at this collective of emerging Murano glass artists. Prices like these are how Murano glass collections begin: beads start at €30 and rings at €7.

OROVETRO MURANO Map p118 — Glass

☎ 041 73 66 78; www.orovetro.it; Fondamenta Vetrai 45, Murano; ⊗ 10am-6.30pm Mon-Sat; 🏛 Colonna

Not all Murano glass chandeliers require baroque ballrooms. These dramatic modern designs in black, red, and acid-green glass could turn studio bedrooms into boutique hotel suites and dens into swanky lounge-bars. Prices begin under €1000 for limited-edition lighting; architect-designed chandeliers with more waving arms than Kali hit five digits.

NASONMORETTI Map p118 — Glass

☎ 041 527 48 66; www.nasonmoretti.com; Fondamenta Manin 52, Murano; ⊗ 10am-6pm Mon-Sat; 🏛 Colonna

Unexpected asymmetrical shapes and striking two-colour combinations have been NasonMoretti's hallmark since the 1950s. Today, third-generation glass designers layer heavy crystal over neon-coloured glass for vases that look like isotopes trapped in ice. Prices start at €44 for signed, hand-blown drinking glasses.

RAGAZZI & CO Map p118 — Glass

☎ 041 73 68 18; Ramo da Mula 16, Murano; ⊗ 9.30am-5.30pm Mon-Sat; 🏛 Museo

The signature bullseye design here is an abstraction of traditional Muranese *millefiori* (thousand-flower) patterns, and bullseyes cluster by the hundreds into tiny oval plates and square steel-topped key chains; prices start at €38.

TOFFOLO GALLERY Map p118 — Glass

☎ 041 73 64 60; www.toffolo.com; Fondamenta Vetrai 67a, Murano; ⊗ 10am-6pm Mon-Sat; 🏛 Colonna

Classic gold-leafed goblets and mind-boggling miniatures are the trademarks of this Murano glass-blower, but you'll also find some dramatic departures: chiselled cobalt-blue vases, glossy black candlesticks that look like Dubai minarets, and highly hypnotic pendants.

EATING

top picks

What's your recommendation? www.lonelyplanet.com/venice

EATING

The visual blitz that is Venice tends to leave visitors bug-eyed, weak-kneed and grasping for the nearest *panino* (sandwich) or plate of *risi e bisi* (risotto broth with peas). But there's more to La Serenissima than simple carb-loading. For centuries Venice has gone far beyond the call of dietary duty, and lavished visitors with wildly inventive feasts. Europe's most outrageous dinner party was held in Venice back in 1574 in honour of Henry III of France, featuring 1200 dishes, 300 bonbons, and napkins made of spun sugar. Unless you're a visiting head of state, you probably won't be required to eat that much in one sitting in Venice – but you'll have your pick of vast, impressive *cicheti* (traditional Venetian bar snacks) spreads at happy hour, decadent pastries at Venetian bakeries, and hot chocolate rich enough for French monarchs and Aztec gods, at Caffè Florian (p199).

'Local food!' is the latest foodie credo, but it's nothing new in Venice. Surrounded by garden islands and a lagoon's worth of seafood, Venice offers local specialities that never make it to the mainland, because they're served fresh the same day in Venetian *bacari* (old-style bars) and *osterie* (pub-restaurants). A strong sea breeze wafts over the kitchens of the lagoon city, with the occasional meaty dish from the Veneto mainland and traditional local options of rice and polenta in addition to classic Italian pastas. But side dishes of Veneto vegetables often steal the show, and early risers will notice Venetians risking faceplants in canals to grab *radicchio trevisano* (bitter red chicory, a ruffled red leafy vegetable) and prized Bassano del Grappa asparagus from produce-laden barges.

Venice's cosmopolitan outlook has kept the city ahead of the locavore curve, and makes local cuisine anything but predictable. Don't be surprised if some Venetian dishes taste vaguely Turkish or Greek rather than strictly Italian: with trade routes bringing imported tastes to Venice for over a millennium, Venetian cuisine is a highly refined fusion of flavours. Spice-route flavours from the Mediterranean and beyond can be savoured in signature Venetian recipes such as *sarde in saor,* traditionally made with sardines fried in a tangy onion marinade with pine nuts and sultanas. The occasional exceptional ingredient from another part of Italy sneaks in, such as Tuscan fillets, Campania *mozzarella di bufala* (fresh buffalo-milk mozarella) and Sicilian blood oranges.

But no matter what's on the menu, many Venetians remain fiercely loyal to local wines. No Venetian feast would be complete without at least one *ombra*, or glass of wine; for best local choices, see the boxed text, p200. *Ombra* literally means 'shade', and the nickname apparently comes from wine stalls in the shade of the Campanile di San Marco where gondoliers once took breaks between fares. Lunchtime is a fine excuse to pop a cork on some *prosecco* (sparkling white wine), the Veneto's beloved bubbly, and start working your way methodically through the extensive seafood menu: tender octopus salad, black squid-ink risotto, and *granseola* (spider crab).

WHERE TO EAT

Bad advice has circulated for decades about how it's impossible to eat well and economically in Venice, which has misinformed day trippers clinging defensively to congealed and reheated pizza slices in San Marco. Little do they realise that for the same price a bridge away, they could be dining on *crostini* topped with scampi and grilled baby artichoke, or tuna tartare with wild strawberries and balsamic reduction. Luckily for you, there's still room at the bar to score the best *cicheti* and reservations are almost always available at phenomenal eateries – especially at dinner, after the day trippers depart.

Once you know what to look for, Venice becomes a foodie treasure hunt. To find the best Venetian food, get lost down side alleys and hidden *campi* (squares), and dodge restaurants immediately around San Marco, near the train station and along main thoroughfares. Beware any menu dotted with asterisks indicating that several items are *surgelati* (frozen). Lasagne, spaghetti Bolognese and pizza are not Venetian specialities, and when all three appear on a menu, avoid that tourist trap.

Look for places where there's no menu at all, or one hastily scrawled on a chalkboard or laser-printed in Italian only, preferably with typos. This is a sign that your chef reinvents

CICHETI: VENICE'S BEST MEAL DEALS

Even in unpretentious Venetian *osterie* (pub-restaurants) and *bacari* (bars), most dishes cost a couple of euros more than they might elsewhere in Italy – not a bad mark up, considering all that fresh seafood and produce brought in by boat. But *cicheti*, or Venetian tapas, are some of the best foodie finds in the country, served at lunch and from around 6pm to 8pm with sensational Veneto wines by the glass. *Cicheti* range from basic bar snacks (spicy meatballs, fresh tomato and basil bruschetta) to wildly inventive small plates: think white Bassano asparagus and plump lagoon shrimp wrapped with pancetta (at All'Arco, p188), or *crostini* with soft local salami and Tuscan truffled pecorino (try I Rusteghi, p182).

Prices start at €1 for tasty meatballs and range from €3 to €6 for gourmet fantasias with fancy ingredients, typically devoured standing up or perched atop stools at the bar. More-filling *cicheti* such as *panini* (sandwiches or filled bread rolls), *crostini* (a slice of bread topped with seafood or meats, vegetables and cheeses) and *tramezzini* (sandwiches on soft bread, often with mayo-based condiments) cost €1.50 to €4 if you eat them at the bar, Venetian style. For *cicheti* with ultrafresh ingredients at manageable prices, seek out *osterie* along side lanes and canals in Cannaregio, Castello, San Polo and San Marco, and check out our top picks for *cicheti*, p189.

the menu daily, according to market offerings. Timing is crucial: your favourite meals may be eaten standing up at 6.30pm, the moment *cicheti* are put out at many *bacari*, washed down with an *ombra* for under €15.

WHAT TO ORDER

Although increasingly fish and seafood are imported, many Venetian restaurant owners pride themselves on using only fresh, local market produce, even if that means getting up at the crack of dawn to get to the Pescaria (fish market; see p85). Eateries that make an exceptional effort in sustainable local sourcing are listed in the GreenDex (p299).

Timid diners who stick to tourist menus are bound to be disappointed – but adventurous diners who order seasonal specialities (see right) are richly rewarded, and often spend less too. *Cicheti* are fresh alternatives to fast food worth planning your day around, but you'll also want to treat yourself to one leisurely sit-down meal while you're in Venice, whether it's in a back-alley *osteria* (pub-restaurant) or canalside restaurant.

No one expects you to soldier through three courses plus antipasti and dessert, but no one would blame you for trying either, given the many tempting *piatti* (dishes) on the local menu. Consider your options. Antipasti (appetisers) vary from lightly fried vegetables to lagoon-fresh *crudi* (Venetian sushi) such as sweet prawns, or a traditional platter of cured meats and cheeses.

Primi (first courses) usually include the classic Italian pasta or risotto; one Venetian speciality pasta you might try is *bigoli*, a thick wheat pasta. Some Venetian restaurants have adopted a hearty Veronese speciality: gnocchi, small potato dumplings. Another tra-

ditional Venetian option is polenta, white or yellow cornmeal formed into a cake and grilled, served semisoft and steaming hot. As the Venetian saying goes, '*Xe non xe pan, xe poenta*' ('If there's no bread, there's still polenta'), a charming way of expressing a Zen-like lack of anxiety or concern.

Secondi (second or main courses) are usually a meat or fish dish. One common *secondo* is *fegato alla veneziana*, liver lightly fried in strips with browned onion and a splash of red wine – but if you're not an offal fan, you can find standard cuts of *manzo* (beef), *agnello* (lamb) and *vitello* (veal) on most menus. Committed carnivores might also try *carpaccio*, a dish of finely sliced raw beef served with a sauce of mayonnaise, crushed tomato, cream, mustard and Worcestershire sauce dreamed up by Harry's Bar (see p199) and named for the Venetian painter Vittore Carpaccio, famous for his liberal use of blood-red paint.

Contorni (vegetable dishes) are more substantial offerings of *verdure* (vegetables). For vegetarians, this may be the first place to look on a menu – and meat-eaters may want to check them out too, since *secondi* don't always come with a vegetable side dish. Go with whatever's fresh and seasonal.

Dolci (desserts) are often *fatti in casa* (house-made) in Venice, including tarts and cookies – but if not, *gelaterie* (ice-cream shops) offer tempting options for €1 to €2.

SEASONAL SPECIALITIES

Lagoon tides and changing seasons on the nearby garden island of Sant'Erasmo bring a year-round bounty to Venetian tables. Below are star seasonal ingredients in Venetian cuisine, and restaurants that do them justice in signature dishes.

Winter

Anatra (wild lagoon duck) Drizzled with wild blueberry sauce at Bea Vita (p190).

Fritole (sweet fritters) Get them hot from vendors around major *campi* during Carnevale (p17)and Festa della Madonna della Salute (p20).

Granseola (spider crab) A feast for the eye and the tastebuds when served atop beetroot tagliolini in the shell at Vecio Fritolin (p184).

Moscardini (baby octopus) Ideal in seafood salads at Pronto Pesce Pronto (p186).

Radicchio trevisano (bitter red chicory) Grilled as a side dish to a juicy steak at Ristorante La Bitta (p183).

Spring

Bisi (peas) Essential ingredient in *risi e bisi*, a risotto broth with peas often served with ham and parmesan cheese, and heartwarming at Enoteca ai Artisti (p183).

Bruscandoli (wild hop buds) Excellent in risotto as an inspired alternative to the usual *bisi* at Osteria La Zucca (p186).

Castraure (baby artichokes) Best when fresh from Sant'Erasmo, served tender and steaming off the hotplate at All'Arco (p188), with or without seafood accompaniment.

Moeche (soft-shell crabs) Devoured whole and lightly fried with a touch of sea salt, washed down with sprightly Soave at Anice Stellato (p190).

Summer

Peoci (mussels) Poached in white wine and served atop pasta at Enoteca Il Volto (p182).

Sardele (sardines) A legend as *sarde in saor,* Venice's tangy marinade with pine nuts, onions and sultanas, at Ristoteca Oniga (p183).

Sardone (anchovies) Served flappingly fresh with no trace of the usual oiliness at Al Fontego dei Pescatori (p189).

Seppie (cuttlefish) Swim in their own black ink alongside polenta at Osteria da Alberto (p190).

Autumn

Barbon (red mullet) Yields legendary *bottarga* (dried caviar paste) shaved atop pasta at Antiche Carampane (p185).

Canoce (mantis prawn) A highlight of the Venetian seafood platter at Al Covo (p192).

Capasanta & canastrelo (large and small scallops) Kicks up its scrumptious red foot atop black squid-ink pasta at Trattoria Corte Sconta (p191).

Sfogio (sole) Grilled to highlight delicate flavours at Trattoria da Ignazio (p186).

PRACTICALITIES
Opening Hours

If you have your heart set on a particular restaurant, call ahead to book a table – often you can get a table when you walk in off the street, but during high season, it's better not to chance it. If your stomach growls between official mealtimes, cafes and bars generally open from 7.30am to 8pm and serve snack all day, and some stay open late as pub-style hang-outs. Restaurants and bars are generally closed one day each week, usually Sunday. In this chapter, opening times are mentioned only where they vary substantially from the norm, as stated here.

Prima colazione (breakfast) is eaten between 8am and 10am. Italians rarely eat a sit-down breakfast, but instead bolt down a cappuccino with a *brioche* (croissant) or other type of pastry (generically known as *pastine*) at a coffee bar before heading to work.

Pranzo (lunch) is served from noon to 3pm. Few restaurants take orders for lunch after 2pm. Traditionally, lunch is the main meal of the day, and many shops and businesses close for two or three hours to accommodate it. Relax and enjoy a proper sit-down lunch, and you may be satisfied with *cicheti* for dinner.

Happy hour takes place from around 6pm to 8pm. *Cicheti* are served at the bar, and in some places can easily pass as a meal. See the boxed text, p179, for details of where to find the best.

The evening meal, *cena* (dinner), is between 7pm and 11pm. Opening hours for *cena* (dinner) vary, but many places begin filling up by 7.30pm and few take orders after 10pm.

How Much?

Restaurant lunch menus often cost the same as dinner in Venice, where most day trippers make a mad dash on lunch places but clear out before dinner. That said, many bars serve filling, gourmet *cicheti* at lunch and with *aperitivi* (predinner drinks). Between meals, pizza *al taglio* (by the slice) is a lacklustre option, since slices often sit out awhile and are hastily reheated – better to hang around until you can get a hot slice from the oven, or hold out for *cicheti*. Another alternative is to head to an *alimentari* (deli) where they'll make a *panino* for €3 to

PRICE GUIDE

This price guide is indicative only. We define a basic meal as a main dish, glass of house wine, and *pane e coperto* (bread and cover charge for sit-down meals).

€€€	over €40 a meal
€€	€20 to €40 a meal
€	under €20 a meal

€4, or you can assemble one yourself with foodie fixings (see the boxed text, p185).

For sit-down meals, most eating establishments charge a flat *pane e coperto* (bread and cover) charge ranging from €1 to €6. Factor in a service charge of 10% to 15%, possibly more for outstanding service.

SESTIERE DI SAN MARCO

Eating options in San Marco boil down to a simple choice: good food, or a view. Getting both is nearly impossible in San Marco, especially at a reasonable price – but you can always enjoy Piazza San Marco panoramas over coffee or *aperitivi* (see p199), then spelunk into San Marco's narrow alleyways for a delightful meal at an authentic *osteria* or romantic restaurant. For scenic canalside dining at more down-to-earth prices, try Cannaregio or Giudecca.

VINI DA ARTURO
Map pp68–9   Italian, Steak €€€

☎ 041 528 69 74; Calle dei Assassini 3656; meals €50-70; ⌚ 7-11pm Mon-Sat; ⛴ Santa Maria del Giglio

Everyone in this corridor-sized restaurant comes for the same reason: the steak, studded with green peppercorn, soused in brandy and mustard, or rare on the bone. Your host will happily trot out irrefutable proof that Nicole Kidman actually eats and that director Joel Silver managed to escape *The Matrix* for steak here.

SANGAL Map pp68–9   Inventive Venetian €€€

☎ 041 319 27 47; Campo San Gallo 1089; meals €35-50; ⌚ 10am-midnight Wed-Mon; ⛴ Vallaresso

Venice by way of Manhattan, with daring cuisine that rocks the proverbial gondola, magazine-ready leather and marble decor, and romantic lighting that gives diners a

certain glow…or maybe that's the food. The menu winks at Venetian culinary history with classic dishes like tripe with polenta, but raises eyebrows and expectations with Venetian wheat pasta stuffed with raw scallops and sea urchin and pineapple 'carpaccio' with olive oil ice cream. Dine under the stars on the terrace in fine weather, and line up for lunch specials.

VINO VINO Map pp68–9   Cicheti, Venetian €€

☎ 041 241 76 88; Calle della Veste 2007a; meals €25-40; ⌚ Wed-Mon; ⛴ Santa Maria del Giglio

Navigate the vast selection of *cicheti* and 300 wines with your server's help, or just ask your neighbours what they're having – it's that kind of place. Octopus salad and *sarde in saor* (sardines in a tangy onion marinade) are solid bets for light appetites, or get ambitious with guinea fowl and suckling pig.

DA MARIO Map pp68–9   Venetian €€

☎ 041 528 59 68; Fondamenta della Malvasia Vecchia 2614; meals €20-30; ⌚ Sun-Mon; ⛴ Santa Maria del Giglio

Squeeze in among the motley collection of fisherman's lamps, ceramic pitchers, watercolours, and the locals who made them, and make yourself at home with a generous plate of seafood pasta and wine by the litre. This classic *osteria* seems miles from tourist attractions and the 21st century, yet the Gallerie dell'Accademia and Palazzo Grassi are minutes away.

OSTERIA ALLA BOTTE
Map pp68–9   Cicheti, Venetian €

☎ 041 520 97 75; www.osteriaallabotte.it; Calle della Bissa 5482; meals €15-25; ⌚ lunch & dinner Mon-Wed, Fri & Sat, lunch Sun; ⛴ Rialto

Budget gourmets throng the bar, pairing each round of *cicheti* with a different wine by the glass – there are more than 25 on offer here. The dining room is less busy and tends to stick to basic crowd-pleasing pastas with seafood, though you might find an authentic plate of tripe if you're lucky.

CAVATAPPI Map pp68–9   Cicheti, Venetian €

☎ 041 296 02 52; Campo della Guerra 525; meals €8-15; ⌚ 11.15am-4pm Tue-Sat & 7-10pm Fri & Sat; ⛴ San Zaccaria; Ⓥ

A sleek charmer strong on seasonal *cicheti* and artisanal cheeses, wines by the glass, and that rarest of San Marco finds: a tasty sit-down meal under €10. Get the pasta or

VENETIAN DINING ETIQUETTE

Flattery never hurts, but you'll win over your server and the chef with these four gestures that prove your mettle as *una buona forchetta* ('a good fork', or good eater):

- Ignore the menu – solicit your server's advice about seasonal treats and house specials, pick two options that sound interesting, and ask your server to recommend one over the other. When that's done, snap the menu shut and say, '*Allora, facciamo cosi, per favore!*' (Well then, let's do that, please!) You have just made your server's day, and flattered the chef – promising omens for a memorable meal to come.

- Drink well – bottled water is entirely optional; *acqua del rubinetto* (tap water) is perfectly potable and recommended as an environment-saving measure. Fine meals call for wine, often available by the glass or half-bottle. Never mind that you don't recognise the label: the best small-production local wineries don't advertise or export (even to other parts of Italy), because their yield is snapped up by Venetian *osterie* (pub-restaurants) and *enoteche* (wine bars).

- Try *primi* without condiments – your server's relief and delight will be obvious – Venetian seafood risotto and pasta are rich and flavourful enough without being smothered in Parmesan or hot sauce.

- Go with local, seasonal seafood – no one expects you to order an appetiser or *secondo piatto* (second course), but if you do, the tests of any Venetian chef are fish antipasti and *frittura* (seafood fry). Try yours *senza limone* (without lemon) first: Venetians believe that the delicate flavours of their seafood are best complimented by salt and pepper. In lieu of lemon, try washing down seafood with citrusy Veneto white wines that highlight instead of overwhelm subtle briny flavours. Sadly, cod for the local speciality appetiser *baccala mantecato* (creamed cod) is now scarce, and imported cod from Norway is a less sustainable option. But on the bright side, locally netted shellfish and line-caught fish are delightful and more-sustainable alternatives – see Seasonal Specialities (p179).

risotto of the day, and the sheep's cheese drizzled with honey for dessert.

I RUSTEGHI Map pp68–9   Cicheti, Panini €
☎ 041 523 22 05; Corte del Tentor 5513; mini panini €2-5; ☽ 10.30am-3pm & 6-9pm Mon-Sat; ⚓ Rialto
Outstanding wine selections and *cicheti* featuring exceptional meats – boar salami, pancetta and velvety cured *lardo di Colonnata* that will win you over to lard. Ask fourth-generation sommelier/owner Giovanni to choose your wine, and he'll give you a long look to suss out your character before presenting a sensual Tocai or heady Refosco you won't find elsewhere.

ENOTECA IL VOLTO
Map pp68–9   Cicheti, Italian €
☎ 041 522 89 45; Calle Cavalli 4081; cicheti €2-3; ☽ lunch & dinner Tue-Sat; ⚓ Rialto
Join the bar crowd working their way through the vast selection of wine and *cicheti*, or show up early for a table in the snug wood-beamed back room for seaworthy bowls of pasta with clams with a DOC Soave, or thick steaks adrift in a puddle of juice with a sailor-size glass of Amarone (a robust dry red wine).

CAFFE MANDOLA Map pp68–9   Panini €
☎ 041 523 76 24; Calle della Mandola 3630; panini €2-4; ☽ 9am-7pm Mon-Sat; ⚓ Vallaresso

Panini (sandwiches) are the speciality here, with some inspired fillings on fresh focaccia including tangy tuna and capers or lean bresaola, arugula, and seasoned Grana Padano cheese. Stools provide sweet relief for tired feet if you plan your break around the lunch peak and happy hour.

ALL'ANGOLO Map pp68–9   Panini €
☎ 041 522 07 10; Campo Santo Stefano 3463; panini €1.50-3.50; ☽ 8am-9pm Sun-Fri; ⚓ Accademia
Picture your neighbourhood joint, only with a glass case stuffed with tempting *tramezzini* (sandwiches), chic orange-velvet booths, and an ideal position for people-watching on a buzzing piazza. Stick around for *spritz* (prosecco-based drink) around 6.30pm, when the local crowd arrives to unwind en masse.

SESTIERE DI DORSODURO

The most sociable spot for dinner, Dorsoduro has bustling restaurants on busy *campi* and sunny canals, and several excellent options within striking distance of the obligatory *aperitivi* in Campo Santa Margherita. When

GOURMET MEALS: SOME ASSEMBLY REQUIRED

Picnicking isn't allowed in most *campi* (squares) – Venice tries to keep a lid on its clean-up duties, since all refuse needs to be taken out by barge – but you can assemble quite a feast to enjoy on the terrace or courtyard of your B&B, rental apartment or hotel. For lunch with sweeping lagoon views, pack a picnic and head to Lido beaches or Biennale gardens.

Farmers' Markets

The Rialto markets (7am-3.30pm daily; Rialto) in San Polo offer superb local produce and the legendary Pescaria, Venice's 600-year-old fish market; see p85. For produce fresh from prison, head to Giudecca on Thursday mornings to the produce stall (041 296 06 58; Fondamenta de la Convertiti 712, Giudecca; 8am-noon Thu; Redentore) at Rio Terà dei Pensieri for fruit, vegetables and herbs grown by a cooperative in Giudecca's prison, with proceeds funding job retraining programs. In fair weather, there's also a produce barge pulled up alongside Campo San Barnaba, near Ponte dei Pugni – but a half-kilo is the minimum purchase, you may need to go elsewhere to get that single peach.

Groceries

Billa Supermarket (Map pp94–5; Strada Nuova 3660, Cannaregio; 8.30am-8pm Mon-Sat, 9am-8pm Sun) meets most grocery needs; but the deli selection is better at Coop (Map pp86–7; 041 296 06 21; Piazzale Roma, Santa Croce; 9am-1pm & 4-7.30pm Mon-Sat; Piazzale Roma) which has a branch at Campo San Giacomo dell'Orio. Another central option with a respectable deli is Punto SMA (Map pp78–9; Rio Terà della Scoazzera 3113, Dorsoduro; 9am-12.50pm & 4.30-8pm Mon-Sat; Ca' Rezzonico). For a wider range of fresh-baked bread options, try Mauro El Forner de Canton (p188), and check out the pastry purveyors reviewed in this chapter.

Gourmet Specialities

Aliani (Map pp86–7; 041 522 49 13; Ruga Vecchia di San Giovanni 654, San Polo; Rialto) offers exceptional cured meats, local cheeses, stuffed pastas, balsamic vinegar aged 40 years and *bottarga di muggine* (dried red mullet caviar paste) – and as a bonus, it will vacuum-pack food for travel. For spices, olive oils, nuts, sweets and other specialities from Venice's ancient spice routes, visit Drogheria Mascari (p170). Organic gourmets will appreciate Rio Bio (041 71 89 13; Campo San Giacomo dell'Orio 1628, Santa Croce; 9am-1pm & 4.30-7.30pm Tue-Sat, 4.30-7.30pm Mon; San Stae), which offers a small but select range of certified 'bio' (organically grown) blackberry jams, wines, dried pastas and more.

Wine

For a special toast, ask staff for suggestions at Drogheria Mascari (p170) or Millevini (p165) – but for uncomplicated Veneto table wine, you can fill up an empty water bottle straight from the barrel at Nave d'Oro, the wine dispensary with locations around the city, including in Cannaregio (Map pp94–5) and Dorsoduro (Map pp78–9).

ANTICHE CARAMPANE

Map pp86–7   Venetian €€

 041 524 01 65; www.antichecarampane.com; Rio Terà delle Carampane 1911, San Polo; meals €30-45; Tue-Sat; San Stae

Hidden in the once-shady lanes behind Ponte delle Tette (Tits Bridge), this culinary indulgence is a trick to find, and you may wonder who you have to, erm, know to get a reservation. The sign proudly announcing 'no tourist menu' signals a welcome change: say goodbye to soggy lasagne and hello to lagoon-fresh *crudi* (Venetian sushi), *bottarga* pasta, and *filetto di San Pietro* (steak with artichokes or *radicchio trevisano*).

OSTERIA AL DIAVOLO E L'ACQUASANTA

Map pp86–7   Venetian €€

 041 277 03 07; Calle della Madonna 561b, San Polo; meals €30-35; lunch & dinner Wed-Sun, lunch Mon; Rialto

Mementos climb the walls, recalling a time when the Rialto regulars were slightly less grizzled and the *bigoli* (wheat pasta) and *seppia in nero* (squid in its own ink) here were at the beginnings of their fame. There's always a wait for the cramped tables – meanwhile, blend in at the bar with an order of *nervetti,* or calf's tendon.

TRATTORIA ALLA MADONNA

Map pp86–7 Seafood €€

☎ 041 522 38 24; Calle della Madonna 594, San Polo; meals €25-35; ⏰ Thu-Tue; 🚶 Rialto

A classic restaurant a stone's throw from the Pescaria, with diners packed in like anchovies, waiters in white jackets and black tie expertly navigating narrow channels between tables, and a menu that hasn't changed much since the restaurant opened in 1954. Traditional seafood offerings range from straightforward grilled fish through seasonal specialities like *capelonghe* (razor clams) in a white wine broth to the more obscure *uova di seppia* (cuttlefish eggs) which tastes like sturgeon caviar.

TRATTORIA DA IGNAZIO

Map pp86–7 Italian €€

☎ 041 523 48 52; Calle dei Saoneri 2749, San Polo; meals €25-30; ⏰ lunch & dinner Mon-Sat; 🚶 San Tomà

Dapper waiters serve simply prepared grilled lagoon fish and pasta made in house ('of course') with a proud flourish, on tables bedecked with yellow linens and orchids. On sunny days and warm nights the neighbourhood converges beneath the garden grape arbour.

AL NONO RISORTO

Map pp86–7 Italian, Pizza €€

☎ 041 524 11 69; Sotoportego de Siora Bettina 2338, Santa Croce; pizzas €7-9, meals €20-30; ⏰ lunch & dinner Thu-Tue; 🚶 San Stae; Ⓥ

Manifesto or menu? At Al Nono Risorto, pizzas are listed alongside urgent action alerts: 'No abandoning animals!', 'More rights for gays and domestic partners!' Prices are left of centre, radical-chic servers can't be bothered with petty bourgeois orders, and on sunny days, all of Venice converges on the garden for squid with polenta, the bargain house *prosecco,* and cross-partisan bonding.

OSTERIA AE CRAVATE

Map pp86–7 Italian, Venetian €

☎ 041 528 79 12; Salizada San Pantalon 36, Santa Croce; meals €15-30; ⏰ 9.30am-4pm & 6-11pm Tue-Sun; 🚶 San Tomà; Ⓥ

A mosquito-motif tie loosened by a ravenous British entomologist is Bruno's favourite of the many *cravate* (neckties) hanging from the ceiling, all donated by diners in thanks for fresh pasta. Try the rustic handmade ravioli, and leave room for house-baked desserts.

ANTICA BIRRARIA LA CORTE

Map pp86–7 Pizza, Italian €€

☎ 041 275 05 70; Campo San Polo 2168; meals €12-25; ⏰ noon-11pm daily; 🚶 San Silvestro; Ⓥ

The former bullfight pen became a brewery in the 19th century to keep Venice's Austrian occupiers occupied, and even as a modern eatery it's still obsessed with grilled beef and good beer. Pizza is the way to go here, including such non-touristy versions as the arugula, *bresaola* and Grana Padano pizza. With room for 150, there's hardly ever a wait, and piazza seating is prime for outdoor movie screenings in summer.

MURO Map pp86–7 Pizza €€

☎ 041 524 16 28; www.murovenezia.com; Campiello dello Spezier 2048, Santa Croce; pizza €8-12; ⏰ noon-11pm daily; 🚶 San Stae; Ⓥ

Mellow at lunch, trendy at happy hour, and chic at dinner: this versatile restaurant/bar/pizzeria aims to please with inventive pizzas, seasonal salads that could serve as mains and an above-average selection of beer and wine. Grab a chair in the piazza, or duck into the snug, exposed-brick interior to canoodle in white-leather and striped-silk banquettes.

OSTERIA LA ZUCCA

Map pp86–7 Inventive Italian €€

☎ 041 524 15 70; www.lazucca.it; Calle del Tentor 1762, Santa Croce; small plates €5-10; ⏰ lunch & dinner Mon-Sat; 🚶 San Stae; Ⓥ

Vegetable-centric, seasonal small plates bring spice-trade influences to local produce: zucchini with ginger zing, curried carrots with yoghurt, and a sensational pumpkin flan. Rabbit with *prosecco* and herb-roasted lamb are worthy choices too, but local produce is the breakout star here.

PRONTO PESCE PRONTO

Map pp86–7 Cicheti, Seafood €€

☎ 041 822 02 98; Rialto Pescheria 319, San Polo; cicheti €3-8; ⏰ 11am-7.30pm Mon-Sat; 🚶 Rialto

Even Tokyo sushi chefs would be duly impressed by the perfectly composed bites at this designer deli across from the Pescaria, specialising in well-dressed seafood salads and artful *crudi* drizzled with extra-virgin olive oil that make the most of today's catch. Grab a stool and a glass of *prosecco* with your tangy *folpetti* (baby octopus)

VEGETARIANS & VEGANS IN VENICE

Even in a city known for seafood, vegetarians need not despair: with a little advance savvy, vegetarian visitors in Venice can enjoy an even wider range of food choices than they might at home. Several eateries designated with **V** in this chapter serve a good range of meat-free dishes at all price points. Self-catering is always an option (see the boxed text, p185) for vegans and others with restricted diets, but if you call ahead, specific dietary restrictions can usually be accommodated at restaurants and *osterie* (pub-restaurants).

Venetian menu highlights for vegetarians and vegans:

Primi The first-course menu of pasta, risotto and polenta usually includes ostensibly vegetarian or vegan options featuring such local specialities as wild mushrooms, artichokes, asparagus and radicchio. But even if a dish sounds vegetarian in theory, there may be beef, ham or ground anchovies involved in that rich stock. Ask your server to point out the best options – or better yet, mention your dietary restrictions when making your reservations so that the chef can plan accordingly.

Contorni As you'll notice at the Rialto markets, the Veneto has superb local produce. Seasonal specialities are heavily featured in local menus on the list of *contorni* (side dishes), including roast vegetables and salads that may be plentiful enough to pass as mains.

Pizza Although Venice is not generally known for its pizza, several worthwhile places are noted in this chapter. Vegans can ask for cheese-free *pizza rosso* (red pizza).

Pastries The neighbourhood *forno* (bakery) and *pasticceria* (patisserie) aren't just for breakfast in Venice – look for decadent selections of meat-free options at lunch and happy hour that include cheesy biscuits, savoury tarts and *pizzette* (mini-pizzas).

Cicheti 'Venetian tapas' include many vegetarian small plates, such as *bruschette* (toasted bread) with fresh tomato and basil and other seasonal toppings; *crostini* (open-face sandwiches) with gorgonzola and pear and other tantalising vegetarian combos; grilled, roasted or marinated zucchini, peppers, eggplant and other seasonal vegetables; and decadent fried snacks like *arancini* (fried risotto balls).

Gelato & sorbetto With the possible exception of savoury ice creams served alongside mains at Met (p191), ice cream and sorbet are generally meatless in Venice. Most sorbets are prepared *senza latte* (milk-free), and Grom (p184) and Alaska (p189) will gladly point vegans toward frozen desserts that are *senza uova* (eggless) and *senza miele* (honey-free).

salad and plump prawn *crudi*, or enjoy it dockside on the Grand Canal.

ALL'ANFORA Map pp86–7
Pizza €

☎ 041 524 03 25; Lista dei Bari 1223, Santa Croce; pizzas €8-10; ☻ Thu-Tue; ♨ Riva de Biasio; **V**
Head out the back into the courtyard to indulge in an enormous choice of generous, tasty pizzas over a beer. The crowd pleaser here is the namesake pizza all'Anfora, loaded up with local cured meats, artichokes and asparagus.

ANTICO PANIFICIO Map pp86–7
Pizza €

☎ 041 277 09 67; Campiello del Sol 929, San Polo; pizzas €8-10; ☻ noon-3pm & 7-11pm Wed-Mon; ♨ San Silvestro
Most Venetian pizzerias pander to tourists, but this wood-fired pizza joint is packed with a neighbourhood crowd – be prepared to lunge at open tables when you get the nod, and order decisively.

Basic options like pizza *margherita* (with basil, mozzarella and tomato) or sausage insult the chef's intelligence – go with anchovies, squash blossoms or whatever seasonal topping your neighbours are enjoying.

AE OCHE Map pp86–7
Pizza €

☎ 041 524 11 61; www.aeoche.com; Calle del Tentor 1552a, Santa Croce; pizzas €7-13; ☻ noon-2.30pm & 7-10.30pm Mon-Fri, noon-2.30pm & 7-11.30pm Sat & Sun; ♨ San Stae; **V**
Architecture students and budget-minded foodies converge here for a choice of 70-plus wood-fired pizzas and ale at excellent prices. Extreme eaters order the lip-buzzing *mangiafuoco* (fire-eater) with hot salami, Calabrese peppers and Tabasco sauce, while Palladio scholars stick with the classic white *estiva* with rocket, seasoned Grana Padano cheese and cherry tomatoes.

SNACK BAR AI NOMBOLI

Map pp86–7   Panini €

☎ 041 523 09 95; Rio Terà dei Nomboli 271c, San Polo; panini €3-4; ☽ 8am-8pm Mon-Sat; 🚊 San Tomà; Ⓥ

A snappy Venetian comeback to McDonald's: scrumptious, right-sized sandwiches on fresh, crusty rolls, well packed with local cheeses, roast vegetables, savoury salami, prosciutto, roast beef and other cold cuts. Sprightly greens are more than garnishes in these sandwiches, and condiments range from spicy mustard to wild nettle sauce. Two of these make a filling lunch for €4 to €5, and three is a proper feast deserving of a glass of Brunello on a stool at the bar.

ALL'ARCO Map pp86–7   Cicheti €

☎ 041 520 56 66; Calle dell'Arco 436, San Polo; cicheti €1.50-4; ☽ 7am-5pm Mon-Sat; 🚊 Rialto Mercato

Venice's best *cicheti* daily aren't on any menu: Maestro Francesco and his son Matteo invent them daily with Rialto market finds. If you ask nicely and wait patiently, they'll whip up something special for you on the spot – baby artichoke topped with shavings of *bottarga*, perhaps, or tuna tartare with mint, strawberries and a balsamic reduction. Even with copious *prosecco*, hardly any meal here tops €20 or falls short of four stars – might as well book your return ticket to Venice now.

DAI ZEMEI Map pp86–7   Cicheti €

☎ 041 520 85 46; www.ostariadaizemei.it; Ruga Vecchia di San Giovanni 1045, San Polo; cicheti €1.50-3.50; ☽ 9am-8pm; 🚊 San Silvestro

The *zemei* (twins) who run this corner joint are a blur of motion by 10am, preparing for the onslaught of regulars and the odd well-informed foodie tourist by 11.45am for first crack at *baccalá mantecato* (creamed cod) with green garlic shoots, *crostini* with silky cured lard and arugula *panini,* or gorgonzola with walnuts and a brandy reduction for adventurous vegetarians. Think past the usual *prosecco,* and wash it down with a rustic Raboso or sophisticated Refosco.

MAURO EL FORNER DE CANTON

Map pp86–7   Pastries €

☎ 041 522 28 90; Ruga Vecchia di San Giovanni 603, San Polo; pastries €1-4; ☽ 7am-7pm Mon-Sat; 🚊 Rialto; Ⓥ

A boutique of bread by the Rialto, with golden *grissini* (breadsticks), the ubiquitous

bovoli (snail-shaped rolls), crusty loaves for all your pressing *panini* needs, and for some fibre and a change of pace, wholegrain breads.

PASTICCERIA RIO MANIN

Map pp86–7   Pastries €

☎ 041 71 85 23; Fondamenta Rio Manin 784/5, Santa Croce; pastries €1-3.50; ☽ 6.30am-8.30pm Mon-Tue & Thu-Sat; 🚊 Riva de Biasio; Ⓥ

Pull up a chair along this sleepy canal and watch the occasional gondolier drift past, over freshly baked cheese biscuits, berry tartlets, and in the early evenings, a happy-hour *spritz*.

LA RIVETTA Map pp86–7   Cicheti €

☎ 041 71 84 98; Calle Sechera 637a, Santa Croce; cicheti €1-3; ☽ 9am-9.30pm Mon-Sat; 🚊 Ferrovia

Cabernet Franc comes out of a hose and platters of hearty fare are passed around at the favourite *bacaro* (old-style bar) of salty sailors and neighbourhood eccentrics. Go for mixed plates with thick slabs of salami, translucent sheets of *pancetta* (bacon), and grilled veggies with crusty bread. Angle for a canalside spot, or duck inside to admire the decor of bicycle parts and dusty bottles of English gin drained before the war.

PASTICCERIA RIZZARDINI

Map pp86–7   Pastries €

☎ 041 522 38 35; Campiello dei Meloni 1415, San Polo; pastries €1-3; ☽ 7.30am-8pm Wed-Mon; 🚊 San Silvestro; Ⓥ

'From 1742' reads the modest storefront sign, and inside you'll find the secret weapons that have helped this little bakery outlive America: killer cream puffs and dangerous doughnuts. Troll the biscuit section in search of wagging *lingue di suocere* (mother-in-law's tongues), suggestively sprinkled *pallone di Casanova* (Casanova's balls), and other *dolci tipici venexiani* (typical Venetian sweets) – but act fast if you want that last slice of tiramisu.

GELATERIA SAN STAE

Map pp86–7   Gelato €

☎ 041 71 06 89; Salizada San Stae 1910, Santa Croce; 1/2 scoops €1/2; ☽ 11am-9pm Tue-Sun; 🚊 San Stae; Ⓥ

Simple flavours are anything but at San Stae, where signature ingredients cover Venetian trade routes from Piedmont (Piemonte)

hazelnut to Madagascar vanilla. Happiness is in hand with a €1 vanilla cone, but heaven is €2 for a double with local pistachio.

ALASKA GELATERIA
Map pp86–7   Gelato €

☎ 041 71 52 11; Calle Larga dei Bari 1159, Santa Croce; 1/2 scoops €1/1.60; ⏱ 9am-1pm & 3-8pm; 🚊 Riva de Biasio; Ⓥ

Day trippers in San Marco may settle for vanilla ice milk, but Venetians head to Alaska for outlandish organic *gelato:* one glorious scoop of Venetian roasted pistachio, or a scoop of vaguely minty *carciofi* (artichoke) that sings when paired with a scoop of tangy lemon. The celery/peach combo may strike you as a smoothie gone wrong, but at these prices, you can afford to take culinary risks.

SESTIERE DI CANNAREGIO

Bars along the main thoroughfare between the train station and San Marco serve sandwiches, pastries and snacks, some above average for commuter fare – but for real meal deals, head down side streets to local *osterie* dotting Cannaregio's long *fondamente* (canal banks).

FIASCHETTERIA TOSCANA
Map pp94–5   Venetian €€€

☎ 041 528 52 81; Salizada San Giovanni Grisostomo 5719; meals €40-80; ⏱ lunch & dinner Thu-Mon, dinner Wed; 🚊 Ca' d'Oro

A classic that has long maintained quality, the Fiaschetteria Toscana has sought-after super-Tuscan options on the menu of 600 wines, but it's Venetian where it counts: the wild-caught lagoon seafood menu, especially the *crudi*, seafood risottos and *frittura della Serenissima* (a haul of lightly fried seafood). But you can also choose to rebel against the city's pescatarian impulses with proper cuts of meat, including lagoon game and Chianina steak that makes pampered Kobe seem tough. Leave room for Mariuccia's *rovesciata,* a Venetian take on caramelised-apple *tarte tatin,* and don't miss lunch specials.

AL FONTEGO DEI PESCATORI
Map pp94–5   Inventive Venetian €€€

☎ 041 520 05 38; Calle Priuli 3726; meals €35-50; ⏱ noon-3pm & 7-10.30pm Wed-Sun; 🚊 Rialto

top picks

CICHETI

- **All'Arco** (opposite) Bide your time with *prosecco* (sparkling white wine) while Francesco and Matteo whip up a *fantasia* of lagoon seafood and Veneto speciality produce.
- **I Rusteghi** (p182) *Panini* (sandwiches) and *crostini* (open-face sandwiches) with top-notch cheeses and cured meats direct from a dedicated butcher in Tuscany, with superb wine by the glass.
- **Osteria Alla Vedova** (p190) The bar is well scuffed by regulars vying for fresh meatballs for €1 and top-notch *crostini.*
- **Snack Bar ai Nomboli** (opposite) Rustic *panini* made with freshly baked breads, quality cured meats and cheeses, and crisp arugula.
- **Pronto Pesce Pronto** (p186) Lagoon seafood served with Japanese bento-box flair: try *crudi* (Italian sushi) with estate olive oil, white pepper and sea salt.

Garden dining is the prime seating option and the menu inspiration here, since chef Bruno takes wild herbs and local vegetables as seriously as he takes his seafood. *Bigoli* (wheat pasta) with cuttlefish and fresh mint, pasta with wild asparagus and clams, and prawn risotto made with wild hops are the seasonal dishes to watch for here, but any dish based on an exotic vegetable or sea creature you can't pronounce is a good bet.

TAVERNA DEL CAMPIELLO REMER
Map pp94–5   Venetian €€

☎ 349 3365168; Campiello del Remer 5701; meals €35-40; ⏱ Thu-Tue; 🚊 Rialto

Off the tourist routes and close to any Venetian foodie's heart, you'll find this vaulted cavern that opens onto a secluded square along the Grand Canal. Buffet-style lunches come fully loaded with *affettati* (Trevisana sausages and cured meats) and freshly made pasta for about €20. At dinner, abundant *primi* are served family-style with about a pound of pasta for two, and diners valiantly struggle to leave room for the grilled catch of the day and the obligatory tiramisu. Specials are recited rather than written down, and the sign says: *menú turistico non ghe xe* (there's no tourist menu). Book ahead, or brave the crowds for an *aperitivo* and *cicheti* buffet.

top picks

FOODIE SOUVENIRS

- Il Pavone di Paolo Pelosin (p167) For restaurant-reviewing notebooks.
- Aliani (see the boxed text, p185) Sells delicious *bottarga di muggine* (red mullet caviar paste).
- Cesare Sent (p174) Makes Murano matte-glass *cicheti* plates.
- VizioVirtù (p168) Indulge in *aceto balsamico* (balsamic vinegar) chocolates.
- Venice cooking workshop (p265) Take home newly acquired skills.

ANICE STELLATO

Map pp94–5   Inventive Venetian €€

☎ 041 72 07 44; Fondamenta della Sensa 3272; meals €25-40; ☾ lunch & dinner Wed-Sun; ⚓ Sant'Alvise; Ⓥ

If finding this obscure corner of Cannaregio seems like an adventure, wait until dinner arrives: pistachio-encrusted lamb fillet, wild sea bass with aromatic herbs, and perfectly fried *moecche* (soft-shell crab) gobbled whole. Sustainability isn't an afterthought here, with filtered tap water instead of bottled stuff, and seasonal menu highlights. Tin lamps and recycled-paper placemats on communal tables keep the focus on local food and local company – all memorable.

ANTICA ADELAIDE Map pp94–5   Venetian €€

☎ 041 523 26 29; Calle Priuli 3728; meals €25-30; ☾ Tue-Sun; ⚓ Ca' d'Oro

Dinner is served in the art-filled salon of a recently restored old Venetian home that's been serving food to neighbourhood crowds since the 18th century. Drop by for tea or *cicheti,* or stick around for a meal of €8 to €10 pasta, plus fish or such oddities as *arrosto di cuore* (roast heart). Service is variable, but the people-watching in this Cannaregio corner around happy hour beats dinner theatre.

AI QUATTRO RUSTEGHI

Map pp94–5   Venetian €€

☎ 041 71 51 60; Campo Ghetto Nuovo 2888; meals €20-25 ⚓ San Marcuola; Ⓥ

Watch the historic *campo* come alive over a plate of housemade gnocchi, pasta with squash blossoms and scampi (prawns), or *bigoli in salsa* (wheat pasta with anchovies and onions), with sidewalk seating at this pleasant ground-floor eatery under the Schola Italiana (Italian Synagogue).

OSTERIA ALLA VEDOVA

Map pp94–5   Venetian, Cicheti €€

☎ 041 528 53 24; Calle del Pistor 3912; cicheti €1-3.50, meals €15-40; ☾ lunch & dinner Mon-Wed, dinner Fri-Sun; ⚓ Ca' d'Oro

Culinary convictions run deep here at one of Venice's oldest *osterie,* which is why you won't find *spritz* or coffee on the menu or pay more than €1 for a bar snack of Venetian meatballs – best not to get them started about spaghetti Bolognese. Enjoy superior seasonal *cicheti* at strictly fair prices at the bar, or call ahead to claim a wood table that has weathered a thousand elbows in post-pasta stupors.

BEA VITA Map pp94–5   Inventive Venetian €€

☎ 041 275 93 47; Fondamente delle Cappuccine 3082; meals €15-30; ⚓ Guglie

The back-room eatery in this local bar is quite a find, with amazing specials like risotto with *anatra* (lagoon duck) drizzled with balsamic reduction and wild blueberries. Ask your host for wine pairing suggestions, and you'll be presented with several bottles at a range of prices from €11 to €40, all solid value.

OSTERIA DA ALBERTO

Map pp94–5   Seafood €€

☎ 041 523 81 53; Calle Larga Gallina 5401; meals €15-25; ☾ noon-3pm & 6-11pm Mon-Sat; ⚓ Fondamente Nuove

All the makings of a true Venetian *osteria* – hidden location, casks of wine, chandeliers that look like medieval torture devices – plus fair prices, seasonal *cicheti*, a crispy Venetian seafood fry, and a silky pannacotta with strawberries. Be warned: the kitchen closes early when the joint's not jumping.

DALLA MARISA Map pp94–5   Meat €€

☎ 041 72 02 11; Fondamenta di San Giobbe 652b; meals €8-30; ☾ lunch daily, dinner Tue & Thu-Sat; ⚓ Tre Archi

Go early or late to squeeze into that rare free spot between the elbows of dockworkers and university professors, and choose from a short daily menu of robust, no-nonsense meat-based cooking slapped down in front of you at bargain prices: €8 for a *primo* with house wine and coffee, or €14 with a *secondo* and vegetable side dish. Weekday fixed-price dinners run from €30 to €40 for seasonal specialities such as venison, duck, pheasant and lamb dishes, with the occasional fish and seafood option.

AL CICHETI Map pp94–5 · Cicheti €

☎ 041 71 60 37; Calle delle Misericordia 367; meals €6-10; ⌚ 7.30am-7.30pm Mon-Fri, 7.30am-1pm Sat; 🚊 Ferrovia; Ⓥ

Train or plane food would be an anticlimactic way to end your culinary visit to Venice, so stop by this *bàcaro* near the station to toast your trip with a glass of *prosecco* and the €5 menu of *primi* of the day – warming *pasta e ceci* (pasta with chick peas) or aromatic asparagus risotto if you're lucky.

LA CANTINA Map pp94–5 · Cicheti €

☎ 041 522 82 58; Campo San Felice 3689; cicheti €2-6; ⌚ 11am-9.30pm Tue-Sat; 🚊 Ca' d'Oro; Ⓥ

Talk about Slow Food: top-notch *cicheti* here are made to order on a modest hotplate, so pull up a chair on a barrel outside and enjoy some house-brewed Morgana beer while you patiently await fresh, seasonal bruschette piled high, and hearty bean soups.

OSTARIA AL PONTE Map pp94–5 · Cicheti €

☎ 041 528 61 57; Calle Larga Gallina 6378; cicheti €1.50-4; ⌚ 11am-3pm & 7-11pm Wed-Sun; 🚊 Ospedale

Early arrival, Venetian relatives and a magic spell might get you a tiny table at this red-doored pub 'al ponte' (on the bridge) – otherwise, join the crowd grazing on *cicheti* and sipping *ombre* at the bar. Go Fridays for well-composed bites of *crudi* or anytime for *panini* with decadently marbled salami, *crostini* with baby octopus salad, and other local, seasonal treats.

PASTICCERIA DAL MAS
Map pp94–5 · Pastries €

☎ 041 71 51 01; Rio Terà Lista di Spagna 150a; pastries €0.90-1.50; ⌚ 7am-6pm daily; 🚊 Ferrovia; Ⓥ

Early departures and commuter cravings call for flaky pastries near the train station, devoured warm with a *macchiatone* (espresso stained with milk): apple turnovers, *krapfen* (doughnuts) and the classic *curasan* (croissant).

SESTIERE DI CASTELLO

At the cutting edge of the city and Venetian cuisine, Castello offers extremely varied dining choices: casual *cicheti* at raucous neighbourhood bars and wildly inventive feasts in the city's most secluded, upmarket restaurants. After the high-concept concoctions that cross your plate in Castello, the Biennale down the street might seem comparatively bland – but unlike the culinary avant-garde elsewhere on the continent, Castello chefs never forget that food is meant to be savoured with gusto rather than studied for PhD theses.

MET Map pp100–1 · Inventive Italian €€€

☎ 041 520 50 44; www.hotelmetropole.com; Hotel Metropole, Riva degli Schiavoni, Castello 4149; meals €60-100; ⌚ dinner Tue-Sun; 🚊 San Zaccaria

Michelin stars don't mean much in Venice given that the last French critic Venetians took seriously was Napoleon, and he had armies backing him up – but you'll find locals who would not normally patronise a hotel restaurant concede that Met chef Corrado Fasolato certainly earns his starry reputation. Moonlit lagoon panoramas and mesmerising blown-glass constellations recede once the meals start arriving. Confident and playful takes on local game and seafood dishes include savoury pheasant canneloni and decadent eel-stuffed pasta that makes foie gras seem trifling; mains arrive with red wine and horseradish transformed into sorbet and *gelato*. Bring a hot date, a sense of adventure, and a fat wallet.

TRATTORIA CORTE SCONTA
Map pp100–1 · Inventive Venetian €€€

☎ 041 522 70 24; Calle del Pestrin 3886; meals €40-60; ⌚ 11.30am-3.30pm & 6-10.30pm Tue-Sat; 🚊 Arsenale

The Biennale jet set seeks out this vine-covered *corte sconta* (hidden courtyard) for imaginative housemade pasta and ultrafresh, visually striking seafood. Crustaceans are arranged on a platter like dabs of paint on an artist's palette, black squid-ink pasta is artfully topped with bright orange squash and tender *cappesante* (scallops) sticking out their red feet, and roast eel loops like the River Brenta on the plate with a drizzle of balsamic reduction.

LOCAL VOICE: EUGENIO ORO

Earth, water, fire Being from Vicenza, my tendency isn't to look only to the water but also the land for ingredients. In Vicenza, we use more meat, more herbs and earthy flavours than in Venice, where the cuisine tends to focus on fish, shellfish and crustaceans. But there's also excellent produce here year-round: even in winter, you'll find white truffles, squash and *radicchio trevisano* [bitter red chicory], and warmer days bring asparagus, aromatic herbs, currants and *castraure* [baby artichokes]. I like to bring those earthy and aquatic flavours together in unexpected ways – add the fire of the stove, and it's a kind of alchemy that happens.

The secret ingredient Passion is essential for a chef. The hours are long, and then there's the commute from Vicenza every day to Venice. I usually walk from the train station via the Rialto markets around 8am. We have purveyors that bring seafood directly to us, but I prefer to see what's at the market. By the time I reach the restaurant, I've got the seeds of ideas. At the end of the day, I'm usually catching the late train. I told my wife I'd try it for a year; that was six years ago. [laughs] But this isn't just what I do for work; you can't treat it like a factory job. People may only come to Venice once, just for a day, and if they choose to eat here, it's up to me to make it memorable for them.

From the Lido to lunch You don't need to look hard for inspiration in Venice. On a beach in the Lido, I came up with an idea for a dessert: waves of pistachio mousse atop a sablé biscuit that reminded me of golden sand. Only much tastier.

Chef and culinary alchemist Eugenio Oro, of Trattoria Corte Sconta (p191).

AL COVO Map pp100–1 Inventive Venetian €€€

☎ 041 522 38 12; www.ristorantealcovo.com; Campiello della Pescaria 3968; meals €35-50; 🕑 7-11pm Fri-Tue; Arsenale

All the markings of a classic Venetian trattoria – low-beamed ceilings, exposed brick wall, regulars installed in the corner – but with twists on typical dishes. Caprese salad gets the Covo treatment with basil and *mozarella di buffala* served with a heavenly cherry tomato gelée, squid-ink pasta with clams and squash blossoms, and Adriatic tuna with five sauces. Prices are understandable given top-quality, lagoon-fresh ingredients, and offset by reasonably priced, limited-production wine. Venice Marathon runners will appreciate the abundant €47 prix-fixe menu: *primo,* main, dessert/cheese and cover.

IL RIDOTTO Map pp100–1 Inventive Italian €€€

☎ 041 520 82 80; www.ilridotto.com; Campo SS Filippo e Giacomo 4509; meals €35-50; 🕑 noon-3pm & 7-11pm Fri-Tue & 7-11pm Thu; San Zaccaria

From an open kitchen the size of a closet comes a parade of tasty small plates: a dollop of savoury Tuscan bread pudding, Venetian *crudi* composed into a glistening mosaic, a silky pistachio flan. Mains are comparatively anticlimactic and pricey, but antipasti like the lobster-nectarine salad and inventive *primi* such as gnocchi stuffed with wild herbs make an inspired meal. There are only five tables, set close together, which makes reservations essential and haphazard service puzzling – but ever-present chef/owner Gianni Bonaccorsi is warm and attentive, and the decor of exposed brick and gossamer veils sets the scene for modern Venetian romance.

OSTERIA DI SANTA MARINA

Map pp100–1 Inventive Venetian €€€

☎ 041 528 52 39; Campo Santa Marina 5911; meals €30-50; 🕑 lunch & dinner Tue-Sat, dinner Mon; Rialto

Don't be fooled by the casual piazza seating and simple dark-wood interiors: this restaurant is saving up all the drama for your plate. Given the à la carte prices, you might as well go for the €55 fixed-price menu or the all-out adventure of the €75 tasting menu, where each course brings two bites of reinvented local fare – a prawn in a nest of shaved red pepper, black squid-ink ravioli stuffed with *branzino,* artichoke and soft-shell crab with squash *saor* (Venice's tangy marinade). Dessert is a must, especially housemade *gelati* and hot chocolate pie.

TAVERNA SAN LIO

Map pp100–1 Inventive Venetian €€

☎ 041 277 06 69; www.tavernasanlio.com; Salizada San Lio 5547/46; meals €25-40; 🕑 7-11pm Tue-Sat; Rialto

Modern without losing Venice's essential quirkiness, the seafood dishes are delicately handled here: go with the seasonal choice of scallops with thyme, pink pepper and saffron or housemade sea bream ravioli with a mint-pesto sauce, paired with the sprightly house pinot grigio. Low wood tables encourage diners to lean towards one another conspiratorially, amoeba-shaped lamps set the mood for free-form conversation, and huge windows let you in on the catwalk action outdoors.

ACIUGHETA ENOTECA

Map pp100–1   Cicheti, Italian €€

☎ 041 522 42 92; Campo SS Filippo e Giacomo 4357; meals €25-35; ☽ daily; 🕮 San Zaccaria; V
Never mind the pizza menu: why choose just one dish when you could go for a range of mini-pizzas, meatballs, *crostini* and other *cicheti* with a good glass of wine? You can stand at the marble bar with the locals, or if you come early or late enough, you might grab a designer seat in the exposed-brick back room amid the throngs of regulars.

TRATTORIA DA PAMPO

Map pp100–1   Cicheti, Venetian €€

☎ 041 520 84 19; Calle Chinotto 3, Sant'Elena; meals €20-30; ☽ lunch & dinner Wed-Mon; 🕮 Giardini
Even though this restaurant is opposite a park in the quietest end of the city, this place boasts *'dal pampo non c'é scampo'* (there's no getting away from Pampo) with reason – the *ombre* and *cicheti* are irresistible happy-hour lures. During the Biennale, flocks of American performance artists and German gallerists descend on outdoor seating, attack plates of seafood risotto and *polenta con seppie in umido* (with squid in a tomato-onion stew), and fly off to openings in a cloud of gauzy black crêpe.

CONCA D'ORO Map pp100–1   Pizza €

☎ 041 522 92 93; Campo SS Filippo e Giacomo 4338; meals €15-20; ☽ lunch & dinner daily; 🕮 San Zaccaria; V
Pizza is not a local speciality, in case you hadn't guessed from the cardboard pies you'll find at eateries pandering to the tourist trade around San Marco – but this place is the exception. This local joint right behind San Marco brought pizza to Venice in 1960, and has been slinging generous thin-crust pies with creative toppings ever since. They're not especially quick about it, so relax and enjoy the sun in the piazza and the Italian ska blaring on the stereo.

PIZZERIA ALLA STREGA

Map pp100–1   Pizza €

☎ 041 520 33 77; Barbaria delle Tole 6418; pizzas €7-12; ☽ 7pm-midnight Tue-Sun; 🕮 Ospedale; V
Late hours and dozens of creative pizza toppings are the secrets of Alla Strega ('the Witch') and its mysterious powers to satisfy picky eaters of all ages. With mod castle decor and a collection of witch dolls keeping a beady eye on proceedings, you might expect the back door to lead to Hogwarts Station – but instead you'll find an enchanting garden where you can keep cool while eating your Calabrian pepper–laced Inferno pizza.

BACARO RISORTO

Map pp100–1   Cicheti €

☎ 041 528 72 74; Campo San Provolo 4700; cicheti €1.50-4; ☽ Mon-Sat; 🕮 San Zaccaria
A shoebox of a corner bar just over a footbridge from Piazza San Marco offering quality wines and abundant *cicheti*, including *crostini* heaped with *baccalà mantecato*, soft cheeses or melon tightly swaddled in prosciutto, and even the occasional sushi.

AL PORTEGO Map pp100–1   Cicheti, Venetian €

☎ 041 522 90 38; Calle de la Malvasia 6015; cicheti €1.50-3; ☽ 10am-3pm & 6-10pm Mon-Sat; 🕮 Rialto
Beneath the portico that gives this *bacaro* its name, Al Portego is a walk-in closet that somehow manages to distribute *cicheti* and wine to overflowing crowds in approximate order of arrival. Reservations are necessary to secure a tiny table for sit-down meals of pasta with scampi or swordfish with a drizzle of aged balsamic vinegar.

PASTICCERIA DA BONIFACIO

Map pp100–1   Pastries €

☎ 041 522 75 07; Calle degli Albanesi 4237; pastries €1-4; ☽ 8am-8pm Fri-Wed; 🕮 San Zaccaria; V
Just around the corner from the Palazzo Ducale and down a narrow alley, Venice takes a turn for the decadent at Bonifacio with a selection of *pizzette* (mini pizzas), petit-fours, and traditional Venetian biscuits including *zaletti* (cornmeal biscuits with sultanas), topped off with Bonifacio's signature Americano cocktail (sweet vermouth, bitters, and soda).

AROUND THE LAGOON

A sunny day spent drifting around the lagoon only gets better with a leisurely island meal. You're in luck: first-rate options abound on Giudecca; Burano has its own destination restaurant; Murano offers sandwiches and *gelato* to refuel while glass-shopping; and Torcello and the Lido offer casual fare in splendid natural settings. But if you're touring the lagoon in low season between November and March, pack a lunch – many restaurants close then, especially on the Lido.

GIUDECCA

HARRY'S DOLCI

Map p112   Inventive Venetian €€€

☎ 041 522 48 44; www.cipriani.com; Fondamenta San Biagio 773, Giudecca; meals €80-120; ☽ 10.30am-11pm Wed-Mon Apr-Oct; ⚓ Palanca

The sun-washed Tiffany-blue sun canopy along the waterfront is the home away from home for the designer-sunglasses crowd. The service is low-key and decor retro (think bistro chairs and subway tile), though the prices have more than kept up with inflation. Still, for the €15 price of *dolci* (sweets) – about the price of Lido beach-chair rental – you could linger long enough to write novels with full approval of wait staff.

I FIGLI DELLE STELLE

Map p112   Pugliese, venetian €€

☎ 041 523 00 04; www.ifiglidellestelle.it; Fondamenta delle Zitelle 70, Guidecca; meals €20-35; ☽ noon-3.30pm & 7pm-midnight Tue-Sat, noon-2.30pm Sun; ⚓ Zitelle; Ⓥ

Declarations of love at Venice's most romantic restaurant are slightly suspect: are you sure that's not Pugliese chef Luigi's velvety, heart-warming pasta and soup talking? A creamy fava bean soup with chicory and fresh tomatoes coats the tongue in a naughty way, and the lagoon-fresh mixed grill for two with langoustine, sole and fresh sardines is quite a catch – though given the cuisine and waterfront views of San Marco, this is a surprisingly reasonable date.

MISTRÀ Map p112   Venetian, Ligurian €€

☎ 041 522 07 43; Giudecca 212a; meals €15-30; ☽ lunch & dinner Wed-Sun, lunch Mon; ⚓ Redentore

top picks

GARDEN DINING

- **Trattoria Corte Sconta** (p191) Stylish courtyard eatery hidden among ancient houses, perfect for escaping paparazzi.
- **Trattoria da Ignazio** (p186) A sociable scene under the grape arbour with attentive service.
- **Al Nono Risorto** (p186) The crowd gets raucous under the wisteria of this canalside courtyard.
- **Al Fontego dei Pescatori** (p189) Gourmets hold court in the shady courtyard over seafood and garden-fresh fare.
- **La Favorita** (opposite) Songbirds tweet for leftovers at this sunny retreat just off the beach.

Take an authenticity trip to Giudecca for seafood served over a gondola-building workshop. Shipwrights troop in from the boatyards downstairs around lunchtime for generous plates of briny clam pasta and genuine Genovese pesto, and toss back scalding espresso over predictions for upcoming regattas. Dinner features more seafood specialities, at more-up-market prices. To get here, look for No 211 on Fondamenta di San Giacomo, take the narrow passage beside it, and follow the Mistrà signs.

LA PALANCA

Map p112   Venetian €€

☎ 041 528 77 19; Fondamenta al Ponte Piccolo 448, Giudecca; meals €20-25; ☽ lunch Mon-Sat; ⚓ Palanca

Lunchtime competition for canalside tables is stiffer than the race for regatta bragging rights on Giudecca, but the views of the Zattere make *tagliolini ai calamaretti* (narrow ribbon pasta with tiny calamari) taste even better. At €6 to €8 for full plates of pasta, you'll be paying half what diners are paying along the waterfront in San Marco.

AI TRE SCALINI

Map p112   Venetian €€

☎ 041 522 47 90; Calle Michelangelo 53c, Giudecca; meals €15-25; ☽ lunch Fri-Wed, dinner Tue-Wed, Sat & Sun; ⚓ Zitelle

Belly laughs hurt after generous plates of pasta and seafood here, but that doesn't stop the neighbourhood from lingering over lunch in the garden, or date-night dinners with wine flowing straight from the barrel.

AL PONTIL DEA GIUDECCA
Map p112   Classic Venetian €€

☎ 041 528 69 85; Calle Redentore 197a, Giudecca; meals €15-25; ⏱ noon-3.30pm Mon-Fri; ⛴ Redentore

Asking for a menu here is like asking for one at your grandma's house. You'll have one of the three daily specials and like it – really – and by the time lunch is over you'll feel like you should offer to help tidy up.

LIDO DI VENEZIA

TRATTORIA ANDRI
Map p116   Classic Venetian €€

☎ 041 526 54 82; Via Lepanto 21, Lido; meals €30-40; ⏱ 1.30-4pm Wed-Sun; ⛴ Lido

While others tan the middle of the day away, foodies head for a leisurely lunch at this canalside restaurant. The menu focuses on simply prepared seafood: shrimp salad, grilled fish and a Lido-light *fritto misto* (fried seafood). Wash it down with well-priced wines and housemade sorbets, and see if you can make it back to that beach chair.

LA FAVORITA Map p116   Seafood €€

☎ 041 526 1626; Via Francesco Duodo 33, Lido; meals €20-35; ⏱ lunch Wed-Sun, dinner Tue-Sun, closed Jan–mid-Feb; ⛴ Lido

Spider-crab *gnochetti* (mini-gnocchi), fish risotto and *crudi* at non-celebrity prices helped La Favorita earn its name. Book ahead for the wisteria-filled garden, where songbirds refuse to be outsung by the ringtones of movie moguls here for the Venice International Film Festival.

DA TIZIANO
Map p116   Pizza, Cicheti €

☎ 041 526 72 91; Via Sandro Gallo 96, Lido; pizzas €6-8.50; ⏱ lunch & dinner Tue-Sun; ⛴ Lido; Ⓥ

Keeping it low-key on the Lido, this local hang-out serves decent pizza at fair prices, and respectable *cicheti* to a regular happy-hour crowd. If movie stars drop by, that can't be helped – this is the handiest pizzeria to the Palazzo della Mostra del Cinema.

MURANO

BUSA ALLA TORRE Map p118   Seafood €€€

☎ 041 73 96 62; Campo Santo Stefano 3, Murano; meals €35-50; ⏱ lunch daily; ⛴ Faro

Watch Murano-glass-mad shoppers rush past as you raise a glass to Lele, your host for extravagant lagoon feasts. Take a seat on the piazza off the canal and work your way through the seafood menu, from crispy, lightly fried *moeche* (soft-shell crab) to sea-bass ravioli in *granseola* (spider-crab) sauce.

GELATERIA AL PONTE
Map p118   Gelato, Panini €

☎ 041 73 62 78; Riva Longa 1c, Murano; snacks €2-5; ⏱ 9am-5pm Mon-Sat; ⛴ Museo; Ⓥ

Toasted prosciutto-and-cheese *panini* and *gelato* give shoppers a second wind, without cutting into Murano glass-buying budgets – sandwiches run at €3 to €5 and ice creams €2. Service can be slow at tables out front and in the back room, so if you're in a rush, order at the bar.

BURANO & MAZZORBO

TRATTORIA AL GATTO NERO
Map p121   Buranese €€

☎ 041 73 01 20; www.gattonero.com; Fondamenta della Giudecca 88, Burano; meals €30-40; ⏱ noon-3.30pm & 7.30-10pm Tue-Sun; ⛴ Burano

Once you've tried the homemade tagliolini with spider crab, whole grilled fish, and perfect house-baked Burano biscuits, the ferry ride to Burano seems a minor inconvenience – a swim back here from Venice would be worth it for that decadent langoustine risotto alone. Call ahead of the steady stream of visiting dignitaries and star chefs, and plead for canalside seating.

ALLA MADDALENA
Map p121   Game, Seafood €€

☎ 041 730 151; Fondamenta di Santa Caterina 7c, Mazzorbo; meals €30; ⏱ 8am-8pm Fri-Wed; ⛴ Mazzorbo

Just a footbridge away from the photo-snapping, lace-shopping crowds of Burano is a seafood oasis on the leafy island of Mazzorbo. Relax by the canal or in the garden out the back with pescatarian pastas or, during hunting season (autumn), enough wild game to satisfy Hemingway.

Open for lunch and *cicheti,* and for pre-booked group dinners.

TRATTORIA-LOCANDA AL RASPO DE UA

Map p121   Venetian €€

☎ 041 730 095; www.alraspodeua.it; Via Galuppi 560, Burano; meals €20-30; ☻ lunch

Lazy lunches alongside the piazza let you watch the lace-shopping frenzy from a safe distance, over a plate of delicate prawn pasta made in the sparklingly clean, hyper-efficient kitchen. Linger over *vin santo* and *essi buranelli* – postprandial spirits served with the classic s-shaped Burano biscuit. For a sleeping review, see p226.

TORCELLO

RISTORANTE AL TRONO DI ATTILA

Map p121   Venetian €€

☎ 041 73 00 94; www.altronodiattila.it; Fondamenta Borgognoni 7a, Torcello; meals €20-30; ☻ daily, closed Mon Nov-Mar ⚓ Torcello

Good cheer and great prices make this spot the pick of the four canalside restaurants lining the path from the vaporetto stop to Torcello's Santa Maria Assunta cathedral. Pull up a chair under the pergola in the charming garden and linger over *risotto di pesce* (fish risotto, €20 for two people). Like the other neighbouring restaurants, this place generally opens for lunch only, unless you book ahead for a group dinner.

ENTERTAINMENT

top picks

What's your recommendation? www.lonelyplanet.com/venice

When the siren sounds for *acqua alta* (high tide), Venetians dutifully close up shop and head home to put up their flood barriers – then pull on their boots and head right back out again. Why let floods disrupt your evening's entertainment? Archival photos from Venice's 1966 deluge show a gondola pulled right up to a bar, and the bartender casually serving the gondolier a drink in hip-high water. It's not just a turn of phrase: come hell or high water, Venetians will find a way to have a good time.

Visitors who stay to see the city unwind after a long day of entertaining day trippers get to know the Venice behind the masquerade mask. At concerts and lounge clubs, you'll see Venice hit its groove as a cellist digs deep for a Vivaldi grace note or a DJ scratches out a swaggering hip hop–Fellini mix. To really blend in and *Venexianàrse* (make yourself Venetian), pick up some Venetian dialect, cookery or painting skills in a short course. For feats of athletic prowess, try rowing standing up *(voga alla veneta)*, or exercise your vocal chords cheering on the local football team (they need all the help they can get).

To consider all your evening options, check out the Shows & Events insert in the tourist office's bimonthly *La Rivista di Venezia,* the monthly *VeNews* at news-stands and the free *VDV (Venezia da Vivere)* distributed randomly around the city and online. In winter many places close up earlier than in summer when the city's late-night venues, beach clubs and jammed events calendar make good on playwright and librettist Goldoni's famous Venetian boast: '*Semo a Venessia, sala! No ghe nasse gnente, e ghe xe de tutto; e a tutte le ore, e in t'un bater d'occio se trova tutto quel che se vol.*' (We're in Venice, you know! Nothing grows here, yet here there's everything, and at all hours, in the blink of an eye, you can find everything you want.)

DRINKING

No rules seem to apply to drinking in Venice. Happy hour from 6pm to 7pm? More like twice daily, from 11am to 3pm and 6.30pm to 8.30pm – plus a bonus round at 8am for hardworking fishermen. No mixing spirits and wine? Venice's classic cocktails suggest otherwise, including *spritz* made with *prosecco*, soda water and bittersweet Aperol or bitter Campari. No girly drinks? Tell that to burly boat-builders enjoying a frothy *prosecco*.

This makes knowing what to order where a little tricky. Price isn't an indicator of quality – you can pay €2 for a respectable *spritz*, or live to regret that €15 Bellini (ouch). If you're not pleased with your drink, leave it and move on to the next *bacaro* (old-style bar). Venice is too small and life too short to make do with ho-hum hooch. Most *osterie* (pub-restaurants) and *enoteche* (wine bars) sell good stuff by the glass or half bottle, so you can discover new favourites without committing to a bottle. Even budding oenologists should solicit suggestions from bartenders, who accept the challenge of finding your new favourite Venetian tipple as a point of local pride. Don't be shy about asking fellow drinkers what they recommend, either; happy hour is highly sociable in Venice. *Cin-cin!* (Bottoms up!)

Where to Drink

For a proper Venetian *giro d'ombra* (roving happy hour), start at 6.30pm at boozing hot spots clustered around the Rialto Market area, Campo Santa Margherita in Dorsoduro, Campo Zanipolo and Campo Maria Formosa in Castello and Fondamenta degli Ormesini in Cannaregio. If you're prompt, you might beat the crowds to the bar for fine Veneto wines for as little as €1.50 and get *cicheti* (snacks) while they're fresh.

For a selection of *osterie* and *enoteche* renowned for their food as well as their drink, check out p178. To line your stomach with coffee, pastry and pasta before you pour on the wine, check out the cafe-bars in this chapter, and skip cappuccino for a stronger, local-favourite espresso drink: *macchiatone* (espresso with a 'big stain' of hot milk). The historic baroque cafes ringing Piazza San Marco serve coffee and hot chocolate with live orchestras, which might help your heart rediscover its rhythm once you get the bill. But this is Venice, and a little decadence is always in order.

Opening Hours

Bars (in the Italian sense, ie coffee-and-sandwich places) and cafes generally open from 7.30am to 8pm, although some stay open after

VENETO VINO

Whether you're a certified cellarmaster or really more of a beer drinker, the Veneto is sure to surprise your tastebuds with the dazzling versatility and heavenly virtues of the lowly grape. Don't be surprised if you haven't heard of most of these Veneto labels or varietals before: many of the Veneto's best offerings head directly from the cellar to Venetian tables, and precious few are exported. Small-production Veneto wineries often can't be bothered with such external validation as the official DOC (*denominazione d'origine controllata;* quality-controlled) and elite DOCG (*denominazione d'origine controllata e garantita;* guaranteed quality) designations, because state-imposed requirements can cramp the winemaker's creativity – and besides, many of the Veneto's best vintners pre-sell their productions to Venetian *osterie* (pub-restaurants) and *enoteche* (wine bars).

Consider a Venice visit your golden opportunity to try wines you simply won't find elsewhere (see the boxed text, p200), and keep an open mind. Ordinary varietals can take on extraordinary characteristics in unusual Veneto growing conditions that range from marshy to alpine, so that Merlot could turn out to be the most adventurous choice on the menu. Try the wines we mention, but don't stop there – venture into Veneto wine country around Verona (p252) and Conegliano (p253), and let your tastebuds be your guide.

8pm and turn into pub-style drinking and meeting places. Pubs and bars in the nocturnal sense are mostly shut by 1am, though a few soldier on until around 2am.

SESTIERE DI SAN MARCO

Legendary cafes and bars make worthy splurges around Piazza San Marco, and cocktail hour arrives in style at snazzy lounges. Meanwhile, in the long shadow of San Marco's monumental attractions, espresso drinks are served in hidden garden cafes and DJs work the room with catchy dancehall beats.

AURORA Map pp68–9   Bar
☎ 041 528 64 05; www.aurora.it; Piazza San Marco 48-50; ⏰ 8pm-2am Wed-Sun; 🚢 Vallaresso, San Marco

Keeping Piazza San Marco up past its bedtime, this plucky venue takes over where polite *caffè* orchestras leave off around 8pm, with cocktails, local DJs and art openings. Aurora keeps a low profile during the day, doling out *gelato* (ice cream) and pricey *cappuccini* (cappuccinos) – but its €2 cocktails are the lifeblood of Sunday nights, and sporadic Thursday art events draw Venice's shy artistes out of their garrets.

HARRY'S BAR Map pp68–9   Bar
☎ 041 528 57 77; Calle Vallaresso 1323; cocktails €10-18; ⏰ noon-11pm; 🚢 Vallaresso, San Marco

Aspiring auteurs throng the bar frequented by Ernest Hemingway, Charlie Chaplin, Truman Capote, Orson Welles and others, enjoying a signature €18 Bellini

(Giuseppe Cipriani's original 1948 recipe: fresh-pressed peach juice and *prosecco*) with a side of reflected glory. Despite the basic bistro decor, this is one of Italy's most expensive restaurants – stick to the bar to save financing for your breakthrough film.

TORINO@NOTTE Map pp68–9   Bar
☎ 041 522 39 14; Campo San Luca 4592; ⏰ 8pm-1am Tue-Sat; 🚢 Rialto

Freeform, eclectic and loud, Torino adds an element of the unexpected to post-dinner drinks in otherwise staid San Marco. On any given night you can enjoy a €2 to €4 drink with a live band, a spontaneous college-student singalong or a DJ set of vintage reggae records.

CAFFÈ FLORIAN
Map pp68–9   Cafe-Bar
☎ 041 520 56 41; www.caffeflorian.com; Piazza San Marco 56-59; ⏰ 10am-midnight Thu-Tue Apr-Oct, 10am-11pm Thu-Tue Nov-Mar; 🚢 Vallaresso/San Marco

If the Torre d'Orlogio (Clock Tower) ever breaks, you can always tell the time by observing Florian's daily rituals, established since 1720: lovers canoodle over late breakfasts in plush banquettes until noon, uniformed waiters serve gooey hot chocolate on silver trays in lieu of lunch, and the orchestra strikes up a dance number to accompany the popping of *prosecco* corks and the illumination of San Marco's portal mosaics at sunset. There's a €6 music surcharge for piazza seating, so you may as well get your money's worth and tango.

ENTERTAINMENT DRINKING

top picks

VENETO HAPPY-HOUR WINES

- **Prosecco** The sparkling white that's the life of any Venetian party
- **Refosco dal Peduncolo Rosso** Intense and brooding, a Goth rocker that hits the right notes
- **Tocai** A dazzling, well-structured white worthy of Palladio
- **Raboso del Piave** Very James Bond – brash when young, brilliant with age
- **Amarone** A profound, voluptuous red: the Titian of wines

CAFFÈ QUADRI Map pp68–9   Cafe-Bar

☎ 041 522 21 05; Piazza San Marco 120; tea service €16-20; ⏰ 9am-11.30pm Tue-Sun; 🛳 Vallaresso, San Marco

Powdered wigs seem appropriate attire in this bodaciously baroque salon. A cafe since 1683, it became a Hapsburg hot spot under the Vivarini brothers during the 19th-century Austrian occupation. Venetians with long memories still veer instinctively towards the Florian, missing out on decadent desserts like baked ice cream and the €16 hot chocolate service with *panna* (whipped cream) and Venetian cookies. Reserve ahead during Carnevale, when the Quadri is packed with costumed revellers partying like it's 1699.

MOSCACIEKA Map pp68–9   Cafe-Bar

☎ 041 520 80 85; Calle dei Fabbri 4717; ⏰ 11am-midnight Mon-Fri; 🛳 Rialto

Minds boggled by a surfeit of San Marco splendour deserve a rejuvenating drink in this upbeat, unpretentious pub, where the bar is pieced together from broken tiles, tables are tucked under exposed-brick Gothic arches and a giant cartoon fly toasts your health on the ceiling. House specials are scrawled on chalkboards, but the guys in black T-shirts working the bar can recommend something from the range of wines, beer, cocktails and sandwiches.

PALAZZO FRANCHETTI CAFFÈ

Map pp68–9   Cafe-Bar

☎ 041 240 77 11; www.istitutoveneto.it; Campo Santo Stefano 2945; ⏰ 9am-6pm Mon-Fri; 🛳 Accademia

Only in Venice could directions to a cafe sound like a fairy tale: pass through the wrought-iron gate and the ivy-covered courtyard garden, step inside the golden Gothic palace, and tell the guard you're there for espresso. After a visit to the Accademia, this cultural centre's newly inaugurated cloister cafe is the ideal sanctuary from the crowds, admiring the greenery through glassed-in archways.

TEAMO Map pp68–9   Cafe-Bar

☎ 347 366 50 16; www.teamo.it; Rio Terà della Mandola 3795; ⏰ 8am-10pm; 🛳 Sant'Angelo

Sunny tearoom by day, sleek backlit bar by night, and full-time fabulousness. Arrive by 7pm for first choice of *cicheti* at the bar and lookers in the leather banquettes – this bar swings both ways, so there's something for everyone.

B BAR Map pp68–9   Lounge-Bar

☎ 041 240 68 19; Campo di San Moisè 1455; ⏰ 6.30pm-1am Wed-Sun; 🛳 Vallaresso, San Marco

Pose as glitterati for the night at the gold-mosaic B-Bar, where top-shelf cocktails are thoughtfully served with bar nibbles and a piano player plays softly so as not to upstage VIP guests like you. There's an entire menu of creative twists on the classic Venetian *spritz,* such as the bittersweet Rialto (*prosecco*, gin and a splash of grenadine).

BACARO Map pp68–9   Lounge-Bar

☎ 041 296 06 87; Salizada San Moisè 1348; ⏰ 9am-2am; 🛳 Vallaresso, San Marco

Good looks and smarts too: the bar at Bacaro is a shimmering mosaic oval that reflects well on you. The business-casual clientele in for an afternoon espresso gets elbowed out by the *spritz*-swilling literary crowd after events at Mondadori next door, and holiday romances, going very well indeed, drift in around midnight for a three-hour nightcap.

CENTRALE Map pp68–9   Lounge-Bar

☎ 041 296 06 64; www.centrale-lounge.com; Piscina Frezzaria 1659b; cocktails €9-12; ⏰ 7pm-2am Wed-Mon; 🛳 Vallaresso, San Marco

Under moody Murano-chandelier lighting, you might spot Juliette Binoche, Spike Lee, Charlize Theron, and sundry Italian moguls within these exposed-brick walls. Meal prices are high and the optional bodyguard service seems a bit much, but Centrale draws late-night crowds for mojitos, midnight snacks, chill-out DJ sets and occasional live jazz.

SESTIERE DI DORSODURO

Even in the dead of winter and the heat of summer, you can count on action in Campo Santa Margherita, Venice's nightlife hub.

The oblong, unruly square is edged with restaurants and bars, and it also hosts a regular weekday fish market, the odd flea market, and kids playing games invented on the spot. At happy hour the eclectic crowd includes students, hipsters, Biennale curators, and local residents. Nearby, a more strictly student crowd hangs out at a couple of popular bars along Calle dei Preti near the Chiesa di San Pantalon.

A legendary summer drinking option is El Chioschetto, bathed in sunshine on Le Zattere.

AI DO DRAGHI Map pp78–9   Bar

☎ 041 528 97 31; Calle della Chiesa 3665;
🕙 7.30am-2am Fri-Wed; 🚊 Ca' Rezzonico
'Permesso!' (Pardon!) is the chorus inside this historic *bacaro,* where the standing-room-only crowd spills out onto the sidewalk and tries not to spill drinks in the process. If you can squeeze inside, past the tiny wood-beamed bar, there's more seating out back, or just let the crowd carry you to tables outside on the *campo* (square).

CAFÉ NOIR Map pp78–9   Bar

☎ 041 71 09 25; Calle San Pantalon 3805; 🕙 7am-2am Mon-Fri, 5pm-2am Sat, 9am-2am Sun; 🚊 San Tomà
Morning brings the crowd that was here late last night back for espresso, only a little worse for the wear after all those top-shelf €6 to €8 cocktails. Architecture students, musicians and travellers converge for *spritz* in the *calle* (street), where the quickest way to start a conversation is to state any of the following: Calatrava is overrated, Albinoni is underrated, and *spritz* with Aperol is better than with Campari.

CANTINONE GIÀ SCHIAVI

Map pp78–9   Bar
☎ 041 523 00 34; Fondamenta Maravegie 992;
🕙 8.30am-8.30pm Mon-Sat; 🚊 Zattere

Good lungs and long arms are instrumental in procuring orders during Cantinone's cheerfully chaotic happy hour, when the entire neighbourhood descends for *pallottoline* (small bottles of beer) with *salame crostini* (open-face sandwiches with salami) and marinated artichokes. Students, gondola builders and Accademia art historians mingle on the quay out front, parting to greet the neighbourhood *nonna* (grandmother) and fetch her a glass of Soave.

EL CHIOSCHETTO Map pp78–9   Bar

☎ 348 396 84 66; Fondamente Zattere al Ponte Lungo 1406a; 🕙 7.30am-5pm Nov-Mar, 7.30am-1am Apr-Oct; 🚊 San Basilio
Down by the Zattere docks in front of Università di Ca' Foscari buildings, tables sprawl out around a bar kiosk that looks like a news-stand but serves a mean *spritz.* Slacking students keep the place busy year-round, but mid-May to mid-September is prime time for DJs, live bands and the occasional sunset party boat trip down the Giudecca Canal (including beverage €15).

IL CAFFÈ ROSSO Map pp78–9   Bar

☎ 041 528 79 98; Campo Santa Margherita 2693;
🕙 7am-1am Mon-Sat; 🚊 Ca' Rezzonico
Sunny piazza seating is the place to recover from last night's revelry and today's economic-crisis headlines, until the cycle begins again at 6pm with *spritz* cocktails and overflowing student crowds. Locals affectionately call this no-name joint *caffè rosso* because of its red sign, and it earns the nickname nightly with inexpensive *spritz* with a generous splash of bright-red Aperol.

IMAGINA CAFÉ Map pp78–9   Bar

☎ 041 241 06 25; www.imaginacafe.it; Rio Terà Canal 3126; 🕙 9am-2am Tue-Sun; 🚊 Ca' Rezzonico
Emerging artists on the walls, comfortable booths and a vast display of Aperol behind the bar attracts a steady creative, gay-friendly crowd that should probably start paying rent. Piazza tables are usually nabbed by locals and their little dogs, all basking in the sun and the admiration of passers-by.

TEA ROOM BEATRICE

Map pp78–9   Tea Room
☎ 041 724 10 42; Calle Lunga San Barnaba 2727A;
🕙 10am-6pm 🚊 Ca' Rezzonico
After a long day's sightseeing, Beatrice offers a welcome alternative to espresso

bolted at a bar. Rainy days are good for iron pots of green tea and almond cake in the Japanese-themed tearoom, and sunny days are for iced drinks and salty pistachios on the patio.

SESTIERI DI SAN POLO & SANTA CROCE (SANTA CROSE)

Happy hour begins at 8am at the Rialto, where fishermen who've been hauling in the day's catch since 3am are due for a drink by their version of midday, before heading back to their Pescaria posts to sling squid for chefs and slow foodies until lunchtime. Around noon, lawyers and artisans converge on backstreet *osterie* behind the Ruga del Speziali for *cicheti*, *prosecco* and an espresso chaser, adding a definite upside to the Venetian workday. By the time the sun dips below the lagoon, Venetians have reclaimed the Rialto from souvenir vendors and staked out their spots with a *spritz* or an *ombra* on the Campo Cesare Battisti and waterfront docks. To take your pub crawl off the beaten path, head to hot spots in San Giacomo dell'Orio or Fondamenta Rio Manin.

AI POSTALI Map pp86–7   Bar
☎ 041 71 51 76; Fondamenta Rio Marin 821, Santa Croce; ☽ 6pm-2am Mon-Sat; 🚊 Ferrovia

Jazz provides a backbeat to buzzing conversation until the wee hours, and local musicians have been known to break into impromptu jam sessions around midnight. Long ago, off-duty mailmen once had the run of the place – hence the name – but now the hipper half of Santa Croce vies for seats along the canal and an unconventional *spritz* served with an olive.

AL MERCÀ Map pp86–7   Bar
☎ 393 992 47 81; Campo Cesare Battisti 212-213, San Polo; ☽ noon-3pm & 4-9pm Mon-Sat; 🚊 Rialto

Discerning drinkers throng this upbeat bar for top-notch *prosecco* & DOC wines by the glass at €2 to €3.50, and scrap dinner plans in favour of *cicheti*, starting at just €1 for meatballs and mini-panini. Arrive by 6.30pm for the best selection of snacks and easy bar access, or mingle with crowds of stragglers stretching to the Grand Canal docks – there's no seating, and it's elbow-room-only at this little gem of a bar.

ANCORÀ Map pp86–7   Bar
☎ 041 520 70 66; Fabbriche Vecchie, San Polo 120; ☽ 9.30am-2am; 🚊 Rialto

Minimalist maestro Tadao Ando would approve of this chic bar tucked under the ancient porticos of Rialto waterfront ware-

---

GIRI D'OMBRE: THREE BOOZY VIEWS OF VENICE

Dorsoduro

The quintessential Venetian *giro d'ombra* (roving happy hour) starts at Cantinone Già Schiavi (p201) with an *ombra* (glass of wine) or *pallottoline* (small bottles of beer). Make a pit-stop for a mixed plate of cold cuts, marinated veggies, and cheese with a house wine at Osteria alla Bifora (p184) or head straight to a *spritz* at Il Caffè Rosso (p201) or Imagina Café (p201), all in Campo Santa Margherita, and by the time you arrive at Impronta Café (p184), you'll be ready for grilled polenta with mushrooms – and maybe a bracing espresso.

Rialto

The perfect *giro* for lazy drinkers, since all your hooch options are within a couple of blocks. Start at I Rusteghi (p182) for small bar bites and big full-bodied reds (don't even think about asking for a *spritz* here) served on low courtyard tables. Drift over the bridge to Al Mercà (above) for an *ombra* of DOC *prosecco*, pull up a seat in the piazza to linger over your next glass at Muro Vino e Cucina (opposite), then roll over to Sacro e Profano (opposite) before the last of the night's speciality pasta is dished out.

Cannaregio

Cover the waterfront bar-hopping all the way, starting with meatballs and a glass of the good stuff at the bar at Osteria Alla Vedova (p190). Head onward and upward along Rio Tera della Maddalena, through the Ghetto, and across the next bridge to Al Timon (p204) for some well-earned *crostini* and a sit-down *ombra* along the canal. Your next move is a tough choice: beer at nearby Osteria agli Ormesini (p204), or risotto and reasonable wines at handy Bea Vita (p190)? Experienced pub crawlers (you know who you are) already know their answer: both.

houses, stripped down to bare bricks and spiffed up with square iron tables for two, hidden on an indoor balcony. Jazz, Grand Canal views, *prosecco*, raw oysters, organic produce and modern romance are house specialities.

ANTICA OSTERIA RUGA RIALTO
Map pp86–7   Bar
☎ 041 521 12 43; Ruga Rialto 692, San Polo; ⏰ 6.30pm-midnight; 🚊 Rialto
Although seafood salads and the classic *fritto misto e pattatine* (lightly fried lagoon seafood and potatoes) – Venice's answer to fish and chips – earn this *osteria* (pub-restaurant) a loyal following, drink is the common bond at this place by night's end. The back room doubles as a gallery of local emerging artists, and the occasional live-music set fills the narrow alleyway with revellers all the way to the Grand Canal.

BAGOLO Map pp86–7   Bar
☎ 041 71 75 84; Campo San Giacomo dell'Orio 584, Santa Croce; ⏰ 7am-midnight Sep-Apr, 7am-2am May-Aug; 🚊 Riva de Biasio
Creaky wood floors and mood lighting indoors and candlelit tables outside on the *campo* adds romance from another era to leisurely happy hours on this picturesque square, aided and abetted by a couple of bustling hot spots around the corner on Calle del Tentor.

DO MORI Map pp86–7   Bar
☎ 041 522 54 01; Sotoportego dei do Mori 429, San Polo; ⏰ 8.30m-8pm Mon-Sat; 🚊 Rialto
Lurking surreptitiously behind the kiosk-strewn tourist thoroughfare to the Rialto is this backstreet *bacaro* that dates from 1462 but doesn't look a day over five centuries old, with gleaming, gargantuan copper pots hanging rather ominously overhead and incongruously dinky, dainty sandwiches called *francobolli* (postage stamps). Make sure to arrive early for the best selection of *cicheti* (€3 to €4) and local gossip (free).

EASYBAR Map pp86–7   Bar
☎ 041 524 03 21; Campo Santa Maria Mater Domini 2119, Santa Croce; 🚊 San Stae
Leave it to Venice to give the usual sports bar crossover appeal. The sleek bar makes

this the watering hole of choice for Università di Foscari architecture students, while bargain *ombre* (glasses of wine) for €0.90 and football matches on TV reel in the masses.

MURO VINO E CUCINA Map pp86–7   Bar
☎ 041 523 74 95; Campo Cesare Battisti 222, San Polo; ⏰ 9am-3pm & 5pm-2am Mon-Sat; 🚊 Rialto
No velvet rope here, though it's the kind of snazzy urban place you'd expect to find one, given the aluminium bar, sexy backlighting and see-and-be-seen picture windows. Prices are friendly too, with wines by the glass starting at €2, respectable cocktails from €5, and €1.50 to €3.50 *cicheti* at the bar. The upstairs restaurant is swanky, but low tables out in the *campo* are more happening than any VIP lounge.

SACRO E PROFANO Map pp86–7   Bar
☎ 041 523 79 24; Ramo Terzo del Parangon 502, San Polo; ⏰ 11.30am-1pm & 6.30pm-1am Mon-Tue & Thu-Sat, 11.30am-2pm Sun; 🚊 Rialto
Musicians, artists, esoteric philosophers and the odd nutter make the crowd at this hideaway under the Rialto exceptionally fun to be around over drinks. Once you're drawn into conversation, you may wind up settling in for a generous plate of pasta or chicken curry, or getting invited along to a ska show – the place is run by a former Venetian ska band leader, which explains the trumpets on the wall.

TAVERNA DA BAFFO Map pp86–7   Bar
☎ 041 520 88 62; Campiello Sant'Agostin 2346, Santa Croce; ⏰ 5pm-2am; 🚊 San Tomà
Named after Casanova's licentious poet pal Giorgio Baffo and lined with his explicit odes to womanly curves, this upbeat bar draws a chatty young crowd with respectable *spritz* and imported beer. In summer, arrive early to stake your claim on outdoor tables and the bartender's attention.

CAFFÈ DEI FRARI Map pp86–7   Cafe
☎ 041 524 18 77; Fondamenta dei Frari 2564, San Polo; ⏰ 8am-8pm; 🚊 San Tomà
Take your espresso with a heaping of history at the century-old carved wooden bar, or recover from sensory overload of I Frari with a sandwich, glass of wine and easy conversation at dinky indoor cafe tables.

CAFFÈ DEL DOGE

Map pp86–7   Cafe

☎ 041 522 77 87; www.caffedeldoge.com; Calle dei Cinque 608, San Polo; ✆ 8.30am-8pm Mon-Sat, 9am-1pm Sun; 🚤 San Silvestro

Sniff your way to the Doge, where hyperactive coffee connoisseurs slurp their way through the menu of speciality import coffees from Ethiopia to Guatemala, all roasted on the premises. The decor is more like a laboratory than a classic Venetian cafe and the looped video ad seems like hype, but these beans have earned an international following.

SESTIERE DI CANNAREGIO

Commuters and day trippers thunder down the Strada Nuova thoroughfare from the Rialto to the train station, missing out on some of the happiest hours to be had in Venice along the *fondamente* (canal banks) of Cannaregio. The Fondamenta della Misericordia sounds like an unlikely happy-hour hot spot, keeping less intrepid drinkers at bay and leaving more room among the locals at the bar and prime seats for live-music sets. Beer is Cannaregio's drink of choice, especially in summer, and in some neighbourhood bars you'll have your pick of imports and worthy local microbrews.

AL TIMON

Map pp94–5   Bar

☎ 346 320 99 78; Fondamenta degli Ormesini 2754; ✆ noon-3pm & 6-2pm Tue-Sun; 🚤 Guglie

Pull up your director's chair along the canal and watch the nightly parade commence. Paint-spattered bohemians join famished students and the stray Japanese hipster bingeing on *crostini* (open-face sandwiches) at the bar, and quality hooch keeps the evening nicely lubricated until the wee hours.

IL SANTO BEVITORE

Map pp94–5   Bar

☎ 041 71 75 60; Calle Zancani 2393a; ✆ 7.30am-midnight Mon-Sat; 🚤 Ca' d'Oro

San Marco may have his glittering cathedral, but here at the shrine of the 'Holy Drinker', there's your choice of blonde beers and red ales, canalside seating or indoor spots to watch the footy match on TV, afternoon internet access and the occasional live band at night.

OSTERIA AGLI ORMESINI

Map pp94–5   Bar

☎ 041 71 58 34; Fondamenta degli Ormesini 2710; ✆ 6.30pm-2am Mon-Sat; 🚤 Madonna dell'Orto

While the rest of the city is awash in wine, beer is the drink of choice here, with 120 mostly foreign brews. The scene spills into the street over happy-hour *panini* (sandwiches) – but try to keep the hilarity down a decibel, or the neighbours and management get testy.

PARADISO PERDUTO

Map pp94–5   Bar

☎ 041 72 05 81; Fondamenta della Misericordia 2640; ✆ 7pm-1am Wed-Sun; 🚤 Madonna dell'Orto

'Paradise Lost' is a find for anyone craving a cold beer canalside on a hot summer's night, with occasional live music acts. Over the past 25 years, Italian jazz great Massimo Urbani, troubadour Vinicio Capossela, and Keith Richards have played the small stage at the Paradiso. On Sundays, jam sessions hosted by two independent local labels alternate with local art openings.

UN MONDO DI VINO

Map pp94–5   Bar

☎ 041 521 10 93; Salizada San Canciano 5984a; ✆ noon-9pm Tue-Sun; 🚤 Rialto

Get there early for first crack at the fresh and largely unfried bar noshes – marinated artichokes and mussels if you're lucky – and a few square inches of ledge to help you balance your overflowing plate and glass of wine. There are 45 wines offered by the glass here with prices ranging from €1.50 to €4, so take a chance on whatever the bartender recommends.

ARDIDOS

Map pp94–5   Cafe-Bar

☎ 041 894 61 83; Campiello dei Fiori 2282; ✆ 7.30am-11.30pm; 🚤 Ca' d'Oro

As you might guess at a glance at these mist-coloured walls, exposed wood details, and sprawling octopus of a chandelier, owner Beatrice is a designer from Milan. The candlelit courtyard offers a suitably chic spot for sipping Veneto wines with a proper Milanese plate of salami and cheeses, but the real surprises are the superior selection of coffee from around the world and fresh fruit smoothies.

CAFFÈ COSTA RICA

Map pp94–5   Cafe-Bar

☎ 041 71 63 71; Rio Terà San Leonardo 1337; 🚤 San Marcuola

Sudden detours en route to the train station are caused by enticing aromas wafting out of this little storefront lined with burlap coffee bags. Since 1930, the Marchi family has been importing beans from Costa Rica and other speciality coffee locales, roasting them fresh daily on the premises, and grinding them on the spot to suit coffee connoisseurs.

SESTIERE DI CASTELLO

Around sunset, Castello converges along the waterfront and the Giardini for the *passegiato* (evening stroll), then disperses to the *campi* (squares) for *aperitivi* (pre-dinner drinks). Cafes in Campo Santa Maria di Formosa, Campo di Bandiera e Mori, and Campo Zanipolo become prime drinking spots by night – though for cocktails with views of islands and glowing Palladio monuments across the lagoon, you might splash out at designer hotel bars along the Riva degli Sciavoni.

BAR TERAZZA DANIELI Map pp100–1   Bar
☎ 041 522 64 80; www.starwoodhotels.com; Riva degli Schiavoni 4196; ☾ 3-6.30pm; ☲ San Zaccaria
Gondolas glide in to dock along the quay, while across the lagoon the white marble edifice of Palladio's San Giorgio Maggiore turns into gold in the waters of the canal: the late afternoon scene from the Hotel Danieli's recently restored balcony bar definitely calls for a toast. Arrive after lunch, and linger the

afternoon away over a *spritz* (€10) or cocktail (€18 to €22) – preferably the sunset-tinted signature Danieli cocktail of gin, apricot and orange juices, and a splash of grenadine. Drinks come with complimentary nibbles and the occasional celebrity sighting.

ENOTECA MASCARETA Map pp100–1   Bar
☎ 041 523 07 44; Calle Lunga Santa Maria Formosa 5138; ☾ 7pm-2am Fri-Tue; ☲ Rialto
Hang out by the outdoor bar for *cicheti* and an *ombra* of organic wine for under €10, or head inside for a €3 *ombra* and a €15 *taier misto* (platters of cured meats and cheeses) that could pass for a light meal for two.

L'OLANDESE VOLANTE Map pp100–1   Bar
☎ 041 528 93 49; Campo San Lio 5658; ☾ 10am-2pm & 5pm-12.30am Mon-Sat, 10am-2pm Sun; ☲ Rialto
Go home happily hoarse after another chaotic night at the Flying Dutchman, where study-abroad students mingle easily and laugh loudly with local eccentrics over cheap beer. Outdoor seating is highly prized, though you might be sharing it by last call.

OBILLOK Map pp100–1   Cafe Bar
☎ 041 528 46 39; www.obillok.it; Campo Santi Giovanni e Paolo 6331; ☾ 11am-8pm; ☲ Ospedale
Devastatingly handsome and artfully Venetian, with oversized baroque flourishes

---

VENETIAN DRINKING ETIQUETTE

Mind the signs At vaporetto stops you'll notice a posted warning that anyone strutting around town bare-breasted may be subject to a fine, which is actually an auspicious sign: any town that feels obliged to regulate public nudity is bound to be a fun place to drink.

Look sharp Obviously you don't have to worry about drinking and driving in Venice, but since many of the best bars are along slippery *fondamente* (canal banks) with no guard rails, steady footing and quick reflexes may come in handy.

Pay for the privilege Most bars reserve the restroom (*bagno*, pronounced *bon* yo) for paying customers, but not all places have one – when in urgent need, look for the 'WC' sign before you order. For free bathrooms, try fancy hotel lobbies.

Think on your feet Drinks at a table can cost twice as much as at the bar so, if your sightseeing schedule is ambitious, factor aching feet into your daily budget.

Tip accordingly For attentive service, you can leave small change on the bar as you leave, or add up to 10% to your bill at a swankier sit-down lounge.

Make way Once you've procured your drink at a busy bar, you can squeeze through the crowds by announcing 'Permesso!' (Pardon!) Grey hair has its advantages: anyone over a certain age gets first dibs at the bar.

Keep it down Since noise reverberates across cobblestone *campi* (squares) and narrow *calli* (alleys), try to keep it down to a dull roar.

stamped on the walls, Titian red chairs, and a sculpted-brass bar where beer is served in leaning glasses. Looks aside, the *macchiatone* is among Venice's best, and the mean *spritz* and sweet jazz pull in the crowds at happy hour.

PARADISO Map pp100–1 — Cafe-Bar
☎ 335 622 30 79; Giardini della Biennale 1260; ⏰ 9am-7pm; ☵ Biennale
Curators woo shy artists on mod couches and star architects hold court under sun umbrellas, even between Biennales. The scene is fuelled by a steady stream of coffee and cocktails that cost less than you'd expect given the designer chairs, waterfront location and lack of competition – this is the only cafe within reach of anyone in stilettos at the Biennale.

QCOFFEE BAR Map pp100–1 — Cafe-Bar
☎ 041 528 97 58; Fondazione Querini Stampalia 5252; ⏰ 10am-7pm Tue-Thu, 10am-9pm Fri & Sat, 10am-6pm Sun; ☵ San Zaccaria
One drink grants you access to two modernist master architects through the Querini Stampalia bookstore. Rainy days are right for hot chocolate in Mario Botta's neoclassical cafe, with white walls framed in black polished-concrete floors, and a harmonious repeating-rectangle theme. Outside, Carlo Scarpa's clever, Mid-East–inspired concrete irrigation channels bring Venice's canals indoors, adding industrial-cool to your *spritz* in the sunny garden.

ZENZERO Map pp100–1 — Cafe-Bar
☎ 041 241 28 28; Campo Santa Marina 5902; ☵ Rialto
Lightning bolts can scarcely compete with the eye-opening powers of Zenzero's espresso, paired with freshly baked profiteroles (cream puffs) and other treats that tend to disappear in a flash. If the caffeine jolt you've received here hasn't worn off by sundown, return for top-shelf *aperitivi* in the *campo*.

AROUND THE LAGOON

To enjoy leisurely drinks in style with lagoon views and the occasional sidelong glance at a movie star, a couple of swanky bars make the short vaporetto trip to Giudecca or the Lido worthwhile.

HARRY'S DOLCI Map p112 — Cafe-Bar
☎ 041 522 48 44; www.cipriani.com; Fondamenta San Biagio 773; ⏰ 10.30am-11pm Wed-Mon Apr-Oct; ☵ Palanca
The ultimate island retreat for the designer-sunglasses crowd, with the same classic cocktails as sibling venture Harry's Bar, served under a Tiffany-blue sun canopy along the Giudecca Canal. Service is low-key and the indoor cafe is paved with what looks like vintage subway tile, so don't go expecting luxury – but you're welcome to luxuriate in the sun over house-made *dolci* (sweets) and coffee (€15) until an idea for your next brilliant novel strikes you.

COLONY BAR Map p116 — Lounge
☎ 041 526 59 21; Hotel Des Bains, Lungomare Marconi 17; ⏰ 9am-1am daily; ☵ Lido
Ah, this is Lido living: celeb-spotting and cocktails on a historic 1900 *stile liberty* (Liberty style) veranda elegantly secluded by maritime pines. Your drink tab will easily match your beach cabana rental for the day, but you'll enjoy five-star perks – fawning service, top-shelf hooch, even lobby wi-fi access – without paying the room rate.

NIGHTLIFE
CLUBBING

In central Venice, every footstep reverberates along the *calle* (alleyway), and noise restrictions nix any hope of a dance-club scene – though you might luck into the occasional 'Silent Night' rave in the Campo San Polo, where crowds dance in apparent silence to special playlists downloaded to their MP3 players. Things look up in summer, when beach clubs open on the Lido, and half a dozen bars erupt into action at Jesolo, about an hour's drive northeast of Venice. (Jesolo is commonly called Lido di Jesolo (p254), not to be confused with the nearby Venetian island of Lido di Venezia.) For club entry, expect to pay anything from €5 to €20, which may include the first drink.

Getting to Jesolo by public transit is easy enough: ATVO bus 10a from Piazzale Roma takes about 70 minutes to Jesolo, and costs €3.80 (return €6.70). The problem is getting back – the last bus usually leaves at 11.20pm in summer. If you find a taxi, you are looking at €80 or more, depending on traffic.

To reach clubs located away from the town and main beach, factor a local taxi into your night-out budget.

Mestre and a couple of small towns on the mainland also have a handful of clubs and community centres with live music and DJs. Most are in far-flung parts of the city most easily accessible by car, though night buses do run sporadically from Mestre to Venice. Otherwise, you're at the mercy of Mestre taxis.

AURORA BEACH CLUB Map p116
☎ 335 526 80 13; www.aurora.st; Piazzale Bucintoro, Lungomare D'Annunzio 20x, Lido; ⏰ 9am-2am, May–mid-Sep; 🚢 Lido

After a taxing day unwinding on a Lido lounge chair, there's nothing better than unwinding on a four-poster beach bed. At this bold beach venue, days flow into nights with a parade of diversions: a free library of books and magazines, designated beach sport and chill-out zones, live music sets, cocktail bars, open-air cinema and weekend DJ sets that will keep you on the dance floor until you face-plant on the sofa.

IL MURETTO
☎ 393 410 11 20; www.ilmuretto.net, in Italian; Via Roma Destra 120d, Lido di Jesolo; admission from €20; ⏰ 11pm-4am Wed & Fri-Sun Apr-Sep; bus 10a, taxi

An army of DJs spins mostly house music at one of the hippest summer dance locales set inland from Jesolo and the beach (you will need a car or taxi to get here). Word gets around about events being held here; flyers can be seen floating around bars from Venice to Padua. Club-hoppers will find other hot spots located on the same road, but those who party late at Muretto get to watch dawn arrive through the open roof.

MARINA CLUB
☎ 0421 37 06 45; www.marinaclubjesolo.com, in Italian; Via Roma Destra 120b, Lido di Jesolo; admission free; ⏰ 8pm-4am Apr; bus 10a, taxi

Breezy gazebos and candles set the scene for summertime patio parties at the Marina Club, which isn't actually on the waterfront; it's near a canal and just down the road from Il Muretto. This club is a sprawling estate with multiple lounges, gardens, restaurants, occasional live music acts and weekend DJ sets that coax sun-bronzed crowds off their lounges. Entry is free but dress stylishly to pass bouncer scrutiny around midnight.

TERRAZZAMARE
☎ 0421 37 00 12; www.terrazzamare.com, in Italian; Vicolo Faro 1, Lido di Jesolo; admission €15; ⏰ 6pm-4am Tue-Sat Apr-Jun, nightly Jul-Sep; bus 10a, taxi

All the style you'd expect from an Italian beach club, with bronzed regulars in enormous glasses sprawled on lipstick red designer club chairs well past sunset and matched pairs of pale Biennale-goers making out behind art installations. With open cabanas on a raised platform, dance scenes on the sand below and occasional DJ duels, the Terazza earns its claim to fame as a 'theatre-bar'.

KNOW BEFORE YOU GO
To see what's next on the bill in Venice, check out these handy websites:
- APT (www.comune.venezia.it) Venice's official tourism website offers listings and discounted online bookings through the Venice Connected service.
- A Guest in Venice (www.aguestinvenice.com) Hotelier association provides information on upcoming exhibits, events, and lectures.
- Agenda Venezia (www.agendavenezia.org) Venice's cultural foundation lists all events happening in Venice on any given day.
- Biennale di Venezia (www.labiennale.org) The official biennale website has programmes for the art and architectures showcases and Venice Film Festival premieres, plus additional Biennale-supported theatre, dance and performances.
- Venezia da Vivere (www.veneziadavivere.com) A savvy insiders' selection of upcoming music performances, film screenings, nightlife and more.
- Music in Venice (www.musicinvenice.com) A thorough programme of upcoming concerts by Venice's most acclaimed and established music groups, with a secure online booking service.

ULTIMA SPIAGGIA DI PACHUKA
Off Map p116

☎ 348 396 84 66; Spiagga San Nicolò, Lido;
🚊 San Nicolò

Between planned development work and Mose barrier construction, summer beach party nights are becoming more sporadic at this legendary 'Last Beach' on the far side of the Lido, with word of free live music events and late-night DJ sets passing via flyer and word of mouth – but that only makes them worth finding. Keep an eye out for flyers around Campo Santa Margherita, and ask what's happening at Pachuka.

CASINOS

Fortunes have been won and entire empires lost for centuries in Venice's *ridotti* (gambling houses). Try your luck if you dare, as long as you're at least 18 years old – they do check identification.

CASINÒ DI VENEZIA Map pp94–5

☎ 041 529 71 11; www.casinovenezia.it; Palazzo Vendramin-Calergi 2040, Cannaregio; admission €5, with €10 gambling token & discounted parking at Piazzale Roma €10; ⌚ 3pm-2.30am Sun-Thu, 3pm-3am Fri & Sat; 🚊 San Marcuola

No opera can match the drama that's been unfolding at Venice's gaming tables since the 16th century: Richard Wagner survived the 20-year effort composing his stormy Ring cycle only to expire at the Casino in 1883. To take on the high-stakes tables here, jackets are required and strong constitutions advisable. Wagner's rooms have been turned into a museum, but the real draws here are the roulette wheels and marathon blackjack sessions. Hotel guests can usually get a coupon for free entry from their concierge, and a free shuttle ferry runs every 10 or so minutes between the Casinò di Venezia and a stop on the Grand Canal, located near Piazzale Roma (see Map pp86–7).

VENICE CASINO off Map p64

☎ 041 529 71 11; www.casinovenezia.it; Ca' Noghera, Via Triestina 222, Tessera; admission €5, with €10 gambling token €10; ⌚ 11am-2.30am Sun-Thu, 11am-3am Fri & Sat

Caribbean poker, slot machines, and 'American-style games' are the draw at this casual casino, where there's no dress code and even the winners seem low-key.

This sprawling casino is located near the airport, and has roughly an airport's worth of charm.

THE ARTS

In Venice, you can purchase tickets for concerts, theatre, and other major arts events at HelloVenezia ticket outlets (☎ 041 24 24; www.hellovenezia.it), located near key vaporetto stops and ACTV public-transport ticket points. For blockbuster events like the Biennale or La Fenice operas, you'll need to book ahead online at the appropriate website or www.vivaticket.it – though you might luck into last-minute discounts at Weekend a Venezia (http://en.venezia.waf.it).

MUSIC

Never mind the costumed hawkers sheepishly sporting knee breeches and drumming up opera business in front of the Accademia – Venice's music scene is vital and varied, ranging from Vivaldi played with radical verve to improvised jazz that swerves into bossa nova. Venice is the place to hear baroque music and opera in their original and intended venues, with notes reverberating in the frescoed Ospedaletto (p107), soaring to Tiepolo ceilings in Grand Canal palaces such as the Ca' Rezzonico (p80) and filling the salon at Casa di Goldoni (p90). Music becomes a religious experience surrounded by Venetian art masterpieces in Venetian churches, and you might even luck into a concert at the Basilica di San Marco (p65).

A handful of eateries and bars sporadically host live music, usually jazz, blues, reggae and *leggera* (pop). Bars with musical interludes include Paradiso Perduto (p204), El Chioschetto (p201), Torino@Notte (p199), Il Santo Bevitore (p204), and Antica Osteria Ruga Rialto (p203). But don't expect to roll in late and still catch the show: according to local noise regulations, bars are supposed to end concerts at 11pm.

In summer, occasional concerts are organised in Jesolo – watch the local press especially in July and August, when international acts like Franz Ferdinand sometimes show up to perform free beach concerts. In Mestre's Forte Marghera area, the big annual draw is Marghera Estate Village (www.villagestate.it, in Italian), a programme of nightly live music from June through August that recently featured Venetian salsa by BatistoCoco, Venice's own Ska-J, twangy Veneto country and bluegrass bands, and the obligatory Madonna, Beatles and Bob Dylan tribute bands with Venetian accents.

Tickets for classical and baroque music concerts can usually be purchased in advance online at musicinvenice.com, at Hello-Venezia ticket outlets (☎ 041 24 24; www.hellovenezia .it) and may also be purchased in advance at the venue. For jazz and other live-music gigs, you generally pay at the door. Bigger concerts are sometimes held at the PalaGalileo concert hall (Map p116) behind the Palazzo della Mostra del Cinema on the Lido.

COLLEGIUM DUCALE Map pp100–1

☎ 041 98 42 52; www.collegiumducale.com, in Italian; Palazzo delle Prigioni; adult/student & senior €25/20; ☺ shows start 9pm; ⚑ San Zaccaria
Spend a perfectly enjoyable evening in prison with this six-member chamber orchestra, whose grace notes in Bach and Albinoni performances escape through the high, barred windows of the converted cell. Opera singers occasionally perform arias with the group, which can get loud in the reverberating stone chamber; ears not trained by blasting MP3 players might prefer concerts in nearby Chiesa di Santa Maria Formosa (p109), where the acoustics are kinder.

INTERPRETI VENEZIANI Map pp68–9

☎ 041 277 05 61; www.interpretiveneziani.com; Chiesa di San Vidal 2862, San Marco; adult/student €24/19; ☺ doors open 8.30pm ⚑ Accademia
Everything you knew about Vivaldi from elevators and mobile ring-tones is proved fantastically wrong by Interpreti Veneziani, which plays Vivaldi on 18th-century instruments as a soundtrack for living in this city of intrigue – you'll never listen to *The Four Seasons* again without hearing summer storms gathering over the lagoon, or echoing footsteps hurrying over footbridges to a late-night winter rendezvous.

LABORATORIO OCCUPATO MORION

Map pp100–1
☎ 041 520 84 37; http://morion.samizdat.net; Calle di Morion 2951; ☺ 9pm-1am Wed, 9pm-2am Fri & Sat; ⚑ Celestia
When not busy staging alternative art biennales or environmental protests to the Mose project, this counter-culture social centre throws one hell of a dance party, with performances by bands from around the Veneto. Events are announced on the blog (in Italian) and, in situationist fashion, with wheat-paste posters thrown up around town.

VENICE JAZZ CLUB Map pp78–9

☎ 041 523 20 56; www.venicejazzclub.com; Ponte dei Pugni 3102, Dorsoduro; admission incl first drink €20; ☺ doors 7pm, set begins 9pm, closed Aug; ⚑ Ca' Rezzonico
Jazz is alive and swinging in Dorsoduro, where the resident Venice Jazz Club Quartet improvises funky tributes to Miles Davis and Charles Mingus and grooves on Italian jazz standards. Drinks are steep, so starving artists booze beforehand and arrive by 8pm to pounce on free cold-cut platters.

THEATRE, OPERA & DANCE

Venice is the home of modern opera and the legendary, incendiary Teatro La Fenice, one of the world's great opera houses. Theatre and dance performances are staged year-round, but especially in summer, during Biennales, and during the International Festival of Contemporary Dance, usually held the first two weeks in June – for listings and venues, check out the Biennale website (www.labiennale .org).

Advance ticket sales are often available at HelloVenezia ticket outlets (☎ 041 24 24; www.hello venezia.it), online or by phone from the theatre, or at the theatre box office one hour before the show.

MUSICA A PALAZZO Map pp68–9   Opera

☎ 340 971 72 72; www.musicapalazzo.com; Fondamenta Barbarigo o Duodo 2504, San Marco; tickets €50; ☺ doors 8pm; ⚑ Santa Maria del Giglio
Hang onto your wineglass and brace for impact: in these intimate palace drawing rooms, the soprano's high notes might make you fear for your glassware, and the thundering baritone is felt in the base of the spine. The drama unfolds over 1½ hours of selected arias from Verdi to Rossini, with 70 guests and their drinks trailing singers in modern dress as they pour their hearts out in song, progressing from receiving-room overtures to heartbreaking finales in the bedroom.

TEATRO FONDAMENTA NUOVE

Map pp94–5   Theatre & Dance
☎ 041 522 44 98; www.teatrofondamentanuove .it; Fondamente Nuove 5013, Cannaregio; tickets adult/student & senior/season pass €12/10/20; ⚑ Fondamente Nuove
Expect the unexpected in Cannaregio's experimental corner: dances inspired by

water and arithmetic, freeform jazz and improvised electronica, British performance art in Italian, and a steady stream of acclaimed artists from Brazil to Finland playing to a full house of 200.

TEATRO GOLDONI Map pp68–9   Theatre

☎ 041 240 20 14; www.teatrostabileveneto.it, in Italian; Calle Teatro Goldoni 4650b, San Marco; tickets €7-30; ☺ box office 10am-1pm & 3-7pm Mon-Wed, 10am-1pm Thu; 🚇 Rialto

Named after the city's greatest playwright, the city's main theatre has an impressive dramatic range that runs from Goldoni comedy to Shakespearean tragedy (mostly in Italian), plus ballets and concerts. The box office opens Friday and Saturday when there is a performance.

TEATRO JUNGHANS Map p112   Theatre

☎ 041 72 06 35; www.veneziainscena.com; Piazza Junghans 494a, Giudecca; performances €5-20; 🚇 Redentore

Cutting-edge theatre takes on a literal meaning at this three-sided stage, nicknamed Teatro Formaggino (Little Cheese Theatre) because it looks like a wedge of cheese. The experimental theatre seats 150, but you're not expected to just sit there: Teatro Junghans offers workshops on costume design in August, mask-acting in July and September, and *commedia dell'arte* (archetypal improvisational comedy) in August and September. If you'd rather leave that sort of thing to the professionals, check the online calendar for performances when the company is in residence.

TEATRO LA FENICE Map pp68–9   Opera

☎ 041 78 66 11; www.teatrolafenice.it; Campo San Fantin 1965, San Marco; tickets from €20; 🚇 Santa Maria del Giglio

Venice's immortal 'Phoenix' opera house has risen twice from the ashes of devastating fires, but the tiny stage seems charmed: Rossini, Bellini and Verdi all premiered major operas here. Tours are possible with advance booking by phone (☎ 041 24 24), but the best way to see La Fenice is in full swing with the *loggione* (opera buffs that pass judgment on productions from on high in the top-tier cheap seats). In the off-season look for symphonies and chamber music concerts at La Fenice or operas staged at the charming, diminutive 17th-

century Teatro Malibran (Map pp94–5; Calle del Teatro 5870, Cannaregio; tickets €10-95; 🚇 Rialto).

CINEMA

Movies in Venice are generally in Italian or dubbed into Italian, with a notable exception: films are premiered in their original language during the Venice International Film Festival (p19). Cinemaphile Venetians opt for movies over sleep, cramming a year's viewing habits into a few weeks – even if the movie is a dud, the crowd scene before and after is not to be missed. The same can be said for free summer movies screened in Campo San Polo.

CASA DEL CINEMA Map pp86–7

☎ 041 524 13 20; www.comune.venezia.it; Palazzo Mocenigo, Santa Croce 1990; annual member's pass adult/student €25/20, premieres €6/5; 🚇 San Stae

This film archive and research centre occasionally puts on film nights featuring classics, pre-release previews and events with filmmakers. For most events you'll need a member's pass. Show up early for prime seating.

CINEMA GIORGIONE MOVIE D'ESSAI

Map pp94–5

☎ 041 522 62 98; Rio Terà di Franceschi 4612, Cannaregio; adult/student €7/5; 🚇 Fondamente Nuove

Screenings of Oscar winners and recently restored classics share top billing at this modern cinema in the heart of Venice. There are two screens (one tiny) and as many as three screenings a day (roughly 5pm, 7.30pm and 10pm).

MULTISALA ASTRA Map p116

☎ 041 526 57 36; Via Corfù 9, Lido 30126; adult/senior & student €7/5; ☺ shows 5.30-10pm 🚇 Lido

When you start feeling the burn on the beach, catch a show instead in this dark, air-conditioned recently remodelled cinema. The program is planned by the Venice municipal film commission, so subtitled arthouse films occasionally share the marquee with blockbusters dubbed into Italian.

SUMMER ARENA Map pp86–7

Campo San Polo; ☺ Jul-Aug; 🚇 San Silvestro

In summer, ancient Campo San Polo becomes the forward-thinking Summer Arena, with open-air cinema, concerts and theatre performances. This space is wide-open to ideas year-round, so watch out for political rallies and flash-mob silent raves.

SPORTS & ACTIVITIES

Boating is the sport of choice in Venice, with the Italian passion for football falling a distant second. The same goes for the great Italian sport of cycling, which is banned in Venice (p258) except for the Lido, though the Veneto offers easy routes through pretty patchwork flatlands and tougher challenges into the Dolomite foothills (p255). Running is gaining popularity in Venice, though most locals stick to jogs through the Giardini and few attempt the mad dash from the Brenta riverbanks to San Marco via pontoon bridges during the Venice Marathon (p20). To test your mental mettle, check out additional courses on p265.

Rowing & Sailing

If this improbably floating city has one standing lesson to offer, it's that imagination makes anything possible – including rowing standing up *(voga alla veneta)*, which is the closest non-Messiahs may get to walking on water. Regattas run from spring through fall and sailing is a year-round passion, especially *vela al terzo,* in traditional, shallow-hulled lagoon vessels with triangular main sails. To get your feet wet (but hopefully not soaked) in Venice's nautical scene, consider rowing classes (p265), look into sailing tours of the Venice lagoon (p271) and consider a boating trip up the River Brenta (p232). If you've brought your own boat, sailing maps are available from Mare di Carta (p168), but be advised that yachting is virtually impossible in this tricky shallow lagoon.

Football

Football is a comparatively lesser passion here than in the landlocked regions of Italy – though the fancy-dress Calcio Storico match in full costume is a Carnevale event not to be missed. Venice's location makes for interesting logistics when AC Venezia (☎ 041 520 68 99; www.veneziacalcio.it, in Italian) plays at home in its island stadium. Periodically rumours arise of funds for a new stadium to be built on the mainland – but in the meantime the team plays at the Stadio Penzo (off Map pp100–1) on Isola di Sant'Elena, a sizeable island on the backside of Castello.

Known as the *arancioneroverde* (orange, black and greens), Venezia was founded in 1907 and sent on to win major championships during WWII. After the war, Venezia was reclassed into Serie B (second division), and in recent years has shifted into Serie C (third division), where the team rallied to win a championship.

Match tickets are available at Stadio Penzo and from HelloVenezia ticket outlets (☎ 041 24 24; www.hellovenezia.it). They can cost around €15 to €20, depending on the seat. Getting a ticket on the day is rarely a problem. On match days, special ferry services run between Isola del Tronchetto's car parks and Sant'Elena, and all buses arriving in Venice are diverted first to Tronchetto to disgorge loads of fans sporting AC Venezia's club colours.

lonely planet Hotels & Hostels

Want more sleeping recommendations than we could ever pack into this little ol' book? Craving more detail — including extended reviews and photographs? Want to read reviews by other travellers and be able to post your own? Just make your way over to **lonelyplanet.com/hotels** and check out our thorough list of independent reviews, then reserve your room simply and securely.

SLEEPING

top picks

- Novecento (p217)
- Bauer Palladio Hotel & Spa (p224)
- Oltre il Giardino (p220)
- Domus Orsoni (p222)
- Palazzo Soderini (p223)
- Locanda Ca' del Console (p223)
- Ca' Angeli (p220)
- Locanda Barbarigo (p217)
- Palazzo Abadessa (p222)
- Charming House DD.724 (p218)

SLEEPING

Waking up in a *palazzo* (palace) to the sound of the lagoon gently lapping at the *fondamente* (canal banks) and a gondolier calling 'Oooeeeeee!' is an unforgettable experience, and more affordable than you might think. High-end hotels aren't your only option for memorable stays in prime locations, as many Venetians have recently opened historic homes as *locande* (guesthouses), B&Bs, *affittacamere* (rooms for rent) and holiday rental apartments.

Whoever keeps circulating the rumour that Venice doesn't have enough beds to go around and offers no rooms under €200 is about a decade out of date, and has yet to hear of an invention called the internet. Since only about a third of Venice's visitors stay overnight, the odds are good that if you go online right now and check availability, you'll be able to find accommodation in Venice proper – even on short notice, and sometimes for a special deal. Many more palaces have opened their doors to guests in the past decade, and coupled with a dip in tourism resulting from global recession, you may actually have your pick of memorable places to stay in Venice.

Mainland Mestre is a miles distant second-best to an enchanted evening in Venice, but with this book and a computer, you won't have to settle for anything less than accommodation in central Venice. For more than 400 accommodation options in addition to the ones reviewed in this chapter see www.lonelyplanet.com. The APT tourist board (www.turismovenezia.it) lists 200-plus B&Bs, 250-plus *affittacamere*, and 275-plus apartments to rent in Venice proper. For still more choices, try the websites of the Associazione Veneziana Albergatori (Venice Hoteliers Association; www.veniceby .com, www.veneziasi.it; ☎ in Italy 199 173309, from abroad 39-041 522 22 64; ☯ 8am-10pm Easter-Oct, 8am-9pm Nov-Easter). If you show up in Venice without a hotel reservation, don't despair: Associazione Veneziana Albergatori has booking offices at the train station (Map pp94–5), in Piazzale Roma (Map pp86–7) and Tronchetto car parks (Map p64).

Hotels are also known as *alberghi* or *locande*. Like a *pensione*, a *locanda* is usually a smaller family-run establishment somewhere between a B&B and lower-end hotel. Many hotels offer rooms with 'Venetian-style' furnishings, which might include antiques and Murano glass chandeliers, but usually means modern remakes of baroque furnishings, including lacquered bedsteads with gilt flourishes, bow-legged nightstands, and hulking armoires. Not all hotels in Venice are grand: some are cramped, drafty, and frayed around the edges, with lackadaisical service. Though we've excluded such undesirable properties from this chapter, you'll find many in this category on the web, sometimes with glowing reviews – buyer beware. Budget and midrange places around the train station tend to be uninspiring, and not that well positioned for sightseeing. Dorsoduro and San Polo offer a good smattering of interesting hotel options, ranging from hip boutique hotels to *pensioni* straight out of a Venetian mystery novel. For luxury indulgence, there are beachside Lido resorts and historic San Marco hotels along the Grand Canal.

Unlike sprawling hotels, many Venetian B&Bs and room rentals *(affittacamere)* offer homestyle hospitality that could be the highlight of your trip. But unless specifically mentioned in this chapter, don't get your hopes up for eggs and bacon at breakfast. *Affittacamere* generally don't offer breakfast, and Venetian laws have strict rules for dining establishments that prohibit most B&Bs serving much beyond packaged croissants. When in Venice, breakfast as Venetians do: stop by a bakery or coffee bar en route to your destination, and enjoy your pastry and cappuccino at the bar for a couple of euros. B&Bs in Castello and Cannaregio offer good value in authentic neighbourhoods, often surprisingly convenient to the sights of San Marco.

Hostels are also known as *foresterie*. Travellers who love a bargain should show up early to claim bunks with canal views at the youth hostel on Giudecca or private rooms at the palatial Palazzo Zenobio and frescoed Foresteria Valdese. University housing usually opens to tourists in summer only, though the Residenzia Junghans in Giudecca offers year-round accommodation to all at student prices.

RATES & DEALS

The best rates are in Venice's low season, typically November, early December, January (except New Year's) and the period between Carnevale and Easter; you might also swing deals in the heat of July to August. When business is slow, many hotels will offer more competitive deals. Always ask if there are special rates available midweek, for longer stays or for last-minute bookings.

Travellers on their own have the best chance of finding dorm beds in high season, otherwise few hotels have any single rooms – and they're often cramped and unpleasant. Some places offer special rates on double rooms used as singles, which is usually two-thirds to three-quarters of the price two people would pay for a double.

Prices in reviews in this chapter may indicate a range if they change significantly from season to season. Where possible, the range indicates the upper rate you would pay in low and high season: 'single €40 to €60, double €80 to €130' means a single might cost €40 at most in low season and a double €130 at most in high season. Where this is not the case, assume the prices are the year-round average rate. Rates cited here should be considered a guide, since hotels change them seasonally, and many hotels offer discounts for booking online.

When you make your booking, you may be asked to provide a credit card number or pay a deposit (usually one night's stay) to secure your reservation. Confirm your arrival time at least 72 hours before your arrival – or the hotel may think you've changed your plans, and cancel your reservation.

AMENITIES

Many accommodation options in Venice are in historic buildings – great for period charm and views, not so great for space

---

LONGER-TERM RENTALS

For longer stays and groups of three or more, renting an apartment is an economical option that gives you the freedom to cook your own meals. Generally, flats are let by the week or month.

ApartmentsApart (www.apartmentsapart.com) Offers flats for rent by the day, starting at about €50.

Guest in Italy (www.guestinitaly.com) Has apartments and B&Bs ranging from €100 to €350 a night, though you may have to fill out a booking form to see the prices on some places.

HomeExchange (http://homeexchange.com) Features more than 50 Venice properties whose owners are interested in a holiday house-swap – the most commonly requested exchanges are in London, New York and Paris. Sign-up for the year costs US$100; individual house exchanges are free.

Interhome (www.interhome.co.uk) Has a selection of mostly small flats (about 50 sq metre) which sleep three to four (a little cramped) for around UK£730 to UK£1100 a week.

Venetian Apartments (☎ 020-3178 41 80; www.venice-rentals.com; 403 Parkway House, Sheen Lane, London SW14 8LS) Arranges accommodation in flats, often of a luxurious nature. Two- to four-person apartments start at around €895 per week.

Venice Apartments Italy (☎ 041 241 16 97; www.venice-apartments-italy.com) Has more than 28 apartments of varying size and quality. Prices range from €720 for two people per week to €1750 for five per week.

Other sites featuring rentals in Venice proper include these:

BB Planet (www.bbplanet.it)

Bianco Holidays (www.apartmentinitaly.com)

RentalinItaly (www.rentalinitaly.com)

Venice Apartment Rental (www.veniceapartment.com)

If you plan to stay for a month or more, you'll want to seek out longer-term rental, which you might find through Craigslist Venice (http://venice.it.craigslist.it) or word of mouth. If you don't mind sharing with students, check out the Università Ca' Foscari notice boards (Map pp78–9; Calle Larga Foscari, San Polo), where you might find rooms in a shared apartment for about €300 to €600 a month (usually the low-end places are in mainland Mestre). To rent a studio for yourself, expect to pay €800 to €1200.

and convenience. Expect rooms to be on the small, snug side, even in big hotels. On the upside, most hotels and B&Bs have sociable public areas, such as salons, libraries, lounges, courtyards and roof terraces. Unless otherwise stated in a review, guestrooms come with private bathrooms, often with a shower rather than a bathtub and both a toilet and bidet.

Citywide wi-fi is now available in Venice for a modest fee, but you may not be able to receive the signal through heavy stone or brick walls – for best internet access options, look for properties with the 🖥 (internet) and 🛜 (wi-fi) symbols, or head to an internet cafe (p268). Business centres are not very well equipped or well staffed, even in swanky hotels, since the assumption is you're here for pleasure. Even though you're surrounded by water in Venice, only a few large hotels have a pool or beach – mostly on the Lido, at hotels marked here with a 🏊 icon.

GETTING TO/FROM YOUR HOTEL

The less luggage you take with you to Venice, the better. Getting suitcases to your hotel can be a challenge, especially if there are footbridges between the hotel and the nearest vaporetto stop. Pick-up/drop-off service from the train station, airport or bus is generally only offered by high-end hotels, but if you're travelling with lots of luggage and your hotel or B&B is on a canal and has a water door, you might consider a water taxi from Piazzale Roma or Ferrovia (p261). Smaller hotels and B&Bs may not have lifts; accessible options are highlighted by the tourism bureau and Venetian travel services specialising in accessible travel (see p274).

If your travel plans allow, try to arrive during daylight hours to give yourself time to find your hotel. Searching for your hotel at night can be daunting: the streets are

dimly let and very confusing to newcomers, and you may find no-one to ask for directions. Crime rates are very low in Venice, but the city's narrow, dark alleyways can seem intimidating until you've had a chance to walk them by day. If an after-dark arrival is unavoidable, get good directions to your hotel and a detailed map before you leave for Venice.

SESTIERE DI SAN MARCO

Roll out of bed and you're surrounded by landmarks in San Marco, especially if you happen to be staying in a historic *palazzo*. Deals are rare here, and rooms facing the Grand Canal are prime real-estate for honeymooners – book well ahead, and bring deep pockets. B&Bs away from Piazza San Marco offer more space and style at a better price than big hotels, where rooms can be surprisingly small.

GRITTI PALACE Map pp68–9   Luxury Hotel €€€
☎ 041 79 46 11; www.hotelgrittivenice.com; Campo Traghetto 2467; d €500-2500; 🛥 Santa Maria del Giglio; ⊠ 🖥

You might not ever get around to sightseeing if you stay at the Gritti, the landmark 1525 doge's palace long celebrated as the highlight of any Grand Tour. Modern hotels may be bigger, but the Gritti remains the grandest hotel along the Grand Canal with 90 individually decorated guestrooms featuring period-perfect Murano chandeliers, silken draperies and hand-painted antique furnishings. Luxury specialist Starwood has recently taken over operations, adding efficient staff and inspired Venetian spice-route cuisine from Chef Daniele Turco in the canalside restaurant.

HOTEL MONACO & GRAND CANAL
Map pp68–9   Luxury Hotel €€
☎ 041 520 02 11; www.hotelmonaco.it; San Marco 1332; s €115, d €180-240; 🛥 San Marco/Vallaresso; ⊠ 🖥

Venice's favourite Ridotto p135 c 1648 is now a solid bet for a glamorous stay along the Grand Canal, thanks to a 2004 overhaul by Milanese architect Piero Lissoni. The revamped Ridotto wing features distinctly modern junior suites in celadon and deep brown, while Monaco wing standard rooms offer more predictable peaches-and-cream Venetian elegance framed in walnut scrollwork. When the main hotel is full, you might be assigned a smaller, darker room in the adjacent annexe, not quite worth the posh price tag. Hit cocktail hour in the groovy glass-front bar on the terrace with Grand Canal views.

NOVECENTO Map pp68–9   Boutique Hotel €€
☎ 041 241 37 65; www.novecento.biz; Calle del Dose 2683/84; d €140-260; 🚇 Santa Maria del Giglio; ⊠ 🐾 💻
World travellers put down roots in nine bohemian-chic rooms with Turkish kilim pillows, Fortuny wall coverings and 19th century scallop-shell carved bedsteads. Guests linger over breakfast in the garden under an Indian sun parasol, take hotel-arranged cookery courses, and mingle around the honesty bar.

HOTEL FLORA Map pp68–9   Boutique Hotel €€
☎ 041 520 58 44; www.hotelflora.it; Calle Bergamaschi 2283a; d €150-200; 🚇 San Marco, Vallaresso; ⊠ 🐾 💻
Down a lane from glitzy Via Larga XXII Marzo, this garden retreat quietly outclasses brash top-end neighbours with memorable stays in an ideal location. All 43 guestrooms feature antique carved beds piled with soft mattresses and fluffy duvets, but prime options include the opulent gilded No 3, and No 32 which opens onto the leafy garden.

HOTEL LOCANDA FIORITA
Map pp68–9   Pensione/Locanda €€
☎ 041 523 47 54; www.locandafiorita.com; Campiello Nuovo 3457; s/d incl breakfast €85/145; 🚇 Accademia; ⊠ 🐾 💻
Take breakfast outdoors on this lovely hidden *campo* (square), and you'd never guess bustling Campo Santo Stefano is around the corner. Rooms are in traditional Venetian style, with timber ceilings and damask bedspreads; ask for spacious No 1 overlooking the *campo* or No 10 with a private terrace.

LOCANDA BARBARIGO
Map pp68–9   B&B €€
☎ 041 241 36 39; www.locandabarbarigo.com; Fondamenta Duodo o Barbarigo 2503a; s €70-160, d €85-180, tr & q €170-220; 🚇 Santa Maria del Giglio; 🐾 📶

Your *palazzo* hideaway awaits beneath the arcade of the historic Palazzo Barbarigo, just off the Grand Canal. These cosy rooms have outsized baroque swagger, with damask walls, gilded mirrors, bow-legged vanities and fanciful chandeliers. Angle for the snug corner room in a lemon-lime colour scheme with views over a side canal, or the little yellow garret room with a wrought-iron bed and exposed timber beams.

BLOOM/7 CIELO Map pp68–9   B&B €
☎ 340 149 88 72; www.bloom-venice.com, www.settimocielo-venice.com; Campiello Santo Stefano 3470; d incl breakfast €90-180; 🚇 Accademia; ⊠ 🐾
Fraternal-twin B&Bs occupy two upper floors of a historic home overlooking Santo Stefano right across the *calle* (street). Bloom features splashy baroque decor schemes in crimson, cobalt and lemon silk damask with gilded beds and cathedral-window views. 7 Cielo (aka Seventh Heaven) is artfully romantic, with sleek tubs in shimmering Murano glass-tiled bathrooms and designer beds setting a honeymoon mood. Take breakfast on the sunny top-floor terrace.

LOCANDA ART DECO Map pp68–9   B&B €
☎ 041 277 05 58; www.locandaartdeco.com; Calle delle Botteghe 2966; d incl breakfast €75-170; 🚇 San Samuele; 🐾
Rakishly handsome cream-coloured guestrooms with comfy beds, custom wrought-iron bedsteads and parquet floors. Take your breakfast in the loft under the rafters, ask helpful hotel staff to arrange in-room massages and private gondola tours, and toss back a *spritz* (*prosecco*-based drink) in adjoining Campo San Stefano like a flapper fleeing Prohibition.

LOCANDA ANTICO FIORE
Map pp68–9   B&B €
☎ 041 522 79 41; www.anticofiore.com; Corte Lucatello 3486; d €70-140; 🚇 Sant'Angelo; 🐾 💻 📶
Local colour is the draw in this cosy B&B in a quiet courtyard, from the arty mother-daughter owners to the eight Venetian-style guestrooms spread out on the top two floors. Ask for the top-floor green canal-view room or the sweet yellow room tucked under the eaves.

LOCANDA CASA PETRARCA

Map pp68–9   Pensione/Locanda €

☎ 041 520 04 30; www.casapetrarca.com; Calle delle Schiavine 4386; s/d €95/125, without bathroom €70/112; 🚊 Rialto; 🔀

A family-run place with six unfussy, sparkling rooms in an ancient apartment building, this is one of the nicest budget places in the San Marco area. From Campo San Luca follow Calle dei Fuseri, take the second left and turn right into Calle delle Schiavine.

HOTEL AI DO MORI Map pp68–9   Hotel €

☎ 041 520 48 17; www.hotelaidomori.com; Calle Larga San Marco 658; d €50-150; 🚊 San Zaccaria; ❎ 🔀

Artists' garrets in an enviable location at bargain rates. Book well ahead to score an upper-floor room with wood-beamed ceilings, parquet floors and views over the Basilica. Rooms with a view cost the same as those without, so ask for No 11 with a private terrace overlooking Piazza San Marco.

SESTIERE DI DORSODURO

Between the modern art museums on the northeast bank of Dorsoduro are splashy designer boutique hotels, while on the Zattere side, you'll find laid-back *pensioni* with Giudecca Canal views – while some great values are hidden in between on neighbourly *calli* (streets).

CA' PISANI HOTEL

Map pp78–9   Boutique Hotel €€€

☎ 041 240 14 11; www.capisanihotel.it; Rio Terà Antonio Foscarini 979a; d €160-456; 🚊 Accademia; 🔀 🖳

An ideal spot right behind the Accademia to hide from paparazzi, yet still get the star treatment. Custom-decorated in a retro-glam style, this hotel has definite star quality with Jacuzzi tubs, art deco walnut marquetry sleigh beds, and all the latest technology hidden behind clever cabinetry so as not to kill the mood. Rooms in the eaves (31 is one of the best) feature sloping timber ceilings, and are handy to the steam bath and terrace with outdoor shower that rather naughtily overlooks the Salute Church.

PENSIONE ACCADEMIA VILLA MARAVEGE

Map pp78–9   Pensione/Locanda €€€

☎ 041 521 01 88; www.pensioneaccademia.it; Fondamenta Bollani 1058; s/d €140/229; 🚊 Accademia; 🔀

Once you step through the gate of this 17th-century garden villa just off the Grand Canal, you'll forget you're just a block from the Accademia and a couple more from Palazzo Grassi. Buffet breakfasts are served on the lawn in summer; at night, garden swings for two promise romance under the stars. All rooms are comfortably furnished with parquet floors, pale walls and modern bathrooms – but a few are a cut above, with four-poster beds, wood-beamed ceilings, and even glimpses of the canal. Thelma is a superior double with its own patch of greenery, named after a regular who loved reading in the garden.

CHARMING HOUSE DD.724

Map pp78–9   B&B €€€

☎ 041 277 02 62; www.thecharminghouse.com; Ramo de Mula 724; d incl breakfast €200-410; 🚊 Accademia; 🔀 🖳 📶

Make like Peggy Guggenheim and hole up in your own art-filled, modernist-chic Venetian bolthole, with lavish breakfast buffets in the library and a movie-viewing room. Guestrooms are designer-sleek yet cosy; splash out for the superior double with a bathtub, and balcony overlooking the Guggenheim's garden.

CASA REZZONICO Map pp78–9   B&B €€

☎ 041 277 06 53; www.casarezzonico.it; Fondamenta Gherardini 2813; d/tr/q €150/180/220; 🚊 Ca' Rezzonico; 🔀 🖳

'La Serenissima' lives up to its name at this tranquil B&B, with handsome antique bedsteads and parquet floors in whitewashed rooms. Opt for a room peeking over the quiet canal, and unwind over breakfast or drinks in the courtyard garden.

LOCANDA SAN BARNABA

Map pp78–9   B&B €€

☎ 041 241 12 33; www.locanda-sanbarnaba.com; Calle del Traghetto 2785-6; d from €120; 🚊 Ca' Rezzonico

The stage is set for romantic intrigue at this 16th-century *palazzo*, where the

1st-floor salon features unusual monochromatic 19th-century frescoes, and corner cupboards cleverly conceal a hidden staircase. Ask for the romantic 'Poeta Fanatico' room under the eaves or 'Campiello', which offers suggestive views of a neighbouring bell tower (campanile) through a skylight. Superior rooms feature 18th-century frescoed ceilings, and one has two balconies over the canal. Downstairs, in the garden, are sun umbrellas, patio seating and a 24-hour bar for happy endings.

LA CALCINA Map pp78–9   Hotel €€

☎ 041 520 64 66; www.lacalcina.com; Fondamenta delle Zattere ai Gesuati 780; s €90-120, d €110-220; 🚊 Zattere; 🖵
An idyllic seaside getaway, with a roof terrace, ground-floor restaurant and several antique-filled guestrooms facing the Giudecca Canal and Palladio-designed Il Redentore. To channel your inner writer, request No 2 where John Ruskin stayed while he wrote The Stones of Venice in 1876.

CA' SAN TROVASO

Map pp78–9   Pensione/Locanda €€
☎ 041 277 11 46; www.casantrovaso.com; Fondamenta delle Eremite 1351; s/d €95/125; 🚊 Zattere
All the Venetian flourishes you'd expect – damask-draped walls, white-lacquered baroque beds, terrazzo alla Veneziana (Venetian chipped marble) floors – in an easygoing seaside atmosphere five minutes from the Accademia. Rooms are cosy and rosy, and the most coveted ones overlook the canal. By day sunbathers flock to the small, sunny communal altana (roof terrace).

HOTEL GALLERIA

Map pp78–9   Pensione/Locanda €
☎ 041 523 24 89; www.hotelgalleria.it; Campo della Carità 878a; s €60-95, d €95-160; 🚊 Accademia
The bargain-hunter's Holy Grail: a family-run hotel in a 17th-century mansion smack on the Grand Canal, mere steps from Ponte dell'Accademia, with updated bathrooms. Nos 7 and 9 are small doubles overlooking the Grand Canal, No 8 has stile liberty (Liberty style) furnishings with Grand Canal views, and Number 10 sleeps five, with an original frescoed ceiling and two Grand Canal–facing windows.

ANTICA LOCANDA MONTIN

Map pp78–9   Pensione/Locanda €
☎ 041 522 71 51; www.locandamontin.com; Fondamenta di Borgo 1147; d €100-160, without bathroom s €40-70, d €75-120; 🚊 Accademia; 🖵
Artists can stop suffering for their art at Locanda Montin: sleepless nights are highly unlikely in tranquil rooms facing the garden. After feasting in the downstairs restaurant where Brad Pitt, David Bowie and Yoko Ono have dined, head up the back stairway and pass through the art-filled salon to eclectic guestrooms where Ezra Pound, Modigliani and Gabriele D'Annunzio have stayed. Works by D'Annunzio grace the walls of No 12, and even Modigliani couldn't pull a long face in rooms 5 and 8, where balconies overlooking the canal keep the inspiration coming.

PENSIONE SEGUSO

Map pp78–9   Pensione/Locanda €
☎ 041 528 68 58; www.pensioneseguso.it; Fondamenta delle Zattere ai Gesuati 779; s €50-160, d €70-190, without bathroom s €40-122, d €65-180, all incl breakfast; 🕙 Mar-Nov; 🚊 Zattere
An authentic pensione in a 1500 mansion worthy of a Donna Leon mystery novel, with antique hat racks, spooky mirrors, lead-glass windows, even staff dressed in formal attire. Almost all 34 rooms have canal views, and 24 have ensuite bathrooms; there's a restaurant just for guests, and the staff will pack you a picnic upon request.

CA' DELLA CORTE Map pp78–9   B&B €

☎ 041 71 58 77; www.cadellacorte.com; Corte Surian 3560, Dorsoduro; d incl breakfast €75-150; 🚊 Piazzale Roma; 🔀 🖵 💻 🛜
Live like a Venetian in this 16th-century family home 10 minutes from Piazzale Roma and Campo Santa Margherita, with guestrooms overlooking the courtyard, a frescoed grand music salon, and breakfasts on the top-floor terrace overlooking terracotta rooftops. English-speaking staff will arrange concerts, plein-air painting lessons, rowing and boating trips, and more.

PALAZZO ZENOBIO

Map pp78–9   Pensione/Locanda €
☎ 041 522 87 70; www.collegioarmeno.com; s/d/tr/q €65/100/120/140, without bathroom €30/56/80/100; 🚊 Ca' Rezzonico
A gilded 1690 palace that formerly housed a school for Venice's Armenian community

recently opened its doors to scholars and guests for a nominal fee. Accommodation is spare but the palace's trompe l'œil frescoed ceilings are splendid, and its overgrown formal garden among Venice's largest and loveliest.

SESTIERI DI SAN POLO & SANTA CROCE (SANTA CROSE)

Most lodging in the area clusters near the train-station end of Santa Croce and around the Rialto in San Polo, ranging from budget student bunks to high-end hotels. In between you'll find some historic family homes now open to guests as top-value B&Bs, including a few with Grand Canal views.

HOTEL PALAZZO BARBARIGO

Map pp86–7   Luxury Hotel €€€

☎ 800 3746 83 57; www.designhotels.com; San Polo 2765; €320-490; ▨ San Tomà; ☒ ▢
Not your grandmother's Grand Canal getaway, the Palazzo Barbarigo is Venice's splashiest new-design hotel. The traditional water gate entryway has been turned into a watering hole, with a deco-inspired bar and strategic lighting schemes that bring to mind an airport club lounge – but the 18 guestrooms get modern low-key luxury just right, with sumptuous velvets and contemporary, curvaceous furniture that call out the occasional silken tassel or gold fringe. Ask for junior suites overlooking the Grand Canal, or standard rooms overlooking Rio San Polo.

LE SUITES DI GIULIETTA E ROMEO

Map pp86–7   Boutique Hotel €€

☎ 041 72 28 33; www.bertoliresort.com; Campo San Cassian, San Polo 1858; r incl breakfast €130-350; ▨ Rialto Mercato; ☒ ▢
The scene is set for modern romance in six individually designed guestrooms featuring in-room Jacuzzis, and beds lit from underneath so that furniture floats in an *acqua alta* pool of light. The contrast between the contemporary decor and the historic setting can be jarring, as with the Mirror room's fluorescent lighting – but when the Pink room's chandelier sends light cascading across the mosaic wall, fancy takes flight.

OLTRE IL GIARDINO

Map pp86–7   Boutique Hotel €€

☎ 041 275 00 15; www.oltreilgiardino-venezia .com; Fondamenta Contarini, San Polo 2542; d €150-250; ▨ San Tomà; ☒ ▢
Live the designer dream in guestrooms brimming with historic charm and modern comforts: marquetry composer's desks and flatscreen TVs, candelabra and colourful minifridges, 19th-century poker chairs and babysitting services. This house was bought in 1922 by Alma Mahler, composer Gustav's sometime wife, free spirit and muse to the bohemian set – and the romance and inspiration persists. Light fills all six high-ceilinged bedrooms; though Turquoise is sprawling and Green occupies a private corner of the walled garden, Grey has a sexy wrought-iron bedstead under a cathedral ceiling.

AL PONTE MOCENIGO Map pp86–7   B&B €€

☎ 041 524 47 97; www.alpontemocenigo.com; Santa Croce 2063; d from €120; ▨ San Stae; ☒
A doge of a deal right off the Grand Canal, steps from the San Stae vaporetto stop and a 10-minute walk through crooked *calli* to the Rialto. Swanky boudoir guestrooms with chandeliers hung from high wood-beamed ceilings are often spacious enough for gymnastic routines, even with four-poster beds, gilt-edged armoires and salon seating. Ask for rooms overlooking Rio San Stae or the private courtyard.

CA' ANGELI Map pp86–7   Boutique Hotel €€

☎ 041 523 24 80; www.caangeli.it; Calle del Traghetto della Madonnetta 1434, San Polo; s €95, d €105-125, all incl breakfast; ▨ San Silvestro; ☒
Brothers Giorgio and Matteo inherited this Grand Canal mansion and converted it into a hotel and antique showplace, with original Murano glass chandeliers, namesake angels dating from the 16th century and a restored Louis XIV sofa in the Grand Canal–side reading room. Spacious room No 1 has Grand Canal views and a whirlpool bath; No 5 has a superb terrace. Breakfasts are made with organic products, and served in the dining room on antique plates.

LOCANDA ARCO ANTICO

Map pp86–7   Hotel €

☎ 041 241 12 27; www.arcoanticovenice.com; Corte Petriana 1451, San Polo; s €45-120, d €60-180; ▨ San Silvestro; ☒ ▢

Under the Gothic archway and through the courtyard, this 16th-century *palazzo* offers charming hideaways footsteps away from the Grand Canal at a fraction of San Marco hotel rates. Guestrooms feature handsome dark woods, cream and yellow brocades, marquetry dressers and exposed wood beams – but best of all is the sunny upper room overlooking the courtyard.

PENSIONE GUERRATO

Map pp86–7   Pensione/Locanda €

☎ 041 528 59 27; www.pensioneguerrato.it; Ruga due Mori 240a, San Polo; d incl breakfast €140, without bathroom €95; 🚇 Rialto Mercato; 🔁

In a landmark building that once served as a hostel for knights heading off on the Third Crusade, these recently updated guestrooms haven't lost their sense of history – ask for ones with frescoes or glimpses of the Rialto markets and Grand Canal. Ask English-speaking staff for insider advice on local restaurants and artisans.

CA' SAN GIORGIO

Map pp86–7   Boutique Hotel €

☎ 041 275 91 77; www.casangiorgio.com; Salizada del Fontego dei Turchi, Santa Croce 1725; d €75-110; 🚇 San Marcuola; 🔁

Talk about first impressions: head through the courtyard, past the 14th-century well and up a stone staircase, and you'll emerge in a sunwashed reception area with exposed brickwork, beamed ceiling and 15th-century columns. The guestrooms are more modern than medieval, with yellow and blue bedspreads, upholstery and curtains, and mosaic-lined bathrooms. The room to get is the Altana, a cosy suite under sloping ceilings with rooftop views.

ALBERGO CASA PERON

Map pp86–7   Pensione/Locanda €

☎ 041 71 00 21; www.casaperon.com; Salizada San Pantalon 84, Santa Croce; s €50-90, d €85-100, all incl breakfast; 🚇 San Tomà; 🔁

In true eccentric Venetian style, guest-rooms here are located in a maze of staircases and corridors, paintings cover the walls salon-style, and resident parrot Pierino greets guests in the lobby. This hotel is hidden down the *calle* from I Frari and around the corner from Campo Santa Margherita, with basic yet personable rooms – ask for Room No 5, featuring a terrace overlooking I Frari.

STUDENT STAYS

In summer only, Esu (☎ 041 72 10 25; www.esu venezia.it), the city's student administration agency, opens its residences to students and academics visiting town. Singles, doubles and triples are available and guests also get access to university *mense* (refectories): from mid-July to mid-September, singles/doubles are available for around €30/50 at Residenza Maria Ausiliatrice (Map pp100–1; Fondamenta San Gioacchin 454, Castello), Residenza Abazia (Map pp94–5; Fondamenta Misericordia 3547, Cannaregio), Residenza Jan Palach (Map p112; Giudecca 186) and Residenza San Tomà (Map pp86–7); Campo San Tomà 2846, San Polo).

HOTEL ALEX Map pp86–7   Pensione/Locanda €

☎ 041 523 13 41; www.hotelalexinvenice.com; Rio Terà 2606, San Polo; d €60-112, tr €80-150, q €100-190, without bathroom s €35-54, d €40-84, tr €60-114, q €80-144, all incl breakfast; 🚇 San Tomà; 🔁

Along a secret local shortcut between I Frari and Campo San Polo, this hotel offers 19 spare, sunny rooms with lacquered furnishings and updated bathrooms on three floors. Some upper rooms have a balcony or terrace overlooking two canals.

HOSTEL DOMUS CIVICA

Map pp86–7   Hostel €

☎ 041 522 71 39; www.domuscivica.com; Campiello Ciovare Frari 3082, San Polo; s/d € 38/64; 🕙 June-Sep; 🚇 Piazzale Roma; 🔁 💻

A women's dorm during the school year, this spot welcomes visitors as a hostel in summer, with shared facilities that include a living room with TV and free internet access. Simple, clean dorm rooms are equipped with single beds, desks and sinks, and there are five bathrooms per floor. There's a 12.30am curfew, and light sleepers should bring earplugs – the hallways reverberate, as do the church bells across the street.

SESTIERE DI CANNAREGIO

Late arrivals may settle for tourist-class hotels along Venice's busy main drag from the train station, but just a few steps away down quiet *calli*, cheerful hotels and designer B&Bs await discovery.

PALAZZO ABADESSA
Map pp94–5   Boutique Hotel €€€

☎ 041 241 37 84; www.abadessa.com; Calle Priuli 4011; d €145-325; 🚊 Ca' d'Oro; ❌ 🔀 🖳 🛜

Evenings seem enchanted in this opulent 1540 Venetian *palazzo*, with owner Maria Luisa fluffing pillows, plying guests with cake between meals, and fulfilling wishes like a fairy godmother. Sumptuous guestrooms feature plush beds, handmade silk damask walls, and 18th-century antique vanities; go for baroque and ask for one with original ceiling frescoes. Enjoy cocktails in the garden until you're whisked off on the hotel's boat to your specially reserved opera seats.

CA' POZZO Map pp94–5   Boutique Hotel €€

☎ 041 524 05 04; www.capozzovenice.com; Sotoportego Ca' Pozzo 1279; s €90-180, d €100-320; 🚊 Guglie; 🅿 🔀 🖳 🛜

Biennale-bound travellers find a home away from their home-design magazines in this design shrine near the historic Ghetto. The minimalist decor reflects artistic priorities: oversized abstract art, undersized televisions, and exposed ceiling beams for historical context. Several guestrooms come with balconies, two are built to accommodate disabled guests, and spacious room 208 could house a Damien Hirst entourage.

DOMUS ORSONI
Map pp94–5   Boutique Hotel €€

☎ 041 275 95 38; www.domusorsoni.it; Corte Vedei 1045; s €80-150, d €100-250, tr €120-280, all incl breakfast; 🚊 Tre Archi; 🔀 🖳

Five stylish rooms sprawl out over this low Venetian house in a tranquil back lane. Breakfast is served in the garden by the Orsoni mosaic works, located here since 1885 – hence the mosaic fantasias glittering across spacious guestroom bathrooms, walls and headboards. Even the single room is a shrine to art-glass chic, with gold-leafed niches in the mosaic backboard, mosaic-inlaid teak floors and a mosaic side table.

LOCANDA AI SANTI APOSTOLI
Map pp94–5   Pensione/Locanda €€

☎ 041 521 26 12; www.locandasantiapostoli.com; Campo dei Santi Apostoli 4391a; d incl breakfast €70-350; 🚊 Ca' d'Oro; 🔀

Stay in the centre of the sightseeing action near the Rialto in a serene gated garden getaway, with floral drapes and upholstery in 11 cheery guestrooms. Most have *terrazzo alla Veneziana* floors, some have exposed wood-beam ceilings, and all are simply furnished – the chief difference is that 'deluxe' rooms peek over the Grand Canal. Prices vary wildly by season; check the website for deals.

LOCANDA LEON BIANCO
Map pp94–5   Boutique Hotel €€

☎ 041 523 35 72; www.leonbianco.it; Corte Leon Bianco 5629; d incl breakfast €80-250; 🚊 Ca' d'Oro; 🔀

Turner used to paint at this canalside hotel, and you can see what he saw in the place: sloping *terrazzo alla Veneziana* floors, heavy wooden doors, and hulking antique furniture that hasn't changed much since Turner's day. Three slightly larger 'deluxe' rooms overlook the Grand Canal, including No 4, a corner room with wrap-around postcard views – but bring your earplugs for canalside rooms, because the Rialto markets opposite starts at 4am.

RESIDENZA CA' RICCIO
Map pp94–5   Boutique Hotel €

☎ 041 528 23 34; www.cariccio.com; Campo dei Miracoli 5394a; s €70-90, d €95-130, all incl breakfast; 🚊 Fondamente Nuove; 🔀 🖳

Down the street from Casanova's house in a convenient yet hidden location is the Riccio family's lovingly restored 14th-century residence. Seven rooms on the two top floors look out onto a courtyard and feature simple wrought-iron beds, wood-beamed ceilings, terracotta tiled floors and whitewashed walls.

HOTEL ROSSI Map pp94–5   Hotel €

☎ 041 71 51 64; www.hotelrossi.ve.it; Lista di Spagna 262; s €56-72, d €80-95; 🚊 Ferrovia; 🔀

Simple wood-trimmed, whitewashed rooms offer a break from Venice's sensory overload. Late arrivals and early departures will appreciate the location near the train station, down a quiet lane off busy Rio Terà Lista di Spagna. Ask about cheaper rooms with shared bathrooms and low-season rates.

ALLOGGI GEROTTO CALDERAN
Map pp94–5   Pensione/Locanda €

☎ 041 71 53 61; www.casagerottocalderan.com; Campo San Geremia 283; dm/d/tr/q €25/85/90/112; 🚊 Ferrovia; 🖳

Cheap and chipper, this hotel is handily located over a bookshop near the train station in lively Campo San Geremia. Rooms are compact with clean bathrooms, in-room internet access, and twee coverlets; some rooms have traditional Venetian rosebud-painted headboards and bow-legged bedstands.

HOTEL VILLA ROSA Map pp94–5 Hotel €

☎ 041 71 65 69; www.villarosahotel.com; Calle della Misericordia 389; d from €70; 🚊 Ferrovia; 🛜

This peachy-keen hotel trimmed with blooming window-boxes is a cheery sight off the busy Lista di Spagna, near the train station. The comfortable candy-coloured rooms have Murano glass lamps, flocked baroque wallpaper and eclectic charm, and the ones with private terraces or beamed ceilings are extra sweet. A complimentary continental breakfast is served in the cosy, wood-beamed reception or outdoors on the patio, and there is wi-fi available too.

SESTIERE DI CASTELLO

For luxury with lagoon views, grand hotels along the Riva degli Schiavoni have reeled in visitors for two centuries. But bargain-hunters, take note: some Castello lodgings are closer to Piazza San Marco than ones with a San Marco address, often at a fraction of the price. For even better rates, walk another 10 minutes from the Piazza towards the Arsenale, where rates plummet up to 50%.

HOTEL DANIELI Map pp100–1 Luxury Hotel €€€

☎ 041 522 64 80; www.starwoodhotels.com/luxury; Riva degli Schiavoni 4196; d €319-2800; 🚊 San Zaccaria; 🏠

As eccentric, luxurious and exuberant as Venice itself, the Danieli has attracted artistic bohemians, minor royalty and their millionaire lovers for over a century. The hotel sprawls along the lagoon next to the Palazzo Ducale in three landmark buildings: the 14th-century *casa vecchia* (old house), built for Doge Enrico Dandolo, with frescoed, antique-filled rooms; the *casa nuova* (new house), with cosier Venetian-style rooms and gilt to the hilt; and the Danielino, a stark Fascist edifice with a multimillion-euro 2008 modern-luxe interior redesign by Jacques Garcia, preserving original bathtubs and chan-

deliers but adding hand-rubbed Venetian-plaster walls, crimson silk curtains and blissful beds with dramatic damask headboards.

PALAZZO SODERINI Map pp100–1 B&B €€

☎ 041 296 08 23; www.palazzosoderini.it; Campo di Bandiera e Mori 3611; d incl breakfast €150-200; 🚊 Arsenale; 🏠 🛜

Whether you're coming from cutting-edge art at the Biennale or baroque masterpieces at the Ducal Palace, this tranquil all-white retreat with a lily pond in the garden is a welcome reprieve from the visual onslaught of Venice. Minimalist decor emphasises spare shapes and clean lines, with metal-edged furniture and bare walls, and an unexpected blue lobby sofa for the element of surprise. The three rooms have all the mod cons: TVs, wi-fi, mini-bars, air-con and heating.

CA' DEI DOGI Map pp100–1 B&B €€

☎ 041 241 37 51; www.cadeidogi.it; Corte Santa Scolastica 4242; s €90, d €130-210, all incl breakfast; 🚊 San Zaccaria 🏠 🖵

Even the Bridge of Sighs at the neighbouring Prigioni Nuove can't dampen the high spirits of the sunny yellow Ca' Dei Dogi, with guestroom windows sneaking peeks into the convent cloisters next door. The streamlined modern rooms look like ships' cabins, with tilted wood-beamed ceilings, dressers that look like steamer trunks, and compact mosaic-covered bathrooms – ask for the one with the terrace and Jacuzzi. Staff can arrange concerts, boating trips and sunset gondola rides.

LOCANDA CA' DEL CONSOLE

Map pp100–1 B&B €€

☎ 041 523 31 64; www.locandacadelconsole.com; Calle Trevisana 6217; s €110, d €120-160, all incl breakfast; 🚊 Rialto; 🏠 🖵 🛜

Live the life of ease and intrigue of a visiting dignitary, like the 19th century Austrian ambassador who once lived here. An elegant salon leads to eight tastefully restored rooms with exposed beams, stucco, frescoes and period furniture from the consul's heyday, plus updated bathrooms. Two rooms look onto a canal, but all are spacious and welcoming, and owner Signora Marina makes every guest feel duly honoured.

LA RESIDENZA Map pp100–1   Hotel €

☎ 041 528 53 15; www.venicelaresidenza.com; Campo di Bandiera e Mori 3608; s €50-100, d €80-180; 🚇 Arsenale; ⊠

Sleep like the dead in the comfort of this grand 15th-century mansion, presiding over a *campo* that was once the site of public executions. Generous-sized rooms are furnished in Venetian style, with cream lacquered wardrobes and beds with boldly striped bedspreads. The upstairs reception is a chandelier-lit salon garlanded with 18th-century stucco, with a grand piano guests gather around at happy hour.

LOCANDA SANT'ANNA

Map pp100–1   Pensione/Locanda €

☎ 041 528 64 66; www.locandasantanna.com; Corte del Bianco 269; d incl breakfast €100-125, without bathroom €70-85; 🚇 Giardini; ⊠ 🖳

Escape the madding crowd on a quiet *campiello* (small square) on the sleepy side of Castello, where tourists are scarce, boats drift past and seagulls circle aimlessly all day. Antique vanities, marquetry bedsteads and parquet floors add character to spacious whitewashed rooms, some with views of Isola San Pietro. The panoramic terrace is ideal for sunny days, and the reading room makes a welcome retreat when lagoon mists roll in.

HOTEL RIVA Map pp100–1   Pensione/Locanda €

☎ 041 522 70 34; www.hotelriva.it; Ponte dell'Angelo 5310; s €80-90, d €100-120, without bathroom s €60-70, d €80-100; 🚇 San Zaccaria; ⊠ ⊠

At the juncture of two canals, this is a prime location to drift off in an upholstered baroque bedstead to the whistling of passing gondoliers, awakening under high wood-beamed ceilings to the tolling bells of nearby San Marco. True to Venetian priorities, all rooms have Murano glass chandeliers and only some are air-conditioned – but the prices are hard to beat.

LOCANDA SILVA Map pp100–1   Hotel €

☎ 041 522 76 43; www.locandasilva.it; Fondamenta del Rimedio 4423; s €45-80, d €60-130, all incl breakfast; 🚇 San Zaccaria

Along a quiet canal five minutes' walk from Piazza San Marco, this family-run hotel has 23 cheerful, gleamingly clean guestrooms with plain blonde-wood furniture. Ask for sunny canalside rooms, and lounge on the

giddy 4th-floor rooftop terrace peeking at San Marco's bell tower.

ALLOGGI BARBARIA

Map pp100–1   Pensione/Locanda €

☎ 041 522 27 50; www.alloggibarbaria.it; Calle delle Cappuccine 6573; s €40-100, d €60-120, all incl breakfast; 🚇 Ospedale

Located in an authentic Venetian neighbourhood near the Fondamente Nuove, this *pensione* isn't easy to find – but that's part of its charm, and so are the intrepid fellow travellers you'll meet over breakfasts on a shared balcony. All six rooms are white, bright and roomy, with tiled floors and rates that rarely hit the quoted maximums.

FORESTERIA VALDESE Map pp100–1   hostel €

☎ 041 528 67 97; www.diaconiavaldese.org/venezia; Palazzo Cavagnis 5170; dm per person €23-24, d from €78, all incl breakfast; 🚇 Ospedale

Holy hostel: this rambling palace retreat owned by the Waldensian church has 1st-floor guestrooms with 18th-century frescoes by Bevilacqua, and one floor up guestrooms have canal views. Dorm beds are available only for families or groups; book well ahead.

AROUND THE LAGOON

Take a breather from the palatial grandeur of Venice at seaside *stile liberty* villas on the Lido, country getaways on Sant'Erasmo and Torcello, simple *pensioni* on Burano and Murano, and bargain lodging on Giudecca. For destination vacations, try luxury hotels in a nunnery on Giudecca, a madhouse on Isola di San Clemente or a seaside Lido landmark.

GIUDECCA

BAUER PALLADIO HOTEL & SPA

Map p112   Luxury Hotel €€€

☎ 041 520 70 22; www.palladiohotelspa.com; Fondamenta della Croce 33; d €296-490; 🚇 Zitelle; ⊠ 🖳

Splash out in a serene Palladio-designed former cloister with San Marco views, private solar-powered boat service and a superb spa. These premises once housed nuns and orphans, but now offer heavenly comfort in 37 rosy, serenely demure guest rooms, many with garden terraces or Giudecca Canal views. Head downstairs for local organic breakfast buffets and ecofriendly spa treatments like the milk, honey and rose bath (€90) with complimentary sauna, Jacuzzi and marble steam-room access.

RESIDENZA JUNGHANS
Map p112   Hostel €

☎ 041 521 08 01; www.residenzajunghans.com, in Italian; Terzo Ramo della Palada 394, Giudecca; s/d €40/70; 🚊 Palanca

Save cash and wax nostalgic about school in this bargain modern dorm residence with instant camaraderie, Ikea desks and school-marmish rules: payment in advance, quiet after 11pm, and locked gates at 1.30am. Ask for deals by the week.

OSTELLO VENEZIA Map p112   Hostel €

☎ 041 523 82 11; www.ostellovenezia.it; Fondamenta delle Zitelli 86, Giudecca; dm incl breakfast €21-26; 🚊 Zitelle

Calming canal views make hostel bunks seem miles away from the stampeding crowds and inflated prices of San Marco, yet all the sightseeing action is just a vaporetto hop away. Sheets, blanket, and a pillow are provided in the bunk price, but you'll need to arrive promptly at the 3.30pm opening time to claim that perfect bunk by the window; reserve ahead for one of two viewless private rooms. Check-in is from 3.30pm to 10pm, check-out is at 9.30am.

LIDO DI VENEZIA
HOTEL DES BAINS
Map p116   Luxury Hotel €€€

☎ 041 526 59 21; www.desbainsvenezia.com; Lungomare Marconi 17; s €128, d €230-420; 🌙 Apr-Oct; 🚊 Lido; 🅿 🔀 🖳 🛜 🛥

'Ooooh-ahhhh' is an understandable reaction to crossing the threshold of this Belle Epoque hotel, setting the standard for seaside grandeur for a century. Oversized keys dangle above the original ebony front desk, illuminated by a chandelier that's gargantuan even by Murano standards. Upstairs are guestrooms bigger than Venetian apartments, with original deco furnishings, a soothing cream and white colour scheme and tall windows with views of the gardens, pool or Adriatic. Management is in flux at writing, and the rear building is being converted to luxury condos – visit now for your glimpse of not-yet-bygone Venetian glory.

ALBERGO QUATTRO FONTANE
Map p116   Hotel €€€

☎ 041 526 07 26; www.quattrofontane.com; Via Quattro Fontane 16; s €140-210, d €188-520; 🌙 Apr-Nov; 🚊 Lido; 🅿 🔀 🖳

Strange but true: this Alpine chalet is just a stone's throw from Lido beaches, and its shaded gardens and tennis court swarm with Hollywood stars during the Venice Film Festival. Celebrities are nothing new to this inn with a chequered floor and a chequered past as a casino frequented by royalty in the 16th century, and a tavern beloved of Robert Browning and his 19th-century bohemian crowd. Rooms are vast and unabashedly retro in the 1970s A-frame annexe; the original building offers tighter, more traditional quarters with charming wrought-iron beds. Bicycle rental, laundry and babysitting services available.

VILLA MABAPA Map p116   Hotel €€

☎ 041 526 05 90; www.villamabapa.com; Riviera San Nicolò 16; d €109-380; 🚊 Lido; 🅿 🔀 🖳 🛥

Lounge the Lido day away in a garden villa dating from the 1930s, about 100m from a private beach. Rooms in the main building are elegantly appointed in stile liberty and deco furniture, with languid views across the lagoon to Venice and dining in the garden. Private motor boats transport guests 10 minutes across the water to sunset cocktails in Venice.

HOTEL VILLA CIPRO Map p116   Hotel €€

☎ 041 73 15 38; www.hotelvillacipro.com; Via Zara 2, Lido; s €70-160, d €80-170; 🚊 Lido; 🅿 🔀

A world away from the narrow streets of Venice but only a few blocks from the vaporetto stop, this pine-shaded villa offers spacious rooms with high ceilings ornamented by Murano chandeliers and tall windows, some with balconies overlooking the gardens. Breakfast is served in the courtyard, and cocktails at the vintage bar or in the gardens; the beach is two blocks away.

CA' DEL BORGO Off Map p116   Hotel €€

☎ 041 77 07 49; www.cadelborgo.it; Piazza delle Erbe 8; s €65-140, d €70-140, tr €90-180; 🚊 Lido; 🔀 🅿

Turn back the clock six centuries to Venice's seafaring glory days at this historic hotel on the maritime end of the Lido. All rooms feature Murano lamps, upholstered beds, period furnishings, and parquet floors with antique rugs, but the blue room under exposed-timber eaves is best for nautical nostalgia. Private motor-launches provide transport to and from Venice.

MURANO

HOTEL AL SOFFIADOR Map p118   Hotel €
☎ 041 73 94 30; www.venicehotel.it; Calle Bressagio 10, Murano; s €50-65, d €53-89; 🚊 Faro; ❌ 🖳
Save cash for glass with stays at the 'Glassblower,' a breath away from several glass factories and showrooms in the centre of Murano. Rooms are unfussy and well-kept, with bathrooms recently spiffed up with new fixtures and marble sinks. There's a restaurant downstairs and patio out back where you can enjoy breakfast in peace – in the quiet hours before and after the showrooms open, you'll be alone with your thoughts and the glass-blowers on Murano.

BURANO & TORCELLO

LOCANDA CIPRIANI
Map p121   Boutique Hotel €€
☎ 041 73 01 50; www.locandacipriani.com; Piazza Santa Fosca 29, Torcello; s & d per person €100-130, half-board €150-180; 🕙 closed Jan; 🚊 Torcello
Not much has changed since this rustic wine shop was transformed into a country inn in 1934 by Harry's Bar founder Giuseppe Cipriani. You won't see Ernest Hemingway hauling in his hunting trophies or working on his manuscripts, but you can still enjoy hearty pastas and *anatra* (wild duck) by the *fogher* (fireplace) or under the rose pergola in the garden. The six spacious rooms are more like suites, with stocked libraries and easy chairs in lieu of TVs for a true literary retreat. Half-board at the restaurant here is a far better deal for starving artists than Harry's Bar.

LOCANDA AL RASPO DE UA
Map p121   Pensione/Locanda €
☎ 041 73 00 95; www.alraspodeua.it; Via Galuppi 560, Burano; s €45-55, d €85-95; 🚊 Burano; ❌
Skip the mad dash for vaporettos back to Venice at sunset, and stay for a socia-

ble dinner on the sidewalk of Burano's main strolling street and a good night's sleep just up the back stairs. The panelled guestrooms are cheerfully chaotic and artistically inclined, with mismatched furniture and original abstract paintings and landscapes. For an eating review, see p196.

Minor Islands
ISOLA DI SAN CLEMENTE
SAN CLEMENTE PALACE
Map p116   Luxury Hotel €€€
☎ 041 244 50 01; www.sanclementepalacevenice.com; Isola di San Clemente; s/d €370/410; ❌ 🖳 🛥
Mad for luxury? Check into this rose-coloured high-end hotel and former madhouse, which takes up most of the island with 205 rooms and suites, two swimming pools, splendid gardens, tennis courts, a golf course, and a full-service spa specialising in seaweed-based beauty treatments. Yes, the rooms are padded, but with silk damask, and Italian marble bathrooms come with tubs and custom-blended soothing aromatherapy products to restore calm after Biennale art binges and wild Murano shopping sprees. Lagoon views abound, and there are four complimentary private shuttle boats running regularly to San Marco.

SANT'ERASMO
IL LATO AZZURRO Map p64   Hotel €
☎ 041 523 06 42; www.latoazzurro.it; Via Forti 13, Sant'Erasmo; dm €25-30, s €50-55, d €70-80; 🚊 Sant'Erasmo Capannone
Sleep among the artichokes on Venice's garden isle of Sant'Erasmo in a red-roofed country villa, 25 minutes by boat from central Venice. Spacious guestrooms with parquet floors and wrought-iron beds open onto a wrap-around veranda. Meals are largely homegrown, organic and fair trade, bicycles are available, and the lagoon is down the lane – bite-prone guests should bring mosquito repellent. Ask about nature excursions, archaeological digs, and opportunities for artists to stay overnight for free in exchange for performances.

VENETO EXCURSIONS

As though Venice weren't enough of a draw, the Veneto countryside is dotted with walled medieval towns, rustic farmhouse bistros and cities brimming with Unesco World Heritage Sites. Easy day trips let you visit more villas along the Brenta Riviera than a Venetian socialite c 1600, glimpse your own emotions mirrored in Giotto's early Renaissance frescoes in Padua, be uplifted by Palladio's gracious architecture in Vicenza, and toast star-crossed lovers Romeo and Juliet with a glass of Amarone (robust, dry red wine) in Verona. Wine-tasting excursions, skiing trips to the Dolomites, and beach clubs along the Adriatic Coast make worthy adventures, even with the timeless temptations of Venice just across the lagoon.

Until the 15th century, the Venetian countryside was divided into a series of competing city-states, the most important of which were Padua (Padova), Vicenza and Verona. But as Venice evolved from a Byzantine backwater to maritime trading empire, Venice's dominion extended from Constantinople to Croatia, and inland to Lombardy. This was not easy land to attack or take by surprise: along the northwestern flank of the Veneto are the splendid but daunting Dolomite foothills and one of Italy's great northern lakes, Lago di Garda, while to the north and south, La Serenissima could see ships approaching a mile away from the beaches of the Adriatic. The region's southern boundary is marked by the country's mightiest river, the Po, which empties into the Adriatic. From Brenta River villas to fortified hill towns across the Veneto, palaces became emblazoned with Venice's emblem: the winged lion of St Mark, resting on an open book.

Yet despite its fame and influence, the Veneto isn't quite an open book. The region's former city-states retained much of their character through the centuries, and their distinct identities are expressed in art and architecture. With so many masterpieces, the Veneto's splendours are constantly being revealed from under the veil of restoration: Palladios in Vicenza and the Riviera Brenta, Giottos in Padua, Mantegnas in Verona. Some private villas and palaces are now open to the public, offering tantalising glimpses of heaven in Tiepolo ceilings and Veronese frescoes around Vicenza.

Geographic differences of just a few kilometres can actually be tasted in the food and wine. After a few days in Venice, your tastebuds may be trained to recognise Venetian culinary standards like *bigoli* (wheat pasta), *baccalà mantecato* (creamed cod) and *risi e bisi* (risotto with peas) – but the further you head inland, the heartier and more savoury these dishes become. No matter how well you know Italian food and wine, the Veneto countryside offers unexpected delights. Several of Italy's most prized wines are available only at small wineries in the Valpolicella and Soave regions, and there's only one way to settle age-old debates over who does fish, wild duck, and local-speciality meats like beef and horsemeat best: eat your way across the Venetian countryside. Once you do, you'll be back – it may not always be visible, but the Veneto has a way of leaving its Mark on you.

VENETO VILLAS & COUNTRY ESTATES

If leaving the marvels of Venice behind seems like hedonist heresy to you, you're not alone. Historically many Venetians rarely left their *sestiere* (neighbourhoods), and some were loath to even leave the island where they lived – given Venice's reputation as a trading empire and entertainment capital, Venetians knew that sooner or later the world would come to them. Only world-class attractions and the combined talents of Palladio, Veronese, and two generations of Tiepolos could convince Venetians to take the party inland.

On an easy day trip or overnight foray, you too can discover what drew Venice's tastemakers to these stretches of countryside: frescoed gaming parlours, contemplative gardens, Bacchanalian boudoirs, country fairs, free-flowing wine, literary hideaways and hearty rustic cuisine. After a day drifting from villa to villa along the Riviera Brenta (p231), you can see how the social season stretched almost half the year in 16th to 19th century Veneto country villas – for 300 years, it's a wonder anything got done back in Venice. Let yourself lose track of time and centuries and go on an architectural treasure-hunt of Palladian villas (p235) south of Vicenza, or make a beeline to the

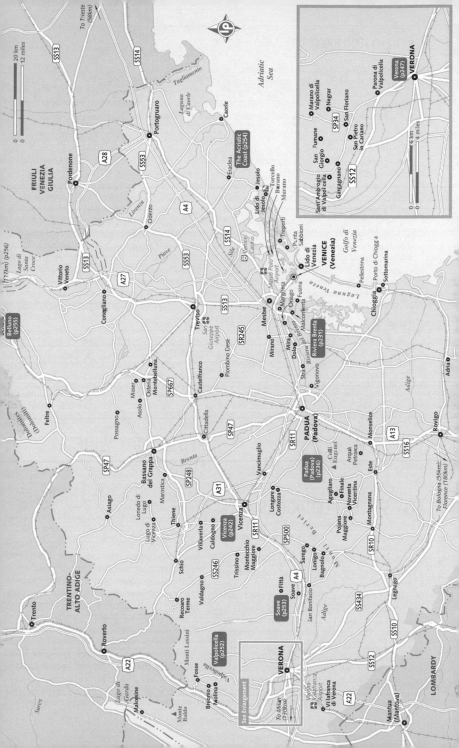

VENETO ITINERARIES

One Day

Drift along the Riviera Brenta (opposite) on an easy bike ride or in a *burchiello* (flat-bottomed boat), sipping *prosecco* (sparkling white wine) en route and stopping at a few of the 80 grand Veneto villas along the riverbanks like a Venetian socialite c 1600. Don't miss Palladio's happily misnamed La Malcontenta (opposite), the Tiepolo frescoes and hedge mazes of Villa Pisani Nazionale (p232), and the Shoemaker's Museum at 18th-century Villa Foscarini Rossi (p232).

Two Days

Brenta boat trips end in Padua, where you can spend the night in the serene Belludi37 (p241) overlooking the Basilica del Santo (p239), the shrine of St Anthony of Padua, patron saint of miracle cures and lost and found objects. But don't miss the small wonders next door in honour of St George: the frescoed Oratorio di San Giorgio (p239) and the Titian-filled Scoletta del Santo (p239). With advance booking, you can see Padua's crowning glory: Giotto's frescoed Capella degli Scrovegni (p236) – otherwise, head for the historic centre to linger at a *caffè* in Padua's arcaded twin piazzas (p240) or tour its ground-breaking university (p238), including Galileo's lecture hall and the six-tiered Anatomy Theatre. After lunch, take the 15- to 30-minute train ride to Vicenza, and spend the afternoon watching sunlight ripple across the soaring facades of Palladio's palazzi (p242) and illuminate the storybook Villa Valmarana 'ai Nani' (p245), covered floor to ceiling with fantastical frescoes by legendary father-son painters Giambattista and Giandomenico Tiepolo. Enjoy happy hour in the long shadow of Palladio at the 12th-century wine bar Antica Casa della Malvasia (p246), and spend the night in a designer-chic palace, the Relais Santa Corona (p247), on a Palladio-lined street.

Three Days

Take your sweet time the next day getting to Verona, where mornings mean Mantegnas at Basilica di San Zeno Maggiore (p247), afternoons call for window-shopping in Via Mazzini and leisurely coffee breaks in the Piazza delle Erbe (p251), and summer evenings bring opera to the ancient Roman Arena (p249). *Romeo and Juliet* was set on Verona's romantic balconied backstreets, and you shouldn't leave town without trying the local love potion: voluptuous deep-red Amarone (p251). Bunk in for the night (p251) if you're here for opera, or head back to Venice by train to awake to the inimitable Venetian chorus of gondoliers and the gentle percussion of waves lapping the *fondamente* (canal banks).

---

most dazzling villa of all: the Villa Maser, Palladio and Paolo Veronese's golden monument to the good life outside the charmed hilltop town of Asolo (p234).

CITY-STATE SPLENDOURS

They sparred for centuries, but today Veneto's spectacular city-states are neatly aligned with Venice along a major east-west railway line. First stop is Padua (p236), only 37km from Venice and yet a world apart with its glowing Giotto frescoes, medieval city centre, mystical shrine to St Anthony, politically charged past and historic university. Next up is Vicenza (p242), a marvel of Palladio palaces, frescoed interiors and distinctive cuisine just 32km northwest of Padua. Another 51km brings you to Verona (p247), where divas sing their hearts out at the ancient Roman Arena (p249), Romanesque architecture sets the scene for aspiring Romeos and Juliets, and Amarone stirs passions in historic *osterie* (pub-restaurants).

RED & WHITE WINE COUNTRIES

No matter how you like your wine – red, white, sparkling or distilled into firewater – Veneto's wine country can cure your thirst. As the houses of Verona recede from view and Romanesque castles and rolling vineyards come into focus, you've arrived in one of Italy's most prized grape-growing regions. Wineries are clustered around the castle-topped wine-making town of Soave (p253) and line the valleys of the Valpolicella wine region (p252). But [Verona's hinterlands don't get all the glory: for a DOCG (*denominazione d'origine controllata*; guaranteed quality) drink that tickles your nose, head to the northeastern Veneto to Conegliano (p253). For something stronger, Bassano del Grappa (p246) offers the city's namesake spirits with heady views of a Palladio bridge and glass escape pods by modern master Massimiliano Fuksas.

BEACH & SKI RESORTS

Veneto's resorts along the Adriatic coastline and up high in the Dolomites provide year-round options to get away from the crowds, but still find plenty of company. To the northeast of Venice, the beaches of Lido di Jesolo (p254) brim with beach umbrellas by day and beach clubbers by night. For a mellow seaside scene with houses painted in eye-opening colours, head to Caorle (p254). Mountain air and wildflower carpets revive city spirits in the national park at Belluno (p255), while ski bunnies and Olympians in training head to Cortina d'Ampezzo (p256).

VENETO VILLAS & COUNTRY ESTATES

Gambling away fortunes, seducing clergy, publishing love-letters: by the end of the 16th century, Venice was becoming so trendsettingly outrageous that the only thing left for bored socialites to do was leave, and shock the locals in some unsuspecting country hamlet. So when summer arrived, Venice's social set packed up their *palazzi* (palaces) and decamped en masse to the Veneto hinterlands to relieve their island fever, and dream up new ways to entertain and scandalise their neighbours. For six months out of the year in their splendid frescoed villas, it was mostly fun and games for Venetian nobles – except for the doge (duke) and his spies, who kept track of politicking at parties, gambling problems that could threaten the tax base, and love affairs that might lead to dangerously strategic alliances.

Even today when you push through the double-height doors to Palladian villas along the Riviera Brenta and country estates outside Vicenza, you'll get a heady whiff of intrigues and forbidden romance. You can still reach the Riviera Brenta by boat and view the parade of villas lining its banks at your leisure, much as Venetian nobles did for centuries – though bicycle, bus, train, and car are also options. With a car, Palladio's villas ringing Vicenza are yours for the viewing, including the most splendid Palladian villa of all: the golden Villa Maser, brilliantly frescoed by Paolo Veronese and surrounded by vineyards.

RIVIERA BRENTA

On 13 June, for 300 years, summer officially kicked off with a traffic jam along the Grand Canal as a flotilla of fashionable Venetians headed for the Brenta. Every last ball gown and poker chair was loaded onto Brenta-bound barges for dalliances and diversions that stretched until November. Hearts were won and fortunes lost; vendettas and villas endured.

The party officially ended when Napoleon took over the area in 1797, but 80 villas still strike elegant poses along the Brenta River, including some constructed under Austrian occupation in the 19th century. Private ownership and privacy hedges leave much to the imagination, but four historic villas are now open as museums; others may be open to organised boat and bicycle tours, and splendid villas can be visited around Vicenza (see p242).

The most romantic Brenta villa is the Palladio-designed 1555–60 Villa Foscari (☎ 041 520 39 66; www.lamalcontenta.com; Via dei Turisti 9, Malcontenta; adult/student €10/8; ◐ 9am-noon Tue & Sat, closed 15 Nov-31 Mar; groups of 10 or more can book for other times at per person €8), nicknamed La Malcontenta after a grand dame of the Foscari clan allegedly exiled here for cheating on her husband – though these effortlessly light, sociable salons hardly constitute a punishment. The villa was abandoned for years, but Giovanni Zelotti's frescoes have recently been restored to daydream-inducing splendour, from Fame in the study to the Bacchanalian bedroom with Bacchus and Cupid among trompe l'œil grapevines over the bed. Palladio's grand facade faces the river, with soaring Ionic columns, capped by a classical tympanum, that draw the eye and spirits upward. Modern artists and architects have been invited to create site-specific projects here, and a recent Zaha Hadid installation used Palladio's blueprint as a matrix for a 3D fibreglass sculpture of liquid space.

To appreciate gardening and social engineering in the Riviera Brenta, stop just west of Oriago at Villa Widmann Rezzonico Foscari (☎ 041 560 06 90; www.riviera-brenta.it; Via Nazionale 420, Mira; adult/student €6/5; ◐ 10am-5pm Sat & Sun Nov-Mar, 10am-6pm Tue-Sun May-Sep). The 18th century villa originally owned by Persian-Venetian nobility captures the Brenta's last days of rococo decadence, with Murano sea-monster chandeliers and a frescoed grand ballroom with an upper viewing gallery. Head to the gallery to reach the upstairs ladies' gambling parlour where, according to local lore, villas were once gambled away in high-stakes games. Ignore the incongruous modernised bathrooms and puzzling modern crafts displays in the bedrooms and head into the garden, where an albino peacock loudly bemoans bygone glories amid moss-covered nymph and cherub sculptures. The gatehouse ticket counter doubles as an APTV Info Point (☎ 041 42 49 73) offering brochures on the Brenta.

Across the Brenta from Villa Widmann Foscari and behind the hedgerows is the Villa Barchessa Valmarana (☎ 041 426 63 87; www.villavalmarana .net; admission €6; ⏰ 10am-6pm Tue-Sun Mar-Oct), which was built a century later and now serves mainly as a conference centre – though it must be hard to concentrate on business in that double-height dining room lined with fanciful frescoes.

To keep hard-partying Venetian nobles in line, Doge Alvise Pisani provided a monumental reminder of who was in charge with the 1774 Villa Pisani Nazionale (☎ 041 271 90 19; www .villapisani.beniculturali.it; Via Alvise Pisani 7, Strà; adult/ EU citizen 18-25yr/under 18yr €10/7.50/free, grounds only €7.50/5/free; ⏰ 9am-6pm Tue-Sun Oct-Mar, 9am-8pm Tue-Sun Apr-Sep, last admission 1hr before closing), surrounded by a labyrinthine hedge-maze and pools reflecting the doge's glory.

If the walls of these 114 rooms could talk, they'd name-drop historical figures shamelessly. Here you'll find the gaming rooms where Venice's powerful Pisani family racked up debts that forced them to sell the family mansion to Napoleon; the grand bathroom with a tiny wooden throne used by Napoleon during his 1807 reign as king of Italy; a sagging bed where Vittorio Emanuele II apparently tossed and turned as the head of newly independent Italy; and, in historical irony, the grand reception hall where Mussolini and Hitler met for the first time in 1934 under Tiepolo's ceiling masterpiece depicting the *Geniuses of Peace*. Don't miss outstanding temporary exhibitions in upstairs salons and the gardens, which have ranged from contemporary sculptor Mimmo Paladino's sleeping figures in the reflecting pools to 19th century painter Emma Ciardi's moody views of party stragglers outside Veneto villas at dawn.

Well-heeled Venetians wouldn't have dreamt of decamping to the Brenta without their favourite cobblers, sparking a local tradition of high-end shoemaking. Today, 950 companies in the Brenta region produce 20 million pairs of shoes annually. The lasting contribution of Brenta cobblers is commemorated with a Shoemakers' Museum at the 18th-century Villa Foscarini Rossi (☎ 049 980 10 91; www.villafoscarini.it; Via Doge Pisani 1/2, Strà; adult/12-18yr &

65yr-plus €5/2.50; ⏰ 9am-1pm Nov-Mar, 9am-12.30pm Mon, 9am-12.30pm & 2.30-6pm Tue-Fri, Sat 2-6pm, 2.30-6pm Sun Apr-Oct), a multiroom dream wardrobe of 18th-century slippers, shoes worn by trendsetters Marlene Dietrich and Katharine Hepburn, and heels handcrafted in the Brenta for Yves Saint Laurent and Pucci. The building also has an impressive pedigree: among the many architects involved was Vincenzo Scamozzi (one of the city's leading 16th-century architects), working from designs by Palladio, although the present look results partly from a later neoclassical reworking.

On Sunday and during holidays in June, September and October, guided visits are sometimes organised to further villas in the area as part of the Ville Aperte (Open Villas) initiative – ask the APT in Venice (p274) for more information.

Seeing the Brenta by boat lets you witness an engineering marvel: the hydraulic locks system developed in the 15th century to divert the river to the sea, ingeniously preventing river silt from dumping into the lagoon and turning Venice into a mudflat. Most boats move only at a walking pace, and when water levels are low, views of the surrounding countryside are not as panoramic. But since most villas face the river, you'll be seeing them as Palladio and his contemporaries intended: at a leisurely pace befitting Venetian nobility.

Il Burchiello (☎ 049 820 69 10; www.ilburchiello.it; full-day adult €66-79, 12-17yr €52, 6-11yr €37, under 6yr free, half-day adult & 12-17yr €44-48, 6-11yr €36-37, under 6yr free) is a modern version of the luxury barges that once plied the river Brenta, so you can see the Veneto countryside from the perspective of a Venetian courtier. Watch as 50 villas drift past from cushy velvet couches with a glass of *prosecco* from the on-board bar. Day cruises stop at La Malcontenta, Widmann and Pisani villas; half-day tours (Tuesday, Wednesday, Thursday and Friday) cover two villas. Full-day cruises leave from Venice (Tuesday, Thursday and Saturday) or Padua (Wednesday, Friday and Sunday), with bus transfers to train stations.

I Battelli del Brenta (☎ 049 876 02 33; www.battelli delbrenta.it; half-day tours €44-48, full day €66-85; ⏰ by reservation Tue-Sun Mar-Nov) also offers full-day boat excursions covering three villas, nine swing bridges and five locks along the Brenta, including some cruises on restored wooden *burci* (barges); half-day trips may include optional lunches and transfers to/from Venice or Padua.

The scenic plains of the Brenta Riviera make an easy, enjoyable bicycle ride, and you can speed past those tour boats along 150km of cycling routes. Rental Bike Venice (☎ 346 84 71 14; www.rentalbikevenice.blogspot.com; Via Gramsci 85, Mira; city & mountain bicycle/foldable bicycle hire per day €10/14; ☺ 8am-8pm) is a friendly bike-rental spot accessible by bus from Venice, Mestre or Padua (see website for directions) offering city bikes with baskets, mountain bikes and handy foldable bikes to take on buses, plus free parking, roadside assistance and advice in English on itineraries, local restaurants and shops. Rentals are also available from Center Bike Bartolomielo (☎ 041 42 01 10; www.rentalbikevenice.blogspot.com; Via Mocenigo 3, Mira Porte; bicycle hire per day €10; ☺ Mon-Sat, by reservation only Sun).

ACTV's Venezia Padova Extraurbanc bus 53 leaves from Venice's Piazzale Roma about every half hour, and stops at most key villages along the banks of the Brenta en route to Padua. Train service from Venice's Stazione Santa Lucia stops at Dolo (€2.35 to €3.55, 30 minutes) en route to Padua. By car, take SS11 from Mestre-Venezia towards Padova (Padua), and take the Autostrada A4 toward Dolo/Padova.

Information

IAT tourist office Padua (☎ 049 875 20 77; www .turismopadova.it); Padua train station (☺ 9am-7pm Mon-Sat, 9am-noon Sun); Mira Porte (☎ 041 560 06 90; Villa Widmann Foscari, Via Nazionale 420; ☺ 10am-5pm Tue-Sun Apr, 10am-6pm Tue-Sun May-Sep, 10am-5pm Sat, Sun & holidays Nov-Mar)

Main APT office (Map pp68–9; ☎ information 041 529 87 11; www.turismovenezia.it; Piazza San Marco 71f, Venice; ☺ 9am-3.30pm Mon-Sat)

Festivals & Events

Dolo Mercatino dell'Antiquariato (Antiques Market; Isola Bassa, Dolo) Give your apartment the graces of a Brenta villa with finds from the region's largest antiques market, held in good weather the fourth Sunday of the month, April to October.

StraOrganic (www.comune.stra.ve.it) The Brenta claims bragging rights to local, organic foods and handicrafts in Strà; held last weekend in April.

Riviera Fiorita (www.turismovenezia.it) Party like it's 1627 with baroque costume parties at the Villa Pisani and Villa Widmann, historically correct country fairs, even gelato in baroque-era flavours; held second weekend in September.

Venice Marathon (www.venicemarathon.it) Run like Casanova caught in the act, from Villa Pisani along the Brenta to Venice, with the final legs crossing pontoon bridges; usually held in October, with proceeds funding clean-water projects in Africa.

Eating

Ristorante da Bepi el Ciosato (☎ 041 69 89 97; www .hotelgallimberti.it; Via Malcanton 33, Malcontenta; meals €26; ☺ lunch & dinner) Across the road from La Malcontena is this country bistro that serves fish baked into *pasticcio di pesce* (fish pie) or wrapped in an artichoke crust.

Trattoria Prandin (☎ 049 50 23 70; Via Pertile 124, San Pietro di Stra; meals €15-20; ☺ lunch & dinner) After wandering the vast Villa Pisani, you might feel ready to eat a horse – and that's one of the traditional Veneto meat specialities on the menu at this nearby spot, which also serves superb steak with homestyle roast potatoes.

Sleeping

Villa Rizzi-Albarea (☎ 041 510 09 33; www.villa-albarea .com; Via Albarea 53; d €200-280; P 🐾) One of the oldest of the Brenta villas, this former monastery is now a luxury inn near Dolo, 3km north of the Dolo exit from the A4 autostrada (shuttle service is available from the railway station and Marco Polo airport). Set in 2 hectares of parkland, the mansion offers plush rooms with antique furnishings, private Brenta boat trips, bicycle and car rentals, a traditional china tea service and a rather unusual amenity: the restored church dating from AD 1100, where brides once made pilgrimages to receive nuptial blessings.

AROUND VICENZA

Not to be outdone by their Venetian neighbours, Vicenza's high and mighty began to build impressive country residences of their own as early as the 15th century. But by order of the Venetian Senate, you won't find any moats or fortifications around Vicenza palaces. Venice forbade the gentry of Vicenza and other mainland cities under Venetian control from building castles in the countryside, fearing a landscape dotted with stout forts that might resist the doge's tax-collectors. Instead of trying to dodge the doge, Vicenza's nobility one-upped Venetian nobility with the sheer splendour of their villas, lavishly frescoed and set like jewels into verdant hillsides and sprawling gated parks. Many of the thousands that were built remain, although most are still privately held and inaccessible to the general public.

Northern Loop: Vicenza to Asolo

A road trip from Vicenza takes you through one of Italy's most sophisticated stretches of countryside, past landmarks of modern art and architecture, to the most splendid villa in the Veneto – if not all of Europe. The drive is about an hour and a quarter each way; stop for lunch in Bassano del Grappa (p246) and make a day of it.

On SR211, head northeast out of town toward the walled Castelfranco, which became a desirable and hotly disputed spot among Venetian city-states for a simple reason: the then-rulers exempted anyone prepared to move in from all taxes. The town has an extra claim to fame as the birthplace of the mysterious painter Giorgione. Little is known about his life, and only half a dozen works can be definitely attributed to him. One of his key works, *Madonna and Child Enthroned with Saints Francis and Liberale,* is in the cathedral (9am-noon & 3-6pm) in the centre of town. For more information, hit the tourist office (☎ 0423 49 14 16; Via F M Preti 66; 9am-12.30pm Mon-Fri, 3-6pm Tue, Thu & Fri, 9.30am-12.30pm & 3-6pm Sat & Sun).

From Castelfranco, take SP667 north and then west on SP248 toward Asolo. After about 2km, you'll see a turnoff at Osteria north onto Via Caldretta, which leads 3km north to Maser. There on a vineyard-covered hillside, you'll spot Palladio and Paolo Veronese's golden monument to the Venetian *bea vita* (good life): Villa Masèr (Villa Barbaro; ☎ 0423 92 30 04; www .villadimaser.it; Via Barbaro 4; with/without PalladioCard €3/6; 10am-6pm Tue-Sat & 11am-6pm Sun Apr-Jun & Sep-Oct, 10am-6pm Tue, Thu, Sat, 11am-6pm Sun Mar & Jul-Aug, 2.30-5pm Sat & Sun Nov-Dec, 10am-5pm Sat, 11am-5pm Sun Jan-Feb). Palladio set the arcaded yellow villa into the hillside with a fanciful grotto out back, but inside Paolo Veronese has upstaged the master architect with wildly imaginative trompe l'œil architecture.

Don obligatory slippers at the door and pad through rooms designed for delight: vines climb the walls of the Stanza di Baccho; an alert watchdog keeps one eye on the door of the Stanza di Canuccio (Little Dog Room); and in a corner of the frescoed grand salon, the painter has apparently forgotten his spattered shoes and broom. But amid these party scenes, there's a tender moment: through a series of salon doors, Veronese's self-portrait gazes fondly across crowded rooms at a portrait of his niece. At the wine-tasting room by the parking lot, you can raise a toast to Palladio and Veronese with Maser estate–grown DOC (*denominazione d'origine controllata*; quality-controlled) *prosecco.*

Back on SP248, head west 7.5km just past the turnoff north to Asolo, and you'll spot a sign pointing down Via Castellana 5km south to the Brioni Family Tomb (Via del Cimitero; 9am-7pm), Venetian modernist master architect Carlo Scarpa's latest, greatest work in the San Vita d'Altivole town cemetery. Among the headstones, Scarpa's 1969–78 monument is unmistakable, with its raw concrete bridge to the afterlife rising from Zen-style gardens. Follow stepping stones over water into the domed chapel, where the sarcophagi of the Brioni are housed. Talk about commitment: Scarpa chose to be buried standing up near his clients, along a boundary wall.

Return to Asolo (population 8590), known as the 'town of 100 vistas' for its panoramic hillside location. Picturesque Piazza Garibaldi has a central tourist office (☎ 0423 52 90 46; Piazza Garibaldi 73; 9am-12.30pm Mon-Fri, 3-6pm Tue, Thu & Fri, 9.30am-12.30pm & 3-6pm Sat & Sun) and is framed by tight ranks of golden-hued houses. In the cathedral south of the square, you'll spot a few paintings by Jacopo Bassano and Lorenzo Lotto.

Robert Browning spent time in Asolo, but the ultimate local celebrity is Caterina Corner, the former Venetian queen of Cyprus, who was given the town, its castle (now used as a theatre) and surrounding county towards the end of the 15th century in exchange for her abdication. In the town's Museo Civico (☎ 0423 95 23 13; Via Regina Cornaro 74; adult/senior & under 26yr/ under 6yr €4/3/free; 10am-noon & 3-7pm Sat & Sun) you can see a section devoted to Caterina's life and travels. She promptly became the queen of the local literary set, holding salons that featured writer Pietro Bembo. If you climb north out of town to the Cimitero di Sant'Anna, you can pay your respects to the tombs of other women artistic figures: Eleonora Duse (1858–1924), a major actress romantically and politically linked with nationalist poet Gabriele d'Annunzio, and British traveller and writer Freya Stark (1893–1993), who retreated to Asolo between Middle Eastern forays.

After the hike uphill, you can enjoy a leisurely meal of suckling pig with roast potatoes or tagliatelle with partridge sauce at the antique-filled, family-run Ca' Derton da Nino (☎ 0423 52 96 48; Piazza d'Annunzio 11; meals €20-30; ☽ lunch & dinner Tue-Sat). Lulled by Asolo's charms and hearty fare, you may decide to spend the night. You'll need to plan ahead to snag a room at Hotel Villa Cipriani (☎ 0423 52 34 11; www.villaciprianiasolo.com; Via Canova 298, Asolo; d €200-520), the famed luxury villa overlooking Asolo, but you might find availability at Hotel Duse (☎ 0423 55 241; www.hotelduse .com; Via Browning 190, Asolo; s €55-70, d €110-130), an elegant four-storey hotel smack in the heart of town with hilltop views.

Before heading back to Vicenza, westward to Bassano on SS248, or to Venice (via SP667 to Castelfranco and SR245 to Mestre), you might consider an 11km detour north of Asolo on SP6 to Possagno, birth- and resting-place of Italy's master of neoclassical sculpture, Antonio Canova. One local landmark is the 1832 Tempio (☎ 0423 54 40 40; admission free; ☽ 9am-noon & 3-6pm Tue-Sun), the outsize church that Canova left to his town that looks more like a Roman temple on holiday in the Veneto. Canova made marble come alive, but mastery didn't always come easy: you can see Canova's rough drafts in plaster at the Gipsoteca (☎ 0423 54 43 23; www.museocanova.it; Possagno; adult/student/under 6yr €7/4/free; ☽ 9am-12.30pm & 3-6pm Tue-Sun), in a building completed by modernist master Carlo Scarpa in 1957.

Southern Loop: Vicenza to Noventa Vicentina

A southern loop route of about 110km would take the SR11 west of Vicenza and turn north on the SS246 to Montecchio Maggiore, where high hilltop twin castles tower over the landscape and classical statues wave you into the elegant 1742 Giorgio Massari-built mansion, the Villa Cordellina Lombardi (☎ 0444 90 81 41; Via Lovara 36; adult/ student €2.10/1.80; ☽ 9am-1pm Tue-Fri, 9am-1pm & 3-6pm Sat & Sun Apr-Oct), 3km east of the Duomo (take Via De Gasperi). Despite its easy Palladian graces, this palace has seen its share of hard work: it was used during both World Wars for military purposes, and served as a farm for breeding silkworms. But through careful restoration of the interiors, Giambattista's Tiepolo's fresco *Intelligence Triumphing over Ignorance* remains intact. Impressive Intelligence blows into the room to the trumpets of Fame, as mighty Ignorance is struck by a putto's arrow and tumbles from the ceiling.

From Montecchio Maggiore, turn south and follow the SP500. Three kilometres before

Sarego, you'll find the somewhat dilapidated Palladian complex of Villa Trissino. A couple of kilometres south of Sarego through rolling vineyard country, Lonigo is surrounded by horses, cattle and a trio of villas, the most striking of which is Scamozzi's 1576 domed hilltop Rocca Pisana (☎ 0444 83 16 25; admission €5; ☽ by prior appointment 3-5.30pm Tue Mar-Nov); to get there, follow signs to the Rocca for 2km. About 4km further south, the village of Bagnolo is home to the proud Palladian Villa Pisani Ferri Bonetti (☎ 0444 83 11 04; admission €7; ☽ 10am-noon & 2-6pm Apr-Nov, visits by prior appointment), a 16th-century facade standing tall above rolling lawns and a stream.

From Bagnolo, a series of winding country lanes leads southeast to Pojana Maggiore and another of Palladio's designs just south out of town on the road to Legnago: the frescoed 1550 Villa Pojana (☎ 0444 89 85 54; admission €4; ☽ 10am-12.30pm & 2-4pm Sat & Sun Nov-Mar, 10am-12.30pm & 2-4pm daily Apr-Oct). Three kilometres east in Noventa Vicentina is the 17th-century Villa Barbarigo (☎ 0444 78 85 11; www.comune.noventa -vicentina.vi.it; admission free; ☽ 10am-1pm Tue, Wed & Fri, 10am-1pm & 3-5pm Mon & Thu), which makes a mighty impressive town hall for a small town; beyond the deep porch and two massive tiers of columns, frescoes were recently discovered on the walls of the grand salons and lovingly restored. Just east, the northbound SS247 takes you past Finale (just south of Agugliaro) and its splendid Villa Saraceno (☎ 0444 89 13 71, Landmark Trust in UK 01628-825925; www.landmarktrust .org.uk; Via Finale 8, Finale di Agugliaro; ☽ open to the public 2-4pm Wed Apr-Oct; P ⛵), a restored 16th-century Palladian country villa you can visit for a couple of hours, or stay overnight in (building rental per night £350 to £800) – it sleeps up to 16 people.

About 22km up the road towards Vicenza, turn off west for the ancient and pretty village of Costozza, blessed with several villas. The star attraction is the complex known as the Ville da Schio (gardens admission €5; ☽ 9.30am-7.30pm Tue-Sun), frescoed mansions set against a hillside of magnificent gardens dotted with sculpture. Get your entry tickets to see the gardens from the neighbouring Botte del Covolo wine bar. In the shadow of the Colli Berici hills (some great walking), the village is worth a stroll and wine stop in a handful of *enoteche* (wine bars).

A few kilometres north, at Longare, take the country road heading northeast over the motorway to reach, some 8km away and on the SR11 road, Vancimuglio. Privately owned but observable from the road, the Villa Chiericati da Porto Rigo is weather-worn but winsome, with ivy sneaking up the pillars and wisteria threatening to run up the stairs. From here, it's about 12km west to Vicenza. On your way back into town, don't miss Vicenza's villa masterpieces: Palladio's La Rotonda (p245) and the Tiepolo-frescoed Villa 'Ai Nani' (p245).

CITY-STATES

Venice's neighbours and worthy rivals for travellers' affections are conveniently lined up along a major train route, making it easy for day-trippers to hit just one city or hop from one to the next in one, two, or three days (see p230). Padua, Vicenza, and Verona are listed by proximity to Venice in this chapter, but there's only a half-hour train ride (or less) between them. Choose where to begin based on your own personal interests: Padua inspires breakthroughs with Giotto masterpieces, powerful coffee in arcaded squares, and a history-making university – plus a medical garden and holy relics that could work wonders for your health. Vincenza lifts the spirits with soaring Palladio palaces, hearty rustic cuisine, glowing icons and an enchanted villa frescoed floor to ceiling with the Tiepolos' wildest flights of fancy. Verona sets the scene for romance with spine-tingling opera, balconies begging for elopements, and backstreet *osterie* pouring romance straight from the bottle.

PADUA (PADOVA)

Although it's just 37km west of Venice, Padua (Padova; population 212,500) looks more like Milan left in the dryer too long, with oddly shaped medieval piazzas, a student population keeping it hip, and broad boulevards lined with elegant *stile liberty* (Liberty style) edifices alongside creepy Fascist buildings and postwar cereal-box architecture. Milan's has da Vinci's Last Supper, but Padua boasts the signature work by the artist da Vinci credited as his greatest influence: the Cappella degli Scrovegni (Scrovegni Chapel) by Giotto.

Padua has certainly been through the wringer since its founding in the late 12th century BC, but as you can tell by its art and architecture, reinvention has become its trademark. Romans took over the town from northeast Veneti tribes and renamed it Patavium, but Goths besieged the city, and Lombard invasions wiped it out in AD 602. A fire again destroyed the city in AD 1164, but

the city made a comeback to claim Vicenza and establish Italy's third university in 1222, becoming a magnet for thinkers and artists. Padua remained a rival to Verona and repeatedly challenged the authority of Venice, which settled the matter by occupying Padua and its territories in 1405. Padua's fate remained tied to Venice through Austrian occupation and Italian independence, but the city found singular purpose as Italy's army base in WWI.

As a strategic military-industrial centre, Padua became a parade ground for Mussolini speeches, a Fascist architecture showplace, an Allied bombing target and a secret Italian Resistance hub based at the university. Padua was wrested from Fascist control in 1945, and within a year there was a new industrial zone east of the city, the university was back in session, work began piecing together shards of Andrea Mantegna's frescoes in the destroyed Eremitani Church, and the puzzlework that is Padua began anew.

Almost 200 years before Michelangelo's Sistine Chapel and da Vinci's *Last Supper* came Padua's Renaissance breakthrough: Giotto's moving, modern 1303–05 frescoes in the Capella degli Scrovegni (Scrovegni Chapel; ☎ 049 201 00 20; www.cappelladegliscrovegni.it; Giardini dell'Arena; adult/6-17yr & senior/under 6yr €12/8/1, night session €8/6/1, admission with PadovaCard free; ☒ call centre 9am-7pm Mon-Fri, 9am-6pm Sat). Medieval churchgoers were accustomed to blank stares from flat saints perched high on gold Gothic thrones – but Giotto introduces Biblical figures as characters in recognisable settings, caught up in extraordinary circumstances. Onlookers gossip as middle-aged Anne tenderly kisses Joachim, and late in life gives birth to miracle-baby Mary; exhausted new dad Joseph falls asleep sitting up in the manger, as sheep and angels take the night watch over baby Jesus; and Jesus stares down Judas as the traitor puckers up for the kiss that sealed Jesus's fate.

Dante, da Vinci, Boccacio and Vasari all honour Giotto as the artist who officially ended the Dark Ages in a blaze of glowing colour, and ushered in the Renaissance age of possibility. In the new multimedia gallery, video projections and a full-scale set allow you to enter each scene, and experience how convincing Giotto can be. Giotto's startling humanist approach not only changed how people saw saints, it changed how they saw themselves; not as lowly vassals but as vessels for the divine, however flawed. This humanising approach was especially well-suited for

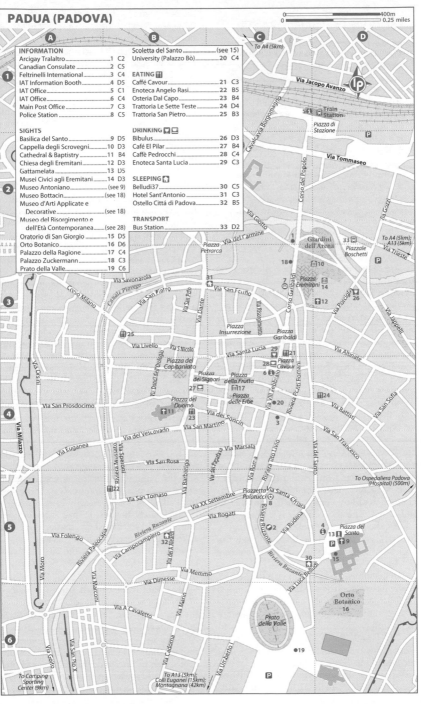

PADUA (PADOVA)

0 — 400m
0 — 0.25 miles

INFORMATION
Arcigay Tralaltro...........................1 C2
Canadian Consulate 2 C5
Feltrinelli International..................3 C4
IAT Information Booth...................4 D5
IAT Office.......................................5 C1
IAT Office.......................................6 C4
Main Post Office............................7 C3
Police Station.................................8 C5

SIGHTS
Basilica del Santo..........................9 D5
Cappella degli Scrovegni.............10 D3
Cathedral & Baptistry..................11 B4
Chiesa degli Eremitani.................12 D3
Gattamelata..................................13 D5
Musei Civici agli Eremitani..........14 D3
Museo Antoniano................... (see 9)
Museo Bottacin........................(see 18)
Museo d'Arti Applicate e
    Decorative.............................(see 18)
Museo del Risorgimento e
    dell'Età Contemporanea.....(see 28)
Oratorio di San Giorgio...............15 D5
Orto Botanico...............................16 D6
Palazzo della Ragione..................17 C4
Palazzo Zuckermann....................18 C3
Prato della Valle..........................19 C6

Scoletta del Santo.................... (see 15)
University (Palazzo Bò)................20 C4

EATING
Caffè Cavour.................................21 C3
Enoteca Angelo Rasi.....................22 B5
Osteria Dal Capo..........................23 B4
Trattoria Le Sette Teste................24 D4
Trattoria San Pietro......................25 B3

DRINKING
Bibulus..26 D3
Café El Pilar.................................27 B4
Caffè Pedrocchi............................28 C4
Enoteca Santa Lucia.....................29 C3

SLEEPING
Belludi37.......................................30 C5
Hotel Sant'Antonio.......................31 C3
Ostello Città di Padova................32 B5

TRANSPORT
Bus Station...................................33 D2

SEE MORE OF PADUA FOR LESS

For 48 or 72 hours (€15/20), a PadovaCard gives one adult plus one child under 14 free use of city public transport and access to 12 of Padua's major attractions, including the Cappella degli Scrovegni (plus €1 booking fee; reservation essential), Musei Civici agli Eremitani, Palazzo della Ragione, Museo del Risorgimento e dell'Età Contemporanea at Caffè Pedrocchi, the cathedral baptistry and the Orto Botanico. The card grants discounts at some Padua restaurants, B&Bs and shops, plus reduced admission at 24 historic sites outside Padua, including Petrarch's House in Arquà Petrarca and Palladio's Teatro Olimpico in Vicenza. PadovaCards are available at Padua tourist offices and monuments covered by the pass.

the chapel Enrico Scrovegni commissioned in memory of his father, who as a money-lender, was denied a Christian burial.

The chapel is a five-minute walk from the train station, but daily visits are by reservation only and booking is required online or by phone at least three days in advance, possibly weeks ahead from April to October; see website for off-season and midweek promotional ticket rates. Chapel visits last 15 minutes, though the 'double turn' night session ticket (adult/child aged 7 to 17 and senior/child under 7 years €12/6/1; open 7pm to 9.20pm) allows a 30-minute stay, and multimedia room visits can last 30 to 90 minutes.

In the adjacent Musei Civici agli Eremitani (☎ 049 820 45 50; Piazza Eremitani 8; museum only adult/child 7-17yr/ under 7yr €10/8/free, admission with PadovaCard or Capella degli Scrovegni ticket free; 9am-7pm Tue-Sun), a converted monastery houses on the ground floor artefacts dating from Padua's pre-Roman history, and, upstairs, notable 14th- to 18th-century works by Veneto artists from Bellini to Canova. The showstopper is a crucifix by Giotto, showing a heartbroken Mary wringing her hands as Jesus's blood drips through the rocky earth, right into the empty eye sockets of a human skull.

On the same ticket you can visit the nearby Palazzo Zuckermann (Corso di Garibaldi 33; 10am-7pm Tue-Sun), home to the Museo d'Arti Applicate e Decorative decorative-arts museum, covering flatware to fashion on the ground and 1st floors, and the 2nd-floor Museo Bottacin, a treasury of finely worked ancient coins, pistols and knives, and medals and badges of dishonour.

When a 1944 bombing raid demolished the extraordinary 1448–57 frescoes by And-rea Mantegna in the Capella Overtari in the Chiesa degli Eremitani (Eremitani Church; ☎ 049 875 64 10; Piazza Eremitani; 7.30am-noon & 3.30-7pm Mon-Fri, 10am-12.30pm & 4-7pm Sat & Sun), the loss to art history was incalculable. After half a century of painstaking reconstruction, the shattered, humidity-damaged stories of Saints James and Christopher have been puzzled together, revealing action-packed compositions and extreme perspectives that make Mantegna's saints look like superheroes.

Follow Via VIII Febbraio to the Palazzo del Bò, seat of Padua's history-making university (☎ 049 827 30 47; Via VIII Febbraio; adult/student & child €5/2; tours 9.15am, 10.15am & 12.15pm Tue, Thu & Sat, 2.15pm, 4.15pm & 5.15pm Mon, Wed & Fri). This institution was founded by renegade scholars from Bologna seeking greater intellectual freedom, and some of Italy's greatest and most controversial thinkers taught here, including Copernicus, Galileo, Casanova, and the world's first woman doctor of philosophy, Eleonora Lucrezia Corner Piscopia (her statue graces the stairs). Guided tours cover Galileo's lecture hall and the world's first Anatomy Theatre, a six-tiered hall built for scientific autopsy in 1594 before biohazards were understood – dissected corpses were dumped into an underground stream.

Ancient Padua can be glimpsed in elegant twin squares framed by arcades, the Piazza delle Erbe and Piazza della Frutta, separated by the triple-decker Gothic Palazzo della Ragione (☎ 049 820 50 06; Piazza delle Erbe; adult/child €4/2, temporary exhibitions €8/5; 9am-7pm Tue-Sun), the city's tribunal dating from 1218. Inside, frescoes by Giotto acolytes Giusto de' Menabuoi and Nicolò Mireto depict the astrological theories of Pietro d'Abano, with images representing the months, seasons, saints, animals and noteworthy Paduans (not necessarily in that order). Unfortunately, the frescoes had to be restored after fire in 1420 and storm damage in 1756, so most of the original work was lost.

South of the palazzo is the city's cathedral (☎ 049 66 28 14; Piazza del Duomo; 7.30am-noon & 3.30-7.30pm Mon-Sat, 8am-1pm & 3.30-8.45pm Sun & holidays), built from a much altered design of Michelangelo's and completely upstaged by the adjoining 13th-century Baptistry (☎ 049 65 69 14; Piazza del Duomo; adult/child €2.80/1, admission with PadovaCard free; 10am-6pm). This Romanesque gem is completely frescoed with luminous Biblical scenes by Giusto de' Menabuoi, a Giotto follower and master in his own right for the cupola depicting hundreds of male and female saints posed as though for a school graduation photo, exchanging glances and stealing looks at the Madonna. The inside of the dome shows Christ Pantocrator holding an open book inscribed with the words *Ego sum alpha et omega* (I am the beginning and the end), and the rear apse wall illustrates his meaning with frescoes that illuminate Biblical stories of creation, redemption and the apocalypse.

The soul of the city is the Basilica del Santo (Basilica di Sant'Antonio; www.basilicadelsanto.org; 6.30am-7pm Nov-Feb, 6.30am-7.45pm Mar-Oct), a key pilgrimage site and burial site of the town's patron saint, St Anthony of Padua (1193–1231). To get here, head from Piazza delle Erbe east along Via San Francesco, and when you hit Via del Santo, turn south and you emerge in the grand square of the same name. Construction of the church nicknamed Il Santo began in 1232, and over the years took on an unmistakable polyglot style: atop a Latin Cross base is the brick Italian Gothic structure, topped by a series of domes and towers that seem to take their cue from the east.

Once inside, you'll notice people clustering along the right transept, where the saint's tomb is covered with requests and thanks for the saint's intercession in curing illness and recovering lost objects. Behind the high altar at the rear of the church radiates a series of nine chapels, mostly decorated in the 20th century. The central chapel is the baroque Cappella del Tesoro (Treasury Chapel), where the relics of St Anthony were transferred in 1745. True to centuries-maintained tradition, parts of him are on show for the edification of the faithful: his chin and grey green tongue, showcased in two separate, exquisitely worked gold monstrances. For the faithful, the tongue became a particular object of veneration, perhaps because in his lifetime he had been a convincing orator and mediator at times of civil strife.

Under vaulted Gothic ceilings frescoed with starry night skies are such notable works as the lifelike 1360s crucifix by Veronese master Altichiero da Zevio in the frescoed Chapel of St James, the wonderful 1528 sacristy fresco of Saint Anthony preaching to spellbound fish by a follower of Girolamo Tessari, and 1444–50 high altar reliefs by Florentine Renaissance master Donatello (ask guards for access). Outside in the Piazza del Santo, Donatello's 1453 equestrian statue commemorating the 15th-century Venetian mercenary leader known as Gattamelata (Honeyed Cat) is considered the first great Italian Renaissance bronze.

Out the east door is the monastery attached to the basilica, with five cloisters. The oldest (13th century) is the Chiostro della Magnolia, so-called because of the magnificent tree in its centre. The Museo Antoniano (049 822 56 56; Piazza del Santo; adult/child €2.50/1.50; 9am-1pm & 2-6pm Tue-Sun) holds a collection of art and religious objects done for the basilica and convent.

Two of Padua's greatest treasures are often overlooked right across the square. The Oratorio di San Giorgio (049 875 52 35; admission incl Scoletta del Santo €2; 9am-12.30pm & 2.30-7pm Apr-Sep, 9am-12.30pm & 2.30-5pm Oct-Mar) was frescoed with the life stories of St George, St Lucy and St Catherine of Alexandria in jewel-like colour by Altichiero da Zevio and Jacopo Avanzi in 1378, and briefly used as a prison by Napoleon – who apparently missed the message of St George's liberation from the torture wheel by avenging angels. Your ticket allows entry next door to the upstairs Scoletta del Santo, with dramatic Titian paintings that include a 1511 portrait of St Anthony calmly reattaching his own foot as an onlooker gasps, and a riveting parable, painted by Titian's brother Francesco Vecellio, showing a doctor discovering a miser's heart is missing, just as a neighbour pulls the bloody heart from a treasure chest.

South of Piazza del Santo, a Unesco World Heritage site is growing. Padua's Orto Botanico (049 827 21 19; adult/student & child €4/1; 9am-1pm & 3-6pm Apr-Oct, 9am-1pm Mon-Sat Nov-Mar) was planted in 1545 by Padua University's medical faculty to study the medicinal properties of rare plants, and served as a clandestine Resistance meeting headquarters in WWII. The oldest tree in here is nicknamed 'Goethe's palm', planted in 1585 and mentioned by the great German writer in his *Voyage in Italy*.

A short stroll southwest leads to the odd, elliptical Prato della Valle, a space long used for markets. A slim canal around this square is lined by 78 statues of sundry great and good of Paduan history, plus 10 empty pedestals: 10 Venetian dogi once stood here, but Napoleon had them removed after he took Venice in 1797.

Information

Feltrinelli International (049 875 07 92; Via San Francesco 7; 9am-7.30pm Mon-Fri, 9am-8pm Sat, 10am-1pm & 3.30-7.30pm Sun) Bookstore and publisher offering books in multiple languages, and an outstanding history section.

TRANSPORT: PADUA (PADOVA)

Distance from Venice 37km

Direction West

Bus Regular SITA buses (☎ 049 820 68 11; www.sitabus.it) from Venice's Piazzale Roma (€3.50, 45 to 60 minutes) arrive at Piazzale Boschetti, 500m south of the train station. Check online for buses to Colli Euganei hill towns (see opposite).

Car & Motorcycle The A4 (Turin–Milan–Venice–Trieste) passes to the north of town, while the A13 to Bologna starts at the southern edge of town. If travelling by car from Padua to the Colli Euganei, see opposite.

Train The easiest way to Padua from Venice is by train (€2.90 to €15.70, 30 to 50 minutes, three to four trains each hour). Trains run from Padua to Montagnana (€3.40, 20 to 60 minutes) via the Colli Euganei towns of Monselice and Este (see opposite). Padua's train station is about 500m north of Cappella degli Scrovegni.

IAT office (Informazione Azienda Turistica; www.turismo padova.it) Padua train station (☎ 049 875 20 77; 🕑 9am-1.30pm & 3-7pm Mon-Sat); Galleria Pedrocchi (☎ 049 876 79 27; 🕑 9am-1.30pm & 3-7pm Mon-Sat); Piazza del Santo (☎ 049 875 30 87; 🕑 Mar-Oct) Never mind the puns: iPadova tours are free audio downloads for your iPod with accompanying PDF maps for four intriguing walking tours through Padua, while Giscover Padova downloads guide you around town via GPS. Both are available online at www.turismopadova.it; click on Soundtouring.

Ospedaliera Padova (☎ 049 821 11 11; Via Giustiniani 1) Main public hospital.

Police station (☎ 049 820 51 00; Piazzetta Palatucci 5)

Post office (Corso Garibaldi 33; 🕑 8.15am-7.30pm Mon-Sat)

Roadside emergency assistance (☎ 116)

Eating

Enoteca Angelo Rasi (☎ 049 871 97 97; www.angelorasi.it; Riviera Paleocapa 7; meals €30; 🕑 dinner Tue-Sun) Come for a glass of wine and *cicheti*, and inevitably you'll pull up a chair by the canal and stay for dinner under the lime trees. Rustic fare is reinvented with a touch of whimsy: creamed cod comes with savoury squid-ink polenta doughnuts, ricotta gnocchi is topped with a decadent zucchini mousse sauce, and cheeses are presented in the form of a clock.

Osteria Dal Capo (☎ 049 66 31 05; Via degli Obizzi 2; meals €25; 🕑 lunch & dinner Tue-Sat, dinner Mon) Rub elbows with locals – literally – over dinner at tiny tables precariously piled with traditional Venetian seafood, local wines by the glass, and a few inspired novelties, such as *caviale di melanzane con bufala* (eggplant caviar with buffalo mozzarella atop crispy wafer bread). Reservations and a sociable nature advised.

Trattoria San Pietro (☎ 049 876 03 30; Via San Pietro 95; meals €30; 🕑 lunch & dinner Mon-Sat, closed Jul) Venice meets Milanese influences behind these kitchen doors, but the results are pure Padua: think Venetian artichokes with Milanese veal, or saffron risotto with seafood. Reserve ahead.

Trattoria Le Sette Teste (☎ 049 66 47 53; Via Cesare Battisti 44; meals €9-15; 🕑 6.30pm-midnight Mon-Sat) Vast plates of pasta (€9) are presented here like a dare, and meaty mains and chocolaty desserts pose serious threats to after-lunch sightseeing plans at the Palazzo della Ragione around the corner.

Caffè Cavour (☎ 049 875 12 24; www.caffecavour.com; Piazza Cavour 10; pastries €1.50-3; 🕑 7.30am-midnight Wed-Mon) Pistachio macaroons, wild berry tarts, and other two-bite indulgences sweeten the expressions of traffic cops bolting espresso at the curved granite bar.

Drinking

Sundown isn't official until you've had your *spritz* (*prosecco*-based drink) in Piazza delle Erbe or Piazza dei Signori.

Caffè Pedrocchi (☎ 049 878 12 31; www.caffepedrocchi .it; Via VIII Febbraio 15; 🕑 9am-10pm Sun-Wed, 9am-1am Thu-Sat) Since 1831, this neoclassical landmark has been a favourite of Stendhal and other pillars of Padua's cafe society for heart-poundingly powerful coffee and *caffè correto* (coffee cocktails). The grand 1st floor is decorated in styles ranging from ancient Egyptian to Imperial, and during the day you can visit the Museo del Risorgimento e dell'Età Contemporanea (☎ 049 878 12 31; Galleria Pedrocchi 11; adult/child €4/2.50; 🕑 9.30am-12.30pm & 3.30-6pm daily), recounting local and national history from the fall of Venice in 1797 until the republican constitution of 1848 in original documents, images and mementos.

Café El Pilar (☎ 049 65 75 65; Piazza dei Signori 8; ◷ 8.30am-1am Mon-Sat) Crush describes the quantity of people you'll have to beat to the bar, the technique the bartender uses, instead of the usual blender, to make signature cocktails, and that pitter-patter Padua inspires by night's end in the piazza.

Enoteca Santa Lucia (☎ 049 875 94 83; Piazza Cavour 15; ◷ 7pm-midnight Mon-Sat) Taking its cue from Milan, Santa Lucia offers upscale wines by the glass (€5 to €10) with a free buffet of local specialities and cheeses 7pm to 10pm nightly. Occupy your battle station at the glassed-in bar for buffet forays with Padua's budget fashionistas, or head inside the ancient stone-walled tavern with the aficionados.

Bibulus (☎ 049 65 41 17; Via Porciglia 32; ◷ 7am-8pm Mon-Fri, 7am-9.30pm Sat) This all-day hotspot near Piazza Eremitani is nicknamed 'the library' because university students practically live here, mesmerised by the orange op-art decor,

seasonal pasta dishes, 15 wines by the glass, and happy-hour buffet, all at philosophy-major prices.

Sleeping

The tourist office publishes accommodations brochures and lists 90 B&Bs and 60 hotels online (www.turismopadova.it).

Through the Koko Nor Association (www.bbkokonor .it; d €60-80), world travellers make themselves at home in the historic heart of Padua in Tibetan-themed apartments, terrace rooms and artists' garrets owned by welcoming, worldly Italian families; ask about informal Italian conversation classes. Additional B&B listings outside Padova are listed on an affiliated website: www.bedandbreakfastpadova.it.

Belludi37 (☎ 049 66 56 33; www.belludi37.it; Via Luca Belludi 37; s €55-80, d €120-150, all incl breakfast; ⚄ 🖳) A sleek boutique hotel with soul: generous beds

---

WORTH A TRIP: COLLI EUGANEI (EUGANEAN HILLS)

Southwest of Padua, the Colli Euganei (Euganean Hills) are a dreamscape of walled hilltop towns, misty vineyards, the occasional castle, and hot springs bubbling through cracks in the earth. The Padua tourist office offers area maps, accommodation, and walking trail and transport information online (www.turismotermeeuganee.it). If travelling by car from Padua to the Colli Euganei, follow the SS16 south for Monselice and Arquà Petrarca, then branch west on the SS10 for Este and Montagnana. Drivers can download an official map and follow the signposted Strada dei Vini dei Colli Euganei (Euganean Hills Wine Road). Worthy stops on a side trip from Padua include the following:

Terme (Natural Hot Springs)

Mountain spring water bubbles up from the Prealps north of Padua, 85°C and rich in mineral salts. For listings of 100 hotels with hot-springs facilities, download the *Terme* guide (www.turismotermeeuganee.it) or stop by tourist offices in Abano Terme (☎ 049 866 90 55; Via Pietro d'Abano 18) and Montegrotto Terme (☎ 049 79 33 84; Viale Stazione 60).

Sonnet City

Italy's great poet Petrarch (Petrarca) spent the last five years of his life in the medieval village of Arquà Petrarca; you can visit his stone house (☎ 0429 71 82 94; Via Valleselle 4; adult €3, admission with PadovaCard free; ◷ 9am-noon & 3-6.30pm Tue-Sun Mar-Oct, 9am-noon & 2.30-5pm Tue-Sun Nov-Feb) and add your thoughts to guestbooks signed by Rilke and Mozart, or pay homage in proper sonnet form to Petrarch's embalmed pet cat. Buses from Padua (€2.70, 55 minutes, three daily) pass through town en route to Este.

Medieval Fortress Towns

The towns of Monselice, Este and Montagnana welcome visitors who arrive by bus (see above) or Padua–Montagnana train (€3.40, 20 to 60 minutes) – but in medieval times impressive fortifications kept out drifters, the French and door-to-door salesmen. Monselice is securely wrapped in five layers of 11th to 15th century fortifications, capped by a restored castle (☎ 0429 7 29 31; Via del Santuario; adult/child 6-14yr/under 6yr €5.50/3/free; ◷ 1hr guided tours 9am-noon & 3-6pm Tue-Sun Apr-Nov). Heading west from Monselice along the Mantua road is Este, where a trail heading north behind romantic castle's romantic ruins leads to the Villa Kunkler, a private home where Byron and Shelley once stayed; there's a marker out front. About 12km further west of Este rise the magnificent 2km defensive perimeter walls of Montagnana, with 24 towers and four gates.

with stirring views of Basilica di Sant'Antonio and helpful staff quick with budget-friendly shopping advice, free drinks, biking itineraries and speciality-food-sampling walking tours.

Hotel Sant'Antonio (☎ 049 875 13 93; www.hotelsant antonio.it; Via San Fermo 118; s €63-69, d €82-94; ⌘) A calm, canalside hotel near the historic city gate, with unfussy, airy rooms, a cafe downstairs (breakfast €7) and some cheaper singles with a shared bathroom (€39 to €42) in the corridor.

Camping Sporting Center (☎ 049 79 34 00; www .sportingcenter.it; Via Roma 123, Montegrotto Terme; camp sites per person/tent €8.30/12; ⌚ Mar–mid-Nov; ℗ ⌘) The only campground in Padua province, this sprawling complex is 15km from the city centre via city bus M from the train station. It offers access to a pool, spa facilities and shops.

Ostello Città di Padova (☎ 049 875 22 19; www.ostello padova.it; Via dei A Aleardi 30; dm incl breakfast €19; ⌚ 7.15am-9.30am & 4.30pm-midnight) Arrive early for your choice of 16 bunk beds, or reserve family rooms with four bunks and private bathroom (€56 to €88) or shared bathroom (€46 to €76). Night owls need not apply: curfew is at midnight, breakfast at 7.15am and checkout at 9.30am. Take bus 3, 8 or 12 from the train station to Prato della Valle and ask for the Ostello.

VICENZA

No wonder Unesco declared Palladio's work in and around Vicenza (population 113,500) one grand World Heritage site: this city is so packed with Palladios that it has a cumulative neoclassical effect on visitors, leaving them giddy and grounded, rational and open to possibilities. Palladio had a strong classical foundation to build on in Vicenza, which was once the Roman town of Vicentia. Gothic mansions and St Mark's lion emblems appeared around town once it was absorbed by the Venetian Republic in 1404, with baroque flourishes added in the 17th century – but Palladio valued clarity over opulence, creating a singular look for Vicenza that has remained through its changing fortunes over the centuries. Vicenza prospered with textile and computer industries after WWII, yet the city remains surprisingly unpretentious, lingering over rustic lunches of local *salumi* (cured meats), game and handmade pasta.

From the train station in the gardens of Campo Marzo, Viale Roma heads into Piazzale de Gasperi. From here, Corso Palladio leads through the city gates into the historic centre.

Vicenza is best appreciated on foot, since it's compact enough to stroll through in an afternoon or a day, depending how awestruck you are by its architectural triumphs. Corso Palladio starts with garden-variety grandeur along a pair of piazzas, but builds to a stunning crescendo as it heads toward the Palladio-lined side streets of Contrà Porti and Contrà di Santa Corona, ending with the Palladian Teatro Olimpico and Museo Civico. Along side streets are a couple of must-see edifices with painting masterpieces, and a short walk south of town are two of the Veneto's finest villas.

The first square you come to along Corso Palladio is Piazza Castello, featuring several grand edifices including the oddly truncated, unfinished Palazzo Breganze on the south side, designed by Palladio and built by Vincenzo Scamozzi. Its couple of outsize columns look strange in isolation, but show the makings of an imposing classical structure. Nearby, in the Piazza del Duomo, is the duomo (Vicenza's official church), rebuilt after Allied bombs destroyed the original in WWII, with only a few artworks salvaged from the wreckage.

The heart of historic Vicenza is Piazza dei Signori, where Palladio lightened the mood of government buildings with plays of light and shadow. Dazzling white Piovene stone arches frame shady double arcades in the Basilica Palladiana (☎ 0444 32 36 81) Palladio designed in 1549 (open only for temporary exhibitions); while on the northwest end of the piazza, white stone and stucco grace the exposed red brick colonnade of the Loggia del Capitaniato designed by Palladio in 1571 and left unfinished at his death.

North of Corso Palladio, three Palladian beauties line Contrà Porti. The finest is the newly restored Palazzo Barbaran (☎ 0444 32 30 14;

MORE PALLADIO FOR LESS

Gluttons for architecture might consider the Palladio Card (www.palladiocard.com, €10), which offers entry to six Palladio landmarks in and around Vicenza for free and six more at a discounted rate for 10 days from first use, including access to Palazzo Barbaran, €2 savings on the combined entry card to Teatro Olimpico and Museo Civico, and €3 off Villa Masèr (p234) entry. For current discounts on villa access south of Vicenza (p235), see the website.

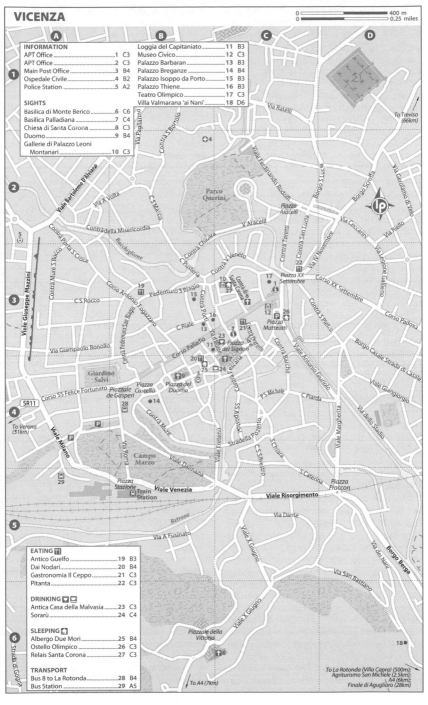

0 400 m
0 0.25 miles

INFORMATION
APT Office.............................1 C3
APT Office.............................2 C3
Main Post Office..................3 B4
Ospedale Civile...................4 B2
Police Station......................5 A2

SIGHTS
Basilica di Monte Berico.....6 C6
Basilica Palladiana...............7 C4
Chiesa di Santa Corona.......8 C3
Duomo..................................9 B4
Gallerie di Palazzo Leoni
  Montanari........................10 C3

Loggia del Capitaniato........11 B3
Museo Civico.......................12 C3
Palazzo Barbaran................13 B3
Palazzo Breganze................14 B4
Palazzo Isoppo da Porto.....15 B3
Palazzo Thiene...................16 B3
Teatro Olimpico.................17 C3
Villa Valmarana 'ai Nani'....18 D6

EATING
Antico Guelfo.....................19 B3
Dai Nodari..........................20 B4
Gastronomia Il Ceppo.........21 C3
Pitanta...............................22 C3

DRINKING
Antica Casa della Malvasia...23 C3
Sorarù................................24 C4

SLEEPING
Albergo Due Mori...............25 B4
Ostello Olimpico................26 C3
Relais Santa Corona............27 C3

TRANSPORT
Bus 8 to La Rotonda............28 B4
Bus Station.........................29 A5

To Treviso
(66km)

Via Ratelli

Parco
Querini

Piazza
Aracelli

To Verona
(51km)

SR11

Campo
Marzo

Piazza
Stazione

Train
Station

Viale Venezia

Viale Risorgimento

Via Dante

Retrone

Via A Fusinato

Piazzale della
Vittoria

To La Rotonda (Villa Capra) (500m);
Agriturismo San Michele (2.5km);
A4 (6km);
Finale di Agugliaro (28km)

To A4 (7km)

Borgo Berga

Strada di Gogna

Contrà Porti 11; www.cisapalladio.org; adult & student €5, admission with PalladioCard free; ⊙ 10am-6pm Wed-Sun), built by Palladio c 1569–70 with a stately double row of columns on the facade and a delightful double-height courtyard loggia that seems to usher in the sunlight. Frothy stuccowork and Giambattista Zelotti's frescoes of gambolling gods lift the roof right off spacious ground-floor galleries. If you use the bathroom under the stairs, take a moment to contemplate through the bathroom window Palladio's clever use of cross-vaulting.

The bank building at No 12 Contrà Porti is Palazzo Thiene (☎ 0444 54 21 31; entrance Contrà San Gaetano Thiene; admission free; ⊙ 9am-noon & 3-6pm Tue-Wed Oct-Apr, 9am-noon & 3-6pm Wed & Fri, 9am-noon Sat May-Sep; book ahead), begun under Palladio's supervision c 1556–58 with rustic stone arches capped by gabled windows and elegant Corinthian pilasters, drawing the eye skyward. Further along the street at No 21, you can't miss Palladio's blinding white, unfinished 1549–53 Palazzo Isoppo da Porto, rippling with eight inset Ionic columns on the 1st floor and crowned with sculpture and pilasters along the attic.

Two blocks east of Contrà Porti is another splendid side street: Contrà di Santa Corona, named after Chiesa di Santa Corona (⊙ 4-6pm Mon, 8.30am-noon & 3-6pm Tue-Sun). Built by the Dominicans in 1261 to house a relic from Christ's crown of thorns, this Romanesque brick church also houses three light-filled masterpieces: Palladio's 1576 Valmarana Chapel in the crypt; Paolo Veronese's *Adoration of the Magi*, much praised by Goethe; and Giovanni Bellini's radiant *Baptism of Christ*, where the holy event is witnessed by a trio of Veneto beauties and a curious red bird.

From the outside it looks like a bank, but a treasure beyond accountants' imagining awaits inside the Gallerie di Palazzo Leoni Montanari (☎ 800 578875; www.palazzomontanari.com; Contrà di Santa Corona 25; adult/student €4/3; ⊙ 10am-6pm Tue-Sun). Ascend past the nymphs along the extravagant stuccoed staircase to grand salons filled with Canaletto's misty lagoon landscapes and Pietro Longhi society satires such as *Tutors of Venier's House*, which shows a sassy child with hand on hip wearing out exasperated tutors collapsed in their chairs. Upstairs is Banca Intesa's superb collection of some 400 Russian icons, gorgeously spotlit in darkened galleries with a recording of soft Gregorian chants setting the scene. Each room elicits audible gasps: bright-eyed saints haloed in silver peer from 16th-century doors; 19th-century

menologies show 99 miniature saints with detailed heads no larger than pencil erasers; and a phalanx of bejewelled, miraculous Madonna icons makes you understand why bags must be left in ground-floor lockers. Such a collection is rare anywhere, especially outside Russia, and public access is generous given the immense value of these works.

Corso Palladio comes to a full stop with Piazza Matteoti, flanked by two Palladian landmarks. Behind a charming walled garden prime for picnics lies a Renaissance marvel: Teatro Olimpico (☎ 0444 22 28 00; www.olimpico.vicenza .it; combined Museo Civico ticket adult/student/under 15yr €8/6/free, adult with PalladioCard €6; ⊙ 9am-5pm Tue-Sun), which Palladio began in 1580 with inspiration from Roman structures. Vincenzo Scamozzi finished the elliptical theatre after Palladio's death, adding a stage set modelled on the ancient Greek city of Thebes, with streets built in steep perspective to give the illusion of a city sprawling towards a distant horizon. The theatre was inaugurated in 1585 with a performance of *Oedipus Rex* but soon fell into disuse – the ceiling caved in and the theatre remained abandoned for centuries until it was restored at last in 1934. Today, Italian performers have vied to make an entrance on this architectural gem of a stage; check online for opera and classical performances, and don't miss Vicenza Jazz concerts here in May.

Save your Teatro Olimpico entry ticket for access to the Museo Civico (☎ 0444 32 13 48; www .museicivicivicenza.it; Palazzo Chiericati, Piazza Matteotti 37/39; combined Teatro Olimpico ticket adult/student/under 15yr €8/6/free, adult with PalladioCard €6; ⊙ 9am-5pm Tue-Sun), housed in one of Palladio's finest buildings, designed in 1550 with a colonnaded ground floor and double-height loggia flanked by vast sun porches. The lavishly frescoed ground floor includes the ultimate baroque party room: the Sala dal Firmamento (Salon of the Skies), with Domenico Brusasorci's ceiling fresco of Diana the moon goddess in her chariot, galloping across the sky to meet the sun. The upstairs painting galleries present works by Vicenza masters in the context of major works by Venetian masters (Veronese, Tiepolo, Tintoretto), Hans Memling's minutely detailed Crucifix, action-packed works by Jacopo Bassano, Elisabetta Marchioni's bodacious still lifes, and Giambattista Piazzetta's swirling, high-drama 1729 masterpiece, *The Ecstasy of St Francis*.

Walk down Viale X Giugno and east along Via San Bastiano, and in about 20 minutes you'll reach the Villa Valmarana 'ai Nani' (☎ 0444 32 18 03; www.villavalmarana.com; Via dei Nani 8; adult/student/ under 12yr €8/4/free; 10am-noon & 3-6pm Tue-Sun Mar-Oct, 10am-noon & 2-4.30pm Sat & Sun Nov-Feb), covered with sublime 1757 frescoes by Giambattista Tiepolo and his son Giandomenico. Giambattista painted the Palazzina wing with his signature mythological epics, while his son painted the Foresteria with fanciful, themed rural, carnival and Chinese rooms. Nicknamed 'ai Nani' (gnomes) for the 17 garden gnome statues around the garden walls, this estate is a superb spot for a summer concert; check dates online.

From Valmarana 'ai Nani', a path leads about 500m to Palladio's Villa Capra, better known as La Rotonda (☎ 0444 32 17 93; Via Rotonda 29; La Rotonda admission €6, gardens €3; gardens 10am-noon & 3-6pm Tue-Sun Mar-Nov, villa 10am-noon & 3-6pm Wed Mar-Nov, groups by prior arrangement). No matter how you look at it, this villa is a show-stopper: the namesake dome caps a square base, with colonnaded facades on all four sides. This is one of Palladio's most admired creations, inspiring villa variations across Europe and the USA, including Thomas Jefferson's Monticello (La Rotonda's current owner, Mario di Valmarana, is a retired University of Virginia architecture professor). Inside, the circular central hall is frescoed from the walls to the soaring cupola with trompe l'œil frescoes. Out front, you can catch bus 8 (€1.50) back to Vicenza.

Also south of the city, the hilltop Basilica di Monte Berico (☎ 0444 32 09 98; Piazzale della Vittoria; 6am-12.30pm & 2.30-7pm Mon-Sat, 6am-7pm Sun & holidays) offers panoramic view of the Palladian city below. The basilica was built in the 18th century to replace a Gothic structure where the Virgin Mary herself is said to have made two appearances in 1426. An impressive 18th-century colonnade runs uphill to the church, roughly parallel to Viale X Giugno. Bus 18 (€1.50) runs here from Via Roma.

Information

APT office (www.vicenzae.org) Piazza dei Signori (☎ 0444 54 41 22; Piazza dei Signori 8; 10am-2pm & 2.30-6.30pm); Piazza Matteotti (☎ 0444 32 08 54; Piazza Matteotti 12; 9am-1pm & 2-6pm) This tourist office can recommend villas worth visiting for architecture, art and natural splendours.

Main post office (Contrà Garibaldi 1; 8.30am-6.30pm Mon-Sat)

TRANSPORT: VICENZA

Distance from Venice 69km

Direction West

Bus FTV (☎ 0444 22 31 15; www.ftv.vi.it) Buses leave for outlying areas from the bus station, located near the train station. Serves many villa hotspots, but not always with great frequency.

Car & Motorcycle The city is on the A4 connecting Milan with Venice, while the SR11 connects Vicenza with Verona and Padua. Large car parks are located near Piazza Castello and the train station.

Train Regular trains arrive from Venice (€4.25 to €11.90, 45 minutes to 1¼ hours) and Padua (€2.90 to €10.90, 15 to 30 minutes).

Ospedale Civile (☎ 0444 99 31 11; Viale Ferdinando Rodolfi 37) Hospital.

Police station (☎ 0444 54 33 33; Viale Giuseppe Mazzini 213)

Eating

Dai Nodari (☎ 0444 54 40 85; Contrà do Rode 20; meals under €10; noon-3.30pm & 7-11pm Mon-Sat) Rustic fare gets hip in the heart of historic Vicenza, packing in local crowds for €7 lunches and €9 dinner menus featuring hearty chicken with wild local mushrooms, followed by Sachertorte, or local-speciality cheese plates featuring the seasoned, grappa-washed Bastardo di Grappa cheese.

Gastronomia Il Ceppo (☎ 0444 54 44 14; 196 Corso Palladio; prepared dishes per 100g €3-5; 8am-1pm & 3.30-7.45pm Mon-Tue & Thu-Sat, 3.30-7.45pm Wed) San Daniele hams dangle over a 30ft counter filled with fresh seafood salads, house-made pastas and speciality cheese. Never mind that there's no available seating: ask counter staff to pair your selections with a local bottle from their shelves for a dream picnic across the street in the Teatro Olimpico.

Antico Guelfo (☎ 0444 54 78 97; Contrà Pedemuro San Biagio 92; meals €35-40; lunch & dinner Mon-Fri, dinner Sat) This culinary hideaway is a hit with slow foodies for its inventive daily market menu, making the most of local specialities in such dishes as Amarone risotto or buckwheat crepes with Bastardo di Grappa cheese. The chef is a specialist in gluten-free cooking, and adapts dishes to any food sensitivity.

Pitanta (☎ 0444 51 35 10; Contrà San Lucia 8; meals €7-15; 7.30am-1am Mon-Sat, 12.30-2.30pm Sun) An authentic *osteria* (pub-restaurant) showing true local pride, from the Vicenza football relics on the wall to the heaping plates of local *bigoli* (thick wheat pasta) with duck sauce for €6 and a glass of respectable house wine for €0.80.

Drinking

Sorarù (☎ 0444 32 09 15; Piazzetta Palladio; ⏱ 8am-8pm Mon-Sat) Drink in the history at this marble-topped bar, serving bracing espresso and cocktails surrounded by pastries made on the premises and tempting jars of candy stashed on carved-wood shelves.

Antica Casa della Malvasia (☎ 0444 54 37 04; Contrà delle Morette 5; meals €35; ⏱ lunch & dinner Tue-Sun) Purveyor of wines since 1200, when Malvasia wine was imported from Greece by Venetian merchants. Today the menu covers 80 wines, including prime Italian Malvasia, plus 100 types of grappa grown just up the road in Bassano del Grappa.

Enos (Contrà Pescherie Vecchie 16; ⏱ 8am-1am Tue-Thu & Sun, 8am-2am Fri & Sat) Hang out under the chandeliers at the cool cocktail bar, or head next door to pick your poison, using a reloadable plastic card, from self-service wine vending machines.

DETOUR: BASSANO DEL GRAPPA

If Vicenza has left you in high spirits, wait until you get to Bassano del Grappa (population 41,900), a small town famed across Italy for its albino asparagus, ceramics, the Diesel fashion label headquarters and the Da Ponte family of Mannerist painters known as the Bassano. But above all, this town is renowned for its namesake grappa – potent digestive spirits Italians will swear is just what the doctor ordered to wash down mountains of pasta. Take the train directly from Venice, or head north from Vicenza on SP248; the town is about 10km shy of picturesque Asolo, and Palladio and Paolo Veronese's Villa Masèr to the east.

From Bassano train station, it's about a five-minute walk west to the edge of the historic centre around the twin squares of Piazza Garibaldi and Piazza Libertà and the APT office. Once you reach Piazza Libertà, follow Via Matteotti north to the Ponte degli Alpini (Ponte Vecchio), the covered bridge straddling the Brenta, designed by Palladio, and Poli Museo della Grappa (☎ 0424 52 44 26; www.poligrappa.com; Via Gamba 6, Ponte Vecchio; admission free; ⏱ 9am-7.30pm), where you can learn the history of Bassano's signature firewater, a favourite drink of Ernest Hemingway (though that could be said of many Venetian drinks).

Although grappa is made all over Italy, the people of the Veneto have been distilling it since at least the 16th century, and by 1601 an institute of grappa distillers was established in Venice. Among the most widely distributed producers is Nardini, which has a laboratory centre 3km south of central Bassano on the SP47 road to Padua. Look right, and you may do a double take: on the lawn, internationally celebrated architect Massimiliano Fuksas parked the Bolle di Nardini, two elliptical bubbles on spindly legs, which look like spaceships. These constructions commemorate the distillery's 225 years of high-flying innovation – and the occasional grappa-induced hallucination – in 2004. Call ahead to visit the Bolle (☎ 0424 22 77 41; www.nardini.it; Via Madonna Monte Berico 7; ⏱ by appointment Mar-Oct), or head for Bassano's historic centre and the Nardini tasting bar (☎ 0424 22 77 41; Ponte degli Alpini 2, Bassano; ⏱ 9am-8pm), alongside the bridge.

But there's more to Bassano than you can see in the bottom of a grappa glass. Attached to the Chiesa di San Francesco on Piazza Garibaldi, the Museo Civico (☎ 0424 52 22 35; Via del Museo 12, Bassano; adult/student incl Museo della Ceramica €4.50/3; ⏱ 9am-6.30pm Tue-Sat, 3.30-6.30pm Sun) showcases among its 500 paintings 17 works by Jacopo Bassano, including his 1545 masterwork *Flight into Egypt*. Bassano shows a farmer dropping his load at the sight of the Holy Family bustling by in a swirl of draperies to keep up with a time-pressed angel, while a dog pauses to sniff the flowers and a boozing guard brings up the rear. In 2009 the museum expanded to better accommodate its library and vast section devoted to the sculptor Canova, including some 2000 drawings, letters, books and plaster casts by the neoclassical master. A separate ceramics collection with more than 1000 porcelain pieces, the Museo della Ceramica (☎ 0424 52 49 33; Palazzo Sturm, Via Schiavonetti; adult/student incl Museo Civico €4.50/3; ⏱ 9am-12.30pm & 3.30-6.30pm Tue-Sat, 3.30-6.30pm Sun Apr-Oct, 9am-12.30pm Fri, 3.30-6.30pm Sat & Sun Nov-Mar) is housed in Palazzo Sturm on the banks of the Brenta.

In Bassano, the Ristorante Ottone (☎ 0424 52 22 06; Via Matteotti 50, Bassano; meals €20-30; ⏱ lunch & dinner Wed-Sun, lunch Mon), just off Piazza della Libertà, has kept up its reputation for rustic fare since 1870, serving up hearty pastas and a local favourite: grilled horse meat. In the shadow of the medieval Bassano castle tower and 200m from the covered bridge, upbeat yellow Hotel Al Castello (☎ 0424 22 86 65; www.hotelalcastello.it; Via Bonamigo 19, Bassano; s €40-60, d €70-100; Ⓟ ❄) offers 11 sunny rooms with parquet floors, some with exposed ceiling beams.

Sleeping

Some 50 hotels in the greater Vicenza area are listed on the tourism board website (www.vicenzae.org), and a dozen B&Bs can be found at www.vitourism.it.

Agriturismo San Michele (☎ 0444 53 37 54; www.agrismichele.it; Strada della Pergoletta 118, off Viale Riviera Berica; d €88-145 incl breakfast; **P**) On the outskirts of town south of Palladio's La Rotonda (p245), this 1700 country estate has been redone in minimalist-Palladian style, with spacious all-white suites overlooking vineyards, olive groves and organic orchards. Enjoy the Jacuzzi amid formal gardens, leisurely meals at the downstairs restaurant and horseback riding through the estate.

Relais Santa Corona (☎ 0444 32 46 78; www.relaissanta corona.it; Contrà Santa Corona 19; s/d incl breakfast €87/104; **P** 🍴 🖥 🛜) A boutique bargain, offering stylish stays in an 18th-century palace ideally located on a street dotted with landmarks. Guestrooms are soothing and soundproofed, with excellent mattresses, minimal chic decor and free wi-fi.

Albergo Due Mori (☎ 0444 32 18 86; www.hotelduemori.com; Contrà do Rode 26; s without bathroom €48, d with/without bathroom €88/55; 🖥 🛜) Right off Piazza dei Signori, on a boutique-lined cobblestone street, this historic 1854 hotel was recently restored to its period charm, with *stile liberty* (Liberty style) bedsteads and antique armoires. There are fans instead of air-con and no TV, but in a nod to modernity there's disabled access and wi-fi.

Ostello Olimpico (☎ 0444 54 02 22; www.ostellovicenza.com; Viale Antonio Giuriolo 9; dm €20; 🕐 7.30-9.30am & 3.30-11.30pm mid-Mar–mid-Nov) A convenient HI youth hostel set in a fine building by the Teatro Olimpico.

VERONA

Though Siena was Shakespeare's initial choice, fair Verona (population 264,200) was where he set his scene between star-crossed lovers Romeo Montague and Juliet Capulet. As usual, the Bard got it right: romance, drama and fatal family feuds have been Verona's hallmark for centuries.

Verona was a key Roman trade centre beginning in 300 BC, with ancient gates and a grand amphitheatre to prove it – and Shakespearean drama seemed to come with the territory. Lombard king Alboin took over Verona in AD 569, only to be killed by his wife three years later. After Mastino della Scala

(aka Scaligeri) failed to be re-elected by Verona's commune in 1262, he rallied the troops and claimed absolute control of the city, until his murder by a conspiracy of Veronese nobility. Under Mastino's son Cangrande I (1308–28), Verona's influence extended to Padua and Vicenza, and the arts flourished: Dante, Petrarch and Giotto all benefited from Verona's patronage and protection. Mastino's great-grandson Cangrande II (1351–59) was a tyrant whose murder by his brother was not widely mourned – but after yet another fratricide, the Scaligeri were run out of town in 1387.

Verona was claimed by Milan, and in 1404 by Venice which managed to hang onto Verona despite Scaligeri-backed uprisings until Napoleon took over in 1797. The city was passed as a war trophy to Austria, then became part of Italy in 1866. Verona served as a Fascist control centre from 1938–45, a key location for Resistance interrogation and transit point for Italian Jews sent to Nazi concentration camps. The city has survived its tragedies; today it's a Unesco World Heritage site, and reprising its role as a cosmopolitan crossroads. Fair Verona continues to attract admirers from afar, many of whom fall in love with the place: one in five children born in Verona has a parent born outside Italy.

Buses leave for Verona's historic centre from outside the train station, south of town. To walk to the centre, head north past the bus station and 1.5km along Corso Porta Nuova to Piazza Brà, take Via Mazzini to Via Cappello, and hang a left into Piazza delle Erbe.

A masterpiece of Romanesque architecture, the striped brick and tuffo stone **Basilica di San Zeno Maggiore** (www.chieseverona.it; Piazza San Zeno; combined church ticket/single entry €5/2.5; 🕐 8.30am-6pm Mon-Sat, 1-6pm Sun Mar-Oct, 10am-1pm & 1.30-4pm Tue-Sat, 1-5pm Sun Nov-Feb) was built in honour of the city's patron saint from the 12th to 14th centuries. Enter through the graceful flower-filled cloister into the vast nave, lined with 12th- to 15th-century frescoes depicting Jesus, Mary Magdelene modestly covered in her curtain of golden hair and St George casually slaying a dragon atop a startled horse. Under the rose window depicting the Wheel of Fortune are meticulously detailed 12th-century bronze doors, including a scene of an exorcism with a demon yanked from a woman's mouth. Painstaking restoration is reviving Mantegna's 1457–59 *Majesty of the Virgin* polyptych altarpiece, painted with such astonishing perspective and convincing textures that

VERONA

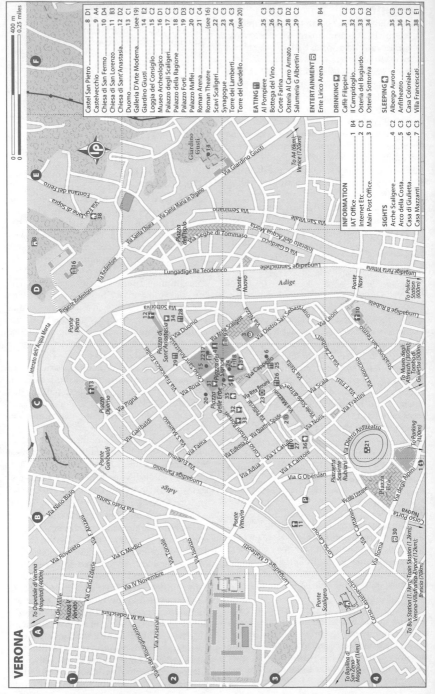

you might believe there are garlands of fresh fruit hanging behind the Madonna's throne. Downstairs is a creepy crypt, with faces carved into medieval capitals and St Zeno's eerily lit corpse in a transparent sarcophagus.

The pink marble Roman Arena (☎ 045 800 51 51; www.arena.it; Piazza Brà, ticket office Ente Lirico Arena di Verona, Via Dietro Anfiteatro 6b; tickets €15-150, tours adult/student/child €4/3/1; ☼ opera season Jun-Aug, tours 8.30am-7.30pm Tue-Sun, 1.45-7.30pm Mon Oct-May, 8am-3.30pm daily Jun-Aug) was built in the 1st century AD and survived a 12th-century earthquake to become Verona's legendary open-air opera house, with seating for 30,000 people. Placido Domingo made his debut here, and the annual June to August opera season includes 50 performances by the world's top names. In winter months classical concerts are held across the way at the 18th-century Ente Lirico Arena.

Off Via Mazzini, Verona's main shopping street, is the legendary Casa di Giulietta (Juliet's House; ☎ 045 803 43 03; Via Cappello 23; adult/student/child €4/3/1; ☼ 8.30am-7.30pm Tue-Sun, 1.45-7.30pm Mon). Never mind that Romeo and Juliet were fictional characters with no resemblance to Veronese nobility, and that there's hardly room for two on the narrow stone balcony, romantics flock to this 14th century house to add their lovelorn pleas to the graffiti on the courtyard causeway, and rub the right breast of the bronze statue of Juliet for better luck next time. Morbid romantics seek out the Tomba di Giulietta (Juliet's Tomb; ☎ 045 800 03 61; Via del Pontiere 35; adult/student/child €3/2/1; ☼ 8.30am-6.30pm Tue-Sun, 1.45-7.30pm Mon), a cloister featuring a red marble coffin long used as a drinking trough, a motley collection of 1st-century Roman amphorae and, upstairs, some frescoes of minor interest, mostly from the 16th century.

Originally a Roman forum, Piazza delle Erbe is ringed with cafes, buzzing with gossip, and lined with some of Verona's most sumptuous buildings, including the baroque Palazzo Maffei, at the north end, with the adjoining 14th-century Torre del Gardello. On the eastern side, you can't miss the fresco-decorated Casa Mazzanti, former home of Verona's history-making Scaligeri clan.

Separating Piazza delle Erbe from Piazza dei Signori is the Arco della Costa, with a suspended whale's rib that Veronese legend says will fall on the first just person to walk beneath it. Veronese cynics are quick to point out that over several centuries, it hasn't fallen once, despite politicians and popes parading beneath it. Nearby, the striped Torre dei Lamberti (☎ 045 803

MORE VERONA FOR LESS

The VeronaCard (www.veronacard.it; 1 day/3 days €8/12) grants access to major monuments and churches and reduced admission on minor sights, plus allows unlimited use of town buses. Cards can be purchased at participating sites and tobacconists. Alternatively, a ticket combining entry to all the main churches costs €5; otherwise, admission to each costs €2.50; see details at www.chieseverona.it.

27 26; admission by lift/on foot €3/2; ☼ 9am-7.30pm Tue-Sun, 1.30-7.30pm Mon) is a watchtower begun in the 12th century and finished in 1463, by which time it was too late to notice the Venetians invading – but it does offer a panoramic city view. Palazzo Forti (Palazzo della Ragione; ☎ 199 199111; www.palazzoforti.it; adult/student €6/5; ☼ 10.30am-7pm Tue-Sun) is home to the new Galleria d'Arte Moderna, with 90 artworks from the 1970s to today and ambitious exhibits showcasing international modern artists such as MC Escher and Sol LeWitt, plus well-curated photography shows in the adjoining Scavi Scaligeri.

Verona's early Renaissance gem is the 15th-century Loggia del Consiglio, the former city-council building, at the northern end of the Piazza dei Signori. Next door where they could keep an eye on conspiring councillors was the Palazzo degli Scaligeri, once the main residence of the Scaligeri family. Through the archway at the far end of the piazza are the Arche Scaligere (Via Arche Scaligere; admission incl Torre dei Lamberti by lift/on foot €4/3; ☼ 9.30am-7.30pm Tue-Sun, 1.45-7.30pm Mon Jun-Sep), the elaborate Gothic tombs of the Scaligeri family where murderers are interred not far from the relatives they'd killed.

Off Piazza delle Erbe to the southwest was once Verona's historic Jewish Ghetto. Tall buildings frame the narrow side street of Via Rita Rosani, named for the Resistance heroine who commanded a band of partisans in Verona until 1944, when she was caught and summarily executed at age 24. On the southeast side of Via Rosani is Verona's newly restored synagogue, where you might find the doors open to Jewish visitors and others who express a sincere interest to Signor Willis, the welcoming synagogue keeper and community historian.

Verona's 12th-century duomo (main cathedral; Piazza del Duomo; combined church ticket/single entry €5/2.5; ☼ 10am-5.30pm Mon-Sat, 1.30-5.30pm Sun Mar-Oct, 10am-1pm & 1.30-4pm Tue-Sat, 1-5pm Sun Nov-Feb) is a striking striped Romanesque building, with polychrome reliefs and the bug-eyed statues of Charlemagne's paladins Roland and Oliver, by medieval master Nicolò, on the west porch. Nothing about this sober facade hints at the extravagant interior, frescoed over the 16th to 17th centuries with angels in the trompe l'œil architecture. At the left end of the nave is the Cartolari-Nichesola Chapel, designed by Jacopo Sansovino with a vibrant Titian *Assumption,* showing astonished crowds pointing at the airborne Madonna.

North of the Arche Scaligere stands the Gothic 13th to 15th century Chiesa di Sant'Anastasia (Piazza di Sant'Anastasia; 9am-6pm Mon-Sat, 1-6pm Sun Mar-Oct, 10am-1pm & 1.30-4pm Tue-Sat, 1-5pm Sun Nov-Feb), Verona's largest church and a showcase for Veronese art. The multitude of frescoes is overwhelming, but don't overlook Pisanello's storybook-quality fresco *St George Setting out to Free the Princess from the Dragon* in the Pisanelli Chapel, or the 1495 holy water font featuring a lucky hunchback by Paolo Veronese's father, Gabriele Caliari.

Southwest from the Piazza delle Erbe along the River Adige is Castelvecchio, the 1354–56 fortress of the tyrannical Cangrande II, so severely damaged by Napoleon's troops and WWII bombings that many feared it was beyond repair. Instead of erasing the Castelvecchio's chequered past with restorations, Carlo Scarpa reinvented the building in the 1960s, building bridges over exposed foundations, filling gaping holes with glass panels, and balancing a statue of Cangrande I above the courtyard on a concrete gangplank. Scarpa's revived Castelvecchio makes a fitting home for Verona's museum (045 806 26 11; Corso Castelvecchio 2; adult/student/child €8/7/1; 8.30am-7.30pm Tue-Sun & 1.45-7.30pm Mon) showcasing a diverse collection of frescoes, jewellery, medieval artefacts and paintings by Pisanello, Giovanni Bellini, Tiepolo, Carpaccio and Veronese, plus wonderful temporary shows ranging from Andrea Mantegna retrospectives to modernist glass.

At the river end of Via Leoni, Chiesa di San Fermo (Stradone San Fermo; 10am-6pm Mon-Sat, 1-6pm Sun Mar-Oct, 10am-1pm & 1.30-4pm Tue-Sat, 1-5pm Sun Nov-Feb) is actually two churches in one: Franciscan monks raised the 13th century Gothic church right over an original 11th-century Romanesque structure. Inside the main Gothic church, you'll notice a magnificent timber *carena di nave,* a ceiling reminiscent of an upturned boat's hull. In the right transept are 14th-century frescoes, including

some fragments depicting episodes in the life of St Francis. Stairs from the cloister lead underground to the spare but atmospheric Romanesque church below.

Southwest from Piazza delle Erbe towards the Ponte Scaligero is the Chiesa di San Lorenzo (Corso Cavour; 10am-6pm Mon-Sat, 1-6pm Sun Mar-Oct, 10am-1pm & 1.30-4pm Tue-Sat, 1-5pm Sun Nov-Feb), a Romanesque church raised in the early 12th century but much altered with Gothic and Renaissance additions. The most unusual element – virtually unique in Italy – are the two cylindrical towers that flank the entrance.

North of the city centre is Ponte Pietra, a quiet but remarkable testament to the Italians' love of their artistic heritage. The two arches on the left date from the Roman Republican era in the first century BC, while the other three were replaced in the 13th century. The ancient bridge remained largely intact until 1945, when retreating German troops blew up the bridge – but locals fished the fragments out of the river, and painstakingly rebuilt the bridge stone by stone in the 1950s.

Over the bridge you'll notice a Roman theatre, cunningly carved into the hillside at a strategic spot overlooking a bend in the river, built in the 1st century BC. Take the lift at the back of the theatre to the former convent above, which houses an interesting collection of Greek and Roman pieces in the Museo Archeologico (045 800 03 60; Regaste Redentore 2; adult/student/child €3/2/1; 8.30am-7.30pm Tue-Sun, 1.45-7.30pm Mon). On a hill high behind the theatre and museum is the Castel San Pietro, built by the Austrians on the site of an earlier castle.

Back down at the Ponte Pietra, head about 200m south along the river and then along Via Redentore and its continuation about 600m, and you'll reach lush sculpted gardens known as Giardino Giusti (045 803 40 29; Via Giardino Giusti 2; admission €5; 9am-8pm Apr-Sep, 9am-sunset Oct-Mar). This garden is named after the noble family that has looked after it and the mansion since opening the garden to visitors in 1591, and it's lost none of its charm over the centuries: the vegetation is an Italianate mix of the sculpted and natural, graced by soaring cypresses, one of which the German poet Goethe immortalised in his travel writings. According to local legend, lovers who manage to find each other in the little labyrinth at the right of the garden are destined to stay together. On the far end of the garden, a short climb is rewarded with romantic, sweeping views over the city.

Information

Emergency Medical Care (☎ 118)

IAT office (www.tourism.verona.it) Verona train station (☎ 045 800 08 61; 8am-7pm Mon-Sat, 9am-5pm Sun); Verona-Villafranca airport (☎ 045 861 91 63; 9am-6pm Mon-Sat, 9am-3pm Sun Apr-Nov, 9am-4pm Mon-Sat, 9am-3pm Sun Dec-Mar); Via degli Alpini (☎ 045 806 86 80; Via degli Alpini 9; 8.30am-7pm Mon-Sat, 9am-5pm Sun)

Internet Etc (☎ 045 800 02 22; Via Quattro Spade 3b; per hr €5.50; 2.30-8pm Mon, 10.30am-8pm Tue-Sat, 3.30-8pm Sun)

Ospedale di Verona (☎ 045 807 11 11; Piazza A Stefani) Hospital northwest of Ponte Vittoria.

Police (☎ 113; Lungadige Galtarossa 11) Near Ponte Navi.

Post office (Piazza Viviani 7; 8.30am-6.30pm Mon-Sat)

Eating

Al Pompiere (☎ 045 803 05 37; www.alpompiere.com; Vicolo Regina d'Ungheria 5; meals €25-40; lunch & dinner Tue-Sat, dinner Mon) The fireman's *(pompiere)* hat is still on the wall, but the focal point at this local hotspot is the vast cheese selection and famed house-cured *salumi* platter. Make a meal of the starters with wine by the glass, or graduate to plates of *bigoli con le sarde* (chunky spaghetti with sardines) or ravioli filled with caramelised onion. Reserve ahead.

Bottega del Vino (☎ 045 800 45 35; www.bottegavini.it; Vicolo Scudo di Francia 3a; meals €60-70; lunch & dinner Wed-Mon) Wine is the primary consideration at this historic *enoteca* (wine bar) with backlit bottles above the bar, and you'll find your sommelier will gladly recommend a worthy vintage for your lobster crudo salad, Amarone risotto or suckling pig – some of the best wines here are bottled specifically for the Bottega.

Corte Farina (☎ 045 800 04 40; Corte Farina 4; pizza €7-12; lunch & dinner Tue-Thu) Argentina meets Verona at this popular pizzeria, which also fires up empanadas (savoury meat-filled pastries) in their ovens. Join famished shoppers fresh from the Via Mazzini along the chic banquette, or grab a spot outdoors for street theatre two blocks from the Arena.

Osteria Al Carro Armato (☎ 045 803 01 75; Vicolo Gatto 2a; meals €20-30; lunch & dinner Tue-Sun) Join the crowd on rough timber benches in this high-ceilinged, down home Veronese *osteria*. There's wine by the glass and hearty local dishes, such as *tagliata di manzo* (thin-sliced beef dish served with rocket) or *pastissada di cavallo*, Verona's legendary horse stew.

Salumeria G Albertini (☎ 045 803 10 74; Corso Sant'Anastasia 39; 8am-2pm & 3-8pm Mon-Sat) This is a picture-perfect deli, featuring all the prepared pastas, cured meats, local Asiago sheep's cheese and wine you could want for an ideal picnic by the river or inside the Roman Arena.

Drinking

Osteria Sottoriva (☎ 045 801 43 23; Via Sottoriva 9a; 11am-10.30pm Thu-Tue) The last of the historic *osterie* that once lined this riverside alley, Sottoriva still draws local crowds to rough-hewn

TRANSPORT: VERONA

Distance from Venice 120km

Direction West

Air Verona-Villafranca airport (VRN; ☎ 045 809 56 66; www.aeroportoverona.it) This is 12km outside town and accessible by APTV Aerobus to/from the train station (€4.50, 15 minutes, every 20 minutes from 6.30am to 11.30pm). Flights arrive from all over Italy and some European cities, including Amsterdam, Barcelona, Berlin, Brussels, Dusseldorf, London and Paris.

Bus The main intercity bus station is in front of the train station, in the Porta Nuova area. Buses serve many provincial localities not served by train. AMT (www.amt.it) city transport buses 11, 12, 13 and 14 (bus 91 or 92 on Sunday and holidays) connect the train station with Piazza Brà (tickets 1hr/1 day €1/3.50). Buy tickets from newsagents and tobacconists before you board the bus. Otherwise, it's a 20-minute walk to historic Verona along Corso Porta Nuova.

Car & Motorcycle Verona is at the intersection of the Serenissima A4 (Turin–Trieste) and A22 motorways.

Train The trip to/from Venice is easiest by train (€6.15, two hours). Verona has rail links with Padua, Vicenza, Milan, Mantua, Modena, Florence and Rome, plus regular services to Austria, Switzerland and Germany (10 daily to/from Munich).

tables under the arcade, with wine by the glass at fair prices, and traditional pork sausages and horse meatballs.

Il Campidoglio (☎ 045 59 10 59; Piazzetta Tirabosco 4; ☯ 11am-2am Tue-Sun) An island of cool in a hidden plaza up a flight of stairs off Piazza delle Erbe, this place serves cocktails strong and tall during the daily 6pm to 9pm happy hour.

Caffè Filippini (☎ 045 800 45 49; Piazza delle Erbe 26; ☯ 8am-2am Thu-Tue) The hippest joint in town has been here since 1901, perfecting the house speciality Filippini, a killer cocktail of vermouth, gin, lemon and ice. Come for coffee in the morning, and don't expect to leave before sundown.

Osteria del Bugiardo (☎ 045 59 18 69; Corso Portoni Borsari 17a; ☯ 11am-10pm Tue-Sun) On busy Corso Portoni Borsari, traffic converges at Bugiardo for glasses of upstanding Valpolicella bottled specifically for the *osteria*. Polenta and *sopressa* make worthy bar snacks for the powerhouse Amarone.

Sleeping

Cooperativa Albergatori Veronesi (☎ 045 800 98 44; www .veronapass.com) offers no-fee booking service for two-star hotels. For homestyle stays outside the city centre, check Verona Bed & Breakfast (www .bedandbreakfastverona.com).

Anfitheatro B&B (☎ 347 24 84 62; www.anfiteatro -bedandbreakfast.com; Via Alberto Mario 5; s €60-90, d €80-130, tr & q €100-150, all incl breakfast) Opera divas and fashionistas rest up in the heart of the action in this recently restored 19th-century townhouse, one block from the Roman Arena, off boutique-lined Via Mazzini. Spacious guestrooms have high wood-beamed ceilings, antique armoires for stashing purchases, and divans for swooning after shows.

Casa Coloniale (☎ 337 47 27 37; www.casa-coloniale .com; Via Cairoli 6; s €50-70, d €80-110, all incl breakfast; ☒) Snag a prime berth off Piazza Erbe in this hip new B&B, where three guestrooms have a single stripe of bold colour marked with the room number in a kind of billiard-ball decor scheme.

Villa Francescati (☎ 045 59 03 60; www.ostellionline.org; Salita Fontana del Ferro 15; dm/single in family room €18/20 incl breakfast; ☯ 7am-11.30pm) A HI youth hostel housed in a 16th-century villa on a garden estate, with helpful staff to book tickets to events and recommend bars. Meals cost €10; there are no cooking facilities. Catch bus 73 (weekdays) or bus 90 (Sunday and holidays) from the train station.

Albergo Aurora (☎ 045 59 47 17; www.hotelaurora.biz; Piazza XIV Novembre 2; s €90-130, d €100-150, all incl breakfast; ☒) Right off bustling Piazza Erbe yet cosy and blissfully quiet, this recently renovated hotel has spacious, unfussy rooms with high ceilings. There are cheaper single rooms without bathroom (€58 to €70). Head to the sunny terrace for drinks overlooking the Piazza.

WINE COUNTRY

A drive through Veneto's southwestern hinterlands is a lesson in fine wine – or if you're travelling without a designated driver, you can reach many key winemaking locations by train or bus, and on pleasant hikes through rolling vineyards. Below are two itineraries based on your drink of choice: red or white. To the north and northwest of Verona are Valpolicella vineyards dating back to Roman times, and east of Verona on the road to Vicenza are the white-wine makers of Soave. With a car, a trip through Valpolicella territory can be combined with detours to Bassano del Grappa (p246) and onward to Asolo (p234) and Villa Masèr (p234). Since nothing complements a well-structured white like Palladian architecture, the Palladio villa loop south of Vicenza (p235) makes a worthy detour from Soave.

RED WINE: VALPOLICELLA

The occasional Romanesque church, 16th-century villa or tiny village punctuate this otherwise unbroken stretch of vineyards, but as you plot your visit, bear in mind that most wineries close on Sunday. By car, follow the SS12 highway northwest out of Verona, veer north onto SP4, and follow the route west towards San Pietro in Cariano to visit the Pro Loco Valpolicella tourist office (☎ 045 770 19 20; www.valpolicellaweb.it; Via Ingelheim 7; ☯ 9.30am-1pm & 1.30-5.30pm Mon-Fri, 9am-1pm Sat). Alternatively, bus 3 departs Verona's Porta Nuova for San Pietro about every half hour (www.apt.vr.it; €2.30, 40 minutes). The tourist office offers maps for walking, biking, and travelling by bus to scenic spots for wine-tasting. If you make an appointment, you can swing by Montecariano Cellars (☎ 045 683 83 35; Via Valena 3, San Pietro; ☯ by appointment Mon-Sat), off central Piazza San Giuseppe, to sample an award-winning DOC example of the most highly prized Valpolicella red: Amarone.

Foodies detour north of San Pietro to the tiny town of Fumane for lunch in a converted 1400s barn at Enoteca Valpolicella (☎ 045 683 91 46; Via

Osan 45; meals €25-35; 🕒 lunch & dinner Tue-Sat, lunch Sun), where the kitchen keeps flavours pure – risotto with wild herbs, game with polenta – so as not to compete with the 700 Italian wines on the menu, including 70 local labels. The Enoteca owners also run the delightful La Meridiana B&B (☎ 045 683 91 46; Via Osan 16/c, Fumane; www.lameridiana -valpolicella.it; s/d incl breakfast €70/90; 🏊) in a 1600s stable, with newly renovated guestrooms – get the garden room with the barrel-vaulted stone ceiling – swimming at a pool 1km away and tasty breakfasts at the Enoteca.

A few kilometres west of San Pietro, Gargagnano is known for Amarone, and if you call ahead you can taste DOC Amarone and lighter DOC Valpolicella reds outside Gargagnano at Corte Leardi Winery (☎ 045 770 13 79; www .cortealeardi.com; Via Giare 15; 🕒 8.30am-7pm Mon-Fri & Sat, 9am-noon Sun, by appointment). A short ride (or well-marked 5km, two-hour hike) west takes you through the hillside town of Sant'Ambrogio di Valpolicella and onward to the picturesque village of San Giorgio, with its fresco-filled, cloistered 8th century Romanesque Pieve di San Giorgio (☎ 045 770 15 30; 🕒 7am-6pm). Halfway between Sant'Ambrogio and San Giorgio is Boscaini Carlo Winery (☎ 045 773 14 12; www.boscaini carlo.it; Via Sengia 15; 🕒 10am-noon & 1.30-7pm Mon-Sat), renowned for award-winning DOC Amarone and Valpolicella, and an especially voluptuous Ripasso available only from the winery. In San Giorgio, Trattoria Dalla Rosa Alda (☎ 045 770 10 18; www.dallarosalda.it; meals €30-35; 🕒 lunch & dinner Tue-Sat, lunch Sun) serves honest local fare, including house-made gnocchi and beef braised in Amarone. It also offers 10 rooms for overnighters (singles/doubles €75/100).

WHITE WINE: SOAVE

You'll never have to look far for a glass of fine white wine in the Veneto, but between Verona and Vicenza, Soave serves its namesake DOC white wine in a storybook setting. This medieval town is the centre of Veneto's wine consortium, so the best Amarone and Valpolicella also pass through Soave's crenellated walls. Hop on the Milan–Venice train from Verona to San Bonifacio (€2.35 to €3.55, 20 minutes) and catch the APTV bus (line 30), or exit the A4 autostrada at San Bonifacio, and follow the Viale della Vittoria 2km north into town.

Soave's fortifications encircled with 24 watchtowers aren't intended to keep visitors away from the good stuff: they were built on a medieval base by Verona's fratricidal Scaligeri family, who ultimately had more to fear from one another than marauding invaders. The Castello (☎ 045 68 00 36; adult/child €4.50/3; 🕒 9am-noon & 3-6.30pm Tue-Sun Apr–mid-Oct, 9am-noon & 3-5pm mid-Oct–Mar) is easily reached on foot (signposted) through gardens and vineyards. Cross the drawbridge on the north side of the castle and pass two courtyards to find the stairway to the Mastio, the central defensive tower that apparently served as a dungeon: during restoration work, a mound of human bones 2m high was unearthed inside.

Just below the castle is megaproducer Cantina del Castello (☎ 045 768 00 93; www.cantinacastello.it; Corte Pittora 5; tour & tasting €8; 🕒 9am-12.30pm & 2.30-6.30pm Mon-Sat, by appointment) where you can tour

---

DETOUR: CONEGLIANO & THE PROSECCO ROAD

The little town of Conegliano (population 37,500) is bubbling over with pride: in 2009, select *prosecco* (sparkling white wine) produced in and around this hamlet was awarded Italy's highest mark of oenological distinction: DOCG (*denominazione d'origine controllata e garantita*), an official guarantee for Conegliano *prosecco*, made with regional grapes according to tried and true methods, that meet the highest quality standards. Conegliano DOCG *prosecco* is one of only 38 DOCG-designated wines in Italy overall – one of four in the Veneto, and the only one not from the hinterlands of Verona.

To sparkling wine aficionados, the announcement came as no surprise. Conegliano is home to Italy's oldest school for oenology, and has long been the toast of the Veneto for its dry, crisp white wines, made from Prosecco grapes, in *spumante* (bubbly), *frizzante* (sparkling) and still varieties. Plot a tasting tour along the Strada di Prosecco (Prosecco Road) from Conegliano to the Valdobbiadene at www.coneglianovaldobbiadene.it, or head to Conegliano's APT tourist office (☎ 0438 2 12 30; Via XX Settembre 61; 🕒 9am-12.30pm Tue-Wed, 9am-12.30pm & 3-6pm Thu-Sun).

If you're taking the train or driving to the Dolomites along the A27 north of Treviso, Conegliano makes a convenient pit stop for premium *prosecco* and self-flagellation – not necessary in that order. Along Via XX Septembre in the centre of town, you can't miss the eye-catching Scuola dei Battuti, covered inside and out with 16th-century frescoes by Ludovico Pozzoserrato. This building was once home to a religious lay group known as the *Battuti* (Beaters) for their enthusiastic self-flagellation. Enter the Duomo through the Scuola to discover early works by Veneto artists, notably a 1492–3 altarpiece painted by noted local master Cima da Conegliano.

underground cellars and sample Soaves ranging from sparkling Brut Soave to superior dessert Recioto di Soave. Across from the church in the old town, Azienda Agricola Coffele (☎ 045 768 00 07; www.coffele.it; Via Roma 5; ☽ 9am-12.30pm & 2-7pm Mon-Sat, by appointment) offers tastings of lemon-zesty DOC Soave Classico and nutty, faintly sweet bubbly DOCG (guaranteed quality) Recioto di Soave. Soave is not known as a complex white, but one trailblazing winery out to change that reputation is Suavia (☎ 045 767 50 89; Frazione Fittà, Via Centro 14; ☽ 9am-1pm & 2-6pm Mon-Fri, 9am-1pm Sat, by appointment), located 8km outside Soave via SP39 in the tiny town of Fittà. By appointment, taste its renegade DOC Monte Carbonare Soave Classico: faintly tropical, with a mineral, ocean-breeze finish.

For rustic local dishes, paired with great deals on speciality wines, in a 140-year-old *osteria*, head to Al Gambero (☎ 045 768 00 10; Corso Vittorio Emanuele 5; meals €20-30; ☽ Tue-Sun) for Soave *sopressa* with polenta or Valeggio-style tortellini tied in love knots. Fancier fare is served in a former 16th-century nunnery at Lo Scudo (☎ 045 768 07 66; Via San Matteo 46; meals €30-40; ☽ lunch & dinner Tue-Sun), where meals are leisurely but you'll want to arrive early and order fast – or miss out on daily fish specials and risotto with Verona's zesty DOP (quality-assured) Monte Veronese cheese.

THE COAST & THE DOLOMITES

Whether you're looking for the next mountaintop to conquer or working diligently toward an advanced degree in beach-bumming, Veneto has your interests covered. If you're into skiing, hiking, or lolling in meadows of wildflowers, you won't want to miss the spectacular scenery and worthy challenges of Veneto's ski resorts in the Dolomites, along the mountain border with Trentino Alto-Adige. When lazy summer days demand less ambitious plans, the Adriatic Coast has your beach umbrella and lounger ready.

In winter ski season and in August, the crowds may seem to follow you to your destination from Venice – definitely check traffic reports before hitting the road, and reserve ahead if you're planning to stay the night. The upside is the festival atmosphere and easy mingling among the good-time crowds of Italians and Northern Europeans on vacation.

THE ADRIATIC COAST

The gentle arc of waterfront northeast of Venice is the Adriatic coast, and it's lined with beach resorts popular with locals and Europeans escaping chillier climates – you can usually tell who's who by the ratio of sunburn to tan. On weekends and sunny days the beaches can get crowded with recliners and stomped sand castles, and may not be everyone's idea of a Mediterranean beach getaway. But at night in local beach nightclubs an Ibiza mood sets in, and DJs work a groove until the crowd abandons hard-won loungers to dance barefoot in the sand.

For Adriatic Coast information, try the Palazzo del Turismo (☎ 041 37 06 01; www.turismojesolo eraclea.it) in Piazza Brescia, Jesolo, or the APT office (☎ 0421 8 10 85) in Caorle. To reach the coast by public transit, take the ferry to Punta Sabbioni or the 70-minute ride on ATVO bus 10a from Piazzale Roma to Jesolo (one-way/return €3.80/6.70). Clubgoers, keep in mind that the last bus usually leaves at 11.20pm in summer, and taxis cost upwards of €80.

Lido di Jesolo, the strand of sand a couple of kilometres away from the main Adriatic beach town of Jesolo is far and away the Venetians' preferred beach. The sand is fine and clean, the water is warm and not too choppy most of the year, and the place hops in summer with nightclubs. DJs and Biennale escapees bring the design-magazine scene to life at Terazzamare (p207); diners catch the garden breezes amid gazebos at the Marina Club (p207); and club kids toast the dawn at Il Muretto (p207). As usual in the Veneto, the most memorable entertainment options are often spontaneous or quasi-organised – so while perfecting a tan on Lido di Jesolo beaches in July and August, keep an eye out for flyers offering free admission to clubs (admission usually €5 to €20) and announcements of free beach concerts. Jesolo (population 23,620) marks the northern end of a long peninsula that becomes Litorale del Cavallino as you head south and culminates in Punta Sabbioni, which together with the northern end of the Lido di Venezia, forms the first of the three Adriatic entrances into the Venetian lagoon.

For a more laid-back beach experience, head 30km northeast of Jesolo to sleepy Caorle (population 11,800), which was a Roman port in the 1st century BC and remains a fishing town today. Independent-minded Caorle resisted Venetian annexation until the 15th century, and retains its own distinct medieval character with the cylindrical bell tower of its 11th-century cathedral. But like Burano, Caorle has modern-art sensibilities and takes pride in houses painted in bold contrasting colour schemes that would make pastel-prone Venetian decorators blanch. Caorle's beaches are also busy in summer, but the whole place has a mellow seaside vibe that sets it apart from jumping Jesolo resorts. The town centre is easy to walk around, with a few hotels and plenty of restaurants offering simple, fresh fish dinners.

BELLUNO

Perched beneath snow-capped Dolomites, Belluno (population 35,600) makes a scenic, strategic base to explore the mountains. The historic old town is its own attraction, with easy walks past Renaissance-era buildings in the long shadow of the Dolomites.

Belluno's main pedestrian square is the Piazza dei Martiri (Martyrs' Square), named after the four partisans hanged here in WWII. At the heart of the old town, Piazza del Duomo is framed by the early-16th-century Renaissance Cattedrale di San Martino, the 16th-century Palazzo Rosso, and the Palazzo dei Vescovi with a striking 12th-century tower.

Northwest of Belluno, the Parco Nazionale delle Dolomiti Bellunesi (www.dolomitipark.it) is a magnificent national park offering trails for hikers at every level, wildflowers from spring into summer and restorative gulps of crisp mountain air year-round. Between late June and early September, hikers walking six Alte Vie delle Dolomiti (high-altitude Dolomites walking trails) pass Belluno en route to mountain refuges. Route 1 starts in Belluno and, in about 13 days, covers 150km of breathtaking mountain scenery to Lago di Braies in Val Pusteria to the north.

Buses arrive at Piazzale della Stazione in front of the train station. Trains from Venice (€5.70 to €6.15, two to 2½ hours) run here via Treviso and/or Conegliano about five times daily. You'll probably have to change along the way, which can add an hour or more to your trip.

In front of the train station on the western edge of town, Dolomiti Bus (☎ 0437 94 12 37; www.dolomitibus.it) offers regular service to Cortina d'Ampezzo, Conegliano and smaller mountain towns.

By car, take the A27 from Venice (Mestre) – it's not the most scenic route, but avoids traffic around Treviso.

Information

Tourist office (☎ 0437 94 00 83; www.infodolomiti.it; Piazza del Duomo 2; ☾ 9am-12.30pm & 3.30-6.30pm Mon-Sat, 9am-12.30pm Sun). From the bus and train station, take Via Dante (which becomes Via Loreto), then turn left down Via Matteotti into the central Piazza dei Martiri to reach this office. The office and its website offer information on skiing, hiking and other sporting activities, including current weather conditions and advisories.

www.infodolomiti.it Accommodation information.

www.webdolomiti.net For information on trekking through the Dolomites.

Eating & Sleeping

To explore hotel, B&B, camping and *agriturismo* (rustic lodging, usually with half board) options in Belluno, the Parco Nazionale and beyond, check www.infodolomiti.it and www.dolomitipark.it.

Azienda Agrituristica Sant'Anna (☎ 0437 2 74 91; www.aziendasantanna.it; Via Pedecastello 27, Castion; r & apt €80-120) Get away from it all in an idyllic stone farmhouse 4km outside Belluno, east of the Piave river near Ponte nelle Alpi. Recently renovated rooms have all the mod cons without losing their rustic charm: iron bedsteads, creaky timber floors and beamed ceilings. Enthusiastic hosts introduce visitors to local culture through Italian classes, hands-on dairy-farming courses and nature hikes. Online deals are available by the week and last-minute.

La Taverna (☎ 0437 2 51 92; Via Cipro 7; meals €20-30; ☾ Mon-Sat) Lead your rumbling stomach off Piazza dei Martiri to top-notch seasonal bruschetta with *prosecco* at Taverna's bar. In the adjoining restaurant, carbo-load for your hike with fresh *porcini tagliolini* (mushrooms with ribbon pasta), or go gourmet with Taverna's seasonal house specialities: wintertime eel with snails or springtime rabbit with zucchini flowers.

Ostello Imperina (☎ 0437 6 24 51; www.parks.it/ost/imperina; Località Le Miniere; dm incl breakfast/half-board/full board €20/35/47; ☾ Apr–mid-Oct) The nearest youth hostel is in the Parco Nazionale delle Dolomiti Bellunesi, 35km northwest of Belluno at Rivamonte Agordino. The hostel is in a converted copper mining centre dating from 1400, surrounded by 50km of hiking trails. Book ahead in April and May. To get there, take the Agordo bus (50 minutes) from Belluno.

Albergo Cappello e Cadore (☎ 0437 94 02 46; www.albergocappello.com; Via Ricci 8; s €45-75, d €90-103; P ☒) A rosy, cosy 19th-century inn just off Piazza dei Martiri. Most guestrooms are monastery-modest, with plain pine bedsteads; splash out for doubles with a Jacuzzi.

CORTINA D'AMPEZZO

The Italian supermodel of ski resorts, Cortina d'Ampezzo (population 6600, elevation 1224m) is fashionable, pricey, icy and undeniably beautiful. The town's stone church spires and pleasant piazzas are framed by magnificent Alps. The mountains encircling Cortina are (clockwise) Cristallo, the Gruppo di Sorapiss-Marmole, Antelao, Becco di Mezzodi-Croda da Lago, Nuolau-Averau-Cinque Torre and Tofane. To the south are Pelmo and Civetta.

Winter crowds arrive in December for top-notch downhill and cross-country skiing facilities and stay until April. Summertime adventurers hit Cortina for climbing and hiking from June until October. Two cable cars whisk skiers and walkers from Cortina's town centre into the mountains, to a central departure point for chair lifts, cable cars and trails. Lifts usually run from 9am to 5pm daily mid-December to April, and resume from June-to September/October.

Ski and snowboard runs here range from bunny to the legendary Staunies black mogul run: starting at 300m, Staunies isn't for the faint of heart or weak of knee. Passes are sold at the ski pass office (☎ 0436 86 21 71; Via G Marconi 15; 1-/2-/3-day pass €36/72/104; ☽ hours vary).

Other winter adventures in Cortina include dogsledding, scaling frozen waterfalls and ice skating at Cortina's Olympic Ice Stadium (☎ 0436 88 18 11; Via dello Stadio; adult/child incl skate rental €10/9), built for the 1956 Winter Olympics.

When the weather cooperates, Gruppo Guide Alpine Cortina (☎ 0436 86 85 05; www.guidecortina .com; Corso Italia 69a) runs rock-climbing courses (three-day course including gear €270) and guided nature hikes (prices vary). In summer, the world-famous Tre Clime di Lavoredo peaks near Cortina crawl with climbers and hikers – mind your sporting etiquette.

From Cortina bus station (Via G Marconi), SAD buses (☎ 0471 45 01 11; www.sad.it) link Cortina to nearby towns and Alto Adige destinations, while Dolomiti Bus (☎ 0437 94 12 37; www.dolomitibus. it) offers service to smaller mountain towns, Belluno and other Veneto locales.

By car, take the A27 motorway from Venice (Mestre), which turns into SS51 around Belluno and heads northwest to Cortina.

Information

Croce Bianca (☎ 0436 86 20 75) Emergency medical aid.

Tourist Office (☎ 0436 32 31; www.infodolimiti .it; Piazzetta San Francesco 8; ☽ 9am-12.30pm & 3.30-6.30pm Dec-Apr)

Eating & Sleeping

Cortina's pedestrian centre is ringed with pizzerias and cafes, which are your best bets for reasonable eats. For additional hotel, B&B, camping, *agriturismo* and *affittacamere* (room rental) options in Cortina, check www.info dolimiti.it.

Oltres B&B (☎ 346 520 31 75; www.oltres.com; d €60-100 Jan-Nov, €100-140 Dec, all incl breakfast; P ☒) According to local legend, Titian was born in this classic 17th-century farmhouse southeast of Cortina, and the wildflower meadows may inspire your own masterpiece. Guestrooms are wood-panelled, cosy and quaint, while bathrooms are updated and spotless.

Hotel Montana (☎ 0436 86 04 98; www.cortina-hotel .com; per person €40-80; ⌨ ☎) Right in the heart of Cortina, this vintage 1920s Alpine hotel hosts snow bunnies and Olympian curling champions alike. In winter, the hotel requires a seven-night minimum stay (Saturday to Saturday or Sunday to Sunday), but call in case of vacancies.

International Camping Olympia (☎ 0436 50 57; www .campingolympiacortina.it; camp sites per adult €4.50-8, tent & car €7-9; P) Set up camp beneath towering pine trees 4km north of Cortina in Fiames. There's an on-site pizzeria, and local bus service to Cortina.

TRANSPORT

Flights, tours and rail tickets can be booked online at www.lonelyplanet.com/travel_services.

AIR

Direct flights to/from major destinations within Italy, Europe and the US are available at Marco Polo airport (VCE; ☎ 041 260 9260; www.venice airport.it), including budget flights run by UK-based EasyJet and Alitalia's Air One. Most direct flights into Venice come from Rome and Milan, with a handful from Naples, Olbia and Palermo. Ryanair's budget flights to/from London Stansted, Dublin, Shannon, and Paris currently use Treviso's San Giuseppe airport (TSF; ☎ 042 231 51 11; www.trevisoairport.it), a 30km, one-hour drive from Venice.

Low-cost airlines are a benefit to travellers, but a burden on the environment and Venice's air quality; to travel with a cleaner conscience, consider a carbon-offset program (see p259). Travel within Northern Italy or from Lugano is often cheaper and more convenient by train (p263), and you'll be cutting back on carbon emissions.

Airlines

More than 40 airlines serve more than 60 destinations direct to/from Venice. Airlines don't bother with shopfront offices in Venice so you'll have to go online, call the following numbers or try a travel agent:

Air Dolomiti (EN; ☎ 199 400044; www.airdolomiti.it) Airline with flights from Monaco to Venice and Frankfurt, Salerno, Monaco and Vienna to Verona.

Air One (AP; ☎ 199 207080; www.flyairone.it) Alitalia-operated airline offers low-cost local flights throughout Italy.

Alitalia (AZ; ☎ 06 2222; www.alitalia.it, in Italian) Flights from Rome, Milan, Sicily and other Italian centres, plus European and US hubs.

BMI (BD; ☎ 0870 607 0555; www.flybmi.com) Flights to Venice from London's Heathrow.

British Airways (BA; ☎ in UK 0870 850 9850, in Italy 199 712266; www.britishairways.com) From the UK.

Cimber (DM; ☎ in Denmark 70 10 84 84, in Italy 02 696 33 595; www.cimber.com) Budget flights from Copenhagen to Venice.

THINGS CHANGE...

The information in this chapter is particularly vulnerable to change. Check directly with the airline or a travel agent to make sure you understand how a fare (and ticket you may buy) works and be aware of the security requirements for international travel. Shop carefully. The details given in this chapter should be regarded as pointers and are not a substitute for your own careful, up-to-date research.

Delta (DL; ☎ in the USA 800 241 4141, in Italy 848 780376; www.delta.com) Flights from New York and Atlanta.

EasyJet (U2; ☎ in the UK 0871 244 2366, in Italy 899 234589; www.easyjet.com) Flights from London Gatwick, Bristol and East Midlands.

Flybaboo (BBO; ☎ in Switzerland 0848 445445; www.babooairways.com) Flights from Geneva to Venice.

Germanwings (4U; ☎ in Germany 0900 191 9100, in Italy 199 404747; www15.germanwings.com) Direct, low-cost flights linking Treviso to Cologne, Salzburg, Prague, St Petersburg, Istanbul, Bucharest and Sofia.

Jet2 (LS; ☎ 0871 226 1737; www.jet2.com) Budget airline that flies from Leeds and Edinburgh to Venice.

Qantas Airways (QF; ☎ in Australia 13 13 13, in Italy 848 350010; www.qantas.com.au) Codeshare flights from Australia to Italy, often via Hong Kong.

Ryanair (FR; ☎ in Ireland 0818 303030, in the UK 0871 246 0000, in Italy 899 678910; www.ryanair.com) Flights from Brussels, Dublin and Shannon, Frankfurt (Hahn), Girona (for Barcelona), Liverpool, London (Stansted), Paris (Beauvais) and Rome to Treviso. Ryanair also flies to Brescia airport, reasonably handy for Verona.

Sky Europe (NE; ☎ in Hungary 06 1777 7000, in Italy 166 205304; www.skyeurope.com) Low-cost flights between Treviso and Prague.

Transavia (HV; ☎ in Netherlands 0900-0737, in Italy 02 696 82 615; www.transavia.com) Low-cost flights from Amsterdam to Treviso and Verona.

TUIfly (X3; ☎ in Germany 0900 109 9595, in Italy 199 192692; www.tuifly.com) Flights from Berlin and other German cities to Venice.

US Airways (US; ☎ in the USA 800 622 1015; www.usairways.com) Direct flights from Philadelphia and Tampa to Venice.

Vueling (VY; ☎ in Spain 902 333933, in Italy 800 787788; www.vueling.com) Flights from Barcelona, Seville and Madrid.

Wind Jet (IV; ☎ 899 809060; www.volawindjet.it) Flights to Venice from Catania and Palermo, and Verona to St Petersburg and Moscow.

Airports

Venice's Marco Polo airport (VCE; ☎ 041 260 92 60; www .veniceairport.it) is 12km outside Venice and just east of Mestre. *Arrivi* (arrivals) at Marco Polo airport is on the ground floor, where you will also find an Azienda di Promozione Turistica (APT) office, car-hire outlets (p262), hotel-booking agencies, bureaux de change, *deposito bagagli* (left luggage) and *bagagli smarriti* (lost luggage).

Check-in and departures are on the 1st floor. You'll find banks, ATMs, cafes and shops on both floors. For transit options into Venice, see below.

Some low-cost airlines, including Ryanair, provide service to Treviso's minuscule San Giuseppe airport (TSF; ☎ 042 231 51 11; www.tre visoairport.it), about 5km southwest of Treviso

and about an hour's drive through traffic to Venice. The arrivals hall has a thinly stocked regional tourist information booth, a lost-luggage office, a bureau de change and several car-hire outlets. Next door, in departures, you'll find an ATM and a couple of tour and airline offices (including Ryanair). Eurobus buses (run by ATVO) connect Piazzale Roma with Treviso's San Giuseppe airport (one way/return €5/9, one hour five minutes). Taxis (€75) can take over an hour in traffic.

BICYCLE

Not that it's feasible with all those foot-bridges, but cycling is banned in central Venice. On the larger islands of Lido and Pellestrina, cycling is a pleasant way to get around and reach distant beaches. Bicycle hire places are clustered around the Lido vaporetto stop (Map p116), including Lido on Bike (☎ 041 526 80 19; www.lidoonbike.it; Gran Viale 21/B; single/tandem/double/family bikes per hr €3/6-18/7/14, single/tandem bikes per day €9/18; 🕙 9am-7pm daily, weather permitting).

GETTING TO/FROM MARCO POLO AIRPORT

To get to Venice from Marco Polo airport, you have four main options: bus, ferry, water taxi and auto taxi. Bear in mind that if you're taking a ferry or water taxi, it's a 10-minute walk down the sidewalk to the airport docks from the arrivals hall. If you take a taxi or bus, you may have to hop on a ferry or walk from the Piazzale Roma depot to reach your hotel in San Marco, Dorsoduro, Castello, Giudecca or the Lido.

Boat

Scenic and convenient, Alilaguna (☎ 041 240 17 01; www.alilaguna.com) offers 60- to 80-minute ferry rides (€13) from the Marco Polo docks into Venice: the A (arancia, or orange) line to Guglie (near the train station) and Rialto; the B (blue) line, with stops at Fondamente Nuove, Lido, San Marco, Zattere, and Giudecca; and the R (red) line to Murano, Lido, Arsenale, San Marco and Zattere. The faster, direct Gold Line to/from San Zaccaria, near San Marco, takes 35 minutes, costs €25 (35 minutes, seven times daily every half hour). Tickets for Alilaguna ferries to Venice can be purchased at the ticket booth in the Marco Polo arrivals hall.

A convenient but expensive option you'll find at the airport docks are water taxis, which can often drop you off right at the water gate of your hotel. Motoschafi Venezia water taxi (☎ 041 522 23 03) is a collective that offers service between Marco Polo airport and Venice for €90 to €100 (possibly more with baggage) for up to four people; ask your B&B or hotel concierge to pair you with fellow arrivals/departures to share the ride.

Bus

This is the cheapest way to go.

ATVO (☎ 041 38 36 72; www.atvo.it) buses, known as fly buses, between the airport and Piazzale Roma leave about every half hour (€3, 20 minutes). Bus stations are in front of the Marco Polo arrivals hall, with ticket machines on the sidewalk. A separate service runs to/from Mestre train station (€2.50).

ACTV (☎ 041 24 24; www.actv.it) bus 5 runs between Marco Polo airport and Piazzale Roma (€1.50, 30 minutes).

Taxi

As a back-up option, Auto taxis (☎ 041 595 20 80) cost around €40 from Marco Polo airport to Piazzale Roma (15 to 30 minutes).

CLIMATE CHANGE & TRAVEL

Climate change is a serious threat to the ecosystems that humans rely upon, and air travel is the fastest-growing contributor to the problem. Lonely Planet regards travel, overall, as a global benefit, but believes we all have a responsibility to limit our personal impact on global warming.

Flying & Climate Change

Pretty much every form of motor transport generates CO_2 (the main cause of human-induced climate change) but planes are far and away the worst offenders, not just because of the sheer distances they allow us to travel, but because they also release greenhouse gases high into the atmosphere. The statistics are frightening: two people taking a return flight between Europe and the US will contribute as much to climate change as an average household's gas and electricity consumption over a whole year.

Carbon Offset Schemes

Climatecare.org and other websites use 'carbon calculators' that allow travellers to offset the greenhouse gases they are responsible for with contributions to energy-saving projects and other climate-friendly initiatives in the developing world – including projects in India, Honduras, Kazakhstan and Uganda. Lonely Planet, together with Rough Guides and other concerned partners in the travel industry, supports the carbon offset scheme run by climatecare.org. Lonely Planet offsets all of its staff and author travel. For more information check out our website: www.lonelyplanet.com.

BOAT

Minoan Lines (www.minoan.gr) and Anek (www.anek italia.com) run regular ferries to Venice from Greece (Corfu, Igoumenitsa and Patras), while Venezia Lines (www.venezialines.com) runs high-speed boats to and from Croatia and Slovenia. But though this may seem like a scenic option, consider big-ship, high-speed transport carefully. Long-haul ferries, cruise ships and speed boats have an outsize environmental impact on tiny Venice and its fragile lagoon aquaculture, exposing Venice's ancient foundations to degradation from high-speed wakes plus leakage of wastewater from the bilge, ballast, and flushing of onboard toilets. Take the lower-impact train instead, and Venice will be most grateful.

Boat Hire

Aspiring sea captains with nerves of steel can take on Venetian water traffic in a rented boat from Brussa (Map pp94–5; ☎ 041 71 57 87; www.brussaisboat.it, in Italian; Fondamenta Labia 331, Cannaregio; ☏ 7.30am-5.30pm Mon-Fri, 7.30am-12.30pm Sat). You can hire a 7m boat (including fuel) that can carry up to six people for an hour (€22) or a day (€140), or make arrangements for longer periods. You don't need a licence, but you will be taken on a test run to see if you can manoeuvre and park; be sure to ask them to point out the four boat petrol stations around Venice on a map. If you'd rather enjoy cocktails on board and leave the sailing to the experts, look into lagoon tours (see p271).

Gondola

A gondola ride offers a view of Venice that is anything but pedestrian, with glimpses through water gates into palazzi courtyards. Official daytime rates are €80 for 40 minutes or €100 from 7pm to 8am, not including songs (negotiated separately) or tips. Additional time is charged in 20-minute increments (day/night €40/50). You may negotiate a price break in overcast weather or around midday, when other travellers get hot and hungry. Agree on a price, time limit and singing in advance to avoid surcharges.

Gondole cluster at *stazi* (stops) along the Grand Canal, at the Ferrovia stop at the train station (☎ 041 71 85 43), the Rialto (☎ 041 522 49 04) and near major monuments (eg I Frari, Ponte Sospiri and Accademia), but you can also book a pick-up at a canal near you (☎ 041 528 50 75).

Vaporetto

The city's main mode of public transport is vaporetto (city ferry). ACTV (☎ 041 24 24; www .actv.it) runs public transport in the Comune di Venezia (the municipality), covering mainland buses and all the waterborne public transport around Venice.

Travel by vaporetto is often scenic, especially at night and in fine weather, but it's not always fast. Walking may actually be a quicker way to get to your destination than all-stops vaporetto lines, such as line 1 down the Grand Canal. Some lines make only limited stops, especially during 8am to10am and 6pm to 8pm rush hours,

WAITING FOR YOUR SHIP TO COME IN

Vaporetto stops can be confusing, so check the signs at the landing dock to make sure you're at the right stop for the vaporetto line and direction you want. At major stops like Ferrovia, Piazzale Roma, San Marco and Zattere, there are often two separate docks for the same vaporetto line, headed in opposite directions. Check dock signage carefully or you could end up on the right vaporetto, heading the wrong way.

The cluster of stops near Piazza San Marco are especially tricky. If your boat doesn't stop right in front of Piazza San Marco, don't panic: it will probably stop at San Zaccaria, just past the Palazzo Ducale. Be sure to get off at San Zaccaria, though, as your next scheduled stop may be the far-flung Arsenale.

so check boat signage. If you're in a hurry, check the digital display or posted schedule for the next limited service – vaporetti are usually quite punctual.

Interisland ferry services to Murano, Torcello and other lagoon islands are usually provided on larger *motonave* (big interisland vaporetto), so those prone to motion sickness shouldn't worry too much about getting tossed about in a small boat. That said, for longer hauls it's always wise to check weather reports beforehand, and bring your motion-sickness medication just in case.

Vaporetti can get crowded, and visitors anxious about missing their stops tend to cluster near exits. If you are standing near an exit, it is common practice on reaching a stop to get off and let passengers behind you disembark before you get back on. Passengers with disabilities are first to embark or disembark, and offers of assistance are welcomed.

TICKETS

Tickets can be purchased from the HelloVenezia (☎ 041 24 24; www.hellovenezia.com) ticket booths at most landing stations, and free timetables and route maps are available at many of these ticket booths. You can also buy single-trip tickets when boarding; you may be charged double with more than one piece of luggage.

Instead of spending €6.50 for a one-way ticket, consider buying a VENICEcard (p266) or a timed pass for unlimited travel within a set time period, which begins when you validate your ticket in the yellow machine located at a ferry dock. Passes are available for tickets for 12/24/36/48/72 hours at €16/18/23/28/33, and for seven days (€50). People aged 14 to 29 can get a three-day ticket for €18 with the Rolling VENICEcard (see p266).

Generally, tickets are stamped with a time when sold to you, validating the ticket for immediate use. If you're planning to use them later, you can request them not to be validated. If your tickets are not validated, you

must validate them in the machines located at all stops before you get on your first vaporetto. If you're caught without a valid ticket, you'll be required to buy one and pay a €60 fine.

ROUTES

From Piazzale Roma, vaporetto 1 zigzags up the Grand Canal to San Marco and onward to the Lido. If you're not in a rush, it's a great introduction to Venice. Vaporetto 17 carries vehicles from Tronchetto, near Piazzale Roma, to the Lido.

Frequency varies greatly according to line and time of day. Vaporetto 1 runs every 10 minutes through most of the day, while lines such as the 41 and 42 only run every 20 minutes. Services to Burano and Torcello are still less frequent. Night services can be as much as one hour apart. Some lines stop running by around 9pm, so check timetables.

Keep in mind that routes and route numbers can change, and not all routes go both ways. Here are key vaporetto lines and major stops, subject to seasonal change:

No 1 Piazzale Roma-Ferrovia-Grand Canal (all stops)-Lido and back.

No 2 Circular line: San Zaccaria-Redentore-Zattere-Trochetto-Ferrovia-Rialto-Accademia-San Marco.

No 5 San Zaccaria-Murano and back.

No 8 Sacca Fisola-Zattere-Redentore-Giardini-Lido

No 13 Fondamente Nuove-Murano-Vignole-Sant'Erasmo-Treporti and back.

No 17 Car ferry: Tronchetto-Lido and back.

No 18 Murano-Sant'Erasmo-Lido and back (summer only).

No 20 San Zaccaria-San Lazzaro-Lido and back.

No 41 Circular line: Murano-Fondamente Nuove-Ferrovia-Piazzale Roma-Redentore-San Zaccaria- Fondamente Nuove-San Michele-Murano.

No 42 Circular line in reverse direction to No 41.

No 51 Circular line: Lido- Fondamente Nuove-Riva de Biasio-Ferrovia-Piazzale Roma-Zattere-San Zaccaria-Giardini-Lido.

No 52 Circular line in reverse direction to No 51.

No 61 Limited stops, weekdays-only circular line: Piazzale Roma-Santa Marta-San Basilio-Zattere-Giardini-Sant'Elena-Lido.

No 62 Limited stops, weekdays-only circular line in reverse direction to No 61.

N All stops night circuit: Lido-Giardini-San Zaccaria-Grand Canal (all stops)-Ferrovia-Piazzale Roma-Tronchetto-Zattere-Redentore-San Giorgio-San Zaccaria (starts around 11.30pm; last service around 5am).

N A second night service, also known as NMU, from Fondamente Nuove to Murano (all stops) – three or four runs from midnight.

N A third night run, also known as NLN, offers sporadic service between Fondamente Nuove and Burano, Mazzorbo, Torcello and Treporti.

DM (Diretto Murano) Tronchetto-Piazzale Roma- Ferrovia-Murano and back.

LN (Laguna Nord) San Zaccaria Lido Burano Mazzorbo Murano (Faro)-Fondamente Nuove and back.

T Torcello-Burano (half-hourly) and back (7am to 8.30pm).

OTHER SERVICES

Alilaguna (☎ 041 240 1701; www.alilaguna.com) runs limited ferry services to the airport via Murano (line R), Giudecca (line B), San Marco and the Lido (lines R&B), from mainland car parks and bus stations at Punta Sabbioni and Treporti to Fondamente Nuove (line G), and a direct line to San Marco from the Stazione Marittima (line M).

Linea Fusina (Map pp78–9; www.terminalfusina.it; Campo di Sant'Agnese 909c, Dorsoduro) runs a direct line from Venice (Zattere) to the Alberoni beaches on the Lido (one way/return €5/10, 45 minutes, up to five a day); see website for schedules. To get to mainland car parks and camping grounds at Fusina, there's a direct line from Zattere (one way/return €7/12, 25 minutes, up to 15 a day).

CHEAP THRILLS ON THE GRAND CANAL: TRAGHETTI

The next best thing to walking on water is a *traghetto* (commuter gondola), the gondola service locals use to cross the Grand Canal where there is no nearby bridge. It costs just €1, but be prepared for a balancing act: all passengers are expected to stand for the duration of the gondola ride across the canal. *Traghetti* typically operate from 9am to 6pm, although some routes finish by noon, and some don't operate on slow, bad-weather days. Major *traghetto* crossings are marked on the Venice neighbourhood maps.

Water Taxi

Licensed water taxis (☎ 041 522 23 03, 041 240 67 11) are a costly way to get around Venice, though they may prove handy when you're late for the opera or have lots of luggage or shopping in tow. Prices can be metered or negotiated in advance. Official rates start at €8.90 plus €1.80 per minute, €6 extra if they're called to your hotel and more for night trips (10pm to 7am), luggage and for each extra passenger above the first four. Even if you're in a hurry, don't encourage your taxi driver to speed through Venice – this kicks up *motoschiaffi* (motorboat wakes) that expose Venice's ancient foundations to degradation and rot (p37).

Make sure your water taxi has the yellow strip with licence number displayed. If approached by a craft without this sign, don't take it. Illegal water taxis have been known to whisk unsuspecting tourists off to places they don't necessarily want to go (a cousin's glass shop in Murano, for example) and charge staggering sums for the privilege. Illegal water taxi drivers are a special problem on the Isola del Tronchetto, approaching freshly parked tourists and offering 'the only way' to get to central Venice by boat – not true, since vaporetto 2 calls here regularly.

BUS

All buses serving central Venice terminate at the bus station on Piazzale Roma, though bus service is available on the Lido. Major bus lines providing service to Venice's Piazzale Roma:

ACTV (Azienda del Consorzio Trasporti Veneziani; ☎ 041 24 24; www.actv.it) Runs buses day and night from Piazzale Roma for Mestre and surrounding areas, as well as buses up and down the Lido. Tickets cost €1 (or a book of 10 for €9) and are valid for one hour from the time you validate them in the machine on the bus. You can buy tickets at the main bus station in Piazzale Roma (Map pp86–7), and from many news-stands and *tabaccherie* (tobacconists). Some timed vaporetto tickets and passes are also good for ACTV buses; see p266.

ATVO (Azienda Trasporti Veneto Orientale; ☎ 041 520 55 30) Operates buses to destinations all over the eastern Veneto. Tickets and information are available at the ticket office on Piazzale Roma (Map pp86–7).

Eurolines (www.eurolines.com) The main international carrier, with connections to other major bus lines across Europe. Eurolines' website provides links to the sites of all the national operators. In Venice, Eurolines tickets can be bought from

Agenzia Brusutti (Map pp86–7; ☎ 041 38 36 71; Piazzale Roma 497e, Santa Croce). Buses run several times a week from London, Paris, Barcelona and other European centres.

CAR & MOTORCYCLE
Driving to Venice
Venice is 279km from Milan, 529km from Rome, 579km from Geneva, 1112km from Paris, 1135km from Berlin, 1515km from London and 1820km from Madrid. The main points of entry to Italy are the Mont Blanc tunnel from France at Chamonix, which connects with the A5 for Turin and Milan; the Grand St Bernard tunnel from Switzerland, which also connects with the A5; and the Brenner Pass from Austria, which connects with the A22 to Bologna.

Once in Italy, the A4 is the quickest way to reach Venice from east or west. It connects Turin with Trieste, passing through Milan and Mestre. From Mestre, take the Venezia exit and follow the signs for the city. Coming from the Brenner Pass, the A22 connects with the A4 near Verona. From the south, take the A13 from Bologna, which connects with the A4 at Padua (Padova).

Once over the Ponte della Libertà bridge from Mestre, cars must be left at the car park at Piazzale Roma or Tronchetto; expect to pay €20 or more for every 24 hours. Parking stations in Mestre are cheaper. Car ferry 17 transports vehicles from Tronchetto to the Lido.

Hire
The car-rental companies listed here all have offices on Piazzale Roma and at Marco Polo airport. Several companies operate in or near Mestre train station too.

Avis (Map pp86–7; ☎ 041 523 73 77)

Europcar (Map pp86–7; ☎ 041 523 86 16)

Expressway (Map pp86–7; ☎ 041 522 30 00)

Hertz (Map pp86–7; ☎ 041 528 40 91)

Parking
If you're determined to drive across the Ponte della Libertà from the mainland to Venice, you'll find car parks in Piazzale Roma or on Isola del Tronchetto. But fair warning: visitors who drive across the bridge into Venice pay a hefty price in parking fees and traffic frustration. On summer days and holiday weekends, day trippers may spend less time seeing the sights than the back end of another vehicle on

the Ponte della Libertà, making little forward progress and unable to go back. Traffic has been known to get so jammed that the police shuts the city off from the mainland.

To avoid the hassle, park in Mestre, and take the bus or train into Venice instead. Nearly all street parking is metered in Mestre, but car parks in Mestre are cheaper than in Venice. Remember to take anything that looks even remotely valuable out of your car, since thieves prowl local car parks.

Serenissima (☎ 041 93 80 21; Viale Stazione 10, Mestre; per day from midnight-midnight €6, weekends & holidays €10; ☽ 24hr) One of several car parks near the train station in Mestre.

Garage Brega (☎ 041 92 64 78; Piazzale Favretti 1, Mestre; per day covered/outdoor €12/6) 350m from Mestre train station.

Garage Europa Mestre (☎ 041 95 92 02; www.garage europamestre.com; Corso del Popolo 55, Mestre; first day €14, per additional day €12) ACTV bus 4 to/from Venice stops right outside the garage.

Autoremissa Comunale (Map pp86–7; ☎ 041 272 72 11; www.asmvenezia.it; Piazzale Roma; compact car per day in low/peak period €24/28, car over 185cm €27/31; ☽ 24hr) Discounts available with online reservation; free six-hour parking for people with disabilities.

Garage San Marco (Map pp86–7; ☎ 041 523 22 13; www.garagesanmarco.it; Piazzale Roma; per 12hr/24hr €24/30; ☽ 24hr) Guests of certain hotels get discounts; 900 spaces.

Parking Sant'Andrea (Map pp86–7; ☎ 041 272 73 04; Piazzale Roma; per 2hr or part thereof €4.50; ☽ 24hr) 100 spots; best for short-term parking.

Tronchetto (☎ 041 520 75 55; www.veniceparking.it; Isola del Tronchetto; per 24hr €21; ☽ 24hr)

ILLEGAL PARKING
If you return to your car to find that it's no longer there, call the local police (vigili urbani) on ☎ 041 274 7070. They dump towed cars in one of three mainland depots. It'll cost you around €100 for the towing, €40 a day in the pound and the parking fine.

MONORAIL
Venice's People Mover monorail (APM; www.apm venezia.com) is currently under construction, and planned to be in operation by early 2010. Designed by the architect Francesco Cocco, this elevated monorail will whisk passengers from Tronchetto car parks to Piazzale Roma

via the Stazione Marittima ferry terminal in just three minutes. The low-emissions, low-noise trains can carry up to 50 passengers at a time, with scheduled departures every three minutes in peak periods.

TAXI

Auto taxis (☎ 041 595 2080) to the mainland operate from a rank in Piazzale Roma (Map pp86–7).

TRAIN

Prompt, affordable, scenic and environmentally savvy, trains are the preferred transport option to and from Venice. Trains run frequently to Venice's Stazione Santa Lucia (signed as Ferrovia within Venice) from locations throughout Italy and major European cities; vaporetti (city ferries) stop right outside the station. Train tickets can be purchased at self-serve ticketing machines in the station, online at www.trenitalia.it, in the UK at Rail Europe (☎ 0844 8484064; www.raileurope.co.uk), or through travel agents.

Validate your ticket in the orange machines on station platforms before boarding your train. Failure to do so will almost certainly result in embarrassment and a hefty on-the-spot fine when the inspector checks tickets on the train.

Venice can be reached by rail from major points in France, Germany, Austria, Switzerland, Slovenia and Croatia. Intercity (IC) trains are fast services that operate between major cities in Italy, Eurocity (EC) trains offer service to European centres, while slower regional trains make more interim stops between Italian transit hubs. Eurostar Italia (ES) provides *pendolini* (high-speed trains) that can zip along at 300km/h; trains have comfortable seats with tables and handy outlets for laptop computers and other equipment. Even in first class, you may be sharing your table or compartment with other passengers.

Almost every train leaving from Stazione di Santa Lucia stops in Mestre (€1, 10 minutes); tickets to Mestre are available from machines and from station *tabaccherie*. Venice is linked by train to Padua (€2.90 to €15.70, 30 to 50 minutes, three to four each hour) and Verona (€6.15 to €25.20, 1¼ to 2½ hours, two each hour). Regular trains run further afield to Milan (€14.50-38.50, 2½ to 3¼ hours), Bologna (€8.90 to €35.20, 1¾ to 2¾ hours), Florence (€21.50 to €54.50, 2¾ to 3¾ hours) and many other cities.

Orient Express

The Venice Simplon Orient Express (☎ in UK 0845 077 2222; www.orient-express.com) runs between London and Venice via Paris, Innsbruck and Verona on Thursday and Sunday (late March to November; two days/one night, about 30 hours). The one-way fare (most take a plane for the return trip) is UK£1867, including steward service, chef-prepared meals, and Bellinis. Special offers and packages with stays at the Hotel Cipriani sweeten the deal.

Train Stations

When getting train tickets, be sure to specify Venezia Santa Lucia (VSL; Map pp94–5), which is the train station in central Venice. The station has a rail-travel information office (☺ 7am-9pm) opposite the APT office and a deposito bagagli office (☎ 041 78 55 31; per piece first 5hr €4, next 7hr €0.60, thereafter per hr €0.20; ☺ 6am-midnight) opposite platform 1.

On the mainland (which is a 10-minute train ride from central Venice), Venezia Mestre station offers rail information, a hotel-booking office and a deposito bagagli office (041 78 44 46; per piece first 5hr €4, next 7hr €0.60, thereafter per hr €0.20; ☺ 7am-11pm).

DIRECTORY

BUSINESS HOURS

In general, shops open from 9am to 1pm and 3.30pm to 7pm (or 4pm to 7.30pm) Monday to Saturday; for more information on shopping hours, see p162. Most supermarkets open from around 9am to 7.30pm Monday to Saturday.

Banks tend to open from 8.30am to 1.30pm and 3.30pm to 5.30pm Monday to Friday, but hours do vary, and a few open on Saturday morning.

For Eating opening hours see p180; for Drinking, see p198.

CHILDREN

This fairy-tale city defies all adult reason - but it makes perfect sense to kids, whose imaginations run riot here. Top Venice destinations for kids are listed on p85; prime activities for the active kids include these:

Grand Canal trip With gondolas, palaces and curious lagoon birds, this is a storybook boat ride – just be sure to get timed tickets (see p260), so you can hop off any time to explore or take bathroom breaks.

Itinerari Segreti (Secret Tours, p67) Secret passageways, spooky prisons, and the true story of Casanova's great escape will send kids' imaginations into overdrive at the Palazzo Ducale.

Watching artisans at work Explore the back streets of San Polo and Santa Croce, and discover artisans creating glass mosquitos at I Vetri A Lume di Amadi (p170), marble-paper jewellery at Cartè (p169) and etchings pulled right off the antique press at Veneziastampa (p171).

Gondolas galore Glide through the canals on a full-scale gondola, glimpse gondolas being built at Squero San Trovaso (p82) then head to Gilberto Penzo (p168) for model-boat kits so kids can bring home their own gondolas.

Collecting Italian comic books Stock up on Hugo Pratt's Corte Maltese mysteries and more at Solaris (p172).

Exploring the Lido by tandem bicycle Hit nearby beaches or cycle (p258) all the way to Malamocco (p116) to discover a shrunken version of Venice.

Getting crafty Kids inspired by Venice's artisans can make their own Carnevale masks at Ca' Macana (p167) or assemble their own bead necklaces at La Bottega di Gio (p171).

Rocking out with classical musicians Arrive early at Interpreti Veneziani concerts (p209) so the kids can get up close and personal with classical music.

Boating around the lagoon Picnic on board a real Venetian *bragasso* (barge), romp through a desert island, and roam bright Burano with Terra e Acqua, p271.

Discovering hidden treasure Kids can score their own piece of Venice's history at summer flea markets (*mercati delle pulci*) or antique teddy bears at Il Baule Blu (p171).

Lazing along the Zattere Venice's stone boardwalk is a prime spot for lazy sunny days, watching ships float past with ice cream at Da Nico (p184).

Practicalities

Special discounted rates usually apply for children under 12 years on public transport and at museums and other sights.

Some of the major hotels in Venice offer baby-sitting services, though you should request a booking well in advance if you want an English speaker.

On weekends take the train instead of a car into Venice to avoid getting stuck in traffic. Since you'll be walking a lot, bring a stroller for little ones, and don't be shy about accepting help over bridges.

Viva Venice, by Paola Scibilia and Paolo Zoffoli, and *Venice for Kids*, by Elisabetta Pasqualin, are packed with illustrations, games, legends, anecdotes and suggestions on what to do. For more advice on travelling with kids, check out Lonely Planet's *Travel with Children*.

CLIMATE

Muggy midsummer (July and August) isn't the most comfortable time to visit Venice. Average daytime temperatures can hover around 27°C or higher, humidity is high, prevailing southern winds (the sirocco) are hot, and as water levels drop, the canals can smell a tad ripe.

In spring, the weather is often crisp and clear and the temperatures pleasant, though you might run into rain from April and into June. In July and August the humidity can bring cracking storms in the evening, which make a thrilling sight reflected in the lagoon and gives you a fresh perspective on Tintoretto's stormy canvases and the ominous violin crescendos in Vivaldi's *Four Seasons*.

In winter, the city and lagoon are occasionally enveloped in mist, which can be damp and chilly but makes for very dra-

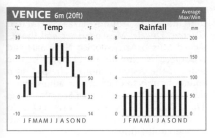

| VENICE 6m (20ft) | | Average Max/Min |

matic photos. The first half of winter brings heavier rainfall, with flooding most likely in November and December. December and January are the coldest months, with average temperatures hovering between 0°C and 7°C, often with the unexpected benefits of clear, crystalline skies. Because of the city's position on the lagoon, snow is a rare and spectacular sight.

COURSES

You too can learn to *Venexianàrse* (become Venetian). With some advance planning, you can pick up some key skills during your visit that will allow you to see life through local eyes.

To research other speciality classes in Venice or bone up on Italian culture before your trip, check out the Istituto Italiano di Cultura (IIC; Italian Cultural Institute; www.esteri.it), a government-sponsored organisation that promotes Italian culture and language. On the official website, click on Ministry, then on Diplomatic Network and Cultural Institutes to locate an institute branch near you. Branches can be found in Australia (Sydney and Melbourne), Canada (Montreal, Vancouver and Toronto), the UK (London and Edinburgh), Ireland (Dublin) and the USA (Los Angeles, New York, San Francisco, Chicago and Washington, DC).

Cooking

Cook a seafood feast fresh from the Pescaria (p85), with the season's best produce and sommelier Sara Sossiga's wine pairings at Venice Table (www.venicevenetogourmet.com; 2–8 people incl meal & wine €130) .

Language & Learning

Istituto Venezia (Map pp78–9; ☎ 041 522 43 31; www .istitutovenezia.com; Campo Santa Margherita 3116a, Dorsoduro; 4hr per day, 1-week intensive €160). Learn Italian

and pick up a few choice words in Venetian for happy-hour toasts. For advanced learners, one- to four-week courses cover such local obsessions as cooking, wine and Venetian art history.

Venice International University (Map p116; ☎ 041 271 95 11; www.univiu.org; Isola di San Servolo) Earn credit as you learn more about Venice from this uni which has credit recognition arrangements with several universities in the Netherlands, Spain, China, USA and Japan. Recent seminars have explored Titian's masterpieces, Venetian musicology, minority communities in Venice, Venice's tense church-state relations and the fall of Venice and the rise of the Ottomans in Constantinople.

Rowing

Row across the Giudecca Canal standing up, Venetian style, with instructors from the Associazione Canottieri Giudecca (Map p112; www.canottieri giudecca.com, in Italian; Fondamente del Ponte Lungo 259, Giudecca; per hr €10). Referrals for instructors can also be found at Maredicarta (p168).

The Arts

Bottega del Tintoretto (Map pp146–7; ☎ 041 72 20 81; www.tintorettovenezia.it; Fondamenta dei Mori 3400; 30-hr 5-day course inc lunch & materials €360) Make your own masterpiece with painting, etching and sculpture courses at the studio that once housed Tintoretto's workshop; see also p152.

Ca' Macana (Map pp78–9; ☎ 041 522 97 49; www .camacana.com; Calle delle Botteghe 3172, Dorsoduro; workshop depending on class size about €60, workshops Wed & Fri 3pm) Create Carnevale masks in a 2½ hour workshop here. Classes focus on either the art of papier mâché sculpting or painted-mask decoration; see p167.

Fondazione Giorgio Cini (Map p112; ☎ 041 271 02 80; www.cini.it; Isola di San Giorgio Maggiore) Get ahead of the art curve with courses, seminars and special workshops on contemporary art forms ranging from Venetian abstraction to South Indian dance; check website for upcoming offerings. See also p115.

Friends of Venice Club (☎ 041 715 877; www.friend sofveniceclub.com; 7-day course UK£250) Become an opera diva or perform a benefit concert with Friends of Venice.

Istituto Europeo di Design (☎ 041 277 11 64; www .ied.it; Isola La Certosa; 75-hr courses €2800, accommodation €900) Design it yourself at this institute which offers three- to four-week English-language summer courses in fashion design, photography and graphic design, in addition to year-long programs and accredited masters degree coursework.

CUSTOMS REGULATIONS

Duty-free sales within the EU no longer exist, but goods are sold free of value-added tax (VAT) in European airports. Visitors coming into Italy from non-EU countries can import, duty free: 1L of spirits (or 2L wine), 50g perfume, 250mL eau de toilette, 200 cigarettes and other goods up to a total of €175. Anything over this limit must be declared on arrival and the appropriate duty paid. On leaving the EU, non-EU citizens can reclaim any VAT on expensive purchases.

DISCOUNT CARDS & PASSES

An International Student Identity Card (ISIC; www.isic .org) can get you discounted admission prices at some sights (such as the Scuola Grande di San Rocco) and help with cheap flights out of Italy, but ISIC benefits are limited in Venice. Only a handful of bars, restaurants, cinemas and shops offer discounts with this card.

Similar cards are available to teachers (ITIC) and nonstudents aged under 26 (IYTC), issued by student unions, hostelling organisations and some youth travel agencies. These cards also carry a travel-insurance option.

Chorus Pass

The association of Venice churches offers a Chorus Pass (☎ 041 275 04 62; www.chorusvenezia.org; adult/child/family €9/6/18; ☽ visits Mon-Fri 10am-5pm) for single entry to 16 historic Venice churches anytime within one year, including I Frari, Chiesa di Santa Maria dei Miracoli, Chiesa di San Sebastiano, and Chiesa di Madonna dell'Orto. Otherwise, admission to these individual churches costs €3 to €3.50. Passes are for sale at church ticket booths; proceeds from the pass support restoration and maintenance of churches throughout Venice.

Civic Museum Passes

Available from the APT tourist office, the Civic Museum Pass (www.museicivicivenziani.it; adult/child €18/12) is valid for six months and covers single entry to 11 civic museums, including Palazzo Ducale (the Secret Tour, p67, costs extra), Ca' Rezzonico, Ca' Pesaro, Palazzo Mocenigo, Museo Correr, and Museo del Vetro (Glass Museum) on Murano. Short-term visitors may prefer the San Marco Museum Plus pass (adult/child €13/7), which covers four museums around Piazza San Marco (Palazzo Ducale, Museo Correr and the attached Museo Archeologico Nazionale and Biblioteca Nazionale Marciana) plus one more of the visitor's choice. The pass also entitles bearers to discounts on admission to the Palazzo Ducale Itinerari Segreti (Secret Tour), Museo Fortuny and Torre d'Orlogio (Clock Tower). Families get a discount on second adult admission.

Other Combined Museum Tickets

For art aficionados planning to visit the Gallerie dell'Accademia, the modern and Asian art collections at Ca' Pesaro, and the Franchetti art collections at Ca' d'Oro, a combined ticket is available (adult/child €12/6.50) for a savings of €9 on adult admission. The combined ticket is good for three months, but during special exhibitions it may not be available. A ticket to the Gallerie dell'Accademia entitles the bearer to reduced entry fees at the newly reopened Palazzo Grimani, for a savings of €6.50 on adult admission.

A combined ticket to the Palazzo Grassi and Punta della Dogana costs €20 for a savings of €10 on adult admission, but you have to be quick about it: the ticket is only valid for three days. Visitors to the Peggy Guggenheim collection can take a further €3 discount on the combined pass within three days of their visits.

Rolling VENICEcard

Visitors aged 14 to 29 (identification required) should pick up the Rolling VENICEcard for €4, which entitles them to buy a 72-hour public transit pass for €18, discounted access to museums, monuments and cultural events, plus discounts on food, accommodation and entertainment. You can get the card at tourist offices, ACTV public-transport ticket points and HelloVenezia (☎ 041 24 24; www.hellovenezia.com; ☽ call centre 8am-7.30pm daily) ticket booths. The Rolling VENICE map lists all the locations where the card entitles you to reductions.

VENICEcard

With a VENICEcard Transport & Culture Pass (3-day junior/senior €66/73, 7-day junior/senior €87/96; ☽ call centre

8am-7.30pm daily), you get unlimited use of APTV vaporetti and buses during the given period, free entry to Venice's 11 civic museums (excluding the Accademia, Guggenheim, Grassi and Punta della Dogana) and 16 churches, plus reduced-price tickets to cultural events and special exhibitions.

VENICEcards can be purchased at the San Marco tourist office, at HelloVenezia (☎ 041 24 24; www.hellovenezia.com) ticket booths at the Ferrovia, Porta Romana, and Ferrovia vaporetto stops, or in advance at a 15% discount online.

ELECTRICITY

The electric current in Venice is 220V, 50Hz, and plugs have two round pins, as in the rest of continental Europe. Several countries outside Europe (such as the USA and Canada) use 110V, 60Hz, which means that some appliances from those countries may require a transformer.

EMBASSIES & CONSULATES

Most countries' embassies in Italy are located in Rome; you can find your country's embassy online at www.esteri.it: click on Diplomatic Network, then the Embassies, Consulates & Trade Offices tab to search for your country by name in Italian (UK is Regno Unito and USA is Stati Uniti).

A limited number of countries maintain consulates in Venice:

Austria (Map pp86–7; ☎ 041 524 05 56; Fondamenta Condulmer 251, Santa Croce)

France (Map pp100–1; ☎ 041 522 43 19; Ramo del Pestrin 6140, Castello)

Germany (Map pp68–9; ☎ 041 523 76 75; Campo Sant'Anzolo 3816, San Marco)

Switzerland (Map pp78–9; ☎ 041 522 59 96; Campo di Sant'Agnese 810, Dorsoduro)

The Netherlands (Map pp68–9; ☎ 041 528 34 16; Ramo Giustinian 2888, San Marco)

UK (☎ 041 505 59 90; Piazzale Donatori di Sangue 2, Mestre)

The nearest US consulate (☎ 02 29 03 51; Via Principe Amedeo 2/10) and Australian consulate (☎ 02 7770 42 17; Via Borgogna 2) are in Milan. The Canadian consulate (Map p237; ☎ 049 876 48 33; Riviera Ruzzante 25) is in Padua.

EMERGENCY

There's a handy police station branch (Map pp68–9; Piazza San Marco 67) in San Marco, and a larger police station (Map pp100–1; ☎ 041 270 55 11; Fondamenta di San Lorenzo 5053, Castello) a bit of a walk from the centre. The city's head police station (Questura; Map pp86–7; Santa Croce 500) is off the beaten track in the ex-convent of Santa Chiara, just beyond Piazzale Roma.

Useful numbers in an emergency can be found on the inside front cover of this book.

GAY & LESBIAN TRAVELLERS

Homosexuality is legal in Italy and well tolerated in Venice and the Veneto. ArciGay (www .arcigay.it), the national gay, lesbian, bisexual and transgender organisation, has information on the GLBT scene in Italy. The useful website www.gay.it (in Italian) lists gay and lesbian events across the country, but options in Venice are slim. Head to Padua for a wider range of gay-friendly nightlife, and the nearest GLBT organisation, ArciGay Tralaltro (Map p237; ☎ 049 876 24 58; www.tralaltro.it, in Italian; Corso Garibaldi 41).

HOLIDAYS

For Venetians as for most Italians, the main holiday periods are summer (July and especially August), the Christmas–New Year period and Easter. Though you might find travel deals in late summer, August can be hot and much of the country closes up shop while everyone heads to the beach. Restaurants, shops and most other activity grinds to a halt around Ferragosto (Feast of the Assumption; 15 August). For information on the city's many festivals and other events, see p17. The following is a list of national public holidays:

Capodanno/Anno Nuovo (New Year's Day) 1 January

Epifania/Befana (Epiphany) 6 January

Venerdí Santo (Good Friday) March/April

Pasquetta/Lunedí dell'Angelo (Easter Monday) March/April

Giorno della Liberazione (Liberation Day) 25 April is the anniversary of the 1945 Allied Victory in Italy that ended German occupation and Mussolini's regime.

Festa del Lavoro (Labour Day) 1 May

Festa della Repubblica (Republic Day) 2 June

Ferragosto (Feast of the Assumption) 15 August

Ognissanti (All Saints' Day) 1 November

Immaculata Concezione (Feast of the Immaculate Conception) 8 December

Natale (Christmas Day) 25 December

Festa di Santo Stefano (Boxing Day) 26 December

INTERNET ACCESS

If you plan to carry your notebook or palmtop computer with you, you should also bring a universal adaptor to convert your appliance to the correct voltage and three-prong grounded plugs to local two-prong outlets. You might consider bringing a grounded power strip, which allows you to plug in more appliances and protects your computer from the power fluctuations that frequently occur in Venice's older buildings – the combination of old wiring and all that water keeps electricians plenty busy with basic maintenance.

Internet Cafes

Bring your passport on your first visit, as under Italian antiterrorism laws you cannot use these centres otherwise. Some of the following places offer student rates, reduced rates for several hours prepaid, and cut-price international calls. Many keep regular shop hours, so don't count on checking email after dinner or on Sundays.

Grace (Map p112; ☎ 041 522 36 93; Fondamenta Sant'Eufemia 517, Giudecca; per hr €5; ☼ 9.30am-1pm & 3.30-7.30pm Mon-Fri) Also offers computer repair and photo printing services.

Internet Corner (Map pp100–1; ☎ 041 277 05 15; Calle del Caffettier 6661a, Castello; per hr €7; ☼ 10am-10pm Mon-Sat, 1-9pm Sun) Near Zanipolo, with printing services; open late and on weekends.

Internet Point Gallery Bottega (Map pp68–9; ☼ 041 241 30 19; Campo Santo Stefano 2970, San Marco; per

20min €3; ☼ 10am-midnight summer, 10am-10pm winter) Near Ponte dell'Accademia; open late and on weekends.

Internet Point San Barnaba (Map pp78–9; ☎ 041 277 09 26; Campo San Barnaba 2759, Dorsoduro; per 20min €3; ☼ 9am-1.30pm & 3.30-7pm Mon-Sat) Computer posts and printing services in a toy store, with a friendly cat that likes to sleep on warm keyboards – fair warning to those with allergies.

Net Gate (Map pp78–9; ☎ 041 244 02 13; Crosera San Pantalon; ☼ 9.30am-7pm Mon-Sat) Friendly service with fast connection and several terminals; also offers printing, photocopying, and mobile phone sales and services.

Planet Internet (Map pp94–5; ☎ 041 524 41 88; Rio Terà San Leonardo 1519, Cannaregio; per hr €8; ☼ 9am-11pm) Photo printing and photocopying services close to train station; open late.

Venetian Navigator (Map pp100–1; ☎ 041 277 10 56; Calle Casselleria 5300, Castello; per hr €7; ☼ 10am-10pm summer, 10am-8.30pm autumn-spring) Close to Piazza San Marco, with wi-fi access, CD and DVD burning, and scanning and printing services; open weekends and evenings.

VeNice (Map pp94–5; ☎ 041 275 82 17; Lista di Spagna 149, Cannaregio; per hr €8; ☼ 9am-11pm) Printing services handy to the train station; open late.

World House (Map pp100–1; ☎ 041 528 48 71; www .world-house.org; Calle della Chiesa 4502, Castello; per 31-60min/3hr €8/18; ☼ 10am-11pm) Open late and on weekends near Piazza San Marco; CD burning, printing, and fast connection.

LUGGAGE

Getting from the vaporetto stop to your hotel can be difficult if you're heavily laden. *Portabagagli* (porters) operate from several stands around the city. At the train station and Piazzale Roma, they charge €18 for one item and roughly €6 for each extra one for

---

WI-FI ACCESS

Venice launched an ambitious UK£9 million citywide wi-fi access plan with much fanfare in 2009. Ten thousand kilometres of high-speed cable have been laid throughout the city, with the noble goal of providing access at 20 to 100 megabits per second free to residents and at a flat rate of €5 per day for visitors.

Yet you may be hard pressed to find a single wi-fi hot spot that actually works near you, since signals often do not circulate from one room to the next through thick old stone walls. Even in hotels that advertise wi-fi you may have to go to the lobby to get access. Staying at a locally run B&B is actually a better bet for free, fast in-room wireless access than a big hotel, where access often requires prepayment and a Byzantine log-on process; technical assistance is scarce even in business centres. Some, but not all, internet cafes offer wi-fi access.

Another option is to buy a PCMCIA card pack with one of the Italian mobile phone operators, which gives wireless access through the mobile telephone network. These are usually prepaid services that you can top up as you go.

transport within Venice proper. Prices virtually double to transport bags to the Lido or Giudecca. Points where porters can be found include the train station (☎ 041 71 52 72), Piazzale Roma (☎ 041 522 35 90), Piazza San Marco (☎ 041 523 23 85) and the Ponte dell'Accademia (☎ 041 522 48 91).

MAPS

You should be able to get by with the maps in this book, but some detailed maps on sale might also come in handy. A good one is the wine red–covered *Venezia* produced by the Touring Club Italiano (1:5000). If you plan to stay for the long haul, *Calli, Campielli e Canali* (Edizioni Helvetica) is a wise investment. This is the definitive street guide, listing every obscure side street and minor canal, and will usually allow you to locate to within 100m any Venetian address you need. Posties must do a course in it before being sent out to deliver the mail.

Street Names

The *Venezianizzazione* (Venetianisation) of street names has created no end of trouble: grammatical and orthographic inconsistencies abound. The city's *nizioleti* (street signs) sometimes post a Venetian name on one street corner only to rename it in standard Italian a block away. Usually if you say the name out loud, you'll find that they sound more similar than they look in print – for example, Zanipolo (Venetian) and San Giovanni e Paolo (Italian). Street signs may not always be consistent with what you'll see on business cards, websites and maps. In this book, you'll find a mix of standard Italian names and, where the Venetian version is more commonly used, Venetian names.

Street Numbering

Venice has its own style of street numbering, which was introduced by the Austrians in the 19th century. Instead of a system based on individual streets, each *sestiere* (neighbourhood) has numbered buildings. However, numbers aren't always consecutive, so searching out an address can be frustrating – be sure to confirm the location beforehand so that you don't wind up wandering the streets unnecessarily. You should be able to check locations on maps in this book, your hotel website or Venice Xplorer (www.venicexplorer.net). Most streets in Venice are named, so where possible we have provided street names as well as the *sestiere* number.

MEDICAL SERVICES
Medical Cover

All foreigners have the same right as Italians to free emergency medical treatment in a public hospital. EU citizens (and those of Switzerland, Norway and Iceland) are entitled to the full range of health-care services in public hospitals free of charge, but you will need to present your European Health Insurance Card (EHIC). Australia has a reciprocal arrangement with Italy that entitles Australian citizens to free public health care – carry your Medicare card. Citizens of New Zealand, the USA, Canada and other countries have to pay for anything other than emergency treatment. Most travel-insurance policies include medical coverage.

In an emergency, head for the *pronto soccorso* (casualty section) of any *ospedale* (hospital). Unless it's an emergency, you won't be able to see a doctor without an appointment. If your country has a consulate in Venice, staff there should be able to refer you to doctors who speak your language. If you have a specific health complaint, obtain the necessary information and referrals for treatment before leaving home.

The Italian public health system is administered by local centres generally known in Venice as ULSS, and known elsewhere as Azienda Sanitaria Locale (ASL), Unità Sanitaria Locale (USL) or Unità Socio Sanitaria Locale (USSL). Under these headings you'll find long lists of offices; look for *Poliambulatorio* (polyclinic) and the telephone number for *accettazione sanitaria* (medical appointments). Call this number to make an appointment, or if you don't speak Italian ask someone at your hotel to help you.

The following medical services may be of use to travellers. Opening hours vary, though most are open 8am to 12.30pm Monday to Friday, and some open for a couple of hours on weekday afternoons, and on Saturday morning.

Guardia Medica (☎ in Venice 041 529 40 60, in Mestre 041 95 13 32, in Lido 041 526 77 43) This service of night-time-callout doctors operates from 8pm to 8am on weekdays and from 10am the day before a holiday (including Sunday) until 8am the day after.

Ospedale Civile (Map pp100–1; ☎ 041 529 41 11; Campo SS Giovanni e Paolo 6777, Castello) Venice's main hospital; for emergency care and dental treatment, ask for the *pronto soccorso* (casualty section).

Ospedale Umberto I (☎ 041 260 71 11; Via Circonvallazione 50, Mestre) Vast modern hospital on the mainland.

Pharmacies

Most pharmacies in Venice are open from 9am to 12.30pm and 3.30pm to 7.30pm, and are closed on Saturday afternoon and Sunday. Information on rotating late-night pharmacies is posted in pharmacy windows and listed in the free magazine *Un Ospite di Venezia* (see p274).

MONEY

As in 12 other EU nations (Austria, Belgium, Finland, France, Germany, Greece, Ireland, Luxembourg, the Netherlands, Portugal, Slovenia and Spain), the euro is the currency in Italy. Each participating state decorates the reverse side of the coins with its own designs, but all euro coins can be used anywhere that accepts euros.

Euro notes come in denominations of €500, €200, €100, €50, €20, €10 and €5, in different colours and sizes. Euro coins are in denominations of €2, €1, 50c, 20c, 10c, 5c, 2c and 1c.

Changing Money

You can exchange money in banks, at post offices or in bureaux de change. See the inside front cover for exchange rates at the time of going to print. The post office and banks are reliable, but always ask about commissions. Keep a sharp eye on commissions at bureaux de change, which sometimes exceed 10% on travellers cheques.

You'll find most of the main banks and several ATMs in the area around the Ponte di Rialto and San Marco. One bank with an ATM that's convenient to both the train and bus stations is the Monte dei Paschi (Map pp86–7; Fondamenta San Simeon Piccolo, Santa Croce).

Several exchanges are located by the train station, Rialto and San Marco, including these:

American Express (Map pp68–9; ☎ 041 520 08 44; Salizada San Moisè 1471, San Marco; 🕓 9am-5.30pm Mon-Fri, 9am-12.30pm Sat) The ATM works with Amex cards.

Travelex Piazza San Marco (Map pp68–9; ☎ 041 528 73 58; Piazza San Marco 142, San Marco; 🕓 9am-6pm

Mon-Sat, 9.30am-5pm Sun); Rialto (Map pp68–9; Riva del Ferro 5126, San Marco) To reclaim value-added tax (VAT) from purchases over €200, bring completed forms and local receipts here.

Credit/Debit Cards

Major cards such as Visa, MasterCard, Maestro and Cirrus are accepted throughout Italy. They can be used in many hotels, restaurants and shops. Cards can also be used in ATMs displaying the appropriate bank link sign. Some banks may allow you to obtain cash advances over the counter with MasterCard or Visa, but be aware that this is a lengthy process, and check charges with your bank beforehand to avoid any nasty surprises later. Most banks now build in a fee of around 2.75% into every foreign transaction. In addition, ATM withdrawals attract a fee, which can range from a flat fee to 1.5% of the withdrawal.

If your card is lost, stolen or swallowed by an ATM, you can call toll free to have an immediate stop put on its use.

Amex (☎ 800 914912)

Diners Club (☎ 800 864064)

MasterCard (☎ 800 870866)

Visa (☎ 800 819014)

NEWSPAPERS & MAGAZINES

A wide selection of national daily newspapers from around Europe (including the UK) is available at news-stands all over central Venice, and at strategic locations like the train and bus stations. The *International Herald Tribune, Time*, the *Economist, Der Spiegel* and a host of other international magazines are also available.

Italy has several important dailies published in major cities, including Milan's *Corriere della Sera* (with a good Venice insert; in English at www.corriere.it/english), Turin's right-leaning *La Stampa* (www.lastampa.it, in Italian) and Rome's centre-left *La Repubblica* (www.repubblica.it, in Italian, some features also in English). This trio dominates the newspaper scene nationwide, publishing local editions up and down the country.

Two papers focus on the local scene: in business since the early days of the Italian Republic in 1887, *Il Gazzettino* (www.gazzettino.it, in Italian) brings out separate editions in each province across the Triveneto area (the Veneto, Friuli Venezia Giulia and Trentino). If you're in Venice and want decent national and foreign news but with solid local content, this is probably the paper you want. Competition comes from two tabloids, *La Nuova Venezia* (http://nuovavenezia.gelocal.it) and *Il Venezia* (www.ilvenezia.it).

VeNews (www.venezianews.it; some features and listing in English) a monthly magazine, has information on the latest events, cinema, music and the like, along with a hodgepodge of articles.

ORGANISED TOURS

Consult *Un Ospite di Venezia*, available from tourist offices, for details of tours of Venetian churches and sights. The Azienda di Promozione Turistica (APT) has an updated list of authorised guides who can take you on a private walking tour of the city. Many museums, such as the Palazzo Ducale, can organise guided tours at a price.

Free tours are offered by a couple of museums, including the Museo Archeologico and the Libreria Nazionale Marciana, and the nonprofit heritage organisation Associazione Sant'Apollonia (☎ 041 270 24 64; http://assap.provincia. venezia.it, in Italian) offers tours from April to October at churches off the beaten tourist track, including the Cattedrale di Santa Maria Assunta in Torcello. Travel agencies and hotel-reception staff can also recommend a range of city tours to match your interests. Below are some of the better tour choices currently available.

Allegro in Venice (☎ 041 528 77 78; www.allegroin venice.com; 2hr-tours €20-35) Creative excursions include a 7.30am tour (for sightseeing without the crowds) and a Running Venice tour for joggers who like to sightsee on the go. Popular evening tours include a happy-hour pub crawl covering local-favourite bars and prime pickings of *cicheti* (snacks), and the night-time tour chasing ghosts and legends from the 1500s with raconteur Manuel Vecchina, based on tales vividly recounted by Alberto Toso Fei in *Venetian Legends and Ghost Stories* (www.venetianlegends.it).

Azienda di Promozione Turistica (APT; ☎ 041 529 87 11; www.turismovenezia.it) APT tourist offices run guided tours ranging from the classic gondola circuit (per person €39) to a 'spicy tour' with tales of Casanova dalliances and society scandal in the Rialto's former red-light district (per person €20).

Basilica di San Marco mosaics tour (☎ reservations 041 241 38 17; ☽ 10am-noon Mon-Fri) Learn to spot key saints and see biblical stories unfold in 8500 sq metres of mosaics on the daily free tour of the mosaics in the Basilica di San Marco. Tours depart at 11am daily from April to October in a

range of languages: in Italian Monday to Saturday, in English Monday, Thursday and Friday, and in French Thursday.

Città d'Acqua (☎ 041 93 68 33; www.veniceitineraries .com; Centro Internazionale Città d'Acqua, Officina Viaggi, Via Col Moschin 14, Mestre; per person with minimum 40-person group €70-75, with minimum 10-person group €90-95; ☽ 10am-4.30pm by reservation) Maree Veneziane (Venetian Tides) tours explore areas of the lagoon not usually glimpsed by visitors; an up-close-and-personal look at distant island communities, nature preserves established through environmental initiatives, and the effects of *acque alte* (high tides) and new marine technologies. Tours cover island monasteries not usually open to the public, or island-hop from Giudecca to Malamocco on the Lido, Le Vignole and Arsenale, with stops at local watering holes.

Folo cruises (☎ 049 807 8032; Via Mantegna 11, Brugine) Sail off into the sunset on a double masted, 1946 fishing *bragozzo* (Venetian barge), for three-day trips (per person from €2000, for six to 10 people) or on-board cooking tours. You sleep in selected villas and *palazzi* in Venice or around the lagoon, spend the day sailing the lagoon and eat seafood lunches on board.

Laguna Eco Adventures (☎ 329 722 62 89; www.laguna ecoadventures.com; 2½-8hr trips per person €40-150) Sail away into the lagoon blue in a Venetian *sampierota*, a narrow twin-sailed boat small enough to slip into canals but purpose-built to glide along open water. Boats accommodate five people maximum, so it's just you, the lagoon birds, and the wind at your backs. Customisable itineraries range from a circuit of outlying lagoon desert islands and Lido beaches to an easy drift along Venice's canals at sunset. Reserve ahead and check weather forecasts, since all trips are subject to weather conditions.

Terra e Acqua (☎ 347 420 50 04; www.terraeacqua.com; 4-9hr trip incl lunch €70-120) Take a wild ride through the lagoon with skipper Cristina della Toffola, a wealth of information about rare lagoon wildlife and juicy historical titbits, including nunneries closed due to scandal during Venice's notorious baroque party-era. Itineraries are customised, and can cover abandoned plague-quarantine islands, fishing and birdwatching hot spots, Burano, Torcello, and other lagoon architectural gems. Cristina makes a mean fish stew and *spritz* (*prosecco*-based drink), served on board at picturesque island mooring spots, and takes the utmost care to preserve the fragile lagoon ecosystem en route. Trips accommodate up to 10 people on a sunny, sturdy *bragozzo* (Venetian barge), which makes trips sociable and easy going for those not accustomed to boats. Reserve well ahead and bring your SPF30 sunscreen.

Friends of Venice Club (☎ 041 71 58 77; www.friend sofveniceclub.com; courses and excursions from €75) Get to know Venice from the inside out, with a range of English-language courses including seasonal Italian cookery, chamber music and choral performances in a local *palazzo* (palace or mansion), rowing standing up Venetian-style across the Giudecca Canal, and plein-air drawing and painting all around town. Instructors are patient and genuinely enthusiastic about showing you the Venice they know and love.

Venicescapes (www.venicescapes.org; 4-6hr tour incl book 2 adults/additional adult/under 18 US$150-275/50/25) Intriguing walking tours run by a nonprofit historical society (proceeds support ongoing Venetian historical research) with themes such as 'A City of Nations', exploring multiethnic Venice through the ages, and 'A Most Serene Republic', revealing how Venice kept the peace through politics and espionage.

Walks Inside Venice (☎ 041 524 17 06; www.walks insidevenice.com; 3-4hr tour €55-70) Spirited tours run by three local women lead four to eight people on afternoon treks through the city's hidden backstreets to major monuments, off the tourist track through the Cannaregio district, or on grand tours of Venice with detours to Murano and the cemetery island of San Michele.

POST

Poste Italiane (☎ 803160; www.poste.it), Italy's postal service, has improved over the past few years, though mail is still slow and package delivery service remains unreliable. *Francobolli* (stamps) are available from post offices and authorised tobacconists (look for the official *tabacchi* sign: a big 'T', often white on black).

The cost of sending a letter by *via aerea* (airmail) depends on its weight, size and where it is being sent. Officially, letters sent within Italy should arrive the following working day, those posted to destinations in Europe and the Mediterranean basin within three days, and those to the rest of the world in four to eight days.

The **main post office** (Map pp68–9; Salizada del Fontego dei Tedeschi, San Marco; ⏰ 8.30am-6.30pm Mon-Sat) is near the Ponte di Rialto, in the former trading house where German merchants once traded downstairs and struck deals upstairs in their living quarters. Stamps are available at windows in the central courtyard.

Poste restante is known as *fermo posta* in Italy. Letters marked in this way will be held at the Fermo Posta counter in the main post office. In Venice, you can pick up your letters at window 16; take your passport along as ID. Poste restante mail should be addressed as, for example: John SMITH, Fermo Posta, Posta Centrale, 30100 Venice, Italy.

RADIO

The state-owned RAI-1, RAI-2 and RAI-3 (www.rai.it) broadcast all over the country and abroad. They offer a combination of classical and light music with news broadcasts and discussion programmes.

There are various local stations, with two based in Venice proper: Radio Venezia (www.radio venezia.it) has news and music, and Radio Vanessa (www.radiovanessa.it, in Italian) presents anything from operettas through '60s hits to Italian pop. If your Italian is good and you enjoy alternative news and views, try Mestre-based Radio Base (www.radiobase.net, in Italian), part of the national Radio Popolare network.

You can pick up the BBC World Service on short wave at 6.195MHz, 7320MHz, 9.410MHz, 12.095MHz and 15.485MHz depending on where you are and the time of day. Voice of America can be found on short wave at 1593MHz, 9685MHz, 11,835MHz, 15,255MHz and 17,555MHz.

SMOKING

Since early 2005, smoking has been banned in all closed public spaces, including in bars, offices, trains and airports. Smoking isn't banned in all hotel rooms, but smokers will definitely have to look harder to find accommodation where it is allowed in Venice.

TAXES

VAT (value-added tax) of around 20%, known as Imposta di Valore Aggiunto (IVA), is slapped onto just about everything in Italy. If you are a non-EU resident and spend more than €155 on a purchase, you can claim a refund when you leave. The refund only applies to purchases from affiliated retail outlets that display a 'tax-free for tourists' (or similar) sign. You have to complete a form at the point of sale, then have it stamped by Italian customs as you leave. You can request an immediate cash refund at major airports and Travelex (see p270); otherwise it will be refunded to your credit card. For information, pick up a pamphlet on the scheme from participating stores.

TELEPHONE

If you're calling an international number from an Italian phone, you must dial 00 to get an international line, then the relevant country and city codes, followed by the telephone number.

Costs

Cell phone calls can be expensive in Venice, especially with roaming charges – so many Italians prefer to send text messages or use land lines whenever possible. A *comunicazione urbana* (local call) from a public phone costs €0.10 every one minute and 10 seconds.

For a *comunicazione interurbana* (long-distance call within Italy) you pay €0.10 when the call is answered and then €0.10 every 57 seconds. A three-minute call from a payphone to most European countries and North America will cost about €2. Australasia would cost €4. Calling from a private land line is cheaper, but beware hotel surcharges on phone calls. For international calls, you might get a better deal at one of the call centres cropping up around town, which often operate in internet cafes (p268).

Country & City Codes

When calling Venice land lines, even from within the city, you must dial the ☎ 041 city code; local mobile numbers have no initial 0. To call from outside Italy, first dial the Italy country code: ☎ 39.

Italian mobile phone numbers begin with a three-digit prefix such as 330, 335, 347 or 368. Free-phone or toll-free numbers are known as *numeri verdi* (green numbers) and start with 800.

For directory assistance numbers see the inside front cover.

Mobile Phones

GSM and tri-band mobile phones can be used in Italy with the purchase of a local SIM card at Vodafone and Telecom Italia Mobile outlets across the city. Be sure to check with your provider before you leave home, though, as some phones may be code blocked.

US mobile phones generally work on a frequency of 1900MHz, so for use in Italy your US handset will have to be tri-band.

Unless you plan to live in Italy, it probably won't be worth your while to buy into a mobile phone contract. You'll need your passport to open any kind of mobile phone account, prepaid or otherwise.

Public Phones

Many orange Telecom payphones only accept *carte/schede telefoniche* (phonecards), though there are pay phones that accept coins around Santa Lucia train station, Piazzale Roma, Campo Santa Margherita and Piazza San Marco. There's also a bank of telephones (Map pp68–9) near the post office on Calle Galeazza.

Phonecards

You can buy phonecards (€2.50 or €5) at post offices, tobacconists and news-stands, and from vending machines in Telecom offices. Snap off the perforated corner before using it. Phonecards have an expiry date – usually 31 December or 30 June, depending on when you purchase the card.

Stick to Telecom phone cards rather than the overpriced 'international calling cards' available in vending machines in Marco Polo airport, which charge €1 per minute for local calls. Unstaffed Telecom offices where you can buy Telecom cards can be found on the corner of Corte dei Pali and Strada Nuova in Cannaregio (Map pp94–5); Calle San Luca 4585, San Marco (Map pp68–9); and at Santa Lucia train station (Map pp94–5).

TIME

Italy (and hence Venice) is one hour ahead of GMT/UTC during winter and two hours ahead during the daylight-saving period, which runs from the last Sunday in March to the last Sunday in October. Besides the UK, Ireland and Portugal, most other Western European countries are on the same time as Italy year-round; New York (Eastern Time) is six hours behind Italy. To compare with other time zones, see www.worldtimezone.com.

TIPPING

A 10% tip is customary at restaurants where a service charge is not included, and you can leave small change at cafes and bars. Tipping water-taxi drivers is not common practice; hotel porters are tipped €1 per bag.

TOILETS

Most bars and cafes reserve the restroom for paying customers, so sudden urges at awkward moments call for a drink-buying detour – but be sure the place actually has a toilet before plunking down your cash. Look before you sit: even in women's bathrooms, some toilets don't have seats. Public toilets (€1) are scattered around Venice near tourist attractions (look for the 'WC Toilette' signs), and are usually open from 7am to 7pm.

TOURIST INFORMATION

The useful monthly booklet *Un Ospite di Venezia* (A Guest in Venice), published by a group of Venetian hoteliers, is distributed in many hotels. In tourist offices, ask for *La Rivista di Venezia*, a bimonthly free magazine with articles in Italian and English, with a handy *Shows & Events* listings insert. Another useful listings freebie in Italian and English is *Venezia da Vivere* (www.veneziadavivere.com), which you can check out online, and may find it in printed form in bars. The Venice section of *Corriera della Sera* (www.corriere.it) is also useful for current and upcoming events.

Tourist Offices

Azienda di Promozione Turistica (APT; ☎ 041 529 87 11; www.turismovenezia.it) has several branches that can provide information on day trips, transport, special events, shows and exhibits in the city.

Official APT outlets for tourist information include these (open daily):

Infopoint Giardini (Map pp68–9; Venice Pavilion, San Marco; ☺ 10am-6pm)

Lido (Map p116; Gran Viale Santa Maria Elisabetta 6a, Lido; ☺ 9am-12.30pm & 3.30-6pm Jun-Sep)

Marco Polo airport (Arrivals Hall; ☺ 9.30am-7.30pm)

Piazzale Roma (Map pp86–7; Santa Croce; ☺ 9.30am-1pm & 1.30-4.30pm Nov-Mar, 9.30am-6.30pm Apr-Oct)

Piazza San Marco (Map pp68–9; ☎ 041 529 87 11; Piazza San Marco 71f, San Marco; ☺ 9am-3.30pm Mon-Sat) Main tourist office.

Stazione di Santa Lucia (Map pp94–5; Cannaregio; ☺ 8am-6.30pm)

TRAVELLERS WITH DISABILITIES

With all the footbridges, stairs, and scant guard railings along canals, Venice might not seem like the easiest place to visit for travellers with disabilities. But the city has been making a more conscientious effort lately to provide access to key monuments, after the considerable embarrassment of paying millions for the Calatrava Bridge without considering its wheelchair accessibility. A disabled assistance office (☺ 7am-9pm daily) is located in front of platform 4 at Venice's Santa Lucia station, and further information on accessibility and assistance in Venice is provided at Informahandicap (see opposite).

One useful tool for disabled travellers navigating Venice is a map available from APT offices with city areas shaded in yellow, indicating that they can be negotiated without running into one of Venice's many bridges. Some bridges along major thoroughfares (such as the route from the train station to the Rialto) are equipped with *servoscale* (lifts), which are marked on maps. You can (in theory) get hold of a key from tourist offices to operate these lifts. APT offices also distribute a series of smaller route maps entitled *Accessible Venice*, with sights descriptions and notes on accessibility.

With wheelchairs, it's often easier to get around town via vaporetto, which have access for wheelchairs. Passengers in wheelchairs travel for free on the vaporetto and some larger lagoon ferries also offer discounted access.

Five bus lines are adapted for wheelchair users: line 2 (Piazzale Roma to Mestre train station), line 4 (Piazzale Roma to Corso del Popolo in Mestre), line 5 (Piazzale Roma to Marco Polo airport), line 6 (Tronchetto and Piazzale Roma to the mainland) and line 15 (a mainland service running between Marco Polo airport and Mestre).

The city of Venice is also developing a project for the sight-impaired, including tactile maps that literally give a feel for the city and its extraordinary layout. Information (in Italian only) is available at www2.comune.venezia.it/letturagevolata.

Organisations

Accessible Italy (☎ 378 94 11 11; www.accessibleitaly.com) A San Marino-based nonprofit company that specialises in holiday services for the disabled, ranging from hiring wheelchairs in Venice to helping to arrange fully accessible Italian weddings. Proceeds from paid services help pay for accessibility improvements sorely needed throughout Italy.

Allegro in Venice (☎ 041 528 77 78; www.allegroinvenice.com; 2hr tour €20-35) Provides excellent information about accessible hotels, monuments, concerts and events, and runs Easy Access Venice tours introducing people with disabilities to the delights of the city, including the Basilica di San Marco, Palazzo Ducale, I Frari, and Scula Grande di San Marco.

Holiday Care (☎ 0845 124 9971; www.holidaycare.org.uk; 7th fl, Sunley House, 4 Bedford Park, Croydon, Surrey CR0 2AP, UK) Provides listings of hotels with disabled access, suggestions on where to hire equipment and tour operators experienced in managing Italy's accessibility issues.

Informahandicap (www.comune.venezia.it/Informahandicap, in Italian); San Marco (Map pp68–9; ☎ 041 274 81 44; Ca' Farsetti 4136, San Marco); Mestre (☎ 041 274 61 44; Piazzale Candiani 5, Mestre) The website has details on hotels that can accommodate guests with disabilities, tips for getting around the city and other information.

VISAS

Citizens of EU countries, Iceland, Norway and Switzerland do not need a visa to visit Italy. Nationals of some other countries, including Australia, Brazil, Canada, Israel, Japan, New Zealand and the USA, do not require visas for tourist visits of up to 90 days.

All non-EU nationals entering Italy for any reason other than tourism (such as longer-term study or work) should contact an Italian consulate as they may need a visa. Non-EU nationals planning to stay a while should also insist on having their passport stamped on entry since they could encounter problems when trying to obtain a *permesso di soggiorno* (residence permit) without a passport stamp.

For more information and a list of countries whose citizens require a visa, check the website of the Italian foreign ministry (www.esteri.it). The standard tourist visa issued by Italian consulates is the Schengen visa, valid for up to 90 days. This visa is valid for travel in Italy and in several other European countries with which Italy has a reciprocal visa agreement (see www.eurovisa.info for the full list). These visas are not renewable inside Italy.

Permits

EU citizens do not need permits to live, work or start a business in Italy, but are advised to register with a police station *(questura)* if they take up residence. Non-EU citizens coming to Venice for work or long-term study require study and work visas, which must be applied for in your country of residence.

WOMEN TRAVELLERS

Of the major travel destinations in Italy, Venice has to be the safest for women given the low rate of violent crime of any kind in Venice proper. Chief annoyances would be getting chatted up by other travellers in Piazza San Marco or on the more popular Lido beaches, easily quashed with a *'Non mi interessa'* ('I'm not interested') or that universally crushing response, the exasperated eyeroll. Following are a couple of women's organisations worth noting:

Centro Anti-Violenza (☎ 041 269 06 11; Villa Franchin, Viale G Garibaldi 155a, Mestre; ☺ 9am-6pm Mon-Fri Jul-Aug, 9am-8pm Mon-Fri rest of year) A women's centre offering legal advice, counselling and support to women who have been attacked, regardless of nationality. All services are free. Take bus 2 from Piazzale Roma.

Centro Donna (☎ 041 269 06 30; www.comune.venezia.it/c-donna, in Italian; Villa Franchin, Viale G Garibaldi 155a, Mestre; ☺ 9am-1pm Tue, Wed & Fri, 9am-5pm Mon & Fri Jul-Aug, 9am-6pm Mon-Fri rest of year) Located in the same building as Centro Anti-Violenza, this centre has a multilingual library, a women's history photographic archive, and a series of cultural events focusing on women's struggles, breakthroughs and contributions, including women's arts projects for the Venice Biennale.

WORK/STUDY

Immigration laws require non-EU foreign workers to have *permesso di lavoro* (work permit), usually obtained through their employers in Italy. While you're at it, you'll need a *codice fiscale* (tax file number) to be paid for most work in Italy. Non-EU citizens coming to study long-term may also need a *permesso di soggiorno* (residence permit) and/or *permesso di lavoro* (work permit).

University students or recent graduates might be able to set up an internship with companies in Venice. The Association of International Students for Economics & Commerce (www.aiesec.org) has branches throughout the world that help member students find internships in their fields.

Art students and graduates might consider arranging an internship with the Peggy Guggenheim Collection through its art schools. The gallery takes on foreign students to staff the museum and its facilities for up to three months.

English-speakers will find Italian a beautiful language to listen to and an easy one to start speaking. Of all the Romance languages Italian claims the closest relationship to Latin, and because English has been heavily influenced by Latin, there are many basic resemblances between the two languages.

Italian has about 65 million speakers worldwide. For historical reasons it has many regional dialects, some of which are so different from standard Italian as to be considered distinct languages in their own right.

You'll find that Italians really appreciate travellers trying their language, and when even a simple sentence sounds like an aria it can be difficult to resist striking up a conversation! If you want to learn more Italian than we've included here, pick up a copy of Lonely Planet's comprehensive but user-friendly *Italian* phrasebook or *Fast Talk Italian*.

Lingo in Venice

Italian in Venice comes with its own unique flavour. Standard Italian, with its roots in the Tuscan dialect of Dante, is spoken by pretty much everyone but often with a strong local lilt.

Influenced by Venexian (one of several dialects making up what linguists refer to as Venet, the language of the Veneto region), Venetians clip and chop consonants to some extent, or they become softer. *Ciao bello!* (Hi handsome!) becomes *Ciao beo!* in the local tongue. There are also some spelling deviations from standard Italian, namely the common double consonants in Italian words are dropped in written Venexian (eg *sottoportico* becomes *sotoportego*). See p269 for more details on various possible spellings of street names in Venetian and standard Italian, and the boxed text on p278 for a list of useful words in Venexian.

Many locals stick grimly to their dialect, while others tend to mix Venexian with standard Italian – at times giving Italian speakers from other parts of the country the impression that they understand everything, only to be confounded halfway through a sentence.

Documents from the time of the Republic (predating unification) show a disconcerting mix of Italian and Venexian. Only with the process of standardisation and universal schooling that occurred through the course of the 20th century have dialects (or mixes of dialect and standard Italian) been clearly relegated to a secondary place in Venice – as elsewhere in Italy.

SOCIAL
Meeting People

Hello.
Buongiorno.
Goodbye.
Arrivederci.
Please.
Per favore.
Thank you (very much).
(Mille) Grazie.
Yes./No.
Sì./No.
Do you speak English?
Parla inglese?
Do you understand (me)?
(Mi) Capisce?
Yes, I understand.
Sì, capisco.
No, I don't understand.
No, non capisco.

Could you please …?	Potrebbe …?
repeat that	ripeterlo
speak more slowly	parlare più lentamente
write it down	scriverlo

Going Out

What's on …?	Che c'è in programma …?
locally	in zona
this weekend	questo fine settimana
today	oggi
tonight	stasera

Where are the …?	Dove sono …?
clubs	dei clubs
gay venues	dei locali gay
places to eat	posti dove mangiare
pubs	dei pub

Is there a local entertainment guide?
C'è una guida agli spettacoli in questa città?

PRACTICAL
Question Words

How?	Come?
What?	Che?
When?	Quando?
Where?	Dove?
Who?	Chi?

Numbers & Amounts

0	zero
1	uno
2	due
3	tre
4	quattro
5	cinque
6	sei
7	sette
8	otto
9	nove
10	dieci
11	undici
12	dodici
13	tredici
14	quattordici
15	quindici
16	sedici
17	diciasette
18	diciotto
19	dicianove
20	venti
21	ventuno
22	ventidue
30	trenta
40	quaranta
50	cinquanta
60	sessanta
70	settanta
80	ottanta
90	novanta
100	cento
200	duecento
1000	mille
2000	duemila

Days

Monday	lunedì
Tuesday	martedì
Wednesday	mercoledì
Thursday	giovedì
Friday	venerdì
Saturday	sabato
Sunday	domenica

Banking

I'd like to …	Vorrei …
cash a cheque	riscuotere un assegno
change money	cambiare denaro
change some	cambiare degli
travellers cheques	assegni di viaggio

Where's the	Dov'è il
nearest …?	… più vicino?
ATM	bancomat
foreign exchange	cambio
office	

Post

Where is the post office?
Dov'è la posta?

I want to send a …	Voglio spedire …
parcel	un pachetto
postcard	una cartolina

I want to buy …	Voglio comprare …
an aerogram	un aerogramma
an envelope	una busta
a stamp	un francobollo

Phone & Mobile Phones

I want to buy a phone card.
Voglio comprare una scheda telefonica.

I want to make …	Voglio fare …
a call (to …)	una chiamata (a …)
a reverse-charge/	una chiamata a
collect call	carico del destinatario

Where can I find	Dove si trova …
a/an …?	
I'd like a/an …	Vorrei …
adaptor plug	un addattatore
charger for my	un caricabatterie
phone	
mobile/cell	un cellulare da
phone for hire	noleggiare
prepaid mobile/	un cellulare
cell phone	prepagato
SIM card for	una carta SIM per
your network	vostra rete telefonica

Internet

Where's a local internet cafe?
Dove si trova un punto internet?

I'd like to …	Vorrei …
check my email	controllare le mie email
get online	collegarmi a internet

Transport

What time does the … leave?	A che ora parte …?
bus	l'autobus
ferry (large)	la motonave
ferry (speedboat)	il motoscafo
plane	l'aereo
train	il treno
vaporetto	il batello/vaporetto

What time's the … bus/vaporetto?	A che ora passa … autobus/batello?
first	il primo
last	l'ultimo
next	il prossimo

Are you free? (taxi)
È libero questo taxi?
Please put the meter on.
Usa il tassametro, per favore.
How much is it to …?
Quant'è per …?
Please take me to (this address).
Mi porti a (questo indirizzo), per favore.

FOOD

For more detailed information on food and dining out, see the Eating chapter (p177).

Can you recommend a …?	Potrebbe consigliare un …?
bar/pub	bar/pub
cafe	bar
restaurant	ristorante

breakfast	prima colazione
lunch	pranzo
dinner	cena
snack	spuntino/merenda
eat	mangiare
drink	bere

Is service/cover charge included in the bill?
Il servizio/coperto è compreso nel conto?

EMERGENCIES

It's an emergency!
È un'emergenza!
Could you please help me/us?
Mi/Ci può aiutare, per favore?
Call the police/a doctor/an ambulance!
Chiami la polizia/un medico/un'ambulanza!
Where's the police station?
Dov'è la questura?

HEALTH

Where's the nearest …?	Dov'è … più vicino?
(night) chemist	la farmacia (di turno)
dentist	il dentista
doctor	il medico
hospital	l'ospedale

I need a doctor (who speaks English).
Ho bisogno di un medico (che parli inglese).

Symptoms

I have (a) …	Ho …
diarrhoea	la diarrea
fever	la febbre
headache	mal di testa
pain	un dolore

GLOSSARY

Listed below are useful Italian terms. Some of these have particular local meanings in Venice (and sometimes elsewhere in the Veneto), and are marked (Vz). Other local terms in Venetian dialect are also included and these are marked (V).

abbonamento – transport pass valid for one month

acqua alta (s), acque alte (pl) – high water (flooding that occurs in Venice, especially during winter, when the sea level rises)

ACTV – Azienda Consorzio Trasporti Veneziano; Venice public transport (bus and vaporetto) company

affittacamere – rooms for rent (sometimes cheaper than a *pensione* and not part of the classification system)

AIG – Associazione Italiana Alberghi per la Gioventù; Italian Youth Hostel Association

alimentari – grocery shop

alloggio – general term for lodging of any kind; not part of the classification system

altana – traditional Venetian roof terrace

altar maggiore – high altar

andata e ritorno – return trip

aperitivo – apéritif, early-evening drink

APT – Azienda di Promozione Turistica (local tourist office)

arco – arch

autonoleggio – car hire

autostazione – bus station/terminal

bacaro – (V) traditional Venetian bar or eatery

bagagli smarriti – lost luggage

batello – generic term for all types of Venetian ferry

battistero – baptistry

biglietteria – ticket office

biglietto (s), biglietti (pl) – ticket

binario – platform

bucintoro – doge's ceremonial barge

calle (s), calli (pl) – (Vz) alleyway

campanile – bell tower

campo – (Vz) square, piazza

cappella – chapel

carabinieri – police with military and civil duties

carnet – book of tickets

Carnevale – carnival period between Epiphany and Lent

carta marmorizzata – marbled paper

cartapesta – papier-mâché, used to make Carnevale masks

casa – house

centro storico – (literally 'historical centre') old town

chiaroscuro – (literally 'light-dark') the use of strong light and dark contrasts in painting to put the main figures into stronger relief

chiesa – church

chiostro – cloister

cicheti – (V) traditional bar snacks

consolato – consulate

contorno – side order

convalida – validation (of train ticket, for example)

coperto – cover charge (in restaurant)

corte – (Vz) blind alley

CTS – Centro Turistico Studentesco e Giovanile (student/youth travel agency)

cupola – dome

deposito bagagli – left luggage

digestivo – after-dinner liqueur

doge (s), dogi (pl) – leader, duke

ENIT – Ente Nazionale Italiano per il Turismo (Italian State Tourist Office)

enoteca (s), enoteche (pl) – wine bar

ES – Eurostar Italia; very fast train

espresso – express mail; short black coffee

fermo posta – poste restante

ferrovia – railway

fiume – river

fondamenta – (Vz) street beside a canal

forcola – (V) wooden support for gondolier's oar

foresto – (V) stranger, foreigner (non-Venetian)

fornaio – bakery

gabinetto – toilet, WC

gelateria (s), gelaterie (pl) – ice-cream shop

intarsia – inlaid wood, marble or metal

isola – island

IVA – Imposta di Valore Aggiunto (value-added tax)

lago – lake

largo – (small) square; boulevard

lido – beach

locanda – inn, small hotel

lungomare – seafront road or promenade

malvasia – tavern (named after the wine imported from Greek islands once controlled by Venice)

marzaria – (V) shop-lined street in heart of Venice

merceria – haberdashery shop, see also *marzaria*

motonave – big, interisland ferry on Venetian lagoon

motorino – moped

motoscafo (s), motoscafi (pl) – motorboat; in Venice also a faster, fully enclosed ferry and water taxi

nave (s), navi (pl) – ship

oggetti smarriti – lost property

ombra – (Vz) small glass of wine

orario – timetable

ostello (per la gioventù) – (youth) hostel

osteria (s), osterie (pl) – pub-restaurant

pala d'altare – altarpiece; refers to a painting (often on wood) usually used as an ornament before the altar

palazzo (s), palazzi (pl) – palace, mansion; large building of any type, including an apartment block

panetteria – bakery

panini – sandwiches

passeggiata – traditional evening or Sunday stroll

passerella (s), passerelle (pl) – raised walkway

pasticceria – cake/pasty shop

pendolini – high-speed trains

pensione – guesthouse, small hotel

pescaria – (V) fish market

piano nobile – main floor

piazzetta – small piazza

pietà – (literally 'pity' or 'compassion') sculpture, drawing or painting of the dead Christ supported by the Madonna

pinacoteca – art gallery

poltrona – airline-type chair on a ferry

ponte – bridge

portabagagli – porter

portico – covered walkway, usually attached to the out-side of buildings

porto – port

posta aerea – airmail

primo piatto – first course

pronto soccorso – first aid, casualty ward

prosecco – sparkling white wine from the Veneto region

punto informativo – information booth

questura – police station

ramo – (Vz) tiny side lane

rio (s), rii (pl) – (Vz) the name for most canals in Venice

rio terà – (V) street following the course of a filled-in canal

ruga – (V) small street flanked by houses and shops

sala – room, hall

salizada – (V) street, the first type in Venice to be paved

salumeria – delicatessen

scala mobile – escalator, moving staircase

scalinata – staircase

scuola (s), scuole (pl) – literally 'school'; religious confraternity

secondo piatto – second or main course

servizio – service charge (in restaurant)

sestiere (s), sestieri (pl) – (Vz) the term for the six 12th-century municipal divisions of Venice

sirocco – hot south wind

spiaggia – beach

spiaggia libera – public beach

spritz – classic Venetian apéritif consisting of one part sparkling white wine, one part soda water and one part bitters

squero (s), squeri (pl) – gondola-building and repair workshop

stazio (s), stazi (pl) – gondola jetty

stazione – station

stazione marittima – ferry terminal

strada – street, road

tabaccheria, tabaccaio – tobacconist's shop, tobacconist

terrazzo alla Veneziana – Venetian flooring

tesoro – treasury

traghetto – ferry; commuter gondola that crisscrosses the Grand Canal

trattoria (s), trattorie (pl) – cheap restaurant

Trenitalia – Italian State Railways, also known as Ferrovie dello Stato (FS)

ufficio postale – post office

ufficio stranieri – foreigners' bureau (in police station)

vaporetto (s), vaporetti (pl) – Venetian passenger ferry

vetrai – glass-makers

via – street, road

vigili del fuoco – fire brigade

vigili urbani – local police

voga alla veneta – Venetian form of rowing that involves standing up

BEHIND THE SCENES

THIS BOOK

The 6th edition of this guidebook was updated by Alison Bing. The previous edition was updated by Damien Simonis. This book was commissioned in Lonely Planet's London office, and produced in Melbourne by the following:

Commissioning Editor Paula Hardy

Coordinating Editor Maryanne Netto

Coordinating Cartographer Ross Butler

Coordinating Layout Designer Aomi Hongo

Managing Editor Liz Heynes

Managing Cartographers Shahara Ahmed, Herman So

Managing Layout Designer Sally Darmody

Assisting Editors Kim Hutchins, Tasmin McNaughtan, Jeanette Wall

Cover Naomi Parker, lonelyplanetimages.com

Internal image research Aude Vauconsant, lonelyplanet images.com

Project Manager Rachel Imeson

Language Content Branislava Vladisavljevic

Thanks to Sasha Baskett, Lucy Birchley, Daniel Corbett, Annelies Mertens, Katie O'Connell, Trent Paton, Lyahna Spencer

Cover photographs Architectural detail, Venice, Italy, Ryan Fox/LPI (top); Gondoliers on the Grand Canal at sunset with Santa Maria della Salute in the background, Venice, Italy, Cosmo Condina/Aurora Photos (bottom).

Internal photographs p4 (#1) 4Corners/Amantini Stefano; p5 (#6) AA World Travel Library/Alamy; p6 (#2) 4Corners/SIME/Scatà Stefano; p8 (#3) Grand Tour/Corbis/ Guido Baviera; p10 (#3) 4Corners/SIME/Kaos02; p11 (#2) Ibex Images/Alamy; p12 (#4) Alamy/Michael Morrison; p12 (#1) AFP/Getty Images/Patrick Hertzog/Staff; p127 (#8) CuboImages srl/Alamy; p129 (#2) Alamy/Peter Erik Forsberg; p130 (#4) SIME/Baviera Guido; p132 SIME/Fantuz Olimpio. All other photographs by Lonely Planet Images: p2, p125 Jon Davison; p3 Christopher Groenhout; p4 (#2) (#5), p5 (#3) (#4), p7 (#5), p8 (#1), p9 (#5) (#6), p10 (#4), p11 (#1), p126 (#7), p127 (#4), p128 (#1) (#5), p130 (#2), Krzysztof Dydynski; p6 (#1) (#3), p7 (#4), Juliet Coombe; p8 (#2) David Tomlinson; p9 (#4) Russell Mountford; p12 (#2) Glenn Beanland; p128 (#3) Diana Mayfield; p131 (#8) David Tomlinson.

All images are copyright of the photographer unless otherwise indicated. Many of the images in this guide are available for licensing from Lonely Planet Images: www.lonelyplanet images.com.

THANKS
ALISON BING

Mille grazie e tanti baci a le mie famiglie a Roma and stateside – the Bings, Ferrys and Marinuccis; superstar

---

THE LONELY PLANET STORY

Fresh from an epic journey across Europe, Asia and Australia in 1972, Tony and Maureen Wheeler sat at their kitchen table stapling together notes. The first Lonely Planet guidebook, *Across Asia on the Cheap*, was born.

Travellers snapped up the guides. Inspired by their success, the Wheelers began publishing books to Southeast Asia, India and beyond. Demand was prodigious, and the Wheelers expanded the business rapidly to keep up. Over the years, Lonely Planet extended its coverage to every country and into the virtual world via lonelyplanet.com and the Thorn Tree message board.

As Lonely Planet became a globally loved brand, Tony and Maureen received several offers for the company. But it wasn't until 2007 that they found a partner whom they trusted to remain true to the company's principles of travelling widely, treading lightly and giving sustainably. In October of that year, BBC Worldwide acquired a 75% share in the company, pledging to uphold Lonely Planet's commitment to independent travel, trustworthy advice and editorial independence.

Today, Lonely Planet has offices in Melbourne, London and Oakland, with over 500 staff members and 300 authors. Tony and Maureen are still actively involved with Lonely Planet. They're travelling more often than ever, and they're devoting their spare time to charitable projects. And the company is still driven by the philosophy of *Across Asia on the Cheap*: 'All you've got to do is decide to go and the hardest part is over. So go!'

editor and intrepid fellow traveller Paula Hardy; Venezia intelligentsia – Francesca Forni, Cristina Bottero, Rosanna Corrò, Giovanni d'Este, Francesco e Matteo Pinto, Davide Amadio and Marina Sent; and to editorial co-conspirator Damien Simonis. Thanks also to the Melbourne mavens Imogen Bannister, Herman So, Rachel Imeson, and Mary-anne Netto, and to the foodie vanguard – Raj Patel, Cindy Hatcher, Cook Here & Now, Slow Food Viterbo. *Ma sopra tutto:* Marco Flavio Marinucci, for anything and everything.

OUR READERS

Many thanks to the travellers who used the last edition and wrote to us with helpful hints, useful advice and interesting anecdotes:

Karen Hazlewood, Harald Kubel, Shirley Lim, Ugo Serandrei, Emanuela Tasinato

ACKNOWLEDGMENTS

Many thanks to the following for the use of their content: Venice Vaporetto map © Actv SpA 2009.

SEND US YOUR FEEDBACK

We love to hear from travellers – your comments keep us on our toes and help make our books better. Our well-travelled team reads every word on what you loved or loathed about this book. Although we cannot reply individually to postal submissions, we always guarantee that your feedback goes straight to the appropriate authors, in time for the next edition. Each person who sends us information is thanked in the next edition and the most useful submissions are rewarded with a free book.

To send us your updates – and find out about Lonely Planet events, newsletters and travel news – visit our award-winning website: lonelyplanet.com/contact.

Note: We may edit, reproduce and incorporate your comments in Lonely Planet products such as guidebooks, websites and digital products, so let us know if you don't want your comments reproduced or your name acknowledged. For a copy of our privacy policy visit lonelyplanet.com/privacy.

Notes

Notes

Notes

INDEX

A

accommodation 213-26,
  see also Sleeping *subindex*
  addresses 269
  costs 215, 216
  online resources 215
  rentals, long-term 215
  smoking policy 272
  student 221
acque alte 34, 36
activities 211, *see also*
  individual activities
addresses 269
Adriatic Coast 254-5
affittacamere 214
air travel 257-9
  airlines 257
  airports 258
  carbon offset schemes
    259
  to/from airports 251,
    258
Ala Napoleonica 135
Albinoni, Tomaso 46
Aldine Press 47
Amarone 252-3
ambulance, *see inside front
  cover*
Ando, Tadao 44, 57, 71, 141
Antico Cimitero Israelitico
  116-17
antiques, *see* Shopping
  subindex
architects
  Ando, Tadao 44, 57,
    71, 141

000 map pages
000 photographs

Codussi, Mauro 55
da Ponte, Antonio 52,
  87-8
Longhena, Baldassare
  55-6
Palladio, Andrea 55-6,
  108, 114, 242, 244-5
Sanmicheli, Michele 55
Sansovino, Jacopo 55
Scamozzi, Vincenzo
  114, 232
Scarpa, Carlo 56-7, 157,
  159, 234
architectural walking
  tour 54
architecture 51-8
  baroque 55-6
  contemporary 57
  neoclassical 55-6
  Renaissance 54-5
  Romanesque 53
  stile liberty (Liberty
    style) 56
  Venetian Gothic 53-4
  Veneto-Byzantine 52-3
Architecture Biennale
  19, 106
Archivio di Stato 145-6
area codes, *see inside front
  cover*
Arquà Petrarca 241
Arsenale 105-6, 157
arsenaloti 106
Art Biennale 18-19, 104,
  106, 157-8
art galleries, *see* Sights
  subindex
arts & music festivals
  La Biennale di Venezia
    18-19, 104, 106, 157-8
  Marghera Estate Village
    208
  Suggestivo 19
  Venezia Suona 18
  Venice Videoart Fair 19
arts, the 38-51, 208-10,
  see also individual arts,
  Arts *subindex*
  courses 265
Asolo 234
ATMs 270

B

B&Bs, *see* Sleeping
  subindex
Baffo, Giorgio 48
Bagnolo 235
Baptistry 238-9
bars, *see* Drinking *subindex*
Basilica del Santo 239
Basilica di Monte Berico 245
Basilica di San Marco 65-6,
  133, **66**, **8**
Basilica di San Zeno
  Maggiore 247-8
Basilica Palladiana 242
Bassano, Jacopo 40-1, 246
Bassano del Grappa 246
bathrooms 205, 273-4
beaches 116, 231, 254-5
Bellini, Jacopo 39
Bellini, Gentile 39
Bellini, Giovanni 39
Bellotto, Bernardo 42
Belluno 255-6
Bembo, Pietro 47
Biennale 18-19, 104, 106
Biennale Pavilions 104,
  157-8
boat tours 232, 271-2
boat travel 258, 259-61
  ferry services 261
  gondolas 77, 259
  scams 261
  traghetto 261
  vaporetto 259-61
  Vento di Venezia 123
  water taxis 261
boatyards, *see* Sights
  subindex
Bolle di Nardini 246
books 23, 47-9, *see also*
  literature
bookshops, *see* Shopping
  subindex
Bottega del Tintoretto
  152, 265
boutique hotels, *see* Sleeping
  subindex
Bridge of Sighs 52, 131, **132**
bridges, *see individual
  ponte*, Sights *subindex*

Brioni Family Tomb 234
Burano 119-20, **121**
  accommodation 226
  food 195
Burano lace 120
bureaux de change 270
bus travel 258, 261-2
business hours 264, *see also
  inside front cover*
  drinking 198-9
  eating 180
  shopping 162

C

Ca' Dario 82, 141, 131
Ca' d'Oro 96, 129, 153
Ca' Farsetti 139, 129
Ca' Foscari 129
Ca' Macana 265
Ca' Pesaro 88-9, 127, 148,
  5, **127**
Ca' Rezzonico (Museo del
  Settecento Veneziano)
  80, 131, 145, **8**, **130**
cafes, *see* Drinking *subindex*
Caliari, Paolo, *see* Veronese
Campanile 72, 134
camping 242
Campo Santa Margherita
  144
Canal, Antonio 41-2, 110
Canaletto 41-2, 110
Cannaregio, *see* Sestiere di
  Cannaregio
Canova, Antonio 235
Caorle 254-5
Capella degli Scrovegni
  (Scrovegni Chapel)
  236, 238
car rental 262
car travel 262
carbon offset schemes 259
Carnevale 17
Carriera, Rosalba 41
Casa di Goldoni 90
Casanova 30, 103
Casinò degli Spiriti 152
casinos 208, *see also*
  Nightlife *subindex*
Castelfranco 234
Castello, *see* Sestiere di
  Castello

000 map pages
000 photographs

GREENDEX

GOING GREEN

The following venues were selected for their commitment to sustainable travel. We've highlighted pubs and restaurants with express commitments to local producers, artisans' studios and venues supporting Venice's vital arts traditions, and fair trade and community nonprofit ventures. We've covered accommodation pioneering Venice's recycling, water conservation and alternative energy efforts. For more tips on travelling sustainably in Venice, see the Getting Started chapter (p16). If you think we've omitted someone who should be listed here, email us at www.lonelyplanet.com/contact. For more information about sustainable tourism and Lonely Planet, see www.lonelyplanet.com/responsibletravel.

MAP LEGEND

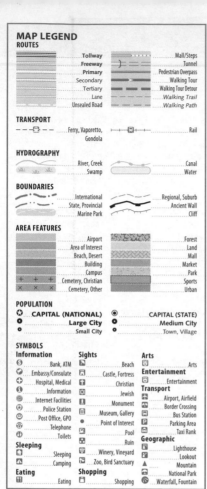

ROUTES

Tollway	Mall/Steps
Freeway	Tunnel
Primary	Pedestrian Overpass
Secondary	Walking Tour
Tertiary	Walking Tour Detour
Lane	Walking Trail
Unsealed Road	Walking Path

TRANSPORT

Ferry, Vaporetto, Gondola — Rail

HYDROGRAPHY

River, Creek — Canal
Swamp — Water

BOUNDARIES

International — Regional, Suburb
State, Provincial — Ancient Wall
Marine Park — Cliff

AREA FEATURES

Airport — Forest
Area of Interest — Land
Beach, Desert — Mall
Building — Market
Campus — Park
Cemetery, Christian — Sports
Cemetery, Other — Urban

POPULATION

○ CAPITAL (NATIONAL) — ⊙ CAPITAL (STATE)
● Large City — ○ Medium City
● Small City — ○ Town, Village

SYMBOLS

Information
- Bank, ATM
- Embassy/Consulate
- Hospital, Medical
- Information
- Internet Facilities
- Police Station
- Post Office, GPO
- Telephone
- Toilets

Sleeping
- Sleeping
- Camping

Eating
- Eating

Sights
- Beach
- Castle, Fortress
- Christian
- Jewish
- Monument
- Museum, Gallery
- Point of Interest
- Pool
- Ruin
- Winery, Vineyard
- Zoo, Bird Sanctuary

Shopping
- Shopping

Arts
- Arts
Entertainment
- Entertainment
Transport
- Airport, Airfield
- Border Crossing
- Bus Station
- Parking Area
- Taxi Rank
Geographic
- Lighthouse
- Lookout
- Mountain
- National Park
- Waterfall, Fountain

Published by Lonely Planet Publications Pty Ltd
ABN 36 005 607 983

Australia (Head Office)
Locked Bag 1, Footscray, Victoria 3011,
☎ 03 8379 8000, fax 03 8379 8111,
talk2us@lonelyplanet.com.au

USA 150 Linden St, Oakland, CA 94607,
☎ 510 250 6400, toll free 800 275 8555,
fax 510 893 8572, info@lonelyplanet.com

UK 2nd fl, 186 City Rd, London, EC1V 2NT,
☎ 020 7106 2100, fax 020 7106 2101,
go@lonelyplanet.co.uk

Mixed Sources
Product group from well-managed forests and other controlled sources
www.fsc.org Cert no. SGS-COC-005002
© 1996 Forest Stewardship Council
FSC